Religious Encounter
and the
Making of the Yoruba

African Systems of Thought

General Editors
Charles S. Bird
Ivan Karp

Contributing Editors
James W. Fernandez
Luc de Heusch
John Middleton
Roy Willis

Religious Encounter and the Making of the Yoruba

J. D. Y. Peel

INDIANA UNIVERSITY PRESS   BLOOMINGTON & INDIANAPOLIS

Publication of this book is made possible in part with the assistance of a Challenge Grant from the National Endowment for the Humanities, a federal agency that supports research, education, and public programming in the humanities.

This book is a publication of

Indiana University Press
601 North Morton Street
Bloomington, Indiana 47404-3797 USA

http://iupress.indiana.edu

Telephone orders 800-842-6796
Fax orders 812-855-7931
Orders by e-mail iuporder@indiana.edu

First paperback edition 2003
© 2000 by J. D. Y. Peel
All rights reserved

Library of Congress Cataloging-in-Publication Data

Peel, J. D. Y. (John David Yeadon), 1941–
Religious encounter and the making of the Yoruba / J. D. Y. Peel.
p. cm.—(African systems of thought)
Includes bibliographical references and index.
ISBN 0-253-33794-1 (alk. paper)
1. Missions—Nigeria—History—19th century. 2. Christianity and culture—Nigeria—History—19th century. 3. Nigeria—Church history—19th century. 4. Yoruba (African people)—Religion. I. Title. II. Series.
BV3625.N5 P44   2000
266'.009669'09034—dc21
00-037031
ISBN 0-253-21588-9 (pbk.)

2 3 4 5 6 08 07 06 05 04 03

FOR DAVID, TIM, AND FRANKO

contents

ILLUSTRATIONS

ACKNOWLEDGMENTS

This, my third book on the Yoruba, draws a greater trail of personal and intellectual indebtedness, going back more than thirty years, than I can readily acknowledge. The idea gelled and serious archival research began in the late 1980s, assisted by two grants from the British Academy. The Nuffield Foundation funded a further spell of field and archival research in Nigeria in 1994. A grant to support a full year's study leave in 1996–1997, which allowed me to complete the bulk of the writing, was provided by the Research Enablement Program, a grant program for mission scholarship supported by The Pew Charitable Trusts, Philadelphia, Pennsylvania, U.S., and administered by the Overseas Ministries Study Center, New Haven, Connecticut, U.S. To all these bodies I render my sincere thanks.

On the subject of this book I have over the years gained especial benefit from the writings and the friendship of two notable scholars, Jacob Ajayi and Robin Horton, who will each be able to see how much I have depended on their seminal contributions to the fields, respectively, of nineteenth-century Yoruba history (and especially the history of Yoruba Christianity), and the theorization of religious change in Africa. Whether or not they agree with all my judgments, I hope that they can each feel that lines of work that they inaugurated have been not unworthily taken forward here.

This is in part a study of the origins of the Yoruba intelligentsia, and it would have been much thinner if I had not had the good fortune to spend some years as a student, lecturer, or academic visitor at the University of Ibadan and the University of Ife (now Obafemi Awolowo University). On my last visit, in 1994, I received generous help and support from (at Ibadan) Jacob and Christie Ajayi, Tunde Agbaje-Williams, Bolanle Awe, and LaRay Denzer, and (at Ife) Tunji and Funmi Oloruntimehin and Femi Ojo. In Lagos and Ibadan, church people and descendants of the early Yoruba clergy in Lagos also responded warmly to my requests for information and documentation. Here I mention especially the Very Rev. Sope Johnson, Canon S.

W. Doherty, Mrs. Kemi Morgan, and Mrs. Ibidunni Sandey. I greatly wish I had been able to pursue these enquiries further.

Many colleagues and friends have contributed to the shaping and detail of the book, saving me in some cases from errors and misjudgments or adding refinements to the arguments, in conversations and seminar discussions or in comments on draft chapters. Of these suggestions and comments I wish I had been able to take more on board; but it is already a long book, perhaps too long, and for its remaining deficiencies I alone must be responsible. Here my debt is greatest to Tom McCaskie, learned, perspicuous, and the truest of friends; and to Karin Barber, the undoubted *aṣaju* of Yoruba cultural studies outside Nigeria. Throughout the long period of archival research in Birmingham, Karin Barber and Paulo Farias, Tom McCaskie and Lynne Brydon, and Jill Oliver offered me hospitality on many occasions and made a greater contribution to the completion of the book than they probably realize. Of my colleagues at the School of Oriental and African Studies (SOAS), Richard Rathbone, Richard Fardon, Louis Brenner, and Paul Gifford have been generous and astute readers of chapters in draft. Akin Oyetade has always been ready to advise on matters of Yoruba language. In one way or another Keith Hart, Caroline Ifeka, Murray Last, John Lonsdale, Peter Morton-Williams, Michelle Gilbert, Sandra Barnes, Ruth Marshall-Fratani, Matthews Ojo, Andrea Cornwall, Laura Lloyd, and Hermione Harris all gave help which is sincerely appreciated. To Sophie Baker I give warm thanks for the patient support she has given an often self-centered author in the closing stages of the book's writing. The confidence in the manuscript shown at a critical stage by John Middleton and Ivan Karp was an enormous boost.

Less easy to pinpoint has been the help received from members of the various seminars where it has been my pleasure to present work in progress or draft chapters of the book. Here I especially value comments made at two meetings of the Satterthwaite Colloquium on African Religion and Ritual, held annually in the beautiful surroundings of the English Lake District; at the African History Seminar at SOAS, the West Africa Seminar at University College London, the Centre of West African Studies at Birmingham, and the Sociology of Religion Seminar at the London School of Economics; at two meetings held under the auspices of the North Atlantic Missiology Project, in Edinburgh and at the Institute of Historical Research in London; at Africanist seminars at Northwestern and Emory Universities and at the University of Maryland; and at the gathering in Nashville of those who had received grants from the Overseas Ministries Study Center in 1997.

Anyone who works on the papers of the Church Missionary Society owes an enormous debt to their custodians. Here first thanks are due to Ben Benedikz and Christine Penney, successively in charge of the special collections at Birmingham University, where the CMS papers are now kept, who were always so helpful and efficient; to Rosemary Keen, who was the CMS archivist when I first worked on the papers of the Yoruba Mission in the 1970s and has done more than anyone else to facilitate scholarly use of them; and finally to Ken Osborne and Colin Rowe, respectively current archivist and librarian at the CMS headquarters in London. Finally, I would like to acknowledge the helpfulness and good humour of Sina Osunlana of the Kenneth Dike Library at the University of Ibadan, which made several weeks of work on the family papers held there one of the most agreeable periods of the whole research.

J. D. Y. P.
London
November 1999

Religious Encounter
and the
Making of the Yoruba

1

NARRATIVES OF RELIGION AND OF EMPIRE

The large-scale adoption of Christianity has been one of the master themes of modern African history; and as the third millennium beckons, it may well prove to be of world historical significance too, contributing to a decisive shift in Christianity's geopolitical placement, from North to South.[1] This study of the first sixty or seventy years of the mutual engagement of Christianity and the Yoruba people of southwestern Nigeria deals with a small but noteworthy segment of this process, and while it depends on missionary records of exceptional richness and interest, an essential key to their interpretation comes from what has been written on the Yoruba in the twentieth century. In a sense, this was where this inquiry began, in questions that seeded themselves over three decades ago during a year's field study of two independent African churches in Ibadan, the Yoruba metropolis.[2] The lines of T. S. Eliot fit the case of anyone who goes back later to explore the early part of a process first known at a later stage: "the end of all our exploring / Will be to arrive where we first started / And know the place for the first time." So it is that this book is written equally as anthropology and as history.

But while its aim is anthropological, its mode and form are historical, in

1

that it both deals with the past and makes narrative central to how it does so. The reasons for this have equally to do with theory, substance, and method. On the first count, it is held that the telling of stories is essential to how human beings constitute themselves and their communities.[3] No anthropology that would give its due to history, whatever other theoretical objectives it might have, can ignore this. On the second, the narratives of Christian conversion and inculturation, and of the formation of the Yoruba as a people, which are the linked themes of this book, have to be seen in terms of the various "grand narratives" that are told to make intelligible the recent history of the world and Africa's place within it, such as the rise of capitalism, European colonialism, modernization, globalization, and so on. We have to ask, for example, how far these Yoruba narratives—processes of religious change and ethnogenesis respectively—are to be seen as mere local pendants to these master narratives, and how far as movements with their own distinct sources and dynamics. The third reason arises from the nature of the source material, which is itself mainly narratives, principally the journals of missionaries—accounts of their experiences and activities, composed in the light of the great story which they wanted to write into the lives of the Yoruba. Hence arose problems of method: how to make the best use of this source, and how to write an account that would be faithful to it. For these journal narratives are more than just evidence of the past; they are constitutive of a continuing subject matter. Narrative, then, is our concern, in three connected modes: (1) the complex sequence of past events which is our subject matter, the actions of missionaries and Yoruba in "making history" together, (2) the journals which both belong to and comment on that history and provide the bulk of evidence for (3) the representation of that history which is essayed in the pages that follow.

CHRISTIAN CONVERSION AND OTHER GRAND NARRATIVES

The challenge of producing a cogent account of religious change in any part of Africa over the last two centuries lies in how to blend the three narrative themes which are pertinent to it: missionary endeavor, colonization, and the endogenous development of African societies. Each of these offers a template by which certain key relationships are highlighted and (by the same token) others are pushed into the background. A generation ago, at the end of the colonial period, Christian mission and European colonialism in Africa seemed so closely and obviously connected that their relationship did not seem to pose particularly interesting problems. To most historians and social scientists, it made sense enough to explain the connection in terms of the instrumental appeal of Christianity to Africans under colonial conditions and of the institutional power of Christian missions, particularly as the main providers of colonial education; and it was quite widely expected that mainstream Christianity, at least, would fade in importance in a modern, independent Africa. Among European historians, Terence Ranger was exceptional for his concern to give religion its complex due in the history of Africa, from the pre-colonial right through to the post-colonial periods.[4] For nationalism meant not only modernization but also the recovery of tradition and a search for continuity with the pre-colonial past. Among those who did maintain an interest in religion, the leaders of the new Nigerian school of history—J. F. Ade Ajayi and E. A. Ayandele— were by the 1960s calling for "African church history" to replace the older "mission history," and in their classic studies of nineteenth-century mission they placed less emphasis on its links with colonialism than on its genera-tion of the African elite which would come to overthrow it.[5] In a parallel movement, during the same period the mission-founded churches attracted much less academic attention than the independent churches and prophet movements founded by Africans who had broken away from them, for they were taken to be culturally more authentic and a genuinely nationalist form of expression.[6]

A third expression of this emphasis on African religious continuities was Robin Horton's short but highly influential article, "African Conversion," which sought to explain why so many Africans had, over the past century or so, turned to more monotheistic faiths.[7] It proposed that the conversion of Africans depended on their movement from life in confined, small-scale set-tings, symbolized by local or ancestral spirits, into a wider social sphere, sym-bolized by the Supreme Being of traditional belief. The theory is Afrocen-tric in the sense that the basic form of indigenous cosmology—its "two-tier" structure, divided between the local spirits whose cult fades with the increase in social scale and the Supreme Being who gains at their expense—is its es-sential starting-point. "Conversion" is then conceived of less as the outcome of an encounter between two cultures or religions than as a matter of cog-nitive and practical adjustment to changes in social experience, within the terms of an existing paradigm. Because the world religions are widely present, and have highly articulated doctrines of the Supreme Being, they are listened to with interest and gain adherents; but neither missions nor colonialism are integral to it. Missionaries might serve as "catalysts" to the process, but the theory is so set up as to explain Muslim as well as Christian conversion or, indeed, an increase in the saliency of the Supreme Being in an indigenous idiom. And while colonialism may produce an "increase in social scale" that results in conversion (and has in fact done so), the theory does not treat colonialism as a necessary condition of conversion. It discounts the common view that colonial power was the main factor inducing con-version, that Christianity was adopted because it was taken to be "the reli-gion of the conquerors."

It was a great merit of Horton's theory that it placed recent religious change, attributed all too easily just to external forces, in the long span of African history, and as such it chimed with the flowering of nationalist historiography in the 1960s and 1970s. Its bracketing together of Islam and Christianity—which is how the two exogenous monotheisms have often appeared to African eyes—was a liberating challenge to their academic compartmentalization. A theory as simple, elegant, and lucid as this proved good to think with, and not just among Africanists. Yet it left several important features of religious change beyond its purview. As Fisher pointed out with respect to Islam (but the point applies to Christianity too), it ignored the distinct cultural dynamics of the world religions themselves, which produce real effects even where their initial adoption has a strongly local rationale.[8] The missionaries and their messages cannot be excluded so radically from the picture. Moreover, the theory embraces little sense of the uneven power relations and the bitter conflicts that have often attended on religious change, which arise from the fact that religions are not just ways of explaining and modifying experience but are formative of communities and the power structures within them.[9]

The 1980s brought a revival of interest in colonialism. If this made sense for an Africa whose first decades of independence had proved very disappointing, it was also grounded in a greatly changed scholarly climate, where "post-colonial" literary theory had become fashionable, and the "subaltern studies" school of Indian historiography drew fresh attention to colonialism as a social and cultural phenomenon.[10] And with this there came a fresh realization of just how important missionaries had been in both creating and representing the colonial and post-colonial worlds of Asia and Africa—especially Africa.[11] Two notable contributions, by V. Y. Mudimbe and by Jean and John Comaroff, have renewed the emphasis on the close relations between missions and colonialism. The missionary program, writes Mudimbe, was so much "more complex than the simple transmission of the Christian faith" that it was difficult "not to identify it with cultural propaganda, patriotic motivations and commercial interests"; and that more than other kinds of colonialists, the missionary was "the best symbol of the colonial enterprise."[12] In similar vein, the Comaroffs insist that "the study of Christianity in Africa is more than just an exercise in the analysis of religious change."[13] Yes; but it is *at least*, and irreducibly, that. Whatever else one wants to say about the social impact of Christian missions in Africa—and there is a great deal to be said, as the Comaroffs show at great length—the story will be radically incomplete if its effects are not adequately tied into the religious project which brought the missionaries in the first place.

The Comaroffs present a detailed and historically specific case for the role of their main subject—British evangelicals active in the northern hinterland of South Africa from the mid-nineteenth century—in the colonial project:

> The impact of Protestant evangelists as harbingers of industrial capitalism lay in the fact that their civilizing mission was simultaneously symbolic and practical, theological and temporal. The goods and messages they

brought with them to Africa presupposed the messages and meanings they proclaimed in the pulpit and vice versa. Both were vehicles of a moral economy that celebrated the global spirit of commerce, the commodity, and the imperial marketplace.[14]

This picture of consistency and fit, both within missionary messages and between their project and the secular projects of their age, certainly conveys something of the reality, but it is too simple. To illustrate the point briefly, the redemptive sacrifice of Christ—which stood at the very heart of evangelical preaching—does *not* imply double-entry bookkeeping or vice versa. Yet elsewhere the Comaroffs themselves rightly acknowledge the "diverse and frequently contradictory designs" of different missionary groups, of their ambivalent relations with secular forces like settlers and administrators, of the "fundamental contradictions" between their views and the outcomes of imperial politics, even of clashes between the acts and the professions of missionaries "since . . . consciousness is never free from contradiction."[15] However valid this last general point may be, there is at hand a more specific explanation of at least some of these contradictions. Religions, and world religions in particular, are bearers of messages from the past to the current situations in which they operate. This anchorage in a temporal otherness, mediated by narratives and other vehicles of "collective memory," both gives strength to religious motivation and renders inadequate any attempt, such as we find in functionalist theories of religion (including their Marxist variant), to tie particular religious manifestations into a purely synchronic set of determinations.

This applies with especial force to the affinities claimed between evangelicalism and its age-mates capitalism, scientific rationalism, and other strands of early modern European culture. Evangelicalism was indeed a product of the age of the Enlightenment, and individual evangelicals were profoundly shaped by many of the secular beliefs and values of their age. But though the Enlightenment ideal of civilization had significant Christian roots, it was cast as a project for this-worldly felicity achievable through the application of reason. Evangelicalism had such different premises and aims—the sinfulness of human nature, eternal salvation—that it could never be entirely comfortable with the "worldliness" of the secular accomplishments of Europe, even if it was often expedient to wrap itself in a *mission civilisatrice* in Africa. But though the links between Christian mission and "civilization" were extremely powerful and consequential, they were historically contingent and subject to strains.[16] The double irony of Christian missions since the early nineteenth century is that they have become progressively estranged from the dominant culture of the societies that sent them, while they have often succeeded in their target areas less for their own reasons than for the reasons of those they have evangelized.

Mudimbe's argument for the colonial character of missions has rather different premises and opens out into a wider spectrum of historical comparisons. Where the Comaroffs argue that evangelical missions serve to sustain modern capitalist colonialism mainly through a myriad of mundane, material practices, Mudimbe sees their colonial character as more general, intrinsic, and connected with their *religious* objective: to refashion inwardly people whom they define as pagans and savages, to rework whole cultures according to divine law. Conversion is control at its most complete, and it is this which makes mission colonialist to the core: "missionary speech is always predetermined, preregulated, let us say *colonized*. . . . The missionary does not enter into dialogue with 'pagans' and 'savages' but must impose the law of God that he incarnates. . . . Consequently 'African conversion', rather than being the outcome of a dialogue—unthinkable *per se*—came to be the sole position the African could take in order to survive."[17] That this view is greatly overstated will be shown repeatedly in the pages that follow. But it is worthwhile to probe the conditions under which it might be more or less true by making some comparisons—a course to which Mudimbe himself, rather against the tenor of his general argument, draws us.

Because Mudimbe's concept of the missionary as the most complete kind of colonialist derives from an "episteme"—marked by the opposition of savage/civilized, pagan/Christian—that is by no means limited to that kind of colonialism which accompanies capitalism and modernity, he is able to give as instances of it three men who belong to very different epochs in the history of mission in Africa. They are Giovanni Romano, who worked in the Lower Congo from 1645 to 1654; the Yoruba Samuel Ajayi Crowther (c. 1806–1891); and the Belgian Placide Tempels, active in Central Africa from 1933 to 1962.[18] These historically wide-ranging comparisons draw attention to aspects of African mission which tend to be neglected when all the emphasis is placed on mission's links with other agencies of modern colonialism. Romano's Catholicism was closer to the Middle Ages than the Enlightenment, which places him cognitively much nearer to the BaKongo than a nineteenth-century European missionary could have been;[19] Mudimbe takes this even further with the remark that "as a missionary, [Romano] could have accomplished the same type of work with St. Boniface [c. A.D. 680–754]."[20] Mudimbe's point here, as I take it, is that Boniface's kind of Christianity shared many assumptions with the paganism it opposed and that the work of mission rested on a more even balance of cultural power between evangelist and evangelized than in later times. Perhaps the comparison can be taken even further. As an Anglo-Saxon evangelist to the Friesians and Saxons of Northern Germany, Boniface could preach in virtually his own language to pagans of a cultural background very close to his own—which was also the situation of Crowther in relation to his fellow Yoruba. Is that kind of mission still colonialist or, since Boniface's mission *was* connected with the Frankish colonization of the then still pagan Saxons, was this a different kind of colonialism, something more akin to pre-colonial state formation in Africa? Here rulers were often attracted to the world religions—Islam as well as Christianity—for the cultural support they offered to their attempts to consolidate executive power.[21] In this the recognition of similarity goes the other way too: European medievalists have been struck by the nineteenth-century African parallels to the early "convert kings" of Germanic Europe.[22] Here the argument starts to loop back in Horton's direction, for in these cases conversion tends to be strongly conditioned by the perspectives of the evangelized.[23]

These cross-temporal and cross-cultural comparisons carry several implications: they underscore that synchronic links between missions and colonial orders are contingent; they highlight certain similarities between aspects of mission across large gaps of time and space; and they suggest that any overall mission situation is shaped by those whom a mission seeks to convert as well as by the power behind the mission. If a mission is an aspect of colonialism, then its relationship may fit rather loosely with its secular organs—indeed such looseness is especially characteristic of modern missions. There are three reasons for this, the first two of which are closely related.

The first is that they were not integral organs of the colonial state, unlike Catholic missions under the earlier empires of Spain and Portugal, which justified themselves, at the ideal level, as instruments to promote the spiritual ends of the Church.[24] But since the higher rationale of the later European empires was the secular notion of civilization, colonial states took a more instrumental view of them, using them and supporting them where their activities coincided with colonial *raison d'état,* but keeping them at arm's length or even restricting them if that suited better (as in some Muslim areas of Nigeria). It was the cultural imperatives of British rule in India which first required this "uncoupling" of the Christian and the colonial projects; and it found additional support in the growing secularism of the public cultures of all European countries as the nineteenth century wore on.

The second reason arises from changes in mission itself. "Modern" missions, those of the kind which have so greatly affected contemporary Africa, emerged in the late eighteenth century in Protestant northwestern Europe, and then outside the ranks of the official state churches.[25] They were an outgrowth of the seismic cultural and social shifts which culminated in the industrial revolution and a democratic political order. Their religious roots were in the Evangelical Revival, whose originality lay more in its ethos and organization than in its essentially Reformation theology: "pneumatic" as well as biblical, emotional as well as ascetic, charismatic against formal, popular and individualistic, outgoing rather than "gathered."[26] The missionary societies exemplified a new kind of social action which evangelicalism helped into being, based on voluntary association and the mobilization of public opinion—typically through appeals to a mix of conscience and self-interest—to effect change in the public sphere. Here the great cause was the antislavery movement, in which individual evangelicals were well to the fore, and which led directly to the missionary engagement in West Africa—first in

Sierra Leone (founded by English philanthropists in 1787) and then, following the liberated slaves back to their homelands, to what is now Nigeria.[27] These societies, funded by the subscriptions of thousands of private supporters, took into their evangelistic practice as a normative standard the turning of individuals to Christ ("conversion") which had been enshrined in the spread of evangelicalism at home. While this did not resonate with most African converts, it did mark a stage in the spread of the culture of modernity by promoting the idea that the decisions of individuals are critical in changing social worlds.[28] So successful an innovation was the idea of mission organized by voluntary association that, pioneered outside the establishment, it was soon taken up by evangelicals in the Church of England, who founded the Church Missionary Society (CMS) in 1799, one of whose premier fields is the subject of this book.[29]

The third reason has to do with the recipients of mission, who in the end are the most important of all. The European colonial empires passed, and mission too is transient—for it is either rejected or it passes into a local church—so what endures are its effects on the local religion scene; that is, the further development of a religious history antecedent to it. Just how strongly an existing culture will put its stamp on mission Christianity will depend both on the circumstances of its reception and on the dynamism of its own tradition. In the present case, several factors worked to strengthen the hand of the Yoruba in their encounter with evangelical Christianity. First, the lines of the engagement were established over some fifty years before the British, influential though they were, had established more than a fringe territorial presence in Yorubaland. The CMS mission had to make its way amid a welter of independent polities, often at war with one another, and to operate under terms largely established by them. In this, it was often at odds with other agents of European influence (such as merchants) and could not count on the physical support of the British authorities at Lagos. Second, it faced an indigenous religious culture of unusual vitality, adaptiveness, and tenacity (as is shown in the exceptional extent of its survival in Brazil and Cuba compared with the religions of most other slave groups). Third, it found a doughty rival already in place in the form of an Islam well adapted to local conditions—which gave the Yoruba, to an extent enjoyed by few other African peoples, an effective choice between the two monotheisms. And finally, there was the circumstance, arising from the presence of so many Yoruba ex-slaves in Sierra Leone, that "native agents" were prominent in the mission, its key players in fact, right from the outset. In this too, the Yoruba experience has been atypical. These men were the quintessential cultural middlemen, adapting Christianity and transforming Yoruba identity in a single seamless process.

Of the various interwoven narratives that we have been considering, that of local religious change has to be placed at the core. In spatial terms, this is the site of the action: it is where mission does or does not make a difference, it is where colonialism and capitalism do or do not produce any concrete effects. Theoretically, religion too has to be at the center of the picture; if it is not, then any study of the social influence of missionaries runs the risk of reading like Hamlet without the Prince of Denmark. Yet even the most resolutely local study of Christian conversion should also open out into a consideration of the longest *durée* of all, that of the world religions themselves, those great vehicles of trans-historical memory, ceaselessly re-activated in the consciousness of their adherents. For it is not just the external analyst of missions who may find it illuminating to compare missionaries in Africa such as Romano or Crowther to St. Boniface, but missionaries themselves. A German agent of the CMS likened himself to "Bonifacius" to a his audience in Ibadan in 1854, and an African pastor, William Allen, full of solemn pride at his ordination in 1865, thought back to "the days of good bishop Cyprian," the leader of an earlier African church.[30] These self-reflections, like the many occasions when mission agents called up Biblical precedents for themselves, were not just fragments of Christianity's collective memory but tokens of its historicity, the peculiar cultural principles of its realization in time. Here we are taken back to Fisher's critique of Horton, that in his concern to ground conversion in *African* history, he neglected the specific ways in which it also belonged to Christian or Muslim stories. If a metaphor is needed, our history in concrete terms is less like a chain or a ladder, whose links or steps represent phases of economic, cultural, and political change which all correspond, than a multi-colored woolen cord, with component fibers of different lengths—Yoruba, colonial, Christian, and other—that give it structure by pulling both together and against one another.

ACTS OF THE APOSTLES

All missionary societies require their agents in the field to keep them informed by means of letters and reports. What makes the CMS archive an especially rich source is that for most of the nineteenth century its agents were also expected to write journals or "journal extracts" for dispatch to its headquarters at Salisbury Square in London. Here they were circulated among the members of the so-called Parent Committee to inform its policy decisions and were edited and excerpted for publication in the periodicals through which the CMS kept in touch with its friends and subscribers at home and around the world. The system was settled by the 1830s, when the efficient Dandeson Coates was the lay secretary, reached its peak during the years when the Rev. Henry Venn was clerical secretary (1841–1873), and resulted in a much fuller documentation for the CMS than for its evangelical siblings, the Baptist, the London, and the Wesleyan Methodist missionary societies. Though it was apparently never specified in a general regulation, what was wanted comes out clearly in Coates's letter to a missionary off to New Zealand in 1832:

9

> Of all the circumstances that occur under your observation, those most especially which depict the Native Character, and the tenor of all your conversations and intercourse with the Natives, let a faithful and minute Journal be constantly kept and transmitted to us. Such Journals are the ground work of future suggestions and plans for yourselves and other labourers in the field. Without them we should not know accurately the state of the Mission: and without the habit of this observing and recording what happens, you would yourselves often be ignorant of your own position.[31]

Yet the CMS wanted more than an accurate ethnography of the mission field. This external gaze had to be complemented by an internal one, consonant with evangelicalism's concern for the Christian's state of religious *feeling*. As the clerical secretary exhorted a missionary to India in 1834:

> Let us learn, from your Journals, all your views, all your feelings; we cannot tell how things are without full Journals; and do not fear writing under the idea that you are telling us the same thing over and over again; we need that if nothing else is to hand.[32]

These journals are sometimes just that—full day-by-day accounts of a missionary's activities and impressions, such as Henry Townsend's account of his first exploratory visit to Abeokuta from Sierra Leone, but mostly they are "journal extracts." Though varying in length and quality, these are documents that typically run to some twenty to thirty foolscap pages, with perhaps two or three entries a week, covering a period of three or six months. The exact conditions of production of these journal extracts are elusive; they must have been written up from a prior record such as an actual journal, but of these none has survived.[33] No doubt the choice of entries was governed by what was felt to be particularly interesting, so their overall effect must be to make mission life sound more eventful than it really was. Daniel Olubi complains in one of his earliest letters of "want of suitable matters to write about," and J. A. Lahanmi writes frankly in 1884 that "one's effort to write a journal is greatly dwindled when he has nothing cheering, nothing of success to say—so is the case with me when I have a general view of my work among the heathen population of this township."[34] Clearly, the composition of these journals was a literary accomplishment, as well as the principal means by which one's labors would be judged. The German missionary Charles Gollmer praises his Yoruba scripture readers for their "little weekly journals" (these must have been the raw material for the worked-up journal extracts), which sounds as if he exercised some supervision over them, but in general it is unlikely (and in most cases it was impossible) that African-written journals were supervised by the senior Europeans.[35] On the other hand, we know that in the 1880s the African agents in Ibadan were helping one another prepare their journals for dispatch to London.[36]

Besides journals, there are letters, "annual letters" and (in a handful of cases) private diaries. The letters in the archive are predominantly from Europeans, since it was mostly with them that the secretaries in London corresponded on personnel, financial, and personnel matters. By the late 1850s "annual letters"—reports on each agent's work over the past year—had come in: at first to no set format, but soon on a standard four-page form, with a section for a statistical return of the station. When in the late 1860s European agents were forced to withdraw to Lagos, they discontinued writing journals, and thereafter only African agents wrote them, continuing in some cases till after 1900. By then, several circumstances were making them redundant: communications with London were much better; the mission was becoming a church, which the CMS controlled less closely; and minutes of committees and local church councils replaced narratives of missionary activity as the staple of the archive. Published CMS sources add little to these unpublished ones, since mostly they are derived from them.[37] Such published missionary lives as exist only add modest amounts to the information contained in the archive, and above all in the journals.[38]

The journals are the pride of the archive for a final reason, which has already been implied: the bulk of them were composed by African agents of the mission. Of the 86 authors of documents in the CMS archive before 1880, 47 (55 percent) were Africans. Though only some 47 percent of individual documents were written by Africans, a great many of those written by the leading Europeans were short business letters, and I reckon that over 60 percent of journals come from the pens of Africans. After 1880, when Europeans were writing only letters with a few longer reports, some 80 percent of the most valuable material is provided by Yoruba authors. The result is that the student of the Yoruba is in the uniquely fortunate position, compared with other regions of Africa, that the great bulk of his material regarding the initial encounter of religions comes from natives of the society. For these Yoruba missionaries to their fellow Yoruba, writing these journals was not just their literary apprenticeship. They were the first works of the modern Yoruba intelligentsia, which opened up into a diverse literature of cultural self-reflection that continues vigorously down to the present.

These journals need to be read in two complementary ways: as sources of information about the world which produced them and as narratives which are of intrinsic interest. Of the latter, more shortly. The information contained in the CMS archive falls under four main headings: the activities, and particularly the evangelistic encounters with non-Christians, of the missionaries themselves; the life of the Yoruba Christian congregations, of which the missionaries had pastoral charge; the broader social setting, that is, the towns and villages where the mission operated; and the political situation throughout the region, where frequent wars affected mission activity.[39] While the great value of the CMS archive for all aspects of Yoruba history has long been recognized, so far more use has been made of it as a source for political and (recently) socio-economic history, rather than where its main intrinsic strength lies, which is for what it contains about religion.[40] Yet it is just here that the reportage of the CMS journalists must be most suspect. So how far can the journals be trusted?

A hermeneutic of deep suspicion can hardly be more appropriate than where virtually all the evidence about one religion comes from its sworn enemy, and all the testimony of religious encounter comes from one of the parties to it. Still, even in this extreme situation—actually quite common in the history of Christian mission[41]—there are promising precedents: two detailed and sympathetic studies of European heresy are based entirely on the records of Catholic inquisitors dedicated to its extirpation.[42] The least of our problems is the expression of robust prejudice, more than enough to upset the ecumenically correct, such as the frequent description of Muslims (always "Mohammedans") as "followers of the false prophet" or of *orişa* priests as "deceivers of the people." Here at least we know where we are. The real challenge is to allow for the effects of the missionaries' selective interest in what they saw, the rubrics governing their reportage, and the psychological, even ontological, assumptions that lay behind them.

The most far-reaching of these was a syndrome of values which marked the outlook of evangelical missionaries on "other cultures." The implied irony here is deliberate, since the point is that they did not recognize them as *cultures* in our sense. In this they were impeded by the mix of individualism and Christian universalism, underpinned by associationist psychology, which they brought to their task. Holding that all individuals, as children of God, were equally capable of salvation, they could not but think that if the Bible and the Holy Spirit, the supremely powerful joint means of salvation, became available to those "in darkness," they must have their due effect. If they did not, some allowance might be made for the inherited drag of the past (e.g., the negative effects of the slave trade); but they saw "heathenism" almost as a kind of absence, not as something with a durability of its own, embedded in an all-encompassing system of thought, style, and ethos.[43] In a nutshell, what they lacked was any concept of "culture." Without such a holistic view of what they were up against, they did not feel that there was any organizing principle that they needed to understand as a means to break its hold over those whom they wished to convert.[44] If this inability to conceive of the cultural other as a whole went for the Europeans, the situation hardly arose for African missionaries. Despite their experience of estrangement and their sense of religious difference, they were still so much "of" their society that, like insiders, they tended to see it in part rather than as a whole viewed from the outside.

So what were the effects for the representation of indigenous Yoruba religion in the CMS journals? What is missing are precisely the kinds of data that are deemed essential for a modern ethnographic study of religion: "thick" descriptions of rituals, extensive vernacular texts, exegeses of myths and symbols, etc. Instead, what we learn about indigenous religion comes in the form of fragmentary observations that are often linked to the intervening presence of the evangelist himself. Yet despite the obvious drawbacks of information of this kind, it does permit an account of Yoruba religion that comes closer to its mundane reality than many modern anthropological studies which rely heavily on the culturally dense material provided by *orisa* festivals, Ifa texts, and the normative exegesis of local experts.[45] For it provides us with (1) a very large number of observations of (2) religion in daily contexts of use, (3) made by men who (unlike anthropologists) had lived long years in the communities they described and had a routine familiarity with their ways; and all this (4) at a time when "Yoruba traditional religion" was less precisely *that* than part of the communal furniture, an omnipresent facility which nearly everyone turned to for protection and empowerment. Moreover, (5) the data was collected under broadly similar rubrics over many decades in several communities which varied in the specific detail of their cults, so that comparisons over space and time can do much both to check bias and to give a context to individual cases.

Much of what we learn about *orisa* cults occurs in narratives of religious encounter, and is thus combined both with recapitulations of the missionaries' arguments against them and with reports of the pagans' responses to them. The careful reader must never forget that these often vivid reports have transmuted the original open-ended dialogues into an essentially monologic form, where the narrator gives himself the last word. The poetics of this I will consider shortly; here the issue is how far this has affected the evidential value of the narratives. If we can make a distinction between contextual information and the reported voices of others, the latter are no doubt more problematic, because there is always a potential motive to justify oneself by distorting the voice of an opposed other. So we may well doubt whether the missionaries "won" arguments with pagans as often as they appear to have done. The best grounds for thinking that a real degree of multivocality is preserved within these highly interested texts is that the reported objections of pagans to Christian arguments often seem so intelligible and cogent. A more subtle problem with the journal narratives as evidence of pagan opinion is that they usually derive from verbal exchanges initiated by missionaries. While such discursive explicitness comes easily to the professionals of a scriptural, conversionist religion, it must to some extent distort the outlook of the lay adherents of a religion which discouraged it by a norm of ritual secrecy, and to some extent by a reliance on non-verbal means, performance and symbols, to "say" things. It also means that the accounts of traditional belief given by missionaries tend to rely a great deal on those indigenous interlocutors whose own specialism was interpretation, namely *babalawo,* or diviners—with long-term consequences for how "Yoruba traditional religion" has come to be viewed.[46]

A final indication that the journals have real integrity as records of religious encounter is that sometimes they do, as it were, speak against their authors. Since the missionaries wanted to vindicate themselves as evangelists, it is impressive that they often record the hostility, indifference, or mockery with which their preaching was received, and casually disclose their own responsibility for some of those responses (e.g., their uninvited intrusion on domestic rituals or harsh denunciation of *oriṣa* to their devotees' faces). They wanted to record success, but repeatedly they had to acknowledge their slow rate of progress and the difficulties they faced: these were, after all, things that the CMS authorities much wanted to know. The speculative character of the reasons that they gave is sometimes so transparent that we are free, from other evidence they provide, to assess them for ourselves.

When we move from a concern to extract information from the journals about the world they represent there to a concern with their qualities as composed texts, we do not thereby abandon a historical and anthropological inquiry for some post-modernist literary project where nothing exists beyond the text, of which an infinite number of "readings" is possible. The relationship between the text and the world, between writing and living, remains crucial. But this is now to be examined from the opposite end, in terms of the links leading forward from the text to the world it goes to shape, rather than those that lead back from the text to the world it represents. The journals achieve this through being narratives: stories of missionary activity, which gain a larger significance from being anchored outside the immediate context both retrospectively (in terms of historical antecedents, both personal and Biblical) and prospectively (in terms of their hopes and intentions for the future). They relate to the process of mission itself in the manner of a synecdoche: they represent episodes of mission both as things in themselves and at the same time, if more implicitly, as segments of, or models for, the whole intended process. In recounting these episodes and setting them in a longer time span, their authors confirm their own agency as missionaries and push forward the practical project of mission: telling becomes doing.

The generic character of the CMS journals is well brought out by comparing them to another form of writing by mission agents. These are the private diaries kept by a handful of Africans, which share the daily entry format of the journals but were not written for others to read, so are barely even a genre, insofar as that term refers to conventions which enable an author to meet the "patterned expectancy" of an audience.[47] Here is an example in paraphrase, one week in the life of Oyebode, a young Ibadan schoolteacher, in 1877:

AUGUST 27. Heard that the chiefs are fighting with the *Arẹ* [head-chief of Ibadan]. Mr Peeler [a Sierra Leonian returnee] came to ask the price of Mr Olubi's colt.

AUGUST 28. Olubi [leader of the mission] came over with the *Balogun* of Atadi [an Egba chief]. Made heaps in farm and planted them with tobacco.

A rumour circulated of the Ijebu kidnapping people in the Ibadan farms, but it was only two men fighting.

AUGUST 29. Went to see Akiele, Oni and others [Christians].

AUGUST 30. Thursday evening service, sermon from I Sam. 4:10–11. Asked his father [Kukomi, the Christian lay leader] for a "dry tree" [to make planks?] and "begged" him for Saka [by his name a Muslim]. A man hurt himself falling out of a tree.

AUGUST 31. Went to Kudeti [the mother church of Ibadan, where Olubi was pastor] for prayer meeting. Mrs Olubi made a jumper for Adegunju. Laperi came. Rain in evening.

SEPTEMBER 1. Worked in farm. Went with Samuel Johnson [catechist at Oyebode's church] to see Ogunola [powerful woman; a wife of the Arẹ?] who gave them some dried meat, while the Arẹ gave one head of cowries. The Egba [with whom Ibadan was sliding into war] said to be making canoes to escape. An Egba slave, escaped to Ibadan, said they were running short of provisions, and that many others would follow.

SEPTEMBER 2. At Sunday service, Johnson preached from II Sam. 10:15–16. "Orisa Ogiyan day [one of the main festivals of Ibadan]: joy and merriment pervade the town."[48]

When this is compared with almost any of the journals, several differences stand out: the prosaic quality of the entries—rumors of war, visits of friends, exchanges of presents, work on his farm, common mishaps, the weather; their lack of complete intelligibility (because entirely self-addressed); and the absence of any overall narrative. In fact, this diary might be considered a perfect example of "chronicle," where events are recorded as they occur, day by day or year by year, without any attempt to impose any longer-term meaningful configuration upon them. It has been argued that, as such, chronicle is closer to human life than narrative, since narrative imposes a pattern on events which chronicle leaves as raw material. But that would imply that the imaginative configuration of events over time—the essence of narrative—is not itself part of life, something integral to action.[49] That it hardly figures in the diary entries is due partly to their format and partly to their purpose. Narrative depends on being able to take a retrospective vantage point, but the diary form makes narratives of all but the shortest time span difficult to achieve. Even so, these brief diary entries contain some of the basic elements of narrative configuration: the rumor of Ijebu kidnapping is later disconfirmed by the news that it was only men fighting; the report of what is happening with the Egba is knitted together with fragments of cause and expectation. It is significant, however, that these entries both refer to reports and interpretations of action from elsewhere, already narrated. But even Oyebode's terse, unelaborated references to visits and presents point to long-term social relationships. Here the diary seems intended less as a representation than as an instrument of his life, a mnemonic aid to the continuous narrative self-monitoring that effective human lives require and which, perhaps, evangelicalism especially imposes on its adherents.

The journals read on the surface like a much expanded version of the diary quoted above, but they were written for an audience with no privileged local knowledge, and they were much more concerned with the public than the private life of their authors: in particular they were meant to show him acting and thinking like a missionary. So there is a high proportion of entries which describe episodes of proactive evangelism and a general tendency to increase their significance by presenting them in the light of the long-term project of the mission or of relevant Biblical precedents. The aspiration to take a longer view that the daily entry format allowed was clearly expressed by S. W. Doherty, an African evangelist, as he began copying out his chosen journal extracts at the end of the year:

> A year of toil and labour has now come to a close. The merchant man takes stock of the goods he has in his store; the bookkeeper sits down quietly before his employer and begins to cast up account for the year, to see whether there is profit or loss; and thus also the toilsome farmer, having reaped, reckons up carefully what the produce of his farm would bring him. . . . Much more earnest would they be who have the cure of souls.[50]

There was a marked tendency to make the entry for one day stand as an exemplary narrative vignette of mission. An English agent, Joseph Smith, at one point explicitly adopted the practice of giving his entries a title such as might be found in a missionary magazine, such as "Go and do likewise" or "A voice from the reign beyond."[51] Though this did not become standard practice, it is significant that years later an African agent independently tried the same device, with headings like "Return of a lost sheep."[52] By narrating their experiences in these terms to a readership familiar with the Bible, they both confirmed their identity as missionaries by and assimilated their actions to historically given templates of missionary action.

In reading the journals we often get a sense of the author straining to lengthen the narrative span, thus breaking free from the limitations imposed by the daily entry format. Sometimes this seems to happen almost spontaneously, when an incident or episode belongs to a sequence which runs over several days or weeks. Here a narrative structure emerges, partly from the author's growing hindsight, partly from his sense of likely outcome. Oyebode's diary furnishes two striking instances: the harrowing story of his wife's death from the effects of childbirth, which for a while excludes everything else; and the story of a fight which breaks out in an Ibadan compound, leading to a man's death and the execution of the killer a week later.[53] This episode was so traumatic that he noted the text for the next service after it was over, a precedent from Scripture: "Master, carest not that we perish? . . . And the wind ceased, and there was a great calm" (Mark 4:35–41). Journeys and evangelistic tours (known as "itinerations") provided welcome material since their movement over space directly evokes a longer time span. Another way of lengthening the time span was to draw, not on the author's own current experience, but on memories of time past, stretching behind immediate events like the tail of a comet: the historical background to some incident, testimonies of past deliverances given at a prayer meeting, an inquirer's story of her religious quest, memories triggered by a visit to a ruined town site, the antecedents of a quarrel among the chiefs, the brief biography of a deceased convert.

The journals sought not only to represent the course of mission, but also to convey a conviction (which often flew in the face of the evidence) that the missionaries controlled events. Narrative, which is the very embodiment of discursive control since the narrator is free to decide how it will end, then becomes a kind of down payment on the mission's eventual success in practice. After their initial, naïve enthusiasm ("Sunrise in the Tropics") had receded, the CMS missionaries knew they were in for a long haul. Their journals did not deny their difficulties and the resistance that they met, their own recurrent feelings of failure and despondency, but sought to redeem them through narratives of being tested by suffering, of errors corrected, of the precedents for hope and perseverance and so forth. Not for nothing was "For who hath despised the day of small things" (Zechariah 4:10) such a favorite text with missionaries: by identifying the small struggling communities of Yoruba Christians with the Jewish Temple in its reconstruction, they asserted the enactment of a divinely mandated success story.

The African agents of the mission were particularly attracted to the use of Biblical precedents as instruments of discursive control. They applied them both to themselves (St. Paul, of course, serving as the exemplary missionary)[54] and, more instructively, to various Yoruba types: Herod,[55] Felix,[56] Cornelius, and (above all) Nicodemus. Here discourse might open straight into evangelistic practice and not be confined to the journal reports of it. Thus Samuel Doherty, on tour in the Oke Ogun, concluded an encounter with a *babalawo* by recounting to him the story of how Nicodemus—the type of a sympathizer of high religious status—came to see Jesus (John 3:1–13).[57] At Ibadan, whose chiefs usually took little interest in Christianity, James Okuseinde was once surprised by the attendance of one influential warrior who said that he would have become a Christian if his position had allowed it. "Then I related to him the story of [the centurion] Cornelius [Acts 10]. May his eyes of understanding be opened that he may see the way of salvation."[58] But often there was not this degree of hope, and it had to be enough to note that the prophets and apostles of old had also faced disappointment. Year after year Samuel Pearse had no option but to record the slow progress of the Gospel at Badagry, especially among the indigenous Egun people. In 1859 he turned to the book of Isaiah to convey their indifference: the house of God was deserted "as a cottage in a vineyard, as a lodge in a garden of cucumbers."[59] Nine years later, he concluded his annual letter with the words of Simon Peter: "Like the Galilean fishermen, we have toiled all night and caught nothing."[60] Yet even here, amid seeming failure, the text has a redemptive potential: the miraculous haul of fishes was in the offing.

A good many of the journal entries report events which fall into one of two classes: episodes (often of local politics or religious practice) which the author has witnessed or learned from eyewitnesses, and religious encounters which the author himself initiated in the course of his evangelism. These tend to employ different means of narrative control. In the first, where the writer has had no hand in the shaping of the events themselves, control is asserted purely in the *telling* of them, typically by the device of "sealing" the narrative with a text or prayer which judges and/or propounds a scenario of redemption. So "How are the dark places of the earth full of the habitations of cruelty" (adapted from Psalm 74:20) closes Samuel Johnson's account of the deposition and murder of Efunsetan, the women's chief of Ibadan, as well as James White's account of the killing of a woman accused of witchcraft at Ota.[61] Another common seal text—"And men loved darkness rather than light because their deeds were evil" (John 3:19)—again employs that cardinal missionary metaphor, of darkness versus light, which was so often taken up in the ejaculatory prayers which serve a similar function. Charles Phillips the elder ended a very discouraged assessment of the prospects at Ijaye with a prayer for "His happy period of time when the people of Ijaye will be better enlightened."[62] "May the Lord open their eyes and hearts to hear the Gospel," "Oh Lord, open then the eyes and understanding of this people to know thee the only true God" and the like are so common that referencing them seems almost superfluous.[63] These prayers of the African clergy for the "enlightenment" (*ọlaju*) of their compatriots would be so well fulfilled that this concept generated the ideology of progress and development that is general among the modern Yoruba.[64]

In the second class of narratives, where the religious encounters were set up by the missionaries themselves, the telling and the doing are much more closely intertwined. Where (as often) Biblical texts are quoted, they are now likely to be internal to the encounter described, rather added later in the recounting. Here is another example from Okuseinde's journal:

> On a visit of condolence to an Ibadan chief, he meets the head of the Ogboni cult and several elders. They start to speak reproachfully of Mele [a recent convert] "that he who had been a great man in the town and held an important position" should have turned Christian. Okuseinde responds by praying *Ki Ọlọrun k'o la wọn l'oju* [That God would open their eyes] and quoting Jeremiah 9:23–24, "Let not the wise man glory in his wisdom,

neither let the mighty man glory in his might." At this they say they won't abuse the Christians again.[65]

This narrative is so pared down to Okuseinde's central point that we may doubt how full an account it is of the encounter which gave rise to it. But what does come over clearly as a hard external given is the attitude of the Ibadan chiefs to the conversion of a prominent man, and, behind that, the radical opposition between two sets of values, amply confirmed by other testimony. It is this feature of religious encounter which gives rise to what we may treat as the archetype of this kind of engaged narrative: a tripartite structure in which a missionary initiative leads to a local response, which the missionary picks up on with further comment, invitation, encouragement, rebuke, prayer, and so forth, to move things further in a Christian direction. An example from Daniel Olubi (who was especially fond of this format in his journals):

> He visits some farms near Ibadan, one with twelve slaves owned by the chief *babalawo*. [Evidently he hoped that slaves would be more inclined to hear the Word than their warlord masters]. The head slave listened to his address, and in reply quoted a proverb: *Ẹnit' o mọ ọna Ọfa, ko gbọ 'fa; ẹnit' o gbọ 'fa, ko mọ ọna Ọfa* [Our masters who can hear, don't want to; we slaves who do want to hear, aren't able to]. Olubi concludes with their prayer [which he implies was also his own]: "God have mercy on us and grant us ways to come to thee."[66]

The dialectical structure of such little stories shows them to be discursive models for the entire missionary project as well as small moments of it. Here discourse and practice come close, though they can never be merged. Mission was intended to be governed by a script, ultimately derived from Scripture, but it also had to respond to practical contingencies that could not be controlled. The reassertion of discursive control in the narratives served to restore faith in mission itself.

So far, attention has focused on two aspects of the archive: the information contained in the journal narratives, and the generic conventions of the narratives themselves. A third feature needs to be briefly highlighted: the multiple voices of the various authors. Partly these arise from race and cultural background—whether African or European, English or German, Saro or home-grown Yoruba, Egba or Oyo—partly from what can only be ascribed to personality or individual interest, such as (to name three of the most noteworthy African writers) Samuel Johnson's fascination with the history of his people, James White's sensitivity to the importance of art in Yoruba life, or W. S. Allen's ear for the stories of ordinary Ibadan folk. How personal interests intersected with the need to convey a given reality within the narrative form required by the mission is best explored through the several accounts of one episode in the life of a Yoruba town.

Its subject is the brief career of Akere, a "prophetess" of the *orìṣa* Yemoja, the goddess of the river Ogun at Abeokuta, where the mission then had its main station. She appeared around the middle of 1855, inspired to offer healing and fertility through the medium of water blessed in Yemoja's name. This attracted large crowds, some from towns many miles away, who continued flocking to her for several months until the chiefs withdrew their support in March 1856. These bare facts of her career appear in four separate accounts, two from European missionaries (J. A. Maser, a German, and Isaac Smith, who was English) and two from Africans (Samuel Crowther, junior, and Thomas King, a Saro but of local origin), and there does not seem to be any reason for doubting them, as far as they go.[67] Though the episode is exceptional, in the sense that nothing quite like this occurs elsewhere in the CMS journals, there is nothing in it which is culturally implausible. In fact the closest parallel within Yoruba religious history that I can think of is the Aladura "revival" which took place at Ilesha in 1930–1931: here too an inspired figure—Christian this time—sanctified the water of a stream and drew large crowds of people in search of healing and fertility.[68] All four authors tell the main story in one chunk, as the topic of one day at the height of the craze, not through fragments told passim over many days. Maser's account is briefest and the least wrought as a narrative, but it has the main points of the others: the priestess a stranger of obscure origin; large crowds over many months; many from other towns, including some Christians; the blessing of water to give fertility and healing; much money collected and profits for her chiefly supporters. The accounts of the Africans, King and Crowther, are richest in detail—the priestess's name, more about the ritual of healing itself, a fuller picture of who attended—and each in a separate entry a few months later recorded her decline and fall.[69]

When we move from the facts of Akere's career to their interpretation, the accounts of the witnesses become more speculative and more diverse, because more dependent on their respective subject positions. They concur that a big factor in her success was her backing by influential chiefs who got revenue from it, but they do not tell us who or how. Crowther elaborates by arguing that the cessation of war had taken away the chiefs' revenue from selling slaves, while the new produce trade was not yet fully established: an explanation (and implicit projection) which fitted neatly with the official CMS line on how civilization would come to West Africa. Smith draws the naïve inference from the mercenary side of Akere's activities that "the system of idolatry" must have been "tottering" if its devotees needed to be supported by such means. He concludes by referring to Ogunbona, the mission's staunchest supporter among the chiefs, who was energetic in promoting cash crops for export and had refused to go and witness Akere's healings. Maser handles the embarrassment of the participation of some lay Christians with the suggestion that it would do good in the long run, because she would be shown up to be an impostor. What is common to all these interpretations, despite their differences, is that they give additional significance to the episode by the tendentious projection of desired outcomes.

Any event's significance is enhanced by looking backward as well as forward. Here King and Crowther differ significantly from their European colleagues, in ways that are linked with the fact that they take Akere more seriously as a religious figure and condemn her more roundly. The Europeans incline to treat the whole thing as not worth serious attention, as if it was just what might be expected of heathenism: Maser calls her a "false prophetess"— a conventional dismissal—and Smith emphasizes the irrationality of belief in her ("the great superstition of the day, viz. the absurdities of Yemoja"). The Africans portray her as more actively fraudulent: King castigates her as "this public cheat," and Crowther as a "daring impostor," imposing on the "stupidity and credulity" of the public. Crowther's indignation must owe something to professional rivalry: the dispensary he ran in Abeokuta lost many clients because of Akere's activities. Yet he also gives her an ambiguous compliment when he writes: "Little did we expect to hear of another Pool of Bethesda in these our days." The allusion is to John 5:2–9, where Christ cures a cripple who was unable to reach the healing waters of the pool when they surged. Obviously he intends to be ironical, but Akere is still clearly given a *religious* precedent (and there is no suggestion in the Gospel that the Bethesda water cure was not genuine). The further point of the analogy, as in many later analogies drawn by missionaries (especially the African ones) between Yoruba pagan and ancient Jewish practice, is to argue that the old religion would surely lead on to the new, the Yoruba/ Jewish to the Christian.

King uses the past in a different way from Crowther, but to a complementary practical effect. He concludes his account by observing how "verifying" in relation to the whole episode is a Yoruba proverb: *Otito de oja, o ku ta; owo l'owo li a nra eke* ("When truth is offered for sale in the market, it finds no buyer; but lies are bought with cash in hand"). Now while the African journal writers often quote Yoruba proverbs, this one is here used in an unusual way: to seal the narrative, the function for which Bible texts or prayers were normally used. In this King seems to be implying two things. The obvious one is that proverbs, nuggets of ancestral wisdom, can be as much vessels of perennial moral truth as Biblical texts. Less obvious and more significant is that, in using Yoruba wisdom against Yoruba heathenism—something that only a Yoruba evangelist could have the knowledge and nerve to do—King implies that the new religion can be continuous with the best of the Yoruba past, not merely a break with it. Thus the Akere episode is settled in relation to precedents as well as to consequences, extending the narrative range of the journal entries well beyond the events of 1855–1856. The precedents offer two opposed relations of past and present which effective mission must always find ways of combining: the continuity implied by King's Yoruba proverb and the change suggested by Crowther's Biblical analogy.

THE TALE TO BE TOLD

In any work of history or anthropology there has to be an adjustment, or better an affinity, between the aims of the writer and the character of the data. The historian tends to be more constrained since he cannot usually manufacture data through questioning people, but has to depend on what the past has left him to work from. My aim in what follows is an account that places the encounter of religions at its center and then grounds it as deeply as possible in the diversity of nineteenth-century Yoruba experience.

Any investigation of Yoruba religious change has to deal with an awkward asymmetry between the stages of its actual development and the stages of our coming to know it. As in other instances of "culture contact" between Europeans and indigenous peoples, the way we are inclined to tell the story— first Yoruba society/culture in its anterior state, then the European impact leading to colonization, and finally a synthesis in which the indigenous and the introduced come to some kind of terms—does not correspond to the order in which we come to know it. Unless there are pre-contact documents, monuments, or artifacts, the main bulk of the evidence of the anterior state must be documents of the contact itself, produced by the European intruders (or, advantageously in the Yoruba case, their local associates). This is where historical inquiry has to start, working its way back to reconstruct the actual sequence from pre- to post-contact. It is in the truest sense a scandal, particularly for members of the colonized society, that the primary means to know the pre-contact past are documents arising from their contact with or conquest by outsiders. This dependence may be reduced by the evidence of oral traditions or modern ethnographic data; but as collected these are still strictly post-contact data, and their relationship to the pre-contact past will always be problematic. *All* knowledge of the past rests on inference, but the lines of inference are shorter—the risks of anachronism less—for the period of contact, where for the first time there is abundant contemporary evidence. This, then, has to be the first point of access to the knowledge of the pre-contact past.

So historical anthropology faces a situation where what it chiefly *wants* to do—write orthogenous histories of those peoples which Europe first encountered in its imperial expansion—is most problematic; while the kind of history most compatible with the evidence—because it goes with the grain of it—is one of European intrusion. In the literature as a whole, the result is a spectrum of differing balances struck between the two extreme options— histories of Third World regions or peoples in which a varying prominence is given to the impact of European power. Toward one pole stand such works as, say, Wallace's *Death and Rebirth of the Seneca* or Sahlins's corpus on Hawaii, where Anglo-American settlers or Captain Cook come in as powerful agents but whose essential subject matter is still the transformation and/or survival of local cultures.[70] Toward the other pole might be placed the Comaroffs' study of the Tswana, which constructs its narrative as the working out, on a South African terrain, of a British project: we have "British Beginnings" and "Africa Observed" (by the British) before we get to "African Worlds," and then "Through the Looking Glass" (the passage of missionaries to "the field") before the British and the Tswana finally start their "long conversation."[71] This narrative balance is appropriate for a study which takes "the colonization of consciousness" as its central focus. For the problem that the evidence is biased toward what Europeans did and thought is soon compounded by another, of the construction of the narrative. All these situations involve the confluence of two narratives: one of outreach from the colonizing center, one of a local history in the colonized periphery. The site of their confluence is the periphery, which is where the subsequent narrative proceeds, whether its major theme is conceived of as incorporation (into the world system), domination, penetration (of capitalism) on the one side, or as inculturation (into local systems of meaning), domestication, selective adaptation on the other. Whatever is selected as the narrative's major theme, and for whatever reason—availability of evidence, theoretical predilection, intellectual fashion, and so forth—it will not be very plausible if a good deal of the other perspective is not brought in too. But the fact remains that it is usually harder to tell the tale from the local side, because that means starting it from before the initial contact and, in Walter Benjamin's phrase, "brushing against the grain" of most of the evidence. The student of the Yoruba is in the fortunate position that the writings of the African agents of the CMS mission enable him to go a long way in doing that.

The pre-contact baseline of an indigenous society's history is commonly presented in a highly static way, as a given structure or system of categories or *way* of life; if there are processes, they tend to be cyclical or normal to the system, its reproduction or expansion. Change, or at least the changes which become the master themes of later history, is regarded as starting with the European impact, however inflected it is by indigenous cultural categories. Several reasons may foster such a view: the evidence may actually suggest this; there may not be enough temporally specific evidence to present it otherwise than in very general terms; endogenous developments—if there is evidence of them—may pale into historical insignificance after the far-reaching effects of colonial impact; the identification of the post-contact period as one of progress, modernity, and so forth may, in retrospective contrast, make it seem like that; the idealization of traditional culture by indigenes or its structuralist analysis by anthropologists equally tend to enshrine the static. But in the Yoruba case it would be neither necessary (for lack of evidence) nor justified (since the evidence clearly tells us otherwise) to see things in these terms.

Rather, if we take our cue from the African journal writers who provide most of the evidence, we are soon brought to realize that our attempt to understand does not start at the beginning, but has to plunge *in medias res.* Putting it another way, we come in on people in a predicament, in the middle straits of something.[72] It is the vision with which Dante begins his great Christian epic—"Half way along the path of this life, I realized in a dark wood that I had lost the straight way."—but the essential point is of theoretical value, since it underscores so strongly the basic conditions of human agency. Where we come in on the middle of individual lives—as the historian does in relation to the writers of the CMS journals, and they in relation to the Yoruba people whose lives they give us access to—we cannot understand them unless that we pick up on their pasts. The concept of predicament also implies that we regard them as exercised about their futures, about their goals, and about the means to attain them. John Bunyan's *The Pilgrim's Progress* likewise starts with a man who is walking "through the wilderness of this world"; he lies down and dreams; he sees a man who cries out "What shall I do?" Bunyan's hero, like our Yoruba evangelists, recognizes himself in scriptural precedents, so the grounding of all projects in memory, where every individual's subjectivity is constructed of an arch linking past and future, is thus forcefully placed at the center of our attention.[73] And beyond this, there is the collective dimension, since the memories of individuals must always be anchored in their sense of belonging to social groups, and of participating in the public and shared experiences of a wider community.

These remarks have a particular application to the evidence of the Yoruba agents of the CMS. They were always aware that they stood in the middle of a process of tumultuous, unprecedented change, of which they personally were conspicuously victims, emblems, and interpreters. The first wave of them were "liberated Africans" returned from Sierra Leone (Saro), themselves or their parents earlier taken into slavery in the course of the warfare which engulfed the Yoruba heartland in the 1820s. Memories of this time break into their narratives of later experiences, as when the catechist James Barber, traveling down to Lagos in 1855, passed through Iperu, the place where he had been first held as a slave after the destruction of his own town; he is led to reflect on the value of slaves.[74] T. B. Wright's recollection was triggered by a Sunday School outing to the Lagos beach, when his having to settle the children in the boat "called to my mind those afflicting times, when we were shipped in the same way intending to be carried to Brazil from whence we had no hope of return."[75] Personal dislocation and the loss and re-formation of communities were such widespread experiences that they came readily into the life stories of ordinary people and were exploited by missionaries to support their own views as to how things should be remade for the future. And beyond the reach of these personal memories were stories of the "old days," running back to the time when Oyo was at its apogee under King Abiodun and the slave trade with the Europeans was uncontested.[76]

The real tale to be told, then, does not have a European beginning or start with the intrusion of Europeans, even though it mainly depends on evidence from European sources at a point when Euro-Yoruba relations were entering a new and more intimate stage. Those relations had then existed for several hundred years and conditioned Yoruba society in significant ways, even though they were mostly indirect: the physical contact of Europeans and Yoruba had been intermittent and limited to the coast. Bayart's concept of "extraversion" had some application to pre-colonial as well as to post-colonial Africa:[77] one significant effect was that practices by which external culture, whether material or spiritual, might be selectively absorbed according to local agendas were already in place. So although this study deals with the operation of a missionary society in the latter half of the nineteenth century, the eventual focus of the narrative is more on the appropriation than the transmission of its message. The process by which many Yoruba became Christian, or Christianity became a major element in the Yoruba religious repertory, has thus to be placed in the prior development of Yoruba religion itself. As we shall see, processes of religious change, especially some deriving from the prior presence of Islam, were already in train when the missionaries arrived. There too they had to join in ongoing arguments and seek to turn them their way.

The chapters are organized as follows. Chapter 2 ("Yorubaland at War") presents a narrative overview of what might be called the Yoruba "long nineteenth century," the narrative framework for what comes later. At the same time it anticipates its own telos, since its story line is deeply shaped by the authoritative account given of it at the end of the century by our witness-in-chief, the Rev. Samuel Johnson. In Chapters 3 ("Living in an Age of Confusion") and 4 ("Making Country Fashion"), dealing respectively with society and religion, I seek to present the principles of action and thought which generated and animated that history. As much as possible, they are written to convey the sense and flavor of the incidents and episodes reported in their concrete specificity by the CMS journalists, in order to underscore the point that they are primary: they need to be appreciated as evidence for knowing what Yoruba society was before they can be treated as instantiations of a Yoruba culture somehow knowable independently of them. Chapter 5 ("The Mission and the Powers") parallels Chapter 2 in that it is a narrative overview, this time of the political history of the Yoruba Mission between 1845 and 1912 within the context of regional politics. Like Chapter 2, it also serves the reference function of introducing people and places that recur in the later chapters.

Chapters 6–9 at last come to grips with the encounter of religions itself, the substance of the missionary project reviewed in Chapter 5. The fundamental matter, too much taken for granted in a great many mission histories, of exactly what was preached to the heathen and how, is addressed in Chapter 6 ("Preaching the Word"). Here the initial emphasis has to be on the gap between the evangelists and the evangelized: not just their very differing notions about what they took "religion" to be, but their contrary social values and cosmological beliefs, the cross-purposes and misunderstandings evinced in the encounter. Chapter 7 ("Engaging with Islam") takes this further onto a terrain complicated by the mix of agreement and opposition between three religions, and it picks up on the question (broached at the end of Chapter 4) of Christianity's relation to the ongoing dynamic of Yoruba religious change. In contrast, Chapters 8 ("The Path to Conversion") and 9 ("Leaf Becomes Soap") deal with the two sides of how that gap started to be closed: by Yoruba becoming Christians and Christianity becoming Yoruba. But though they stand in dialectical succession to the two preceding chapters, their range is virtually concurrent in time. In this central section, it is important that the reader should hear as much as possible of the voices of our witnesses, not just because their evidence is sometimes problematic, and we sometimes need to weigh their silences and reticences, but also because they were so important as cultural agents themselves in shaping modern Yoruba consciousness. So my preferred mode of composition has been to select those journal entries that served best to point the line of the argument; present them (whether verbatim or in paraphrase) at some length; and then to make the argument largely through their explication: by comment, contextualization, and critical assessment; by drawing out their implications; and by comparing them with other voices in the archive.

In the last two chapters the teleology latent in all the foregoing is at last addressed. In speaking so far of "the Yoruba" as a collective subject with a long pre-contact history, I have adopted a designation that is, strictly speaking, a fiction. For despite the links and affinities which do enable us to treat this group of peoples as a single historical unit, they did not know themselves by a common name—until, that is, they came to adopt the name chosen for them by the founders of the Yoruba Mission. Chapter 10 ("The Making of the Yoruba") is an essay in the intellectual history of the modern Yoruba: it examines how the African agents of the mission succeeded in giving dynamic substance to the notion of a shared Yoruba identity, and that as a direct corollary of the project of Christian evangelism. Finally, Chapter 11 ("Looking Back"), connects the whole history to the present from which it sprang and attempts some assessment of what it means now for the ongoing reality of Yoruba life.

2

YORUBALAND AT WAR

It was in the 1820s that the old order of Yorubaland fell decisively apart, with the accelerated decline of the long-dominant regional power of Oyo and the destruction of many old communities in its wake. One immediate consequence of the wars and raids was the enslavement of tens of thousands of people, some of whom ended up as Christian converts in Sierra Leone. Although the political landscape of Yorubaland was permanently redrawn, none of Oyo's successor states was able for long to erect a stable system of regional power relations around itself—none, that is, except the British in Lagos, a growing presence after midcentury, who finally in the 1890s used their overwhelming force to resolve the stalemate. While it would be an exaggeration to speak of a state of continuous war over the whole country, wars were widespread and sometimes prolonged, if of varying intensity, and hardly anywhere was untouched by them. Some of the most distinctive social forms of the age—the new title system of Ibadan, and the ideal of the "big man" as warrior[1]—were direct adaptations to the saliency of war. War was a prime motor of other social and economic changes.[2] This 70-year period saw the establishment of the missions in Yorubaland. Their presence was an indirect effect of the break-up of the old order, and they were closely implicated in the train of events which led up to the imposition of colonial rule. For the first half-century of the mission, the reality or the possibility of war was a constant backdrop to its activity.

BEFORE THE WARS: OLD YORUBALAND

Yorubaland was a regional system of mostly small polities, among which one, Oyo, or "Yoruba Proper," embracing roughly half the land area and half the population, had long been dominant.[3] It merged into the non-Yoruba areas round its margins, notably the kingdom of Benin to the east, Nupe and Borgu to the north, and the polities of the Ewe-Aja-Fon cluster (including Dahomey) to the west, with all of which the adjacent Yoruba states shared particular trade, religious, or political ties.[4] Yoruba country may be regarded as the central portion of a wider zone extending roughly from the Volta basin in the west to the Niger valley in the east, an *oikoumene* where Ile-Ife carried prestige and there was a diffusion of Yoruba cults such as Ifa and Ogun.[5] This was bounded by the markedly different cultures of the Akan to the west and the Igbo to the east, an area where the cowry became the medium of exchange rather than gold or manillas.[6] Despite their shared linguistic and cultural traits and regard for Ile-Ife as the origin of their most sacred traditions, the speakers of "Yoruba" dialects did not as yet share a common and distinctive name: they knew themselves as Egba, Ijesha, or Awori, or else just by the name of their *ilu*, or "town." Perhaps one reason why there was no name to distinguish Yoruba speakers as such from others was just this combination of more local identities, which sufficed for immediate political purposes, with a wider *oikoumene* of peoples who realized that, despite their language differences, they shared a similar cosmological foundation to their lives. The "Edo speakers" (as we now know them)[7] and the "Gbe speakers" (as it has been proposed to call the Ewe-Aja-Fon group)[8] equally had no overarching identity based on similarity of dialect. What is striking is that, of all these three major language groupings, only the Yoruba have developed a unified ethnic identity based on language. The nature of their engagement with the missions provides a large part of the answer.

The Yoruba-speaking area itself straddled the forest (to the south, and broadening eastward) and the savannah (to the north, but coming closer to the coast in the west).[9] As we shall see, this ecological contrast was to have far-reaching consequences for the political geography of Yorubaland, and so also eventually for the distribution of religious variety. The system of eco-zones reaching from the coastal lagoon belt through rain forest to savannah encouraged a north-south pattern of trade routes for the exchange of the natural products of the different zones. Near the borders of the ecozones or on interstate boundaries, there tended to grow up markets for long-distance trade, such as Ikorodu and Ejinrin on the north shore of the lagoon,

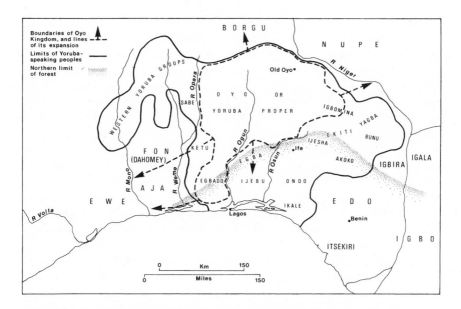

Figure 2.1. Yorubaland in Its Region: Sub-groups and Neighboring Peoples

Apomu and Omirinmirin in the northern forest, and Ogodo on the Niger. States too seem to have clustered near the ecozone boundaries.[10] To the north the desert and to the south the ocean gave access to a sphere of transcontinental trade.

The reasons for the emergence of this regional order by the end of the sixteenth century are sketchy and uncertain, but they surely involved, as with its collapse some three centuries later, some interplay between changed conditions on the coast and in the interior.[11] For its most salient feature was the replacement of Ile-Ife, which had flourished in the forest for several centuries before 1500, by Oyo, situated far to the north with access to the Niger valley, as the dominant Yoruba power. The opening of the Atlantic trade brought new opportunities, which seem to have advantaged smaller kingdoms nearer the coast, such as Ijebu and Owu, at the expense of Ife.[12] Benin extended its influence along the lagoon system to the west, as far as Lagos and the Awori country, as well as among the small kingdoms in the interior to its northwest, for which it was a conduit of the coastal trade.[13] Ilesha, only twenty miles from Ife, grew after 1600 to become the main buffer state between the spheres of Benin and Oyo, forest and savannah.[14] But although Ife shrank to a shadow of what it must have been at its height, it retained its reputation as the scene of the cosmogony and as the entire region's most prestigious sacred center.

Oyo had existed for some centuries before it became the great power of Yorubaland, founded (according to legend) by Oranyan, an Ife prince.[15]

Early in its history it was overshadowed by the Nupe, who around 1500 sacked Oyo-Ile and displaced the capital for several reigns to Igboho, further to the west.[16] But by the early seventeenth century the old capital (strategically nearer the Niger trade routes) was reoccupied, and Oyo entered what Law calls its "imperial period." Since Oyo's power rested on its cavalry, its dominion was largely limited to the open savannah country, where cavalry could operate freely and horses were less prone to disease. To the northeast, Oyo's influence ran some way into Igbomina and the fringes of Ekiti, but here it met counter-influences from Benin, Ijesha, and the Nupe. In general, the forest Yoruba looked toward Benin more than to Oyo,[17] and only the small towns of the Egba to the south were Oyo tributaries.[18] The main direction of Oyo's expansion from its "metropolitan provinces" was to the southwest, where it established colonies among the Egbado and Anago and controlled the trade route to the coast at Ajase (Porto Novo).[19] This was crucial to the basis of state power, since the horses which were imported from the north across the Niger were paid for by the export of slaves (many of whom probably came from the far interior). So Oyo's expansion, though mostly well in the interior, was critically dependent on the Atlantic slave trade, as that burgeoned in the seventeenth and eighteenth centuries.[20] Dahomey, itself a direct supplier to the slave trade, was made tributary by the 1740s, and the *Alafin* Abiodun (1774–1789) extended Oyo's power further among Dahomey's Gbe-speaking neighbours.[21]

The polities of this Yoruba-speaking world varied greatly in both size and structure: from the "mini-states" and village groups of the northeast, southeast, and far west[22] the small kingdoms of Ekiti and the loose confederations of the old Egba; and the middle-sized kingdoms with a focused capital such as Ijesha, Ijebu, or Ondo to the "empire" of Oyo with its vast capital, its heartland comprising many towns organized in provinces, and tributary states beyond. Yet all this variety was built up from a repertory of basic social forms spread throughout the area: nucleated settlements or "towns," households grouped locally in neighborhoods or quarters, lineages with a strong agnatic bias, age- and gender-based associations, societies for special occupational and cultic interests, and leadership positions given public recognition by means of titles.[23] Variation from town to town should be seen more as the contingent responses to varied historical circumstances solidified into local practice than as the outcome of different values. For, as the lineage traditions of long-settled towns show,[24] even before the nineteenth century there was much small-scale migration within Yorubaland; and while this led to much cultural diffusion (of religious cults, of crafts, of titles, etc.) there is no doubt that the migrants came already endowed with the practical knowledge of the same basic social forms.

The foundational concept of Yoruba political sociology was the term *ilu*, commonly translated as "town" or "community." The Yoruba have long been known as an "urban" people, living in large permanent nucleated settlements.[25] But mere size was not the essential thing. The largest towns, such as Ibadan or Abeokuta, which were estimated to have had populations of up to 100,000 in the nineteenth century, were recent products of the wars, and most historic *ilu* were much smaller, in the 5,000–20,000 range. What made a settlement (of whatever size) an *ilu* in the eyes of its citizens was its social quality: it was distinguished from farm settlements (which might be quite large, and people might spend most of their time there) by being the site of their homes, the graves of their forebears, and the festivals of their gods. In English we speak both of "towns" (nucleated settlements) and of "kingdoms" (sovereign territories) in relation to Yoruba realities. But Yoruba did not make this conceptual distinction: like the *polis* of Ancient Greece, an *ilu* was both "town" and "polity," with typically the latter named after the former. The political field of Yorubaland, though involving territories and border posts and "sub-tribal" identities, should still be conceived of as a system of relations between *ilu* as point sources of power, like a galaxy of stars of greater or lesser magnitude with shifting fields of gravitational pull between them.[26]

The political design of a major *ilu* pivoted on the position of its "king" (*ọba*), whose very title often designated him as the symbol and possessor of the town, like *Aseyin* of Iseyin or *Elẹkọle* of Ikole. A fully-blown *ọba* was a quasi-divine personage, and one of his essential functions was to mediate with the deities (*orişa*) to ensure his people's well-being. The king's palace (*afin*) was ideally the focus of the town's layout; a complex of buildings, courtyards, and shrines set in an extensive walled enclosure, from which the king rarely emerged except for major festivals. The *afin* had a large resident population of royal wives, slaves, messengers, priests, eunuchs, functionaries, strangers, and other dependents.[27] The title of the Oyo king was *Alafin* ("Lord of the palace"). In what is probably the most formally perfect town layout to be seen today—that of Ilesha, which tradition holds was modeled on Oyo-Ile's—the roads radiate out from the *afin* like the spokes of a wheel and continue beyond the town gates to the frontiers of the kingdom. Thus the whole disposition made a forceful political statement about the centrality of the *ọba* in the order of things, an order which had a cosmological dimension as well as a charter in its source and exemplar, Ile-Ife.[28] The hastily settled, disorderly towns, some of them with no *ọba*, which were formed by the refugees in the early nineteenth century presented a sharp and deeply felt contrast with this normative order.

The paradox of the *ọba*'s position was that he symbolized the unity of the *ilu* and at the same time stood in complementary opposition to the chiefs or titleholders (*ijoye* or *oloye*, from *oye*, "title"). They drew their character both from the particular lineage, residential, or occupational interest groups from which they were drawn, and from their status or ranking in the title system as a whole. The most senior group of chiefs was widely known as *iwarẹfa*, usually six in number, the "elders" of the town as a whole, who conferred directly with the *ọba*. The senior of them was usually a kind of "first commoner" of the town—like the *Baṣọrun* at Oyo or the *Ọbanla* at Ilesha—who had on occasion the obligation to speak for the people against the *ọba*, and who would play a key role during the succession. Below the *iwarẹfa* there were invariably chiefs who served as quarter heads, or as leaders of the men of their quarters as a militia (hence often generically called *ẹlẹgbẹ*, "band leaders," or *ologun*, "war leaders"). In the quarters themselves there were often further holders of minor titles under the quarter heads, and in the larger kingdoms there were usually also palace-chiefs, who held ritual offices or performed personal services for the *ọba*. Titles were typically both grouped to emphasize collective solidarity in relation to their function and also rank-ordered within the group, which underscored status distinctions between them.

By means of its title system the community achieved a two-way flow of control, resources, and information between its center (the *ọba*) and its periphery (the household heads, or *bale*). At all levels of the hierarchy that ran through the chiefs, power consisted most essentially in the control of people. Material resources (including cowries, the great converter of everything into anything else)[29] had their point in that they could be used to attract and keep the support of human beings. The correlative values ran consistently through Yoruba culture and social practice: to have many children was the great concern of every adult, and childlessness had no peer among personal misfortunes, especially for women. Polygyny was the outcome of the almost equally insistent competition among men to enlarge the size of their followings: many wives meant not only more children, but a greater circle of affines from whom political support might be recruited.

Power and dependents, title and power, were reciprocally linked. Titles might be conferred as a recognition, and serve as an expression, of power otherwise attained (as by a successful hunter, farmer, or warrior); but an established title also conferred power, since it gave its holder the presumptive support of a given constituency, and, by virtue of its place in the title system, a certain access to resources distributed from the center. For power flowed upward (or inward from the periphery) as well as downward (or outward from the center). So while the relative power of any titleholder from the *ọba* downward was a direct expression not only of his position in the title system but also of the size of his following, its continued loyalty had to be maintained by his effective representation of, and redistribution to, it. As a result, Yoruba kings and chiefs were severely limited in how far they could, in the strict sense, *exploit* their own subjects.

So how did they derive the resources necessary for them to maintain the Yoruba chiefly ideal as a man of generosity? In a phrase, by exploiting strangers. Here, individual Yoruba communities must again be seen in the context of the wider regional system. The resources needed to prime the pump of local hierarchy came from the community's success in using its natural endowments and situational advantages in assuring to itself a disproportionate share of the regional resource flow. This is why the location of trade routes and markets was so critical for the existence of Yoruba states— traders (as strangers) would pay for the local protection which they needed, prestigious goods could be accessed, tolls could be levied—and the resources so derived were used to underwrite the status of those able to offer themselves as the local powers. This depended on the ability of chiefs to back up protection by force, and so ultimately on the numerical strength of their followings. For a community to grow in numbers faster than its rivals was alike the means and the token of its success. Though free migrants were drawn to successful towns, the accelerated means to success was the involuntary transfer of people as slaves. Like other forms of tribute and booty from the conquered or subordinate towns, slaves also played a critical part in maintaining the status system within communities. Slaves captured in war went disproportionately to the *oba* and chiefs, swelling their households over those of lesser men; and slaves, being people with no local kin, were exploitable as free subjects were not.

END OF AN EMPIRE

"Metropolitan dissension, provincial disaffection and Muslim rebellion" is Robin Law's succinct summation of the main features of Old Oyo's demise.[30] The precise manner of their interplay is less easy to determine. The coincidence in the third quarter of the eighteenth century of prolonged conflict between the *Alafin* and the *Basorun,* head of the senior line of chiefs, with Oyo's growing involvement in the coastal trade has suggested that the access of new resources seriously destabilized relations within the capital.[31] *Alafin* Abiodun's death in 1789 led to a recrudescence of quarrels between his successor Awole and his chiefs, disputes into which several important provincial rulers were drawn. The most important of these was Afonja, ruler of Ilorin, who was also the *Are-Ona-Kakamfo,* or commander of the military levies from the subordinate towns. When Awole was deposed (c. 1796), Afonja made a bid to be chosen *Alafin* and, when this was unsuccessful, seceded. Over the next few years Ilorin carved out an independent territory for itself from the northeastern corner of the kingdom, while at Oyo the debilitating struggle between successive *Alafin* and the chiefs continued. In 1817 Afonja, though not a Muslim himself, decided to enhance his support by calling up the growing Muslim interest.[32] He invited to Ilorin an influential Fulani cleric, known to the Yoruba as Alimi, who soon proclaimed a jihad against pagan Oyo, which won widespread backing among Muslims, both Yoruba and non-Yoruba, and provoked a revolt among slaves of northern origin. Afonja's warbands, known as *jamaa,* ranged further and deeper into the Oyo kingdom, the young Ajayi Crowther being one of their victims. Around 1823 Afonja was killed in an insurrection of his Muslim allies, and Alimi's son Abudusalami took charge of Ilorin, declaring his allegiance to the Sokoto Caliphate. By this time Oyo's eastern provinces had fallen away altogether, and refugees were flooding to the forest regions south and east, beyond the borders of the old kingdom.

Developments at the coast had equally far-reaching effects, which by the 1820s combined with those in the north to redraw the regional map radically. From the 1790s Lagos began to eclipse Oyo's client kingdom of Porto Novo as the chief outlet of the slave trade. This brought Ijebu into greater prominence as a supplier and by the 1810s led to intensified slave raids in her hinterland. When some Oyo traders were kidnapped at Apomu, a market town under Ife on its borders with Owu and Ijebu, the Oyo demanded that their local ally, Owu, take action: Apomu was sacked and Ife defeated. Ife then made an alliance with Ijebu and together they defeated Owu (c. 1817), an ominous feature of this war being the use of guns for the first time in Yorubaland—acquired by the Ijebu from the Europeans. The allies then laid siege to Owu, an ancient and well-fortified town, which they finally took (c. 1822).[33] By that time their army was greatly augmented by refugees and warriors from the chaos enveloping the Oyo kingdom. This combined force of Ifes, Ijebus, and Oyos then turned its attention to the small Egba towns, once subject to Oyo, and destroyed nearly all of them (1823–1824). (Once again, and in greater numbers, some of those enslaved would eventually become CMS agents). The shattered Egba eventually regrouped on the western edge of their territory, at a new settlement, Abeokuta, while the sites of two of the old Egba towns, Ibadan and Ijaye, were occupied by displaced Oyos. Meanwhile Dahomey was finally able to throw off Oyo suzerainty, and it started a career of expansion into Yoruba-speaking lands. For the rest of the century the southwestern Yoruba, where Oyo's influence had lately been so strong, would be a bone of contention between Dahomey and Abeokuta.

Oyo-Ile itself lingered on for another decade. The first eyewitness accounts of it by Europeans in 1826–1830 describe a "large, dull city," tumbledown and semi-deserted, with the people apathetic in the face of the Fulani encroachments; yet the road up from Badagry through Egbado, the old conduit of Oyo's coastal trade, was still secure and peaceful.[34] Not for long: in 1831–1833 the Fulani of Ilorin finally reduced Oyo to tributary status and overran nearly all the provincial towns in the north and west. A last attempt to throw off the Fulani failed, the *Alafin* Oluewu was killed and Oyo's remaining inhabitants fled south (c. 1836). A son of *Alafin* Abiodun named Atiba, who had once professed Islam at Ilorin, secured enough support from Oyo's surviving senior chiefs and warriors to be recognized as *Alafin* and established himself well to the south at a place called Ago Oja, which eventually became known as the new Oyo. Here he and his successors recreated as much as they could of the palatial pomp of the old capital. But in the face of the threat from Ilorin, practical measures were also needed. Astutely recognizing the new centers of power, Atiba conferred high Oyo titles on the two principal warlords: Oluyole of Ibadan was made *Başọrun*, and Kurunmi of Ijaye *Arẹ-Ọna-Kakamfo*. A working alliance was thus set up among the Oyos displaced to the south, which proved its worth when the Ilorins were defeated at Oshogbo, decisively checking their southward advance (c. 1838). Ibadan was now revealed as the fulcrum of the Yoruba country.

NEW TOWNS, NEW WARS

In the 1840s the politics of Yorubaland settled to a new agenda. Internally, it revolved around the attempt by Ibadan to establish its regional hegemony and the responses of the other Yoruba states to this. While the vacuum left by Old Oyo's collapse certainly provided its primary condition,[35] Ibadan's project was genuinely original: though of mainly Oyo traditions, it was a community of a very different social character and its "empire" came to straddle the savanna/forest divide, the first major Yoruba power to do so. Externally, Yoruba politics had to respond to the ending of the slave trade, effectively concluded by the British annexation of Lagos in 1861 after a decade of consular rule.[36] Lagos depended for its revenue on taxing the new staple of "legitimate trade," palm oil, which the British (and missionaries above all) hoped would replace slaves. But palm oil had the paradoxical effect of fueling wars in the interior, since it created demands for labor which, under prevailing social conditions, had to be unfree. Palm oil for guns became the key equation of the Yoruba political economy. Ibadan was the main producing power of the interior because it was also the main military power, but it did not have access to the coast; so her coastward rivals, Abeokuta and Ijebu, found it an irresistible tactic of war to cut the trade routes between coast and interior. Since this threatened the revenue base of the Lagos Colony, the long-term logic of the situation was for the interests of Lagos (the imperialist bridgehead on the coast) and Ibadan (the imperial power of the interior) to converge.[37]

The new powers need some introduction, and particularly the three states which figured in the first great dénouement, the Ijaye War of 1859–1862: Ibadan, Ijaye, and Abeokuta. All were born in the agonies of the collapse of the old order and made from much the same cultural materials, yet the institutional outcomes showed great and lasting differences. Because all three places had early mission stations, we at last come on to times and places which can be documented from rich contemporary evidence.

Ibadan had its origins in the mixed force of Ifes, Oyos, and Ijebus which destroyed Owu and sacked the old Egba towns.[38] An early Ife leadership was soon swept aside in factional fighting, and with the numerical predominance of Oyos among the new arrivals, the Oyo elements took control. Still, Ibadan remained the most heterogeneous of all Yoruba towns, with relatively little local concentration of people of particular origins, so that hardly any prior communal organization could take root in the new town. People settled as the followings of warriors or in small groups of kin and dependents, or as

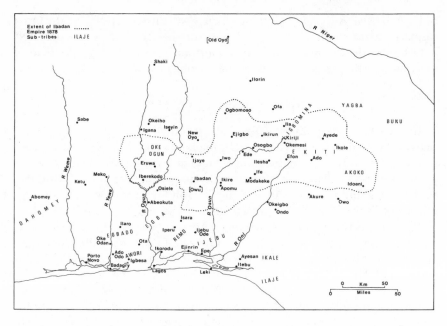

Figure 2.2. Yorubaland in the Nineteenth Century

individuals attaching themselves as clients to warlord patrons. The compounds in which they settled were clusters of buildings with a single gated entrance leading to a large central courtyard and (in the case of the large ones) the residence of more than one household. Though compounds typically had an agnatic core, they included non-kin affiliates, and not all agnates might elect to live together, so it is too simple to treat every compound as the direct residential equivalent of a "lineage."[39]

Above the level of compounds or households, there was no system of administrative quarters as existed in the older Yoruba towns. The named districts of Ibadan are merely locations, and were very often named after a notable chief or early resident (Oke Oluokun, Agbeni, Oke Foko). That itself indicates how much the key local leader in the early days was the *baba-ogun*, or war-leader—men such as Olunloyo, who was the patron of the Christians at Kudeti—and the extent to which the political relations of the whole town were coterminous with those between its leaders in war. They were the men with the largest followings, bound to them by personal loyalties and with some internal command structure. Skilful management of his "warboys," by a judicious mix of control and reward, was the foundation of any chief's career.[40] But even in anti-institutional Ibadan, titles—relatively stable positions in a power structure—emerged early on. They took the form of a chain of military offices, whose senior title was *Balogun* [War-captain]—unless the leader used an Oyo title like *Baṣọrun* or *Arẹ-Ọna-Kakamfo* instead—followed by *Ọtun*

[Right-hand], *Osi* [Left-hand], *Ẹkẹrin* [Fourth], and so forth. Titles were filled by the consent of the leaders, and worked roughly by promotion from lower to higher grades as vacancies occurred. Periods of fairly collective leadership alternated with the hegemonies of surpassing war leaders, such as *Baṣọrun* Oluyole (c. 1835–1847), *Balogun* Ibikunle (1851–1864), *Baṣọrun* Ogunmola (1865–1867), and *Arẹ* Latosisa (1871–1885). Civilian titles were at first few and random, but by 1850 the long absences on campaigns of the military chiefs made it clear that something more systematic was needed to maintain routine order at home, and a similar "ladder" under a *balẹ,* or civil head, was developed. None of these titles was hereditary within a lineage, and Ibadan developed an ethos that any enterprising warrior might make his way to the top there.

Ijaye might have turned out much like Ibadan, but for the fact that it was more purely an Oyo town, and that it was for three decades completely dominated by one man, Kurunmi, who held the Oyo title *Arẹ-Ọna-Kakamfo.*[41] Ruthless in eliminating rivals, he succeeded in engrossing to himself sources of power which were at Ibadan diffused among the war-chiefs or even not held by them, such as the headships of major cults, especially of Sango. All fines, tolls, and tributes flowed through Kurunmi's hands and he allowed no one else to store gunpowder.[42] The corollary of the power which terror had such a part in creating was the "generosity" with which he feasted the people on every fifth Jakuta day, sacred to Sango. Until they had tasted living under it, missionaries were full of praise for Ijaye's orderliness, compared with unruly Ibadan.[43]

Abeokuta presents a different picture again.[44] In their old homes the Egba had lived in small townships, probably of only a few thousand people in many cases, which were governed by petty *ọbas* and councils of chiefs, otherwise the elders of the *Ogboni* society. These small towns were grouped into three federations each headed by a premier *ọba,* among whom the *Alake* had a certain paramountcy. As a result of the wars of the 1820s the pan-Egba military organization (under chiefs called the *Ologun*) assumed greater importance under *Balogun* Sodeke, who led the Egba to Abeokuta. It was Sodeke who received the first missionary envoys in 1842–1843 and invited them to set up in Abeokuta. The three groupings of Egba were joined by a large body of survivors from the destroyed Owu, who made up a fourth grouping in the town. In contrast to Ibadan, Abeokuta's quarters were the old townships transplanted, with their members' loyalties and much of their organization. Though most had lost their *ọbas* they were still governed by councils of elders (*Ogboni*) and warrior-chiefs. The township *Balogun,* or war-chiefs, were key figures since it was through them that Abeokuta as a whole raised its army. So precarious was Abeokuta's situation in its early years—threatened by Ibadan to the east and Dahomey to the west—that a strong pan-Egba military leadership would seem essential. But after Sodeke's death in 1845, it often did not get it. The personal rivalries of chiefs combined with chronic factionalism between townships and tensions between the military and civilian or *Ogboni* groups of chiefs to produce frequent political stalemates and sometimes the pursuit by individual townships of virtually their own foreign policies.

It soon became clear to the Egba that both security and opportunity lay in the control of the trade routes between Abeokuta and the Lagos lagoon. In the early 1840s they fought the Awori towns which threatened this objective, taking Ota and besieging Ado. A complex set of hostile alliances was thus activated, for Ado was tributary to Porto Novo, now the ally of Dahomey. Then Lagos and the British came into play. In 1845, King Akitoye of Lagos was prevailed upon by the British to abolish the slave trade, and his nephew Kosoko (whose mother was from Ota and who had close contacts with the slavers at Porto Novo) put himself at the head of the slave-trade party and expelled Akitoye. Akitoye fled to Abeokuta, where he had maternal connections, and then to Badagry on the western lagoon (then under strong Egba influence).[45] Opinion at Abeokuta was divided, but the overall logic of her situation won out: an alliance with Akitoye and the British against the Kosoko/ Dahomey connection. The return of the repatriates from Sierra Leone, the establishment of the missions, and the defeat of the Dahomean invasion in 1851 consolidated it. The British drove Kosoko from Lagos and restored Akitoye. When in 1853 Kosoko made a last bid to get back, the Egba sent a force to help the British consul repel him. Egba power now extended right down to Lagos.

Meanwhile the two powers of central Yorubaland, Ibadan and Ijaye, were consolidating themselves. The towns were only twenty miles apart, and they eyed one another with suspicion, despite the theory that they were jointly authorized by the *Alafin*—now at his new capital, known at this time as *Ago d'Oyo* [The Camp that became Oyo], itself only a few miles north of Ijaye— as joint protectors of the Oyo against the Fulani threat. It is hard to tell just how seriously the new warlords took this notion or the mystique of Old Oyo (sedulously fostered by the *Alafin* Atiba) in which it was grounded. Certainly the prestige of Oyo titles was very real in the new towns, and the division of spheres of influence between Ijaye and Ibadan closely followed that between the westward *Ẹkun Ọtun* and the eastward *Ẹkun Osi* provinces of the old empire. Ibadan was starting to move even farther east by the 1850s, initially to block Ilorin's expansion toward Ijesha and northern Ekiti and in support of easterly Oyo towns such as Ede and Ikirun, but later by the prospect of booty and slaves. By 1858 Ibadan was so swollen with newly taken slaves that its social cohesion was felt to be at risk, and it took measures to absorb them more effectively.[46]

Ijaye was also expanding, though its sphere—largely the depopulated savannah lands of the northwest—did not yield such rich rewards as Ibadan's eastern hinterland. Still, Kurunmi mounted a successful expedition for plunder against the far west Sabe kingdom in 1855, and Ijaye, like Ibadan, extended its town walls in the 1850s.[47] There was a sense of growing rivalry between Ibadan and Ijaye which the *Alafin* Atiba sought to damp down, though he clearly (if discreetly) inclined to Ibadan. It was Atiba's death in 1859 which precipitated the showdown. Kurunmi challenged the legitimacy of the succession of Atiba's son Adelu, and the quarrel soon spread, since some of Ijaye's tributary towns made a bid to transfer their allegiance to the new *Alafin*. Ibadan's intervention led to an angry response from Kurunmi, and the Ibadan chiefs decided on war. After some delay, the Egba, fearful of Ibadan's growing power and resentful of their past ill-treatment at her hands, came in as allies of Ijaye.[48]

Ijaye's fall in 1862, after a long siege during which Kurunmi himself died, left Ibadan as the dominant Yoruba power.[49] It also created an alliance between the Egba and Ijebu which would ultimately be one decisive check on Ibadan's ambition to lead the Yoruba world. Ijebu, the ancient kingdom lying between Ibadan territory and the lagoon, was perhaps the least affected by the collapse of Old Oyo.[50] The basis of its power was precisely its strategic position athwart both the east-west routes along the lagoon and those running from coast to interior. By the mid-nineteenth century, Ijebu Ode's great slave market, its control of the lagoon ports, its firm foothold in Ibadan itself (in Isale Ijebu quarter) and the far-ranging activity of individual Ijebu as traders all made Ijebu the most formidable power of the south. Ijebu had never been strongly expansionist, despite its involvement in the campaigns that had destroyed Owu and the old Egba towns. The cardinal principle of its policy was to maintain the integrity of its borders and outlets, which it achieved by two means. The first was the close internal integration of the kingdom;[51] the second was an inveterate suspicion of strangers and an adamant refusal to allow Europeans, particularly missionaries, to settle. So it was that their common hostility to Ibadan brought into alliance those two Yoruba powers which respectively gave the warmest welcome and offered the strongest resistance to the missions: Egba and Ijebu.

The direct route from Ibadan to Lagos lay along what can be called the "Remo corridor" through the western portion of Ijebu to the port of Ikorodu, whence across the lagoon to Lagos. The Remo were Ijebu in custom and dialect but with some distinctions that marked them off from the towns closer to Ijebu Ode, and they recognized the authority of a "sub-paramount" ruler, the *Akarigbo*.[52] The Remo towns had always tried to loosen the hold of the Ijebu paramount ruler, the *Awujale*, over them, and in the 1850s Ibadan won the support of Ipara, the key to the northern end of the corridor. With Ijaye eliminated, the focus of hostilities between Abeokuta and Ibadan shifted to this crucial artery of trade, as Ijebu Ode moved to reassert control over Remo. The two sides settled to a protracted run of engagements in Remo, but without decisive outcome.

The British, who in 1861 had annexed Lagos in order better to protect commercial interests, now became directly involved. The active ingredient here was the energetic Captain Glover, whose management of Lagos affairs stretched over a decade and who, as "Goloba," entered popular Yoruba consciousness as few other colonial officials have done. Interventionist by disposition and eager to extend British commitments despite much parliamentary opposition to further imperial expansion in West Africa, Glover broke decisively with the earlier Egba/missionary bias of British policy. When in 1865 the Egba refused to end their siege of Ikorodu, Ibadan's ally at the southern end of the Remo corridor, Glover sent troops and drove them off with rockets. Peace was formally made in mid-1865 and the camps in Remo were broken up, but the fundamental issues—Ibadan's desire to get unrestricted access to the coast and the reluctance of Egba and Ijebu to give it her—remained unresolved. Relations between Lagos and the Egba continued to deteriorate: when the Egba set up a customs post near the mouth of the river Ogun, Glover retaliated by annexing Ebute Meta on the Lagos mainland. In late 1867, anti-British feeling among the Egba reached the boiling point, and in the incident known as the Outbreak, or *Ifọle* ("breaking of houses"), the missionaries—taken, despite their protests, as proxies for the Lagos administration—were expelled from Abeokuta.[53] The first act of the long drama of British involvement in the politics of the Yoruba interior was over.

IBADAN: ZENITH TO STALEMATE

While the Egba were thus engaged with Lagos and Dahomey, Ibadan's attention was turned again to the east, where her armies seemed to roll all before them.[54] The ground for Ibadan's *Drang nach Osten* had been prepared by the flood of refugee Oyos from as far back as the 1820s, which had transformed the ethnic composition of towns that had once been in the northern orbit of Ife and Ilesha. No group of these Oyo refugees had a more disturbing impact than those which were accommodated at Ile-Ife.

Despite the social memory of its earlier glories and its continuing prestige as a cult center, Ife's actual political importance within the region at the outset of the nineteenth century seems to have been modest.[55] But from the 1810s onward, particularly with the elimination of her rival Owu, its influence started to revive: in the mid-1830s she was able to repel Ijesha attacks and, after intervening in civil disturbances in Ondo, gain an outpost at Okeigbo on the Oni river to the south. The Oyo migrants now moving into the area seem at first to have been a positive factor for Ife, since as allies they augmented her military strength. Yet before long these Oyo began to have a destabilizing effect on Ife's internal politics: a succession of *Ọni*, who look to have sought to buttress themselves with Oyo support, had ominously short reigns. About 1847 the *Ọni* Abeweila attempted a resolution by creating a separate settlement for the Oyo migrants, adjacent to Ife, called

Modakeke. Their resentment unallayed, the Ifes attacked Modakeke but were defeated and forced to abandon their ancient town, which lay deserted for the next nine years (1849–1858). Since Modakeke was a natural ally of Ibadan, Ife had no choice, after its restoration in 1859, but to submit to Ibadan overrule.

The real gateway power to the east was the Ijesha. Over the centuries they had periodically thrown back the assaults of Oyo cavalry, but by the late 1860s they came under renewed pressure, and their formidable capital, Ilesha, was sacked for the first time in its history in 1870. With Ilesha now reduced to tributary status, Ibadan forces at first ranged with little effective resistance into Ekiti and beyond. Sometimes they exploited local disputes, but usually their attacks were unprovoked. The forces ranged against them were the militias of small towns, marshaled under elegbe chiefs who had experience of local conflicts but were no match at all for what had become a professional army. What eastern Yorubaland meant for Ibadan was expressed by the Are Latosisa in memorably plain words: "[The Ekiti] are our wives, our slaves, our yams, our palm oil. . . . *I will eat them up!*"[56] But what had begun for Ibadan as a seemingly easy way to provision herself for her ongoing struggles in the older theaters of war against more seasoned opponents such as Ilorin, Ijebu, and Egba ended by adding yet more members to the grand coalition against her.

By the 1880s the Ibadan army was operating a hundred or more miles from home—it took five days to get to the war camp at Kiriji—and a large part of it was absent for years at a time. At its greatest extent Ibadan's "empire" covered well over 15,000 square miles, stretching over two hundred miles from end to end, and must have counted upward of two million subjects. The conquest of new areas led to the enslavement of many of their inhabitants. Afterward, if a town was not permanently abandoned by the survivors, it was required to pay tribute, and generally to support Ibadan's interests, including offering hospitality, supplying troop levies, and providing porterage for Ibadan's forces when they wanted it. Ibadan overrule was irksome less because it was close than because it was often so arbitrary: yearly tribute was less of a problem than the irregular exactions of Ibadan's agents.[57] Local oba and chiefs were usually left in place, though Ibadan might take a hand in their selection. Above them there was a two-way system of formal control. Each subordinate town was placed under one of the Ibadan chiefs, known as its *babakekere* ("little father"), through whom it offered its tribute and who represented it at Ibadan—often he was the chief who had first conquered the town. This system was very similar to one long used at Old Oyo and in some other kingdoms.[58] In addition, a local representative was appointed, called an *ajele,* resident in the town itself, to keep an eye on local events and guard Ibadan's interests. The *ajele* was not necessarily an Ibadan man, and was often highly predatory on his own account, especially in the eastern, non-Oyo, parts of Ibadan's domain.[59] The system of control was deeply personalized, an extension of age-old patterns of authority in small communities.

Despite Ibadan's military prowess in the interior, and its resultant growth in population and productive capacity, the Egba and Ijebu still refused to allow it free access across their territories to the coastal markets. The late 1860s brought another drawn-out blockade, which the Lagos authorities could not ignore because of its implications for the colony's revenue base. So Governor Glover tried a radical new initiative: the opening of a route to the interior via the developing ports of the eastern lagoon and thence northward through Ondo, which would circumvent Ijebu and Egba entirely.[60] Now, for the first time, the British were drawn decisively into the local politics of eastern Yorubaland. An initial task was to reconstitute Ondo itself as the main polity along the line of the proposed road, without which there would have been no security: its capital, Ode Ondo, had been deserted for many years as the result of a civil war. A more stubborn problem was the existence of Okeigbo, a town of mixed refugees under Ife control within Ondo's northern borders, a product of the same time of civil war; but this had to be left, which galled the Ondo chiefs rather as Modakeke did Ife. So the "Ondo road" was opened in 1872 and was consolidated in 1875 by the establishment of a new CMS mission station at Ode Ondo, far away from their previous operations. As early as 1879 large numbers of traders from both Lagos and the interior were using the route.

The new route certainly helped Ibadan in the face of her old enemies to the south and west, but it also created opportunities for her victims in the east. Ijesha repatriates in Lagos had for some years been scheming how to help their countrymen in the interior against Ibadan. The origin of their organization went back to a Christian prayer group also known as the Ijesha Association. Its leading light was a Brazilian returnee called Philip Jose Meffre, an elder of the congregation at St Paul's Breadfruit (of whom more will be said in later chapters). At first, their objective was simply to see mission work extended to their own country. But by the mid-1870s, when Ilesha had been made tributary to Ibadan, they had come to the view that military enhancement was needed and applied to the Governor of Lagos for training. By 1876 the group had renamed itself the Ekitiparapo [Ekiti—the people of the highlands—together] Society, apparently to broaden the regional base of its appeal. But what really put it into business was the uprising against Ibadan rule that broke out in 1878. Now the Ekitiparapo had plenty to do to support the cause, by lobbying and representation in Lagos and by supplying the forces in the interior by means of the Ondo road. Ijesha traders were soon to be found in numbers in the eastern lagoon and in 1881 founded a new settlement there named Aiyesan [The world gets well], which was a vital staging post for supplies.

The uprising started at Okemesi, and spread quickly in Ekiti and Igbomina: Ibadan *ajẹlẹ,* messengers, and sympathizers were killed or expelled. In the first pitched battle near the Oyo town of Ikirun, Ibadan was still able to inflict a heavy defeat on a mixed force of Ekiti and Ijesha and their Ilorin allies. But they regrouped on home ground at Otun-Ekiti, and by 1880 they had started to gain the upper hand. They were joined by the Ijesha freebooter Ogedengbe, the most famous of a number of warriors from eastern parts who had learned the art of war, Ibadan-style, from service as slave warboys to Ibadan chiefs. He now took over leadership of the Ekitiparapo forces, which moved to make their base in the hilly country near Imesi-Ile, close to the northeastern Oyo towns loyal to Ibadan. The two camps at Kiriji, on hills about a mile apart facing one another across a valley, were to remain there for more than a dozen years. They became sizeable towns and must have resembled what Ibadan had been like in its early days: there were markets, crafts, and farms nearby, and many of the inhabitants were non-combatants, including women and children. It went on so long partly because the engagements settled down to a kind of routine, but, more important, because the standoff at Kiriji was merely the main thread of a knot of antagonisms extending all over Yorubaland.

When in 1882 the Ife contingent at Kiriji switched sides to the Ekitiparapo, Ibadan's Modakeke allies attacked Ife and the town was abandoned again, this time to remain derelict until 1894. The people decamped either to Okeigbo, which the *Ọni*-Elect, Derin Ologbenla, had made his base, or to Isoya, a few miles south—both of them locations which controlled trade routes to the coast. In the west, the Egba renewed their hostilities against Ibadan, and even the cautious Ijebu joined the alliance against Ibadan. Ijebu's main problem was always how to respond to the growing volume and variety of the trade between Lagos and the Yoruba interior in such a way as to maintain her own political integrity. By the late 1880s the *Awujalẹ*'s policy of tight frontier control, equally wary of both Ibadan and the British in Lagos, had been reasserted—which would only finally be broken when the British invaded Ijebu in 1892.

The governor of Lagos was increasingly looked to as the arbitrator of the interior conflicts. A first round of attempts to resolve them was made in 1881–1882, when delegates from the interior came to Lagos. In 1884–1885 the senior CMS missionary at Abeokuta, the Rev. J. B. Wood, went twice on behalf of the governor to Kiriji. Another attempt in 1886 (with two African agents of the CMS, Rev. Samuel Johnson of Oyo and Rev. Charles Phillips of Ondo, serving as principal negotiators) won more success, because of growing fatigue on both sides and the death of Latosisa, the ruler of Ibadan. This time a partial peace was concluded and there was some dispersal of forces from Kiriji. But the conflicts in some other theaters of war—Ife versus Modakeke and Ibadan versus Ilorin—proved more intractable. They were only settled when the British decided that direct intervention was unavoidable and Governor Carter made his tour of Yorubaland in 1893 to "break up the camps" and to conclude treaties which enshrined the authority of the governor of Lagos. That was made much easier by the impression made throughout Yorubaland by the British invasion of Ijebu the year before, carried out in order to break Ijebu control of the Lagos-Ibadan road.[61] After Ijebu, there was little need for recourse to the iron fist: Ogedengbe was detained by force at Ilesha in 1893[62] and Oyo was briefly bombarded in 1895,[63] but not much besides.

So colonial rule came to the Yoruba. They mostly acquiesced—whether from a feeling of exhaustion with the wars, or from a hearty regard for British power, or because they did not see where British "protection" would lead before it was too late to oppose it. This peace would also, by and large, be confirmed by growing prosperity. Within a few years and for several decades to come, the colonial order would come to be seen as providing essential conditions for economic developments—expanding systems of production and consumption, trade and transport—in which the Yoruba were eager to become involved.

WHICH NARRATIVE? WHOSE STORY?

When I began writing this chapter, my intention was a simple, not to say naïve, one: to give a narrative history of nineteenth-century Yorubaland that would serve as an adequate reference backdrop to the more detailed analysis of social and religious relations which was to follow. What was in my mind was something rather straight and factual, perhaps like the news on the BBC World Service, or the lists of locally significant events for each town compiled under the direction of Professors J. F. Ade Ajayi and A. A. Igun for the 1963 Nigerian census, to help the enumerators gauge the ages of elderly people: a relatively theory-free account of the major events and trends and enough of their interconnectedness to make them intelligible. It seemed important to provide the reader with an account that was disinterested, in the sense of being fairly independent of what I wanted to argue about the nature and consequences of the CMS intervention in Yoruba history. It seemed too that the main problems in achieving this would be practical and evidential: how to simplify a complicated and many-stranded story without distorting its essential elements, and how to handle those many aspects which, in our present state of knowledge, were still obscure.

But what became progressively evident in the writing was how impossible it would be to give such a neutral account. The mostly secondary studies that I was drawing upon were deeply permeated by certain schemes of emplotment, or thematized story lines. The source was not far to seek: the looming presence behind this literature of its main progenitor, the Rev. Samuel Johnson, who (as we have just seen) played a major role in the negotiations which brought the wars to an end.[64] This is doubtless largely because Johnson's *History of the Yorubas* is easily our most important source of information for pre-colonial Yoruba history (and particularly for before the nineteenth century); but its great influence is also due to the compelling quality of its narrative structure.[65] The collective subject of Johnson's story still barely knew itself as such, beyond the ranks of those influenced by the missions. Johnson gave the notion of a Yoruba people real historical substance by making them the subject of a powerful story of growth, decline, and recovery. Old Oyo inherits the cultural mantle of ancient Ife and builds itself up to a great state, culminating in the reign of *Alafin* Abiodun; it falls through a combination of internal disputes and external foes (especially the Muslim Fulani), and a period of chaos and dissolution ensues; but a successor state to Oyo emerges in Ibadan, which becomes the focus of a new, emergent "Yoruba" order into which the non-Oyo Yoruba (i.e., erstwhile non-"Yoruba") are drawn. At the same time, a key part is played by the missions, who bring enlightenment and progress to the country—values which, while particularly linked with Christianity, have gone beyond it to become public values which all Yoruba recognize.

This *History*, completed in 1897 within a few years of the end of the wars, had to wait until 1921 to find its public: a "pre-Nigerian" book which only saw the light of day well into colonial Nigeria. Subsequent work of all kinds, from patriotic local histories written by amateurs to the writings of academic historians, have imitated, amplified, and supplemented Johnson's vision of Yoruba history rather than replaced it with a radically different narrative paradigm. They have placed it in its later Nigerian context, and they have redefined it within the project of nationalist historiography. But Johnson's pan-Yoruba vision, grounded in the symbolic heritage of Ife, expanded from the Oyo to take in all the Yoruba-speaking sub-groups and wedded to the modernizing values introduced by the missions, has remained the basis of Yoruba cultural politics.

The cogency of Johnson's narrative derives not just from its literary qualities but also from the extent of its social embodiment, from its installation at the core of the modern Yoruba sense of themselves as a people. The title of Toyin Falola's collection of essays on Johnson—*Pioneer, Patriot, and Patriarch*—is more than an accolade to a mere historian. Life is not art, nor is history (qua event-sequences in time) the same as history (qua stories about them), but there is a mutually shaping interplay between them. Johnson's representation of the Yoruba past would be validated in the political and cultural practice of the Yoruba in the decades after his death in 1901. It is too simple, and in any case inappropriate, to see this as the Yoruba enacting a "script" written for them by Johnson, for historical action is always largely a matter of improvisation in response to circumstances, and Johnson's influence depended, significantly, on the further evolution of Yoruba ethnicity under the conditions provided by the Nigerian state. So while I hope that what I have written as a background *histoire evénementielle* may serve as such, it is also a particularly vivid reminder of that maxim which anthropologists know only too well—for many it is all they know about history—and that historians too readily forget: that all history is in a sense the history of the present. It follows that it needs be read as part of the cross-temporal reality of Yoruba society and as something which the encounter of religions to be analyzed in later chapters will be needed to explain.

3

LIVING IN AN AGE OF CONFUSION

Any large-scale account of human action has to involve both "history" and "sociology": a narrative of the collective subject's passage through time and an analysis of how that subject is constituted. The former is often regarded as a "dynamic" dimension and the latter as a "static" one. And while it can be readily conceded that they are *just* dimensions, aspects of what is concretely a complex, undecomposable unity, the problem stubbornly remains of how to write about either without the distortion of not simultaneously writing about the other. The commonest response is to attempt it sequentially: history first, sociology second, or vice versa. The choice of sequence may depend on essentially literary criteria, or it may be theoretically motivated, as with the structuralist history developed by Marshall Sahlins.[1] There, the aim being to reconcile history and anthropology by showing that history is "organized by structures of significance," the sociology (in the form of the system of cultural categories) is presented first, as a precondition of historical action. I see the choice as more of an expository problem: put history before sociology, and the narrative may not be fully intelligible; put society or culture first, and it may well appear as too given and reified, too independent of historical agency at all. The latter seems to me the more insidious dan-

47

ger, so here it has been history first—though as I have said, the narrative comes already saturated with cultural value. And so to sociology.

THE AGE OF CONFUSION

The aim of this chapter is to describe the social relations of the nineteenth-century Yoruba towns in which the missionaries set to work, as well as something of the lived experience of their people. The main thread of the analysis will be the attempts of Yoruba to recover and to redefine community. In constructing such an account—which would seem to have to be largely about "structures"—we are soon brought back to narratives, often with an overtly political content. I do not here mean the journal narratives of the missionaries themselves, which provide us with most of our information about social conditions, but the stories of others that they report and that serve to constitute the social relations that they form. No CMS journalist was more alert to the importance of stories as vehicles of social and moral reflection than W. S. Allen, catechist at Ibadan; and it is three narratives reported by him that take us to the heart of social experience in the "Age of Confusion."

First is a real-life story told to him while on his rounds in 1885 by the headman (*bale*) of a house, in explanation of why it had been deserted by all its other members:

> There had been two young men, one from this house, the other from one nearby. [Allen does not name them, but for ease of reference let me call them Omole and Idowu.] They ate and drank together, and were such close friends that they would even wear one another's clothes. Idowu fell grievously sick and accused Omole to his face of poisoning him. Three years before, they had drunk *okigbe* together, a medicine to confer invulnerability against weapons, from which time Idowu had had stomach trouble. Omole denied having administered any poison with the medicine, wept bitterly and departed. Three days later Idowu died. His father brought his body to Omole's house, causing all the residents to run away. The father said he would not take the body away unless Omole was killed and laid alongside his son. They appealed to the chiefs, who ruled that the father must take back the body, but that Omole had to pay 100 bags of cowries (£50) for his life.[2]

This story is so poignant that it is perhaps superfluous to ask why Allen recounted it. But Ibadan was then in dire straits from the Kiriji War, and the story must have served to underscore how much it needed the light of the Gospel. More to our immediate purposes is how effectively the story discloses some of the basic principles of social action: the search for protection, the importance (but also the frailty) of friendship, the obligations of lineage, and the demand for recompense.

The next two stories both offer generalized moral reflection on the breakdown of public order and social trust which many felt had engulfed the Yoruba country. Once in 1873 an old man asked if he could make some comments after Allen had finished his public preaching. He couched them in the form of a fable or parable (*owe*):

There was a man with three sons, called Poison, Fire, and Covetousness, who quarrel over their respective powers of destruction. Poison says that if he is put on an arrowhead, any living thing he is shot at will die; but his father replies that God has made an antidote. Fire says he can burn through whole towns, destroying everything in his way, but his father says there is water to stop him. Covetousness wins the contest, saying "I shall always be in man's heart and make them lust after things which does not belong to them and will cause them to commit every sort of sin." To this the father replies: "There is nothing to oppose you . . . and this is the sin which is reigning in this our country such as war, kidnapping, stealing, etc."[3]

This moral and social commentary was often expressly linked to reflection on the history of the past few decades. In two successive weeks of January 1878, Allen, again at his outdoor preaching stand in the town, addressed his listeners on the Ten Commandments. It was in the middle of the campaigning season in the first year of the Kiriji War, so his audience was chiefly composed of women, old men, and children. On the 20th his sermon on the "first table" of the commandments: "Honor thy father and thy mother"—an apt text for times when the obligations of lineage were under heavy pressure— won particular approval.[4] On the 27th, he went on to the "second table," and when he had finished, an old man asked if he could add some remarks:

He said that God had made man to be upright, and had given him four attendants: friends, respect, truth, and merriment. But each had his negative counterpart—enemies, disrespect, falsehood, and dejection—which remained behind when the former had gone. "And it is impossible to have those which were gone reclaimed" went on the old man, "[but] without it we cannot keep these command[ments]. Our grandfathers have kept [them], and there was peace and happiness in their days, but since the reign of Afonja Are-Ona-Kakanfo . . . everything began to upset, nowadays it is worse and this is what brings the Yoruba country to such a state as it is."[5]

Afonja, the rebellious ruler of Ilorin who had played a key role in Old Oyo's downfall, here stands as the personification of disloyalty and disorder.[6] In antithesis is the *Alafin* Abiodun, who often came up when people recalled (or perhaps imagined) former times of order and prosperity.[7] So Samuel Johnson did not break fresh ground when he ended his great *History* with a prayer for a restoration of the country "as in the happy days of ABIODUN."[8]

Their own days, by contrast, Yoruba people saw as an "Age of Confusion."

David Hinderer sensed this on his first visit to Ibadan in 1851, reporting on his return to Abeokuta: "I could tell you about the history of the obba l'Oyo [*sic*]—Kings of Yoruba—even before the time of confusion—an emphatic term for time of war—you would only be surprised it is not worse."[9] Near Ilesha in 1858, he encountered the same outlook (this time from people who feared an Ibadan attack): "A very common notion is that from the commencement of the slave linching [*sic*] wars to this time, a god of confusion reigned."[10] *Orisa* priests were reported as saying the same kind of thing. A Sango priest at Ibadan angrily retorted to Hinderer's call to turn to God with the words: "The world is like a worn-out and cast-off garment, it is too old for God to care about, he has abandoned it and therefore everyone must do as he pleases."[11] An elderly Obatala priest—they typically had milder personalities than Sango devotees—seated before his house in Lagos, told Maser in 1858 that "the world was spoiled and turned upside down, like the seed of a fignut."[12] The *orisa* held responsible above all for spoiling and confusing things was Esu;[13] and a *babalawo* in Ibadan expressly attributed the troubles of the times to God's release into the world of Esu (confusion) and Ogun (war) in order to punish men for their disobedience—as well as to the supply of guns and powder by Europeans![14]

The experience of confusion—of communities racked by internal conflict or destroyed altogether, of families broken up, of large-scale displacement, of radical changes in personal circumstances, of the norms of social life challenged or overthrown—was fundamental to Yoruba lives in the nineteenth century. An Ijesha Christian, looking back in old age to the destruction of his village, described how its inhabitants fled, "people, animals, chickens, loads and all" (*tenia, teran, tadie, teruteru*), leaving all desolate when "parents knew their children no more, nor did the wife see her husband again" (*olomo ko mo omo, aya ko ri oko mo*).[15] Yet the Yoruba struggled to hold onto what they could of old identities and patterns of living. Even when displaced and parted from kin, reduced to pure individuality, they carried the springs of social identity with them, in their "familiar names," the *oriki orile* which defined their community of origin, "tribal marks" (*ila*) cut into the face, food taboos (*ewo*) associated with lineage or cult membership, and, often, the sense of a protective personal destiny (*ori*). Wherever they were driven, they sought out others who shared or recognized these personal markers, as they did in the distant exile of Brazil, Cuba, or Sierra Leone; and where they could, they aimed to reconstitute their communities.

At Abeokuta, where this ideal was realized most fully, the old *ilu* of the Egba forest, which became the "townships" of the new city of refuge, continued to command the primary loyalty of ordinary Egba. Their stubborn ancestral piety is well illustrated in the case of an elderly war-chief at the deserted site of Emere, northeast of Abeokuta, who had built a hut over his father's grave, frequently visited it, and hoped to attract enough of his townsmen to rebuild it.[16] He was not successful, because raids by the forces of

Ibadan or Dahomey kept Egbaland in such chronic insecurity that people preferred to keep their homes in Abeokuta. Even there, remorse about the past could stir amid the politics of the present. When in 1853 the Egba began to think that they might again choose an *Alake,* the first since their settlement at Abeokuta a generation before, a diviner told them "that their murder and non-burial of the last Alake was cause of all calamities of the past thirty years."[17] So the Ake people went to the ruins of Old Ake, about twenty miles away; each township of the Egba Alake brought a sheep, a cloth, and a bag of cowries; and together they made reparation, disinterring the bones and putting them in a coffin for reburial. Back in Abeokuta, Oro kept the women indoors for two days while the funeral took place, to settle the late *Alake's* spirit. Some months later the first *Alake* of the new dispensation was installed.

The persistence of the old identities at Abeokuta brought recurrent problems, as an episode in 1851 involving no less than four townships shows:

A "boy belonging to Toko people" was delivered to the senior Emere war-chief (*balogun*) under the pretence that he was stray. This *balogun* passed him to his equivalent at Kesi, who forwarded him to Somoye, *Balogun* of Iporo, who was also a major figure at the pan-Egba level. Somoye kept the boy for a while and then, when he was short of cowries, sold him down to Lagos. Here the boy was seen by a relative, who reported to the Itoko back in Abeokuta. They retaliated by capturing some Emere and Kesi people. Since it was strictly forbidden to fire muskets in disputes in Abeokuta, the parties set to with stones. When Sagbua, the senior Egba chief at the time, tried to break it up, he too was stoned. At this, people started to get frightened at where it might lead, and the affray was broken off.[18]

This chain of events shows how the principles of action might just as easily undermine as support one another. For while the solidarity of the townships on behalf of their members and the networks of dispersed family members were mutually sustaining, they also threatened the viability of Abeokuta as a whole. Less obvious was their corollary, the exposed position of apparently unattached individuals such as the boy, who was converted first into an item of gift exchange and then into an export commodity. Both circumstances and opportunities drew the war-chiefs into practices that undermined the stability of the pan-Egba community which they were commissioned to defend.

In Ibadan, the reconstitution of old communities was impossible, though people from an area might cluster together or seek out a patron from their old town to attach themselves to. Sometimes they even gave recognition to their refugee *ọba,* like the people of five adjacent compounds, all from Old Ikoyi, who "to keep their nationality distinct . . . reigned a king at Ibadan who is honoured in the quarter"[19]—but this found no formal expression in the new town's overall government. Indeed, after the rapid population

Figure 3.1. A view of Ibadan toward the central ridge, probably from
Kudeti mission compound to the south. *Church Missionary Gleaner,*
April 1904.

growth of the 1850s there was some sign of a different concern, about the
threat to social cohesion presented by its sheer heterogeneity. It was the aboriginal deity Oke'badan, named after the hills around which Ibadan was built,
which gave voice to this concern, complaining early in 1859 that lately its
worship had been neglected:

> "Its desires were gone into": oracular consultation clarified the sacrifices
> required and public collections were made. Then Oke'badan declared
> that Ibadan was too large, and that the Oyo people brought by the wars
> should return to rebuild their old deserted towns. There were "too many
> strange people who were brought here lately by the warriors" (i.e., slaves
> from Ekiti) who might rise up and destroy the town, so Ibadan should de-
> sist from further campaigns. Oke'badan also made two more requests: that
> "Egungun are no more to be seen in the town," and that likewise all pigs
> were to be removed from Ibadan.[20]

Hinderer saw all this as an intervention in the dispute then going on
among the leading war-chiefs about whether the Oyo towns should be rebuilt. In essence this was a debate about a fundamental issue for the Ibadan
leadership: was its real objective to rebuild the Oyo polity or to create something quite different, its own brand of imperial republic? But the oracle also
seems to be concerned about the quality of social relations within Ibadan,

arguing against excessive heterogeneity and inequality and for the reduction of aggravating cultural difference. Oke'badan's hostility to Egungun and
pigs is most easily interpreted this way. There was cause to dislike Egungun—
masked ancestral spirits—because their parading round the town often led
to violent clashes between their several bands of followers; and the hostility
to pigs was perhaps a gesture to the growing body of Muslims in the town.
There was certainly a great massacre of pigs,[21] but otherwise Oke'badan's
advice was ignored. Ibadan's turbulence would become one of her hallmarks.

So the problems ran deeper than the yearning of the displaced to re-
assemble their communities according to well-accepted principles of social
life. For these communities were themselves under pressure: the chaos, the
danger and, for some, the opportunities presented by the wars threatened
their moral foundations. In other words, issues of collective identity (membership of lineages, cults, and towns) were connected with changes of power
and status within the community. Both were called into question—first by
historical circumstances which made them seem unviable or insufficient, then
(in the usual way of social reflexivity) by many members of the society, and
finally by motivated outsiders such as Muslims or Christians who offered their
own alternative models of identity and conduct. But the new moral world
which the missions pressed with such confidence on the Yoruba had itself
to be tested against *their* requirements.

FELLOWSHIP: FRIENDS, COMPANIONS, CO-WORSHIPPERS

Like all other human societies, nineteenth-century Yoruba was a compound of "horizontal," or egalitarian, and "vertical," or hierarchical, relations, which mutually generated and challenged one another. To show this
clearly, it is helpful to abandon a convention of exposition which is both
deeply rooted in European social thought and well-hallowed in Yoruba
ethnography.[22] This starts with kinship and lineage, and on this basis then
proceeds to public or political institutions, along lines marked out in such
evolutionary models of the development of human society—lineage to
state—as those of Maine and Morgan; and these tend to carry the further
assumption that kin-based society is to be equated with the absence of inequality. Now the fundamental contrast here, perhaps most widely known in
the formulation of Tönnies, between gemeinschaft (supremely realized in
kinship) and gesellschaft (typified in voluntary association), can also be found
in Yoruba social thought as the antithesis of *ajọbi* [being born together] and
ajọgbe [residing together]. Here too primacy is given to kinship, or *ajọbi,* even
though the necessity of *ajọgbe,* or associational life, as a makeweight to it, is
insisted upon.[23] The advantage of going against the sequence presented in
sociological myth, Yoruba as well as European, is that it makes clear the irreducible nature of *communal* relations (even when, as often, they are
metaphorized in the terms of kinship); it enables us to approach sociality in

its purest, egalitarian form as fellowship; and it removes a barrier to appreciating that kinship was one of the most potent sources of inequality. Perhaps most important, in terms of the theme of this book, it opens the way to exploring the importance of religious fellowship for the Yoruba sense of community.

Let us take our cue from the parable of the old Ibadan man quoted earlier on: first of all he put "friends" as the thing which had been lost in the troubles of the times. It is striking how often the CMS journalists refer to friends, both to individuals (including many pagans) whom they describe as their own personal friends and to pairs or groups of friends and companions that come to their notice in the community. The private diaries of R. S. Oyebode and W. S. Allen are even more telling on this point, with their many entries recording the visits and the exchanges of presents with which they kept their friendships in good repair. Oyebode's father, David Kukomi, the "father" of the congregation at Aremo in Ibadan, brought his friend Israel Atere to be a Christian: they were like David and Jonathan, says Hinderer.[24] Close friends had an emotional importance equaled by no other relation besides a man's mother—more than fathers, wives, and brothers—and the two are brought together in a telling entry in Samuel Johnson's journal:

> With his own friend Oyebode, he calls to condole with a man who often attends church with a friend, in deep grief over his mother's death. "To be plain," he said, "I can instance my mother's death as quite out of place. She is my backstay, and it would be better if my father had died rather than she. When I am home or about in war, she takes care of my wives and children, and she is everything to me whilst my father is not. . . . " Johnson concludes by noting that "his attendance at times [at church] seems to secure his friendship with this our member."[25]

Equally, the deaths of friends often gave rise to a rare intensity of grief:

> Allen's colleague and friend at Aremo church, the scripture reader Thomas John, suddenly dies of fever on 22 March 1870. Next Sunday Allen preaches from Hebrews 13:14, "We have no continuing city here." It makes a great impression on the congregation. "It was difficult for me to go on. I had several times [to] stop and give way to tears when looking at Mr John's place and found him no more with us. . . . " He feels his loneliness keenly: "Two men shall be in the field, the one shall be taken and the other left."[26]

Despite the Christian context, the emotional tenor of this is thoroughly Yoruba: the death of a friend evokes the fragility of the community's existence ("no continuing city").

For friendships were not purely a personal matter between the individuals: it would be generally known of Omole that he was Idowu's friend, so that their friendship became part of the texture of public life:

When Captain Glover had composed the affairs of Ondo back in 1871–1872, his personal messenger had been an Oyo man called Obayomi, who settled in Ondo. By 1875 Obayomi had become very influential—"a very good looking man by nature . . . he seemed to be one of the princes of that place"[27]—and a close associate of the most powerful warlord of the town, Edun, who in that year was made *Lisa,* the first of the non-royal High Chiefs. The two of them, united by political interest as well as by personal "chemistry," dominated Ondo in these years, though by 1878 things had cooled a little between them.[28]

Still, early in 1880 the *Lisa* and "his beloved friend Obayomi" fell out badly over the latter's treatment of a woman whom *Lisa* called his sister. *Lisa* hit him with the flat of his sword. "All the respects which he had accumulated among the Ondos generally have all gone away. They said to him, we have done enough for you."

A month later news came that Obayomi had fallen ill on his farm—probably from the smallpox then raging—and had asked that, in the event of his death, his children be taken care of and not sent to Ibadan lest they be enslaved. Nine days later he did die, and *Lisa* asked the mission to bury him. Phillips and Young first demurred as he wasn't a Christian, but *Lisa* insisted he had been Glover's messenger and should be buried by his own people (i.e., the *oyinbo,* or "white men"). *Lisa* called the King of Ondo and all the five other High Chiefs to each give a goat to Obayomi's wives for the funeral, and sent his two sons to the mission according to their father's wish.[29]

In fact the bonding power of friendship within the community was underscored by the fact that it could transcend *ilu* boundaries. Ogunbona, the missionaries' patron at Abeokuta, was known as a friend of Ajobo (who rose to be *Balogun* of Ibadan), which may well have been a factor in Ajobo's benevolence to the Ibadan church.[30] When a later *Balogun,* Ajayi Ogboriefon, died in 1879, the above-mentioned *Lisa* of Ondo sent a keg of powder, three demijohns of rum, and a ram to help bury him, in memory of their friendship, which so pleased Ibadan's ruling chief Latosisa that he reciprocated with valuable gifts himself.[31] There was also a very public agenda here, in that it was strategically essential for Ibadan to maintain her coastal access by the Ondo road, and the *amicitia* of these warlords played a vital part in enabling it to be done. We might well suppose that this kind of fellow feeling among the war-chiefs of different towns, parallel to the emerging "supra-tribal" sentiments of Christian clergy and teachers, laid some foundation for modern Yoruba consciousness.

Friendship readily found more formal expression in gangs or clubs (*ẹgbẹ*). *Orẹdẹgbẹ* [friends become a club], which is a common name for social clubs nowadays, expresses an enduring cultural disposition of the Yoruba. After childhood, *groups* of friends were always gender specific. Those of men (who had much more free time than women) were more likely to be seen in pub-

Figure 3.2. Akesan market, Oyo. *Church Missionary Gleaner,* April 1904.

lic recreation, as with old men playing the board game "warry" (*ayọ*) under the shade trees in the market, or young men drinking together in palm wine booths. Women married much younger than men did, and their friendship groups (except of the most casual kind) seem different in two ways: they were typically realized through associations which had other ends, particularly commercial and religious, and (as an aspect of this) they were less age specific than the men's. Two good examples are the group of women, mostly petty traders working from the fronts of their houses in Lagos, who rallied round a worshipper of Ibeji (the deity of twins) when the evangelist M. F. Willoughby engaged her in unwelcome argument in Lagos in 1870,[32] or the Sango women whom Samuel Pearse disturbed (to the great annoyance of some of them) while they were getting ready the feast in honor of their god in Badagry in 1863.[33]

The solidarity of male age-peers was strikingly manifest in the common practice by which groups of young men, once as large as forty, came to see the missionaries, out of curiosity to see what they were about rather than from any sense of need.[34] For groups of male peers had a directly political relevance which women's groups lacked. The ethos of mutual support, the emphasis on an essential equality of condition and the controlling solidarity of "moving together" which we find in informal friendship groups were taken up in several kinds of formal public association. Foremost here was the age-grade organization which was found in many parts of Yorubaland, notably in Ijebu (the *rẹgbẹrẹgbẹ*, which were designated with a distinct name at four-year intervals), and in Ekiti and the northeast. Very widely, (e.g., Ijesha, Ondo) the young men who formed the militia were constituted as an *ẹgbẹ*, their leaders being quarter-chiefs called *Ẹlẹgbẹ* (a word often synonymous with *Ologun*, "war-chief," but which can also mean just "companion").

Other associations of men were either occupational (like hunters' or craft guilds) or were of a general secular and civil character, being concerned with maintaining the town's internal order rather than its external defense. Here the fellowship of elders, rather than of young men, was central, and a religious dimension starts to appear. The Ogboni cult or society was most prominent at Abeokuta, but it crystallized principles of authority general throughout Yorubaland. Sanctioned by the power of the earth, the Ogboni as elders stood closest of living people to the ancestors who were the springs of the community as a moral order. The material symbols of their authority, the small double-figured brass staffs called *ẹdan*, had a fearful effect when they were sent to summon an offender or lay an interdict on a debtor.[35] The social ethos of Ogboni was rather of a small-town conservatism, concerned with the routine control of women and young men but also to restrain the aggrandizement of individual men, or large trans-generational flows of wealth. Individuals might join Ogboni to enjoy its immunities, but they might also be compelled to join, since joining involved membership fees, redistributed to existing members. But the chief stroke by which Ogboni leveled wealth and created solidarity was by burying its members, which entailed the large payment of fees to the society which were largely spent on the funeral feast: the wealth of the living was converted into honor for the dead. J. A. Maser held it responsible for the fact that, as he correctly observed, "there are no rich families in Abeokuta, no aristocracy."[36]

The executive arm of Ogboni at Abeokuta was Oro, the cult society of the collective ancestors, whose instrument, the bull-roarer, sounded with its "huzzing and humming"[37] to confine women indoors when it had business to do. This included the execution of condemned criminals and witches, but also major public sacrifices, deliberations, and palavers. Oro's activists were young men, but they acted at the behest of elders, according to a normative prescription which prevailed even where, as at Ilesha or Ondo, neither Ogboni nor Oro existed in the form they did at Abeokuta. Oro's secrecy, anonymity, and lack of individuation were strongly evocative of the collective solidarity of fairly small and homogeneous communities. Oro also existed in some Oyo towns, such as Iseyin, Ijaye and Ibadan, but here its scope was limited by stronger chiefly authority, and its punitive functions were often taken over by Egungun, a more personalized form of ancestral cult whose form encouraged individual self-promotion and often rowdy rivalry between groups of supporters. It was presumably this potential which made it necessary for Egungun to be headed by a senior chief or a high-profile elder.[38] In many references to Oro, in contrast, no specific leaders are mentioned, other than (by implication) the senior Ogboni. Egungun sometimes adopted a style of provocative confrontation[39] which was quite alien to Oro's way, despite their similar ideological role: to expose the living to the power of the dead and so to underwrite community. Crowther seems to have had both cults, but especially Oro, in mind when he wrote of "an established religion of government, which is the worship of the dead or their deceased ancestors."[40] Similar expressions were used of Egungun: "a national god of the Yorubas,"[41] "a thing which the Yorubas take to govern their town and [their] wives."[42]

We have moved by a series of gradations from the spontaneity of friendships, through the fellowship of more formalized *egbe,* to *egbe* charged with the institutional needs of the community. By steps the essentially egalitarian character of fellowship is compromised by inequality, expressed in the taken-for-granted language of age and kinship. *Egbe* are models of community to the extent that they stress commonality of condition, which is why they are ideally age specific, since this eliminates the most uncontested source of hierarchy in Yoruba culture. Hence the solidarity, equally of Ogboni (qua elders) or of the young men who carry out their decisions through Oro or as warriors. But the articulation of these two levels of solidarity brings into play the foundational inequalities, those of age and the parent-child relationship. The indignant voice of the elders of Ado-Odo, a self-consciously conservative little town, protesting at the presumption of their young warriors, put it succinctly: "Are they not our children? They want to know too much. It is not for them to govern but to carry out the plans and wishes of the elders. We were warriors in our earlier years, so they must wait for their time to rule."[43]

Everywhere the ideal charter of community involved sharing a relationship with forebears, to whom elders stood nearest. Thus the Egba conceived of themselves as "children" (*omo*) of Lisabi and the Ijesha of Obokun. Neither of these figures was reckoned to be literally the ancestor of the mass of their "children." But both evoked aspects of patriarchal authority: Lisabi as champion and protector (he was the warrior who led the Egba against Oyo oppression in the 1770s),[44] and Obokun (founder of the Ilesha royal lineage) as the archetype of every subsequent ruler.

The Yoruba preference for a "co-filiative" rather than a fraternal idiom of fellowship or citizenship, as has been adopted in the European tradition, led to certain terminological problems when the missions wanted to express notions of religious "brotherhood." *Orisa* cults worked analogously to communities, in that their members thought of themselves as together the children of a deceased or more-than-mortal person. European Christianity moved readily from the notion of "children of God" to one of "brotherhood of man," but directly fraternal idioms are not so suited to express ideas of religious fellowship in Yoruba, since siblings are always strictly rank-ordered by age. Unlike the English terms "brother" and "sister," sibling terms in Yoruba are age related and gender neutral: *egbon* [senior sibling], *aburo* [junior sibling].[45] Still looking for an idiom of Christian fellowship that did not employ the co-filiative one of *oriṣa* cults, the missionaries moved outside *kinship* altogether, and used terms based on *ara,* "person, resident." The semantic range of *ara* overlaps with that of *ọmọ* ("child"), though they are often used contrastively: a citizen of Ibadan can be called *ọmọ Ibadan* or *ara Ibadan,* but *ọmọ* has the clear connotation of belonging by descent.[46] So "brethren," or "brothers and sisters," in a religious sense came to be rendered *arakunrin, arabinrin* (i.e., *ara* qualified by gender).[47] The awkwardness of European Christianity's lacking a term both warm and ungendered to express religious fellowship was not easily shaken off.

INEQUALITIES AND CONTROLS

So the *ẹgbẹ,* whose egalitarian solidarities were enlisted on behalf of the community, stood in contrast to kin groups, yet came to draw on their inescapably inegalitarian idiom: parents superior to children, husbands to wives, children ranked by age, and wives by seniority. The kin group, especially the locally co-resident section of a lineage or the agnatic core of a compound (*idile*), was still the individual's primary source of social identity, the main place he was known as coming *from.* Precisely because friends and *ẹgbẹ* were voluntary (which gave them much of their affective importance), they could not generate the binding attachments of the lineage. Though a son might want to succeed his father in a friendship,[48] *ẹgbẹ* in general did not have that unlimited temporal extension which was presupposed by lineage commitments. Thus, lineage membership had a double-edged quality: just as it was expected to protect and represent its members through its *baale,* or head, it also had large powers to control and even exploit them. Here its inegalitarian internal structure showed itself strongly.

Crimes, debts, and funerals were three classes of events where the ineluctable side of kinship showed itself. Compounds policed themselves internally and were to a large extent held responsible for their members' behavior outside, sometimes with fearsome consequences. At Ibadan in 1851, a young man was beheaded for stabbing someone to death; he gave a defiantly unrepentant speech and (specifically because of that) his family were all sold into slavery.[49] In 1870, two members of a compound offended: a woman while cooking carelessly had started a fire which destroyed nearly 200 compounds, and her son had infringed public policy at the time by kidnapping two people at Abeokuta. Their local chief ordered that both of them with their whole household be sold as slaves to buy gunpowder.[50] It does not affect the point that both these punishments were arbitrary as well as severe and depended on the mood of the public and the chiefs, for the uncertainty added to the prevailing sense that household members were bound to hang together. Where the interests of powerful chiefs were at stake, these features were accentuated. The *Lisa* of Ondo, suspecting the adultery of some of his wives,

59

had his men sack the houses of the suspects.[51] When the lover of one of the *Arẹ* Kurunmi's wives managed to flee Ijaye, Kurunmi demanded that a substitute from his family be killed in his place.[52] On another occasion he fined the father of an unfaithful wife (who was herself, as usual, put to death) eighty heads of cowries—which he paid up, since he didn't dare abscond in case the rest of the family suffered.[53] Nor was collective responsibility limited to those cases where a punishment was imposed by the authorities. At Ota in 1855 a man was killed in a dispute about kola trees (a valuable economic crop). His killer ran off to Abeokuta, but the victim's family threatened vengeance on his family. So the killer's family sent a message to him to return, saying they had paid the indemnity. He came back unsuspecting and was himself killed by his companions (with whom his family must have colluded).[54]

Debt was a widespread feature of this increasingly monetized society. The most common reasons why people went into debt were to raise trading capital, to pay for divination and medical treatment, to pay fees to chiefs if they got into legal trouble, to redeem relatives from slavery, and, perhaps most commonly, to pay for funeral expenses. Debt put a lot of pressure on both parties: it gave rise to threats or attempts at suicide by creditors as well as debtors.[55] People in debt were less than fully free, in that they risked themselves being sold to pay their debts (a fate most likely to befall those who had few local kin).[56] Much Yoruba suicide seems to have been motivated by public shame, which must have been further stoked up by the fact that it was not just kinfolk but communities which could be held liable for their members' debts. Two incidents from Abeokuta show how easily the debts of individuals could come to embroil their communities:

> In 1854, a young woman, the niece of a church member, was seized in the street by men sent by none other than Ogunbona, the Christians' patron but here acting in his capacity as *Balogun* of Ikija, on account of a debt owed by her townsman to a man of Ikija. The debt was the sum paid by the Ikija man for his wife, who had left him to go with an Ilawo man. While missionary intervention got the young woman freed, Ogunbona insisted he still needed a substitute from Ilawo to secure the debt's repayment.[57]

In the second case two kinds of community intersected:

> Relations were always tense between the Awori town of Ota and the Egba farm villages which extended to within a few miles on its northern side. One of these villages was Sunren, founded by Christians from Abeokuta. In 1875 a low-intensity war broke out between Ota and Sunren, triggered by the kidnap of a girl from Igbein township in Abeokuta because of a debt by another Igbein person. But since she was also a Christian living at Sunren, John Okenla, the *Balogun* of the Christians, felt he had no option but to act by counter-kidnap to get her back.[58]

In both of these cases collective liability could not have worked without the control which a community could exercise over its members through its own internal status hierarchy.

Where the backstop liability of kin or community broke down or was missing, debt became highly problematic. At Ondo in 1878, Charles Phillips encountered a very sick, elderly man thrown out into the street and jeered at; and when he went to complain, the chiefs told him that anyone who helped someone in such a case became liable for his debts.[59] Such a conspicuous abrogation of normal decency amounted to a public expulsion of the debtor from his compound—and we can only guess at the circumstances which lay behind it. A cognate case was the practice (reported from Abeokuta) by which a deceased debtor's body was wrapped in a mat tied to a horizontal pole supported in the air by two posts. Anyone who buried the body would become liable for the debt. Again, the account doesn't make the background clear: was it a recognized way for the family to disown the dead man, or was it authorized by the local Ogboni to put pressure on the debtor's family, who would be troubled by the restless ghost of the unburied man?[60]

Substantial debts were normally secured on the person of an *iwofa*, or "pawn," someone who was bound to work for the creditor until the loan was repaid. An adult might pawn himself, but mostly children or adolescents were pawned by their senior relatives. Pawnship was held to be to be quite distinct from slavery—*Afotele ko je ki a pe iwofa li eru* [Whatever has been said before, a pawn is not to be called a slave] went one saying[61]—and the giver of the loan (who took the pawn) could be regarded as a doing a favor to the person in need.[62] But these were views of beneficiaries of the system, of senior people in the kin group who were able to exploit their juniors and of those other seniors who through pawns could swell the size of their personal followings. Substantively the condition of a pawn might not differ very much from that of a slave: the great mass of both categories would be engaged in farm labor, though the pawn's prospects and security were greater, since he stayed in his own community where he had kin. But the accidents of life and the times might annul such relative advantages:

A boy, Sangolowomu, ran to the CMS missionary at Oyo, George Meakin, to escape being beaten by his master, a Sango priest. He had been pawned for five heads of cowries by a man who had died at Ijaye, and his mother was missing, presumed dead. But his master claimed he was a slave and gave him as such to the *Alafin* Atiba. Meakin went to fetch him, but the *Alafin* said he had to redeem him or else teach him to make snuff or gunpowder. Later he was sold to Egbas and taken to Abeokuta. Here he went to the CMS compound and was redeemed by Townsend, whom Meakin had alerted. Meanwhile his mother turned up from Ilorin where she'd been trading, now wealthy and a Muslim. Though duly thankful, she wanted the boy back, but he preferred to stay with Townsend. She succeeded in getting the priest heavily fined for his treachery.[63]

In any case, even the ordinary condition of a junior's subordination to senior relatives might feel very oppressive, as with a young man who wanted to stay with Adolphus Mann at Ijaye, "being tired of serving a relative of his as a kind of slave."[64] His relatives came to take him back, and the case went to the Are Kurunmi; but he owed no one money and was not a slave, so Kurunmi let him go.

It is no accident that funerals figure so often in the CMS narratives and that they gave rise to large expenses which were one of the major reasons for putting young people into pawn. One of his pagan friends explained to Olubi the motive of funeral expenditure as "to be applauded of men, if even we have to put our children in pawn for it, and this is praiseworthy."[65] Funerals were defining occasions in the flow of community life, points at which the deceased were finally recognized for what they had been and confirmed as ancestors. Celebrations of the patriarchal and gerontocratic principles of Yoruba life, they redefined kin groups through assertive acts of power over those of lower status. A dead man's wives were reassigned to new husbands within the lineage, a determination sometimes accompanied by much distress and conflict:

> James Okuseinde attended the reallocation of wives after the death of his kinsman Sodeinde. Quarrels broke out among the sons over the choice. To stop them "the Ogbonis present produced two brass images [edan] which were laid on a mat and the production of which is generally understood as putting an end to all strife. Two kola nuts were splitted upon it as a sort of ceremony and eaten."[66]

That was an Egba occasion, so the Ogboni, as elders, were there to assert the need for communal amity amid circumstances very prone to fuel individual rivalries. Sometimes patriarchy went too far (or perhaps the Ibadan chiefs were less governed by it):

> A woman hanged herself by her head-tie from a tree. She wanted to be the wife of one of her former husband's sons, and not of the man she was assigned to. [This implies she was one of the younger wives, probably a very young woman, and wanted to marry a man close to her own age, the son of a much senior wife, rather than the husband chosen for her]. But her parents and relatives ignored her wishes, one of them saying "Die if you may, you will never be his wife." Because a suicide polluted the entire town, the matter went to the Are Latosisa, who confiscated their houses and would have killed the man who uttered the fatal words if the family had not paid dearly to get him off.[67]

Yet the most categorical exercise of power at funerals was not the pawning of children or the reassignment of wives, but the sacrifice of slaves to appease the spirit of the deceased. The relative exploitability of pawns, wives, and slaves was mainly a function of the degree of their strangerhood or externality to the community. Whereas pawns were typically retained in their home town, many wives (as well as being strangers to their husband's compound, like pawns) were strangers to the town because they were slaves, and slaves, as a condition of their being so, were strangers. The use of slaves in sacrifice was merely the sharpest expression of the principle that the young and the stranger were there to be used to ensure the survival and reproduction of the social order.

THE MAKING AND THE MEANING OF SLAVES

Slavery was an institution of pervasive importance in nineteenth-century Yorubaland, a painful memory or a feared possibility for virtually everyone, and a quotidian reality in every community and most households.[68] Though the status of "slave" (eru) could be contrasted sharply with that of free person (omo, "child"), their common setting in such a patriarchal social order means that it is more realistic to treat them as standing at different points on a single continuum of autonomy-dependency. To soften the pain of the condition and reconcile him to it, James Johnson reported, a slave might be addressed as omo odo ("young child") rather than eru.[69] Slaves had become so by being ejected or torn from their own communities, thus losing the protection that went with membership of their own kin group. It was this lack of the free person's normal social resources which was the essential feature of the slave's condition in Yorubaland, the prerequisite of everything that was done with her/him.[70] Yet there was a gradient from the extreme vulnerability of the newly taken slave through various degrees of social incorporation as the slave settled into his captors' community. Despite this, slaves did bitterly resent their condition, which condemned them to a kind of perpetual juniority for their lifetimes if they did not get themselves out of it. They *were* held as property and would be inherited on their owner's death. Where a free person might be pawned to meet his senior's funeral costs, a slave might be sold again.[71]

People fell into slavery in various ways. It was a heinous offense to sell one's own kin into slavery, which at Abeokuta might merit the severest sanctions of Oro;[72] but people might be sold for serious crimes, especially those likely to imperil the community, and it might arise from heavy, insoluble debt. At Ijaye, the Are Kurunmi once enslaved a boy for putting the town in danger by insulting a mask of Egungun, the ancestral cult which he took very seriously;[73] and a father sold off his pawned son for twice absconding, an action which he feared might bring the whole family into trouble by provoking retaliation.[74] But the vast majority of slaves were the victims of war, though they came in various ways. There were bulk acquisitions through major campaigns, such as the destruction of the old Egba towns in the mid-

1820s, Ibadan's sweep in western Ekiti in the mid-1850s, or the sack of Ile-sha in 1870. So many slaves were taken that, after Ibadan chiefs and warriors had taken their fill, large numbers were left to be sold on: a mission party traveling up to Ibadan from Lagos in 1856 passed lots of Ekiti teenage boys being driven down to the coastal markets (one infers from the sex ratio here that female captives had been largely retained in Ibadan as wives).[75]

The large throughput of slaves in the militarily successful towns created a niche for specialist slave dealers. Kurunmi had his own, whom the cate-chist Charles Phillips once called to see:

> Entering the house of "Are [Kurunmi]'s immediate dealer in human traffic," he met a man with chains on his legs, who at once fled into a back room, terrified from his English clothes that he had come to buy him. The master of the house was consulting Ifa, and Phillips heard the diviner prom-ise him children. Phillips asks him if he'd truly like to have children. "What do we come for in the world? Is it not to have children and plenty of money?—Yes, would you like to sell the children after grown up?—No! How can one sell his own children?—But do you think or have you ever heard from your ancestors that any human being [was] ever born with the sign of slave?—No!—How come you to put chains?—It is not I but Are."[76]

The very normality of slavery and its continuity with other forms of so-cial dependency obviated the need for much by way of justification. Slaves were the soldier's reward, the anticipated outcome of going to war. Wars which the chiefs saw as strategically necessary became difficult to prosecute if they yielded no slaves for the troops.[77] Olubi was told by Odulana, the chief warrior of his quarter, when he taxed him about Ibadan militarism: "Who can give up war in the Yoruba country when one can enrich himself [i.e., by taking a slave] in a day?"[78] Phillips describes the departure of the Ijaye army for its Sabe campaign in 1855: in the street by the Arę's palace, women held out numberless images of their orişa, offering to the soldiers "propitious bless-ings for preserving their lives as well as to catch many slaves."[79] Many of these women must have been slave wives of the soldiers; and however we imagine their mixed feelings—fear for their husbands' safety? empathy for those who would come to share their own fate?—they knew that an influx of fresh slaves and new wives would push up their own status. To Phillips's reproaches, the Ijayes justified the war by historical precedent rather than theoretical argu-ment: "The people whom we are going against are not Yoruba [i.e., not Oyo].... They are the people our forefathers used to catch and sell as their prey, even from the time of [the Alafin] Abiodun."

The general breakdown of regional security created other openings for the capture of slaves. When states were at peace, they regarded it as a seri-ous offence for their respective citizens to kidnap one another,[80] but when war was in the offing, the authorities would announce that the enemy's farms were open for kidnapping. This kind of raiding for captives was known as *sumọmi*, distinct from regular war (*ogun*).[81] Bands of men, from a handful of companions to parties of several hundreds, would then set off to waylay travelers or raid farm hamlets:

> William Moore, pastor of the Egba town of Osiele, was traveling to Abeokuta when he passed an old farmer in tears. His harvest of maize, which he was due to sell to market women who had come out from Abeokuta, had been seized by a party of some 400 men off to kidnap on the Ijebu farms. The kidnappers killed the men and captured the women and children of two Ijebu villages, but later were ambushed by the Ijebu, and some three-quarters of them were killed. What had encouraged them to go was that three weeks earlier some sixty men had gone to kidnap on the Ibadan-Ijebu road. It had been a success, with a great quantity of trade goods (salt, tobacco, European cloth) and five slaves taken.[82]

Often a much smaller party of men would make a camp in the bush near a road and hope to snatch victims in ones and twos: women going to trade were favorite targets.[83] It was still sometimes an uncertain business, as in another cautionary story told by Moore:

> Four Egbas went off to kidnap Ijebus. Having only caught one victim (who was the particular prize of one of them), they had to stay longer than intended so that the others could get their own. They made a camp, but were unlucky: they feared to jump one group of travelers lest some escape to give the alarm, and were foiled by the size of a convoy 350 strong. They consulted Ifa about their lack of success, and were told to sacrifice sixteen bush-rats and sixty cowries. A day was spent setting traps to catch the rats, during which the captive escaped. They gave up and came home. Later it came to court: should the man who took the captive be compensated by the others because he had lost his prize through staying back to help the others?[84]

The breakdown of normal functions when towns were destroyed eroded social trust as it made slaves. Thomas King's mother was first enslaved when her small Egba town, Emere, was destroyed in the wars of the 1820s:

> After four years in Ijebu, she was sold to Lagos. When her master, who was himself a slave, escaped, she was sold again. Her new master's wife, being Egba too, tried to get her redeemed, but with no success. Still, disturbances in Lagos at this time enabled hundreds of slaves to escape. But they needed "conductors" to guide them to Abeokuta; and "all such conductors reckoned those who were thus brought to the town through their means as their captives and demanded from them as much as they

pleased." So she effectively became a slave again, until some years later she was redeemed by the missionaries, on account of her son Thomas.[85]

As Ijaye crumbled and fell, its people dispersed, some to their conquerors at Ibadan (where many of them had kinsfolk) and some to Abeokuta (which had been their ally). Many went farther afield, coming to James White's attention in Ota, a town under strong Egba influence:

On 9 January 1862, twenty Ijaye women, who had been "seeking some means of subsistence" in the area, rushed to the CMS compound for protection. Egbas had started seizing these women in the streets to make them their slaves, "assigning as their reason that they had authority to catch and sell all such Ijayi people as fall within their power and to purchase ammunition with the money." With the threat of force from Chief *Olikosi*, the Egbas agreed to free Ijaye women who had come from Lagos, but not those from Abeokuta.[86] The ensuing months saw even more kidnapping of travelers on the Lagos-Abeokuta road, and the victims—many of whom were Ijayes—were quickly taken by night to the slave market at Oke Odan.[87]

Here we see two forms of social metamorphosis. The first, the sale of the Ijaye women to buy gunpowder for the Egba, like human sacrifice at funerals, is the conversion of strangers into the means to protect the life of the community. The second, which is also seen in the slave career of Thomas King's mother, is the transformation of allies or protectors into captors and masters. Outrageous though this seemed to the narrators, it was not without *some* cultural support, in that the concept of "father" (*baba*) embraced many facets of domination from the benignly protective to the exploitative, just as the status of slave was continuous with other forms of dependency. An analogous case, though in reverse, was provided by those Ijeshas, desperate from starvation when Ilesha fell after its long siege, who handed themselves over as slaves to the Ibadans. They made a point of giving themselves up to the *Balogun* Ajobo, because of his reputation for "unparalleled liberality."[88] And surely they would have called him *"Baba!"*

Slaves were not set to do any one particular thing, and the only thing they did (or rather that was done to them) that absolutely separated them from the free population was to be sacrificed (which was the fate of only a minute proportion of the total slave population). The vast bulk of slaves did not have different employment from the mass of the free population: if men, they were farmers or craftsmen; and if women, they were wives and pursued trade or a craft. Slaves were normally allowed scope to work for their own benefit as well as for their master's, and a capable and well-placed slave might thus earn enough to buy his freedom, like the Ijesha Peter Apara. About twenty-three years old when he was captured by the Ibadans shortly after the sack of Ilesha in 1870, he was sold first to the *Balogun* of Ife, and then passed, via the slave market of Ejinrin, to a man at Epe on the Lagoon. Only six years later, *o sanwo rira ara rẹ kuro l'oko ẹru* [He spent money to buy himself away from the farm of slavery].[89] But it is impossible to know how typical this was, especially with those slaves who were held in large concentrations of dozens or hundreds, working on the farms of the big Ibadan chiefs.

In a rather different case were those slaves who were taken into the personal retinues of great men and chiefs. Young able-bodied male slaves counted prominently among the warboys of the great chiefs, and as such stood far above the mass of the free population in the power hierarchy. Reflecting on a year (1855) in which military success had brought a huge influx of slaves, Hinderer described Ibadan as having two classes, "the working class and the warriors,"[90] but this did not correspond with the slave/free distinction. In the 1880s, when the Ibadan army was hard pressed by the effects of blockade and their enemies' success, the chiefs at Kiriji used to send their "swordbearers" to press-gang extra recruits from men still in town and to raise money for munitions by looting and arbitrary fines.[91] These thugs were mostly the slaves of senior chiefs. When David Kukomi's farm was pillaged, the Christians sought reparation through their contacts with a slave who was the overseer of a nearby farm of the Arẹ Latosisa's, a man to whom "all the farmers around including our Christians are voluntary clients."[92] The irony is that it was the very source of the normal slave's powerlessness, his lack of local kin, which made slaves the best instrument for the chiefs to use when they wanted to turn the screw on the civilian population: they could carry out an unpopular and (in its way) anti-social policy with less compunction—and they would be sure to add a little exploitation on their own account. Yoruba ọba had always had large numbers of slaves resident in their palaces, and the slaves of the Alafin at New Oyo were notorious: "They go where they like, assault who they like, fire whose houses they like, and farms, and steal from whom they like, and no one dare complain."[93]

Modern arguments about the nature of African slavery had precursors in the vigorous debate which took place in 1879–1880 about the holding of slaves and pawns by agents of the Yoruba Mission itself.[94] The issue was most acute at Abeokuta, which of all the interior stations had the most adherents, had been under an entirely Egba leadership from 1867 until the arrival of James Johnson in 1877, and had adapted itself the most to local customs.

Two main points were made in extenuation of local slavery. The first was practical: that servile or semi-servile labor was the only kind readily available for those who needed it, other than that of one's own children. William Allen, one of the Egba clergy accused of having slaves, who suffered from painful guinea-worm in his leg and needed continuous personal attendance, explained his use of a "slave" thus:

"In this country . . . no labourer could be got for any price for the citizens of this place look at any one who wants to employ them as a real insult to them." He could not get any of his relatives to help. "The motto of this country is, that every cask must stand on its own bottom. These make me to get my own people for myself. . . . They call me their father for what I did for them."[95]

The difficulty of getting wage labor was widely echoed;[96] and in fact women were much more commonly employed as laborers than men—for example as porters and builders' laborers.[97] The grounds for men's dislike of wage labor were astutely divined by Charles Phillips of Ondo: "I would charge unwillingness to work for wages to the family law, which reduces the son or younger brother to the level of slaves to the father or elder brother."[98] Labor for others had to be unfree labor, since it was already defined as such within the age-stratified family unit: the closeness of eru and omo was prefigured. Set in opposition to it was the Yoruba male ideal of adult autonomy, a personal independence that needed both fatherhood and friendship to be fully realized.

The second point made about slavery is implicit in what has just been said. It insisted on the "leniency and gentleness"[99] of Yoruba slavery, a servitude which was reduced to "a tolerable or palatable grievance" by its domestic character.[100] Opinions differed, but did not polarize Europeans and Africans. Hinderer called it "comparatively a very mild servitude,"[101] and Townsend wrote to Venn stressing how different African was from American slavery;[102] but James Johnson always came down vehemently against it, drawing attention to the arbitrariness and brutality it could involve, especially to sick or useless slaves, who might be simply thrown out into the street to die.[103] In the face of these generalities, two contrasting cases serve to mark out the possibilities.

On one side is the affection evident in a "form of manumission" prepared for Sodeinde, the *Oluwo* of Ake (the senior Ogboni of his township, and a man with close Christian relatives):

It declares free "the woman called Kele who resides in my house and who has been as a mother to me. After my death I hope she will continue to live in my house and take care of my children." But if she wants to leave, she may. He thus makes his wishes known, but if anyone troubles her, "I, Sodeinde, imprecate evil on that person and I say that he or she who shall cause such trouble will soon follow me to the other world."[104] [The minatory tone of the final sentence is to deter relatives who might seek to claim as their own any slave set free *without* the payment of redemption money.]

At the other extreme is the case of a woman, a member of James White's congregation at Ota, whom he proposed to redeem with funds left to the mission for this purpose by an Englishwoman:

Joanna Merigbe was owned by a "great chief and priest" at Ota. Though her husband was a pagan she tried to bring up her children as Christians.

When she annoyed her master by refusing to eat meat from the household's sacrifices, he chained her up for several weeks to make her recant. During this time, one of her children died. She now feared that, not being free, her children might be sold away at any time. "Joanna now determined to live without a husband for she says, 'I shall no more be the bearer of such unfortunate beings as slave children.'"[105]

Joanna was clearly not reassured by what is sometimes stated as a convention of Yoruba slavery, that home-born slaves were never sold. Nor should she have been; slaves were always subject to acts of power at their owners' discretion, because they lacked the social support to resist them. And surely this is behind White's judgment that, while it was true that "there are a great many of our people who are very indulgent to their slaves . . . yet the recollection that he is a slave fills his breast with gloominess, discontent and murmurs, and he groans as it were under a very heavy load."

This is evident enough from the responses of slaves, especially the young and newly captive. Suicide was most common then, as with nine of the great flood of Ekiti slaves which was brought to Ibadan in 1855, or the Ijebu man who escaped to Ibadan and, when told by the *Balẹ* he would be returned, struck at five of the *Balẹ*'s men with a knife before turning it on himself.[106] James Johnson put suicide second only to absconding as the thing which might put at risk an owner's investment in slaves (since he would have to pay for expiation of the death).[107] But there was space for hope even in the heart of Ibadan, at Oja'ba market, which in the 1870s newly taken Ekiti slaves used to frequent to look for missing relatives. "Seeing each other here, they would sympathize with each other and those of them who had been in the town before and had redeemed themselves may be able to redeem their own people."[108] If they could, slaves escaped, and as the century wore on more and more of them did so. If they could not get home, they headed for the British settlements—slaves from Abeokuta and the west to Lagos, and those from southeastern areas to Leki—and by the 1880s even Ibadan slaves were starting to leach back eastward. Only in the 1890s did this trickle become a flood.

Finally, there was the use of slaves as sacrificial victims, the extreme case of the consumption of strangers to give life to the community. Formerly current all over Yoruba country, the practice was in decline among the Oyo and Egba in the second half of the century.[109] In Ibadan, it went out as a regular practice in the early 1870s, with the ascent to the paramountcy of the *Arẹ* Latosisa, Ibadan's first Muslim ruler. Back in 1847, *Baṣọrun* Oluyole's death (so it was reported in Abeokuta)[110] had occasioned seventy deaths to appease his spirit. During Ogunmola's fatal attack of smallpox a boy and a girl, loads of cowries, and on the last day a positive hecatomb of sheep and goats were offered up to save him. After his expiry on 29 March 1867, a horse, seven women, and a boy were killed for his spirit.[111] Ibadan's major official human sacrifice was to the *orişa* Oranyan, customary when the army left for war. One was noted in 1854, and another in 1860, when Anna Hinderer recorded the dignity of the young male victim, the solemn atmosphere in the town before the act, and the relief and rejoicing afterward.[112] Others occurred in 1872,[113] and again in 1873, sanctioned reluctantly by the *Arẹ* Latosisa.[114] At the outbreak of war in 1877, there was no sacrifice, but there was a lapse in 1885, after Latosisa's death, when the army's desperation at Kiriji drove them once more to seek to propitiate the *orişa* with a human victim.[115]

The picture for Abeokuta seems broadly similar in the timing of its public decline, but characteristically uneven as regards the different townships: no sacrifices at all are reported for Ake, but several for Igbein and Ikereku.[116] But it was in the east that the practice continued in vigor till the 1890s, and nowhere more than at Ondo. Apart from the woman and the man offered each year to the *orişa* Esu and Oramfe respectively, slaves were killed at the funerals of rich and powerful people, of women as well as of men. As elsewhere, slaves at Ondo were more at risk the newer they were, the closer to being total strangers. The unpleasantness of killing domestic slaves who had formed attachments in the compound led to a practice by which chiefs bought young female slaves expressly to be sacrificed at their funerals.[117] They were made to swear an oath of loyalty to their master and treated as favorite wives, but were not allowed to have children. (The stated reason for this was that a mother could not be killed in front of her child; but equally a woman who had borne a child for a community had already started to become a member of it). When human sacrifice was abolished in Ondo in 1892, the people tauntingly told the *Şọra,* the priest-chief of Oramfe, that if he wanted victims, he should go and get them from the Ikale, Ondo's hostile neighbors to the south.[118]

Human sacrifice might even be the occasion for deciding just who *was* a stranger:

> A human sacrifice [probably to Obalufon] took place in Ikereku township in 1866. The *orişa* people had their eye on a captive Ijesha *balogun,* but Soretire, the chief in whose house he was living, objected and Madam Tinubu ransomed him for eight bags of cowries. "Then it seems a foreigner, a Gambari, was taken."[119]

That perhaps was a small moment in the formation of the modern Yoruba identity: the Ijesha was defined by Egba as "one of us," while a Gambari or Hausa speaker paid for being a "foreigner."[120]

Slaves themselves were not always completely passive in the definition of identity. This came out strongly in the dissension around the funeral of the Ondo warlord Edun, the *Lisa:*[121]

> Since *Lisa* was the most powerful man in Ondo, his death on 13 September 1880 promised a great display. But there was a delay because,

amazingly, they had trouble in getting enough sacrificial victims. (*Lisa* had given orders that he wanted at least 45 people to be killed.) News of his death traveled quickly, and on the 15th there were raids against his farm from Okeigbo, a hostile town twelve miles away, and a refuge for runaway Ondo slaves. With the impending sacrifice, *Lisa*'s slaves became very unsettled, and started to arm themselves. On the 17th fighting nearly broke out between the slaves and the town-chiefs (who felt that *Lisa*'s wishes should be honored). The chiefs suggested that the slaves would be in no danger if they contributed to the purchase of fresh slaves to be killed. But when this proved impracticable, the slaves themselves split into two factions, the older ones planning to assure their own safety by offering up some of the newer ones for immolation. To calm things down, the King reduced the number to be killed to twenty, and on the 20th the funeral went ahead. There were still demands for the full number to be killed, so tension remained high. A month later, fighting broke out again among the slaves, and about 300 of them made a break for Okeigbo and freedom.

So the slaves—or at least those of them who could—used two tactics to reduce their alienness: by defining themselves as insiders in contrast to the newest slaves; and by escaping to Okeigbo, which appropriately was itself a community of strangers, a new town where most people were parvenus, ruled by an Ife prince who was also an Ibadan-style warlord.[122]

The spokesmen of the world religions were strongly against human sacrifice—which is why we have such a full picture of it from Ondo, since Phillips and Young never let the topic rest. Less obtrusive was the Muslim opposition to it at Ibadan. Here the *Are* Latosisa's position was difficult, as the Muslim head of a community most of whose members still held to the value of the sacrifice. When the time came for Oranyan's propitiation in 1873, Latosisa proposed a compromise, a hefty offering of bullocks and horses; but this was not acceptable, so for that year he gave in and sent out to buy a Gambari man. In calling him a Pontius Pilate for giving in to pressure, Allen at least acknowledged that in principle they stood together on the issue.[123] For it was inescapable that Muslims and Christians would oppose the practice, quite apart from its flat incompatibility with the second and the sixth commandments: it rested on a particularistic notion of community to which the ideal of a universal humanity under God was radically opposed.

PATRIARCHY IN POLITICS

Running through the preceding discussion has been the power of the great warlords, men such as the *Are* Latosisa of Ibadan, Ogundipe Alatise of Abeokuta, or Edun, the *Lisa* of Ondo. In treating them as a novel phenomenon of the age, which offered a different kind of leadership from that of

Figure 3.3. A warlord: Ogedengbe of Ilesha after his arrest by Captain
Bower, 1894. Courtesy of Foreign and Commonwealth Office Library.

ọba and hereditary titleholders, recent academic opinion has echoed contemporary views.[124] But how much, and what kind, of novelty, were they? For
the new functions—as bosses, patrons, warlords, "godfathers," and so forth—
were rendered through an extension rather than an abrogation of an existing terminology of male domination, and particularly of the keystone of this
deeply patriarchal culture, the concept of "father," *baba.*

Baba carried connotations of priority, dominance, leadership, or superior
efficacy in any sphere, human or otherwise. *Ẹnit' a ba l'aba, l'a npe ni baba*
[Whoever one finds already in a place, one calls father] goes a much-cited
maxim. A standard way in which proverbs state that one thing is superior to
or the source of another is by using the term *baba:*

> *Ailowo baba ijaiya*
> "Lack of money is father of misery"[125]

> *Igọgọ igi nla ni baba ireta*
> "The trunk of a big tree is the father of invisibility magic."[126]

Powerful deities were "fathers," such as the omnipresent source of confusion, Esu (*Babaode,* "Father of the outside"), or the dreaded smallpox god,

Sopona (*Babaluaye*, "Father, lord of the world")[127]—and in no euphemistic sense either, for fatherhood meant the capacity to punish as much as to protect. The local leader whom young warriors followed to war in Ibadan was their *babaogun* ("war father"), and the patron-chief at Ibadan of a subordinate town was *babakekere* ("little father"). Still widely current in the early twentieth century was a chorus used by groups (implicitly as a challenge to their rivals) to celebrate their powerful patrons: *Tani wipe a o ni baba?* [Who says we have no father?] At Badagry in 1850, a man approached the scripture reader William Marsh, asking to be introduced to his "Babba," which he glosses as "father, master, superior" and says used to be applied to the slave dealers by their followers.[128] The word was likewise used by Yoruba CMS agents to refer both to their superiors in the mission and to those chiefs who protected them:

> Otun the first person in the town gave us a leg of beef [wrote Olubi from Ibadan] and made a little fun on the death of my grandmother-in-law, that he would come to bury the dead, that means to ruin me with enormous expense. I told him that he is our Baba and therefore that he is to provide for us and that we are to enjoy it; upon this he laughed and said that he will do it.[129]

The slight hint of menace in the *Otun*'s joke conveys precisely the potentially negative side of great men, even when they were looked to as protectors and providers.

Common to both the new warlord-style *baba* and the *ijoye* of the traditional gerontocracy was the conviction that communities are by nature hierarchical, their idiom of inequality drawn from kinship. The old way—in which the community's general will was formed by consultation up from the household heads through the chiefs, and given final authoritative expression by the *oba*—is nicely conveyed in two proverbs quoted in the small Oyo-loyalist towns of the Oke Ogun:

> *Okegbadi sunkun ati orun, oninu oba l'o nko*
> "Gbadi Hill cries to reach the heavens, but fears it should offend the king."

> *Ajanaku kuro l'eru omo kekere, enikan ki da apa erin ya*
> "Behemoth is too much for a child's load, one man alone cannot tear off an elephant's limb."[130]

The first of these celebrates kingship as the awesome symbol of the community's will, while the second was quoted by the king of Iganna to emphasize that he could not act alone in an affair of the whole town. Their remoteness from the main theaters of war meant that in towns such as Iganna the gerontocracy stayed so well in place that the young men even hesitated to approach an Egba evangelist because he was considered "the elders' stranger."[131]

The *Alafin* Atiba, attempting to recreate the mystique of Oyo-Ile at Oyo's new site, found a vivid image for hierarchy in the musical box which Hinderer played him: "Oh now listen, there is a master inside that music"—referring to the bass note in the melody—"How wonderful [that] everybody and everything in the world has a master!"[132] Atiba looked with some disdain at the apparently masterless world of Ibadan, where authority was so unstable. For the warlords were often counted symbolically as young men: they had made their way through their capacity as warriors, and their power depended on their wealth, their slaves, and their charms, rather than on the loyalty of constituencies given them by custom and the inherent spiritual powers of elders. That is why two old-style chiefs at Ondo (*Saṣẹrẹ* and *Adaja*), wanting to dissociate themselves from the powerful *Lisa*, told Young "not to mind him—that he is a young man and that he only depends on riches."[133] *Owa* Bepo of Ilesha spoke similarly about the Ijesha warlord Ogedengbe, in a grudging admission of the realities of power: "Young as he is [he was probably in his early fifties], he is my father."[134]

The warrior career was, under nineteenth-century conditions, the premier path to the Yoruba man's ideal of autonomy and self-realization. As a social pattern, however, it generated two great contradictions. First, the peer-group fellowship which played a vital part in the young men's struggle against elders' control was very prone to be undermined by their personal rivalries. The peace of Ibadan was constantly disturbed by fights between young warriors, especially after the military stalemate of the 1880s dried up the supply of slaves and booty. In Ibadan in 1868, for example, a young man was executed for murdering a friend who had taunted him about his personal appearance.[135] Second, a young man could only complete himself by building up his own "people," through acquiring wives and slaves, that is, by becoming a *baba* himself and so replicating the structure which produced his youthful ambition. Though this transit from youth to elder was an age-old cultural given, the institutional outcome in a militaristic town such as Ibadan was significantly different from the association of elders that were the traditional norm of patriarchal government. Relations between these warlord-*baba* were regulated less by norms of propriety and restraint than by the pragmatics of force and resource, as if they were still ego-driven young men. Yet the old ideal was still current, an implicit reproach to the warlords:

Olubi is visited in 1870 by Ope, son of Labosinde, who, like his father, was admired for his kindness, fair dealing, and gentleness to his subjects. When going to the farm or around town, Ope would never take gun or sword, but only a couple of whips—which, however, he never used to flog people but only to give a gentle touch to people or animals to signal his approach. In a fracas between two of his sub-chiefs, people called out *Baba mbọ* [Father's coming] when they saw him, and peace was soon restored. *Baṣọrun* Ogunmola, himself the epitome of a warlord, granted him the title *Baba Isalẹ* [Father of the lower town].[136]

In Abeokuta, the Ogboni chiefs upheld the old ways of collective elderly leadership while the Ologun embodied more of the new way; and at Ondo, where the pre-war title system continued fully operative, the *Lisa* conducted himself as if he was an Ibadan-style war-chief despite holding the senior traditional title of the town after the *Oṣemawe*.

Polygamy was integral to the social order, whether old or new: Hinderer was right to call it "an institution of the state."[137] Its implications for age relations were probably even more far-reaching than for gender, in that the disproportionate holding of wives by wealthy, senior, and powerful men meant a corresponding shortfall of wives for younger and poorer men (except to the extent that this was offset by the retention of more female than male slaves in the community). Since marriage was the essential first step of adult self-realization, control over their children's, especially their daughters', marriages was a powerful sanction in the hands of parents (and as such it would often be used to deter Christian conversion). By delaying the age at which most men could marry, polygamy underwrote the power of the chiefs over young men. The conspicuous polygamy of the warlords—by which I mean their possession sometimes of dozens of wives—gave rise to frustration among wives and temptation among young men. The resultant adultery palavers—they are reported for most of the biggest warlords, such as Latosisa of Ibadan, *Lisa* Edun, or Kurunmi of Ijaye[138]—could throw an entire community into turmoil. Traditional Ondo had a safety valve for relieving some of the social tensions of polygamy, which Phillips called "polyandry": heavily polygamous chiefs gave chosen junior relatives sexual access to their wives; the children were credited to the husband; and, in a further bonus for patriarchy, the licensed paramours were treated as their "menservants."[139] Interestingly, the *Lisa* does not seem to have much availed himself of this arrangement, despite many wives "whom he keeps there for many years and months without notice [and who] always complain of having no children."[140] When some of these were caught in adultery (with the connivance of their mothers) and *Lisa* took revenge by pillage and confiscation, so great was the uproar that it seemed an enemy army was approaching, and the king had to go to his house to beg him to lay off.[141]

The competitive self-aggrandizement of patriarchal warlords, in settings where the regulatory power of custom was weakened and the rewards of success were both great and uncertain, overcast social life in the larger towns. Even at Abeokuta, despite the powerful collective sanctions of Oro, the greater warlords were so ready to take their own political or judicial initiatives that a kind of "privatization" of public interests occurred:

In 1868, a general decision was taken by the Egba chiefs to attack Meko, a town some forty miles to the northwest, for its suspected complicity with Dahomey and Oyo against Abeokuta. To buy them off, the Meko people sent gifts through Ogundipe, the powerful *Balogun* of Ikija, which were shared by several senior chiefs. So Ogundipe refused to take part (though some men of his township went). When the Egba force got badly mauled and its commander was killed, Ogundipe (so it was said) shot off guns to show his satisfaction. The final repulse of the Egba, with considerable losses, was assisted by troops sent by the *Alafin,* apparently contacted by Ogundipe. On its return, the defeated Egba force came close to attacking Ogundipe's house, which would have unleashed outright civil war, but was headed off by the intervention of the Ogboni. Ogundipe recouped some favour by using his influence with Meko to prevent the Egba prisoners being sold into slavery.[142]

Here we see Ogundipe's determined pursuit of his own interests against his community's agreed policy, even to the point of dealing as an independent agent with foreign powers like Oyo. After this, his equally furious assertion of more personal interests—for example, against a wife who ran away to Lagos or to recover a couple of slaves whom he thought rightfully his[143]—may seem bathetic. But Ogundipe and his fellows were actors in "heroic history,"[144] whether in the mode of Achilles sulking in his tent over a slave girl taken from him or of Alcibiades conniving with his city's enemies to restore his fortune. The sociological condition of such heroics is the continuous interpenetration of the personal and the political, which occurs when the basis of power is the capacity to command large personal followings.

Ibadan was the town where public life resolved itself most completely into the colliding ambitions of its great chiefs. The documentation is richest for a series of crises in the 1870s, which led to the successive downfalls of *Balogun* Ajobo, *Iyalode* Efunsetan, Aiyejenku the *Fokọ,* and *Seriki* Iyapo. These upheavals were all steps in the rise to the supreme power of the *Arẹ* Latosisa, who showed consummate skill in turning to his advantage the social forces at work in the system:

> It began in 1870, when Ajobo as *Balogun* won much influence among the defeated Ijesha. Soon he was accused before the other chiefs of keeping to himself presents he had received from one of the candidates for the vacant Ijesha crown. Particularly miffed were the war-chiefs next after him, Latosisa the *Ọtun* and Ajayi Ogboriefon the *Osi,* who had played the main part in the Ilesha fighting. Though Ajobo won widespread popularity in Ibadan through his largesse, a meeting of the senior chiefs in July 1871 demanded the war-staff from him [a sign that he was deposed, which also meant he must die]. Presents sent to appease the chiefs were in vain. Ajobo distributed his wealth among his family, freed many slaves, and arranged his coffin—but escaped by night to Ijebu, thus confirming his reputation as a coward. In October, the *Balẹ* [civil head] also having died, Latosisa assumed overall headship of Ibadan, taking the prestigious Oyo title *Are-Ona-Kakamfo* and making Ajayi the *Balogun.*[145]

This was the first step in Latosisa's ascent, where he pulled himself clear of the ruck of chiefs by heading their general resentment of Ajobo's engrossment of revenue and use of it to win general support in the town. He and his two main allies, younger chiefs with the prestige of a successful campaign behind them, also exploited the flaw in Ajobo's reputation: that, while he was generous with money, he lacked something of the manliness of a true *Balogun*.

Effective chiefship depended on being able to reconcile two imperatives which strained against each another: to stave off the envy of one's fellow chiefs, by fair and open sharing of the assets which came in through Ibadan's prowess in war, and to retain as much as possible for oneself in order to be able to keep the loyalty of one's own "people"—warboys, slaves, and other dependents. Ajobo's failure was on the first of these counts, but a chief's enemies might also exploit resentments against him within his—or in the following case, her—own household:

> Shortly after on returning from the Ado campaign early in 1874, the *Arẹ* Latosisa struck against the *Iyalode* [chief of the women] Efunsetan. She traded in ammunition, and it appears that many of the war-chiefs were in debt to her. In Johnson's account, the *Arẹ* was angry that she did not send him supplies during the campaign and did not come to greet him outside the town walls on his return. When she heard that she was deposed, Efunsetan's first step [as Ajobo's had been] was to send gifts to try to win over the chiefs. Here she had some limited success, since a council meeting rescinded an earlier decision to disgrace her. But the *Arẹ* remained obdurate, and when a few days later the Egungun's voice was heard at night, she knew her fate was sealed.

Yet the *Arẹ* still hesitated openly to take a step which public opinion shied away from. So he exploited the discontents of her adopted son Kumuyilo and others in her house. She was said to be too severe with her slaves, "from her masculine nature." It was said that, having lost her own daughter in childbirth, she forced any of her female slaves who became pregnant to have an abortion. Even if this was only a rumor, it was a highly significant one, since it made Efunsetan out to be the moral equivalent of a witch, a supremely wicked woman.

Efunsetan now spent a wretched time in her house waiting for the blow to fall. Eventually, two of her slaves under Kumuyilo's direction got into her bedroom through the ceiling and clubbed her to death. They put it out that she'd died in the night, but opinion in town was outraged and demanded some restitution. Kumuyilo came close to indicting the *Arẹ* and was himself disgraced. The *Arẹ* was acquitted of any involvement, "to prevent civil war," while the slaves who did the deed were impaled as criminals at Oja'ba market.[146]

Though the warlords were often able to set themselves beyond the norms that bound ordinary people, this case shows several ways in which the values of the community shaped the otherwise ruthlessly pragmatic strategies of these conflicts. Most obviously, there were the norms of female behavior which Efunsetan—an awkward female patriarch[147]—either infringed or was represented as having infringed. Then there were those norms of mutual restraint in disputes and of intra-house solidarity which the *Arẹ* and Efunsetan's betrayers respectively were felt to have ignored. Both of these were part of the older public morality which was now being eroded. Then there were cultural ideals, such as the youth-to-patriarch self-aggrandizement which fueled the actions of all the chiefs. Finally, there was public opinion, of uncertain power but a real presence, especially at moments when the struggles between the principals were set on a knife edge. Why else, on a day in 1877 when Ibadan was in tumult over a conspiracy against the *Arẹ* and it was uncertain where the *Balogun* stood, should a young teacher note tersely in his private diary: "Today is the first time Are entertain[s] the townsmen with country beer"?[148]

The right to define norms was at the heart over the next case, that of Aiyejenku the *Fọkọ* in January 1877:

> He was an elderly man, with a distinguished past: one of Ibadan's first settlers who had even then "entered the town on horseback," he had played a notable role at the siege of Ijaye. "He was never a private man at Ibadan." At meetings of the chiefs, he would speak forthrightly from his long experience, referring to the former rulers he had known. "This the Are . . . never liked to hear, and . . . was ever on the look out for an opportunity of putting an end to this 'historian,'" wrote Johnson. Aiyejenku could be irritable and he did not seek to court the younger chiefs, but on occasion reproved them quite sharply.

Aiyejenku's downfall was set off by a dispute between him and the *Arẹ* over whether the people of Igbajo, a subject town of which Aiyejenku was *babakekere,* should be allowed to depose their king. He was overruled at a public meeting, and his offer of some slaves in appeasement was rejected. His enemies went further and stripped him of his right, arising from his earlier exploits as a warrior, to levy the tolls at the Abeokuta gate. Fighting broke out and his quarter was devastated. At first the intention seems to have only been to strip him of most of his wealth and slaves, and the *Arẹ* made as if to distance himself from his most vocal enemies. He was allowed for a while to take shelter with his old friend, Chief Tajo. But when his slaves started to regroup, it was resolved he must quit town or die. Tajo knew he could shield him no longer, and Aiyejenku retired to his own house and shot himself.

The *Arẹ* judged it fit to be magnanimous once this thorn was removed. When Aiyejenku's people sent to the mission to ask for a coffin—for he had been its good patron—Olubi felt it prudent to ask the *Arẹ*'s permission. It was so allowed: "Make it as fine as you can for them." Some months later, the *Arẹ* even gave a bull to Salako, Aiyejenku's son, for him to sacrifice to his late father's spirit.[149]

The insufficiency of the Igbajo dispute by itself to explain Aiyejenku's fall was acknowledged at the time: when the crisis broke, Olubi wrote that he could see "no really decided or actual crime" on his part. His real offense was inveterate opposition to the *Arẹ*, or "taking the town from the head-chief by giving veto to proposals." As with Efunsetan, the enemies outside also sought out malcontents inside his house: he was accused of "greediness to his sons," for not buying them horses! In fact the coalition against Aiyejenku, skillfully orchestrated by the *Arẹ*, appears to have been shot through with the resentment of the warboys at the ornery self-assurance of an old warrior who had taken on much of the style of the traditional elder. He was, wrote Johnson, "like a king in his own quarter of the town, where he was ac-knowledged, loved and venerated," and his deployment of his historical knowledge to back up public arguments—an essential prerogative of the elder—was obviously galling to the *Arẹ*, who was a much younger man. For despite the gravitation of every warlord toward being a patriarchal *baba*, Ibadan's military character meant that the youthful warboys needed always to be courted and rewarded. This fundamental political reality was neglected by Aiyejenku and grasped by *Arẹ* Latosisa.

Aiyejenku's removal served to accentuate the atmosphere of jealousy and distrust among Ibadan's political elite, both among rivalrous aspirants to higher titles and in the community at large in the face of the *Arẹ's* growing power. Another crisis developed over the next few months, its central figure being Iyapo the *Seriki* (head of the junior line of warriors):

Iyapo was the son of *Balogun* Ibikunle [d. 1864], and so belonged to a new wave of youthful leaders, the *mọgaji*, or recognized successors to the head-ship of the great houses established by the first generation of Ibadan's war-lords. Iyapo fell foul of the *Arẹ* for keeping back some plunder from Aiye-jenku's house and for treating his whole quarter, Ayeye, as one compound under him as *bale*, so that the *Arẹ's* writ effectively did not run there. Moves to impeach him were started in February, but the *Arẹ* and his clique backed down when they saw his resolution, fearing "lest he should spoil the town." Some bags of cowries patched things up for the time being.

Later in the year the chiefs fell out badly with the *Arẹ* over his conduct of the war with Abeokuta and his buildup of a special corps composed of slaves from his own house. In October most of the senior war-chiefs (in-cluding both Iyapo and the *Balogun*, Ajayi Ogboriefon) met in the Og-boni house to hatch a plot to overthrow the *Arẹ*. Some chiefs lost their nerve and leaked the plan to the *Arẹ*, but nothing was openly admitted, and for a while the situation was too uncertain for him to act. But by play-ing on the potential for rivalry between *Balogun* Ajayi and *Seriki* Iyapo, he was able to win over the *Balogun,* and so to strike against Iyapo. Sensing the movement of things, the other chiefs shifted to the *Arę*'s side and he was able to rearrange the titles in the *Seriki*'s line, to isolate him from his colleagues. It was when the *Ǫtun Seriki* [second in his line] was expelled from town for declining to replace him as *Seriki* that Iyapo knew just how implacable the *Arę* was. He set his house in order and on 17 November took his own life.

Thereafter the *Arę* was the undisputed, but resented, master of Ibadan till his own death at the Kiriji camp in 1885.[150]

That this was high politics of a particularly ruthless kind must not lead us to ignore its strong domestic base. The model for political *authority* was still the patriarchal household head, and this was set in opposition to the notionally egalitarian relations between age-mates or household heads which defined political *community.* In the above sequence, both Iyapo and Latosisa used patriarchal models to enlarge their political base: Iyapo by treating his whole quarter *as if* it was a single compound under his fatherly control ("and his people loved him because of the protection he gave them"),[151] and the *Arę* by organizing his own slaves—there must have been several hundred of them—as a corps under his son as commander. This corps was feared as a possible step toward a permanent hegemony of the *Arę*'s house, and after Iyapo's fall the *Arę* made sure that the other household heads in Ayeye quarter were removed from any dependency on the house of Ibikunle.[152] There was a certain etiquette about these downfalls, which was intended to remove great warlords without destroying their houses: if the offending patriarch killed himself, his house would escape pillage and his slaves redistribution, and his heir would be able to maintain the line. For everyone saw the great houses as the building blocks of the community and the vehicles of its traditions. This finds clear expression in the historiography of Ibadan, in Johnson's relish at the patterns of replication and retribution which he discerned in their histories, and in Akinyele's delight in the *oriki* which were the means by which a house's ancestral qualities were made real in the imaginations of its members.[153]

GREAT MEN AND THE SUPERNATURAL

These conflicts generated intense feelings of insecurity. This was a society in which people at all levels feared what their rivals or "enemies" (*ǫta*) might do to them—if not openly, then by witchcraft, evil charms, or poison.[154] Good fortune excited envy, and that was externalized as witchcraft. It was dangerous to provoke anger, which was likely to rebound in some form of hurt or harm, and where people thought they had given offense, they were prompt to "cool" or appease the other person by giving presents or by prostrating. This is what Ajobo, Efunsetan, and Aiyejenku did when they saw they were in trouble, since what went for ordinary folk went also for the high and mighty. Indeed, the higher someone was, the higher the stakes were in the struggles of life. They could do more damage—an elder's curse carried more power than a child's abuse—but they were much more susceptible to danger from their enemies:

> The chief reason why chiefs in this country, especially kings, wish themselves long life is because plots are often formed against them, either by their brothers of the same father but different mothers or by their chiefs, hence there is often civil war among them to which they often fall victims. And therefore when the title is given to one, although he accepts it with joy, he must now resort to Mohammedan and heathen diviners for charms to bury in his house, to hang to the roof of his house or round his body for protection.[155]

Those general remarks were made at Iganna in the Oke Ogun, and as if in pointed illustration of them, it was reported from Ondo:

> In 1884 the succession of the new High Chief *Adaja* was bitterly opposed since he had followed his close relative in what was supposed to be an open title. The authorities yielded to the pressure of his powerful family in order to avoid violence in the town. When he entered the chieftaincy house, he dug up all the corners of the rooms to remove "every bad medicine and charm." But it was to no avail: he died barely a year later.[156]

If it was like this in relatively peaceful places such as Ondo and Iganna, how much more was it true of the political crucibles of Ibadan and Abeokuta. This was the stuff of hot gossip in the community: the young R. S. Oyebode wrote in his private diary that he had "heard that the Are has been thrice to Abeokuta to consult with Ogundipe and that he bought all Aje's witchcraft [which here must mean *oogun*, charms] before his death."[157] But this was a perfectly serious part of a warlord's equipment and as unremarkable as his purchase of ammunition. The *Are Onibọn Balogun* (head of the *Balogun*'s guns) at Ibadan attended church for three weeks in 1871 before asking Allen (who had a considerable reputation for his medical skill) if he could help him get effective charms against bullets.[158] The great Ibadan chiefs had their houses spectacularly well protected:

> S. W. Doherty reported he saw "extraordinary things" at the compound of the *Balogun* Ajayi Ogboriefon, which Samuel Johnson took him to view. As you went in, you stepped over a skull half-buried in the ground. There were two others in the courtyard, and others set on 2-foot-high posts spaced at intervals, all to serve as protection. The roofs [high pitched, thatched, coming to within a few feet of the ground] were all covered in Muslim and pagan charms, including a special one tied up with black and white thread which was anointed with palm oil in sacrifice every day.[159]

When Sokenu, one of the senior Egba war-chiefs, died in 1861, three large piles of his charms were exhibited at different gates of the town, and these were said not to be the half of them.[160] The rumor that his death was due to poison through an enemy's collusion with a favorite wife of his—in fact he probably died of a painful chronic ailment—merely reiterated the standard view of the dangers that faced great chiefs.[161]

The paradox was that these same men, who felt themselves so vulnerable to the malice of their enemies that they were ever on the lookout for the best mystical protection available, were themselves regarded as in some ways more than human. A token of this was that the excesses to which they went— in their accumulation of wives, slaves, and wealth; in their overweening acts; in their pride and ambition—were actually widely celebrated in their communities. A prime vehicle for this was their *oriki* or praise-chants, sung around them as they went about the town or at festivals and at their funerals and in memory of them.[162] To go beyond what was the norm for ordinary men— in this culture which so strongly prescribed courtesy and restraint in all social interaction—was to behave more like an *orisa* than a man. Since all cultures restrain the extreme gratification of the ego impulses which they encourage, it is likely that big men and *orisa* were attractive to the Yoruba precisely because they actually did what lesser men, in their positions of relative weakness and dependency, could only yearn to do.

No man embodied this more fully than the *Are* Kurunmi, the absolute ruler of Ijaye for more than twenty years. Over a decade after Ijaye's destruction, an African pastor on tour passed through its overgrown ruins and was shown the remains of Kurunmi's house, whose mud walls must have been fast eroding into the red soil from which they were formed. His guide recalled how much Kurunmi had been dreaded, quoting the saying: *Are npe o, o l'o ndifa; b'Ifa fo ire bi Are fo, ibi nko?* [The *Are* calls you, you say you are consulting Ifa; if your Ifa speaks favorably and the *Are* says contrary, what then?] One of Kurunmi's "nicknames" (i.e., a phrase of his *oriki*) also came to mind: *Irin wewe ti j'ori* [small piece of iron that devours heads].[163] The two features of Kurunmi's rule which are recalled here—his comparability with the *orisa* and the ferocity of his punishments—are repeatedly documented in the journals of the clergy who served there, the German missionary Adolphus Mann and his Egba catechist Charles Phillips.

One of the most outrageous episodes was his response to one of the many cases of adultery among his wives, which they both reported. Phillips gives the more sensational detail: after the guilty wife was killed, Kurunmi "split the woman's belly and took out the heart and liver and ate it raw in the open street before a very large assembly of his town people. This was performed on the front of his own house before his Ogu, his god of iron."[164] Mann's interpretation tends to the psychological: he sees the action as "giving the token of satisfied revenge," the expression of an emotion which terminates in its catharsis, and clinches this view by saying Kurunmi would later take an emetic. Phillips takes a much more Yoruba angle, treating the extraordinary as continuous with the supernatural, and going on to a more general description of the magical sources of Kurunmi's power:

> Kurunmi also takes the heart and liver of people he has had beheaded, dries them by the fire and grinds them into powder to mix into the food and beer which he serves at the public feasts he holds every Jakuta [the day of the Yoruba week sacred to Sango] to gain people's affection towards him. Once a man took out of his soup what he thought was a piece of beef, but found it to be part of the palm of a man's hand. He slipped it in his cap to show the people of his compound. Almost every day Kurunmi plunders some compound and uses the haul for his Jakuta feasts.

Did this really happen? It is a certainly a common Yoruba belief to this day that the most powerful *oogun* ("medicines, charms") are those which contain human body parts, just as human beings were the most powerful kind of sacrificial offering to the *orisa*. Kurunmi must surely have shared this view and it is very likely that he acted on it to consolidate his rule. At the very least, if an Egba catechist thought that such things went on, he must have derived that belief from the common notions of the Ijaye people all around him.

For Kurunmi was spoken of as a god in Ijaye: "He is our god, he has made our town strong," said one man simply to Mann.[165] We may be inclined to ask if remarks like this are to be taken literally or metaphorically. But that is an unnecessary dilemma. For we only need metaphor when we wish to assert some likeness between two categorically distinct or radically discontinuous orders of being. The case is rather that in Yoruba ontology humans (*enia*) and *orisa*, though clearly distinguished from one another in concept, were still seen as occupying different points on a single scale of power or life/spirit, and there were various ways in which they could instantiate, partake of, or be transformed into the divine. So when we read that people swore by *Are* Kurunmi—"Let Are's sword eat me if I have done such and such a thing"—or invoked his "head"—"Are's head will keep you and help you"[166]—we will fail to grasp the full import of what was being said if we treat such idioms, routinely employed to address *orisa*, as "mere metaphors." Underlying such remarks was a worldview—in which the Yoruba were far from unique[167]—in which all phenomena were, to a greater or lesser degree, permeated with spirit and so potential signs or instances of the divine.

Kurunmi's power was moreover bound in with his headship of the cult of Sango. When lightning struck a house—a sign of Sango's anger—its owners had to pay heavy indemnities to the Sango cult for their purification, and many are the references to the profit that Kurunmi derived thereby.[168] But to reduce his cult headship to the mere seizure of a fiscal opportunity would be wholly to underestimate the import of Kurunmi's identification with Sango. Kurunmi did not have by virtue of his title the quasi-divine status of an *ọba:* as *Arẹ Ọna Kakamfo* he was in theory just the commander of the provincial levies of the *Alafin* of Oyo. But in Ijaye as Sango's chief worshipper, he was as it were the eldest "son" of Sango, the royal deity of Oyo whose priests were greeted in Sango's name with the kingly salutation "*Kabiyesile.*"[169] All his acts were in a sense delegations from his "father" Sango, just as the hubristic and lawless acts of Kurunmi's own sons were an extension of their father's power.[170]

Phillips and Mann, though they came to detest him, still showed a remarkable insight into the interdependence of the two sides of Kurunmi's existence: his outward ferocity and his inward fears. He refused an extension of the town to relieve overcrowding unless it was close to the back of his palace because he feared plots; he characterized Ijaye people as famous for farming, fighting, and "telling lies"; he sent spies to the funeral of the popular and much-respected *Balogun* Ogunkoroju to check up if anyone would praise him for being a better man than himself.[171] It got worse as events started to close in on him—several of his sons killed on campaigns, the stabilizing influence of the *Balogun* removed, intimations of the war to come—and Mann wrote:

> Nobody is so much agitated by fears as he himself. He thinks himself in imminent danger, as if all towns conspired against him. . . . Endless sacrifices to prolong his life are the order of the day—and his fears are not appeased.[172]

When Kurunmi died in 1861, the siege was well advanced and Ijaye was rapidly becoming deserted, as its people slipped away in advance of the inevitable.

One cannot but be touched by the loneliness of the deaths of several of these warlords, whose personal followings had been so large. Thomas King was impressed by the stoicism of Sokenu in his last painful illness: "nor dare any one who was about him ask what was the matter with him or console him with words of sympathy."[173] Their very eminence distanced them from close contact with their dependents, and since most of their equals in age and status were their rivals, the close friendships of youth were no longer available. We have the fullest picture of Ogundipe of Ikija, who succeeded his former leader Ogunbona as the mission's chief patron at Abeokuta and stood in the forefront of Egba politics for over thirty years. The English missionary J. B. Wood once called on Ogundipe when he was occupied at his forge at the back of his house—he was in his seventies and still worked as a blacksmith—but could not speak to him because none of his household dare venture into his presence, not even to tell him his *oyinbo* friend was here to see him.[174] When Ogundipe's health was failing, he came to suspect one of his wives of putting poison on his sleeping mat and shot two of them, killing one. A few days later he died, probably by his own hand. And yet, concluded Wood, Ogundipe was "admired, feared and *respected*" in the town at large, for his good sense in public affairs and his fairness and moderation as a judge. He died on 15 August 1887, and the failure of the second rains a few weeks later was attributed by the Egba to his spirit: already he was being credited with the acts of an *oriṣa*.[175]

CONCLUSION: COMMUNITY AND RECIPROCITY

We have been considering the interplay of two kinds of differentiation, that between different communities and the differences of power, status, and wealth within particular communities. Membership of a community—principally the *ilu*, or "town"—was the basis of everyone's social existence, the best guarantee for personal security and the essential setting for individual self-realization. But the *ilu* was not the only, or itself an all-sufficient and uncontested, focus of community. Two other types of community, though of lesser, were of growing importance. The first was entities of higher or lower order in the communal hierarchy, such as at one end "tribes" or identities embracing a number of *ilu* (such as "Ekiti," "Ijebu" and eventually "Yoruba" itself) and at the other the villages or subordinate towns of substantial *ilu*, or in some cases sub-communities within them such as the quarters (*adugbo*) of Ilesha or the old Egba townships within Abeokuta. The second was partial or quasi-communities existing within or across *ilu* boundaries, of which the most important were cult-groups.

I suggested earlier that though egalitarian fellowship is complementary to kinship and has a particular importance in the realization of community, it is readily penetrated by the language of kinship. One reason for this must be that kin relations had a *binding* quality that was absent from friendship, such that people still clung to them if their community fell apart. Another is that the hierarchical order of kin relations was so convenient for the grounding of political obligation. So although for many the first response to the collapse of old communities was to move from the co-filiative ties of being, say, *ọmọ Liṣabi* ["children of Lisabi," i.e., Egba] to being "the Arẹ's people," that is from finding security in lineage to seeking it in a great man's clientage, the clientages soon sought to reclothe themselves in the language of kinship. Even slaves, if they survived and stayed, were destined for eventual affiliation.

A triad of power, status, and wealth marked the leadership of communities. A cardinal difference between the old days and the Age of Confusion was that power and status—in the sense of such normative conditions of leadership as fatherhood, accession by right and due process to a title—tended to become substantially reversed. The least of the triad was wealth, since it was insecure: it could not guarantee itself and eventually it followed power and status. As Efunsetan found out, it did not help to have warlords in debt to you. Yet just because it was so fluid, wealth serves as an invaluable tracer of social relations. In some ways most instructive as to the essential features of the cultural context are not those transfers of wealth which marked changes in positions of power and status, such as occurred at the downfall of great Ibadan chiefs, but those which served to maintain or challenge the bounds of community itself: presents and charity.

One of the most frequently reported kinds of information in the entire CMS Archive concerns the presents exchanged between mission agents and chiefs. They were reported with especial thoroughness by *African* agents (who also, in the few personal diaries that have survived, record carefully the gifts they gave and received in their own personal lives). Presents signified and established moral relationships. They served to define community and, as in the gifts made to "appease anger" by Ibadan chiefs in danger or by litigants to chiefly tribunals, to reassert the donor's membership of it. We can infer that a considerable portion of the disposable wealth of Yoruba towns was more or less constantly circulating to this social end. In a long letter in 1884, the Rev. J. B. Wood described "the system of giving presents" as prevailing "in every grade and condition of society."[176] In the absence of regular taxation, he went on, the chiefs depended on presents for much of their revenue, and the superintendent of the mission was in effect the principal taxpayer of the Christian community, so he had to operate the system "if he would be on good terms with the heads of the town." He detailed a lengthy series of transactions with Ogundipe, which involved the exchange of cowries, cash, cloth, and other things, the net effect of which was to leave a significant material advantage to Ogundipe, but which in return brought a real measure of protection and assistance to the mission. Personally, Wood "abhorred" the system of presents, no doubt because it was incompatible with his universalistic values; but he knew that he had to work within it, and he did not deny that it paid off for the mission.

On the other side was the idea of charity, the religious obligation to give disinterestedly to the poor, irrespective of their status. There were poor people in Yorubaland, most of them the victims of family breakdown or the vicissitudes of war which left them bereft of the support of kin; characteristically they were very young or very old, and were often disabled.[177] Yet begging was very rare: Townsend, visiting Ilorin from Abeokuta, remarked that "[a] blind beggar by the wayside asking alms in the name of the Prophet showed us we were in a country where another religion was professed, [for] there are but few beggars among the heathen."[178] He also acutely noted that where Yoruba did beg, "they regard [alms] as a gift, not a right," and as such they had to be returned at a later date.[179] It was not just that begging was felt to derogate from personal dignity—an able-bodied adult should be able to support him/herself and would be an acceptable addition to the following of a chief—but that disinterested or unreciprocated giving simply made no cultural sense. The point was put with crystal clarity by James White, in a comment on how his wife's charitable acts were viewed at Ota:

> She was often regarded by the heathens as generous to a fault, for, say
> they, kindness ought to be shown only to those from whom we expect a re-
> turn, either personally from themselves or from their relatives nor ought
> they to be shown to strangers with whom we are not acquainted, and the
> question is generally put, and who is to thank you?[180]

This theory was evident in practice, when in 1890 several thousand destitute refugees fled from Iberekodo to Abeokuta to escape Dahomean raids.
The churches set up a relief committee, which met with an unexpected
difficulty:

> From sheer want and without thinking of the future, some accepted what
> was offered readily enough but others could not believe that people would
> give them food and clothing without having some ulterior design to their
> disadvantage and so they would not accept what was offered. . . . Afterwards
> it was found that they were in great want, but from fear durst not say so.[181]

In neither case was gift-giving conceivable outside the moral frame of the
community, which was itself defined as a social entity by the networks of giving and receiving. Beyond it stood strangers, people to be exploited and
feared because they might exploit you. The system of presents was distaste-
ful to a European and the system of charity was incomprehensible to many
Yoruba for reasons that were two sides of the same coin: the former insisted
upon a particularistic notion of community, while the latter rejected it. The
historic importance of Islam and Christianity was that they asked searching
questions of existing definitions of community and proposed significant ex-
tensions of it—and that growing numbers of Yoruba were starting to listen
to them.

4

MAKING COUNTRY FASHION

There are two very different ways in which we can conceptualize the beliefs and practices of the Yoruba about the hidden powers and their relations with the mundane—their "religion"—and both were anticipated in the descriptions of it given by the CMS authors.[1] The first is to see it as a religion of a particular character, homologous but antithetical to Islam and Christianity. Missionaries to the Yoruba, in contrast to those to some other African peoples,[2] were never in any doubt that they faced a *religion* of a character both distinctive and recognizable. They recognized it as "heathenism" or "idolatry," something roughly along the lines of the religions of the Ancient Greeks and Romans (the original "paganism") and of the Anglo-Saxons (ditto "heathenism") or the cults of local idols which the Israelites found in the land of Canaan. Thus it was identified, not merely as a well-known *type* of religion, but as standing at a particular *stage* in the history of religion. For the missionaries this encouragingly implied its eventual supersession by Christianity, along the lines of either the sacred history presented in the Old and New Testaments or the secular cultural history of Europe.

Samuel Crowther the younger wrote a polemical tract about the three religions of Yorubaland to which he attached sketches, as in Figure 4.1. He ex-

Figure 4.1. The three religions. Sketch by Samuel Crowther Jr.

plained them as showing "the heathen bowing down to his god of thunder and lightning called Shango, with his Ifa bowl of palm nuts beside him and the goat's head for sacrifice being against the wall and his calabash of medicines to preserve him from his enemies being also hung against the wall"; then "the Mahomedan sitting in the street praying and counting his beads in the midst of numerous spectators"; and finally "the Christian praying to God in penitence and humility."[3] The religions are held to be infused by distinct values and to represent different cultural options. Each is a whole, a system of religious alterity to the others.

This was not at all the "pagan" Yoruba view. They had no generic concept of religion as a discrete field of human activity or a fortiori of particular religions as bounded entities. The modern Yoruba word for religion—*ẹsin*, from *sin* [to serve], really a variant of *isin* [service]—refers primarily to the world religions which need to so conceive of themselves. Variety within the field of what we call religion was recognized by Yoruba in terms of the wide range of cults, identified by either the deity worshipped or the ethnic origins of the cult. The members of particular cults were described as those who "had" a certain deity, as with *Eleṣu* (Esu devotees, especially those who carried his image round town) or *Oniṣango* (Sango devotees), and the diversity of these cults was an acknowledged feature of community life. "Let the Ifa man worship his Ifa; let the orisha man worship his orisha; and let the slave follow his Shango priestcraft for his food," ran an adage quoted by the Ogboni spokesman of the Ijebu town of Iperu to urge the merits of a live-and-let-live approach to cultic allegiance.[4] A slave appears here as the devotee of Sango, since that was a cult exotic to Ijebu, introduced there by slaves of Oyo origin. Because cults spread from one area to another, it was natural that they were spoken of in terms of their alien provenance and bearers. So from the indigenous viewpoint Islam was known as the religion of the Imale, because its earliest bearers were probably Wangara traders who traveled down the Niger from Mali, and Yoruba Muslims today are still called *Imale;* while

Christianity began as "the white man's religion" or, more exactly, as his "custom" or "fashion" [*asa* or *oro*].

Hence arose the other designation of Yoruba religion, which was really a refusal to designate it *as* "a religion" at all. When referring to such acts as consulting a diviner or making a sacrifice, missionary authors—especially, but not only, African ones—frequently use the expression "making country fashion." The phrase came with the first missionaries from Sierra Leone and is essentially Creole, an African concept in an English expression. Its Yoruba original was probably something like the phrase that Ajisafe used in his *History of Abeokuta* to convey how Egba people would describe the ancient forms of their worship: *A nṣe Oro ilẹ tabi baba wa,* which he translated as "We are performing the Established Customs [*Oro*] of our nation [*ilẹ*=land or country] or [of our] ancestor[s]."[5] The related phrase *asa ibilẹ* [customs of the country] is widely found in Yoruba-language local histories of this century. It also came to serve as the Yoruba rendering of the colonial expression "Native Law and Custom." The phrase "country fashion," then, serves to blur any sharp division between the religious and the non-religious; it implies a shifting and unbounded body of customary practices rather than a definite and integrated "religion." The attraction of our so conceiving the object of study is that it helps stave off the teleology which is so hard—and perhaps in the end impossible—to avoid when we set up our inquiry in terms of an outcome—the widespread adoption by the Yoruba of the Christian or Muslim "religions"—which was not predetermined yet which does much to shape how we describe the prior state of affairs.

"Country fashion" had no obvious or given starting point, such as a central institution or a holy book, so a good way to break into it is with a prosaic example of daily religious practice. What follows is an informal prayer which a man addressed to his charm, on rising in the morning. It was overheard by Adolphus Mann at Ijaye, and is the longest Yoruba text in the entire CMS archive:

> Ki'n má ri ẹjọ Arẹ. Enni t'o ba gbé [pe?], ki t'emi ko má sunan, ki ti oluwa e k'o d'ojude. Ọtta t'o kán mi, o kōku. Ẹssẹ mi ki ngkọ ki 'm má kọ ẹnnu. Ki m' ma ri ẹjọ aladugbo. Ki m' má ri akoba. Ki gbogbo irin mi k'o jẹ alafia. Ki 'n má ri arọn, arọn l'ọtta. Ki ng ri ilera. Ki ng má r'ofo. Ki ng[ohun?] ti ng se k'o mà ṣe dèdé. Kọ ṣe.
>
> "May I avoid any dispute with the *Arẹ.* Whoever it may be who wishes against me, may I come out on top. The enemy who hurts me, may he be a dead man. With my foot may I knock against things, not with my mouth. May I avoid any dispute with my neighbor. May I avoid troublemakers. May all my journeys be in peace. May I avoid sickness, sickness is an enemy. May I enjoy health. May I avoid loss. May everything I do turn out well. So shall it be."[6]

The opening petition, referring with implicit dread to the *Arẹ* Kurunmi, at once sets the tone of what is to follow. The prayer is not a vehicle of moral

reflection or even much of a colloquy with the divine, but a technical instrument for securing practical benefits from the controlling powers oper-
ant through the charm. With its concern about the active malice of enemies
and the risks of getting into trouble with neighbors, the prayer is eloquent
of the insecure and competitive life-world of nineteenth-century Yoruba. The
allusions to journeys and to "loss" (*ofo*) make one think the petitioner may
have been a trader. In its later petitions, the prayer moves from specific social dangers to some of the more general components of a good life. These
are summed up in the state of *alafia*, a term usually translated "peace" but
which has a much broader connotation, to embrace health, success, and
prosperity. A telling detail is how the prayer personalizes sickness in a manner analogous to the human enemies dealt with earlier on.

The ethos and assumptions of this prayer are pervasive throughout
Yoruba religious practice, and are endlessly documented by the CMS journalists. "Peace, health, and children" was the prayer of an Egba woman who
had sacrificed eight animals, much cloth, and cowries to get them.[7] A son of
the late king of Lagos expressed his disappointment that after prayers to Ifa
"to bless him and his family with health, long life, and riches," three of his
people had died and he suffered trading loss.[8] T. B. Wright encountered in
Lagos a company of women with a few men conducting a ceremony for
"Eyinle, god of stream": the substance of their petitions was "Lengthen our
lives, bless us with money and children, and deliver us from danger."[9] This
insistent this-worldliness contrasted sharply with mission Christianity's emphasis on "eternal life," salvation in the world to come. Gollmer tells of the
chief of a small Egbado town who "ha[d] no orisha or idol in the house except Ifa, and therefore he begged me to help him that he, his wives and children may not die but live, prosper and have peace."[10] In Abeokuta, Müller
was once particularly struck by an intent young woman who "did not ask 'Shall
I get children, money and a long life by serving Jesus[?],' [b]ut . . . 'What
must I do to obtain peace and happiness for my soul[?]'"[11] In fact he may
well have drawn the wrong conclusion, for the woman's request was still for
alafia, whose primary connotations were so strongly this-worldly.

A barren woman could not really enjoy *alafia*, and her desire for children
was likely to surpass all other needs:

Willam Moore visits a temple of the *orisa* Obatala at Osiele, where he meets
the priestess and a woman who has come with an oblation. The priestess
wants to hear what Moore has to say, to the impatience of the other woman,
who sneers at him and asks the priestess to get on with her business. After he has spoken about Jesus as the means to the Living God and happiness in the world to come, the woman replies that it is not he that gives
children, but only Obatala. She doesn't care for eternal life, but assever-
ates in a loud voice *omm̞o re mo o nf̞e* [children is what I want], repeating
it so heartily as if to make her wish come true.[12]

No one was more vulnerable than childless, elderly women—of all people they were most likely to be accused of witchcraft, an index of the envy they were presumed to feel at the success of others—and so in greater need of protection. S. W. Doherty overheard the morning prayer of "a very nice and clean old woman" at Okeho:

> Oh thou god Shango, my maker and preserver in life, thou hast caused me to wake again this morning, I thank thee. Thou knowest that I am old and childless, also that I am a widow and have no husband to care for me, send me kind persons to do me favour today and guide me through the day not to fall into any evil.[13]

Here Sango, whom we have already encountered as the sanction of absolutist rule in Ijaye, appears in a mode more general among *orișa*, as a life-giving and protective power.

"Making country fashion" was above all a quest for power. This might take the form of personal endowments, such as health, wealth, and fertility; or (because these good things were felt to depend in large part how you stood with other people) of relational powers, power over other people, or protection from the power of others. In societies like this, an adequate history of religion has to be a political history too, while political history, if it is not to be unpardonably thin, has to have a strong streak of religion in it.[14] More specifically, the political narratives of the last two chapters form an essential backdrop to the mainly "religious" focus of what is to come, for two principal reasons: first, because relations with *orișa* and other unseen powers are modeled on those with chiefs and powerful people, who are often regarded as differing from them in degree rather than in kind; and second, because the point of "making country fashion" was largely to affect power relations in the community. That is why the missions, with their new teaching about the unseen powers and their new political affiliations, were so seriously both a challenge and an opportunity for the Yoruba.

DEALING WITH UNSEEN POWERS: THEORY AND PRACTICE

A long-running but inconclusive argument in the anthropology of religion concerns whether "belief" or "ritual" should take priority in its exposition and analysis.[15] It has been widely argued that a properly comparative or general approach to religious phenomena could not ground itself on belief, or other individually subjective states, since "belief" was not a cultural universal[16] and anyway was much more central to some expressions of religion, notably those of Western Europe since the Enlightenment, than most others.[17] Many social anthropologists sought to avoid the difficulties posed by the category of "religion" in relation to undifferentiated and non-literate societies by speaking of "ritual" instead.[18] Ritual as a concept had two attractions: it seemed universal in religions, and it also served to mark out a particular *type* of behavior, essentially expressive rather than instrumental, as distinctive of them. On this view, ritual or religion is comprised of performances which employ symbols drawn from the repertory of local culture, to express social values and, by expressing them, to evoke commitment to them. But this too created more problems than it solved, above all by ignoring the extent to which religion often has cognitive and practical functions.[19] The Yoruba prayer from Ijaye quoted earlier is in many ways less like a "ritual" than, say, a request for development funds from an aid agency; Yoruba sacrifices are in important ways less like Holy Communion than like Efunsetan's attempts to save herself by giving presents to the Ibadan chiefs. It is better to sidestep the belief/ritual antinomy altogether and address the material with concepts that make no prior determination about its special nature. Whatever else nineteenth-century Yoruba religion was, it was a set of practices: that is how Crowther represented it in his little sketch, and that is just what is implied in our guiding phrase "making country fashion." The term "practice" embraces both what anyone might want to call "rituals" and actions of a more uncontroversially instrumental nature; and it also extends to the identities and public associations that in Yorubaland go with them. The primary task of analysis is to make practice intelligible, which depends on putting together two further sorts of information: about the context or circumstances of action, and about the theories or principles which govern it.

The major premise of all Yoruba religious practice was that the material, phenomenal world is continuously affected by unseen powers of various kinds and indefinite number. A saying current in Ibadan in the 1860s put it thus: *Abogun ki ri Egun, aboṣa ki ri Oriṣa, ati Imale ti o nfi ori balẹ ko ri Ọlọrun* [The Egun worshipper does not see the ancestral spirit, the Orisa worshipper does not see Orisa, and the Muslim who bows his head to the ground does not see God].[20] As this implies, the powers fell into three major categories: deities (*oriṣa*), sometimes called *imọlẹ;* deceased persons, whether remembered individuals, ancestral spirits belonging to particular compounds, or the collective ancestors of the community; and God. Leaving God aside for the time being, the division evident here, between "gods" and "ancestors" is found widely in the cosmologies of West African peoples.[21] But what is striking about the Yoruba case (though perhaps not peculiar to it) is the extent to which concepts that are distinctly grounded seem to "reach out" to one another, so that they end up sharing many of each other's attributes.

The *oriṣa* were manifest in natural objects: in features of the landscape such as rivers, hills, and large trees; in meteorological phenomena such as thunder, whirlwinds, and tornadoes; in material substances such as iron and stone; and in some wild animals such as the python or the chameleon. But "natural" is not quite the right word here, since what we are really talking about is forces from "out there." That is why an old cannon, used to repel the Dahomean attack in 1851, and even the Igbein church bell, looted during the *Ifọle* in 1867, were later to be found receiving sacrifices in Abeokuta.[22] As possessed by their devotees, the *orişa* were less essentially present in the carved statues which are among the glories of Yoruba art than in their appropriate physical embodiments: river pebbles for Osun, the iron baton of Orisaoko, stone celts for Sango's thunderbolts, any iron object for Ogun, the lump of laterite rock which stood for Esu at a house's doorway. Townsend, in early days at Abeokuta, asked a young convert "What is an orisha?"[23] The boy first named some, then when pressed to say what their nature was, gave a strictly materialist answer: "Orisha is a few cowries, a calabash, a piece or two of wood etc." Townsend concluded that it was "a symbol of an imaginary invisible being. It is difficult to know which of the several things put together is really the Orisha; some people say [it is] the cowries strung together." Cowries were not just the medium of monetary exchange, but also the symbol par excellence of transformative power, and so they were pointedly used as an attachment to religious tokens and images of all kinds, and were a routine component of sacrifices.[24]

But while their material tokens conveyed the natural source of the power of the *orişa*, their anthropomorphic images presented the complementary side of their being: that they behaved analogously to human beings. The stories told about the major *orişa,* and the representation of them in Ifa divination verses, show them quarrelling and loving in a thoroughly Olympian way. Human beings needed to know that they could protect as well as harm, that they might show their anger but they could be appeased. These two sides of the character of the *orişas* are nicely conveyed in the account of a vision seen by a man in a "near-death" experience, told to Samuel Johnson by a *babalawo* in Ibadan:

> He saw "a great, high God . . . enthroned in a spacious place, from top to bottom in white. On his right is the god Orisanla, and on his left the god Ifa, both his counsellors. . . . Before him and in active service are the gods Ogun [war] and Sopona [smallpox]. Ogun is armed with 4000 short swords and he goes out daily on earth to slay, for his meat is to drink the blood of the slain. Sopona also has 4000 viols [*sic*] about him; his also is the work of destruction, bringing in his victims and disappears immediately for others and so continually. As for Sango, he is a very mighty god, and when he is about to go [into] the world, he is always cautioned by Ifa and Orisanla to deal gently with their own special devoted followers."[25]

But even Sango and Ogun were the trusted protectors of countless devotees.

Ancestors start out as something quite different from *orişa,* as known individuals with whom the worshipper has had a personal relationship, perhaps an intimate and affectionate one. Even before death, as elders, they were already credited with power beyond the average, able by their very words to produce effects by curse or blessing; and the crediting of superhuman power to ancestors may well have its source in a simple extension of this. In a seminal paper, Igor Kopytoff argued from the closeness of elders to ancestors that it was misleading to speak of ancestor "worship" in Africa, since it led us to ignore the prosaic quality of the exchanges between the supplicant and his ancestor, rather like how it would have been like in life.[26] The point is well taken, but (at least as far as the Yoruba are concerned) it fails to capture the heightened quality of dealing with the *dead*.

Funerals actually effected a major change in the status of the deceased. The following is C. N. Young's account of the burial rites of a mother-in-law of the *Jomu*, a senior chief at Ondo:

"The people here worship the dead" [he begins in lapidary style, rather as if to put Kopytoff down]. The corpse is wrapped in two beautiful mats, a fine country cloth, and a white sheet. Her children and others stand around with the offerings: a small bitch, a goat, a dried bush-rat, a dried fish, and some kola. The bitch is beheaded and its blood dripped on the forehead, breast and toes of the dead woman, as they pray, "This is your bitch, this is your goat. . . . Do not let us die, let us not meet with any trouble and sickness." They then split the kola and throw the pieces on the ground to divine if the sacrifice is accepted or not. The corpse is then tied in three places and taken to the room in the house where it is to be buried. Then they cry for the dead.[27]

Several of the features of this ritual occurred in a ceremony at Ibadan, performed at the grave of a woman who had been buried three days earlier. A bound goat was laid on the fresh grave, the dead woman's children knelt while a male relative said a long prayer asking her to take care of them, and another man stunned the goat with a club, cut its throat, and sprinkled its blood on the wall by the grave.[28] The Yoruba buried their dead under the earthen floors of their houses, and their graves became domestic shrines.

With great men the transition to ancestorhood was much grander and could be phased in two stages:

King Akitoye of Lagos, whom the British had restored to his throne in 1851 after a bombardment to expel his nephew and rival, Kosoko, died suddenly on 3 September 1853. His body must have been interred almost at once, as was usual. On 20 February 1854, his second burial took place. The "corpse" was a pile of cloth shaped like a body covered with crimson velvet, and the walls were draped with overlapping velvet cloths. Pictures, looking glasses and a cuckoo clock were hung up on display, while the floor was strewn with cowries. After three days Akitoye's son and successor, Dosumu, and those of his party who were free men partially shaved their heads (the slaves fully shaved theirs). Henceforth, Akitoye was counted as an ancestor, and Dosumu prayed to him. Over the next few weeks he was often to be found making offerings to his deceased father.[29]

That is not surprising, for Dosumu's political position was far from secure. His cousin Kosoko, popular and well armed, had not given up his hopes for the throne and, though checked in the mid-1853, still threatened Lagos with his canoes from his base at Epe, seventy miles away on the lagoon. Leopards used to range into the outskirts of Lagos in those days, and when one was killed in August 1854, having attacked two men, Ifa revealed that it had been sent by Kosoko. With his enemy enjoying such a reputation, it is not surprising that Dosumu devoted so much attention to summoning help from the one power whose loyalty could be counted upon, his own dead father.[30]

As regards Kopytoff's argument, the clincher is not that Yoruba authors invariably used words such as "worship" and "sacrifice" to refer to the acts that children performed toward their dead parents, but that the acts themselves and the reasons why they were performed were so similar to those directed at *orișa*.[31] Moreover, most of the "ancestor" worship reported in the CMS papers was not directed at immediately deceased parents, but at figures who were further removed from people once known in life. The collective Oro ancestors, so important at Abeokuta, were neither individuated nor represented visually. In contrast, the masked ancestral figures of the Egungun cult, strong among the Oyo, were both of these; but though they were regarded as embodying lineage ancestors returned to earth, each one did not represent a specific deceased individual. Rather, a particular lineage's ancestors were, so to speak, collapsed into one another and represented together in a form known by its own name as an *egungun*—such as Alapansapa and Oloolu, two of the best known at Ibadan[32]—rather than as historic individuals. In other words, what is named is the representation, not the dead persons so represented. Yet deceased individuals were still approachable through these generalized ancestral spirits. After Samuel Ajayi Crowther's father had died in battle, his senior brother made a lavish funeral for him and "[his] spirit made its appearance under the god [*sic*] Oro." Consulted about the fate of the young Ajayi, lost into slavery, it said he would return to become head of the family.[33] When Kosoko made his unsuccessful assault on Lagos in July 1853, one of the first things he did on landing was to sacrifice to "Egun (his deceased father deified)."[34] In sum, the masked figure was regarded as a supernatural being with a personality of its own, and to that extent is like an *orișa*. The executioner of the Oro cult at Abeokuta was a masked figure known as the "cat of Ijeun" (*ologbo Ijeun*) because the office belonged to that township.[35] Samuel Johnson was far less knowledgeable about Egba than Oyo custom, but his mistake in writing of a "god called Ologboijeun" is understandable in the light of the Yoruba inclination to endow their ancestors with the qualities of *orișa*.[36]

The way in which *orișa* and ancestors were both complementary and convergent takes us to the heart of the pressures that shaped Yoruba practice. Generated by the quest for empowerment as guided by two distinct intuitions—of the enchantedness of nature, and the charisma of elders—the primary form of their relations with human beings were sharply contrasted. The *oriṣa* had as their first function to represent the alien and obdurate forces of nature, powers that were "out there" but prone to intrude with devastating effect on human life. Ancestors, by contrast, were continuous and consubstantial with their descendants, which guaranteed their human approachability. The one stood for realism about the conditions in which life had to be lived, the other represented hope that something could be done about its problems. The "dream ticket" of Yoruba religion was a natural power with the qualities of a parent. To the extent that it was impossible to achieve a lasting high-level synthesis of hope and realism, what emerged was a shifting series of trade-offs: the *oriṣa* were the outcome of moves to humanize alien or "natural" powers, while Egungun and Oro were deceased parents correspondingly enhanced. In a sense this trajectory, from being a power "out there" to being a quasi-person with whom people hoped to establish moral ties, was re-enacted during the annual festival of most *oriṣa:* the rites were begun at its bush shrine, from where the devotees processed into town bearing tokens of the *oriṣa*'s power, which were then solemnly established at shrines in the town (above all at the *ọba*'s palace).[37]

Unseen powers of any kind showed themselves through unusual or extraordinary events. The Yoruba were deeply disposed to interpret accidents and coincidences as signs bearing on their own situation. If such signs seemed to affront the natural order of things, they portended no good. They might be fairly trivial, like the birth of a two-headed kid reported at Abeokuta,[38] or the first appearance at Ondo of the African agents' wives wearing European costume, which led some people to think that women so dressed "can create harm upon the inhabitants of the country."[39] One of the most ominous events was the birth of twins, since multiple births, while appropriate for animals, were viewed with abhorrence in human beings. The custom of killing twins had been abandoned in central and western Yorubaland in the eighteenth century, to be replaced by a cult of twins (*ibeji*) as special beings, but it continued strong in the east.[40] Phillips considered the Ondo to be "more violent and touchy" on the subject of twin-killing than on human sacrifice.[41] They held that a twin birth was an abomination on the land, which if unexpiated would bring sterility to crops and people. The responsibility for dealing with the problem lay with the Idoko, an aboriginal group within Ondo: they took away the mother's wrapper and cooking utensils, plundered the house, removed the twins to be killed, and fined the woman's family.[42] So the pollution was lifted, in a procedure which somewhat resembled that used by the Sango cult for the ritual cleansing after lightning strikes in Oyo country.

On the other hand, a coincidence which seemed to enhance or express the cosmic order was propitious. Ogundipe hailed as "a blessing" the arrival in Abeokuta on the same day in 1871 of a white man from the coast (in the person of Henry Townsend) and a white man from the interior (an Arab trader bound for Lagos).[43] Some accidents were in the fullest sense epiphanies of the divine:

A large boulder, fifty feet in circumference, crashed down from one of Abeokuta's many hills after its base had been cut away by people digging for clay and then further eroded by heavy rain. It fell on a children's play area, but during the night, so no one was killed. People called it "motherly" for sparing the children and wanted to make sacrifice to it. William Allen, quickly at the scene, told them it was God who had spared them and an argument developed. One woman asserted angrily *"oriṣa ni, oriṣa ni* [it is a god, it is a god] . . . tomorrow we shall sacrifice to the motherly rock."[44]

A few years later, a piece of the Olumo Rock—itself regarded as an *oriṣa*, the fortress rock from which Abeokuta was named—fell off, causing great alarm. *Baṣọrun* Somoye sent the bellman round to tell people not to be despondent, and in the evening the bell was sounded again to tell people to make sacrifices at the town walls.[45] Some unusual phenomena were agreed to emanate from powers already known, as albinos were a manifestation of Obatala, the creator-*oriṣa* whose special color was white.[46] Swarms of bees were an appropriate secondary epiphany of Sango, who otherwise showed himself in the terrible form of lightning strikes.[47]

Whether they were portents of impending danger or were themselves evils, such as outbreaks of disease or accidental deaths or the conflagrations which could destroy whole swathes of the town, these signs required practical responses. Those phenomena that could not be read in an ad hoc fashion or assigned a priori to a definite agent called for the diviner. Of the wide variety of oracles, the most prestigious was Ifa, operated by diviners called *babalawo* (lit. "fathers of mysteries"). Of the *babalawo* themselves, more anon; suffice it to say here that their professional mystery was a set of techniques and a body of knowledge which enabled them to reveal "hidden things" (*awo*). Divination aimed to provide answers to two questions: (1) who was the source of the trouble that affected the human object of supernatural attention, and (2) what needed to be done to persuade them to avert the threat to his *alafia*. Two general presumptions underlay all oracular answers: the unseen powers were to be construed in terms of human-like agency, and their anger or ill-will was to be assuaged, typically by giving them presents, in the form of sacrifices.

Which unseen power lay behind a particular incident was often uncertain. When the Ose stream at Ijaye, swollen by rains, swept some people away, many townspeople said the *oyinbo* (Europeans) had done it by putting a charm in the water. But the tyrant of the town, Kurunmi, attributed it to the river itself and sent his bellman to forbid fishing, since "the river took revenge . . . of its children."[48] The public disasters most feared were fires and smallpox. At least in Abeokuta, the white *oriṣa*,[49] Obatala and Obalufon, seem particularly to have been turned to for protection against fire: Müller once out preaching "met a country fashion" in progress, a group of women with pots of water on their heads to give Obatala to drink, as an precautionary measure.[50] A whole range of possibilities was explored at Ota in 1870, after a fire had destroyed most of the town, killing thirty-nine people in its course:

> James White made sure to remind the chiefs of the sacrifices made only a few months earlier to Ale (a local *orisa*) and to Sango, consisting of three cowries and a half-burnt piece of wood for every person. The "heathens" [which must here refer to the most active devotees, rather than to pagans in general] said the fire was due to the neglect of some other god. Others said it was a judgment by the gods of a robbery by one Odunlami, at whose house it had started. The Muslims said it was due to the chiefs having failed to give them a black bullock to offer prayers against fire, when they had predicted it. The Christians said it was God's punishment of Ota for its unbelief and hardness of heart. On 19 March, the King sent round to collect contributions for another sacrifice—to an undisclosed power.[51]

The desperation of the Ota chiefs, faced with a pressing problem and a plethora of possible but dubious solutions thrown at them by interested parties on all sides, is readily understood. Three years later they went through it all again over a smallpox outbreak. This time the Muslims got a cow to do their prayers, then Ifa was tried and, that failing, the water deities Eyinle and Osun were offered a bullock and a cow; finally Oro was supplicated for three whole days.[52] A similar picture emerges in the response of the Ondos to the run of smallpox epidemics which hit them from the late 1870s. When smallpox's "own" deity did not stop it, they turned to some visiting devotees of Sango, and then to the spirit of a former king, Olukolasi, whose dying curse was remembered.[53]

After divination, sacrifice. Sacrifice was at the heart of the devotional relationship in Yoruba religion: to "worship" a deity was to sacrifice (*bo*) to it, the generic word for "sacrifice" (*ebo*) being formed from it. Significantly, one was not said to "*bo*" the Supreme Being, Olorun, since He was not sacrificed to. Instead, Christians and Muslims speak of their "serving" (*sin*) Him. (One could also be said to *sin* an *orisa*, as well as to *bo* it). The verbal root *bo* appears in *aborisa*, the Yoruba word commonly rendered "idol-worshippers" by Christians, as well as in an uncomplimentary term for pagans current among nineteenth-century Muslims, *ibogibope* ("worshippers of wood and palm-trees").[54] The act of sacrifice was much more central than the act of prayer, since prayers merely expressed what people wanted from their relationship with their god, whereas sacrifice actually constituted the relationship. Just as the giving of presents made and reaffirmed the civil community, so also through sacrifice did the reciprocal bonds between men and the gods become most real.

The most critical kind of sacrifice was called *etutu,* one made to propitiate or appease the anger of a god, as manifested in disasters like those described above. Smallpox was so bad in Ondo in 1895 that after earlier attempts to propitiate the god had failed, "the fetish priests went still further . . . by asking the king himself to do a sort of penance by sitting exposed under the sun . . . from noon until nightfall."[55] The unusual duty prescribed to the *ọba* here suggests that the Ondo people still felt that the curse of their deposed *ọba* Olukolasi was the source of the epidemic. Elsewhere, the anger of a former ruler might call forth the greatest of all sacrifices, that of a human being. When a new *Olowu* was installed at Owu township in Abeokuta in 1855, a man and a horse were killed as *etutu ọba,* "to propitiate the spirit of the late Olowu so as to allow his successor to reign in peace."[56] In domestic contrast stands what a *babalawo* prescribed after his wife's ominous dream:

> An expiatory sacrifice was to be made of *agidi* (maize pudding) covered with fowl's feathers, the blood of a fowl sprinkled over, some cowries stuck in and "Ifa powder" sprinkled over the top. She had to place this at a spot where three paths met after waving it three times in the air. Then she was to return to be blessed by the *babalawo.* After three days there would be a drizzle of rain, in which she must wet herself.[57]

The materials used here, while not untypical of Yoruba sacrifices to this day, are now beyond detailed symbolic exegesis, save that the crossroads location suggests that the *etutu* was directed at Esu, source of confusion, and that the contact with "the gentle rain from heaven" expresses both the "cooling" (*itutu*) of the god and the relief of the woman.[58]

A much fuller picture of the social context of making an *etutu* appears in William Moore's narrative of a day in the small Egba town of Osiele. Its subject was the attempt to cure the illness of the chief, Akashi, who (while not a baptized convert) had certainly become a Christian fellow-traveler:

> Much drumming and celebration took place as a bullock was sacrificed to Ogiriyan "to pacify its anger that it may not put an immediate end to the chief's existence in this life." Akashi's former daily worship of Ogiriyan, which he'd done in a shrine opposite the entry to his compound, had lapsed twelve years before. But he fell ill at the Egba war camp at Olokemeji during the Ijaye war with asthma and then a stroke which deprived him of speech. His relatives consulted Ifa, which said Ogiriyan was the cause. They then took one of his bullocks—the Ogiriyan people rejected the first one chosen because it was too small!—for the sacrifice. Then, "[after] having sat down to eat and drink, the people rose to play the orishas, extol[l]ed and magnified [them] in dances all over town, especially when a convert to Christian[ity] is seen. . . . Then the Ogriyan [would] be highly spoken of as a mighty god from whose power the Olorun . . . was not able to deliver Akashi though he putteth his trust in him."[59]

What stands out here is that sacrifices, even those arising from one man's problem, tended to involve a much wider network of people than the individual and the unseen power who had affected him: here most prominently Akashi's relatives and the members of the Ogiriyan cult, though they made sure that effectively the whole town was drawn in. It seems probable that Akashi's defection from the cult had rankled with many, and that his illness enabled popular opinion, given authoritative projection by Ifa, to force him to acknowledge Ogiriyan once more. The devotees went further, publicly promoting their god(s) by dramatic presentation of their images ("play the orishas"[60]), by singing their praises in *oriki*, and by disparaging their rivals—in this case particularly the Christians and their God, Olorun. Indeed it might be said that praise was the essential accompaniment to sacrifice as the means of establishing a relationship with one's god.[61] And again the parallels between behavior directed at *oriṣa* and at chiefs and important figures in the community are very close.

Most emergency sacrifices, like this one, presumed that a regular relationship with the *oriṣa* was already in place, which could be activated at the diviner's indication. Devoted worshippers gave their *oriṣa* attention every day, and often a sacrifice every four days.[62] Not all private worshippers were active members of the cult-groups which existed for most of the major *oriṣa*. It was common for cult-groups to hold a substantial celebration of their *oriṣa* every sixteen days, at which its praises were sung and danced, a sacrifice was made, and a meal shared. The *oriṣa*'s favor was tested by divination—in the simplest form, kola was broken and thrown—and its acceptance of the sacrifice was announced with a formula like *Eṣu a gba a* ("Esu will take it") or "[Obatala] will surely take the sacrifice."[63] Annual festivals (*ọdun*) were the most elaborate, those of the major *oriṣa* being given public recognition by the town's authorities and articulated with others in an official ceremonial cycle. Here the *ọba*, or a chief acting on his behalf, would offer sacrifice on behalf of the community as a whole. In contrast were domestic *ọdun* where all the *oriṣa* associated with the family or worshipped by members of the compound would be cleaned, dressed, and set out in order in the courtyard of the house, so that the household could annually renew its bonds with its massed spiritual resources.

THE ORIṢA: CULT-GROUP AND COMMUNITY

So far, this account of "country fashion" has been rather a static one, paying small regard to how it varied from one community to another or changed over time. To appreciate its dynamism, the devotees of the *oriṣa* need to be brought more fully into the picture, for they were the principal means by which cults expanded. Though the *oriṣa* cults have always been regarded as the centerpiece of Yoruba religion, participation in them was quite uneven and different cults called for different degrees and modes of individual involvement. Abstractly, we can distinguish four levels of involvement (which in practice merged into one another): (1) no regular attachment except as a spectator at festivals or a sharer in sacrifices offered at the worship of *oriṣa* within the compound; (2) a personal relationship with an *oriṣa*, dating from dedication at birth or later adoption and involving daily or periodic worship of it as a protector; (3) continuous active involvement in the *oriṣa*'s cult-group in the community, with regular attendance at its periodic festivals and public witness for, and identification with, the *oriṣa;* and (4) serving as a recognized leader or professional, whether as a titled officeholder in the cult or as a priest (*aworo*) who had been possessed by the *oriṣa*.

I have already mentioned that cult members speak of their fellowship in terms of their together being the "children" of their *oriṣa*. In many cases this arose from their regard for that deity as their protector from birth or even before it: "By Sango I was begotten and by Lakijena I was brought forth, and them will I ever serve," was the fervent declaration of a woman at the yearly festival of Kesi, her township in Abeokuta.[64] A child would be regarded as the special gift of the *oriṣa* which the mother had worshipped in order to conceive and have a safe delivery. Names given at birth by parents or relatives—*abiṣo,* "spoken at birth," they were called—often indicated that the *oriṣa* was credited with giving this help—and frequently too it was one already associated with the family. Ogun and Ifa, followed by Sango, Osun, Esu, and Obatala, seem to have been the ones most commonly alluded to in personal names, whether explicitly, as in *Ogunbiyi* [Ogun begot this one], *Fagbohun* [Ifa heard my voice], *Oṣunlana* [Osun opened the way]; or by means of a symbol, as in *Salako,* referring to the white cloth (*ala*) of Obatala, or *Bamgboṣe,* referring to the ceremonial baton carved as a double axe (*oṣe*), used in Sango worship.

So cult attachments were connected with lineage in several ways. One of their main functions was to sustain family reproduction: they were expressed in kinship idioms, and they were largely passed on through family ties. Many cults were "owned" by a particular lineage, in that their headship was vested in it, and its members served as the core of the worshippers. A cult headship or priesthood was a significant resource for the lineage, and someone might well be lined up to take the office, as with a young weaver active in the Erinle cult (and himself already known as Erinle) at Ijaye[65] or the man whom the Ogboni chiefs at Ikereku in Abeokuta wanted to install as *Bamoku,* head of that township's most important civic cult, of Obalufon.[66] Even at the level of individual devotion, practiced in compounds or at the little local *oriṣa* houses which were scattered all over Yoruba towns, a worshipper would often look to find someone to take care of her *oriṣa* after her death. It would be of concern to the compound as a whole to find someone to keep up each of its significant cults for the sake of its collective welfare. Yet despite all this, there was, as Bascom put it in his classic study of cult-groups carried out in Ife in the late 1930s, "no identity between the sib [his term for lineage] and the worshipping group."[67] Because individuals might be directed by divination, at a crisis point later in their lives, to serve a particular *oriṣa*, adherence was not reducible to a hereditary relation, as it was between a person and his ancestors. Just as people might choose which *oriṣa* to worship, so there was great variation in the general amount of attention which different individuals gave to the *oriṣa*.

By far the most important social factor affecting involvement in *oriṣa* cults was gender: the great bulk of active and regular worshippers were women. This is one's aggregate impression from a myriad of casual references by the CMS writers to *oriṣa* worship and is also sometimes stated as a general observation. During the clampdown on Christian activities in some of the Abeokuta townships in 1850, the chiefs announced that the restrictions would hold "till every woman has again made her orisa, and every man his Ifa."[68] A similar association of women with the *oriṣa* and men with Ifa was made by Daniel Coker, writing of Ido island near Lagos in 1873: "The women worship Songo and Agba, they are more ignorant than the men. The men do not worship any god, they hold Ifa in great reverence and believe in charms for protection and success in their ways."[69] Women's devotion to the *oriṣa* was emphasized at their marriage and was focused on the birth and survival of their children. "Before marriage takes place sacrifices must be made to the gods by whose auspices she is supposed to have been born and protected; the young woman must also purchase some gods to worship in her husband's house in order to get children, wealth and peace," wrote Crowther from Abeokuta in 1848.[70] It was even expected of the prospective husband that he would help to equip his fiancée in this way, as a token of his concern for her: a young Christian inquirer was told by his prospective father-in-law, a *babalawo*, that the engagement was off unless he took up his own Ifa again and bought *oriṣa* for his fiancée.[71] So it was the women of the household who chiefly cared for the gods who cared for them, a quotidian devotion of which our disapproving missionary witnesses only give us tantalizing glimpses: in a house in Abeokuta "the idols put into two lines and the piazza beautifully adorned with cowries";[72] a woman at Ota, whose small parlor is half full of her various *oriṣa*, but whose special devotion is to Sango because he was propitious to her mother at her birth and who has a little boy dedicated to Ogun;[73] and a priestess's house in Lagos which the evangelist finds shut up while the *oriṣa* are cleaned and dressed by the men in preparation for their festival.[74]

Women also preponderated in the public worship of the *oriṣa*, though not to such an extent as within the compound. Men tended to hold the headships of major cults, such as the *Ṣọra* (Oramfe at Ondo), the *Aromọna* (Sango at Ibadan), or the *Alaye* (Orisa Onifon, the local equivalent of Obatala, at Ilesha). Terminology is confusing here, since these titled heads are often called "priests" but were not, as a rule, *aworo*, or possession priests who had been called to their deity's service and offered access to its power through trance. Possession by an *oriṣa* used a sexual idiom: irrespective of the gender of either the human or the god, the devotee or priest was said to be "mounted," becoming as the god's "wife."[75] Most of the half dozen cases reported by CMS witnesses refer to women, though they included one male sent by Oya, goddess of the tornado and wife of Sango;[76] and the two possessed devotees of Sango were one of each sex.[77] Possession could be accompanied by prophetic messages from the deity, as in a case from Ondo:

> The Obatala women [writes Charles Young in 1875] were up all night drumming, shouting and dancing. There was great commotion when one of them fell to the ground naked, crying, and "uttering too many serious words in a voice feigned which startled all of them with much fear—that she has been to the next world and thereby instructed by the deity to come and warn all standing of certain evil that is intended to befall them if they do not quickly fetch one goat with which to pacify the mind of the orisa to drive away the evil, [or] those of them that have asked for children will be deprived of them and such a one should abstain from drinking palm wine."[78]

This revelation appears to have arisen in the context of the normal periodic public worship of Obatala by his mainly female devotees, with a similar outcome to those which might have followed from an Ifa divination. Very different in form, being both more individual and more sustained, was the case of a woman "possessed with the spirit of divination" who pestered Samuel Johnson at the compound where he lodged on his way through Oshogbo in 1883: she had been so affected for five days, and was treated with "respect, or should I say dread . . . venerat[ed] as a god" by the residents.[79]

As here, possession was only the most dramatic manifestation of a general feature of *orisa* cults which is vital to understanding their appeal and their spread: the strong identification which existed between the *orisa* and their devotees, not only in their own eyes but in the estimation of others. Apart from their extravagant praise of their *orisa* at its festival, perhaps the most striking form of this was the practice by which devotees, most often women, took the image of their god around in public, offering blessings in its name and receiving cowries in return. This was most commonly done in the name of Esu, but it is also recorded for Sango, Ogun (especially in his manifestation as a python), Ibeji, Obatala, Sopona, and Egungun.[80] Usually they went in ones or twos, but sometimes in a group, as with the fourteen Sopona women who "did" Osiele and met under a tree at the end of the day to divide up their takings.[81] Sometimes it did get rather close to extracting money with menaces, as with an elderly Sango priest who stationed himself by a road in Abeokuta, with a rope stretched across it which passersby had to lift, and an array of ritual axes (*ose*, symbol of the thunderbolt) spread out before him: people did not *have* to give anything, but if not they would get "Sango's frown instead of his smile."[82] Missionary observers sometimes called these devotees "beggars" and the offerings "alms," but while they would yield a modest income, this was not the primary nature of the transaction. The cowries were given as a sacrifice to the *orisa*, in expectation of favors of the usual kind: it was a relationship of exchange like any other.[83] Because the devotee stood as the *oriṣa*'s proxy, just as in another way the possessed *aworo* did, an *Elesu* [Esu-worshipper, literally "possessor of Esu"] could actually be called Esu herself,[84] and since the deity and the devotee were so closely identified, the sacrifice offered to the deity would also be, without any contradiction or impropriety, the devotee's income. As a Buruku priest in Ibadan indignantly put it to a critical missionary: "The chiefs have their sources they get money from to live, the Mohamedans have their living by selling charms, my own portion, like all the babalawos, is to make country fashions and sacrifices for the people, and from this I eat."[85]

So while gods and humans start off as categorically distinct, ritual and divine action works to bring about various kinds of exchange, transition, and identification between them. These transactions were thought to go either way, from god to man or from man to god. The epiphany of an *oriṣa* might be seen in a human being's extraordinary good fortune:

> W. S. Allen was visited at Ibadan by "a man well noted for war and kidnapping," who spoke about his many deliverances from danger. Once he had climbed a tall *iroko* tree by a liana rope to get a squirrel he had shot. The rope snapped and he was trapped up the tree for three days and nights. The third night he had a vision he would be released in the morning. Next day a fierce storm arose and blew over a tree twelve feet away against the *iroko*, which enabled him to get down. People were amazed. "He himself said it was his orisas that delivered him, many people worshiped him and asked blessing from his orisas."[86]

Whatever the literal truth of this soldier's tale, the attitudes revealed in the last sentence of Allen's narrative ring true: if the man was not to be treated as an *oriṣa* himself, at least he could give the blessing of the *oriṣa* who had shown him such signal favor.

People regarded as close to the *oriṣa*, even if by more conventional indications, were treated with respect and accorded privileges. A small but telling indication of this is the double epithets which missionaries sometimes used to describe the few highly committed *oriṣa*-worshippers whom they converted: "a notorious idolator and popular woman" at Abeokuta, "a zealous idolator and a man of great note" at Ota.[87] Occasional vignettes show how their self-esteem was sustained by both the signs of their *oriṣa*'s favor and the regard of their fellow-worshippers:

> A priestess [wrote Johnson from Ibadan] stopped to rest at the covered stall of a Christian woman, on her way back "from a festival or from a ceremonious visit." She was "in her best and she carried on her back her orisa in a large leather bag ornamented with beads and wore strings of small cowries round her neck. Proud of her priestly dress, she considered her-

self worthy of respect and above every remonstration." She was annoyed when the Christian woman told her she was serving a dumb idol to no profit, and told her own story. She had been a "believer" at Ilorin and taken a Muslim name, but misfortune showed up her mistake. Later at Lagos she had married a Christian, who had taken her idols away. But now she was back to her former religion, and all had gone well with her.[88]

One of the most widespread privileges accorded to notable *orisa* devotees was to be allowed to pass through toll gates without being required to pay the usual few cowries. Allen came across an *orisa* woman citing this concession to a group of listeners in an Ibadan compound as a token of her powers and of the respect in which she was held,[89] and it was said that the mere display of the ceremonial red leather bag of the Sango cult, called *laba,* "serves as a passport for anyone who takes it when he is allowed free passage through the gate of any town."[90] Initiates of the prestigious (and expensive) cult of Orisa Oko, recognized by the red and white clay beads above their forehead, were immune from debt seizure as well as tolls, and could even cross battle lines with impunity.[91]

So devotees got significant social rewards in the community at large from the awe in which their *orisa*'s powers were held. Their relationship with their god was strictly reciprocal, not just in the *do ut des* of devotion itself—sacrifice one way, protection the other—but in the mutual constitution of both parties to the relationship. On the one side, the gods made men in the sense that they presided over their coming into the world; on the other, men made the gods in the sense that their existence in the world depended on their recognition, worship, and promotion in the community by their devotees. These two assertions may not seem commensurate, since the first is a frequently stated indigenous view, while the latter looks like the pronouncement of a external sociologist. But in fact, the latter too is how the Yoruba saw, and said, it: the admission by an Ogboni chief that the Egba "made" their *orisa*[92] merely echoes the phrase "*se Oro,*" which lies behind the expression "making country fashion."[93] Karin Barber has shown us how vital it was for the devotees to make the name of their god good in the eyes of the community: for if *they* did not praise him, who else would believe in his power?[94] This was an uncertain and competitive world for gods as well as for human beings, in which the *orisa* had at least as many failures as successes. As Ogiriyan's exuberant followers at Osiele showed, devotees disparaged their rivals when they extolled their own god. People responded variously: some would accumulate gods of all kinds, as if to get maximum possible coverage, others might take the line of an old woman at Ijaye who "thought the orishas are nothing but her Shango alone has value."[95] It is from the interplay of people and communities looking for solutions to their problems, and cult members looking for new opportunities, that the spread and diversification of *orisa* cults takes its rise.

DIFFERENT GODS, DIFFERENT TOWNS

We get a good impression of the number, variety, and distribution of the cults to which Yoruba had access from the lists of "idols" that are reported as being given up by converts. Mostly only one or two *orisa* are mentioned in each case, but sometimes up to half a dozen or more are. Here is a selection of some of the longer ones:

1. Ifa, Odu, Sango, Agemo, Obatala, Elere, Ogun, Ososi, Elegbara, Yemoja, Orisa Oko, Osanyin, Osogbo, and Iweren (a man at Ota).[96]
2. Ifa, Iweren, Osanyin, Elegbara, Osun, and Yemoja (another man at Ota).[97]
3. Obatala, Esu, Omolu, Buruku, Osun, Bosiya, Yewa, and Yemoja (a woman at Abeokuta).[98]
4. Sango, Obatala, Osun, Esu, Ibeji, and Yemoja (another woman at Abeokuta).[99]
5. Sango, Osanyin, Oya, Osun, Elegbara, Aje, and Obatala (a woman, probably Oyo-Yoruba, at Badagry).[100]
6. Ori, Elegbara, Ifa, Odu, Sango, Osun, Ososi (a man at Ibadan).[101]
7. Bayonni, Ori, Osun, Ogiriyan, and Orisa Olufon (a woman at Ibadan).[102]
8. Obaluwaye, Osun, Esu, Orisa Ikire, Orisa Adatan, and Oya (an Ife woman at Leki).[103]
9. Olojo, Osun, Ogun, Osu, Ogiriyan, and Sango, with his Ifa and Esu still to come (an Ijesha *babalawo* and Brazilian returnee, at Badagry).[104]
10. Orisa Asalu, Osun, Agbure, Olode, Ogun, Osanyin (a man from Ilesha).[105]
11. Ifa (3), Osun, Ogun, Oluwa, Obatala, Orisa Oloko (the seven first male converts at Ondo, all Ondo themselves except for one Ekiti).[106]
12. Osun (3), Obatala (2), Ogun, Ibaokoigbo, Ibeji (the first four female converts at Ondo, being one Ondo, two Ekiti, and one Egba).[107]

This list is arranged regionally, by people's place of origin rather than where they were converted, since it is that which mainly determines what *orisa* they worship. It goes roughly in an arc from the southwest, at the Awori town of Ota (nos. 1 and 2), then north to Abeokuta (nos. 3 and 4), northeast to Ibadan and the Oyo-Yoruba (nos. 5, 6, and 7), further east to Ife and Ilesha (nos. 8, 9, and 10) and finally east again and southeast to Ondo and Ekiti (nos. 11 and 12). Large areas of Yorubaland—Ijebu, Ketu and points west, much of the east—are missing.

All major types of *orisa* are present here, including most of those which have a claim to be considered "pan-Yoruba." There is Ifa or Orunmila, the

Figure 4.2. An *oriṣa*-house of Yemoja, Abeokuta. S. S. Farrow, *Faith, Fancies, and Fetich* (1926).

principal god of divination, and Esu or Elegbara, the trickster deity associated with entrances and crossroads, who always had his portion of every sacrifice. Then there is Obatala or Orisanla, the *oriṣa* of human creation, author of harmony in the community, and a range of other deities linked to him—local variants, generically called *oriṣa funfun* ("white deities")—such as, in this list, Ogiriyan, Orisa Ikire, Orisa Adatan, Obalufon, and Orisa Asalu. There are river deities, always considered female: Yemoja (of the River Ogun),[108] Osun, Yewa, Oya (the Niger), and Oluwa. There is a range of well-known gods with special functions or distinctive characters, such as Sango (thunder), Ogun (iron and war), Sopona alias Omolu or Obaluaye (smallpox), Buruku (an *oriṣa* of western, non-Yoruba origin), Osanyin (healing), Aje (wealth), Ososi (hunting), Orisa Oko (farming). There are the two personal cults of Ori (individual destiny) and Ibeji (twins). Odu and Iweren are minor cults connected to Ifa, Osu and Bayoni to Sango. The remainder are more miscellaneous or uncertain, some probably of very local appeal.

From this list the truly pan-Yoruba *oriṣa* of wide appeal appear as remarkably few in number: Ifa, Esu/Elegbara, Obatala and his variants, Osun, and Ogun. One or two others were widely recognized but were not the general object of much personal devotion, such as Oduduwa, treated as a female counterpart to Obatala in the southwest and in central areas as the founder of Ife and overall ancestor.[109] Sango, who (except for Ifa) is mentioned far more often in the journals than any other *oriṣa*, had his heartland among the Oyo, and had spread with Oyo's political influence to the Egba and down to the southwest, but was alien to Ife and the eastern Yoruba—until, as we shall see, the late nineteenth century. Significantly, the only Sango worshipper from the east in the fourteen specimen cases is the Ijesha *babalawo*, a much-traveled man.

In fact, we might roughly classify the *oriṣa* into three groups: (1) those found throughout Yorubaland, (2) those limited to a particular town or small area, and (3) those found over a wide area but not all over Yorubaland. As to group (3), there is a very broad regional distinction to be made, albeit very fuzzy along its edges, between a central/northern/western zone, mainly in the savanna and long subject to Oyo rule or influence, and an eastern/southern zone, mainly in the forest. To the first of these belonged not only Sango but Orisa Oko, Ososi, Osumare the rainbow god, Buruku, Oya, and Yemoja; Ibeji was found only here,[110] and apparently Ori too. Specialized smallpox gods like Sopona seem more common here, as does Osanyin, especially in the far southwestern corner. In fact most of the highly distinctive and personalized *oriṣa* who dominate general accounts of Yoruba art and religion are limited to this zone. The religion of the eastern/southern zone was internally more heterogeneous: it did not have such a range of region-wide *oriṣa*, and beyond the small pan-Yoruba core, most of its deities were quite local. Of the pan-Yoruba deities, only Ogun (whose main cult center was at Ire-Ekiti) found greater support in the east, not just from individuals, but as the focus of major public festivals at Ondo and elsewhere.[111] But the boundary between the two zones was permeable and shifting, and became more so when the collapse of the old order pushed Oyo people and cults south and east into the forest regions.

It follows from this that for a realistic study of Yoruba religion in practice we should take the local cult complex, rather than a supposed Yoruba-wide pantheon, as our unit of analysis.[112] When the cults are viewed as part of a system of religious provision for the community, rather than in relation to the demands of individual cult members, the functionally distinct properties of each *oriṣa* are highlighted. In this, Ibadan and Ondo, the one an Oyo town close to the savanna, the other deep in the southeastern forests, make an instructive contrast.

Daniel Olubi, the Egba pastor of Ibadan for over thirty years, wrote there were three principal gods with rites in which "the whole town" was engaged: first Orisa Oko ("god of the farm"), worshipped for the New Yam in mid-July, when "every gate and street are full of soup and pounded yams" and people would even pawn their children to put on a good feast; second Ogiyan, in September, at whose festival men, women, and children would whip one another with canes to please the goddess and win her favor; and third Oke'badan ("Ibadan Hill"), during whose preceding vigil "all the religious

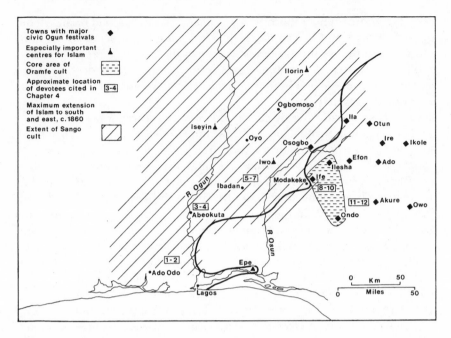

Figure 4.3. The Regional Spread of Cults

females spend the whole night singing and dancing over town."[113] Olubi omits what was probably the deity most widely worshipped by individuals in Ibadan, one whose priests commanded great influence with the chiefs, namely Sango; but Sango did not represent a general interest of the community. The relevance of Orisa Oko to farming speaks for itself. Ogiyan, as one of the white *oriṣa*, shared Obatala's concern for communal amity; the whipping, a marked feature of its cult in Abeokuta, too, was a form of sacrifice (and perhaps also a cathartic ritual display of aggression).[114] Oke'badan we have met already, an oracular *genius loci* from well before the time when Ibadan was taken over by Oyo elements in the 1830s.

The cycle of major annual festivals at Ondo can be put together from many references in the journals of the African clergy.[115] It opened in late July with the sacrifice of a woman, "to appease the rage of Esu . . . against the production of their farms."[116] A few days later occurred *Ọdun Ọba* ("the king's festival"), at which the *Oṣemawe* offered a sacrificial meal to the royal ancestors and received the tributes of his subjects; his chiefs danced before him and there was a general exchange of presents. In late August came the Ogun festival, at which the military companies (*egbẹ*) of the town's quarters paraded through the town, heavy with protective charms and drawn swords. In September or early October came the climax of the cycle, the festival of Oramfe: all strangers (except Ife people and the *oyinbo*) were sent away for seven days, the town fell quiet, and the *Oṣemawe* stayed in his palace; then a man was sacrificed to the god and the New Yam could be eaten. Oramfe was a deity that hailed from Ife, where he was associated with the sky and credited with sending thunder—but without the distinctive trappings and practices of the Sango cult.[117]

On the surface these two cycles of civic religion look quite different, except that both occurred between the end of June, when food was plentiful from the first rains, and the end of December, after the harvest from the second rains and before the military campaigns of the dry season. But the basic concerns of civic religion were uniform: a successful farming year, social harmony in the community, mutual regard between king and people, the goodwill of ancestors and/or the spirits of the land—all to keep death in abeyance. These concerns were intertwined, but exactly how they were distributed between the locally available *orisa* allowed for much flexibility. Orisa Oko makes obvious sense as the deity of the New Yam, as at Ibadan; but elsewhere that most material condition of continued life might be attached to Ogun—present in the farmer's cutlass and hoe—or to one of the white *orisa,* such as Obalufon.[118] At Ondo, Oramfe's association with cosmic renewal may have seemed to fit him to occupy that niche. It is rarely possible to give a detailed historical explanation of just how a particular community's cult complex came about, but we can discern some of the general principles involved.

Community interests called for *orisa* to be found whose special traits gave confidence that they could answer to the problems recurrent in key areas of life—farming, hunting, war, trade, disease, and so on—so there emerged a degree of functional specialization in relation to these niches among the deities of a locality. And because the *orisa* were regarded as being like persons, these functionally distinct traits were glossed or overlaid with such human features as gender, kin and seniority relations to one another, and preferences as to food and costume, which added to their distinctive character. On the other hand, because their individual devotees, who were decisive in "making" them, had much the same all-purpose requirements of them—in a word, *alafia*—the *orisa* were pushed back toward a common norm of performance: Sango (fierce and male) also gave his devotees children, and Osun (gentle and female) also protected hers from their enemies. The *orisa* were thus subject to a continuous to and fro of differentiation and convergence.

Local cult complexes could be stable for long periods, as the case of Ondo shows over more than a century, but they were still subject to two great forces of change: movements of people and vicissitudes of circumstance. In the nature of things, the *orisa* were always failing their supplicants. Individuals could respond, with the *babalawo*'s help, by turning to other *orisa*—with such a plenitude of unseen powers, no very elaborate theodicy was called for— but the aggregate of preferences must have always have inclined toward cults which offered, in addition to a sense of control over natural circumstances, expressive and social rewards above the average, as Sango did. At the community level an existing cult might be revived by an inspired adept addressing herself anew to perennial problems, such as Akere, the prophetess of Yemoja who enthralled Abeokuta in 1855.[119] Yet Yemoja, the native river deity of Abeokuta, was apparently outstripped in her appeal, even in Abeokuta, by Osun, the main river deity of central and eastern Yoruba country.[120] When a cult moved into a new area, it might take on quite new attributes or lose old ones because its niche was already occupied by one already there. When the Ikole-born warlord Esubiyi founded Ayede in midcentury, he introduced the cult of Yemoja, which he had taken up in Ibadan.[121] She became something she never had been at home, the principal royal oriṣa, and her relations of kinship and affinity with other oriṣa were adjusted to take account of local cultic realities. Another case of west-to-east migration brought Orisa Oko to a small Ekiti town; but because Ogun was already serving as the farming god, it had to settle for an all-purpose role, centered on healing and protection.[122] Conversely, when Sango moved west from Oyo country into the Ketu and Sabe kingdoms, which already had Ara as a male thunder deity, his latecomer status was expressed in his being regarded as the wife of Ara.[123]

Mostly we are only in a position to see the outcomes of these movements, but in the case of Sango at Ondo, there is direct evidence, not just of migrants taking their own oriṣa with them, but of a bid by professional (or quasi-professional) devotees to take advantage of acute local need to extend their cult. In the 1870s, with Glover's new road, Ondo became much more open to novel religious entrepreneurs, both from Lagos and from the north. Devotees of Esu and of Ogun manifested as a python made a stir, but were both ejected from town on the *Lisa*'s orders.[124] Sango made a much more effective show of it—not surprisingly, for this imperial cult of Old Oyo had adapted remarkably well to the needs of the Age of Confusion. The reasons are various. His cult had a very distinct organization—unlike, say, Ogun, who was the deity of all who worked with iron but had few specialist priests of his own. But Sango had its own powerful cult leader in each town; its *mọgba*, or possession priests; and many active devotees of both sexes.[125] No cult deployed such sanctions as Sango's, authorized as it was to levy heavy indemnities on compounds struck by lightning, to propitiate Sango's anger. Its public displays were spectacular, especially when the priests went about the town with bowls of fire on their heads and blew fire from their mouths while their attendants called the royal greeting *Kabiyesi!* "and charged [the onlookers] with sacrifices."[126] Confident in the power of their fearsome god, Sango's devotees conducted themselves in public far more assertively than any other cult.

With this background among the Oyo-Yoruba, Sango cultists became active in Ondo in the late 1870s:

Sango was first noted in 1877, when Phillips commented that he was "worshipped here by only a few but is looked upon with some degree of contempt by the mass of the people."[127] But just over a year later, in the first reference to the epidemic which was to ravage Ondo for nearly two years, he commented on the death of a respectable woman from smallpox, after much had been given "to the Songo priests . . . as fees for propitiating the disease."[128] Throughout 1879 and into 1880 smallpox claimed its victims.[129] There was much desperate consultation among the Ondo chiefs, who were prepared to entertain all suggestions.

One of them came from a Sango priest, a former slave of the Ondo king, who in mid-1879 told them "that he was sent by the god Sango to make a sacrifice that the mortality caused by the smallpox might be checked." They gave him a horse, which was sacrificed on the road to Okeigbo to drive the smallpox away, as well as a bull and a ram on which the Sango people feasted. Later he called at the mission, and to Phillips spoke scathingly of Ondo credulity—"They are deceiving themselves and like to be deceived"—and added that "the smallpox said it will continue to rage till it has destroyed all the witches and charmmakers in the country."[130] An Ondo man present at this discussion "made a great palaver with him" about it, but Sango continued to appeal.

Another Sango devotee, this time from Lagos, got money from the *Lisa* to do something about the smallpox, before he died of it himself; and late in 1879 "many worshippers" were attracted to its festival, at which gaily painted images and "beautiful red prints" were on display.[131] In February 1880, the Ondo chiefs made yet another attempt, the sixth or seventh, ritually to expel the smallpox from town, this time southward to Oke Aye.[132] By the end of that year, the epidemic must have passed, as references to it vanish from the CMS journals.

So Sango, a cult unconnected with smallpox on its home ground, rapidly made its way during the epidemic. The Sango priest's opportunism is undeniable, but his cynical attitude toward exploiting the Ondos did not rest on a secular foundation: there is no reason to doubt his belief in his access to smallpox as a personal being or in his spiritual interpretation of the epidemic. Since he did not speak of Sango to Phillips, we cannot know if he was coming to regard him as a "god of smallpox," which was what his recommendations meant in Ondo eyes. For not only were the chiefs prepared, more than once, to spend big money on the solutions proffered by the Sango priests; but many individuals attached themselves to the new cult, whether to gain personal immunity through Sango's protection or to enjoy its social and material advantages. But the cult did not last. Late in 1884 there was another outbreak of smallpox; Chief *Oyegbata*, a Christian sympathizer, fell ill but recovered; and a coalition of young men and some of the chiefs—hardly any of them Christians—moved against the smallpox cults. Sopona and Sango were abolished, and their idols and paraphernalia destroyed.[133]

In these perplexities, there was one cult which stood apart from all others: that of Ifa and its priest-diviners, the *babalawo*. The Yoruba knew many forms of divination, but Ifa was by far the most widespread and most prestigious.[134] The oracular messages were presented in sets of verses (*ęsę*), grouped under sixteen main headings (*odu*), which each had a certain overall character in terms of what they portended for the client. The *ęsę* were narratives of archetypal occasions when clients with problems (including *orişa*, kings, and fabulous figures) had consulted Orunmila, the deity of divination, who had specified what sacrifices were needed and to whom. The stories concluded with the client's response, and its outcome for his life. The *babalawo* manipulated Ifa's sacred palm nuts (*ikin*) to determine which *odu* was relevant to the client's problem and then recited some of the *ęsę* which fell under it. Once the relevant *ęsę* was chosen, there was a further determination of the steps the client needed to take, by means of casting lots (*ibo*) to questions put in a yes/no form.

Uncommon qualities were required in a *babalawo*. Memory, intelligence, and self-discipline were necessary for him to acquire the knowledge of *ęsę* which was fundamental to his practice, as well as the psychological insight and worldly experience needed for dealing with clients. Though sons might follow their fathers, the profession was not hereditary, but depended on boys with aptitude and inclination being apprenticed to an established *babalawo* from an early age. Further development depended on association with one's professional peers and on wide-ranging travel to study with noted *babalawo*, especially at Ile-Ife and other centers of the cult. They often added medical practice to their divination.[135] *Babalawo* were thus the intellectuals of Yoruba society, the people most able to take a long-term and supra-local view of things, adept at the analysis of novel situations in terms of precedents, and prone to the rationalization of the cultural materials—myths, proverbs, *oriki*, maxims, fables, historical fragments—which were built into the *ęsę Ifa*. If there was a keynote to the Ifa cult, it was control: control of circumstances through knowledge of the relevant precedents for action, a control which itself depended on the *babalawo*'s own self-control. Unlike the other major *orişa*, Ifa or Orunmila did not possess his priests, and, again unlike the other cults, they were nearly always male.[136]

Ifa had its laity as well as its professionals: it was easily the most widespread personal cult among men. Men were initiated into Ifa at any age—but especially at birth, or at the age of the baby's teething, or at adolescence—and received a set of dedicated palm nuts (*ikin*), which were kept in a small vessel and, like the image or material token of any other *orişa*, received daily devotion and gave protection. Further stages of initiation might take place later in life, giving deeper degrees of access to the mystery and power of Ifa.[137]

Women usually received help or protection through the Ifas of their men-folk. In a small Ijesha town, a woman returned from the farm and, before greeting anyone, went straight to prostrate to her husband's Ifa for her safe journey.[138] A more elaborate case from Ota:

> Siba's wife does not conceive, so he spends much money to have himself initiated to Ifa. During the ceremony, the *babalawo* tells of the time when Ifa himself had a barren wife, but made her fruitful by large sacrifices. Divination reveals that four fowls and other things are needed to make the sacrifice. They are handed over to the *babalawo* "who after presenting them to Ifa and offering a prayer for their acceptance touched the fore-head of the wife with the fowls and afterwards took them home."[139]

Ifa was not merely a very distinctive cult in itself, but also cultivated a unique relationship to the ensemble of the other *orișa*. Through divination, it played the key role in directing individuals to their appropriate *orișa,* thus making itself the linchpin of the religious system; and the narratives of the *ẹsẹ Ifa* tirelessly aggrandize Orunmila against the other *orișa* for his superior wisdom and reliability. This sense of superiority was moreover grounded in Ifa's special relationship with God: the *babalawo* invariably described Ifa as God's messages or messenger,[140] and as "the mediator between God and man, hence its name Orunmila (heaven's reconciliation)."[141]

Now while Ifa's endorsement of sacrifices as the essential means of rec-onciliation with the *orișa* puts it at the heart of "country fashion," this claim to a privileged relationship with God gives Ifa a foot in the other camp: it creates a bridge to the world religions. And in fact Islam has a significant presence in the *ẹsẹ Ifa*. Many of the references to it are somewhat hostile, suggesting an early rivalry between the Muslim *alufa* and *orișa* priests; yet Ifa could also declare that a child was to be a Muslim.[142] But by the mid-nineteenth century, professional ties between *babalawo* and Muslim *alufa* could be cordial—as a *babalawo* told an African pastor: "each of us babala-wos has a Mohammedan friend and each Mohammedan priest, so much as I know of those at Abeokuta, makes friends with babalawos in order to have their help in difficult matters of divination."[143] Ifa's openness to the world beyond the *orișa* may well go back to its very origins. For it is virtually cer-tain that Ifa derives its formal properties from the system of divination by "sand-writing" practiced in the Islamic world, which diffused widely into Sub-Saharan Africa and so far beyond the frontiers of Islam as to seem entirely autochthonous.[144] But Ifa's origins are not required to sustain the essential point that needs to be made about Ifa: that it was fundamentally concerned with reconciling the far and the near; not merely heaven and earth, but also ancient sacred precedent and the messy actuality of the Age of Confusion, in which outsiders and their religions were a growing presence.

GOD IN YORUBA BELIEF

Belief in a Supreme Being, associated with heaven or the sky (*ọrun*), who stood as the ground of being or the ultimate author of things, was general among the Yoruba. His common name was Olorun ["Lord of heaven," "Owner of the sky"], which is always and unavoidably rendered in English as "God." Christians and Muslims readily spoke of their God as "Olorun," and had no trouble or hesitation in identifying Him with the Being so described in indigenous discourse. Some instances of talk about God:

> *Ọlọrun, iwọ ni o ma gba mi o!* [God, it is you who will save me]: a spontaneous exclamation made by a *babalawo* in the street.[145]

> *Sisọ ni tirẹ, riro ni tiwa, ṣugbọn ṣiṣe t'Ọlọrun ni* [Yours is to speak, ours is to think about it, but to do it is God's]: said by a Sango priest in response to Hinderer's preaching at Ibadan.[146]

> *Tani le ba Ọlọrun ja? Gbogbo ẹniti o ṣe buburu yi, Ọlọrun a bi wọn* [Who can fight against God? All those who did that wickedness, God will punish them]: sententious remarks by a war chief about the people involved in the Abeokuta *Ifọle* of 1867.[147]

> *Ti Ọlọrun li emi nṣe* [I am doing God's business]: a *babalawo* in Ibadan justifying himself.[148]

> *Ki Ọlọrun ki o wo o ju ni lọ o!* [May God look after it better than we do]: quoted as a remark that people will make to the mother of a new baby.[149]

> *Ọlọrun mbẹ* [God exists]: said by an Ibadan war chief, laden with charms, after listening to an evangelist.[150]

> *O ku yiyọ Ọlọrun* [Greetings to you on God's saving you]: how a man might be greeted on returning from war.[151]

It is a large part of the problem in examining the place of God in Yoruba worldviews that reports of what people *said* bulk so much more largely than reports of practice—inescapably so, since the vast bulk of practice was directed at the *orisa*. And it is the relationship between Olorun and the *orisa* which has been the central focus of academic discussion. The literature is dominated by one book, the Rev. E. Bolaji Idowu's *Olódùmarè: God in Yoruba Belief,* which seeks to show that, although God received little direct worship, He nevertheless figured prominently in traditional religious consciousness. Idowu's approach is both very Yoruba and very Christian: it is Yoruba in its assertion that Yoruba belief in God was both ancient and indigenous; and Christian in its insistence on the absolute distinction between God and the *orisa*.[152] In this it continues a hermeneutic tradition begun by the Yoruba missionary clergy, which was aimed at maximizing the area of possible agreement between Christianity and Yoruba culture.

The historical evidence, however, suggests that the Yoruba understanding of God was not as definite, unchanging, and uniform, nor did it hold Him to be as distinct from the *oriṣa* as Idowu maintains. His contention that, in addressing the *oriṣa*, people were essentially directing their prayers to God through His ministers or deputies, is one that was often upheld by pagans in response to missionary attacks on idolatry. Thus Chief Sagbua of Abeokuta replied to Henry Townsend, asking him why he still worshipped *oriṣa* when he believed all things ultimately came from God: "Messengers we appoint them to be. I hold Shango's feet, Ifa and Egungun, that they should help me beg God to give me all things I need."[153] Or as a *babalawo* insisted: "God made us and commanded us to make the petty gods and worship them and send them with sacrifices to him."[154] Another *babalawo* compared the relationship between God and the *oriṣa* to the government of Ibadan:

> Balle the head chief over all, then Balogun, Otton, Osi etc [*sic*], they all get power, they have their own people, Balle cannot claim any of their own children but still they submit to Balle. In like manner God [is] the highest, but the Orisas . . . have their worshippers and no Orisa can allow any of his children to follow God [directly].[155]

Most remarks of this kind are, significantly, the rationalizations of *babalawo*, defending customary practice against missionary criticism. It is impossible to tell just how central God was to the thoughts of ordinary people when, in the routine course of their lives, they worshipped their *oriṣa*.

These texts all presuppose the categorical distinction between God and the *oriṣa* that is stated in modern dictionaries: an *oriṣa*, says Abraham, is "any Yoruba deity apart from *Olorun*."[156] God is not *a* god; He belongs in a class of one. But there was another view, which significantly came from the east. Reporting on his preaching in the market of Okemesi, on the borders of Ijesha and Ekiti, an African evangelist—who of course accepted the categorical distinction between God and the *oriṣa*—complained that "there were many people who could not distinguish between orisa (idol) and God the Supreme Being."[157] The same view occurs in a potted account of Ondo religion given by Charles Phillips in 1889, in response to a inquiry about local religious beliefs sent out through the CMS.[158] Part of his answer to a question about the Supreme Being can be summarized thus:

> The name generally in use for God is "Orisa," which they connect with the idea of a creator. The Ondo say, *Oriṣa yi o da wa ni aiye* ("Orisa who creates us into the world"); and the Ilaje [a people of the creeks to the south] say, *Oriṣa n'o buru iwa* ("Orisa who originates being"). Another name is "Oduduwa," meaning "the author of existence," which conveys the fatherhood of God, as in the phrase *Emi ọmọ Oduduwa* ("I am a child of O."). "Both these names represent God as a personal being. But the name Olorun, used for God among the Egbas and Yorubas, seems to be recently imported into the Ondo language." The Ondo do not use "Olorun" for a personal being: on a cloudy day they say, *Oju Ọlọrun ko sian loni* ("The face of God is not

good today"). Of a fortunate man they say, *Ọlọrun rẹ da a tan* ("His God created him completely"). . . . The Ondo only have vague traditions about the creation, but they say: "When the Oduduwa sent man into the world, he gave him a fowl and a quantity of dust tied up in a bag. He threw the dust on the water and set the fowl on top, and where the fowl scratched the dust became dry land."

The first thing to deserve comment here is the use of *Oriṣa* to denote the Deity in a singular, as well as in a generic, sense. The fact that terms cognate to *Oriṣa* are widely found to denote the Supreme Being, not only among the eastern Yoruba but among neighboring peoples, from the Itsekiri (*Oritse*) and Edo (*Osa*) to the southeast to the Gbe-speakers to the west (*Lisa*),[159] suggests that *Oriṣa* is the ancient term throughout a broad linguistic region, and that its use as a generic term is relatively recent. The word *imọlẹ* (or *umọlẹ* in eastern dialects), which continues in currency as a synonym of *oriṣa*, looks as if it was the old generic term for "subordinate deities."[160] While we can only speculate about the historical context of *Oriṣa*'s shift of reference, we can, I think, infer one aspect of what probably happened. Since of all the later *oriṣa* it is Obatala or Orisanla who came closest to the attributes of the presumed original Orisa/God,[161] it seems that Orisa became an "overburdened symbol"[162] and fragmented into a range of refractions or local cultic variants, the so-called white *oriṣa*.

The evidence for blurred, shifting, and contested boundaries between God and the *oriṣa* goes further, particularly in eastern Yorubaland. The *oriṣa* Oramfe enjoyed great prestige around the Ife-Ilesha-Ondo triangle. His festival was the fulcrum of the Ondo sacred year. Though Phillips calls him "god of the soil" in his 1889 letter, presumably because the New Yam was eaten then, this is misleading, since Oramfe was associated above all with the sky. His cult was big at Ibodi, a small town between Ife and Ilesha, where "the devotees . . . propitiate the God of heaven; as such they sprinkle ashes in a circular form, 3 or 6 feet from the compound entrance, looking to heaven and saying a prayer for each member of the family, splitting kola in the circle."[163] At Ife in the 1930s Oramfe's status was the subject of open disagreement: "By some informants he is identified with *Ọlọrun*, the sky-god who stands above all other orishas, while for others he constitutes a separate orisha."[164]

A further deity of this kind was Olojo [Lord of the day], who also had a major festival at Ife, but who comes first to our attention in Ilesha:

When George Vincent urges the people of Omofe quarter to worship God, they say that "all of them . . . worship God." Vincent asks how, and they reply that at daybreak they say, *Ọlọjo oni, o ma gba o!* [Lord of the day, you will save us]. To further questions they say that God gave *Ọlọjo oni* as "the daymaster, that is the angel of whom the Lord put the care of the day to his hand."[165]

Ọlọjọ oni is expressly stated by Idowu to be an epithet of Olodumare, as he calls God.[166] So again what we seem to find is an aspect of God being worshipped directly as an *orisa*.

Then there is Oduduwa, whom the modern consensus treats as a kind of god/man, the "ancestor of the Yoruba race," the quasi-historical founding king of Ife.[167] Yet nineteenth-century conceptions of Oduduwa appear to be more variable than of almost any other deity.[168] In the southwest, where there was a great shrine of Oduduwa at Ado Odo, the *orisa* was always represented as female, "the great goddess of the Yoruba country," and was closely linked with Obatala.[169] It was also at Ado that James White was told by the chiefs that Oduduwa was "the same person as 'Olorun' whom we call God."[170] In central and eastern Yorubaland, Oduduwa is spoken of as an ancestor, usually male, but also sometimes as God too: both characterizations appear in Phillips's account of Ondo beliefs. But the most compelling testimony along these lines comes from the report by Phillips's catechist, C. N. Young, of an argument he had with the ruler of Okeigbo, Derin Ologbenla:

> When Young spoke to Derin of "the way of worshipping the true God," he got a most irritated response. "The Ifes know it and that is Oduduwa. I said what do you mean to say by the word Oduduwa, do you mean to say that is the God of heaven—or do you mean this name to be one of your orisas? He said he meant the being who made the earth and the heavens and formed all members upon man. I said, you have not known him as you ought, he said what do you mean? and at this time he was in a fit of passion; when he said presently if he [Derin] call upon him [Oduduwa], he will answer him. . . . I said no, it is beyond what you can venture to say or do. . . . Thence he said he is an Ife by origin and that all nations both white and black originated from Ife. And as he was in passion and would not admit any view as the right one but his, I was asked to give up."[171]

This could hardly be more plainly said. And Derin was not just an Ife, but a member of the Ife royal lineage; and not just a royal, but shortly to be elected *Ọni* himself, Oduduwa's earthly successor. The conclusion that these evidences point to is that, while Oduduwa was described as an *orisa*, s/he was also treated as an aspect of the Supreme Being, particularly in the capacity of ancestor.

Last to be considered is Olodumare, which Idowu treats as the most authentic and "ancient, unique name" of God.[172] The exact etymology of the word is uncertain. Its key component is either *odù*, meaning "principal," "chief," or "heading" (as in the *odù Ifá*, or the first element in *Odùdúwà*), or *òdù*, meaning "a large, deep vessel" or "largeness, fullness," preceded by a possessive prefix "*Ol-*." "Almighty," as in the Christian phrase *Oluwa Olorun Olodumare* ("Lord God Almighty"), which has become the conventional modern rendering, may not be too far off the mark. Idowu's preference

119

for *Olodumare* is partly because that word is widely used in Ifa verses ("the Odu corpus," as he calls it) to refer to the Supreme Being and because he thinks—correctly, I believe—that the currency of *Olọrun* has been greatly boosted by Muslim and Christian influence. Yet the evidence of informal religious discourse in the nineteenth century suggests not merely that *Olọrun* was the popular term, but that it enjoyed a stability of reference which the more esoteric *Olodumare* lacked. In fact there is only a handful of references to *Olodumare,* compared with many to *Olọrun.* The "official" version is present: a *babalawo* at Owu in Abeokuta, mentioning Obatala and Ifa, said that "if anyone were to go to heaven now, he would surely find these deities in the presence of God the Olodumare";[173] and Phillips gives it as an Ondo belief that a dead man's soul goes straight to "the Almighty (Olodumare)" to be judged.[174] But more "heterodox" representations also circulated. Some young women at Ota, petty traders and worshippers of Esu, told James White that "Olodumare . . . made Olorun, but you have left Olodumare to serve Olorun," thus implying Olodumare and Olorun (God) were not the same person.[175] Then there was the devotee of Sopona at Osiele, who was provoked by missionary probing on the relations between God and the smallpox *orịṣa,* to burst out defiantly "that if anybody hear this term Olodumare which signifies Almighty, that person must understand it to be smallpox"; at which "she gave a song and they all shouted together."[176]

If there is one rule of analysis to bring to this situation, it is to refrain from pronouncing, usually on the basis of some pet theory or external requirement, which of these conceptions must be discarded as "wrong." For it is precisely the variety and disagreement that indicates that serious theological thought was going on. Yoruba people in the nineteenth century should not be seen as mechanically reproducing some received doctrine (and sometimes making mistakes, like faulty photocopiers), but as struggling to capture, in the idioms and with the materials available to them, their experience of the world that lay beyond mundane perception. The girls at Ota may well have been trying to make sense of White's preaching about the divinity of Christ—God, but also the Son of God—and the remark did lead him to think they were "impressed with the plurality of persons in the Godhead." We should probably interpret the Sopona woman's claim as seizing on what to her was an obscure but impressive-sounding epithet, not securely attached to her idea of God (whom she and her friends had been calling *Olọrun*), in order to aggrandize her own special *orịṣa,* Sopona. She was calling Sopona "the greatest"—somewhat in the manner of a sincere but misguided supporter of Newcastle United or the Chicago Bears—rather than making him out to be the Supreme Being. These remarks were highly situational, but the more general variety of religious conceptions surely shows the relevance of some of the perennial large issues of theology: is God a creator or an ancestor, is He unitary or plural?[177]

As the *orịṣa* systems tended to differ between the eastern and the central/

western zones of Yorubaland, so also did prevailing conceptions of God. A more complex overlap of God and the *oriṣa,* and the widespread use of *Oriṣa* for God, was found in the east, beginning from Ife where, apart from Obatala/Orisanla, there were three *oriṣa* widely considered as aspects of God: Olojo, Oduduwa, and Oramfe. In the center/west, there was a much sharper distinction between God and the *oriṣa.* Here God was *Olọrun,* the term which Phillips thought was recently introduced to Ondo by the Oyo and Egba, and whose present popularity Idowu attributes to the influence of Muslims and Christians. So we may infer that a major factor defining the difference between the two zones was the presence or absence of Islam. Between the two zones, and their associated conceptions, the *babalawo* played a mediating role. Upholding Ife as the site of the cosmogony and the source of human society, as well as the most prestigious center of their mystery, they moved with assurance into the sphere of Oyo and became intimate consultants to its rulers and chiefs from the *Alafin* downward.[178] Here too, if they yet existed, the *babalawo* encountered Islam, probably from as early as the seventeenth century; or, perhaps more likely, Ifa was itself born, fusing a largely indigenous religious content with a new type of divining system adapted from Islamic "sand-writing." If Islam offered techno-mystical knowledge that was very attractive, it also presented a challenge to their Ife-centric cosmology. Ifa can be seen as a recasting of the *oriṣa* system to meet some of the more trenchant Muslim criticism of it, which must have focused on the relationship between God and the *oriṣa.* The Supreme Being was given a distinctive, perhaps ancient, but certainly Ife-derived name, *Olodumare;* and Olodumare was separated off from the *oriṣa,* clearly defined as a creator, not an ancestor like Oduduwa. And though in Ifa the *babalawo* reworked the *oriṣa* system, they still took care to put some space between their particular *oriṣa,* Orunmila, and the rest of them. His name alludes to God's abode (*ọrun,* "heaven") and he is represented as being God's special messenger—perhaps as Mohammed is by Muslims?—and as such more powerful than the other *oriṣa.*

So the "traditional religion" of the Yoruba does not really present itself as a single, given, separate entity. What it designates concretely is a congeries of cultic practices, actuated by some common principles, but varying a great deal over space and over time. It was a terrain of constant questioning, contestation, and exploration, which gave much opportunity for new cults to break in, though their success in doing so permanently depended on their being able to meet existing criteria of religious need and the social rules for cultic coexistence. Two cults stood apart from the rest—Ifa and Islam—which, I have suggested, may be more closely connected in their Yoruba origins than the labeling of one as part of "country fashion" and the other as a world religion may lead us to think. Islam, in the zone where it was present (albeit only as the religion of strangers and a small minority of Yoruba), seems to have fostered significantly different conceptions of God and human destiny than those that prevailed in the zone from which it was absent. Ifa not only offered the most systematic philosophy of Yoruba experience, but also claimed for itself a place as primus inter pares of all the cults on the basis of its special relationship with God, for whom its preferred name was Olodumare.[179] So when Christianity arrived in the "high noon" (ọsan gangan) of Yoruba religious history, it not only came in on an open and dynamic system of belief and practice, but found there were currents with which it could swim and hope to turn its own way.

5

THE MISSION AND THE POWERS

A mission is a certain kind of power in the land, a power both specific and limited. While it is the specific qualities of the mission's impact—that is, above all, in the fields of religion and culture—on Yoruba society that are our primary concern, this could not have occurred if the mission had not first been able to establish itself as a power in a more generic sense, among the other powers that occupied the social terrain. The most important of these powers were the towns or kingdoms (*ilu*) in which the CMS wanted to set up its stations. For until the 1890s, outside Lagos and its dependencies, the Yoruba Mission operated as an autonomous agent in a zone of independent states, where its presence had to have the sanction of the local authorities. So there can be no adequate assessment of a mission's religious impact without a prior analysis of the political setting in which it operated, and of the negotiations through which it established a local place for itself.

It was an essentially political calculus which first governed the response of Yoruba rulers to the requests of missionaries to be allowed to set up locally; and it was expressly to them as Europeans (*oyinbo*), as bearers of "the white man's religion," that they responded. This calculus, as of other nineteenth-century rulers in Africa, had two main strands: (1) a search for allies in the ongoing regional power struggle, and (2) a desire for "cultural enhancement."[1] The perceived power of Europeans was central to both these objectives, which were more intimately interwoven in their understanding than they might be in a Western view. For the pragmatism of their search for power did not preclude that it should extend beyond the limits dictated by Western practical rationality. They wanted not only allies and technology, but also access to the hidden sources of the white man's power. This also gave them an interest in the specific character of missionaries as European *priests:* men who professed expertise in the world of "spirit" or the hidden sources of power (*awo*) and so were comparable with the religious specialists that they already knew, such as diviners and Muslim *alufa.*

Exactly what kind of Europeans and what kind of priests the missionaries were, and so what kind of power a mission was and what it might bode for any community that received it, were issues that exercised Yoruba rulers for many decades. African rulers everywhere were quick to realize that allowing a mission to operate nearly always carried consequences which they could not entirely control, costs as well as benefits. The mission was bound to some degree to challenge the normative order of the community, and (to the extent that it succeeded in making converts) to create a degree of alienation in a section of the population from its institutions. The responses of African rulers to this risk depended on a cost/benefit analysis specific to their several situations. They ranged from the resolute refusal of the king of Dahomey and the *Awujalẹ* of Ijebu even to admit missions, or Asante's policy of admitting them but not allowing to make any converts,[2] through the limited sponsorship of the *Kabaka* of Buganda (which had such unexpected and far-reaching results)[3] to the positive promotion of Christianity (but on his own terms) by Khama, king of the Ngwato.[4] Most Yoruba rulers fell somewhere in the middle: prepared and in some cases eager to have missions, but, as far as they were able, anxious to mitigate their solvent effects. We might see them as involved in a continuous learning process, but with a lesson that was always changing and that varied from one town to another.

SUNRISE WITHIN THE TROPICS: 1845–1861

The mission started in earnest in 1846, when Henry Townsend and Samuel Crowther finally got to Abeokuta, after several months in Badagry owing to the death of Sodeke, the Egba leader who had originally invited them. The third member of the party, Charles Gollmer, stayed behind in Badagry, to build up the station there. At Abeokuta the mission went rapidly ahead, owing to the presence of a fair number of well-disposed Saro returnees, who provided the nucleus of the early congregations, and the active support of some key chiefs. These included Okukenu, known by his title *Ṣagbua,* the senior Ogboni chief of Ake (the premier Egba township) and, in the absence of an *Alake,* the chief spokesman of the town; and three of

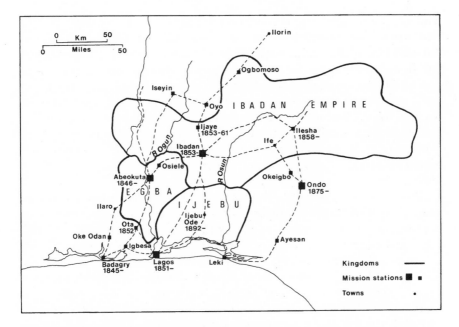

Figure 5.1. Mission Stations and Main Routes before 1892

the leading war-chiefs, Somoye, Ogunbona, and Apati, who vied intensely over who should receive the missionaries first.[5] The main station was at Ake, and by the end of 1847 others were set up around the sprawling town. In these early years, the CMS occupied a key mediating position in an Egba-British alliance, a role dramatized in the gifts—a Bible from Queen Victoria and a steel corn mill from Prince Albert—which the missionaries presented to Chief Sagbua in 1849.[6] While the mission's progress was not without local challenge, the role of the missionaries in the defense of Abeokuta against the Dahomean assault in 1851 consolidated their hopes that here they might indeed see "sunrise in the tropics."

Badagry stood in marked contrast. Despite Gollmer's boarding school, the indigenous Egun (Popo) people were indifferent to mission, the converts being drawn from an immigrant and largely transient Yoruba population. Struggling to adjust to the changes in the Atlantic trade, caught in the cross-pressures of the Egba-Dahomey conflict, and drawn into the dynastic rivalries of Lagos, Badagry proved so stony a field that a year after the British had installed the consular regime at Lagos, Gollmer moved there (1852). Badagry became a mission backwater, with no more resident European missionaries, though it would see the staunch, and far from ineffective, labors of Samuel Pearse (1859–1874), who eventually dedicated its church to St. Thomas, because it was "a place hard to be persuaded."[7] At Lagos, however, the numbers of Christians grew with the town's rapidly expanding population. The head station at Faji in Lagos's more open "east end" was soon outstripped by the "west end" mission, situated in the most crowded area of Saro resettlement, which came to be known as Breadfruit and developed into one of the most dynamic churches in the entire Mission.[8] To these was in 1854 added a third station at Ebute Ero at the north tip of the island, an area of mainly indigenous Lagosians.[9] Meanwhile the Awori town of Ota, where Lagos's sphere of influence overlapped with Abeokuta's, accepted a mission in 1852—no doubt partly because it was so vulnerable that it felt it could not refuse. But it still proved "a very hard and almost barren soil," wrote James White on retiring from the long years of his ministry there (1854–1879).[10]

The great events of 1851—the Egba defeat of Dahomey and the British restoration of Akitoye to the throne of Lagos[11]—brought missionaries to the attention of rulers across a wide swathe of Yorubaland. In the early and mid-1850s missionaries received many messages—often given extra weight by accompanying "symbolical letters" (aroko)—from kingdoms in the interior, professing friendship and sometimes asking for a white man to settle with them.[12] Crowther's visit to Ketu in 1853 was in response to one such long-standing invitation.[13] These invitations meshed with the CMS plan that Abeokuta should be merely the first of a chain of stations stretching into the far interior (so it was that David Hinderer was initially commissioned to learn Hausa).[14] The next link in the chain would obviously have to be Ibadan. So Hinderer visited Ibadan from Abeokuta for five months in 1851,[15] secured the agreement of the chiefs to a mission, and after a year's furlough in England during which he married Anna Martin, returned to set up the mission for which he would be remembered.[16] Once Ibadan had agreed to have a white man—he was seen primarily as such, rather than as a missionary per se—its rival Ijaye did not want to lose out on any possible advantages, and in 1852 its ruler Kurunmi sent a message asking for a visit.[17] Townsend went to reconnoiter and explain, and early in 1853 the newly arrived Adolphus Mann was sent to open a station, which would last till Ijaye's destruction eight years later.

Can we say what exactly these rulers had in mind when they invited the missionaries to come to their towns? Some interest groups did *not* want them: the network of allies and partners of ex-king Kosoko of Lagos who were reluctant to abandon the overseas slave trade, which ramified to Abeokuta, Ijebu, and Ota; the Muslim authorities of Ilorin; and the Muslim party in some other towns. Where opinion was positive, we tend to assess it in terms of a purely secular-pragmatic rationality, like Henry Townsend when he candidly admitted to Venn that he did not think the chiefs were at all interested in the spread of the Gospel, since it would overturn "the system of lies" on which their authority rested:

> They want us without our religion. They want us on account of the people
> in Sierra Leone [i.e., as potential repatriates], because they see that through

us they are likely to keep open the road to the sea and obtain trade and be well supplied with guns and powder for sale or war as may be required.[18]

This is fair enough, as far as it goes. But we get a fuller picture from the comprehensive wish list which the *Alaketu* of Ketu presented to Gollmer at a private meeting in 1859:

> 1, that he and his people may have peace in their town and country; 2, that he may not see sudden death at his place; 3, that he may not have fire in the town; 4, that he may not see war, either from Dahomey or Abeokuta; 5, that he may soon ascend his throne and have full power; and that he hoped we would assist him to get the necessary things suitable for a king, such as a crown; 6, that he may be able to open the road to the river Opara to facilitate commerce seaward.[19]

As a set of personal and political objectives for a newly established Yoruba *oba* these make complete practical sense. It was when the *Alaketu* got round to asking something quite specific of his visitor that another element of thinking came in. For after explaining his policy goals, the *Alaketu* asked Gollmer to pick one of twenty sticks, each of which represented one of his twenty wives (who had come to greet the CMS party earlier). Gollmer was supposed to have "eyed" one of the wives, who had earlier done some mischief, and thus was taken to have superior power to tell good and evil. In thus being invited to select one of the sticks, he was being treated like a diviner or a Muslim *alufa* (or perhaps his powers were just being tested). In other words, while the *Alaketu* might not have been interested in Gollmer's "religion," he was interested in his spiritual powers.

A common opening claim made by the missionaries was that "we [are] come to make [your] country good," as Townsend told Kurunmi on his first visit to Ijaye;[20] or, as Gollmer announced in Badagry, "To make your country stand the same as white man's country—this is the reason why we come here, and why we wish to preach the word of God to you."[21] The missionary theory was that this would come about through the adoption of their ethical teaching: when people at Iseyin welcomed Mann on his first visit, saying that "we make the town good," he replied that "the town will be good if the hearts of the people become good."[22] But Yoruba thinking also anticipated a more direct link between religious cause and social effect: the spiritual techniques of the man of God were regarded as having an intrinsic efficacy. So when the most committed of the early chiefly supporters of the mission at Abeokuta, Ogunbona, asked to have a chapel at his house, it put Crowther in mind of the idolatrous Micah in the Book of Judges (17:13), who also wanted a priest of God in his house, saying that "Now know I that the Lord will do me good, seeing I have a Levite to my priest."[23] Nor was this sentiment confined to such declared friends of the mission: a few months after the Dahomean defeat, a woman possessed by an *orisa* announced to the Egba that they should offer sixteen cattle to "the white people and the Mohammedans" for having saved the town.[24] This linking of the missionaries with the Muslims (who would certainly have made their contribution by offering prayers and making charms) rather implies that the *olorișa* regarded them as having helped by their prayers as well as by their skill at removing bullets.

In the early years the most widespread hope entertained of a resident missionary was that he would bring protection. Again, we should not be too hasty to explain this in too rationalist a fashion, as if it was simply a conviction that any town with a European living in it would be able to count on British intervention to help it if attacked. At this stage, very few chiefs had ever seen a white man before, and can only have had vague ideas about how they might act in the politics of the interior. Rather the white man was treated as a mixture of prestige object and protective charm, and his specifically missionary character was ignored. Thus J. T. Kefer, within a few months of arriving in Abeokuta in 1853, heard himself alluded to in a song: "White man become two, the walls of our town are now strong."[25] In some places there were objections to missionaries influencing people, but satisfaction at the missionary presence per se: once when Kefer was preaching, a man came to drive away his hearers, but yet insisted "I have not come to interfere *with you.*"[26] Even Kurunmi, who treated Mann's preaching with an indifference close to contempt, was still anxious to have a missionary in Ijaye. When after a quarrel Kurunmi thought Mann was going to leave, he sacrificed a pig to prevent it, since "it is not good for the town that a white man forsake it who has once settled."[27]

Like a charm, too, a white man was of ambivalent potential. In the small and vulnerable town of Isaga, west of Abeokuta, Joseph Smith was welcomed as a token of peace when he went in 1859—but some people worried, on seeing a white man, whether something was wrong. Some months later, with rumors of a Dahomean attack, he felt that if he had shown signs of leaving, he would have precipitated an exodus.[28] The white man's status as an ambivalent magical power, and the jealousy between towns over having one, are well conveyed in Hinderer's first letter after his return to Ibadan from leave in 1853:

> He found that his first patron, Chief *Agbakin,* had died in his absence, and that the Muslims had persuaded many of the chiefs that if they received him back in the town, "their lives would be cut short." Many were afraid even to shake hands with him, and said they had buried charms in the road to prevent him coming again from Abeokuta.
>
> The Egba chiefs had opposite reasons for not wanting their rival Ibadan to have such an asset as a resident white man, and sent a bluffing message that if Ibadan wanted peace, it should not let him settle. Kurunmi [who, as noted, wanted *his* own white man] used the same threat as the Ibadan Muslims: that their lives would be cut short if they received Hinderer again.[29]

Once admitted, a missionary would then be clearly identified with the town
or its ruler: Townsend was known as "Sodeke's white man" and *Oyinbo Alake*
["The white man of Ake" or else "The *Alake*'s white man"].[30] These two views
of the white man, as the *ọba*'s prestige object and as something like a powerful charm, were both expressed in the song with which Hinderer was welcomed when he first visited Ilesha, after many solicitations from the *Ọwa*:

> *Oibo Ọwa, o ma gun, aiye gun rebete*
>
> "Now that the *Ọwa*'s white man has come up, the world will come out
> straight"[31]

With time and experience, of course, the enchantment attaching to white
men would dissipate—and nowhere sooner than at Abeokuta and Lagos,
where they were best known and their impact was greatest.

The later 1850s was a period of optimism and expanded activity for the
missionaries. At Abeokuta, their patron Sagbua was in 1854 installed as *Alake*,
the first paramount to be installed in the new town; and though his powers
were confined, it did help to secure for the CMS mission a privileged position close to the center of the Egba polity.[32] His prestige enhanced for having negotiated the agreement which enabled the Egba to lift their siege of
Ado,[33] Townsend became the confidant and secretary of the ruling circle of
chiefs, particularly in their dealings with the British Consul in Lagos. The
mission was buoyant with a steady stream of inquirers and converts, and
among the Egba there was a rising swell of interest in the benefits to be had
from exporting agricultural produce. The components of the CMS formula
to "make the country good"—Christianity, civilization, and commerce—
seemed all to be working together according to plan.[34] This decade saw a
sharp and continuing rise in the production of palm oil, as if secreted from
thousands of pores throughout the countryside. The CMS set itself to encourage cotton growing by setting up an Industrial Institution, which distributed gins and bought the prepared cotton.[35] Crowther's sons, Samuel
junior and Josiah, were employed for several years for this work; and though
by 1859 the Institution's commercial losses led to the CMS's withdrawal from
direct involvement in the trade, private traders quickly took over, working
more flexibly with a range of products. In 1856 the first of several European
merchants, the Italian Giambattista Scala, settled at Abeokuta, basing himself first in the CMS compound at Ake.[36]

No chief was more eager to develop cash crops than the mission's most
committed patron, Ogunbona of Ikija, who experimented with ginger and
arrowroot, as well as cotton, of which he was one of the largest producers.[37]
Ogunbona was famous as a proponent of new consumption styles which con-
joined the older prestige values of chiefship with the symbols of "civilization."
He was the first to build a storey-house (hence his sobriquet *Agboketoyinbo*,
"He who lives upstairs like a white man") and ordered a splendid silk and
velvet gown, which cost no less than £21, or 1,000 lbs. of cleaned cotton.[38]

In 1854 he realized an ambition he had long nursed, to invite all the Europeans and missionary agents, both CMS and Wesleyan, to a European-style dinner at his house. Townsend the Englishman and King the Egba gave very different (but not incompatible) accounts of it. Townsend presents a strongly visual tableau:

> Thirteen sat down to table, Ogunbona being flanked by Chief Sagbua and *Basorun* Somoye on one side, and Mrs Townsend, to carve the meat, on the other; and the meal was witnessed by thirteen friends and retainers of each chief. The mission's cook had been lent for the occasion. The table groaned under a great weight of crockery, set out to make a display. After the main course, Ogunbona served to his fellow chiefs the foreign delicacies of sugar and pickle, to take from the palms of their hands. The occasion was a great success, and Crowther said a blessing at the end.

Townsend's emphasis on the outward show of the occasion seems to betray a certain misgiving, for it fits with his frequent lament that his converts lacked the true "religion of the heart";[39] but he still concludes cautiously that "the attempt made to do it after our model will, I think, tend to advance civilized life."[40] King's account focuses on something that Townsend omits entirely, Ogunbona's speech defending the mission against its Egba detractors:

> He says there should be no more molestation of Christians or interference with funerals, and that no one should call the religion "abukon" (disgrace). If they say this, people are reproaching chiefs such as Sokenu, Basorun, Sagbua and himself, "because many of their children and wives are book people." Looking at the chiefs sitting there with their state umbrellas, he asks if it is a disgrace to so sit in the assembly? "Having frankly declared himself as a book man, he then asks the other senior chiefs if they are not so also too? They reply affirmatively. . . . He was scarcely ever seen so highly gratified as on that occasion."[41]

What King is most concerned to register is the public expression of commitment to the Christian cause by the senior chiefs of his community.

The mission pressed on to consolidate its broader cultural project in other ways. The Industrial Institution started to turn out sawyers, carpenters, bricklayers, and printers. When a tower was added to Ake church in 1858—it was easily the tallest building in Abeokuta—people shook their heads and exclaimed, asking what it cost and what it was for. But still it made a strong assertion, overtly of the presence of the "book people" in the town, implicitly of the craft skills which had made it possible.[42] In 1853, the CMS founded a Training Institution for the secondary education of mission agents. The principal was to be R. C. Paley, a Cambridge graduate, but he died within three weeks of arriving in Abeokuta,[43] and it did not really take off until taken over by G. F. Bühler (1857–1864), a devoted and liberal teacher who had a profound impact on his pupils. (They would include some important fu-

Figure 5.2. Rev. Henry Townsend and other missionaries at the Church
Missionary Society compound, Lagos, who were probably gathered for
a meeting of the Finance Committee, c. 1860. Courtesy of the Church
Mission Society, London.

ture clergy, such as Samuel Johnson and Charles Phillips). Townsend's special enthusiasm was printing, and he set up a press, which mostly produced
service sheets, hymn pamphlets, and so forth.[44] In 1859, he brought out the
first edition of Nigeria's first newspaper, *Iwe Irohin* [News Sheet], in order
to encourage "the practice of seeking instruction and information by reading," which he felt was strange even to well-educated and intelligent Africans.[45] There may also have been a deeper motive, not explicitly articulated
by Townsend: to foster that sense of individual inwardness, of solitary self-
motivated quest, so integral to the evangelical sensibility, which he felt was
lacking in the outlook of even devoted Egba Christians.

The successes of Abeokuta encouraged the Yoruba Mission to plan a further push into the interior; the Niger Expedition of 1857 and the overland
trek of one of its members, Daniel May, back to the coast through Kabba and
Ekiti revived the old hopes for a chain of stations to the Niger.[46] The CMS
Parent Committee was ready to commit fresh human resources. Despite the
terrible mortality of newly arrived Europeans, by 1853 there were as many
as eleven white missionaries and wives in Abeokuta.[47] In 1860, six new mission agents came out (the most ever in one year) and the total of fifteen men
then in post represented the zenith of European missionary numbers. But

already the problems of the next three decades were starting to appear. New stations were opened in 1858 at Oyo and Iseyin and placed under young European agents, Meakin and Hollinhead; but a combination of medical problems and local difficulties, aggravated by the outbreak of the Ijaye War, led both to pull out after barely two years. Plans for the densely populated country east of Ibadan did not go much better. In 1859 Hinderer made a tour east from Ibadan as far as Ilesha, through a land tense with the expectation of war, to meet rulers and to see where he might best place the African agents—teachers or scripture readers—whom he had gone to Sierra Leone to recruit for the purpose.[48] Ife, Modakeke, Oshogbo, and Ilesha were the places he chose; but only David Vincent at Ilesha seems to have stayed in post for longer than a year. The outbreak of war made it impossible to build up stable congregations or to give the agents adequate support and supervision from Ibadan.[49] Yet African agents would be the lifeline of the mission over the difficult years ahead.[50]

ABEOKUTA, IBADAN, AND LAGOS: 1861–1874

The Ijaye War brought to a head the contradictions in the external politics of the mission. The political thinking of the CMS was shaped by two main forces: a desire for moral simplicity, to identify the instruments of Providence amid the welter of competing worldly interests; and a need (since it could not deploy force) to cleave to those secular powers which would best support its evangelistic project. Until the mid-1850s, there was a happy concordance such that the CMS could regard Great Britain, Abeokuta, and the party of King Akitoye at Lagos as together supportive of the mission and its promotion of Christianity and civilization—in sum, as the forces of light. On the side of darkness were Abeokuta's enemies (notably Dahomey), the party of Kosoko at Lagos, Portuguese slave traders, and any of their allies. But once the British had made themselves responsible for Lagos and the CMS was extending itself in the Yoruba interior, this simple set of equations no longer worked out. The CMS found itself at odds with former friends, internally divided as to where to commit itself, and (as always) operating in communities that were internally divided about *it*.

The assumption that the interests of Abeokuta, as perceived by the Egba, or those of the Yoruba Mission as such, must coincide with those of Lagos, as seen by the consul or its merchants, was soon challenged. Lagos could not restrict itself to being "the Abbeokutan seaport."[51] The consul had to treat with the deposed Kosoko, who had good contacts with Ijebu and all along the lagoon, for he had to maximize the flow of trade through Lagos. While Townsend and Gollmer were on furlough in England in 1855, there was even a petition from Lagos merchants to disallow their return to West Africa, on the grounds of their malign influence on local politics.[52] Over the next decade the merchant view of what was in Lagos's best interests came to hold sway, decisively so in the tenure of the trader William McCoskry, who served as the last acting consul and the first acting governor (1861–1862). He communicated these views to Richard Burton, who after visiting Abeokuta in 1861, added his own Islamism and negrophobia to mount a wholesale attack on the missionary/humanitarian project.[53]

By then the Ijaye War was well under way, and the CMS mission, which had stations in all the three main combatant towns (Ibadan, Ijaye, and its ally, Abeokuta), was in the thick of it. Each missionary tended to identify strongly with his host community, and they fell to arguing against one another in their letters to London. Townsend insisted that "the Egbas are the power that represents progress and advancing civilization, and it is to be feared if they should be conquered, our cause or rather that of God would suffer at least for a time immensely."[54] Hinderer could not but agree that "wicked Ibadan" was the aggressor, but felt Townsend's reports in *Iwe Irohin* were unfair, and in the war's later stages was bitter at his Abeokuta brethren's support for the blockade which was causing great hardship at Ibadan.[55]

So how did the cooling of relations between the British and the Egba affect the position of the mission within Abeokuta? This was internally the most complex of all Yoruba towns, and though the missionaries often spoke of Abeokuta as a unitary collective agent, their own support was highly skewed within it. The primary cleavages were between the different townships, and between the two main categories of chiefs, the Ogboni and the Ologun, or war-chiefs, of which only the Ologun were organized at the pan-Egba, as well as the township, level. Intersecting with these in fluid and unpredictable ways were the followings and alliances of big men, and such emergent status or interest groups as traders or Saro returnees. It makes sense that the mission's initial backers came mainly from among the Ologun rather than the Ogboni,[56] and from the premier township, Ake (of which Sagbua was the senior Ogboni chief, the only such among them), since the mission's primary local relevance was in the context of Abeokuta's external relations. In contrast, the Ogboni, who articulated the values of the local community, were deeply involved in the widespread persecution which had occurred in late 1849, and sporadically since.[57] Here there also came into play such interests as those of the Egba allies of Kosoko, who were particularly strong in certain townships, such as Igbein.

The protracted endgame of the Ijaye War, when Abeokuta and Ijebu fought to limit Ibadan's outlet to the coast, left the British even less inclined to take the side of Abeokuta against the great war polity of the interior. Both the Egba and the British started using trade blockades to put pressure on one another. But what finally shattered Egba trust in their old ally was Governor Glover's use of rockets to force them to abandon their siege of Ikorodu, the lagoon terminus of the Ijebu Remo route to Ibadan (1865). All this ate away at the influence of the CMS mission in Abeokuta. In 1861, the *Alake* Sagbua had given a speech in which he distinguished three kinds of white men:

> Missionaries are good men who 'teach book' and who dissuade people from slavery and sacrifice, exhorting them to live in peace and quiet. . . . Warmen are also good men; their trade is to fight, and yet they fight for order, not to gratify their passions. . . . As for merchants, they come to get what they can; they care for nothing but cowries; they trade with a man and his enemy—in fact (raising his voice) they are liars and rascals.[58]

But now the "warmen" had apparently joined the merchants. In fact the missionaries already felt themselves affected by the declining regard for white men,[59] and the rockets at Ikorodu made things much worse. For a week after the attack, they did not dare venture outside the mission compound, and when they did, they were often told to go preach in Lagos instead.[60] In other ways, too, their position was weaker: their strongest backers among the chiefs, Ogunbona and Sagbua, both died in the early 1860s; and the third member of the old triumvirate, *Baṣọrun* Somoye, had to court other interests. Though Ogunbona's successor as *Balogun* of Ikija, Ogundipe, continued as their firm friend, he was often at odds with the other chiefs. And as Abeokuta's external interests, for which the Ologun were responsible, swung against the British, so too the missionaries lost one of the main structural bases of their support in the town.

Then a new force appeared on the Egba political scene, at once the offspring and the rival of the missionaries. There was a body of Saro returnees, many of them in some sense Christian but not fully "mission people," some of them disconnected on account of polygamy, often with commercial interests in Lagos. Angry with Glover's treatment of Abeokuta, they cherished some ideal of it as a modern state—and on that account might be considered the earliest precursors of nationalism in Nigeria. In 1865 one G. W. Johnson, known as "Reversible,"[61] offered himself as secretary to the *Baṣọrun* and chiefs—a position Townsend had long occupied—and with others (notably a Wesleyan Saro called Turner) set up the Egba United Board of Management (EUBM). This operated as an advisory panel to the chiefs, and pursued a number of projects intended to modernize Abeokuta: tolls on the river Ogun to create a source of public revenue, a government school, a postal service to Lagos. The missionaries' response was ambivalent. Maser was frankly dismissive—"these men have the idea that civilization is a thing by itself and able to stand without Christ"[62]—but Townsend took a longer, more canny, view:

> These . . . men are thus forcing on civilization and English customs, teaching the people the use of writing and printing, and bringing about the adop-

tion of written laws. They are doing what we cannot, for we cannot use the means they do to accomplish their purposes—I am trying to influence them; I cannot command them.[63]

Egba-British relations frayed further in 1866–1867, with mutual challenges over the boundaries between their respective spheres on the lower Ogun River. In June 1866, a German missionary, C. F. Lieb, was assaulted by Bada, a warrior of Igbein township, who had been prominent in raids on the river traffic. The case was not handled by the Igbein authorities with the sympathy that missionaries had come to expect: "We are tolerated but not protected," wrote Maser in his journal.[64] As if a taboo had been lifted, the missionaries now became subject to "repeated insults" as they went about the town, and there were arson attacks on church buildings.[65] It came to a head in the movement known at the "Outbreak" or *Ifole* ("Breaking of houses"), which exploded on the weekend of 12–13 October 1867.

The first news of it was the town bellman bringing a message from *Baṣọrun* Somoye to say that the missionaries and Saro might attend their churches, but that the native converts must go to Lagos, if they wished to serve God.[66] Maser—the senior CMS missionary in town, for Townsend was in England on leave—sent a plea to Somoye to reconsider, but one of Somoye's slaves, who followed him to the schoolroom with some armed men, repeated that "the business of God could no longer be attended to." Ogundipe was next contacted: the decision had been made without him, but he still advised against holding services that day. Later in the morning, armed men fenced off all the main churches. In the afternoon, mobs began to plunder the churches and the mission houses, except for Ikija, where Ogundipe's men kept the marauders away. There was then a lull, and meetings. When Ogundipe—who had a difficult path to tread between Egba anger and his support for the missionaries—told them that it had been done to show their feelings about Glover's acts, they replied that it was well known that they did not condone them, and that if the Egba were tired of them, they should be allowed to leave. A large gathering at the *Baṣọrun*'s some days later evinced much bitterness:

> It was said that the Egba had been the first to receive and protect white men, but had taken more injuries from them than the Ijebu and the Dahomeans who had not, or than the Ibadans who had even captured one.[67] The missionaries had said there would be no more war, but they had endured many wars. Besides, asserted Akodu the *Seriki,* a senior pan-Egba war-chief, "it was written in the Bible that Christian teachers should leave a town after they had been in it 21 years, and we had been 21 years in Abeokuta and it was time for us to go." There was some murmuring at this, but Akodu asked Secretary ("Reversible") Johnson to confirm it. From Johnson's uneasy silence, Maser concluded that he had briefed Akodu.

The missionaries repeated their desire to leave; some asked them to stay awhile; and there was talk of some going after their stolen goods had been returned. The chiefs' intentions seemed unclear and divided. A militant party led by Solanke, the leading war-chief of Igbein, kept up the pressure by threatening the houses of Christians (four in the Ake compound were set alight), and *Baṣọrun* Somoye even advised the Ake chiefs to be ready to defend their township against Solanke. Two further Sundays passed without services, and on Monday, 30 October, the European staff of all three missions—Methodist and Baptist as well as CMS—finally left Abeokuta, escorted by the messengers of Somoye and Ogundipe to ensure their safe passage to the coast. Many Egba Christians, fearful of their position, went with them, and others followed over the next few weeks.

So the *Ifọle* was a characteristically Egba affair: ambiguous, unevenly supported, even hesitant. While in the outcome the persecution was directed at Europeans rather than Christians, as Ajayi has suggested,[68] there does seem to have been some initial attempt to proscribe Christianity, though it was half-hearted and soon abandoned. There were *some* attacks on Christians, and the catechist William Allen reckoned he narrowly escaped being killed by the mob at Igbein.[69] A telling feature of the *Ifọle* was the extent to which the Ologun and the Ogboni chiefs reversed roles in relation to the Christians. Because it arose as an aspect of Abeokuta's external politics, it was Ologun chiefs who played the main part in the *Ifọle*, subject to the usual divergences between the interests of different townships. In contrast, in the days after the pillage, the Ogboni were reported (said Maser) to be opposed to the missionaries' departure; and while this was partly because they resented the augmentation of Ologun power which was always the result of war, it probably also indicates how well integrated many Christians had become in their local township communities. The main consequence of the *Ifọle* for Christianity at Abeokuta was to drive that process much further. For it meant that the church was to be without European missionaries for nearly a decade—the Saro pastor of Osiele, William Moore, being left as its only ordained priest. Its congregations needed to be rebuilt under the leadership of the African agents, who more than ever needed the goodwill of local chiefs. So when Allen, two years after the *Ifọle*, erected a new church building at Igbore, which was to replace the destroyed one at Igbein, he got the local Ogboni and Parakoyi chiefs to lay the first balls of mud at the base of the walls, according to the proverb: *Ẹni mọ, ki wo o* [What someone builds, he cannot demolish].[70]

Ibadan came to a similar outcome, but by quite a different route. Its mission did not enjoy Abeokuta's advantage of a substantial number of Christian repatriates, nor was it the jewel of the CMS's cherished project of Christianity and civilization. Where "Christian Abeokuta," as it became known for a while in England, was endowed with the image of a town beleaguered by savage enemies such as Dahomey, Ibadan's reputation, both deserved and self-celebrated, as the expanding military power of the Age of Confusion, made it much more problematic as the subject of a narrative of Christian redemption. Over his seventeen years as missionary there (1853–1869), David Hinderer put his stamp as firmly on the Ibadan church as Townsend had done at Abeokuta, but to an opposite effect. The mother church of Abeokuta was at the leading township, Ake, and it was clearly if discreetly associated with attempts to give the Egba polity a more solid center. Moreover, Townsend, by personal inclination as well as by Anglican precedent, aspired to place himself and his mission close to the leading chiefs. That he succeeded so well made the rupture of the *Ifọle* the more traumatic. The Ibadan mission, in contrast, derived its religious strength precisely from holding itself apart from the political center. Spatially the three stations—Kudeti (the mother church) to the south, Aremo to the east, and Ogunpa to the west—stood on the periphery of the vast town, more or less equidistant from Oja'ba ("*Baṣọrun*'s Market") at the center, which was where the Muslims had their Friday mosque. Though Hinderer could not have operated (especially in the early years) without powerful chiefly patrons, as well as the sanction of the chiefs as a whole, he never sought to stand close in their counsels.[71] Aside from the element of pure personal inclination, Hinderer's stance stands closer to the Württemberg Pietism in which he was raised, with its marked polarization of Christian spirituality and the way of the world, than to evangelical Anglicanism's tradition of seeking influence in the circles of power.[72] It entirely fits that it was in Ibadan that Bunyan's *Pilgrim's Progress* was translated into Yoruba and used as devotional reading.[73]

The contrast between the two Christian communities showed up most starkly in their attitudes toward converts going to war. Missionaries abhorred war, less on general grounds (for they were not in principle pacifist), but because it was so bound in with slave taking and a nexus of social values deeply inimical to their preaching. Hinderer's distaste for the military ethos of Ibadan was so strong that he risked the political viability of the mission by expressing it. When the army returned from its successful Ekiti campaign in 1855, "proud and rich" with booty and slaves, he went to greet the *Balogun* and *Ọtun* as was customary, but at first they would not see him because he had not sent to greet them while they were at the war. He begged their pardon and made amends by having some boxes made with presents for them.[74] A few months later, he called to greet Ajobo, one of the greater war-chiefs, to find him with a hundred of his warboys, sitting around eating and drinking.[75] When he urged on them "the advantages of a farmer's life over that of a kidnapper"—a little like a priest admonishing a gang of mobsters to get honest jobs and pay their taxes—they dared not openly ridicule him, because he was Ajobo's friend.

The two incidents show that it was easier for the mission to recommend

Figure 5.3. Missionaries remembered: Portrait of Rev. David and Anna Hinderer hanging in the parlor of Ile Olugbode, Ibadan, 1995. Courtesy of Dr. Ruth Watson.

itself to the chiefs than to the young warriors. Chiefs mostly appreciated the overall strategic benefit of having a mission in the town, and could personally derive material advantages from being its patrons. Taking the view that the converts were the missionaries' "people," they were usually prepared to concede to them (as to the members of some *orisa* cults) some immunities, such as not having to go to war. Since war engaged the sense of honor and provided the main avenue of advancement for young men, Christians were despised for refusing to fight; and, granted the strength of peer-group values, this was very hard for them to bear. For those who could not, two resolutions were possible. One emerged at Abeokuta, where it was easier to condone war as defensive and where the Christians were already much more integrated in the local structures of the community: by 1863 the Christians had formed their own military company of 700 men under a *Balogun,* John Okenla, an Ake communicant who thus became lay leader of all Egba Christians.[76] The other resolution was for Christians to give into social pressure, even against their pastors' teaching,[77] and go to war as individuals, which is what tended to happen at Ibadan. In 1878 many were driven to do so "on account of frequent charges of cowardice and womanliness from heathens," and this probably occurred on a smaller scale earlier.[78] Yet the Ibadan Christians continued to be known as a "quiet people, averse to fame and worldly honour,"[79] a kindly way of saying that they were not fully *of* the community they lived in (which perhaps was not far from what Hinderer wanted).

It follows from all this that, compared with its importance at Abeokuta, the CMS mission was rather marginal to the political history of Ibadan over this period. Its prestige dropped to an all-time low in 1862 when a young English missionary, Edward Roper, was caught in Ijaye when it was finally overrun by the Ibadan forces and technically became the slave of the *Otun Balogun,* who insisted on a ransom. Hinderer was led to write of "our almost abandoned position," with Christians facing mockery and insults in the streets.[80] But as the logic of regional politics became clearer, with the estrangement of Abeokuta and Lagos, the mission at Ibadan acquired a sounder basic guarantee than the favor of chiefly patrons: namely, the need of Ibadan to keep on terms with the British in Lagos. What really made the mission's life difficult in the 1860s was something it shared with Ibadan as a whole, the effects of blockade, which cut it off from essential supplies for months and even years on end.[81] Finally in 1869, Hinderer decided he should leave the station to be run by his African agents. As a white man, he was stuck in the interior, too closely identified with the Lagos government, and unable to move as freely as Africans would be able to, virtually a prisoner of the Egba and Ijebu; he was tired, and his and his wife's health was not good. He had full confidence in Olubi and the other African staff whom he had trained over many years. At a valedictory prayer meeting at Ogunpa church, a young man prayed for his safety:

> Remember Lord, he is often sick and no wonder, the air that he breathes is not that of his own country, the water he drinks is not that of his own country, the food he eats is not his own country's food, it is not prepared by his own mother nor by his own sister. Have mercy upon him, spare him and make him strong."[82]

So within the space of less than two years, the mission stations of both Ibadan and Abeokuta passed into the management of the African subalterns.

Daniel Olubi was the first home-grown Yoruba—as against a repatriate from Sierra Leone—to assume charge of a mission station, and the first to be ordained a priest. He was a kinsman of Ogunbona, who converted in 1848 and became Hinderer's houseboy in Abeokuta.[83] A member of the first mission party of six which opened the Ibadan station,[84] he rose to be Hinderer's right-hand man and his obvious successor at Kudeti. James Okuseinde (another Egba and an older man) took Ogunpa, and W. S. Allen (assisted by a young schoolmaster, Samuel Johnson) took Aremo, which was in fact the largest of the three congregations. The task in front of him, as the leader of a small and unappreciated religious group that had just lost its European *baba,* an Egba in a town that was perennially at war with the Egba, must have been a daunting one, but he set about it with resolve.

The first requirement was to establish a personal relationship with the senior chiefs and to show them that the white man's departure did not imply any faltering in the mission's project. As it happened, Olubi's takeover coincided with a period of relative openness in Ibadan's top leadership between the death of *Başǫrun* Ogunmola (1867) and the rise of *Arẹ* Latosisa (1871), and within the year there was a round of title-filling.[85] Olubi was punctilious in making courtesy visits to the new titleholders, which culminated in a delegation of the entire Christian body—about 400 people—to the new *Balẹ* or civil head of the town, Orowusi, on 11 November 1870:

> So many people were present that Orowusi's compound could not accommodate them, so the audience was held outside in the street. He sat in state on an iron chair (the finest of four left by the Hinderers, which they had presented to him at his installation six weeks earlier) under a tree, with ten wives, forty attendants, and drummers behind him.
>
> First the clergy and teachers greeted him, and then their wives. Then, accompanied by their big harmonium, they sang a Yoruba version of "God Save the King" (*Ǫlǫrun gba Balẹ wa*), specially composed for the occasion. They then read portions of Psalms 20, 45, and 118,[86] and Olubi said prayers for the *Balẹ*. Then, as a kind of interlude, they exhibited Allen's musical box and two dolls which they had brought with them, one as big as a child, the other with eyes that opened and shut. This caused amazement and applause from the onlookers.
>
> Then James Oderinde, the senior lay convert, gave an address. He said that white ants were never without a leader, surrounded by thousands of ants to protect it. None dare attack it, but when man comes he can break it as he likes. So it is with you, our beloved *Balẹ*. No one can lift his hand against you. But God on account of sin can do what he wants. We beg you to listen to his Word through us his teachers.
>
> Orowusi listened carefully and promised protection. Then Allen spoke, to remind people that the dolls were not "oibo gods," and to give a short history of the mission, "pointing to the Christians as those who by God's grace and mercy had been enlightened." They sang the anthem again, and Orowusi gave them gifts before they dispersed.[87]

It is hard to imagine Hinderer ever arranging such a performance as this, a veritable power play, in fact. Two features merit special comment. First, the display of European technical marvels made the strongest claim that Olubi and his African colleagues were *oyinbo,* with access to *oyinbo* power, too; and so they were clearly (mis)understood by some of those present, as the reference to "oibo gods" indicates. Second, the tenor of the whole occasion—especially the national anthem and the loyal address—bade to move the mission to a much closer relationship with the powers of the town than Hinderer had cultivated. In fact, it represents a shift to a more Egba and Anglican view of how the mission should stand in the community, an audacious step in a town where the Christians were so few and where Muslim *alufa* were already close confidants of many of the chiefs. Yet it paid off: the next paramount of Ibadan, the *Arẹ* Latosisa (1871–1885), though himself a Muslim, gave sustained support and protection to the mission, and Olubi's public prestige grew steadily over the years.

So the early 1870s saw the mission checked in its earlier hopes for rapid expansion by the refractory politics of the Yoruba states, forced to rebuild and consolidate in its two main interior stations. Its European personnel were driven back to live in the British territory of Lagos. Their number, which had peaked at around sixteen in 1860, had fallen to about half that by the end of 1874, and would fall to its lowest, at less than half a dozen, by 1880. On the other hand, from the mid-1860s there was a further and accelerating phase of growth in the number of African agents, some of whom would go on to ordination as priests.[88]

Church growth was most evident in Lagos. In 1866, Mann, restless since the end of his Ijaye mission and bitter against what he felt was Townsend's neglect of the Ijaye refugees, founded what became known as Palm Church, later St John's Aroloya, on the eastern side of the town.[89] Rather than the local people (who were Muslims of the poorer kind) it attracted immigrants, especially Ijayes, and later some of the Christian refugees from the *Ifọle*. Most of the Egba, however, settled on the mainland across from Lagos Island, where they formed a new congregation, St Jude's Ebute Meta, whose first pastor was Faulkner, formerly himself of Abeokuta.[90] The leading Lagos church continued to be St Paul's Breadfruit, which had been first been built up in the 1850s by T. B. Wright (then a scripture reader) and Samuel Pearse (then a teacher), with services only in Yoruba.[91] As the numbers of wealthier and better-educated Saro repatriates rose, there developed a demand for services in English too; and during the pastorate of the English missionary Lancelot Nicholson (1863–1872), the church was several times enlarged. A leading parishioner and the church's greatest benefactor was Captain J. P. L. Davies, a merchant and ship owner, one of the wealthiest Lagosians of the day. One source of Breadfruit's dynamism may well have been exactly the interplay between the two sides of its congregation: the "Yoruba," poorer, less educated, many of them from the interior; and the "English," those who belonged to the emergent bourgeoisie of colonial Lagos.

The 1870s saw the efflorescence of "Victorian Lagos."[92] In later years, when racial barriers had hardened, the African elite would look back to the days of Governor Glover as a time of social ease and openness.[93] The missions had provided a major input to its rich cross-cultural mix—through education, music, associational forms, and more—but many European missionaries took an extremely grudging attitude toward its products. In 1873, Breadfruit members took the lead in founding an Association for Promoting Educational and Religious Interests in Lagos.[94] But missionaries such as Maser, Roper, and Mann were anything but pleased at such an initiative from the laity, not least since some of their African colleagues supported it. Maser expressed his misgivings with self-exposing candor:

> Our agents are without the proper sense of looking to those who are placed over them for guidance. The principle of obedience which pervades all Yoruba native Society or which is obtaining among employers in the Government or mercantile Service is unknown to them. They seem to walk the streets of Lagos without masters as sheep without a shepherd and fall an easy prey to designing men.[95]

There were two aspects of Lagos life which white missionaries, especially those who had spent most of their time in the interior, found not to their liking. They could not exercise the same sway over their congregations as they could in places where the converts, often of low social status or socially detached by the fact of conversion, looked up to them as their great patrons in the community. And then they were discomforted by the worldly, masterless, bourgeois life of Lagos, with all its new cultural options. Roper's indignation at the involvement of J. A. Payne in the Association—he being a churchwarden at Faji—was combined with criticism of him for enjoying balls and parties.[96] It was one thing to preach "civilization" in the interior, but the cultural freedom of Lagos led Maser to invoke the supposed discipline of "native society" against it.

FROM BREADFRUIT TO ONDO AND IJEBU: 1874–1892

In 1874 the Rev. James Johnson, born in Sierra Leone of mixed Ijesha/ Ijebu parentage, came to Lagos to be pastor of St Paul's Breadfruit. A formidable dual reputation preceded him: as a committed fighter for African advancement against racial prejudice and as a spiritual disciplinarian, a man of the most unbending evangelical piety, "Holy" Johnson.[97] Both these sides of him were soon evident at Breadfruit. He annoyed many older and laxer members equally by his enforcement of a stricter discipline—particularly over sexual behavior—through a system of Bible classes under trusted lay leaders and by his opposition to the practice, popular with the fashionable bourgeois part of the congregation, of giving children elaborate European names (such as Charles Augustus Aristarchus Fitzgerald Glendower[98]) rather than Yoruba ones. But the devotion of his pastoral ministry, his earnestness for the evangelical ideal of a heartfelt religion, his zeal in promoting lay evangelism and, perhaps above all, his commitment to the advancement of Africans in church and society—all brought him a growing public regard, particularly among the serious young. Though they might charge him with an excess of "race feeling," his European colleagues never impugned his religious caliber, while Africans quickly came to see him as one of their natural leaders.

In 1877, Johnson was appointed to the position of superintendent of the interior stations, based at Abeokuta. This was a new post, intended as a halfway house to something long envisaged by Henry Venn: a Yoruba church led by a Yoruba bishop. That had been opposed—when Crowther was in view as the bishop—by European agents who were unwilling to serve under an African, and who argued that the prestige of the mission in the eyes of the *obas* and chiefs of the interior would suffer if it were not headed by a white man. Crowther had been consecrated in 1864 as bishop of "the countries of Western Africa beyond the limits of the Queen's dominions" and had taken leadership of the Niger Mission, worked by African agents entirely. Yoruba-land outside Lagos was thus theoretically inside his diocese though its main stations at Ibadan and Abeokuta (being under the direction of Europeans) were treated, along with Lagos, as falling under the jurisdiction of the Bishop of Sierra Leone.[99] The absurdity of this situation got worse with the departure of white missionaries from the interior stations after 1867, and by 1875 both Hinderer and Townsend had come round to the view that a Yoruba bishop should take charge: Hinderer suggesting Crowther, and Townsend James Johnson.[100] That Johnson was, in effect, put on probation by being appointed as superintendent rather than bishop—partly, it seems, because of the resistance of some younger European missionaries, and partly because the CMS was starting to lose Venn's commitment to the early African self-government of the church—would have far-reaching consequences.[101]

Johnson threw himself with energy into the challenge of his new post. He made extensive tours of all the interior stations and beyond—north to Oyo and Ogbomosho, northeast to Ilesha, southwest to Ilaro—and (a project particularly dear to him) tried to break in to Ijebu through an approach from Abeokuta to the Remo town of Iperu.[102] His plans for expansion were impeded by fresh hostilities between Ibadan and Abeokuta, and then by the outbreak in 1878 of what would prove the long, final phase of the Yoruba wars. But Johnson's chief preoccupation was with the state of the church in Abeokuta itself. His aim to set up a "native pastorate"—by which the local Christians would take financial responsibility for their own clergy rather than depend on the mission—soon led to conflict with the church elders, since it required the raising of class fees. The need for money brought to the fore another problem: "baptized polygamists, several of whom are of the well-to-do class, wield their money influence over the Church to the serious detriment of its sanctity and the prostration of its dignity by almost everybody from first to last."[103] He took a severe view of the aftermath of the *Ifole*, as "a favourable time for tares in the master's garden,"[104] and compared the moral tone of the Abeokuta church, with its 2,295 members, unfavorably with Ibadan's, which had only 401.

The worst consequence of the Egba church's adaptation to "circumstantial influences" was the prevalence of slaveholding, among both the laity and mission agents. It was Johnson's vigorous attempt to implement a Minute on Domestic Slavery lately drawn up by the CMS which provoked the showdown between him and the Egba.[105] The Egba agents, led by the elderly William Moore and by David Williams, pastor of Ake and son of an Ogboni chief there, felt themselves pilloried, and Johnson in turn felt they had colluded with the Egba chiefs against him.[106] The decade of relative isolation had created a strong climate of resentment against the intrusion of strangers in Egba affairs; and Johnson was spoken of as "the Jebu man." A replay of the events of 1867 looked very possible; an unidentified man called at the Ake mission house saying *Ṣọpọna a pa ọ!* [Smallpox will kill you], and the chiefs advised Johnson to leave. With Johnson's return to Lagos, to resume his pastorate of Breadfruit, a significant initiative in the organization of the Yoruba church was abandoned.[107] The episode was replete with irony: Johnson, the evangelical moralist who longed to see the church become truly native, failed because he high-handedly tried to enforce the mission's standards in a local church which had gone all too native in its struggle to survive since the trauma of the *Ifọle*.

But even as this drama was unfolding in Abeokuta, another initiative was getting under way in an area of Yorubaland yet untouched by the mission. The opening of Glover's "Ondo road" had given rise to the idea of a new Eastern District of the Yoruba Mission. In 1873 Maser and Roper made an exploratory visit to Ondo and found the chiefs favorable, and the following year Hinderer was sent to organize it from a new station at Leki on the eastern lagoon, the farthest dependency of Lagos.[108] The original plan was for a mission worked by African agents under European supervision, but when Hinderer went to Lagos to recruit them, he was disappointed at the listless response he got from the Lagos churches—"I exempt thoroughly the Rev. J. Johnson," he added. One source of interest that alarmed him was that shown by the Ijesha Association, a prayer-cum-politics group based at Breadfruit, whose desire for a missionary for Ilesha was all too evidently linked to strategic objectives against Ibadan. He warned them off, though this was to be one of the most political areas of the mission. Still, Hinderer was able to launch the station at Ondo in May 1875 with two African agents, but his own ill health forced him to retire permanently less than a year later.[109] It was only when the Rev. Charles Phillips took charge in January 1877 that things really took off.

Phillips, the son and namesake of Mann's catechist at Ijaye, had been educated under Bühler at the old Training Institution in Abeokuta. Here he was "born of the spirit," acquiring a religious disposition that was confirmed by the years he spent as teacher and catechist at Breadfruit, latterly under James Johnson.[110] He was never afraid to assert himself,[111] and over the years he acquired an impressive authority throughout eastern Yorubaland: when

M. J. Luke, on his way to Ilesha in 1888, was molested by young men at the Ondo village of Araromi, he got himself free by pleading he was "Mr Phillips' stranger."[112] It is true that Ondo was an easier place in which to operate than Abeokuta or Ibadan. Since Glover had brokered the town's restoration after a civil war, his reputation at Ondo was as positive for the mission as it had been unhelpful at Abeokuta: *E ho Gobana Oyinbo mu 'ba wole o, Gobana o! E ho Gobana Oyinbo pari ote o, Gobana o!* [Hail, Governor, White Man, for bringing our king home! Hail, Governor, for ending the civil war!], sang the women at Maser's visit in 1873.[113] In seeking the chiefs' permission, Maser had expressly "represented the matter to them as a continuation of Captain Glover's work to renew (*ton se*) Ondo"; and C. N. Young, sent by Hinderer as the first agent in 1876, was even asked if the mission house he wanted to build was not for Glover.[114] While the aura of Glover tended to fade once the mission was installed, Phillips still made the most of his connections with subsequent governors of Lagos. To his European colleagues, Phillips might be a "native minister," but to the Ondo chiefs he counted as an *oyinbo*.

For his first few years, Ondo was dominated by a warlord of the Ibadan kind, Edun the *Lisa,* generally supportive of the mission but fickle, whom Phillips had to treat with circumspection. But after the *Lisa's* death in 1880, no subsequent chief, not even any of the *Osemawe,* really took his place, and there came to be a certain flatness in Phillips's picture of the political landscape of Ondo. By the late 1880s Phillips had become one of the most influential men in Ondo, indispensable to the chiefs in their external dealings not only with the governor but with other Yoruba groups, such as the Ijesha (who were constantly passing through) or the Ikale (Ondo's often hostile neighbors to the south). His role as the governor's mediator on the Ekitiparapo side in the negotiations to end the war at Kiriji—Samuel Johnson was his opposite number on the Oyo side—greatly enhanced his prestige. Though this did not at once translate into spectacular results in the religious sphere—Christian numbers grew only modestly for the first decade or more, and his constant reproofs of the chiefs for human sacrifice did not bear fruit till the British intervened decisively in 1892—Phillips was masterful in positioning Christianity for the future "harvest of souls."

Consider his record of his dealings with the Ondo chiefs over the last three months of 1888:

19 Sept. He visits the *Osemawe* for the first time since "the yearly festivals" [of Esu and *Odun Oba,* at which human sacrifice was made] and asks him why they are neglecting the worship of the great God, whom they too acknowledge. The king, driven onto the defensive, remarks that God allows the Christians to approach him by the "straight way" [i.e., without the *orisa* as mediators] but they the pagans . . . have to go "through the way of which the devil [Esu] is the gatekeeper."

27 Sept. He visits a chief and reads him Matthew 6:24 ("No man can serve two masters"). He tells him that their constant recourse to diviners is the result of sin.

2 Nov. A man is publicly executed (clubbed to death) for attacking and wounding five women. Phillips goes to express his approval of it to the chiefs, as a legitimate taking of life, in contrast to human sacrifice.

22 Dec. The Saṣẹrẹ, "the most influential" of the high-chiefs, visits Phillips and they have a religious talk. He asks many intelligent questions. Four of the five High Chiefs pay official visits over the Christmas period "to rejoice with us, as they say."

31 Dec. The new Oṣemawe comes to visit for the first time since his accession. He admires all he sees: the portraits on the walls, English lamps, doors, locks, the clock. In church he hears some hymns sung to the harmonium, "the prayer for heathen kings," the Lord's Prayer, and the Benediction. He wonders especially at the harmonium. "These visits are expensive" [comments Phillips], but serve to create respect and goodwill.[115]

The strategy being followed here—to place the mission close to the political center in a system of reciprocal gifts and visits, so that demands could be made upon it—was the same as that adopted by Olubi at Ibadan in 1870, except that, thanks both to the town and the times, it was much more effective at Ondo. For Phillips was operating from a far stronger position, and knew it: his confident reprimands to the chiefs indicate a man who knew things were going his way and that he had powerful outside backing, both cultural and political. Olubi could not presume in this way, and it was the Muslims who, over the period 1850–1870, had achieved that intimacy with the chiefs which meant that Islam would be the world religion that most Ibadan people would turn to when they wanted one. At Ondo, by contrast, there were no local Muslims when the CMS arrived.

As British involvement in the affairs of the Yoruba interior grew during the 1880s, against a world background of imperialism and the surge of racialist sentiment among Europeans, two distinct attitudes emerged among Yoruba Christians about the ties between the mission and British policy. Situational rather than intrinsic, the adoption of whichever attitude depended on whether the salient Other was seen as the European (as in Lagos) or the "heathen" (as in the interior). Both of these fed into what is now often called "cultural nationalism" (though "Ethiopianism" comes closer to its religio-political agenda), a movement of cultural assertion rooted among those Yoruba most familiar with Euro-Christian culture and most deeply involved in European colonial institutions.[116] While its source in the interior lay in the impetus by African clergy to "inculturate" their preaching, a step toward a more effective evangelism, in Lagos it had less to do with the encounter of

Figure 5.4. Bishop Charles Phillips, Rev. E. M. Lijadu, and elders of the church at Ondo, 1901. Courtesy of the Church Mission Society, London.

religions than with African Christians' experience of racial prejudice, whether in the church or in society at large.

Here it was the humiliating treatment of Bishop Crowther over events in the Niger Mission, followed by his resignation and death in 1891, which seemed emblematic of a wholesale devaluation of African hopes and endeavors.[117] James Johnson was the compelling personal focus of a wave of African counter-assertion, but his position remained ambiguous or qualified: his Ethiopian rhetoric was never matched by a readiness to break decisively from the CMS, and his advocacy of African culture was always limited by the orthodox evangelical piety by which he had been formed. So the political results of Ethiopianism were meager: despite the first secessions from CMS congregations to establish independent churches—of a number of individuals to found the United Native African Church in 1891, and the much larger group who in 1901 seceded from Breadfruit, calling itself Bethel, or the African Church—the mass of CMS Christians stayed in a church organization which European missionaries still controlled at the highest level.[118]

Ethiopianism also failed because its Christian base in Yorubaland was too narrow, being largely limited to Lagos (though of course it connected to similar circles in the Gold Coast and Sierra Leone). But when it came to Christian expansion, the perspective of the interior, where it would have to happen, diverged from that of Lagos. James Johnson in Lagos might urge Africans to differentiate themselves from Europeans, but one of the strongest claims of the African agents of the interior was precisely that, in the eyes of chiefs and people, they were associated with them. Derin of Okeigbo once wanted the intervention of Olubi "as the white man's representative in these parts"[119] (which in a formal sense he was not), and Olubi took care to maintain this impression. When the governor's envoys reached Ibadan on their way to make peace at Kiriji in 1886, Olubi sent two of his colleagues to meet the party at Odo Ona, two miles outside the town, and they accompanied them in before many spectators.[120]

The tensions between the two perspectives became most apparent over the conquest of Ijebu, which for nearly half a century had been a forbidden kingdom for the missionaries. Over the years there had been a number of attempts to gain a foothold—through Remo, through young Ijebu migrants in Lagos or Ibadan—and there were even some secret Christians worshipping in Ijebu Ode itself. In 1889, after much patient diplomacy by James Johnson and J. A. Otonba Payne, the *Awujale* agreed to admit a teacher, who was allowed to instruct children on a palace verandah.[121] This experiment failed after less than a year, when the teacher, suspected of being a British spy, was expelled (in his own words) "as a dog who had been to the leopard in his lair, and had come out safe."[122] As British policy grew more interventionist, the CMS looked to government help in "opening" Ijebu, and in 1891 a new governor, Gilbert Carter, forced a treaty on the Ijebu chiefs to open the roads (which they refused to sign).[123] As British pressure mounted, a significant section of educated Christian opinion in Lagos came out against this imperial harassment of a independent state, identifying themselves with its rulers.[124] The Ijebu were incensed when in February 1892 two European missionaries (Harding based at Ibadan, and Tugwell at Lagos) pushed into their country in the name of this "treaty"; there was some violence by, and against, the missionaries' Ibadan porters; and the Ijebu again closed the road to Ibadan.[125] More than that, they greatly upped the stakes by demanding of the Ibadan chiefs (who were still mostly at Kiriji and in need of munitions) that as the price of reopening the road they should expel Harding and Olubi from Ibadan; and they also sent a man to pronounce a curse on Olubi, whom they regarded as their sworn enemy.[126]

Now Carter had his excuse, and after just over a week's campaign, Ijebu Ode was taken.[127] On May 23rd, the first rumors of Ijebu's defeat reached Ibadan, and soon visitors were flooding to the mission houses to offer their congratulations.[128] Over the next few months there was a rush of new inquirers in the towns of the interior. As often, W. S. Allen caught the tone of popular talk:

> There is one common talk in the mouth of both young and old in the town at present, and that is *Olorun ni a o sin,* 'We will serve the Lord'. This was through the war that had subdued the Ijebus. When considering the troubles and ill-treatments [we at Ibadan] had received from the Ijebus, and how they usually brag and defy the Oyinbos, and that in one day [the Ijebus] were subdued . . . with all their charms.[129]

Ethiopianism could not match this Yoruba reading of the Ijebu defeat, that God was great and seemed to be on the side of the *oyinbo.*

INTO THE COLONIAL ORDER: 1892–1912

The conquest of Ijebu and Governor Carter's tour of Yorubaland in the following year transformed the conditions of evangelism by enabling the mission to expand virtually anywhere it wanted, subject to the availability of personnel and resources. The mission which, outside Lagos, had had to learn to work amid a cluster of independent polities, now became a colonial institution, a defining part of colonial society, though not an organ of the colonial state. At the same time, despite its European leadership, it was more than ever an African enterprise, in that the vast majority of those actually engaged in evangelism were Yoruba, so that the understandings conveyed were those that arose from African needs and questions. Yet these in turn were framed by the constraints and opportunities of the emergent colonial order, which the Yoruba termed *Aiye Oyinbo,* "the Age of the White Man."

The Ijebu, in particular, were given a crash course in colonial power, and proved amazingly ready learners. By the late 1890s, there was talk of a mass movement to Christianity to rival the better-known one concurrently under way in Buganda.[130] The mission took a novel form, in that it was not directly organized by the CMS, but by Lagos Church Missions, an arm of the native pastorate which was the treasured project of James Johnson.[131] To explain the Ijebus' enthusiasm for Christianity simply in terms of a proud and self-reliant people responding to their military defeat by adopting the religion of their conquerors fails to encompass the full complexity of the situation. None of the other kingdoms of the West African forest subdued by force in that decade (Dahomey, Benin, Asante) responded with a mass desire to become Christian and, in any case, an even greater number of Ijebu flooded into Islam, especially in the capital, Ijebu Ode. If we seek a common explanation for the simultaneous rush to Islam and Christianity, as I think we must, it has be in terms of what the two religions shared: as the people said in Ibadan, *Olorun ni a o sin* [It is God we shall serve]. And the conquest facilitated conversion, not just because it discredited the old gods who had failed to protect Ijebu, but because of what it forced on the Ijebu in its aftermath. For as it demolished the old system of tolls and controls which had underpinned Ijebu's position as an entrepôt trading power, it also opened up new commercial opportunities in the expanded Lagos Protectorate and beyond, which young Ijebu seized with alacrity. And as they moved out, they moved into the sphere where the world religions became compelling options. Islam was the principal gainer to the extent that, and where, it already had the most points of contact to reap the benefits of this situation.[132] But Christianity's gains were still enormous. In 1902 Johnson estimated there were 15,000 converts and a further 10,000 "readers,"[133] and by 1910 about a third of Yoruba Christians were Ijebu.

After Ijebu, Christianity's new frontier lay to the east and the northeast, among peoples for whom "the Yoruba" were not themselves but the Oyo (until they learned otherwise in church and school). Ilesha was the main springboard to Ekiti and beyond. Its Christian body had existed in a desultory way since the 1860s, but could only enjoy steady growth when the warriors returned from the Kiriji camp in 1893. Then it got an exceptional boost when the kingmakers chose as *Owa* Frederick Haastrup, a repatriate from Sierra Leone who had been a merchant in Lagos, where he had belonged to Ebute Ero church. As the first Christian *oba* (1896–1901) of any Yoruba kingdom, Ajimoko—so he was named on accession—vigorously promoted Christianity as part of a policy of social renewal and modernisation.[134] In this he was aided by the first Ibadan man to be ordained to the priesthood, R. S. Oyebode, who served Ilesha from 1896 to 1927 and supervised the beginnings of evangelism in western Ekiti.[135]

Throughout eastern Yorubaland a very powerful vector of Christianization was the great reflux of slaves from Ibadan, Abeokuta, and elsewhere, and of ex-slaves and free laborers from Lagos, which took place in the 1890s. Many of these had become Christian in their places of slavery and took their religion back with them when they returned home, thus implanting Christian *ecclesiolae* in advance of the arrival of mission agents. Indeed, this seems to have been the *normal* pattern of Christian expansion into the villages and small towns of Ijesha and Ekiti. Even where these returnees were not Christian, as only a minority were, they would have come back well apprised of the appeal of the white man's civilization and of the reality of his power in the land, and so inclined to take a favorable, or at least a respectful, view of the religion which mediated it. Such a man was the *Oni* Adelekan of Ife, who claimed to remember "Alapako" (Gollmer) in Lagos and had even carried loads for the CMS to Abeokuta.[136] While the phenomenology of religious change in the east was broadly similar to what it had been in Ijebu, its pace was much slower, for it depended on the penetration of colonial institutions—taxation, administration, communications, schools—to regions much remoter from Lagos; and it was not until the early 1920s that mission reports from Ekiti start talking of mass movements.[137]

By this time, the Yoruba Mission had long become colonial in another way. After Bishop Crowther's death in 1891, the episcopal question became pressing. It was decided to create a diocese of Western Equatorial Africa based in Lagos, with a European at its head. Bishop Hill died of fever virtually on his arrival from England, and in 1894 Herbert Tugwell, already a missionary in Lagos, took over. To assuage African opinion (and because there was now too much work for one bishop), the CMS also decided to appoint two Africans as assistant bishops ("half-bishops," they were derisively called in Lagos). The outstanding African cleric, James Johnson, was felt to be too risky an appointment.[138] The men chosen were Charles Phillips of Ondo and Isaac Oluwole, a safe conventional man who had been principal of the CMS Grammar School but was no great evangelist.

The relentless abandonment of the ideals of the long-dead Venn was carried farther in the mission's organization, as a new model was conceived: mission districts to be headed by Europeans, who would manage and superintend the work of African evangelists or pastors working at the local level.[139] This was first effected in the older districts, when J. B. Wood took charge of Abeokuta and Tom Harding of Ibadan, churches that had pulled through the tough times of the 1870s under African leadership. With few exceptions, such as Phillips in Ondo and Oyebode in Ilesha, it simply seemed natural in the newer ones to have a system that paralleled the structure of colonial administration, where the mass of Africans was dealt with by African "middlemen" who in turn were supervised by Europeans. It worked in the commercial sphere too (where indeed it had been invented), and meant that across the different sectors of the colonial order, European principals would deal with one another: the district officer, the superintendent of the mission district, the district manager of the United Africa Company. Daniel Olubi had been the first of his kind, and his death in 1912 marked the end of an era in the history of the Yoruba church.

6

PREACHING THE WORD

The political history of the mission, its achievement over more than half a century, was the complex outcome of a myriad of context-specific inter-actions, each governed by the objectives, strategies, and "knowledges" of the particular individuals and collectivities involved in them. In the next three chapters we move closer in to the heart of the matter, to that engagement of variously motivated persons which must lie at the center of any adequate account of mission. Diverse as these motivations were, they tended to clus-ter in two broad patterns, characteristic respectively of the missionaries and the evangelized. Insofar as evangelistic encounters were set up by the mis-sionaries, according to a schema that derived from their long-term objective of building a local church, we find on their side a relatively uniform adher-ence to one pattern. The Yoruba, in contrast, did not approach these en-counters with objectives specific to them but on the basis of their more gen-eral life goals, and the manner of their engagement varied according to their social position and personal needs. In their mutual encounter, the mission-aries faced a far wider range of social types than did the Yoruba.

The objectives, strategies, and "knowledges" of both groups of agents can be plotted within a single four-cell matrix that also serves to define the "ter-rain" of missionary endeavor. Its first two cells (A1, B1) constitute the practico-

Figure 6.1 THE TERRAIN OF RELIGIOUS ENCOUNTER

A. Internal sphere of human relations	B. External sphere of nature/history	
A1. Society, community: power embedded in social relations	**B1. Techniques, objects: power in and over physical things**	1. Material realm of power
A2. Ethics: theory of how to act before man and God	**B2. Cosmology: theory of how the world "out there" works**	2. Realm of ideas and meaning

material conditions of human existence, realms of power that are social and technical. These were respectively the prime concerns of the missionaries, whose aim was to create a Christian community, and the Yoruba, who were anxious to gain access to new sources of power, of techniques and artifacts that would enhance life. One does not need to speak in Marxist terms of "social relations and forces of production" in order to acknowledge that social and technical conditions are linked at every stage of societal development. Where Marxism tends to cast a baleful analytical shadow is over another aspect of the matrix I wish to present: the relations between the material and the "ideal" aspects of missionary strategies. A paradox of missionaries is that they were idealists who were deeply and unavoidably involved in the material transformation of the societies where they worked. Those who want to make the case for the importance of the material aspect of missionary activity may then be drawn to employ some variant of the base/superstructure model of society, which represents it as a "deeper level" of social reality than mere religious talk. But by eliding so much of what the missionaries actually spent their time doing (and set great store by), this model threatens to make their strategies unintelligible. As with the analysis of traditional religion, the task is to relate practice continuously to its informing theory. So two further cells (A2, B2) constitute the theoretical counterparts to the two areas of practical concern: ethics, or theory about right behavior, and cosmology or "science," theory about how things work in the world and over time.

The matrix can be represented schematically as in Figure 6.1. Before turning to the use of this matrix as a model to clarify real processes, two further points need to be made. First, in practice the contents of the four cells are not always rigidly distinct, but may overlap and merge, particularly across the A/B line. Second, there is a degree of cultural bias in the model, in that its differentiations largely reflect the culture from which the missionaries came rather than the Yoruba view. For example, the internal/external distinction does not correspond exactly with society/nature, and such modes of religious action as sacrifices and charms involve not only the manipulation of physical substances (B1) but also speech, a means of social influence (A1). In general, the model is most useful for analyzing the missionaries' strategy—but then it was they who had set up the encounter, even if they could not control its course and outcome.

So the missionaries and the Yoruba faced one another with quite distinct objectives—respectively to make the Yoruba into a Christian community (A1), and to acquire *oyinbo* power for their own purposes (B1)—and (stripped to its barest essentials) the story of their interaction is of the trade-offs they achieved over time between them. Setting out to persuade the Yoruba to their own objective (A1), the missionaries soon found that they needed both to challenge major elements of the Yoruba outlook on existence (A2, B2) and to concede a great deal to Yoruba objectives (B1); in effect to seek to persuade them that Christianity contained the solution to their problems. Their strategy, like any strategy, was to seek to realize a narrative, which in this case began from their theory of history—an account of how God works out His purposes in the world—the "old, old story" (in the words of the popular evangelical hymn) of the creation, fall, redemption, and salvation of mankind (B2). From this cosmo-historical theory there followed the Christian ethical system (A2), which would provide the blueprint for the creation of a Christian community and the reformation of Yoruba life along Christian lines (A1). From this would flow the enhancement of material capacity, whether collective ("to make your country good") or individual ("children, money, and a long life"), which was the primary religious objective of the Yoruba (B1). If European missionaries shrank from laying as much emphasis on the material benefits of religion as the Yoruba did, it was still there in their preaching, and it was certainly a point which the Yoruba agents, like Olubi when he went to visit *Bale* Orowusi of Ibadan in 1870, emphasized fully.[1] The missionary strategy, then, covered all cells of our matrix, linking them in a sequence (B2>A2>A1>B1) which suggested an argument that Christian sacred history was the key to Yoruba advancement. But though strategies are narratives which seek to impose themselves on the course of events, they must not be regarded as more than models for how things *might* go. Even where one party to an interaction is able to override the wills of others, his strategy is likely to be modified by contingencies. Improvisation is of the essence of real life and of history.

THE PRACTICE OF EVANGELISM

Although Henry Venn had worked out for the CMS a sophisticated theory for the development of the mission into a native church, the actual practice of the missionaries was guided less by a theory of evangelism than by exemplary narrative instances of it, drawn from the Bible itself or from published biographies of missionaries. Two of the most read were those of the famous Henry Martyn in India or W. A. B. Johnson, who had worked for the CMS in Sierra Leone.[2] The Bible was described by Roper as being "by itself . . . a perfect converting book, . . . that with the Power of God accompanying it . . . has a power excluding all other powers,"[3] and no part of it was more directly relevant than the Acts of the Apostles. "The Apostle Paul," wrote Roper in his next letter, "must ever continue to be the true pattern of a missionary."[4] Kefer, newly arrived in Ibadan, wrote in his Journal:

> "Read and studied the Bibel [sic] the whole forenoon, especially the Acts in order to learn from the Apostles how the Gospel must be preached to heathen. St Paul's first and second missionary journeys, Acts 13–18, gave me much light. I never read the Acts so attentively." After dinner, he went out to a remote part of town and preached from Acts 13:4–12 [Christ as the light of the gentiles], and then from Acts 17:29–31 [idols, repentance, and judgment].[5]

Possibly more sermon texts were drawn from Acts 17:16ff.—St. Paul at Athens, a "city wholly given to idolatry," where he sees the altar "TO THE UNKNOWN GOD"—than from any other passage of the Bible. Acts not only gave a sense of how to proceed and what to say, but fostered a boosting identification with the Apostles: "As we sailed along," reported Harding and Tugwell of their journey along the eastern lagoon on the way to Ondo and Ilesha, "we read together Acts 13 [Paul at Antioch], and felt that we were also being sent forth by the Holy Ghost and that He was going to use us."[6] Among Europeans, this impulse to reach back to the apostolic dream time may well have been encouraged by the sense of being radically cut off from their earlier lives that they often felt when starting out. This feeling was well conveyed by Mann, on his way to Ijaye in 1853:

> At the third and last day of the Journey . . . I felt as cut off from everything that hitherto had become familiar to me. The separation seemed to be more marked by this line of long and horrible bush than that which seas and countries made. I did not wish to return and felt myself as if already engaged in the blessed work of seeking for Jesus what is lost.[7]

While they were not evidently subject to this stimulus, the African agents were equally if not more prone to see themselves in terms drawn from the great ur-narrative of the Bible. So Olubi reports proudly of his young colleague Samuel Johnson's preaching forays in Ibadan: "Often he came home with almost the words of the disciple 'And the Seventy returned with joy, saying, Lord, even the devils are subject to us through thy name.'"[8]

At the outset, before a congregation had been gathered and could start to spread its influence in the community, through its school and its members' contacts, missionaries had to be strongly proactive in taking the Word to the non-Christian mass. Above all, that meant going out to preach in the streets and the marketplaces. In his early days in Abeokuta, going from market to market and speaking through an interpreter, Hinderer gave short addresses, often on themes suggested by the immediate surroundings, such as the Rock of Ages near the rocky outcrops of Ijemo, or God as a consuming fire (shortly after a fire at Kesi), or the robe of Christ at a weavers' shed. People's curiosity ensured that he drew large and usually friendly crowds, who on one occasion begged him not to be offended at the insults of a *babalawo* the worse for drink.[9]

Later on, when people had gotten used to the main lines of their preaching (and when *babalawo* and others had developed more systematic responses) they came to prefer to visit compounds, where there were less likely to be hostile interruptions, and more chance for what Hinderer called "conversational teaching," which he thought more effective.[10] In 1859, Gollmer reported on his visiting plan: over three weeks he went to eighty compounds and spoke to nearly 500 people, and over five weeks his scripture readers spoke to a further 1,900. He felt that compound visits enabled preaching to be focused more closely on the immediate circumstances of people's lives. A sick family member "rendered them a little soft to listen to the consolation of God's word," while a house in mourning was receptive to an address on the three questions: Why do we die? Where do we go after death? Who can save us?[11] Part of Olubi's strategy in 1870 to raise the profile of the Ibadan mission was to organize visits to the compounds of the war-chiefs lately returned from the Ilesha campaign. These men were so notoriously disinclined to religious discussion that Olubi's colleagues approached the task with trepidation. Allen fortified himself with a precedent more apt than St. Paul, the words of the Lord to Gideon: "Go in this thy might and thou shalt save Israel from the hands of the Midianites. Have I not sent thee?"[12]

Over time the saliency of street preaching tended to decline, but two other forms of outreach continued to be practiced, especially by the African agents, into the 1890s: "itinerations," or tours of villages and small towns, where the missionary usually stayed at the chief's house and preached to people who gathered there; and "stands," well-chosen spots in the town where the missionary might preach regularly once or twice a week. We first meet Samuel Johnson in his reports of his weekly preaching, after Sunday school, under the *ọdan* trees along Ibadan's "Ikoyi highway."[13] An advantage of this method was that it facilitated a relationship of dialogue between the preacher and an accustomed local audience, as we see from W. S. Allen's account of his opening of a preaching stand at Eleta, a southeasterly quarter of Ibadan, in 1868:

> 5 July. Accompanied by two church members, he rings a bell to summon an audience and speaks from the wall of an old broken *orisa* house as a pulpit.

> Next Sunday he finds people already waiting to hear him. A man asks him, what is the yoke of Satan? He says it is like when a man pawns his son to pay for a sacrifice, which makes the bad worse.

26 July. Four men who have heard him at Eleta come to the mother church at Kudeti to inquire further.

16 August. He preaches again. A man comes and takes ten children of his house away from the crowd. Next day he and Okuseinde go back to find the men of the house discussing how to stop their people attending. They go in and talk to them, and get them to promise not to obstruct.

25 October. He preaches to a hundred people at Eleta. A woman in the crowd interrupts with praise of her deity Ori (personal destiny). Allen refutes her by saying that her Ori is merely made of cowries, and only God who made them should be worshipped.[14]

One striking thing about this sequence of entries, compared with most accounts of street preaching, is that though it documents an initiative of Allen's and is rounded off with a favorite text of his, adapted to assert his control of the situation—"The time of your ignorance God winked at, but now he hath commanded all men to repent" (Acts 17:30)—great prominence is given to the feedback he got from his audience. What he says of his own words is mostly his responses to theirs, rather than what he preached to them. This dialogic format would, of course, be the key to making Christianity Yoruba, and Allen was a particularly skilled exponent of it. It is no accident that it was from the audiences at *his* preaching stands that two of the narratives of moral reflection quoted at the beginning of Chapter 3 were drawn.

By the late 1860s, African preachers in Ibadan such as Allen had become fairly well known for what they were, variously treated with interest and sympathy or with suspicion and dislike. But at the outset, missionary preaching as a social practice was often regarded as incomprehensible by Yoruba. When Young first started public preaching at Ondo, some people "considered us as one having nothing to do, and some thought we are some sort of outcast having nowhere to live in, therefore we have come to live amongst them."[15] It was not that the Yoruba were unfamiliar with the idea of religious specialists publicly making claims on behalf of their gods and pressing their cults on others; but the missionaries were very anxious *not* to be assimilated in Yoruba eyes to *orisa* priests or Muslim *alufa* (with whom they were often compared, and with good cultural reason).[16] They repeatedly sought to discourage this by insisting that unlike *babalawo* or *alufa* they did not take money for their prayers, quoting Christ's injunction to the disciples, "Freely ye have received, freely give."[17] A *babalawo* once commented to Olubi on this difference, and in reply to his drawing a contrast between money and the things of God, spoke about money as the lubricant of all social transactions—as with a man who takes money to a chief over his palaver, and is told *Lọ joko wayi, o tan nu* [Go and sit quiet, it will not go further].[18] In effect the missionaries were refusing to play by the social rules of the game for religious specialists, which presumed that they would offer their services for those who wished to purchase them. This in turn would have implied their acceptance of prevailing Yoruba ideas about the proper ends for religious action, and it was precisely these which they had set themselves to challenge.

The mismatch between Yoruba expectations and CMS intentions does much to explain the variety of reported Yoruba responses to missionary preaching. Coming from outside with the self-image that they were *freely* offering something of transcending value which the Yoruba could not see that they needed, the missionaries felt justified in intruding on situations and asserting their views in ways that often provoked highly negative reactions. Their earnest admonitions on death, judgment, and the eternal consequences of sin not only frightened their audiences but, granted Yoruba views about the material efficacy of speech, sometimes even made them feel that they were being cursed. "*Igede l'eyi* [This is an incantation]" was the response of a *babalawo* at Badagry to Samuel Pearse's dire eschatological warnings.[19] Visiting a small Egbado village, James Johnson preached such a fierce sermon on God's anger at sin that the people were afraid to join with them in prayer; and a "wild and obstinate heathen" shouted at them, "Spoilers of the world, ye! Disturbers of people's peace! You pest [*sic*] us at home and now follow us to our farms."[20] A much more common response to uncomfortable words from missionaries was to stay away, as a woman did because Allen spoke to her so solemnly after she had failed to live up to a promise to come to church that she took it as a curse;[21] or as a man did after hearing Hinderer say (ironically, in a sermon about the goodness of God) "that all who heard the preaching of the word of God and do not believe on it nor do . . . what God requests them . . . have made God a liar."[22]

While missionaries *had,* in a sense, to preach the awful judgment of God against idolatry, because it was so deeply integral to their message, they could also give offense more gratuitously, by the occasion of their preaching. Probably nothing annoyed people more than being interrupted while making sacrifices, the act that was for them the essential means to secure welfare through their *orisa*'s favor and, by the same token, for missionaries the very heart of idolatry. That perhaps why is their accounts of it seem so unapologetic, as if their discourtesy was justified by its higher aim. So Gollmer reported an encounter with a group of worshippers in Igbesa in 1854:

A dozen men and women are singing their god's praises, while a priest sprinkles the blood of a freshly killed goat on those present. Gollmer goes up close and with uplifted hand, tells them that God requires no more sacrifice, on account of the sacrifice of Christ. The singing breaks off, and all faces turn in alarm towards him. The two priests "quietly begged that I would proceed on my way." Gollmer refuses, saying it is time for him "to testify to the truth—to lead you in the right way—God sent us to you and if we were silent God would be wrath with us [*sic*]."[23]

No doubt the sudden appearance of this censorious white man, as if out of nowhere, was highly disconcerting to the people of a small and little-visited Awori town. But situations differed, and when Samuel Cole interrupted some women devotees in Abeokuta, his home town where he was well known, he got a very different response:

> When they see him, "one of them said the talkative man is coming; if you abuse them, they will not vex themselves; then deceive them, they will not cease to come to your house, they are never tired." Cole greets them. They ask him not to disturb their sacrifice: "they are busy now, have you no modesty?" Cole says he will come back later to talk on the folly of worshipping idols: "Will you not allow me to speak to you then? We will hear, said a woman, let him go away, you don't know him, he will try to get you in to speak to you, words which you do not like to hear." They go on with their sacrifice.[24]

Here the women's tribute to the persistence of the missionary is matched by his implicit acknowledgment of their confident devotion to their *orisa*. Out of this mutual recognition of voice, framed by membership of the same community, would eventually re-emerge the practical compromises that mark the generous religious ecology of the Yoruba.

The missionaries' frequent refusal of the social etiquette that governed religious interaction and their reluctance to offer the same kind of practical services as other religious specialists were two sides of the same coin. Yoruba bafflement at their unreasonableness might grow to mighty irritation at their tactless intrusions. "Oh! None of your God botherings—good-bye" was the common reply which Pearse got on his assiduous visiting in Badagry,[25] while White was told by an exasperated Sango woman at Ota that "the Mohammedans do not go about to plague us like you do."[26] The whole emotional register of rejection—evasion, indifference, anger, mockery, contempt, even parody of their preaching by an Obatala priest at Abeokuta (to the bystanders' merriment)[27]—is painfully recorded in the journals of the CMS agents. Perhaps most frustrating was the ironical politeness of *mo gbọ*—"I hear," but said to put an end to the conversation—or the terse withdrawal of an elderly Muslim's *mo tuba* [I retreat], both elicited by the relentless White.[28]

Yet contrary attitudes to missionary preaching were also widely current. The Yoruba were readily drawn to public religious disputation and enjoyed its verbal sallies and repartee:

> William Moore speaks to a group in a blacksmith's shop about the burning lake of fire in hell. A woman challenges him on the grounds that they never saw any traces of it on the ancestors who returned as Egungun. All round the shop people look at Moore to see how he will reply. "Why do you think they always cover their bodies entirely with cloth when they appear?" A hit: everyone laughs.[29]

A degree of skepticism was already written into traditional belief, and Yoruba audiences were well prepared to see the testing and discomfiture of individual religious specialists. Always a robust controversialist, White made the most over the theft of someone's Ifa at Ota: if Ifa cannot stop itself being stolen, he proposed with heavy irony, why don't all the *babalawo* get together to consult Ifa to know the thief, "otherwise Ifa sees and knows nothing"—to which the gathering burst out with laughter.[30] "You speak well!" (*O foo re*) people said jokingly to Joseph Smith, when after some exchanges about idolatry, he told the people at Isaga that they should bring their idols to hear the word of God too.[31]

But on a more serious plane, missionaries often report people counseling them to have patience and telling them not to be discouraged at people's indifference. Attitudes of sympathy for the preacher and interest in his message were often closely juxtaposed with hostile ones. This is well conveyed in Doherty's account of ten days' itineration in December 1878 around a group of villages and farm hamlets in Egbado.[32] He had been sent by his superintendent James Johnson to follow up on the preaching tour they had done in a few months before. In many places the severity of Johnson's preaching had left negative memories—at Agodo people said "this man comes again who told us to throw away our idols and believe in Olugbala [Savior]"—and met him with hostility or mockery. But a few days later at Asa, where he met the people all together consulting Ifa, they gave him a warm welcome. The *babalawo* (who reminded him of Cornelius, the sympathetic Roman in Acts 10:33) said they would readily hear God's word, since last week Ifa had foretold that two messengers would be coming. He was even shown some eggs and bananas which they meant to put in a calabash by the road "to draw the mind of the messengers toward them" (these being foods that Europeans were known to like). Though he spoke sharply against idolatry, they all listened intently, gathered round the Ifa bowl, and later joined in prayer, "May God number us among the people of Olugbala . . . "

In small villages like these, local responses were likely to be fairly unified, whatever their source—a leading figure's interest, the hostility of locally resident Muslims, or whatever—but in great towns like Ibadan a diversity of voices was more usual:

Kefer, while out preaching in Ibadan from Nahum 1:7 ("The Lord is good, a stronghold in the day of trouble"), is interrupted first by a man praising Ifa, who starts waving a sword to break up the crowd, and then by an old man who roars praise to Sango, saying that "Sango will kill him and all who listen to his words." Kefer holds his ground, and with support from the crowd, resumes. The Sango man breaks in again and his son now runs into the crowd with a gun. People try to calm them, and beg Kefer to complete his address. He continues in the open street, to an even larger crowd. Finally a woman comes forward, prostrates and offers him kola, which turns out to be a gesture of appeasement from the Sango man's daughter, afraid that Kefer might retaliate by cursing their house.[33]

The woman's anxiety was clearly grounded in the sense of the gathering that Kefer had been treated offensively and would have grounds for striking back. In Ibadan the interrupters, if not *orisa* devotees, were often young warriors, and they might be told off sharply by their elders, for here again the missionaries found themselves on the right side of the Yoruba sense of public decorum.[34] On one occasion even the mild Hinderer benefited by his audience's reproof:

> While he was preaching in Isale Ijebu quarter, a Muslim and an Obatala man opposed his words about there being only one mediator between God and man. "The assembly was large, they seemed to be moderate. I got hot! But they begged me to teach them softly, for that was the way the Yorubas liked best—I had a lesson—the Obatala man afterwards invited me to his house, he would be glad to see me and hear more at any time, so we parted in peace."[35]

The CMS evangelists had no option but to learn their missiology from the friction of experience. What they had to reconcile was the advantages of dialogue in establishing a relationship with those whom they wished to evangelize with their motivating conviction that they uniquely possessed the Gospel which would save the Yoruba. If what Europeans most needed to learn was the necessity of dialogue (as Joseph Smith put it, "it is sometimes well in going into compounds and introducing ourselves, to talk with people first in their own way, and very often they will soon give us a text from which we can preach, and having produced for us the text, they will the more willingly listen"[36]), an African evangelist might be more concerned that the message would not be mistaken. Summing up his own practice, James White wrote that, while he visited many compounds, he did not care to stop long unless the people were "in a humour to argue, and sober and . . . disposed to listen." This was dialogue too, but of a more combative kind, and there could be only one winner! White went on:

> For I make my motto never to desert my post till I see myself master of the field, and the people are willing to acknowledge themselves beaten. Otherwise I feel generally so mortified that I have not done my utmost in opposing Satan and his agents to the last. But it is one thing to convince and be convinced of error . . . [and] it is another thing to convert and be converted. The former is all that we can do. The latter is more the work of the Holy Spirit, which may God vouchsafe to breathe upon the dry bones of our day."[37]

White's military metaphor is less revealing than his very intellectualist view of what the evangelist should try to do. This was more typical of African than European evangelists—it implies that idolatry was a system of ignorance and error rather than one of wickedness—and it underscores how important it is to understand the message which they sought to impart.

"TRANSGRESSION" AND TRANSVALUATION

Before turning to the message itself, which took an essentially narrative form, we need to look at how the missionaries tried to communicate the elements of that narrative—particular values, concepts, symbols, and so forth—to a Yoruba audience so that they became real and compelling. They did this by establishing connections—typically analogical or metaphorical in kind—between these religious entities and the given experience of the Yoruba. The problem was one inherent in religious communication as such, rather than exclusive to cross-cultural religious transfer, though that is likely to make it harder. For insofar as *all* religion has to do with unseen forces— with what is felt to be transcendental or beyond mundane human experience, with the undefinable or the irreducibly other—there is an inherent problem of how to convey information about such a beyond in terms of what is already known. The problem for the CMS missionaries, coming from a terrestrial beyond, thus differed in degree rather than in kind from that which faces all those who offer knowledge of hidden or heavenly things to a lay public. No wonder that the *babalawo,* who had this function within Yoruba society, seem to have felt an affinity with their missionary rivals.[38]

The relations between heavenly and earthly entities can be worked either way: fetching heaven down to earth or reaching up to earth from heaven. The former has been met already in the Christian and missionary habit of sacralizing experience by identifying it in terms of Biblical precedents: Ake church, resplendent in its new iron roof, was "our Zion";[39] David Kukomi, the leading convert at Ibadan, recreated Bethel in his own compound as a small house of prayer with twelve rocks round it representing the tribes of Israel;[40] Abeokuta, threatened by Dahomey, was like Judah under King Hezekiah facing the Assyrians.[41] This downloading of the sacred past into the otherwise profane present was also deeply implicit in Yoruba practices of social legitimation. But it is a complex movement that starts off in the opposite direction that is our main concern here: that is, where mundane phenomena are used as leads to spiritual truth, but at the same time mundane priorities are reversed to create an other-worldly source of ultimate value. As Birgit Meyer has shown in her fine study of the Bremen Mission among the Ewe, this way of moving from earth to heaven was a standard mode of advocacy in German Pietism, where it was known as *Transgression auf das Himmlische* [Stepping toward the heavenly].[42] The method of *Transgression* has its great exemplar in the Parables of Jesus, where symbols and stories of quotidian simplicity—the grain of mustard seed, the lost sheep—were used to reach up to sublime truths. As any churchgoer knows, forms of *Transgression* are used widely in the sermons of all churches, but its self-conscious

practice is especially relevant to the CMS Yoruba Mission since so many of
its key figures were actually Pietists from southwestern Germany; and it does
appear from their journals that they were especially prone to use it.

So on two days in Ibadan in 1856, Hinderer "transgressed" from a party
of men thatching a house to a heavenly house not made with hands (the
men stopping work to hear him talk); and then from the shade trees where
he preached to "the only true and effective shelter from all earthly woes and
troubles."[43] Then, taking refuge from the sun's heat under a blacksmith's
awning, he responded to the blacksmith's comparing his fire (which he could
put out) with the power of the sun (which was beyond him) by talking about
the nature of fire, and comparing it with the Word of God. Another German, J. C. Müller, mentions it as his practice to give short sermons on mundane objects like "salt," "new yams," "dry wood fit for the fire" or whatever
articles were being sold in the street, which people always found it very interesting.[44] The range of analogies, drawn from the round of daily life, was
potentially endless: provisions bought in a market trigger a short address on
"the bread of life";[45] a fine *etu* cloth being woven on a loom in Ibadan prompts
reference to the Word of God;[46] the dross which the blacksmith rakes off
when he smelts iron is the sin from which the body must be purified;[47] some
ginger lozenges, which the children find very sweet, lead to the sweetness of
the Gospel;[48] a woman washing clothes is the cue for words on sins washed
away by the blood of Christ, and one firing pots on the punishment of hell.[49]

Transgression bespeaks a religious outlook which regarded the phenomenal world as suffused with traces of the divine. Now here there is an apparent area of contact with the Yoruba worldview, which regarded all sensible
phenomena as the products of hidden "spiritual" forces and hence as possible indicators of their disposition toward human beings. That must be one
reason for the reported fascination of Yoruba audiences with preaching based
on *Transgression*. But the character of the linkage between the two spheres
was very different in the two cases. With *Transgression*, the connection was
symbolic, the mundane elements serving as reminders or pointers to a system of values, expressed independently in Scripture, which the preacher
sought to communicate more fully. (Yoruba culture also employed symbolism in this way, as in the items used in *aroko* or "symbolic letters"—sometimes
called "parabolical" by missionaries—which gave physical form to their
sender's intentions.)[50] But in *orisa* cults, the linkage was material, with mundane phenomena serving not merely as signs (though they were indeed that)
but also as real effects of the agency of hidden forces. In the one case human beings seek to move in imagination from earthly things to the beyond,
in the other they are subjected to physical intrusion from the beyond and
have to react to it. *Transgression* may have found "sermons in stones," but river
pebbles were a material embodiment of Osun's power.

Faced with this feature of the Yoruba life-world, missionaries strove to dis-
enchant it, through the severance of the symbolic and causal links between

objects and their particular mystical sources. Here the strongest efforts came from the African agents, who were most aware of the enchanted life-world of their fellow countrymen. Thus an example from Doherty while itinerating in the Oke Ogun:

> At the small town of Awaye, he is welcomed by the *Bale*, who is just about to make offerings to the Isanrin stream, saying, "She is a god and does me much good." Doherty replies with the standard argument that God as the Creator is the only one who deserves to receive such recognition, while the river merely has uses, such as to wash and fish in. When he says that "we" [the *oyinbo*, in whom he implicitly includes himself] do not sacrifice to the Ocean—always associated with Europeans—the *Bale* astutely says there are storms which capsize vessels. Doherty says this is a "natural" quality.[51]

Here it would have been fascinating to have known how Doherty put this last contention in Yoruba, and how the *Bale* understood it, if he understood it at all.

But a greater challenge than a small river in the Oke Ogun was the oil palm (*ope*), foremost among plants of sacred significance, which often figures in Yoruba myths, and whose products were associated with major deities: the fronds (*mariwo*) with Ogun and the nuts (*ikin*) with Ifa. His neighbor's initiation into Ifa—which involved the costly purchase of dedicated palm nuts from a *babalawo*—led White to challenge their sacred character:

> The *babalawo* has gone and White himself is leaving the house, when he sees a woman cleaning palm nuts on the verandah, and "remarked to her how wiser the women are than the men in purchasing a whole basket of palm nuts for less than a shilling, while the men would spend ten pounds and upwards for only 16 palm nuts." She saw the drift of his argument and defended the men. But a warm discussion ensued which lasted until sunset.[52]

So White's sly appeal to female sentiment did not pay off. Olubi adopted a different tack, though still makes polemical use of secular pragmatism:

> His addresses a group of Ijebu men in Ibadan from John 3:16 ("For God so loved the world that he gave his only begotten son"). They hear him attentively, but still insist they need Ifa for deliverance from death. Olubi counters with the argument that for God to delegate his power to Ifa is like the *Awujale* of Ijebu handing his over to a slave. They agree that that is not possible. Olubi then goes on to enumerate all the uses to which the palm tree ("the father and mother of Ifa"), created by God for the use of men, is put. He itemizes some fourteen of them, from palm wine and two kinds of oil for cooking and lighting to the medicines made from its root and bark and the multiple objects of daily life (ropes, fish-traps, baskets,

spindles, sieves, brushes, torches, matches, and building materials) made from its fronds and branches. All this, Olubi rounds off, makes the palm tree a sort of useful slave. He makes his final move: "Would you run after such a person for a blessing?" "*A gbọdọ, a gbọdọ* [we cannot, we cannot]," they reply.[53]

The style of argument employed here—where a persuasive metaphor is used to drive one's opponent into an absurdity—was one much favored by some of the African evangelists, for it depended on a command of Yoruba language and culture greater than a European could possess; and it is hardly accidental that we seem to find the best examples of it in those who show most virtuosity in the composition of journal narratives, such as Moore, White, Pearse, Olubi, Doherty, W. S. Allen, and Samuel Johnson. But the main thrust of their message is to secularize the Yoruba environment, by stressing the forward linkages between material substances and their practical uses and denying their backward linkages with any hidden powers.

This rhetoric of disenchantment was complemented by one of transvaluation, or the inversion of many of the "natural" values of Yoruba life (or indeed of human life in general). Yoruba religion was directed to certain ends—health, prosperity, long life, and so forth, in a word, *alafia*—and it specified certain means to those ends, notably the cultivation of the hidden powers, *orịsa* in particular, which were most able to assist or hinder their attainment. Disenchantment struck at the Yoruba doctrine of the means here, for it insisted that no *orịsa* lay behind the phenomena; and transvaluation challenged its ends, for it made out that the most important human objectives lay beyond earthly existence, not within it.

The analogies employed in *Transgression* (like all analogies) are selected initially because of some similarity between the two terms compared, but this act of comparison already presupposes a categorical difference which is fundamental to its whole religious point. This is the difference between earth and heaven, or mundane existence and the hereafter. So in the standard use of *Transgression,* similarity soon passes over to difference. When a man, probably an Ijebu trader, asked Hinderer to take him to his own country, he replied that he would rather show him "the road to a much better country" (i.e., heaven).[54] When the head of a compound in Ibadan confessed to Okuseinde his disappointment at not getting a chieftaincy title, he offered him "another title, a title to heaven"; and when the man protested he was a elder of the town, he was told the story of Nicodemus.[55] On two different occasions, in different towns, the complaint "*ẹbi npa mi* [I am starving]" was met with words on "the bread of life" or "the bread of heaven."[56] The point of Allen's comparison of the costly *ẹtu*—a prestige cloth worn by chiefs—to the Word of God was that, unlike the cloth, the latter was both priceless and freely available even to the poorest.

The values of Yoruba society were thus inverted, through a rhetoric which exploited terms common to the two cultures. Extreme, idealized contrasts were sometimes drawn by missionaries to highlight what they saw as the values of the true Christian:

> Gollmer describes the death after a painful illness of an elderly female communicant, "poor as regards the things of this world, but rich in God." The old woman's daughter was not a Christian, and Gollmer contrasted the "poor suffering old mother, without a complaint, without a murmur and full of comfort, joy and praise—whilst on the other hand, her young, strong, healthy and idolatrous daughter was full of trouble, gloom and sorrow, and almost angry with her mother for talking so much about God and heaven and for admonishing her to forsake idols."[57]

In similar vein was Gollmer's reflection on the plea of the *balẹ* of a small Ketu town "to help him that he, his wives and children may not die but live prosper [*sic*] and have peace": "Poor blind people, their only desire is to live and their only fear is to die, what a contrast between them and a happy believer who can say 'to die is gain.'"[58] Transvalued, "true peace" was not that condition of all-around well-being which the Yoruba call *alafia* but something quite independent of a person's physical condition, social relations, and material circumstances, truly a "peace which passeth all understanding."

The reader who looks back to the Yoruba prayer quoted early in Chapter 4[59] will not be surprised that such extreme paradoxes as "to die is gain" often led to the frank amazement of Yoruba audiences:

> At Abeokuta in 1849, Müller visited "one of the great men of this town," who asked him to help him get rich. Instead Müller spoke of the temptation that riches might would lead to sin and damnation. "Do therefore never consider the things of this world your gain, for they are your loss. Strive on the contrary to be made rich toward God by believing in his son. These then are riches which will accompany you through death into eternal life." The man was astonished at this doctrine, but some women said that they wanted to hear more.[60]

The Christian practice of praying for one's enemies also gave rise to great surprise, for it implied an inversion of the Yoruba view of prayer as a spiritual technique to protect oneself from all those hostile forces which threatened one's *alafia* and ultimately one's life.[61] As death was the great enemy for the Yoruba,[62] a Christian's "good death" was the decisive proof of the successful implantation of the Christian alternative: to die in calm assurance of eternal life. To be able to say "*Mo dupẹ, ẹru ko ba mi* [I give thanks, I am not afraid]," the last words of Mrs. Puddicombe, the elderly widow of a long-serving mission agent, as reported by Charles Phillips at Breadfruit, was the normative seal of the convert's life.[63] Some years later after moving to Ondo, Phillips himself was sorely put to the test, when three of his four young children died within a week from smallpox. He left no journal for that terrible period, and in his annual letter he simply reported with stoic formality that "the Lord did not leave us alone in our affliction."[64] The text most often used when reporting hard bereavements—"For whom the Lord loveth he chastiseth and scourgeth every son whom he receiveth"[65]—is well compatible with the Yoruba model of the stern but benign father, but only granted the extra Christian condition that the afterlife had a much greater potential than life on earth. The plausibility of transvaluation thus crucially depended on the missionaries' bid to introduce a new temporal framework for Yoruba existence.

THE PLAN OF REDEMPTION

Over the decades of evangelism recorded in the CMS journals, many different texts and topics were used as pathways into the complex task of presenting the Christian religion to the Yoruba. But what gave them coherence and point was above all the redemptive history in which they were placed, for it always underlay their preaching on specific topics such as sin, death, the power of God, true peace, Christ's role as mediator, sacrifice, life eternal, and so forth. Christianity is a religion whose scripture takes a strongly narrative form, and "Scripture History" was part of the core curriculum of the education of CMS missionaries, including the young Yoruba trained at Abeokuta and Lagos.[66] At the very outset of the Ondo mission in 1875, Charles Young, the catechist placed there by Hinderer, opened instruction at his little school by teaching "the alphabet of the Yoruba translation, the Lord's Prayer and the Scripture History in the Yoruba language."[67] The text most widely used, Pinnock's *Analysis of Scripture History,* was essentially an interpretative commentary on the sequence of books which compose the Bible, especially on the Old Testament in relation to the New, designed to show the whole as the working out of a single divine scheme of redemption. It had much to say of prophecies later fulfilled, especially of "the *typical* and *prophetical* intimations of the Messiah" in figures such as Adam or Joseph, and of the Jewish "types" of Christian doctrines or rituals, as the Passover was of the Eucharist or the sacrifices of the Day of Atonement were of Christ's redemptive self-sacrifice.[68] Scripture History was so set up as to give the reader of the Bible not just interpretations of particular episodes but also a general sense of Scripture as the plan of a historical process otherwise mysterious. With a wonderful serendipity, it thus meshed not only with the Yoruba cultural demand for oracular guidance, for the means to impose a moral order on the arbitrary incidents of temporal existence, but also with Ifa's specific reliance on archetypal precedents.

Sometimes the missionaries allude to their preaching of the plan of redemption in a rather summary form. Hinderer, in an Ibadan street, gave "a simple narration of the historical part of God's plan of redemption and an appeal to accept that Salvation freely offered."[69] James White, reviewing his public preaching schedule in Ota, described his perennial theme as "the history of the creation of all things, the fall of man and the consequences thereof, and the interposition of Jesus Christ the Son of God as Mediator"; and in another place as "the history of Creation, the fall, the plan of redemption, the resurrection of the world and the day of judgement."[70] Itinerating in Egba villages, William George gave his hearers the whole story—creation, fall, redemption through Christ's sacrifice, repentance, and salvation—and then got them to repeat the Lord's Prayer.[71] The African agents seem to have been particularly aware that "the historical part" of the divine plan had its roots in a cosmogony, since the story the Bible told here was very different from the cosmological myths of the Yoruba. So when Young taught the Genesis story as literal truth, his pupils at Ondo "were in great astonishment to hear how the whole world came into being [in] only six days with all the things and men that are therein."[72] The paradox is that, while Genesis and science may have been regarded as belonging to rival cosmologies in Victorian England, in Yorubaland the Genesis account of creation was as much part of the white man's knowledge as the theory that electricity is the cause of thunder. Elementary science was taught alongside Scripture History at the CMS Training Institution and deployed with confidence against the Sango people's explanation of thunder in terms of the anger of their god.[73]

Whether in its fuller or more abbreviated versions, redemptive history was always brought to the point in the existential choice facing the individual. Conversely, personal decisions were given weight by their grounding in the cosmo-historical scheme itself, in God's plan of redemption. Thus, in paraphrase, Gollmer's address to an audience in a small town in Egbado:

How God created man, man's fall through sin, and God's wish to restore him. What God wishes for mankind: the Ten Commandments "which seemed to strike [his hearers] much and which quite riveted their attention." He then put three rings on the ground to stand for earth, heaven, and hell, and asked people where they would go when they died. How vain it was to worship idols and offer sacrifices, "as there is one name only under Heaven whereby we can be saved." Pray to Jesus for God's forgiveness for your sins, and they would go to Heaven the good place.[74]

But of all the reported instances of redemptive history, none seems to have had a greater impact on its audience than the "wordless book" which James Read used in his outdoor preaching at Leki in 1877, which abandoned verbal discourse altogether for pure symbolism.[75] This seems to have consisted of something like four double-spread pages, colored in sequence: black (= sin), red (= Christ's sacrifice), white (= sanctification) and gold (= glory in heaven). Read's assistant, Isaac Braithwaite, described its message as "the heart washed by the blood of Christ" and confirmed the great impact it had on audiences: on one occasion a man responded by simply exclaiming, "the truth is come."[76] While the overt message was powerful enough in its simplicity, especially to the young runaway slaves who constituted most of the population of Leki, its impact must have been greatly enhanced by its coincidence with Yoruba modes of signification. Overall, it had much of the character of *aroko,* the "symbolical" or "country" letters used in the solemn communications of chiefs, which deployed a symbolic lexicon of substances and colors to underscore messages by giving material form to their intentions. Missionaries had already made some use of the idiom—particularly using white things, such as the jars of salt and sugar which Hinderer once sent "as a sort of letter" to the Ibadan chiefs in the war camp,[77] or the Bible wrapped in a white cloth which Doherty once gave to the *Balę* of Okeho to reciprocate his offering of water in a white calabash.[78] But the "wordless book" made use of the whole range of the black/red/white color triad, and did so in a way which fitted (albeit simplistically) with enduring Yoruba values: black (*dudu*) as hidden or negative; red (*pupa*) as ambivalent, dangerous, or mediatory; white (*funfun*) as spiritual and positive.[79]

As Victor Turner pointed out,[80] basic symbols such as the three colors derive a strong emotional charge from their multi-referential character, which any user will find himself evoking without intending it. And not only was each symbol enhanced by having more than one reference, but the entire sequence of them was enhanced as well. The story line of Read's "wordless book," which he devised to convey the plan of redemption, can also be read in another way, as a symbolization of the history that the mission was attempting to make at a concrete level. Without doubt, the master metaphor used by the missionaries for their project was of bringing light into darkness; so the black/white opposition could also stand as a color-coding of heathenism/Christianity, African/*oyinbo,* tradition/modernity, past/future, a typological contrast projected onto the course of real cultural change. Red would then signify the struggles and suffering, the self-sacrifice of missionaries and the persecution of converts, which would lead from black to white; and gold the enhanced wealth and power which would result from "enlightenment" (*ǫlaju*). Black-red-white-gold thus vividly encapsulates the course of cultural history which the mission was inviting the Yoruba to adopt.

But while the plan of redemption could be presented in symbolic terms that were congenial to the Yoruba, and its offer of a golden future had a real appeal to people who experienced their present as mired in "confusion," we must not forget that it challenged Yoruba conceptions of the cosmic and moral order in fundamental ways. Before examining the two main complexes of difference in greater detail, which will necessarily take the form of a loosely "systematic" theology, let me present an exchange between an evangelist and a *babalawo* (always their most serious interlocutors) to show how the plan of redemption was introduced as a "narrative" theology to underpin the specific

Figure 6.2. "An African catechist preaching in an African village." Based on the journals of S. W. Doherty in the Oke Ogun. *Church Missionary Gleaner,* September 1876.

points of missionary challenge and to ground the life changes which missionaries hoped would follow:[81]

> Reaching Iganna on a tour of the Oke Ogun, S. W. Doherty first preached from Exodus 20:1–17 [the Ten Commandments] to a sizeable audience before the Ṣabiganna's palace. Later he is reading under a tree opposite his lodging. An old *babalawo* comes to sit by him and admires the book. Doherty asks him for one of his beads, and this leads to a conversation in which he challenges the *babalawo* for "deceiving" people. He replies: "God made us and handed us all over to Ifa and the other gods to take care of us." Doherty responds with "sacred history" from Creation to Redemption, and the needlessness of sacrifice on account of the sacrifice of Christ. He urges the old man to give up consulting Ifa for people or consecrating them to the cult. "If you will put away your book from you . . . ," counters the *babalawo.* But he is silent when Doherty says the book tells him how to conduct his life and how to prepare for the life to come. The *babalawo* asks what he would live on if he renounced his profession, and Doherty says he should farm: "If any should not work, neither shall he eat." "I take these things [money, animals, etc.] from them because I see death, and make them to avoid it by sacrificing for them," he replies.
>
> Next day, the *babalawo* rejoins Doherty while he is talking with a weaver. He opens his Bible again and lights on Matthew 6:19–21 ["Lay not up for yourselves treasures upon earth . . . (but) treasures in heaven"], which he

explains. The *babalawo* says "the word of God is a good treasure where nothing but truth is taught to men," and is positive about having a House of God at Iganna.

On the third day at noon the *babalawo* comes again, so they go and sit under the tree to talk. Doherty expounds John 3:1–13, the story of how the Pharisee Nicodemus, "a ruler of the Jews," came to Jesus, acknowledging that he was teacher sent from God and being told that he must be born again if he would see the kingdom of God.[82]

Many of the leading themes of half a century's evangelism are interlaced in this one narrative. There is the contested parallel between the stranger and the local religious specialists, and their respective sources of wisdom (Bible and Ifa); the centrality of sacrifice in arguments about relations between God and humankind; the transvaluation of the notion of treasure; constant missionary dilation upon death and futurity, so relevant to the temporal re-configuration which they proposed; and the connections made between sacred history and the new lives which Yoruba were asked to live. Doherty's three texts were well chosen to run in a cumulative dialectical sequence. First, the Ten Commandments, which always went down well with Yoruba audiences, since they contain so much of universal morality; second, as if in antithesis to them, verses from the Sermon on the Mount, whose transvaluatory tone so sharply confronts the Yoruba cultural ethos; and finally, the passage from St. John's Gospel, which both asserts the necessity of spiritual rebirth and, with the tacit identification of the *babalawo* and the sympathetically questioning Pharisee Nicodemus, suggests that his journey to Christianity had already begun.

FIRST AND LAST THINGS

As a temporal configuration of the cardinal episodes of human existence, the plan of redemption presented a strictly one-way flow. More than this, the Christian view was teleological, in that it was oriented to a transcendent *end*—the life eternal of the soul redeemed from sin to dwell in the presence of God—which gave direction to the preceding span of each person's existence. In contrast, the normal Yoruba pattern was "archeological,"[83] in that the end was nothing more than a return to the *origins*, which were what received cultural elaboration and social emphasis. Its characteristic cognitive style was most plainly evident in Ifa divination, where the solution to the client's problem was disclosed in an archetypal precedent, and its fullest ritual realization lay in the cult of ancestors. More than that, the typical view was that the new-born were reincarnations of their ancestors, particularly of a recently deceased grandparent, thus identifying the social past and future in a very concrete way.[84] Of course in the immediate flow of quotidian time, what was past and what was in the future could be readily distinguished from one another—for example, by the adjectival phrases *t'o koja* [that is past] and *t'o mbo* [that is coming]—but the past and the future did not exist as distinct and opposed absolutes, as in the Christian and Western view. Rather the same term *lailai*, denoting a kind of "time beyond time," was used to refer to both the past of "once upon a time" and the future of "for ever and ever."[85] Whereas the one-way temporal scheme of Christian sacred history was uniformly and consistently presented by the missionaries, the opposing Yoruba views were less consistent and fixed, as well as somewhat regionally variable. There were important differences between the central/western areas and the east, which correlate with the presence or absence of Islam. The missionaries came in on a situation of flux and contestation, where the ground for what they wanted to say about time and the afterlife had already been to some extent been prepared by Islam. So it makes sense to begin with the east, where prevailing ideas were not only closer to the ancient pattern throughout the region but were still widely present in the center/west as a substrate under the newer notions introduced by Islam.

The prevailing impression of the CMS agents at Ondo—themselves Egba or Oyo by origin—about the attitude of local people toward the afterlife was of their utter lack of interest in it.[86] Phillips reported the views of a man who had started attending services:

> He acknowledged that the Word of God has shed some light into his heart about the future life, but he is afraid to look fully upon the light. . . . The Ondo belief in which he was educated was that there is no heaven elsewhere but within a childbearing woman, where the spirit reenters as soon as it leaves the body to be born again into the world as an infant. This is why they worship their deceased parents in their children."[87]

This substitution of "a woman's womb" for "heaven" (*orun*), as both the destination and the source of life, occurs so often in Ondo that one suspects it was made in response to insistent questioning in order to establish a point of contact with Christian teaching.[88] Conversely, no less a figure than Ondo's principal warlord, the *Lisa*, once interrogated Charles Young about how Christians treated the dead:

> Young replies that the Christians gave the dead nothing. Remarking that "we are not wise, while we considered ourselves the wisest persons in the world," the *Lisa* went on to ask what they call their two big toes. Just toes, replies Young. The *Lisa* laughs, and says that for them the right toe represents the deceased father, and the left one the mother. When they sacrifice to them, they pour some of the victim's blood on each toe before eating the meal with their friends. The *Lisa* then speaks of the killing

of human beings in memory of important people, which leads Young to conclude: "Thus you see how blind and selfish these people are—and I hope the Lord of Heaven will soon open [their] eyes . . . to know the true way of eternal life."[89]

This picture is confirmed and taken further in the general account of Ondo religion which Charles Phillips provided in answer to a missionary questionnaire.[90] The Ondo, he wrote, put in the grave all the things the dead person would need to live as on earth; sometimes they seem to confound the world of spirits with the womb of a woman, saying there is no *ọrun* ("heaven"). They divine to ascertain the prior identity of the newborn; and the dead are credited with great power over the living. At funerals, people will bless the mourners by saying: *Ki oku gba eruku ti ọ l'ẹsẹ* [May the dead gather dust to your feet," i.e., keep you firmly on the ground] or *Ki oku fi ẹhin tilẹ ki o gbe ọ* [May the dead lie on his back to sustain you]. They make offerings to the grave for a few months, and then to their big toes, which represent the dead.

But alongside this strongly cyclical and earth-oriented picture, Phillips gives indications of another set of ideas, where heaven (*ọrun*) and moral redress have greater prominence. Thus they may say of a man "well buried," *O ba Ọlọrun n'ile* [He meets God at home], and of the dead who have injured them: *Ati ọrun de ọrun apadi* [May his heaven become the 'heaven of broken pots']. The soul of a dead man goes to the Almighty (Olodumare) to be judged; if condemned, he will be chained in *ọrun* and not be reborn, but will become an evil spirit. These ideas are not only typical of the world religions, but in a rigorous sense incompatible with the social logic of an ancestral cult. For there it is not individuals' moral careers but their structural position in relation to the living which matters: even the wicked cannot be allowed to become evil spirits (at least in the eyes of their descendants). So what do we make of Phillips's reportage? It is striking that, whereas the first set of ideas appears as grounded in practice as well as discourse (and fully in line with the indications of Ondo belief that occur in missionary reports of actual religious encounters), the latter appears merely in the form of discourse. It seems we should regard the second perspective as a supplement to the first, imperfectly integrated, if not in places downright inconsistent with it, and perhaps more recently introduced. If so, by whom? Since there were as yet virtually no Ondo Muslims, the most likely source is the *babalawo*—whose signature is on Phillips's account in the reference to "Olodumare" as the heavenly judge.

In the central/western towns like Ibadan and Abeokuta, we also find the two perspectives on the afterlife, but here the concept of heaven is much more salient, and the second perspective does occur in the talk of ordinary individuals: yet the first perspective, cyclical and earth-oriented, is still dominant.[91] When William Moore preached about eternal life to an Egba woman who had gone to a shrine of Obatala to be able to conceive a child, it was vehemently expressed by her companion ("two wild women," he calls them):

> They did not want happiness after death, she insisted, but would be pleased to go where their ancestors had gone. Moore says they should not expect the mercy their ancestors might receive, for they had acted out of ignorance. After further exchanges about the condition of the dead, she asserts that "their deceased fathers . . . come out from the world of spirit every year in the shape of Egungun and Oro," to be feasted and given cowries by their descendants, and that "had there [been] any trouble in the world of spirit they would have told them."[92]

The woman's indifference to what her posthumous conditions of existence might be was the corollary of her belief in the ongoing mutual exchanges between human beings and their ancestors: she saw herself going to join them, while they regularly revisited the earth, whether in the form of the Egungun and Oro spirits, or as reborn in the persons of their descendants. Compared with popular Ondo belief, there is a greater time-space allowed here for the dead between death and rebirth: the "world of spirit," otherwise "heaven." (Egungun to this day are known as *ara ọrun*, "denizens of heaven"). Her friend's pressing concern to have a child of her own was not merely a secular aspiration, since a woman who died childless would have no one to feast her spirit during the annual festival when people went to welcome their ancestral spirits by placing food offerings for them in the Oro grove.

The CMS journals from central and western Yorubaland abound with evidence of popular belief that the deceased, in going to *ọrun*, enter a spirit world rather like earth, from which they revisit the living periodically and will eventually be reborn in their descendants. A *babalawo* says he cannot convert until his next life (*aiye atunwa*, lit. "the world/age of return").[93] The neighbor of a young man who died tells Mann at Ijaye that he "must have many fine rooms (of course with wives) in heaven where he has gone, as he loses these enjoyments so undeservedly on earth."[94] W. S. Allen reports two encounters with elderly people at Ibadan: a destitute (and so probably childless) woman in the street calling on God to take her, who answers his query as to where her soul would be with *li ọrun* [in heaven]—but she has no clear idea of what that is; and a man so old that he has none of his age left alive, and says that he is preparing to join his father and mother in heaven.[95] A man about to be executed at Abeokuta for kidnapping says defiantly that when he returns he will at once go off to raid again in Ijebu[96]; and a *babalawo* at Badagry, who knows something of Christianity but has been worsted in debate, says "When I return again to this world, I will be born in white man's country," which implies the belief that the returning soul chose its new destiny (*ipin*) before returning to earth.[97] In line with the close correspondence posited between the earthly and the heavenly realms, it was even said that each town had its own distinct *ọrun:* some "Yoruba" (which here means Oyo) told the Egba William Allen that "they in the interior would have a better world than Abeokuta!"[98]

The missionaries repeatedly challenged the notions of replication and return which ran through these images of the afterlife. For them heaven was a place for moral redress, even status reversal, and assuredly there was no return from it. They met much skepticism when they urged this alternative pattern of cosmo-history on the Yoruba, some of it on the simple but elegant grounds that if no one returned from the other world, how did Christians know what to say about it? Charles Phillips the elder said of critical audiences in Ijaye:

> They daily mocked the doctrine of the future state by saying, since they used to see their forefathers died [*sic*], they never saw one come back to them to tell them the good or bad of the future world. How came you, Oyinbo, to know such doctrine of the future time, that there is good and bad in the next world?[99]

Yet we must not forget that, especially among the Oyo Yoruba (who included Ijaye), it was not Christian missionaries but Muslim *alufa* who first preached heaven and hell. As we know from Crowther's *Vocabulary of the Yoruba Language* (1843) a distinction between two heavens, *ọrun rere* [good heaven] and *ọrun apadi* [heaven of potsherds] had wide currency. Though the exact formulation of this does not sound very Islamic, it is hard not to believe there is some Muslim influence in the very idea of a judgment after death—for Islam was up to two centuries old among the Oyo Yoruba. The *Apena* of the Ogboni cult at Ijaye responded to Phillips's words on the future judgment with "many wicked and shocking questions"—alas, unreported—and then told a story of the *Alafin* Atiba, who in his youth had "tapped the Koran" but later reverted to *orisa* worship. Atiba had told an *alufa*, who scolded him about God's judgment of the wicked, "to go and tell God if he does not have enough firewood to kindle the hellfire, then he should send for more from this earth," meaning that they knew they were wicked and would pay no attention even if angels were sent to preach to them. The missionaries sometimes met a similar defiance:

> Akiogun, a young man at Ota, strongly resisted White's preaching for over eight years. Once he replied to White, "'Cease to frighten me with *ọrun apadi*—a world of potsherds—that is too mild a place for me, seeing *apadi* is brittle. Let God put me, if He pleases, in *ọrun ele* (a world of iron)' . . . by which he meant to show his unmindfulness of the punishment which is reserved for the ungodly." He would not leave the religion of his ancestors or his Ifa.[100]

This attitude of "if it was good enough for my ancestors, it is good enough for me" was really entailed by the old cosmology, as a *babalawo* showed in his angry response to Doherty before an intent crowd in Abeokuta: "You people are great cowards, the fire of hell you so much dread is what we heathens are prepared for, why should we refuse to go there since our forefathers had preceded us to that place?"[101]

So the idea of the afterlife as a site of punishment or reward, and not just as a staging-post between one earthly existence and another, was widespread in central and western Yorubaland. Townsend summed up attitudes in Badagry in 1845: "It is a common saying . . . that they shall meet their forefathers after death and they have some notions of a state of reward or punishment, but it is indistinct and seldom spoken of."[102] A similar picture is given in White's comment on a family at Ota, disconsolate after the death of one of its members: "Poor fellows! . . . though they talk of a good and a bad place, of good people being sent to the former and bad to the latter, yet they do not concern to discover to which of these places they will be doomed."[103] While we cannot treat the search for posthumous moral redress as a universal human inclination, it does seem likely to become more attractive under the conditions of the Age of Confusion, when so many people were torn adrift from their families and communities. Subjected to unprecedented personal strains, people were forced to confront their experiences much more as individuals. The prior existence of a widespread, if vague, belief that the afterlife might offer condign recompense to good and bad individuals provided a platform from which the missionaries could appeal to people's hopes and fears about the future and move them further toward Christianity's configuration of human life as a story which did not repeat itself.

Where the Yoruba were inclined to anticipate the "good heaven" for themselves and their relatives, it fell to the missionaries to urge people to avoid the terrifying alternative by abandoning idolatry and accepting the salvation which was offered to them through Christ. While (as noted above) some pagans laughed off the threat of hell, others were seriously affected by it:

> A neighbour of Daniel Olubi's at Ibadan, who had learned much about Christianity but still strongly rejected it, was on his deathbed. In a lucid interval before dying, he told his family he was among the wicked "who have to stand without the walls of heaven," and desired the Christians to come and pray for him. Olubi went to speak to him, but to the end he stayed faithful to his own god, Orisaoko.[104]

In less extreme instances too, people often seem to have been touched by Christian preaching on death and its aftermath:

> Moore talks with four elderly men sitting under a tree, who at first had laughed at him for preaching "the white man's religion." He emphasizes the folly of spending money on sacrifices to drive away death, which, ever since "our foreparents had lost that happy state," would be in the world till the end of time. If the messenger of death is sent by God, he is not to be

turned away. The old men are now listening with admiration, confirming it from their own experience. Moore sums up his message: "The prudent inquiry of any of the . . . children of Adam should always be what I must do that I may be happy in the world of spirits [which] is our everlasting home," The old men become serious and say: *şişẹ ni* [it is to be done].[105]

The readiness of so many Yoruba to listen responsively to what the missionaries had to say about the telos of human life seems to me to go beyond what a whipped-up fear of hell might warrant. The evidence that Yoruba were already, from Muslim sources, adding elements of heaven/hell to their cyclical or reincarnational scheme suggests that another explanation is needed. The Yoruba, like other populations of pre-colonial Africa, existed in a state of chronic cognitive deficit, forever aware that their stock of knowledge, although extensive, was liable to fail to meet their survival needs or to quell their anxieties. Moreover, since it was above all ancestral knowledge, the precedents for wise action, that their acknowledged experts controlled, in an age of unprecedented change the general sense of deficit must have been especially acute. If the *babalawo* were locally taken as the peculiar masters of the first things of human existence, the missionaries claimed, and were widely accorded, the advantage in respect of its last things.[106]

These contrasts repeatedly came into play in exchanges between the two kinds of religious expert. Sometimes the *babalawo* sought to play to their strength, as with one at Abeokuta who tried to draw a convert, Sally, away from Christianity by saying that they knew more of the origins of all things than the missionaries. When he spoke of new babies as ancestors reborn, she responded with God's creation of the human race from Adam and Eve, triumphantly asking, "So where did *their* first children come from?"[107] On the other side, missionaries challenged *babalawo* for not having anything to say about the last things, or the future as other than the past replicated. So George Meakin at Oyo told a *babalawo* that Ifa had not been able to help those people whose towns had been ruined in the wars, or had been killed or sold as slaves, and that it had not told them of the world to come, referring to the last judgment. The *babalawo* replied, not by telling him he was talking nonsense, but by angrily shouting that then he was ready to go to hell.[108]

For what is really striking is how open many *babalawo* were to missionary criticisms of the very system of which they were the supreme interpreters, and in which, as professional diviners, they had a large material stake.

"Did Ifa ever tell you anything respecting the world to come?" asked Müller of a *babalawo* at Abeokuta in 1849, following it up with a characteristically transvaluatory challenge: "Does Ifa tell you to sell all things and to give them to the poor, and thou shalt have a treasure in heaven?" The *babalawo* admitted he knew nothing about this, but told Müller the origins of Ifa [which, annoyingly, Müller omits to record]. He even went on to say that originally, and in contrast to the present, Ifa priests "were not to aspire after riches nor . . . [own] slaves, and . . . were expected to be benevolent to the poor."[109]

It is hard not to see this as the reflection of a highly transvaluatory missionary ideal—made at a time when the honeymoon between the Egba and the missionaries was still on—rather than any genuine tradition of how things once were. One Egba *babalawo* suggested to Thomas King that their aims and those of the Christian pastor were much the same, but King insisted on the distinction:

> "They predict health and prosperity to those who are capable of making costly sacrifices to ward off . . . any calamity or misfortune, while on the contrary God commands us to warn people to prepare for death and judgement by speedy repentance." When the *babalawo* replies with "the customs of our forefathers," and says they would go to meet them, King asks what removed their forefathers. "Death," says everyone; and after King has spoken further on the inescapability of death, the *babalawo* "begged in the face of all present that . . . we must not be relaxed in telling them about these things."[110]

It is no contradiction that *babalawo* were among both the most astute and zealous defenders of "country fashion," and those most able to see its deficiencies and explore alternatives. They did so in a setting where the old cyclical worldview still made most sense of the social experience of most people, but where there was a growing desire to see it supplemented by ideas of posthumous moral recompense, which represented a kind of reversal, and hinted at a unidirectional patterning of human existence. Particularly in the Oyo and Egba areas, such promptings had been given some shaping by Islam, so missionary preaching about the last things, radical and confronting as it was to many of those who heard it, did not break in as total novelty. But while Islam might sometimes have served as a catalyst, I doubt if it should be invoked too readily; for Yoruba was a complex and ever-changing society and its traditions of moral self-reflection, which the missionaries came in on, were surely indigenous.

Consider the story which Daniel Olubi was told in 1855 by a pagan acquaintance, who had had it from his father forty years before:

> Two men were about to come into the world. The first man went to God and asked that he be blessed with property, and that he lose none of it throughout his life. The second man said to God that he would yield all his property to God, but let him allow him at least to enjoy half of it. God agreed to both requests. The two men came into the world and were very blessed with property. But when the second man came to his height, he began to lose it: half his people died and half his property was consumed. But he was content with what was left. The first man died without losing any of his own, and in the afterlife "was exposed to sun and rain and dews."

The second man then died, and was admitted to a very big house with many people and servants: "everything about him was pleasant and he was in full joy." The first man asked God the reason for his wretched state. "God answered him that when he was on earth, he laid his treasures on earth and enjoyed his time and property in full. But the other man laid half his treasures in the other world, and now he enjoys the treasures he had laid in store."[111]

This reminded Olubi of the parable of Lazarus and the rich man in Luke 16, and also of Romans 2:14–15 ("For when the Gentiles, which have not the law, do by nature the things contained in the law . . . "). The story begins entirely within the framework of the old cosmo-history, in that the two men go to God to be allotted their destiny, or *ipin*, the first stage in the life of a person born (or rather reborn) into the world. The themes of the story— wealth comes from God, it cannot be expected to stay fixed in one place, men should respond to changes in fortune with equanimity—express an enduring Yoruba philosophy of life. But then there is the presumption that appropriate behavior meets its reward in the afterlife; and the strong closure of the narrative seems to exclude the possibility that this is not how it ends. It goes too far to say that this is the Christian worldview anticipated—though that hope can be forgiven Olubi—but not that this is the kind of basis on which the missionaries might plausibly start to persuade the Yoruba of it.

SIN, MEDIATION, AND SACRIFICE

The preceding section has focussed on missionary attempts to change the cosmo-historical presuppositions of Yoruba life (B2 in the model presented at the beginning of the chapter) in order to win them to the temporal scheme of the Christian plan of redemption. These cosmological contrasts were seen to carry ethical implications (A2 in the model), which themselves entailed a certain view of how human beings need to relate to the spiritual powers. Evangelical Anglicanism taught that as a result of the Fall, related in Genesis 3, the central feature of the human predicament is that man stands in a state of sin, a condition which thereafter underlies all particular sinful acts. As man in Adam separated himself from God, so God in Christ opened the path to reconciliation by taking human form and, through His death on the Cross, offering Himself as a redemptive sacrifice to lift the burden of sin. Human beings are not able, by the good acts which God requires of them, to *earn* salvation, but it is still freely available to them if by faith they accept the sacrifice made for them by Christ and live in the assurance of it. In the potent key metaphor of evangelicalism, sinners who accept Christ's promise of redemption are washed clean in the blood of the Lamb—a metaphor derived, as the CMS agents knew well, from the sacrificial rites of the ancient Jews. This theological scheme had enough points of contact with Yoruba ideas about the relations of men, God, and the *oriṣa* to give rise to serious dialogue. Yet the hope, especially of the African evangelists, that these commonalities offered a bridgehead which would readily ease Yoruba into an acceptance of Christianity proved too sanguine. For there was less common ground between the moral structures that underlay such seemingly common notions as "sacrifice" and "salvation" than the mere translation of the words suggests. This comes up at once when we consider the link between sin and that estrangement between God and man which the Judeo-Christian tradition expresses in the narrative of the Fall.

The very notion of "sin," in the sense of Christian theology, which was the foundation for the entire plan of redemption, was exotic to traditional Yoruba thinking. The noun *ẹṣẹ* (which was used to translate it) derives from a verb *ṣẹ*, meaning to offend against someone, and typically refers to specific acts against another agent—human mostly, but including by extension *oriṣa*—which might excite their retaliation. It implied nothing like an intrinsic disposition of human beings. Indeed, it came much closer to "crime" than to "wickedness," where Yoruba would tend to speak, more concretely, of someone as an *ẹni buburu* [bad person] or as a person of particular moral failings. When missionaries spoke of sin as part of the human condition, it seemed incomprehensible to people who thought in terms of specific social acts. Chief Okan of Badagry, when Marsh preached to him about the danger of dying in his sins, asked if he was not good: did anyone speak badly of him?[112] When Mann challenged a public audience in Ijaye—"Can anyone say he has no sin?"—an old man stepped forward to say he had none. Confusion broke out, and in response to Mann's questions, he said "*his* righteousness consists of having obeyed always his parents, in not hating anybody, having no bad thoughts towards his enemies, never having kidnapped . . ." The best that Mann could then do was to tell him, "Fight not your case with a holy God in heaven."[113] But the most telling case involves none other than the senior Christian convert at Ibadan, James Oderinde. When he knew he was going to die, he specially asked for the prayers of the clergy, that he be forgiven his "past sins before conversion, for after conversion I am not guilty of any known sin," as he put it. At that stage of things, Samuel Johnson was not going to confront the theological innocence of a gallant and steadfast old man, so he merely counseled him "to trust solely in the merits of Christ, rather than on his good works after conversion . . . for we are unprofitable servants."[114]

An apparently striking parallel between the two religions can be seen in some of the myths which explain how the estrangement between God and humankind came about—though the differences are ultimately more revealing. In the Judeo-Christian case, it is Adam's disobedience to God's express command, the archetypal sin, which produces the estrangement, resulting in humanity's expulsion from God's presence in Eden. The Yoruba had no single canonical story like this, but a variety of myths, all with the premise that originally "heaven was very near to the earth, so near that one could stretch up one's hand and touch it."[115] As in the myths of many other African peoples,[116] a human offense—a greedy person helps himself to too much food from heaven, a woman's dirty hand touches the clean face of heaven—leads to a withdrawal of heaven/God from its earlier close contact with earth/humanity. The contrast in the direction of the separation—in the Biblical narrative man has to depart from God, but in the African myths God typically withdraws from his close prior involvement with man on earth—corresponds with differences in the kind of mediation between man and God which is subsequently required. In the Biblical myth, the main result of the Fall is sin, which is addressed through the unique act of mediatory sacrifice performed by God incarnate in Christ. The Yoruba myths of divine withdrawal, however, leave it to humankind to close the gap through acts of sacrifice to the *orisa* who are appointed as their mediators with the Supreme Being. Since they (rather than God) are now immediately responsible for specific earthly events, they are the recipients of sacrifices from human beings.

Little enough of these myths figures in the journals of the CMS agents, yet they were continuously presupposed in exchanges between missionaries and the Yoruba about the proper relations of God and man. If Olorun had not existed for the Yoruba, the missionaries would surely have needed to invent Him, so indispensable was He as a common ground in the encounter of religions. From early on it was the view of missionaries of all races that, as Townsend put it, "in the Negro's mind there is no rival to the one true God, for all their gods are mediators between them and God as they suppose."[117] Even the missionary claim that pagans barely knew the God whom they acknowledged might meet with rebuttal, as by a man whom Moore overheard in a village near Osiele, saying to his friend: "There is not a day past [*sic*] in which we never call on the name of (Olorun) the living God, but the book people [Christians] . . . take the matter of God too much upon themselves as if they only know him."[118] The human need for a mediator was a further area of common ground, and one which brought the disputants closer to the point at issue: which kind of mediator was most pleasing to God. "I told them," said James White in a discussion with a *babalawo* in Lagos, "that their notion of a Supreme Being is pretty far correct, and the necessity of a middleman through whom we can communicate with God . . . [who] should be touched with the feelings of our humanity . . . [and is also] sinless and without spot."[119] The arguments turned on whether, as the Yoruba maintained, the *orisa* were mediators with God or, as the missionaries insisted, their cult amounted to the grievous sin of worshipping the creature rather than the Creator. It is a moot point as to whether ordinary people, when they worshipped their *orisa*, actually felt they were dealing with God, only through a mediator; but this was certainly how the system was rationalized in arguments with missionaries. As a man near a shrine of Ososi in Iganna told Doherty,

"God made us and commanded us to make the petty gods and worship them and send them with sacrifices to him. We do not violate God's laws but we keep them daily."[120]

These arguments often took a highly pragmatic character, in which missionaries sought to exploit the sociological metaphors by which relations between God, man, and the rival mediators were figured. Kefer reports a long discussion with a *babalawo* in Ibadan, the brother of his African assistant Thomas Puddicombe, who felt that his status as a priest of Ifa would stand him in good stead with God, just as his family connection made him no stranger to the mission compound. The conversation went on:

[K] "Well, you think you are, because you are introduced."

[B] "Just so it is with God."

[K] "True, but who can introduce us to God and beg us? Your brother or the servants are fit to beg for you by us, because you are men, they are men and we white people are men too. But none of all men, nor of any creature is fit to be mediator between God and us. Sacrifices and charms can do nothing. There must be a mediator who is like God, who has free access to him, and who is not too high for us men, but who is like us that we can approach him. And now look, these are just the glad tidings we have to tell you, that the Son of God came down from heaven. . . . He then made a full sacrifice for our sins and is now again with his father always making intercessions for us sinners; and now whoever . . . calls upon his name shall surely be saved."

[B] "Good word! but Ifa can do the same. He begs for us."

[K] "Well, if he can beg for you, why do you run away from him and make your sacrifice to Sango and then to Esu, and after all you are still frightened and begin again with Ifa, and when death comes, you are shrinking back from the very thought. Why are you so when your sacrifice is an atonement for your sins and your mediator Ifa introduces you to God?"

[B] "It is so as you say. We have no peace and are always in fear. God will not receive our souls, therefore we try it with all our gods."

[K] "Now, friend, believe me. All who try it with this mediator, they do find peace, which last[s] all their lifetime, and even in the hour of death they are rejoicing in their saviour. This happiness I wish you all Ibadan people and to lead you to this our redeemer, therefore we are here."[121]

Kefer's skillful expression of Christ's role as mediator in the terms of Yoruba politics—clients "begging" their chiefly patrons for support—is repeatedly echoed in the journals, often in locally quite specific ways. At Ibadan in 1855, a *babalawo* told Hinderer that "God is great indeed, but like as Bale [the civil head of Ibadan] has towns under him and in all he has Ajeles (Consul) so God has his Ajeles. They are our Orisas, to them we must look as intercessors."[122] While in Ijaye in 1854, Mann found a highly pertinent local analogy for a Sango devotee who visited his compound:

> If a man is to be beheaded by Are [Kurunmi] but has some hope for re-
> lease, all depending on a proper Mediator, will he send his dog to Are? All
> people cried out: no! I asked whom will he send? Some said a chief: well,
> at least a friend! All said: yes! The man listened to the word without being
> provoked and said, by and by we all must believe your word.[123]

But it is really insufficient to regard this as merely being an analogy. It is rather the case that there was a real continuity in the quality of relations from commoners to chiefs and from men to oriṣa. When a blacksmith at Abeokuta said that the Christians were "too bold" in approaching God directly in their prayers, he was merely generalizing from "secular" political practice: no com-moner went straight to the ọba.[124] For the Yoruba, religion and politics were consubstantial, for their ends were essentially the same: the enhancement of earthly existence.

No indigenous mediator was promoted with such conviction as was Ifa or Orunmila by babalawo. The chief babalawo of Ilesha greeted George Vincent "Orunmila a gbe ọ [Orunmila will support you]," telling him that "Ifa is em-ployed [as a] mediator between God and man to tender the latter's sacrifices and oblations to the former, and conveys blessings in like manner."[125] In their aggrandizement of Ifa as an oriṣa above all other oriṣa, the babalawo made much of Ifa's key role in specifying the sacrifices which the supplicant needed to make (to whatever deity) in order to set herself right. The more Ifa or Orunmila was thus elevated as uniquely the messenger of God, the closer the parallel with Christ came to seem, which paradoxically *helped* the task of mission, since it created more of a niche which the Yoruba might be per-suaded Christ should occupy. So a senior babalawo of Ota, who had gone to the ọlọta's palace to present him with a rare medicinal plant, "then went on to show that Ifa is the Saviour of the World and that he is the medium of communication between God and Man, and that nothing is to be added to or taken from the words of Ifa"; to which White replied "that his . . . asser-tion might hold good if only Jesus Christ were substituted for Ifa."[126] The idea of a substitution or continuation was also in Charles Phillips's mind when he opened the chapel at Ayesan in 1884:

> Preaching from I Timothy 2:5, he "showed them that where the Ifa fails,
> there our Jesus begins. For the Ifa is called 'Orunmila' which fully ren-
> dered means 'Heaven only knows the Mediator', and thus teaches us only
> our need for a mediator. But the word of God declares our Jesus as 'the
> only mediator between God and man.' "[127]

It was especially the African missionaries who took this line of argument, which would mark a decisive step in the inculturation of Christian theology in Yoruba.[128]

In both the Yoruba and the Christian schemes, sacrifice played a central role in the work of mediation, and evangelists made use of the parallels to make intelligible the redemptive sacrifice of Christ. The core idea common to both traditions was that through the offering of blood—the stuff of life—future life could be assured. In what was a standard argument, Müller's coming upon a family at Abeokuta making a sacrifice "gave rise to speak on the all sufficient sacrifice of Christ for sin."[129] This demand for a substitution which hardly made sense outside the Christian plan of redemption was sometimes later supported by a historicist argument which drew parallels—here much more substantial ones—between the blood sacrifices of the Yoruba and of the ancient Jews. In a journal entry which refers to a long talk he had with a friendly *babalawo* about the purpose of sacrifice, Meakin mentions that a ritual he had seen in which blood had been sprinkled on the doorposts of a priest of Sango reminded him of the Jewish Passover practice.[130] He makes nothing more of it. But others, and especially some of the African clergy, developed a general theory—combining Scripture History with a home-grown comparative religion—of how blood sacrifice was superseded by Christ's sacrifice. The "origin of sacrifice" was a stock theme for sermons, but no one seems to have returned to it more insistently than James White. "As our people are grossly addicted to sacrifices," he explained. "I have endeavoured to point out the purpose for the institution of sacrifices, their propriety, legality and their abrogation—their ends having been answered; that they were shadows and that Jesus Christ is the substance of them."[131] He once introduced the subject to rebut a *babalawo*'s claim that God had given different religions to different peoples:

> No, replies White, all human beings descend from one man, Adam, and have fallen away from God. "How came to know you to know of sacrifice but by tradition from our fathers [and have] derived the practice from our great ancestor Ham who witnessed his own father sacrificing even after they had come out of the Ark, and he too derived it from Adam our first parent. The head of every family was a priest. Is it not so with you to this day?" Thus sacrifice is of divine origin. Jesus Christ's is the "true Antitype" of it, the perfect sacrifice which wipes away the need for all other sacrifices.[132]

On a later occasion White drew an even more daring parallel with Yoruba sacrificial practice. Using a print of Christ on the cross as a visual aid while out preaching at Ota, he drew his hearers' attention "to some of their own sacrifices where the victims being opened are expanded whole upon the altar, and pointing to the picture of Christ on the cross, I asked them whether there was not some similarity in the mode of offering the victim." He ended as usual with the all-sufficiency of Christ's atoning sacrifice.[133]

Yet all the emphasis on historical continuities and symbolic parallels, while it no doubt served to make the strange seem more real and familiar to Yoruba audiences, could not in the end conceal the far-reaching differences in the import of Christian teaching on sacrifice. Thus R. S. Oyebode's exchange with Chief *Lejofi* of Ilesha:

> On the subject of sacrifice we proved to him from reason the inefficacy of all their sacrifices before God; and that the only perfect and effectual sacrifice was not within our power, but God in his mercy did it for us in sacrificing His Only Son; and all who believe in him is accepted of God. The man was startled.[134]

And well he might be, since what he was being offered was a concept of sacrifice completely transvalued, one which radically inverted Yoruba religious values. Joseph Smith took things further in a dialogue with a *babalawo* at Isaga:

> [S] "God is our maker and preserver and we ought therefore to worship and serve him."
>
> [B] "True, God is great above all things and we cannot approach a being so great, we offer this and that sacrifice to Ifa, and Ifa for us presents them to God. What more? What sacrifice does God want, and how must we offer it?"
>
> [S] "God does not accept such sacrifices as these, but the sacrifices of God are a broken spirit &c. and to obey is better than sacrifice. God wants our hearts, it is his desire that we should repent of our sins and turn unto him, that we may be pardoned and have everlasting life."
>
> [B] "God made us and gave us the idols to worship him through them."
>
> [S] "No, God made man, and man made the idols, therefore man ought to worship God and the idols ought to worship man."
>
> At this the man and the people seemed rather struck.[135]

At this recurrent kind of *aporia*, missionaries' accounts tend to break off, as if they realized that they had come to a point where, granted the prevailing assumptions of both sides, no further fruitful exchange could take place.

A sacrifice may be viewed as a kind of gift, through which the giver intends to lay an obligation on the recipient which will later be returned in a desired form, so the direction in which it is made is crucially indicative of its social character.[136] Yoruba sacrifices were made by human beings to the *oriṣa* in anticipation of benefits, typically on the advice of a *babalawo* as to what should be offered and to whom. Through sacrifice, people sought to draw the *oriṣa* into a closer relationship with them, just as they might do with chiefs, another kind of superior being, through tributes or presents. The religious relationship thus renewed was entirely within the norms of the community. The perfect and complete sacrifice of Christ, in contrast, works the opposite way: here God puts humanity under a limitless obligation to Him and the relationship stands right beyond the norms of any particular community. Though in both cases life is sacrificed to produce future life in return, the nature of the life sought is quite different. With Yoruba sacrifice it was the life human beings know, the deferral of death; but with Christ's sacrifice, for those who accept it, what is offered is eternal life, transvalued life after death. The earthly test of human acceptance of Christ's sacrifice is readiness to be a "living sacrifice," that is to live according to His example thereafter. Thus the forms of sacrifice in the two religious systems rigorously correspond with their contrasting moral and social character.[137]

The records of the innumerable exchanges that the CMS evangelists engaged in leave the reader in no doubt that on many occasions and at several levels a real dialogue took place. Yet two great paradoxes seem to run through it all, which ensured that often the two parties were talking past, rather than with, one another, and that pragmatic calculation of the benefits of interaction and appropriation played as large a role in them as a desire to engage fully with religious otherness. The first arose from the way by which missionary transvaluation took apparently shared and common symbols and concepts and turned them inside out by transposing them to the other world or the afterlife. A religion which thus inverts prevailing social values acquires thereby great leverage to promote cultural change. The second was the fact that the mission sent out very strong but mixed messages to the Yoruba. On the one hand, its overt religious teaching took this markedly other-worldly, transvaluatory form—which rendered it peculiarly baffling (not to say absurd) to those who were well or securely placed in society. Yet on the other, this message was preached by men in enviable possession of techniques and artifacts that enhanced earthly existence, and so, in the Yoruba view, merited serious religious attention. For decades to come these contradictions would be worked at and worried over by Yoruba Christians.

7

ENGAGING WITH ISLAM

Aye l'a ba 'fa, aye l'a ba 'male,
ọsan gangan ni 'gbagbọ wọle de

We met Ifa in the world, we met Islam in the world,
but it was high noon before Christianity arrived.

This well-known adage encapsulates two essential features of the religious
situation of nineteenth-century Yorubaland: first, that it was a triangular encounter of religions in which the missionaries found themselves; and second, that while Christianity was an entirely novel addition to the Yoruba religious repertory when it was introduced in the 1840s, Islam and the
traditional religion had known one another for a long time. So we should
not treat "traditional" religion as a purely indigenous cultural baseline, an
entity wholly independent of Islam. Ifa divination, both in its form and procedures and in the traditions of its origins, shows traces of early Muslim
influence. The adage seems to have an Oyo provenance, and certainly does
not apply to the eastern and southeastern forest regions, where Islam only
came with Oyo (or in parts of the far northeast, Nupe) migrants and was
sometimes preceded by Christianity. As already argued, the contrasts between
discourse about God reported from the central/western and from the southeastern parts of the country strongly suggest that, in the former area, prevailing conceptions of God and of the afterlife show definite traces of Islamic
influence.[1]

The co-presence of *two* world religions, while it complicates the task of description, facilitates that of explanation, for it provides us with something of like kind to compare Christianity with. It enables us to discern more finely what it was about Christianity that the Yoruba responded to: for example, how far it was as a scriptural monotheism or as the white man's religion. The evolving dialectic of similarity and difference, of alliance and rivalry, between Christianity and Islam was played out before a "pagan" audience which offered a vast pool of potential converts, so was powerfully molded by *its* rules of the game, which were simply the norms and criteria of Yoruba society at large. Islam's long prior existence in the Oyo Yoruba heartland had produced some contrasting outcomes for its relations with Christianity. On the one hand, it smoothed the way for the Christian project of incarnating itself in Yoruba culture by its own earlier introduction of a number of concepts belonging to a Judaic religion of the Book, many of which a not-very-grateful Christianity proceeded to appropriate for itself. On the other, it achieved a degree of practical adjustment to Yoruba social norms and cultural values that led some Christians to hail it as a more genuinely African religion than Christianity,[2] and others, rather more numerous, to treat it as little better than the idolatry it opposed.

In placing initial emphasis on the Yoruba context in which Islam and Christianity met and the Yoruba criteria by which they were assessed, we must not neglect that they also faced one another in the light of their own particular historicities; that is, of the principles of their self-realization over time, entertained most consciously by their clerical professionals. The historicity of a world religion, cumulatively acquired (but laid down most definitively in its earliest decades and centuries), is not a thing to be unilaterally imposed in new settings but will still tend to make itself felt over time through negotiation with local circumstances often uncongenial to it. When Christianity and Islam met in West Africa, a frontier zone for both of them, their encounter was deeply colored by their prior understandings of one another. Christianity had long been apprehended by Islam as precursor, a religion encompassed in thought and substantially in practice too, as Islam in its early centuries overran Christian lands and put pressure on their populations, who provided most of its early converts in the eastern and southern Mediterranean regions.[3] Islam was manifest to Christianity as heresy, a subversion of its central doctrine and of the integrity of its Scriptures that it was necessary to expel and push back. By the nineteenth century, these perceptions had not disappeared, but they had been overlaid by a later contingency of Christianity's history: its intimate association with Western Europe's empowerment through science and capitalism and its rise to world hegemony. As a result, Christian missionaries to Yorubaland, where Islam was already a presence, could aspire to reverse the earlier pattern: here Islam was the precursor, so Christianity could be the successor in the elevation of the country from idolatry and backwardness.

The other great contrast between the historicities of Islam and Christianity

concerns their respective cultural strategies, which again derived from civi-
lizational values established in their early years. Graduating to an imperial
ideology within a few years of its founder's death, Islam fused civilization with
religion on the basis of the language of its revelation, Arabic. Christianity,
in contrast, took three centuries on the path to political power, so was unable to fuse religion and civilization (which for long afterward remained stubbornly pagan). Without the secular instruments of power, the diffusion of
the Word depended on its translation into the vernacular languages of the
Classical world: "We do hear them speak in our tongues the wonderful works
of God," said the heteroglot Jews on the day of Pentecost (Acts 2:11). Where
Latin, Syriac, and Gothic led, Yoruba, Setswana, and Luganda would eventually follow. As Lamin Sanneh has tellingly argued, it is the compulsion to
translate its Word which has most distinguished the cultural path of Christianity in West Africa from Islam.[4] The wider import of this was long unappreciated, because Christianity seemed so bound into the whole overwhelming weight of European culture presented with colonialism. But the
connection between Christianity and the European languages of colonial
modernity was contingent compared with the integral bonds between Islam
and its Arabic expression. Even though for centuries West African Islam existed in practice as a complex mix of Islamic and indigenous cultural traits,
Arabic remained absolutely privileged as its medium of religious communication, perhaps the more so because so few Muslims understood it. Koranic
schools started their pupils on memorizing the Arabic text of the Koran, with
an understanding of the language to come later for a diligent few; mission
schools in Yorubaland typically began with the Yoruba Primer (*Iwe ABD*), and
progressed to reading the Bible in the mother tongue. And while Islam, in
putting down local cultural roots, mostly introduced Arabic-derived terms
for its religious concepts, Christianity's inclination was to seek out vernacular expressions for its concepts (and in Yoruba often ended up using terms
which Muslims had already introduced).

The historical courses of the two exogenous monotheisms, as they have
worked their way into the fabric of West African life, show corresponding
differences. Both exhibit a mixture of the local and the universal in their religious idioms and practices, a mix which some of their members see as a
temporary compromise on the path to a better determination of how the
religion should be locally realized. Once Islam had passed from being the
exclusive preserve of the trader-strangers, who had introduced it into the indigenous population, it typically became less scriptural and Arabized, more
responsive to local demand for manipulative techniques which also embodied
"pagan" elements, and reconciled to social practices of an un-Islamic character. It was then subject to pressure from clerics, sometimes with the forceful support of self-consciously Muslim rulers, demanding reform in a scriptural direction. In the terms of Fisher's useful model, Islam moves through
a trajectory of three stages: quarantine, mixing, and reform.[5] These stages

are not rigid, and one society might yield examples of all three orientations at the same time. The Yoruba Islam encountered by the missions was overwhelmingly and conspicuously of the "mixing" kind, with "reform" only at its edges. To start with, the normative model for reform was provided by the official, post-jihad Islam of the Sokoto Caliphate, whose bastion in Yorubaland was the emirate of Ilorin. Only toward the end of the century did another model for reform start to emerge, this time among Muslims in Lagos and Abeokuta. Dubbed "modernizing reform" by Ryan, it sought to move Yoruba Muslims toward a version of their religion that was doubly universalist—more scriptural and Arabic, but also more attuned to the modern world.[6] This latter goal was above all triggered by the challenge of Christianity, which as "the white man's religion" appeared to nineteenth-century Yoruba as the epitome of modernity.

Yet what these modernizing reformers saw as an area where Islam needed to catch up on its rival presented a diametrically opposed problem to Christianity. Where the internal critics of Yoruba Islam were most anxious to upgrade its Islamic credentials, the most persistent demand on Yoruba Christianity has been to prove its African ones. All too well identified with European culture and for many decades less well integrated into Yoruba society then Islam was, Christianity had its task of making itself truly a *Yoruba* religion well cut out. To translate the Bible into Yoruba was not only just the start but was itself the template of Christianity's whole project of realizing itself as an African religion. Before the court of Yoruba opinion, both religions had to meet two main criteria of value: they had to offer means for individual and collective empowerment and they had to offer attractive, viable identities. These two criteria were not always or wholly compatible, and were variably met by the competing monotheisms, which had to find the best trade-offs between them that they could manage.

ISLAM AS PRECURSOR

The theory that Islam first came to the Yoruba down the Niger from the northwest rather than from Hausaland, long suspected on the basis of the word *Imale* ("Malian," "Muslim"), now has clinching support from Stefan Reichmuth's careful study of Songhai loan-words in Yoruba.[7] The thirty-two words so identified include some of the basic terms of the Yoruba Muslim lexicon: *alufa* or *alfa* ("Muslim cleric" or "mallam,"[8] to use the Hausa-derived word now current in Nigerian English), *kewu* ("read Arabic"), *hantu* ("Arabic writing"), *walaa* ("writing board"), *tira* ("amulet"), *saraa* ("alms"), *girigiri* or *jingiri* ("praying enclosure"), *aawe* ("the Ramadan fast"), *iwasu* ("preaching, sermon"). Most of these words ultimately derive from Arabic, but their form shows that they passed through Songhai rather than Hausa. Exactly when these imports occurred is not clear, but it may have been as early as the late sixteenth century, while the *Alafin* were in exile at Igboho and closely involved with Borgu to the north. By the eighteenth century, however, the dominant Muslim influence was coming from the Hausa and other Nigerian peoples (whether as Oyo slaves or as traders) reaching as far as the coast.[9] When Yoruba started to become Muslims is unclear, but clearly their number was substantial by the 1810s, when a contingent of them joined the revolt in 1817 which led to the establishment of Fulani Muslim rule at Ilorin.[10] Ilorin became the hinge that articulated Yorubaland and the states of the Sokoto Caliphate to the north, a major seat of Islamic learning and, except for Lagos, the most cosmopolitan of the Yoruba towns.[11] Missionaries were not allowed to settle there, but on their occasional visits they met traders from as far as Tunis and Constantinople.[12] Ilorin's *alufa* were of highly diverse ethnic origins, but mostly from within today's Nigeria, so Yoruba Islam became subject more to Hausa and Fulani influence.

One might expect that Islam would be distrusted or feared for its role in the overthrow of Oyo and the subsequent upheavals, to the detriment of its spread further south. Muslims did encounter some hostility, even persecution;[13] but Islam was too well established among the Oyo Yoruba not to spread southward with them into the forest belt. It continued to be carried by Muslim slaves of northern origin. In some cases it was promoted by repatriates from Sierra Leone and Brazil, converted there as Christians were;[14] and its reputation as a source of powerful spiritual techniques, if anything enhanced by the successes of the jihadists, remained high among non-Muslims, giving a point of entry for its *alufa*.

The western area, from the Oke Ogun past Abeokuta into Egbado, through which the trade route had run from Old Oyo to the coast, saw the growth of local Muslim communities from before midcentury—at Ilaro led by a scion of the Oyo royal lineage.[15] There was Muslim influence in New Oyo right from its beginning, despite the *Alafin* Atiba's repudiation of his prior Muslim profession and his recreation of the mystique of the monarchy: in 1857, a CMS missionary refers to the hostility of two of the chiefs who "had been taught by Mohamedan alufas."[16] Iseyin, an old provincial town of Oyo, had supported the Muslim side in the civil wars of the 1810s and 1820s and escaped destruction.[17] It later attracted refugees from Old Oyo, and by the 1850s, Muslims were reported to be very numerous there, with many mosques and a quarter of their own called Imale-fe-alafia [Muslims love peace];[18] There was even some pressure on the *Aseyin* to declare himself a Muslim. Iseyin was also a center of Arabic education and attracted Muslims from a wide area: a prominent follower of ex-king Kosoko of Lagos was an exile there in 1853,[19] and a son of the *Are* Latosisa of Ibadan spent four years there at Koranic study in the 1870s.[20] But these movements, and the subsequent influence of Islam, still varied from town to town according to local circumstances. Though it lay much closer to Ilorin than Iseyin or New Oyo, Ogbomoso was described in 1877 as "a very intensely heathen town," with only three mosques (compared to twelve in the much smaller New Oyo).[21]

Floods of Oyo migrants moved southeast to the greater security of the forest towns, radically affecting their ethnic balance and eventually their religious complexion. Iwo, formerly a town within the orbit of Ife, swelled with refugees and by 1858 had a Muslim *Oluwo*, whose palace acquired the distinctive high gables (*kobi*) of the royal Oyo style. The war-chiefs were strongly Muslim, with *alufa* in attendance, and the turnout at the end of Ramadan was spectacular.[22] Iwo would become one of the most Muslim of the larger Yoruba towns. Further east at Ede, the accession in the late 1850s of a young king (*Timi*) who was a keen Muslim had produced a spurt of new Muslim adherents.[23] "Many priests are employed now to teach especially the young," wrote Hinderer, adding that most people were still pagan and the Muslims were unlettered—the sort of situation which must have been standard in the early years of Islam's existence in Yoruba communities.

Islam advanced more slowly in Ibadan than in some of its subordinate towns.[24] Official policy kept its reservations about Muslims into the 1850s: when the above-mentioned Muslim *Timi* of Ede was installed, he was given Ifa to worship by the Ibadan chiefs, but threw it away and reverted to Islam when he got to Ede, thereby incurring the suspicion of his Ibadan overlords. *Başorun* Oluyole, Ibadan's first paramount (c. 1836–1850), was remembered for his demolition of the first central mosque at Oja'ba, but under his short-lived successor, the *Bale* Opeagbe (1850–1851), the Muslim body began to receive recognition.[25] It was comprised not only of Hausa settlers and other Muslim strangers but also of a growing number of Oyos, including some rising chiefs. On his exploratory visit in 1851, Hinderer met the *Bale* in the company of a large number of *alufa*: "He seems to countenance them much and engages them to pray for him," he and his fellow chiefs (few of them yet Muslim) replying *"Amin!"* to their Arabic prayers.[26] When he returned in 1853, he found the Muslims so advanced in numbers and influence that they had persuaded many chiefs that "their lives would be cut short" if the white man was allowed into Ibadan.[27] It did not come to this, but there were other signs of conflict and suspicion as the Muslims grew in influence in the late 1850s.[28] Islam's standing was decisively confirmed when the *Are* Latosisa—his Muslim name was Momo, a contraction of "Mohammed"—assumed the paramountcy in 1871. Yet despite his personal allegiance, he did not forget that he still ruled over a town the vast bulk of whose people held to the *orişa* cults, and he was also prepared to act as a patron to the Christians.

Islam also found an early footing outside Oyo country. There were Egba Muslims before Abeokuta's foundation in about 1830: from his name, Yisa of Itoko, the first pan-Egba *Balogun*, must have been one, and it seems likely that Islam was part of an Oyo style of things, like the new military organization which Yisa headed.[29] Of all the Egba sections which settled at Abeokuta, Owu was the most precocious in Islam, and land for mosques was granted by Sodeke in its earliest days.[30] On his arrival in 1846, Townsend was struck by the many Muslims, which he took as a sign of the religious tolerance of the Egba.[31] Yet as at Ibadan, Islam had not been uncontested at Abeokuta, as Crowther was told during the persecution of Christians in 1849:

> The Mohammedans were sadly troubled by the [Ifa] priests prior to our arrival, [and] their mosques were several times attempted to be pulled down because the Egbas were forsaking Ifa and embracing their religion which the babbalawos did not like to see; [but] since our coming here the Mohammedans have been left alone and the malice of the priests are now directed against us.[32]

Because power in Abeokuta was so diffused among the townships and between the different categories of chiefs, Islam's advance there seems to have been more gradual and piecemeal, less marked by distinct stages linked to the rise of prominent individuals than in the more unified Oyo towns.

Of the two principal vectors of Islam—displaced Oyo, and traders and/or slaves from the non-Yoruba Muslim north (Hausa, Fulani, Nupe, and Kanuri)—it was the latter who had the greatest impact in Lagos.[33] An additional element of some importance was Muslim returnees from Sierra Leone or Brazil. There had been Muslim Hausa in Lagos since the late eighteenth century, but Islam only started to advance among indigenous Lagosians in the late 1840s, so that the movement to Islam was here more nearly synchronous with the operations of Christian missions. It was also deeply linked to the dynastic politics of Lagos. Kosoko, the king of Lagos from 1845 till his deposition by the British in 1851 in favor of his uncle Akitoye, had favored the Muslims. Two of the most prominent of them, the war-chiefs Ajinia (*Balogun* of the Muslims)[34] and Osodi Tapa (a Nupe former slave), were Kosoko's followers; and when Kosoko took refuge at Epe, an Ijebu town on the Lagoon some seventy miles east of Lagos, the Imam of Lagos, a Hausa called Salu, went with him. When Kosoko's people returned in 1862, they were solidly Muslim; and over the next three decades they provided the base upon which Islam would gain the allegiance of the majority of indigenous Lagosians.[35]

So virtually everywhere Christian missionaries went, in northern, central, and western Yorubaland, they encountered Muslims. The east was different: the first Muslims at Ilesha were ex-slaves from Lagos or the Oyo areas who returned in the 1860s, the same time that the first Ijesha Christians did;[36] while as late as 1875, the only Muslims in Ondo were two or three slaves of the *Lisa*'s.[37] Though highly visible, before midcentury Muslims were rarely more than a small minority of the local population, but their *alufa* had a respected niche in the system of religious provision, and by the 1850s some Muslims were rising to positions of secular power from which Islam's influence could be extended. Less obvious was a more diffuse and sometimes unacknowledged influence of Islam. Just as Yoruba Islam presupposed or adopted many features of local culture, so too it put its mark on the expression and practice of Yoruba life at large, well beyond the ranks of confessed Muslims. Thus there arose a degree of "pre-adaptation" to Islam, a phenomenon that might be compared to the bow wave that a large vessel pushes out in front of itself as it cleaves the water.

The elements that entered Yoruba culture over a long period from Islamic sources were not all of a piece. A prime site of some of the most consequential of early borrowing was Ifa divination itself; so it is an irony indeed that this provenance was forgotten so that, as in the adage quoted at the head of this chapter, Ifa could be regarded as the very flagship of traditional non-Islamic religion. Some adopted elements were very directly connected with Islam itself, while some were adopted from those peoples who were its bearers, but we cannot assume that this distinction was recognized by the Yoruba, or that traits deemed "secular" or "accidental" to Islam were less important to its spread. One example, not as trivial as it may seem, was observed by Townsend at Abeokuta in 1847: "Mahomedan costume [turban, loose over-garment and voluminous embroidered trousers] is become very fashionable with the young and gay. . . . This dress is by no means put on as a religious peculiarity."[38]

While Townsend may have been right about the lack of a specific "religious" motive underlying the adoption of Muslim dress, he overlooked its possible religious consequences; for it must have led its wearers to be (very literally) *seen* as Muslims and thus made it more likely that they would internalize this external identification. Here we have an intrinsically secular item that nevertheless signifies Islam. Other cultural items, terms, or concepts, had lost the Islamic trademark that they probably once had and had become part of the religiously unmarked habitus of Yoruba society, such as the terminology relating to horse equipment and various trade goods which came from Songhai with the early *Imale,* or such diverse (and presumptively later) borrowings from Arabic through Hausa as *alubọsa* [onion], *aṣiri* [secret] and *anfani* [benefit, advantage].[39]

Our particular concern here is the conceptual bridgehead offered to Christianity by the prior religious, ethical, and cosmological influence of Islam. The strategy for Christianity was to take full advantage of the semantic ground prepared by Islam while at the same preserving both the fittingness and (where possible) the distinctiveness of the Yoruba rendition of its own system of concepts. Least problematic were ethical concepts introduced by Islam that had become completely naturalized, two of the most widely used and essential to Christian discourse being *alafia* [peace, well-being] and *anu* [mercy, regret]. When it came to more specifically religious concepts, there were more complex choices: to choose an existing Yoruba term, or to create a neologism? If the former, to adopt a Muslim, a pagan, or a religiously neutral term; if the latter, to introduce a European term or to coin a new one from Yoruba elements? The preferred option was to adopt an existing Yoruba term where possible; and then, if there was a choice of terms, recognizing the common stance of the monotheisms against idolatry, to prefer Muslim to pagan ones.[40]

So in one of his boldest decisions, Crowther adopted the term *alufa* [Muslim cleric], not only for "priest" throughout his translation of the Bible (most strikingly, perhaps, in the discussion of Christ's priesthood in Hebrews 7), but for a Christian clergyman or pastor.[41] This was in preference to *aworo* [possession priest of an *orişa*], which was not even used for a prophet or medium of a god in places where it would have suited rather well (such as for the prophets of Baal in I Kings 18, whose actions in cutting themselves with knives and calling down fire might well recall Sango's devotees). For "prophet," another Muslim term was used: *woli* [saint[42]], which would come to have by far its widest Yoruba currency to refer to Christian Aladura prophets. Two of the basic categories of Christian religious action—prayer and preaching—were also expressed in Muslim terms. In his 1843 *Vocabulary*, derived from Yoruba speakers in Freetown, Crowther had translated "prayer" as *irong* (=*irun*), the Muslim term for communal prayer; but by 1850, in his translation of *The Book of Common Prayer*, he had decided that its specific connotations could not be transferred to Christian practice and settled on another Muslim term, *adura*, which denotes individual petitionary prayer.[43] The word for "preaching, sermon" (*iwasu*) was one of the early Songhai loan-words, and it is still the term used by Christians; the modern Muslim term for preaching is *waasi*, also derived from the Arabic *wa'z*, but instead through Hausa.[44] The inference has to be that during the past century, Yoruba Muslim usage has adapted to Hausa influence, while the old Islamic term has been preserved in Christianity.

The avoidance of pagan associations was clearly an overriding concern, so that in translating "power" Crowther preferred *agbara*, a more secular notion [strength, force], over *aşę*, which was used in relation to the efficacy of the *orişa*.[45] For the petition of the Lord's Prayer, "but deliver us from evil," Crowther could not find an indigenous noun that was sufficiently general and absolute to render the full meaning of "evil," and we might have expected him to adopt *l'ọwọ Eşu* [from (the hand of) Esu], since Esu was almost always (even if inaccurately) used by missionaries, both African and European, as the equivalent of Satan or the Devil. But he did not do this, whether for ethnographic accuracy or because he judged it anachronistic that the name of an *orişa* should appear in the Bible.[46] Instead he decided on *tulasi*, a Hausa loan-word meaning "trouble," which in a later edition was changed to the more telling *bilisi* (<Hausa for "Satan"<Arabic *iblis*<Greek *diabolos*), thus getting to the same semantic outcome by a more acceptable route.[47] Sometimes he seems to have felt that even the Muslim term did not suffice, as with *maleka* [angel], to which he preferred an imported neologism, *angeli*—perhaps because ordinary Yoruba Muslims sometimes treated *maleka* as functionally equivalent to *orişa*.[48] But there was no hesitation in adopting the Muslim term *keferi* to denote "heathen."

As the lexicon of Yoruba Muslims diffused into the vocabulary of a people still overwhelmingly non-Muslim, so did Muslim religious conceptions—

though not automatically, since a counteractive process could also occur: Islamic words could get infused with a pagan content, as in the case of *maleka,* Islamic angels re-imagined as *oriṣa.* The most important of those conceptions were of God as a Creator distinct from all other beings and of separate heavens for the good and the bad after death (*ọrun rere* and *ọrun apadi*). An Islamic source for these ideas is implied both by their inconsistency with so much else of Yoruba religious thought and by their absence from (or novelty in) those parts of eastern Yorubaland, especially Ondo, where we know there was no Muslim presence when the missions arrived. What is hard to say is just how current these ideas, and the practices associated with them, were beyond the ranks of Muslims. In 1878 an Egba war-chief was described as no longer making sacrifices to Ifa or the *oriṣa;* he just prayed to God and killed a ram once a year; he showed its skin—it was the twelfth year he had done it.[49] The killing of a ram is a feature of the Muslim *Ileya* festival—commemorative of Abraham's near-sacrifice of Isaac—but the chief was not a Muslim. He just said he did it "because I know God is the source of all goodness," and now he wanted to know how to pray in the name of Jesus.

But a more telling case concerns Akodu, who held the major pan-Egba military title of *Seriki.* He was not, as far as I know, recognized as a Muslim. J. F. King called on him in 1868, to find him sick and sententious over the Outbreak (*Ifọle*) against the missionaries the previous year:

> By his expressions during our conversation, he appears to feel the hand of God upon him in his illness taking vengeance, but he prayed that God may in mercy spare him. . . . God shall call all those who have done those evils [the Outbreak] to judgment. . . . There are two books in the hands of God, in one He writes the names of the wicked; and in the other the names of the good, and that even now God is visiting the wicked from house to house in Abeokuta. . . . One of the attributes he gave to God was "*Ọbangiji, ọba alanu, ọba mimọ, ti ko ni ẹẹri* [Obangiji, merciful king, holy king, who has no filth]."[50]

Apart from the obviously untraditional notion of the two books of judgment—which, however, Akodu relates to punishment in this life, not the next—the most instructive feature of the story is how God is addressed. In four distinct ways it bespeaks Muslim influence. (1) *Ọbangiji* appears as a name of God which King vaguely renders "Lord," probably because it does not make obvious sense in Yoruba, despite the initial element *Ọba-* [king]. In fact, it must surely be a corruption of the Hausa *Ubangiji* [lit. "Master of the house"], used as an epithet of God.[51] (2) The repeated invocation of God as a king is very typical of Yoruba Islam.[52] (3) The epithet *alanu* [merciful] not only incorporates one of the early Songhai loan-words but echoes the standard Muslim address to God as "the Compassionate, the Merciful," known in Yoruba as the *Bisimillahi.* (4) The reiterated references to God as "holy" and clean are again highly typical of Islam.

The last of these bears on the translation of a pivotal text of Yoruba Christianity. When Crowther gave his first Yoruba sermon, in Freetown on January 9, 1844, he preached prophetically from Luke 1:35, "That holy thing which shall be born of thee shall be called the Son of God."[53] In an improvised orthography which looks uncouth to modern eyes, he rendered this as: *"Ohung ohworh ti a o bih ni inoh reh a o ma kpe li Omoh Olorung,"* in contrast to the version which would eventually appear in the Yoruba Bible: *"Ohun mimọ ti a o ti inu rẹ bi, Ọmọ Ọlọrun li a o ma pe e."* It is less the differences of orthography or word order than the translation of the key term "holy" which crucially distinguishes the two versions. Already in his Yoruba *Vocabulary,* published the year before, which includes a translation of the Lord's Prayer, he had acknowledged the lack of an exact Yoruba equivalent for the Greek word *hagiasthētō* ["let it be made holy," "hallowed be"]. His first thought was *ohworh* (in modern orthography *ọwọ*), meaning "respect, honour," but this, he felt, "conveys no idea whatever of setting apart for sacred or holy uses."[54] Later he settled on *mimọ* as the best general word for "holy," which is an adjective derived from the verb *mọ*, meaning "to be clean," and still means "clean" in a secular sense as well as "holy." This rather large semantic shift involved adopting a complex of meanings—holiness, purity, ritual cleansing, and so forth— that were strongly emphasized by Muslims in relation to their own faith.

ISLAM OBSERVED

Unsurprisingly, the CMS agents have much less to say—indeed very little at all—about what went on inside Muslim gatherings (at mosques, Koranic schools, prayer meetings, the private consultations of *alufa*) than about their public appearances and the interface with non-Muslims. They also place a heavy stress on the pragmatic or "magical" side of Islamic rituals; and while this is strongly compatible with the ethos of *orisa* worship and may be expected to have been salient in a popular and, for most of the Muslims the missionaries encountered, a newly adopted Islam, its ethical and theological features are underplayed. Or rather, they appear more often in a polemical or defensive discourse provoked by Christian evangelists than as aspects or implications of reported practice. While most exploration of the social consequences of particular religions has been through their ethical impact,[55] this tends only to emerge in the long term; so it seems unavoidable to start, as the Yoruba did, from the public and pragmatic faces of Islam.

The *alufa* were always impressive when as a group they attended on the *ọba* and chiefs of a town. The most formidable display was at Ilorin, where Islam was the official ideology: some thirty *alufa*, "a fierce and proud looking set of people," sat by the Emir when he received Adolphus Mann.[56] They could be almost as prominent at the courts of "pagan" kings, such as the *Alaketu,* who at Gollmer's visit in 1859 kept turning to a "great mallam who styles himself 'sherriff', a venerable looking Hausa man."[57] While on a visit to Okeho in the Oke Ogun in 1875, Samuel Doherty witnessed the arrival of an *alufa* from the interior:

> The *alufa* asked the king for lodging, but was told to go and lodge with the Muslims in the town; he said that last time he'd stayed with the *Balogun* [the war-chief]. He then sat down in the open air, and said that it was the practice of Muslims to pray before salutation. "He now commenced his whispering prayers [in Arabic] and in conclusion made all present to rub their faces with their hands and repeat aloud 'lafia, lafia,' peace, peace." When the prayers were over, the people were to strike the ground with both hands. He then told the people to bring a goat, a sheep and a covering cloth, "for me to make you a serviceable charm which will exalt you above your enemies and make your name renown[ed]." When he asked the king for a bearer to accompany him to Iseyin, the King said it was too much, but he would give him at least some of it, lest the charm was turned against him.[58]

This brief episode in a small, remote town illustrates several key features of Islam's self-insertion at the public level in Yoruba towns. The *alufa* seeks to establish links with the local authorities and offers powerful techniques for the purposes of state, especially its military needs. He entirely accepts local criteria of need, but offers specifically Islamic means to meet them, and on this basis seeks to set up a pattern of reciprocal exchange between holy man and ruler. The people are induced to share in Muslim religious practice without coercion, yet the presumed power of the *alufa*'s charms makes him feared, which allows him to press his terms in the exchange.

So community leaders came to regard the purchase of the spiritual powers of the *alufa* as a necessary item of public expenditure. They might be invited in to call off excessive rain,[59] or to give prophylaxis against fires, or to stop epidemics.[60] Abnormal astral phenomena—an eclipse of the moon at Iseyin, a comet at Ota—led to anxieties which the *alufa* were felt particularly able to assuage: the *Aseyin* accepted their request for a goat, five heads of cowries, and lots of kola "to make an offering to God as he is not pleased with him, for if he is pleased with him, such sign [the eclipse] might be not seen in the cloud in his days."[61] In these cases, the *alufa* were engaged in a very similar spirit as *babalawo* and other religious specialists were. Indeed, both might be employed for the same project, as when a minor Egba war-chief consulted both Ifa and an *alufa* before going off to raid the Ijebu farms for slaves.[62] Just as the *alufa* would offer their services to anyone—with no evident prejudice against pagan chiefs or rulers or partiality for an Islamic state such as Ilorin against its enemy Ibadan—so too their pagan clients treated them with pragmatic calculation. Kurunmi, for example, paid them for the prayers they said for him and bought charms from them, but when an *alufa* from Oyo was caught making bad charms against Ijaye, did not hesitate to have him put to death—but was circumspect in the manner of it, since it would have been dangerous to shed a holy man's blood.[63]

The prevalence of war gave great occasion for the *alufa*'s services. At a public meeting in an Egbado town in 1878, "much was [said] . . . of the power of Mohammedan charms employed by the Ibadans, and which are believed to have acted as a spell upon Egbas and confused them. A Mohammedan priest presented a counter sacrifice."[64] They might even have had in mind the charm (costing a slave) which was made by the Imam of Iseyin for the *Balogun* of Ibadan, Ajayi Ogboriefon, before the attack on the Ilorin camp at the battle of Ikirun earlier that year.[65] When the Dahomeans were much on Egba minds in 1851, the leading Egba chief, Sagbua, commissioned charms to "tie war," that is, to restrain their enemies, from a Muslim Brazilian returnee.[66] In 1884, the Egba were reported to have given the Muslims 2,000 bags of cowries "to tie the Ibadans at Kiriji"; and at a large meeting held to discuss it, a fabulous precedent was cited to justify the power of the *alufa*:

> Musa [Moses] was a great conqueror. One day he raised a war to destroy a town and in this town was a mother of Mohammed's wife; and she begged her husband that Moses might be prevented from taking that town. The husband raised a subscription . . . 200 bags of cowries [which] was given to a Mohammedan priest of high reputation who prayed to God to confuse Moses that he may not know the town and where he came from. This prayer was said to be heard and Moses had to wander in the wilderness for 40 years, at the end of which Moses asked God if this strange wandering was from Him? But if it be the hand of man, I pray thee Father to blot out the name of that person from the book of life. This prayer was also said to be heard.
>
> One day an antelope came from the bush and entered the town; in vain did people try to kill it, but [it] went straight to this Mohammedan priest. He seeing the daring animal forcing its way toward him, he stretched forth his hand in defence—down he goes and turned to an antelope, and so both ran to the bush. And thus will they deal with the Ibadans at Kiriji![67]

This strange story gives us an unusual insight into the thought-world of popular Yoruba Islam, of Muslims who were still deeply imbued with the outlook of their old religious background. In putting forward a precedent for the mystical power of the *alufa*, it does exactly what the Ifa verses recited by a *babalawo* would do. Moses appears like an Ibadan warlord of the period, as if planning to attack an Ekiti town. The story of the Hebrews' wandering in the wilderness is radically re-signified in a timeless cultural bricolage, where Mohammed becomes the contemporary of Moses. Yet Mohammed himself figures much less prominently than the "Mohammedan priest" or *alufa*, whose powerful prayers to God enable the warrior Moses to be checked. But the real sting of the story is kept for the end, where the *alufa* changes into an antelope, a creature of the bush: in other words, he becomes as an *oriṣa*!

The principal means of the *alufa*'s spiritual power were three—prayer, charms, and a kind of offering called *saraa*—which should be regarded as falling in a series rather than as wholly discrete entities. Charms or amulets (*tira*) were in essence materializations of prayer, since they typically consisted of pieces of paper on which prayers and invocations were written in Arabic, sometimes accompanied by symbolic substances, sewn into a small leather packet. One amulet of Kurunmi's had the invocation *Bisimillahi* written some 80–100 times, with names of God and of prophets such as Abraham set out in lined squares.[68] A woman's *tira* which James White opened had "May God preserve you" written seven times, the paper then wrapped around with black and white thread before being sewn up in leather.[69]

Compare with these the one substantial example we are given of the spontaneous prayer of a Muslim, the chief of the small refuge settlement of Bolorunpelu north of Abeokuta:

> O God of Glory, God of Mercy, who reignest [*sic*] kings, sets one up and abases the other, be please[d] to be with me Ajayi. . . . If any man or woman, black or yellow[70], tall or short, or of whatever description, seek after my hurt by the interposition of angels, old people or my deceased father, compound that person, kick him to the ground, rub his lips to the ground, bore a hole through his lips and tie them to the roof of the house. Give his head a good slapping and make himself to become as a dog to which thou hast given tail and class him among the dumb and senseless. Give me the gown of renown which thou didst give to my late father and make me to become greater than my father. Deku Allah, Deku Allah, Deku Allah. Misimilahi, Misimilahi, Misimilahi. Alahaududulai, Alahaududulai, Alahaududulai.[71]

This prayer combines the name and epithets of God and the repeated Arabic formulas which were written into charms with a set of petitions which also shed light on the spirit in which charms were used. The ferocity of the chief's imprecations, far more impressive than his request for personal glory, forcefully conveys that feeling of embattled encompassment by enemies, enemies who might be anyone at all, which was so much a part of the nineteenth-century Yoruba life-world. The main purpose of amulets, too, was to protect one from one's enemies. Muslim though he was, the chief had lost little of the pagan sense of dangerous mystical powers: angels, elders, and ancestors. What the text refers to as "angels" can only have been *maleka* in Yoruba, which as we have seen was used as an Islamized version of *orisa*, a force of morally ambivalent power.

By far the most complex term in the series is *saraa*. Deriving from the Arabic *sadaqa*, its original meaning was "alms," which it can still bear in Yoruba, especially when it takes the form of a meal offered to the community as a form of thanksgiving to God. But from instances of the word in use in the CMS journals—where it appears more frequently than any other term of the Yoruba Muslim vocabulary except *alufa*—its most common reference in the nineteenth century was something much closer to "sacrifice."[72] A *babalawo*, interrupted while making a sacrifice to Ifa, explains it as "saraha fun Olorun (a sacrifice to God)."[73] In similar vein, a man asks Samuel Johnson, while out preaching, whether God required "sara, gift"—by implication, as the *orisa* needed sacrifice.[74] Then there are cases where individuals are reported as offering or "making" *saraa* in order to obtain the same kind of benefits which one sacrificed to the *orisa* for: a quarter chief at Ibadan speaks of a "great sara given for riches and long life"; and the *Are* Latosisa, before leaving Ibadan for the war camp at Kiriji in 1880, gives presents "perhaps so prescribed by the head [of the] Mahommedans whom we met with him [who] also asked for himself two gowns, white and black, to complete his saras (gifts) to the easy prey over his enemies."[75] So Gollmer described the 15 shillings' worth of cowries given by the *Alaketu* to the Muslims as being "in virtue like a heathen sacrifice."

This assimilation of *saraa* to pagan sacrifices must have been especially compelling where the offerings took the form, not of just of money, but of animals and other material items, some of which would have been used for sacrificial offerings. And since prayer would always be added to these offerings to produce their effect, they resembled charms, which also combined written prayers with symbolic substances. Yet *saraa* did not entirely lose their specifically Islamic character as alms given to holy men or (more prosaically) payment for their religious services: mostly just for prayers, but also for divination or for Arabic teaching. This showed up very clearly when Christian pastors found themselves treated like *alufa*. A staunch Muslim woman at Palma on the eastern lagoon, who had two relatives attending M. J. Luke's church, said she would send him a present, "thinking it is customary with us as with their Mohammedan teachers to receive (sara) presents";[76] and a woman once came up to W. S. Allen after his preaching at Ibadan with some cowries in a calabash, saying "Alufa, sara mi re o! [Teacher, this is my offering]."[77]

Now these two concepts of *saraa*—as payments to *alufa* for their religious services and as sacrifices to God—were not separate in Yoruba thinking, but were held together by the prevailing view that all priests, in a rather strong sense, represented their deities. The devotee of Esu or Sango *was* Esu or Sango manifest, so that the cowries given as a sacrifice to the god were at the same time the priest's reward. The *alufa*'s remuneration could be directly compared to that of *orisa* priests, as by a priest of Buruku to a critical missionary in Ibadan in 1854: "The Mohammedans have their living by selling charms, my own portion like all the babalawos is to make country fashions and sacrifices for the people and from this I eat."[78] And the system lent itself to exploitation in a similar way: Allen witnessed an incident in an Ibadan street when a lay Muslim pretended to be an *alufa,* and so frightened a woman that "she went in and brought cowries for the man (sara as he said)," just as if he had been an importunate *Onisango.*[79] Of course for informed Muslims there was a cardinal difference between the two types of "priest" which was not fully recognized in the common Yoruba view. The *alufa* might receive *saraa* intended as a sacrifice to the deity whose power he gave access to, as its representative; but here the deity in question was God, who in the Muslim view could not be embodied in his devotees in the same way that *orișa* were. Nevertheless, the public role of the *alufa* was initially construed according to the premises of the old religion.

But the heavily instrumental picture I have so far drawn of the Yoruba reception of Islam is only half the story, even if it is the one which is documented most fully by the CMS journalists. For against this orientation, which tended to be individualist (or at least client centered) and hierarchical (in that access to spiritual power was through esoteric religious expertise), was another, which emphasized the moral community of Muslims and the egalitarianism of collective worship.[80] Just as sacrifice to the compound's *orișa* and ancestors implied the commensality of its living members, so too *saraa* had an important communal dimension. William Moore described the *alufa* at Osiele going round the houses of the principal men at the end of Ramadan "to beg money . . . to bless the people in the name of God." Large crowds of people went with them applauding, and with the money collected, the *alufa* "made feasts which they call Saraa for those who attended them."[81] So here *saraa* denotes not so much what the *alufa* took but what they gave to the body of actual or potential Muslims. The contributions given as *saraa* were, in effect, reinvested by the *alufa* in the growth of the Muslim community. A somewhat similar case of *saraa* was reported by Foster from Iseyin in 1879 (though he did not expressly name it as such):

A famous Muslim preacher called Asheru died after a painful illness. Then one of his wives had a dream of him bound with ropes by the hands, feet and waist, and cast into the fire. His sons were alarmed and "cooked largely the following Friday and carried [the food] to their Mosque, by it to beg their co-religionists to assist them in prayer for the forgiveness of their father's sins."[82]

At one level this may be regarded as comparable to a pagan *etutu,* a sacrifice to assuage the anger of a deity revealed in a dream, except that the deity was God and the punishment was placed in the afterlife. But the *saraa* was offered to the community of Muslims, which was thus treated as the mediator between its members and God: *vox populi, vox Dei.*

When we seek to explain the steady growth in the numbers of Muslims after midcentury, it seems undeniable that the power credited to the *alufa* played a significant part in it. At the very least it provided an effective entry to non-Muslim circles by giving practical answers to some of their problems in terms which were culturally acceptable. But the credited power of its techniques is rarely a sufficient condition for the voluntary adoption of a new religion in all its ramifications. In most cases this finally depends on potential converts being prepared to align themselves with the religion's existing adherents. So the key issue is how those impressed by the *alufa*'s techniques were further drawn into association and identification with the body of people around him.

We can see the small beginnings of this process in the way that the *alufa* visiting Okeho got the people to perform certain ritual acts—in effect, to start to speak and act as Muslims—as part of his delivery of Muslim prayer-power for them. But it was probably more effectively done by the encouragement given to the non-Muslim population to participate, without preconditions, in the main Muslim celebrations. Where Islam was well enough established in a town, the end of Ramadan was marked by a grand procession to the prayer ground, usually outside the town walls. At Osiele in 1851 the two principal *alufa,* dressed in their best robes, rode horses in the procession and were accompanied by some eight to ten non-Muslims whom they had hired to ride with them, as well as half a dozen drummers, to whose rhythms the horses danced.[83] With this evocation of military prowess (and the *saraa* feast following) the *alufa* aligned Islam with deeply held Yoruba values of prestige.[84] It was often sourly acknowledged by CMS agents that these occasions, in bringing together Muslims and pagans in shared conviviality, were effective in drawing converts to Islam: "Because natural men have much delight in such religion as consisted only in eating and drinking and rose up to play," as Moore put it. At these feasts pagans might adopt the first outward and visible sign of Islam, the wearing of a turban and clean white apparel, to claim and publicly show fellowship with their Muslim friends.[85] Even if they then declared for Islam, little further was insisted of them, such as rigorous abstention from pagan rituals; and in fact most new Muslims continued to participate in *oriṣa* rites and festivals. An Ibadan woman, afraid of the anger of her *oriṣa* when her son became a Christian inquirer, said: "I want my son to do like the Mohammedans, they worship God and orisas and all amount to the same thing."[86] Samuel Johnson summed up his remarks on the 1880 Egungun festival in Ibadan, begun on the word of the Muslim *Arẹ* from the Kiriji war camp and with the active participation of Chief Tajo, the senior Muslim chief left in town:

> What a mixture of Mohammedanism with heathenism! It amounts to no religion at all. At the Mohammedan festival, the whole town are Mohammedans, and in any heathen festivity, they all took part in it. Such is the nature of the people we have to deal with.[87]

The exasperated tone of the missionaries' comment on this mode of Islamization seems to owe much to their feeling that this was just not the way that conversion to a new religion ought to go. As evangelicals they held firmly to a certain notion of genuineness in religion: it was where a heartfelt inner conviction led to external actions consonant with it. In their own missionary practice, they strove first to create such an inner conviction in their Christian inquirers through instruction and prayer for the Holy Spirit; and they sought to assure themselves of its existence before admitting them as Chris-

Figure 7.1. Mosque at Kemta, Abeokuta. S. S. Farrow, *Faith, Fancies, and Fetich* (1926), taken by Rev. J. F. T. Halligey in 1892.

tians by baptism. But Yoruba Islam seemed to invert this "inside-outward" process: becoming Muslim seemed to be primarily a matter of acquiring external tokens, very much to do with worldly advantage. Convinced, with much justification, of the low level of Arabic education and religious knowledge among most Yoruba Muslims, Christian critics appreciated too little that the process of making Muslims had barely begun with the saying of the *shahada*[88] and the adoption of a Muslim name.

It was to be taken further by instruction and participation in the religious life of the Muslim community: by attendance at the little local mosques that sprang up in Yoruba towns, by listening to the preaching and Koranic exposition, particularly during Ramadan, of notable visiting *alufa,* and, perhaps most of all, by responding to the diffuse symbolic impact of Islamic culture. At Lagos in 1866, the Friday prayers were attended by some 500 to 600 worshippers gorgeously dressed—"a grand sight it was for Africa"—and afterward a sermon was given in Arabic or Hausa, translated into Yoruba.[89] We must not neglect the moral impact of men such as the fluent *alufa* from Ilorin, who attracted hundreds to hear him at Badagry in 1849 and preached "against their selling slaves; of their using their domestic slaves cruelly; of their obliging their wives to provide for them instead of providing for their wives; of their making trade of their writing as charms; and against their general immoralities";[90] or of the "taosiry" (Arabic *tafsir,* Koranic exegesis) which took place after formal prayers during Ramadan at Iseyin in 1881, when the *alufa* took *Sura* 49 as his text, and warned his congregation "for their hard and bad using their slaves . . . to be active in their profession [as Muslims] . . . [and] about using their wives in a roughly [*sic*] manner."[91]

Few Christian clergy were as concerned about the growth of Islam as James Johnson, pastor of Breadfruit from 1874, when the numbers of Muslims in Lagos were rising rapidly. Like others, he attributed it to the fact that Muslims associated freely with pagans, while "Christians are regarded as a people separate from them, as identifying with a foreign people, and the dress they usually assume has become a badge of distinction."[92] But his main response, to press for more literature in Yoruba and to urge Christians to emulate the alleged zeal of Muslims in proselytizing ("Every Mohammedan regards himself as a missionary to his neighbours," he claimed), was much less radical than it seemed, since it did not challenge the missionary conviction that it was assiduous preaching to the heathen which did most to win converts. Johnson did not advocate that the CMS abandon its policy of making a high level of cultural demands on its potential converts, from intensive pre-baptismal instruction to the abandonment of polygamy. The Muslims proceeded quite otherwise: they attracted non-Muslims by practical offers and they made few initial demands on them for cultural renunciation, but they knew how vital it was to keep up preaching to the converted.

THREE-SIDED ARGUMENTS

Of the two main ways in which the Yoruba typified Christianity—as the religion of the white man and as a scriptural monotheism—one divides it from Islam, while the other assimilates it. In large measure they also correspond to two contrasting approaches to how religious change has been analyzed. The former points to a mainly external yet also historically short-term analysis, in which the links between the missions and other agencies of European colonialism are given prime attention; while the latter looks more to the historically long term and the relevance of features that are more intrinsic to the religion. The other major antinomies which bulk large in the explanation of religious conversion—how far it arose from a quest for power and how far from a quest for meaning or for embodying truth as against providing identity—do not align exactly with one another, and seem to cut across the main distinction made by the Yoruba, that is between *whose* religion it was, and *what kind* of religion it was. In a practical setting where new religions are introduced by outsiders, it is perhaps inevitable that they should be first categorized in terms of their bearers: Christianity being the religion of the *Oyinbo,* as Islam had been of the *Imale.* But very soon Yoruba started to look beneath the manifest external differences of the two religions to assess them as variants of one another, as similar and alternative paths to a wider religious identity and the direct worship of God.

This perception was most simply expressed when Christian pastors were greeted in the terms appropriate to the monotheism which the Yoruba already knew: an *egungun* masquerader saluted T. B. Macaulay from a respectful distance with the words "sala-ma-leku" (i.e., the Muslim greeting *as-salaam alaikum*, "peace be on you").[93] It was because both they and the *alufa* were recognized as fellow specialists in the cult of God that they were sometimes offered *saraa*. When Thomas King traveled through Ota in 1852 (before the mission had been established there), the chiefs presented him with a ram "to make my Sunday with," remarking "Is not your mode of worship and the Mahomedans quite alike?"[94] One Ibadan man told Olubi that first the Muslims preached about the day of judgment, and now the "Oibos" [Europeans] had come to confirm it;[95] while another told Okuseinde "You Oibos are like the Mohammedans of Ilorin who count our orishas as nothing" (which incidentally implies that Ibadan's Islam was seen as much less stringent than Ilorin's).[96] Just as Muslim strangers at Ota, before it acquired a significant Muslim community, were sometimes sent to lodge with White at the mission house, so the *Baḷẹ* of the small town of Ilesan in Egbado proposed that Doherty—not at all to his liking—should stay at the head Muslim's house, "as we are alike *alufa*."[97]

These pagan views of the essential affinity of Christianity and Islam were also echoed by many Muslims, though the recognition here was more complex and clouded by religious rivalry. They were sometimes motivated by a desire to fend off unwelcome proselytization by contending that the two religions were much the same. When Doherty visited Eruwa on a preaching tour, a Muslim interrupted his address to say there was already a "house of God" there, implying that if there were Muslims, there did not need to be Christians too.[98] This sentiment comes up often in reports from Lagos in the 1860s and 1870s, when Islam was advancing rapidly. T. B. Wright, a catechist at Oko Faji, was told by four amiable young men that they used to be *orisa*-worshippers but were now Muslims "which . . . is on the same level with Christianity";[99] and when he challenged a Brazilian returnee making walking sticks at the front of his house as to why he was working on a Sunday, the man replied he was a Muslim "which he said is the same with ours."[100] Some other Muslims again told him that he should preach to the pagans "as they had not the light of God whatever . . . , [but] they themselves are in the same level with us."[101] Remarks of this kind fit well with reports of people hovering between the two monotheisms, as if their desire to "worship God" was prior to any pragmatic reason for opting for one rather than the other way of setting about it. A young Christian inquirer at Ibadan found himself opposed by his family, who "told him that if he truly meant to worship God, he must be a Mahomedan but to be an Oyinbo [i.e., Christian] is a thing which they hate, to have a single wife."[102] At Ota in the 1870s White worried that "many of those whom we have convinced [against idolatry] have become proselytes to the false religion";[103] and Maser felt that people in Lagos were "excited [about] what they had better do, to become Christians or Mohammedans."[104]

Discussions between Christian evangelists and Muslims ranged in tone from abusive confrontations to serious attempts to explore their differences within a shared recognition of their common roots. At one extreme was the slanging match which broke out between S. W. Doherty and the local *Lẹ-mọmu* (Imam) when he visited Okeho in 1876:

> After he had preached publicly before the *Balẹ* and chiefs, Doherty's prayers were disturbed by the laughing and talking of hostile Muslims. An altercation followed, in which Doherty charged Mohammed of being a great sinner and impostor, and Christ the only mediator. The argument then moved to the subject of sacrifice [I presume at Doherty's instance, since it was a ground where missionaries felt they could advance their case, against both pagans and Muslims] and Doherty accused the Muslims of making sacrifices, which they strenuously denied. "And what is the meaning of your sara, is it not offering or sacrifice, are you any better than the heathen . . . in this respect?" This sally seems to have provoked the *Lẹ-mọmu* into saying loudly to one of the chiefs, "Do you know that the leopard and the dog cannot meet together, such is the case between us and these people." To this insult, Doherty replied with "By their fruits ye shall know them," and accused them of Satanic principles. At this point the *Balẹ* told them all to be quiet.
>
> Doherty rounds off his account with a confirming Scriptural precedent: "Thus I met with Elymases today."[105]

But there were also less competitive settings—particularly, it seems, where the tide of conversion was not running strongly and Islam was not already well ensconced—where Muslims might show a friendly, at times even collegial, interest in Christianity. A Muslim householder at Ibadan listened to Allen teaching the Lord's Prayer to people in his compound, and "spoke very sharply to the children to repeat after us and to keep in memory what they had learned."[106] It might well center on issues common to religions of the book. A Hausa Muslim visited Meakin at Oyo in 1858, bringing a gift of some eggs. They talked about the diversity of languages, and the visitor said the *alufa* were trying to write Yoruba in Arabic script as Hausa already was. They went on to discuss persecution, and the next day he brought five or six others, and they talked again.[107] The Ten Commandments always won favorable attention:

> While some Ilorin traders were visiting Maser at Abeokuta, a Christian woman called to buy a prayer book. Seeing that Maser "could not converse fluently . . . in the native language," she helped him expound the basics of the Christian religion "with great warmth and zeal." At the Muslims' request she repeated the Ten Commandments, which impressed them greatly.[108]

An elderly Muslim helpfully confirmed Doherty's exposition of the Ten Commandments when he preached at Bolorunpelu;[109] and even the *alufa* of Iwo (who prevented the establishment of a mission there) were interested to hear them in Yoruba from Hinderer's Scripture reader Wilhelm, and asked him to say them again.[110] At a higher level was M. D. Coker's exchange with Aminu, the Arabic teacher of Agbeni mosque in Ibadan, in 1892:

> One Wednesday Aminu calls to see Coker, accompanied by seven converts and two of his scholars. Coker gives him an Arabic translation of St Mark's Gospel. He turns over all the pages to the end, and then back again; and then turning to Chapter Ten, he reads it all through. He knows the meaning of some of the words in Arabic. Coker then reads it aloud from the Yoruba Bible. The *alufa* is pleased to have the book, and their talk goes on for over two hours. The converts listen attentively and sometimes join in. They part having agreed to attend one another's services.[111]

But not far beneath the surface of even friendly encounters, especially where they involved clerics on both sides, ran strong currents of rivalry and reserve. Coker and Aminu did not keep up their ecumenical resolution: on Friday Coker said he was laid low with fever, and on Sunday the *alufa* sent to say that he could not come because of ill health (I suspect because he regarded Coker as having made a polite excuse to get out of it and was probably relieved to get out of it himself). Rivalry quickly came to the fore in the battle of the books which Samuel Johnson had with the *Lẹmọmu* of Ibadan (the "Mohammedan bishop," as he calls him):

> On his way to the monthly prayer meeting at Ogunpa, Johnson sees the *Lẹmọmu* sitting on a hide at the front of his house, accompanied by some *alufa,* with parchments of the Koran around. The *Lẹmọmu* bids Johnson wait, so he can read him some prayers. He takes some pages from the bundle, and Johnson opens his own bag of books to get out his Bible. The *Lẹmọmu* says that two *alufa* will oppose one another, and he will look to who will win the contest. But he's struck with admiration at the gilt edging of Johnson's Bible, and taking it in his hand exclaims to his friends, "'God alone is above them and knows the secret of their wisdom.' But having the presence of mind to find that he was betraying himself [continues Johnson] he said to me, 'But you have all your glories in this world and none in the world to come.' I then said to him, the fact that God honoureth us with great blessings here disproves your argument. 'Him that honoureth me, said he, I will honour.' Is God unrighteous to reward us with evil hereafter if we faithfully serve him, and reward with good those who are unfaithful? He was speechless, and smiling at me promised to give me a kola nut if I call on him on my return."[112]

Whether in reality Johnson's triumph was quite so resounding, we may doubt; but still the focus of the exchange on the relative power of the two religions was common and characteristic. In most such public encounters, faced with the inclination of both pagans and Muslims to emphasize what was common between Christianity and Islam—commonalities which, as we have seen, were also tacitly admitted in the use of Islamic terms to translate so many key Christian concepts into Yoruba—Christian evangelists were anxious to emphasize what divided them from the Muslims. To this end they employed two different, and potentially contradictory, strategies. On the one hand, as in Johnson's narrative just quoted, they asserted the superior power of Christianity, a strategy which implicitly appealed to a *pagan* criterion of religious value, the capacity to deliver this-worldly benefits. On the other, they argued that Islam was inferior to Christianity because in the common practice of Yoruba Muslims it came so close to the paganism which they both looked down on. "But do you compare us to the heathen?" replied some Muslims who had come to visit Gollmer at Badagry, when he charged them with dishonesty, probably over the making of charms.[113] His reply was hardly irenic: "No . . . not exactly. You know more than they of the Will of God but, says the Scripture, the servant that knows his master's will and does it not will receive a double portion of stripes."

These arguments often focused on the low level or the misuse of literacy. Always they were directed toward convicting Muslims of falling short of the standards of a professed religion of the Book and so becoming susceptible to pagan modes of appropriating the power of literacy. In the early days at Badagry, Samuel Crowther the elder showed an Arabic Bible to the local Muslims and taxed them with knowing little of the Koran;[114] his son at Abeokuta challenged two Muslims who attended his dispensary to read an Arabic Prayer Book, and affected a rather manipulative surprise at their ignorance.[115] Gollmer at Badagry asked a man sitting on the verandah of his house what his work was and was shown in a small bag a mass of paper scraps with Arabic writing on them; to the *alufa*'s remark "this book can save me," he spoke of Christ as savior.[116] On another occasion, while Gollmer was visiting Mewu, one of the senior Badagry chiefs, a Hausa *alufa* called with a new charm which the chief bought; he told him that to make such charms was a sin for which God would punish him; and the *alufa* left without a word to say.[117] Friendly Muslims might be hurtfully rebuffed by this militancy: the Arẹ Latosisa's drummer, a Muslim like his master, called on James Okuseinde, but "went away sorrowful" (like the young man in Matthew 19:22) after a denunciation of charm-making as being against God's command.[118] At Abeokuta in 1850, not long after the persecution, a number of Muslims approached Hinderer to say they must be friends, since their two religions were much the same; but Hinderer insisted that in their mode of life they were little different from the heathen.[119] A few years later, in Ibadan, he talked with a Muslim who candidly admitted that the Muslims "must conform a little with the heathen fashion because they are not yet enough in number and power to get on without."[120] The fact that similar charges might also be made by prestigious visiting *alufa* from Ilorin or farther north, suggests that Christian criticism of Muslims for their Arabic illiteracy and their cultural closeness to

Yoruba pagans could touch a raw nerve, at least among the more religiously self-conscious of them. Gbadamosi's verdict, that these theological disputations rarely won Muslims over to Christianity, seems well justified; and by the late 1870s some *alufa* were counseling their adherents to avoid getting into debates with missionaries.[121]

The main theological issues which came up in these disputes between Christians and Muslims concerned, first, the proper rituals for the worship of God and, second, the natures of Christ and Mohammed as proclaimed mediators with God. These two issues were often directly linked in discussion, as in Gollmer's exchange with Muslim visitors in 1847:

> Five Muslims came to admire his garden, asking about one or two strange plants like cabbage and arrowroot. Gollmer used this to introduce the subject of God's goodness in supplying mankind with so many things to eat, even [here suddenly raising the stakes] pig's flesh. He then spoke of the greater freedom of the New Covenant. The discussion then moved on to the relations between God and "Jesus son of Mariam." [This distinctively Muslim designation of Christ suggests that the topic may have been raised by the Muslims, whom I surmise were Hausa of some Islamic sophistication.][122]

Both issues were implicated in an all-enveloping discourse of power. Rituals of worship—*how* God is to be approached—always had a strongly instrumental aspect, which led directly to the issue of the divine nature—*who* God is—because God required that He be addressed properly, in a way appropriate to His nature. By both Muslims and Christians, but perhaps especially by Muslims, God was conceived of as a king, and the Yoruba etiquette of kingship was indispensable to how they figured the task of addressing Him, even though (and perhaps the more because) both religions proposed that He might be directly addressed, which mundane Yoruba *ọba* were not. So the stakes were high, anxiety great. A strong indication is given in the juxtaposed epithets from the invocation of an Egba chief quoted earlier: *Ọba alanu, ọba mimọ* [Merciful king, holy king].[123] "Merciful" implies that the petitioner expects that God will answer his prayers, that he anticipates that God's power will be made available to him; and "holy" acknowledges the awful purity of God, the otherness which worshippers must bridge by conforming to God's requirements of moral and ritual purity.

On both these issues, it appears that Muslims faced the Christian challenge with some confidence. They repeatedly urged the importance of being "clean" (*mimọ*), as required by the ritual of Muslim prayer, in approaching God. Three Ilorin Muslims, passing through Ibadan, responded to James Barber's preaching of Christ as mediator with God by insisting that if men wished to serve one God, they should wash their hands (i.e., perform ritual ablutions before prayer) and abstain from eating pork, an unclean meat;[124] and a Muslim at Abeokuta attacked Christian worship and the impurity of Christians for eating pork.[125] An *alufa* at Ibadan answered a criticism from W. S. Allen with a strong metaphor of ritual impurity:

> There was a high hill and people inhabited its valley. At the top of the hill every dead creature was buried. At the rainy season a stream issued at the bottom. Do you think that the water was pure?[126]

Allen agreed that Adam and Eve brought corruption, but insisted that Christ's sacrifice had the power to wash mankind clean (and by implication, obviated the need for specific rituals of purification). But the standard Christian rejoinder to the Muslim emphasis on ritual purity was to put up the same contrast between Christianity as an "internal" religion and Islam as an "external" one that came into play in their critical comments on the process of Islamic conversion. One of his converts brought a Muslim—an impressive man with followers, literate in Arabic—to see James White at Ota:

> White shows him his Arabic Bible, from which the Muslim translates some verses. He then asks him what he thinks of Christ. "A messenger of God, and more than that, for he had no fleshly father," he replies. White then speaks of Christians as being the adopted sons of God, while the Muslim describes Muslims as "slaves of God." The Muslim then asks why Christians reject Mohammed. Because he did things contrary to God's teachings and propagated his religion by the sword, replies White. The Muslim then turns to his companions and says that "we were clever fellows, if only we would kirun." White asks what "kirun" is. "To wash the hands and feet, and to cry out God is Great," he replies. White says these are only external things; even baptism is only an emblem of the cleansing of the heart.[127]

The theme of cleanliness as a condition of the heart was the regular missionary response to Muslim promotion of their rituals of purification and prayer. God required a pure heart, not outward ceremony, insisted Samuel Cole to one Muslim critic at Abeokuta; and to another, objecting to the eating of pork, he quoted Matthew 15:19, on evil coming from the inside, not from the outside.[128] Oyebode, meeting two Muslims at a Christian's house in Ibadan, spoke in more evangelical terms of "the impotency of the Koran to influence the heart to holiness of life."[129] The point at issue was the relationship between ritual and ethical purity: for the Muslims the former was an expression and evocation of the latter, for the CMS missionaries the former was suspect as tending to displace the "religion of the heart" which they sought to create.[130]

Much that was said concerning the other great issue, the mediatory roles of Christ and Mohammed, echoed centuries of religious polemic. Muslim views of Christ were necessarily more positive than Christian views of Mohammed, in accordance with the historical asymmetry of the two religions, the earlier standing as precursor, the later as heresy to the other. Whereas

Mohammed was a "false prophet" (*woli eke*) to the missionaries, to Muslims Christ was *Anabi Yisa*, "the Prophet Jesus": though his divinity and crucifixion were denied, his virgin birth and divine inspiration were conceded. Some age-old themes of interfaith dispute got an airing—How could a unique and transcendent God have had a son? Was Mohammed foretold in such texts as Deuteronomy 18:15 and John 14:16?—but the main thrust of argument followed an essentially Yoruba agenda: the search for the most effective mediator with God. It showed clearly in a triangular debate reported by Kefer from Ibadan in 1855:

> Near the main mosque in the middle of town Kefer gets into discussion with a number of *alufa*. As usual they object to his presentation of Christ as savior. Kefer tries to show them the need for a mediator "but they wanted then to cooperate with me and began to encourage me to talk only against the Orisas of the Keferi [pagans]." A *babalawo* comes forward and defends the *orisa* with great eloquence. "The Alufa looked at me but I told him, though I have an answer, he may refute the Babbalawo." He tries his best "to enforce the greatness of God, the Creator of heaven and earth, . . . but he made mistakes in the comparison, so that he could make only little impression with his energy." Kefer then takes on the *babalawo,* and tries to show "that the very Orisa system of the Keferi indicates their great desire after a mediator, they mistake it only and make their own which cannot help, instead of receiving Christ whom God has given to the world. In him alone we find salvation and without him Keferi and Imalle [Muslims] will be lost. But God calls them both."[131]

Here Kefer's improvised strategy of argument unrolls to reach a paradoxical conclusion. First, he is dyadically opposed to the *alufa;* then, the monotheists join forces against the *babalawo,* but Kefer craftily steps back to let the *alufa* make the case against paganism; then he re-enters the argument as the real champion of monotheism, but invokes a criterion of pagan religious culture—their acknowledged need for a mediator—to offer Christ as the solution to *both* pagans and Muslims. But there is a conflict of understandings latent in the exchange: where Kefer had chiefly in mind the salvation unto eternal life offered by Christ, the mediation sought by the Yoruba through their *orisa* was needed for the troubles of earthly existence.

So despite the particular doctrinal views held by Christianity and Islam of their respective founders, Yoruba opinion assessed them by a common criterion of likely effectiveness as mediators. An *alufa* at Badagry spoke of Mohammed "as a great favourite of God to whom no favour can be denied, that everything he asks of God must be granted," according a lower status to Jesus.[132] At Ibadan in 1891, a Muslim rebutted F. L. Akiele's urging of Christ as mediator by insisting that "Anabiyisa . . . will not intercede for men but Mohammed the great prophet [will] . . . for all sinners and Anabiyisa too."[133] In a more Yoruba idiom of differential power, a Muslim at Leki called Jesus

"Mohammed's younger brother," thus reducing temporal specificity to a coeval present of religious confrontation.[134] In the struggle to appeal to an audience that was not yet committed to either monotheism but was prepared to listen with sympathy to their mythic representations and knew well enough what it wanted—spiritual friends in high places—Christianity had one definite advantage: it could put forward a more elevated view of Christ, as God incarnate, than Islam did of Mohammed. (It is true that in the heat of argument missionaries sometimes accused Muslims of raising Mohammed to the status of a god.[135] If this unlikely charge was ever justified, then it may be a telling indication of where the pressure of religious competition under Yoruba conditions might lead.) So Christian evangelists made the most of Christ's supernatural conception (not denied by Muslims) and of the miracles described in the Gospels (the Koran, being a revelation to Mohammed, does not report any of him).[136] It follows that, notwithstanding the gulf between missionary Christianity and Yoruba cultural values, Christ was in principle more capable of being represented in terms analogous to an *orisa* than Mohammed was. So it would prove: as early as the 1870s, Christ was being promoted as a functional alternative to one *orisa* in particular, Orunmila, and the Rev. E. M. Lijadu would go so far as to claim in his book *Orunmla!* (1908) that in Orunmila the Yoruba actually had a degree of foreknowledge of Jesus Christ.[137] That Mohammed was not adaptable in this way may be one reason why, particularly in the absence of a strong Sufic tradition, Koranic charms remained so important as a means to access the power of God.

When we compare the peculiar respective strengths of Islam and Christianity as religions competing for Yoruba favor, two factors seem to stand out on each side. For Islam it was the appeal of the spiritual techniques of the *alufa*—their prayers and charms, backed by the prestige of Islam's trans-regional networks and its politico-military clout—and the social openness of Yoruba Muslims toward non-Muslims which eased their self-identification with the Muslim body. For Christianity, it was the appeal of Christ as mediator; and its association with the technological power of its European bearers, eventually to be diffused through the colonial order. The power of European technique was an awkward fact for Yoruba Muslims to contemplate, since they shared the prevailing view that the mastery of the conditions of mundane existence was a prime object and test of religion. Muslim clerics, especially visitors from the north, often called at mission houses to admire their construction and furnishing. In order to reconcile their admiration for the white man's things with their Muslim faith—which of course they saw as a religion of power too—they deployed a remarkably consistent theodicy. "God has allotted Earth's happiness to the white man and reserved heaven's felicity for the Musulman, and this accounts for the Wealth, Wisdom and Skill of the Europeans," was how James White reported it after two *alufa* called to see his house at Ota. Thomas King put identical sentiments—"Terrestrial happiness and worldly skill is the portion allotted by God to white men in this world, but theirs is the heavenly felicity"—into the mouth of Idirisu, a well-known *alufa* at Abeokuta, when he came with his friends to admire Mrs. Crowther's cuckoo clock.[138]

So there is the paradox that the religion whose primary pitch was that it offered moral renewal and eternal salvation to those who accepted its Word, found itself most respected by its rival for its accompanying material culture, which was, in its own eyes, a secondary consequence; while Islam, whose relative success was due to two things which missionary Christianity failed to emulate—its magico-spiritual techniques and its social affability—invoked in its own defense an other-worldly dimension which was probably of small concern to its new Yoruba converts. As they grew more familiar with European technology, Yoruba Muslims lost some of their awe at it and became more able to separate the religion of the *oyinbo* from the rest of their culture. In this, Lagos Muslims took the lead, confident in having become by the 1890s the largest religious group in the British administrative capital. In 1891 Lijadu, then still a teacher, talked with the Muslims in a trade caravan passing northward through Ondo, and noted that "the Mohammedans from Lagos, affecting to be more enlightened than their correligionists of the interior, stood as champions for the rest."[139] At Ibadan the next year Oyebode was discouraged at a man who said he'd heard Blyden describe Mohammed as a prophet of God in a speech in Lagos; and then a woman chimed in to mention "an Englishman who returned of late from Mecca . . . and is making converts in England."[140] Yet these articulate Lagos Muslims, who had most fully taken the measure of Christianity, were also the most subtly influenced by a cultural ideology which would eventually work, and with growing force as the colonial order took hold, to Christianity's advantage. This was the missionary-derived model of cultural progress or civilization, which Lijadu's description of the Lagos Muslims as "enlightened" hints at. Despite its Christian origins, enlightenment, or *ọlaju*, would come to command a general allegiance for its connotation of advancement for individuals and communities. As a consequence the cynosure of Yoruba Muslims would begin to shift from Ilorin to Lagos.

8

THE PATH TO CONVERSION

The primary burden of the two preceding chapters has been on the missionaries' presentation of their case to the Yoruba audiences—both the great "pagan" majority, and the small but growing Muslim minority—whom they wished to bring to Christianity. In the course of this effort, just how different their religious assumptions and objectives were from those sustained by Yoruba culture became clear. Then a triangulation of all three religions took the picture further by showing, first, how in seeking converts both world religions had to address the court of Yoruba opinion; and second, how much Yoruba Islam, over the long process of its adaptation to the local scene, had taken into itself significant features of the religious orientation of the *keferi*.

Now the argument moves on to the analogous process with Christianity, through an examination, first of how the Yoruba started to turn toward it, and then (in the next chapter) of what kind of Christians they became. It may seem paradoxical to approach the issue of the "inculturation" of Christianity—that is, of its rooting in local culture—by means of an analysis of what is apparently an opposite movement—of some Yoruba leaving their local and ancestral cults for a world religion urged on them by outsiders—but two reasons justify this characterization. First, Christianity cannot possibly become

Yoruba without some Yoruba first becoming Christian. Second, although conversion, as it is usually understood, implies some kind of change (and often complete or radical change at that), it can never be understood as a process except in terms of the purposes and judgments of those who undergo it, as well as of the situations or circumstances which prompt it. These purposes and criteria of judgment necessarily *precede* conversion, being drawn from the converts' prior cultural repertory; and since they undergird the decision to convert, they are likely to continue as a substrate of the new beliefs and practices, whatever other novelties may inhere in or follow from the fact of conversion itself.

The concept of "conversion" is not without its difficulties: it is hard to use it comparatively without extending the theological or phenomenological assumptions of a Euro-Christian and Protestant background to historical and cultural settings where they do not apply.[1] Moreover, the interiority of the experience of conversion, psychologically conceived,[2] makes it of problematic value when our subject matter is a large-scale process of religious change where we have little or no evidence about the inner states of the individuals concerned. Here the only *workable* definition of conversion is the process by which people come to regard themselves, and be regarded by others, as Christians. This social identification is what being a Christian most immediately and unarguably *is,* rather than holding certain beliefs or behaving in certain ways specified a priori. Of course Christians in general will tend to display distinctive beliefs and practices—sometimes from a prior adoption which led them to seek Christian identification in the first place, but probably much more often a result of being taught them as a condition of membership, or socialized into them as a consequence of it. By taking social identification as the real thing to be explained we avoid the analytical problems which arise if—as often occurs in practice—Christians maintain or later adopt "non-Christian" beliefs and practices but still insist on regarding themselves as Christians and are so regarded by others.

The argument will relate conversion most centrally to the search for power which was pervasive in Yoruba society, and in general it will move from the more intrinsic to the more contingent links between religion and power, from power inherent in objects to power deployed in social relations, and from the positive appeal of becoming a Christian to its opportunity costs. Conversion is a process which can be complex even at the personal level, and while the complexities of individual cases may be to some extent ironed out when the outcomes are viewed in the aggregate, it is still a highly composite process, brought about by the interplay of many different factors. And of course it is a historical process too, not only in the obvious sense that it unrolls over time but also in that the significance of the factors of conversion is not intrinsic, but depends on the temporal context in which they come into play.

SEEKING POWER: TECHNOLOGY, HEALING, WRITING

That the search for power, individual or collective, was the dominant orientation of the Yoruba toward all religions must by now need no further demonstration. There were both technical and social aspects to this power, but the former—power in and over material things, power as practical knowledge—was primary, an end in itself as well as a means to the latter. The status of *babalawo* and Muslim *alufa* mainly depended on their reputation for being able to give access to sources of power, and the power of Europeans was widely acknowledged through comparisons of them with *orisa* in personal names: twice the name *Fatoyinbo* [Ifa is as great as the white man] comes up in passing in CMS journals.[3] But what we have to explain is how the conviction that there is power in a religion actually leads the adherents of other cults to want to join it, particularly if it insists that they abandon all prior religious identities. And if the power credited to "the white man's religion" was so potent a factor, why were converts still so few in number after fifty years of strenuous evangelism, and disproportionately drawn from the more marginal groups in society?

The missionaries put out a mixed message on the subject of power: the transvaluatory element in their preaching, which deprecated the routine objectives of Yoruba religious action, were at some variance with their claims that the Gospel "would make the country good" and that God would be attentive to the faithful prayers of His people, which seemed to offer additional means to those objectives. In these positive claims, the effects of religious action come about in two quite different ways. The country would be made good, according to the missionary theory, by a process of what we might call culture change: individuals would be remade inwardly by the Gospel, would change their lives and reform their institutions, and prosperity would follow. In that sense, the Bible was "the key to England's power and greatness," and could be so for the Yoruba too. This mode of religious effect, with its emphasis on changing the human subject, was entirely novel to Yoruba thinking. Prayer, on the other hand, moved in a much less mysterious way: it went straight to the divine source of power—"we telegraphed to God," was a way that Allen liked to put it[4]—and produced mediated effects on the subject's environment. The Yoruba came to see it, like the Muslim *saraa*, as analogous to sacrifice, an offering to God which would evoke His favorable response.

The products of European technology were mute though eloquent icons of *oyinbo* power, and also, in Yoruba eyes, a potential argument for the truth of their religion. In principle, even European wonders were attributable to *orisa*, as with the cotton gin which evoked sacrifices to Orisa Oko at Abeokuta in 1855.[5] From the beginning Sango was linked to electricity, by means of two contrary arguments. On the one hand, missionaries sought to secularize lightning strikes by invoking electricity, not Sango, as their cause.[6] The mission at Abeokuta had an electro-magnetic machine which Faulkner said was very useful to explain to Sango worshippers the folly of idolatry.[7] On the other hand, electric power might itself be seen as a manifestation of Sango, much as a swarm of bees was. (The statue of Sango which stands today outside the headquarters of the Nigerian Electric Power Authority in Lagos might be taken as a "symbolic" statement of such a view.) Was something like this in the mind of the young man who told Faulkner that he would hold the handles of the electrical machine from noon till sunset to get a new silk umbrella, as if such sacrificial suffering, a sort of "reversed thunder" perhaps, must reap its reward?[8]

But such possible interpretations were overridden by the insistence that the white man's wonders must be attributed to his relationship with his God. This claim was made most emphatically by the African evangelists, like Olubi and the others when they took the dolls and musical box on their formal visit to *Balę* Orowusi in 1870.[9] At times there may have been no more to this than self-promotion through the display of prestige items or the use of novelties to draw attention. Samuel Crowther junior sought to impress a *babalawo* who had come to visit his dispensary at Abeokuta—after he had refused to let Crowther experiment on his charm—by means of a chemical spectacular, making fire from a mixture of potassium chlorate and sulphuric acid; the man ran away shouting *"Oyinbo! Oyinbo!,"* and offered Crowther five bags of cowries to do it again at the *babalawos'* annual festival.[10] A pyrotechnic performance in support of the authority claims of a religious specialist was not at all alien to the style of Yoruba cults, as witness the tricks with fire performed by Sango priests or the ventriloquism through a puppet which was used in the Osanyin oracle.[11]

The arguments suggested by European technological achievements were various, but the main one was (as always) forcefully put by James White:

> People greatly admired the work of an Egba carpenter, Philemon, who put up the first church roof at Ota. White "tried to show them that the Whitemen are far superior to them in everything, they cannot be inferior to them in matters of religion." Pressed as why they despised the white man's religion, they said it was difficult to give up their fathers' gods. "Why—I said—it is not difficult for you to make use of Whiteman's muskets, powder, cotton, velvet, silk etc. which ages ago our fathers have not known."[12]

Though they may have helped establish a general predisposition to Christianity, arguments of this kind rarely seem to have led to practical conviction in individual cases. Of the many reasons for this, an immediate one was they did not bear on the pressing personal needs which made Yoruba turn to the *orişa*. In the following case the display of an *oyinbo* wonder is connected much more distinctly with Yoruba religious concerns:

In 1876 on a tour of the Oke Ogun, S. W. Doherty takes an artificial snake with him to draw people. Then he preaches from Mark 16:15–20, which includes the verse, "They shall take up serpents; and if they drink any deadly thing, it shall not hurt them; they shall lay hands on the sick, and they shall recover." Next day when he shows it by the verandah of the *oba*'s palace at Eruwa, people run off in fright. He tells them it is "but an art," nothing compared to the steamship or railway, and goes on: "We Africans . . . know nothing of arts and sciences, and yet the least seeming device we call *awo* ["secret"]. . . . Mohammedan charms you would believe but what discoveries do Mohammedans make in our country worth admiring?"[13]

Doherty's audience must have been less impressed by his praise of European technology—what could they care about steamships in Eruwa?—than by his implicit use of the marvelous snake to support a claim to be able to heal and give protection against poison, perennial Yoruba demands on their religious specialists. The Muslims were doing just that with their charms.

Personal protection from enemies seen and unseen, healing and fertility, practical guidance through the uncertainties of life, all summed up in that state of worldly well-being called *alafia*—these were the fruits of power which Yoruba most looked for from Christianity, as from all other cults. At the outset of his Osiele ministry, William Moore described how a woman knelt to beg him for a cure for her husband's bad foot: "She as well as all the people in this country thought that we possessed some power to do marvelous act [*sic*] or are like the Mahomedans here who always pretend healing in the name of God."[14] Moore was a Yoruba, but writes here like any other missionary, with a sincere conviction that Christianity could empower, but not always in the respects or by the means that Yoruba pagans asked of it. The dilemma—which must have been more acutely felt by the African agents—was how far they should adjust to the thaumaturgical demand placed on them by those whom they wanted to convert. It would never be resolved within the official practice of the mission-derived churches and would later fuel religious breakaway movements.[15]

As the foregoing remarks of Doherty and Moore indicate, one of the most pressing demands made on religious specialists was for healing. In the light of the great success of medical work in twentieth-century missions throughout Africa, when relatively simple surgical and pharmaceutical means often produced dramatic results and gave a great boost to evangelism,[16] it cannot be strongly enough emphasized that there were few objective grounds for the Yoruba to attribute superior healing power to Europeans before the colonial period. The extremely high mortality of missionaries, right into the 1890s with the decimation of Bishop Hill's party, spoke for itself. With no effective prophylaxis against such diseases as malaria, typhoid, and yellow fever, they referred almost fatalistically to the "seasoning fever" of the new missionary's first few months (which carried so many of them off). Their "knowledge" was often rudimentary or even made things worse. Sometimes missionaries were even prepared to try local remedies, like Gollmer who, suffering from swollen legs, turned to a Hausa surgeon who administered a cupping, "quite successful but awfully painful."[17] In a round of fatal illness at Abeokuta in 1853, Hensman attributed a severe symptomatic headache to "inflammation of the brain" and applied leeches; he then treated his insomnia with a remedy suggested by some of the mission's African servants, which he mixed with opium; and died soon after, perhaps from an overdose.[18] Smallpox severely affected the families of several African agents—it killed the Rev. T. B. Macaulay—while sleeping sickness, which spread rapidly in the mid-1860s to affect many Christians, completely baffled them.[19]

Yet Yoruba still applied to missionaries for "medicines" (*oògùn*, "preservatives of life in time of war and peace," as Gollmer once well defined them, since it was a wider category which included charms).[20] Initially, both parties were wary. Gollmer opined that "people in general are afraid of our medicines, but sometimes they will ask us for medicines for constitutional defects, or unusual or aggravated diseases for which [neither] we nor they know any remedies."[21] Correspondingly, when the Ake people came to thank Townsend for the care he had shown an Ogboni chief in his last illness, he said he was glad to receive this gesture since "it is a delicate thing to administer medicine to those under the influence of heathenism, they might charge me with his death."[22] This suspicion is understandable, granted the affinity between medicines taken internally and poison—as shown in the story about the invulnerability "medicine" called *okigbe*, cited earlier[23]—and seems to have relaxed as trust in missionaries grew. It was for their surgical rather than their medical skills that missionaries won respect during the Dahomean attack on Abeokuta in 1851 and during the Ijaye War. Mann found that the members of his congregation at Ijaye constantly sought his medical advice, though pagans stopped when he made it plain that his *oogun* did not include charms.[24] In the mid-1850s the younger Crowther attracted many patients to his dispensary at Abeokuta. There was initially such satisfaction at the rapid results from laxative and expectorant medicines that pressure grew on the less treatable conditions, such as pleurisy and venereal diseases, and then, in disappointment, numbers fell.[25] But this dispensary was not an operation which could be long sustained, and it was not typical of the medical role of the CMS mission for the rest of the century, which had to be built on two premises: most of the agents were Africans with no medical training, and there were no specialized medical institutions.

But medical demand was a constant, and so was what Crowther described as "the inseparable connection that has always been believed to exist between medicine and priestcraft."[26] This presented a serious problem to the local congregations, whose members necessarily depended on "country medicine" for their needs. So James White reckoned that some medical knowledge—he picked up quite a lot from medical books—was very helpful for a pastor. With pagans it opened a path for the Gospel, whereas if Christians had to resort to native doctors, the latter might "take advantage of the necessity of the case to [subject them] to their absurd heathen notions" (such as making sacrifices as part of the cure).[27] White knew his limitations and was reluctant to try if he thought his efforts would fail; but he was highly successful at treating external sores and ulcers—very common conditions—with "bluestone and Holloway's Ointment."[28] The most adventurous of these pastor-physicians was W. S. Allen, who appears to have acquired an extensive local reputation in Ibadan as an emergency surgeon: he would be roused in the middle of the night to patch up a young man with severe abdominal gashes from a knife fight or a women wounded by thieves trying to steal her goat.[29] Reading these accounts of treatments one has the impression that they would be seen less as a distinctively Christian kind of healing than as healing acts that happened to have been performed by men recognized as Christians.

So what was the import for the course of religious change of these efforts to heal and be healed? Although no religion was very good at dealing with the most intractable illnesses, or obviously better than any of the others, they all claimed to offer healing and tried to persuade the public that their apparent successes were due to their privileged relations with the divine. "To him this is a miracle," wrote White of a Christian cured of a nasty sore, "and I hope it will have a tendency to confirm him in his belief in Jesus Christ." Yoruba religion was, quite simply and literally, a matter of life and death. In the rivalry between its different cults, just as healing successes were exulted over, so also failures were the more mortifying because they amounted to a kind of public disgrace. The sudden death of Chief Nasi, one of Christianity's early patrons at Ondo, just over a week after he gave up his Ifa, provoked widespread hostility to public preaching in the town.[30] When Afresi, the first indigenous female convert at Badagry, died only four months after her marriage in church, the Christians were stunned, and Samuel Pearse wrote in his journal: "Tell it not to Gath, neither publish it in the streets of Ashkelon, lest the daughters of the Philistines rejoice, lest the daughters of the uncircumcised triumph."[31]

But although the missionaries were largely constrained to engage in this competition by the locally obtaining rules—not least because they were deeply ingrained in the thinking of potential converts—their own, rather different, views of the relationship between religion and healing continued to influence how they responded to cases of illness and death. For the Europeans among them, at least, the link between the divine source of healing power and the illness/cure was less direct and subject-specific than in the Yoruba view. Medicines produced their effects in a universal and automatic way, so that God was less intrinsic to the healing process, separate from the choice of medicine and treatment.[32] He was placed "above" it, as a ground of being, or "after" it as a seal or sanction of the act of healing. African missionaries commonly sought a more intrinsic link between religion and healing. In treating a sufferer with Holloway's Ointment, White says to him "the medicine I use is God's and to render it efficacious I must ask God's blessing upon it," as if he wanted to make God part of the cure yet was not able to surmount the externality of God to the physical treatment he was offering.

As well as secularizing it (or accepting the secular view gaining ground in their own culture), European missionaries tended to make healing a more ethical and less pragmatic affair, in ways which echo two distinct strands in the Christian interpretation of sickness. On the one hand, there was an older view, closer to how the Yoruba saw it, which regarded sickness as a punishment for misdemeanors against the divine. Thus Young's response to the smallpox epidemic in Ondo:

> The reason for [the epidemic] we cannot account for. It is too many [deaths] that I can say. . . . We have to go round always to advise them to abstain from the constant use of fowls and all forbidden things [i.e., for sacrifice to the *oriṣa*]—and not to expose their patients in cold. And we have also warned them against the worship of [smallpox]. We have tried to shew them that pestilence is the rood [*sic;* presumably he means "rod"] of God against disobedience of the nation and country—but they cannot understand us.[33]

While the Ondo looked to offer sacrifices to the *oriṣa* directly responsible for the epidemic, the Christians regarded it as a punishment from God which required a general repentance, above all from idolatry. The claim implicit in this—that sincere Christians could expect more disease-free lives—was certainly hinted at, and even more often inferred, in many individual cases. When Olubi and Allen call on a sick man in Ibadan, they speak of "Christ the Good Physician, the effective cure of the disease of sin"—which becomes a claim to offer bodily healing too, if sin is taken as the cause of sickness—and certainly this is what the man seems to expect: "God, we pray thee. Help us, help us."[34] Okuseinde tells a woman that her sickness is a call from God; her sister, a Christian, tells her sacrifices are useless; from then on she improves and says "If God continues to help me and restores me to health, I shall then come."[35]

On the other hand, the promise of health and healing might be transvalued: Christ is a physician but mostly in a metaphorical sense, more essentially of the soul than of the body. Here missionary utterances could be regarded by Yoruba as annoyingly equivocal:

> Hinderer enters a compound at Ibadan where a man is fatally ill. He expresses sympathy and speaks of Christ as a "physician of body and soul," who asks all to come to him. Those present expect an instantaneous healing. The sick man implores Hinderer to help. When he reiterates "the

infinite worth of their souls above the body," they look disappointed. One man laughs at Hinderer.[36]

In a context of high mortality, the Yoruba demanded healing—the deferment of death—in no ambiguous terms; all religions offered it to them in some form, and people wanted to believe them; but no religion seemed able to offer decisive proof of its power. So healing was less a decisive factor to win people to any of the faiths which competed for Yoruba adherence than it was a terrain where people realized the intrinsic consolations of religious belonging and belief. Within each cult-group and congregation people prayed for their fellows, and in that sense the most potent medicine was prayer.

In seeking for the key to unlock the power of Christianity, Yoruba attention was focused on its character as a religion of the Book. The name by which Christians were most commonly known was *Onibuku*, "Book-people": a man asks of a girl's Christian intentions with the words *Iwọ nfẹ gba buku?* [Do you mean to take book?].[37] In his dying hours, a young male convert at Abeokuta insists on his books being placed beside his bed, so as to show his pagan relatives that he remains a "book-man."[38] The books in question were, first, of course, the Bible; and second, and hardly of lesser importance, the Yoruba reading primer, known as *Iwe ABD* ("The Book of ABC"), which contained religious texts as well as reading exercises. Indeed, since the primer was the book which the inquirer came to first and opened the path to conversion, it was perhaps that which most deserved the designation *buku*.

The intrinsic "magic" of writing is that it allows a stable content to be transmitted across space and time. An Ibadan chief told Okuseinde, after he had read and translated for him a letter from his brother in Lagos, that "he wondered greatly how [he] was able to disclose his brother's mind to him."[39] Add to this expectations based on the magical use of writing in Muslim charms, and the parallels discerned between writing and the marks made by the *babalawo* in the powder on his tray—themselves tokens of powerful messages from the beyond—and the stage is set for a view of the written word as offering direct access to other kinds of power. When Charles Phillips visited Chief *Odunwo* at Ondo, he was "required . . . to read the book to him that his defective hand [might] be healed."[40] After William Marsh had read a letter from his relatives in Sierra Leone to a returnee, the man was so amazed at his being able to tell him "the names of all the persons belonging to my family" that he came back to ask him to "look into your books, and tell me what I am to do in order to be better and see good."[41] The man regarded both letter and books as containing *awo* or secrets—the same concept that the Eruwa people (as reported by Doherty) applied to all wonderful devices—things which needed a more than ordinary power of insight.

Expectations of oracular guidance, along lines already marked out in Ifa and local Islam, were there from the very beginning. Marsh, newly arrived at Badagry in 1845, noted the many applications made to the missionary party for charms made from sacred writing, and goes on:

> The Mahomedans profess to know what would befall the people, as what is the cause of their not being lucky etc., and also, to cure all the ills that might befall them. But to this people I often spoke and showed that all futurities are known to God alone; that power belongs to God only; that none can stay his hand when he would bring to pass his purposes; and that the Gospel is the only remedy for all evils.[42]

There is a subtle ambiguity here, if not in what Marsh intended, at least in how he would have been heard: the phrase "the only remedy for all evils," while it can be understood in a thoroughly non-magical sense, could *only* have been taken by ordinary Yoruba listeners to imply a claim to offer just the kind of mundane empowerment that Marsh rejected in the form in which it was offered in Muslim *tira*. The demand to know the future from the sacred Book always arose from a precise context of need, just as when a diviner was consulted:

> In November 1873, Ibadan was full of delegates from its subordinate towns, come to pay their tribute. Four men from Ejigbo called in at Allen's house "and asked me to look into our Koran and see if the Ibadans are going to [attack] their town, that they may know what to do; and should there be any charms that could be done for them, which would be buried . . . to prevent wars to attack it."[43]

Since it was Islamic divination that the delegates had in mind, writing had two roles to play: the Book would give the diagnosis of the problem, and writing from it, incorporated into charms, would provide the solution. Allen's reply—that the Bible did not foretell such things, but rather "how we are to live in this pilgrimage world"—cannot have been at all what the Ejigbo men wanted to hear.

Bible and primer were often seen as the Christian's personal repository of power, analogous to the dedicated palm nuts (*ikin*) of the Ifa devotee or the image of an *orisa*. So, traveling from Ota to Lagos, White commented on some villagers that "they have heard of the white man's book [which] . . . is not an orisa as many suppose."[44] In the eyes of many converts there was a kind of antipathetic equivalence between Ifa palm nuts and the Yoruba primer—indeed, the very expression "take book" exactly mirrors the phrase used for receiving the Ifa palm nuts, which I suspect was its origin.[45] A young candidate at Abeokuta was refused his fiancée because "he had thrown away his Ifa and taken a book instead (primer which he learned at school)."[46] About to join the Egba forces at the siege of Ado in 1852, a convert who had thrown away his Ifa and charms asked Crowther to prescribe for him "something to depend on during the war"; and was told to take his primer and read from it every Sunday.[47] A slave inquirer at Ibadan, wavering between Ifa and Christianity, finally decided on an empirical test: he left his Ifa out in its earthenware dish, uncovered save for a primer laid over the top; by morning rats had eaten four of the *ikin,* but left the primer, convincing him "that Ifa had no power, not even over rats."[48] As with an *oriṣa* or a charm, the non-Christian could regard the power of the primer as potentially negative: a female convert at Ibadan was accused of using hers to bewitch the man her hostile family had engaged her to marry.[49]

The evident power of Europeans was not matched by the mission's ability or readiness to make it available in the forms or the ways that the Yoruba wanted; and the latter in turn were long inhibited from realizing the power of writing by the framework within which they imagined its use. Some of the differences came out in a conversation between White, a chief, and a *babalawo* at Ota. They had argued before, and on this occasion the chief began by insisting again on Ifa's ability to predict the future:

[W] Ifa cannot speak.

[B] How do you understand from your book what God says?

[W] Why, the words are plain before us.

[B] We are likewise so acquainted with [Ifa] that we know immediately what he means by consulting him.

[W] But your Ifa is always changing. If he says a thing just now and you were to consult him upon the same thing a few minutes after that he will say quite another thing altogether. But our book never changes. Open the same place a hundred times and you will find the same thing. This shows that God and his words are true and Ifa and his words false. But I am inclined to believe the words are your own and not Ifa's.

[B] Well, Ifa gives a distinct prophecy every time he is consulted.[50]

Where the indigenous wisdom of Ifa was secret, pragmatically oriented, flexible, specific in its application, and linked to status, the Word of God as presented by the missionaries was open, ethically oriented, fixed, universal in application, and in principle independent of status. In a society where knowledge was above all the prerogative of the old, nothing was more amazing than that this most basic of the white man's techniques was so readily acquired and used by women and children.[51]

INQUIRERS AND THEIR MOTIVES

While its credited power was the main general ground on which people might be persuaded to leave one cult or religion for another, three other classes of factor are also relevant to the explanation of conversion. These were the expressive or otherwise non-instrumental appeals of Christianity, such as its ethical teaching or its cultural style; the social advantages of belonging to the Christian community, as such; the system of rewards and controls in society at large, which made the costs and the benefits of conversion socially so variable; and the freedom to convert if one wanted to. The interplay of motivations and controls which produced the overall pattern of conversion can only be apprehended through individual case histories, which are barely amenable to statistical analysis or reducible to a single model, though some rough generalization about the weight of particular factors is possible.

The CMS journals mention many individuals who turned up at mission stations as "inquirers," some of whom settled to a course of religious instruction as "candidates," whose ideal end product was baptism, the formal ceremony of admission to the Christian body. Sometimes they came out of curiosity to see the *oyinbo* and their things, and it went no further. They might come singly, or in a group of companions, or be brought by a Christian relative or friend. They might be neighbors, or come to follow up on what they had heard from a missionary's public preaching, or just in response to what they had casually heard about the *oyinbo*'s religion or from Christians they had come across around the town. Quite often inquirers had had some prior, transient contact with Christianity: they had heard a missionary preach some time ago in another place, or had had a relationship with a Christian. Often too, inquirers were strangers of some kind—slaves, new settlers, or traders— or were migrants returned, all of whom were more inclined and more able than native residents to explore new religious options. Meakin commented that at Oyo his neighbors, who were friendly but not inclined to become Christians, continually brought strangers to him.[52]

In reading these accounts we are, as it were, dropping in on moments in individual lives of which we are given only the briefest characterization: we usually learn something of what had gone before but often little of what followed, even of whether the inquiry led to conversion. What the missionary journalists tell us about inquirers is partly their circumstances and partly their motives. The latter are inherently much more problematic as data since they are not open to external inspection. The kinds of motive that the missionaries wanted to hear (and sometimes report)—conviction of the folly of idolatry, consciousness of sin and of the need for salvation, attraction to their ethical principles, and so on—are more like post-hoc justifications for Christian faith than the considerations that would really impel *orisa* followers to explore what the new religion had to offer. A brief instance from Ibadan neatly brings out the contrast between the inward convictions which the missionaries sought and the practical concerns which brought inquirers to them:

A woman comes to James Okuseinde at Ogunpa, Ibadan's smallest CMS station, to give up her idols. He asks her what sign is in her heart. She replies she's a great sinner. He asks again what sign is in her. She tells with many tears of the many sacrifices she has made to *orịṣa*, "but instead of good things, things went wrong with me, no peace with me whatever," so it came to her to forsake them. He encourages her with John 6:37, "him that cometh to me I will in no wise cast out."[53]

It is hardly surprising that it was the pragmatic search for personal *alafia* which most often came to the fore in initial Yoruba inquiries of Christianity, since that was already the most likely reason, readily sanctioned by Ifa, why anyone might want to switch their devotion from one *orịṣa* to another.

Inquirers often had a prior history of religious quest, like the woman at Ijaye whom Mann overheard telling her friend that she had first worshipped her Ori or personal destiny; then, finding no peace, Sango; then tried the Muslims, with no better luck; and finally decided to take the path of the *oyinbo*, to what effect we do not know.[54] Whatever the source of the problem—with women, childlessness came high on the list—it was likely to be aggravated by the cost of the medicines or sacrifices that were certain to be prescribed along the way. Another case from Ijaye:

> Mann speaks for the first time to a woman who has been attending for two months. She had lost her children, and paid money in vain for help from Ifa, to the hunters "who are said to find the good medicine against death in the far distant woods" and to the Muslims. She then reckoned that as all are subject to the one God, she should seek help from those who preach Him and tell people to abandon the *orịṣa*. She was put off by the cool reception she got from Mrs. Bowen at the Baptist Mission, and hearing the lessons as she passed by the CMS station, she called in to try her luck there.[55]

And one from Abeokuta, reported by Thomas King:

> A woman comes to church at the prompting of "various warnings by dreams, and the constant disturbance and restless state of her heart at all times." She had spent four bags of cowries "making Obatala" with no benefit; and was then told she must get herself an Elegbara (Esu). This was an elaborate assemblage: an image with miniature clubs, small calabashes with medicines and strings of cowries attached to it, all of which cost several heads of cowries, seven goats, and other occasional sacrifices. But her heart was still troubled, till she met a Christian woman who comforted her and told her to go to God's house. Here she was "wrought upon" by Proverbs 8:32–36 [and I imagine especially by verse 35: "For whoso findeth me, findeth life, and shall obtain favour of the Lord"] and gave up the Elegbara.[56]

Whether or not Christianity solved these problems in an external sense, one relief it could bring was to break the dispiriting and impoverishing cycle of expenditure on charms and sacrifices which many sick and barren people were driven to. Another of King's contacts was a man brought in from his farm hamlet, still sick and now destitute after having spent thirty heads of cowries for eight animal sacrifices. This prompted a dream in which he saw "a very large assembly of all ranks and ages, all having books in their hands, and who were reading, praying and singing"; his conductor in the dream told him to kneel and pray, and said that he would die if he did not give up worshipping idols.[57] The man gave up his Ifa, but whether he recovered we do not know. But White tells a story which gives another twist to the abandonment of sacrifices: a woman at Ota, convinced of the futility of idols by her Saro landlady, threw hers away, but not before cutting off their decorative cowries, which she used as trading capital—and was eventually able to redeem her two nieces from slavery.[58] In any case, childlessness might perhaps be borne more easily within a new community which did not stigmatize it so severely and offered more of a theology of acceptance of what God had sent.

Many inquirers took a highly experimental, even consumerist, approach to the religious options open to them. Okuseinde reports a typical instance from Ibadan:

> An elderly woman has given up coming to services, "when the object of my attending church with the Christians had been baffled." Her husband had long been sick and much had been spent in vain on sacrifices. A Christian woman suggested they attend; they came and tried to do all what was asked of them [unfortunately unspecified], but her husband still died.[59]

In a similar case from Badagry, the inquirer's strategy was the same, but the issue still unresolved:

> A man was asked by his wife, being childless, to sacrifice a goat to Ifa. He told Daniel Coker that "if . . . the object desired is not got, he will join the Christians and no more worship Ifa, because he is seeing that idolatry is a vain service." It was not successful, and now he attends church.[60]

The notion that religious claims were "verified" by positive answers to prayers was equally strong among Yoruba Christians and their pastors:

> Thomas King admits as a candidate a man who had given up his Ifa. He had first come five years ago, but then fallen away. Travelling from Abeokuta to Lagos, he had been struck by a violent pain and had prayed to God for deliverance, promising to dedicate himself if he pulled through. "How verifying are the words of Psalm 50:15 ['And call upon me in the day of trouble: I will deliver thee and thou shalt glorify me'] to his experience."[61]

In a perfect religious market, where all cults face the same pattern of popular demand and where none is much ahead of its rivals in being able to meet that demand, we would expect an equal movement all ways between the competing cults, only proportionate to the size and saliency of each cult. The CMS journals do indeed provide evidence of such an all-ways movement: from one *oriṣa* cult to another, pagans turning to Islam or to Christianity, either way between the two world religions, both Christians and Muslims turning back to *oriṣa* cults. It was part of Yoruba common sense that all cultic allegiances were provisional:

> An inquirer at Ibadan hands in his Ifa, which his wife had hidden, thinking he would want to return to it. His father had been a Muslim for a time, entrusting his *oriṣa* to a relative to look after, in anticipation of his later taking them up again. The man's wife scolded him for being foolish, but conceded, "He is your god, take it, burn it and eat it and die if you like."[62]

But what we have to explain in practice is a divergence from this pattern of equal circulation between cults. There was a definite overall drift toward the world religions, modest and halting at first, but then beginning to accelerate, first in Lagos from the late 1860s, but in the country at large only from the 1890s. Two sets of considerations seem pertinent to explain it. The first is the world religions' greater capacity than the *oriṣa* cults to retain the commitment of those who joined them. One sound way to defend against preference being transferred to rivals is to make some of the cult's satisfaction internal, or independent of external performance criteria—just as brand loyalty, strictly irrational from a consumer viewpoint, does in modern retail markets. Up to a point, Yoruba were held to their existing cults by feelings of mutual obligation between themselves and their *oriṣa:*

> A warrior hands his Ifa in to Okuseinde, saying "I thank God who showed me the way of salvation." During the Ijesha war he had failed to capture a slave but a fine carved Ifa bowl had fallen into his hands. Showing the bowl to his own Ifa, he said to it, "I cared for you, so you must take care of me from all dangers." A few days later he was shot. But he still kept his Ifa, so that it would draw the shot out of his leg. Then he saw it was no good to save him from trouble in this world or the next. He thought of becoming a Muslim, but his brother, already a Christian convert, suggested he go to the *oyinbo*.[63]

This went further, for the sacrifices which expressed these bonds of mutual obligation between human beings and *orisa* also created, through the sharing of the sacrificial feast, strong feelings of fellowship among cult members. A baptismal candidate at Ibadan withdrew "because he could not bear that his heathen friends partake of his feast and he be unable to partake of their sacrifice."[64]

While all cults strove to foster their members' loyalty through such means, the world religions also had an intrinsic doctrinal advantage, in that they could offer rewards in the next life, which were not susceptible to empirical disconfirmation in this one. While outsiders might well express skepticism about these claims, they could not but have worked toward the retention of members, especially those who had been well socialized into Christian teaching. Hence the importance which the missionaries attached to the careful instruction which candidates for baptism had to undergo. Learning to read, through the Yoruba primer, was a big part of this, and it also seems very likely that the large investment of effort required to become a "book person" (like the labor of learning to recite the Koran among serious converts to Islam) helped to fix converts in their new Christian identity and so reduce the chance of their moving on to another cult.

The other source of the drift to the world religions was still an external appeal but not an immediately pragmatic one. This was their ethical and metaphysical attraction, or the superior answers they were felt to give to questions of meaning posed by the experiences of the Age of Confusion. The relative infrequency with which such motives were expressed by inquirers should not be taken to prove that they were insignificant, since pragmatic motives, specific and concrete, were both easier to articulate and endorsed by the prevailing Yoruba rhetoric of religious choice. That they occur most distinctly in accounts of some of the high-status converts is probably because these were deemed to be people to whom the usual pragmatic motives would be less likely to apply. But that does not prove they were not present in humbler cases, or in cases where no clear motive is indicated, like a young man at Ijaye, a friend of the schoolteacher Andrew Wilhelm:

> He was a weaver, and known as Erinle, because he was the leader of a company of worshippers of that *orişa*. He was "much troubled," attending church regularly and observing the sabbath. There was great pressure on him from his family and friends to desist, for "his rank entitles him to many honours": he was in line for the headship of the cult and for marriage to a daughter of the *Arẹago*, a close friend of Kurunmi, the despot of Ijaye. He left his loom and went off to sit on a lonely rock in the bush for hours. The *Arẹago* told him to respect his family obligations and break off his links with the Christians.[65]

This is what he seems to have done—for he does not appear again in the journals—and we never learn what the focus of his disquiet was.

The most telling cases are from the narratives of a select group of converts— senior, high-status men. The first concerns Erubami at Ota, described as "a zealous idolater and a man of great note in this town . . . as bold as a lion":

> In August 1873 Erubami came to tell White of his desire to give up his idols, and called in repeatedly over the next month. He had first heard the Word of God a quarter of a century before, from Gollmer near Badagry, and later from other people in Ota [but not much apparently from White himself, since otherwise earlier journals would surely have mentioned it]. Feeling "such disgust for his idols . . . that they appear to him

as filth rather than anything else," he wanted them all out of his house, including those which were kept there by others. He handed them over to White—fifteen of them, each one named—in two stages. His relatives were amazed to see it, and came in a party to ask him why he had done it, granted "that he is in good health, has enough to live upon and has children." His answer was that "he has no peace in his mind, that their fathers have erred, that his idols have done him no good and that unless they repent and do as he has done, they would perish in the world to come."[66]

White uses the same language to express Erubami's condition—of not having "peace" of "heart" or "mind"—as of other inquirers whose misery sprang directly from a more material cause, such as being sick or destitute or childless, but in his case it seems to have a less material source. It serves to remind us that the desired condition of *alafia* refers to a holistic state of well-being, in which physical and "metaphysical" elements not only coexisted but interacted with one another.

The same diffuse sense of "dis-ease" pervades the testimony of his life which James Oderinde, already rising to sixty, gave when he was baptized at Kudeti church in Ibadan in 1856:

Originally he had been a worshipper of Yemoja, and had made good money from making and selling images of Elegbara. But he always felt dissatisfied and "no peace came in his heart." He started listening to the claim of the Muslims to have the true religion, and after "a remarkable dream [had] troubled him much," he joined them. Then he suffered great losses, his slaves absconded, his family died, and he sank into poverty. He still had no peace of mind. A friend suggested that he go to the *oyinbo*, then still new in Ibadan. He found it strange that both religions claimed to have the Word of God, but was impressed by the fact "that Mr Hinderer never told him to break with the Mahomedans, while these when hearing of his going to white man forbade him to visit us." This made him come over sooner. Of his three wives one died, and the other two were both baptized. He was smitten particularly by Luke 14:26 ["If any man come to me, and hate not his father, and mother, and wife, and children, and brethren, and sisters, yea, and his own life also, he cannot be my disciple."]. After much discussion, his second wife agreed to leave him—there was no baptism for polygamous men—and "he dismissed her in peace."[67]

As with Erubami the exact nature of Oderinde's primary discontent is not clear, but some kind of revulsion against the *orişa* cults, impelling him toward Islam as the only monotheism then available seems most likely. Though material trouble is not held responsible for this first conversion, the subsequent disasters in his life are implicitly held against his decision to become a Muslim. But his fortunes seem to have sufficiently recovered—wives and at least two sons, who became boarders at the Kudeti school—for us to discount the idea that lack of material *alafia* was what turned him to Christianity. This interpretation seems supported by the text from Luke: one of the most confronting pronouncements of Christ, so radically subversive of the domestic pieties which are written into all "primal" religions, from those of the classical world to the Yoruba cults.

The last case of this kind concerns David Kukomi, the most eminent Ibadan convert of his day, who succeeded Oderinde as the leading lay Christian. Converted in 1859, he was not baptized till 1867, since not until then was he able to set aside all but one of his seventeen wives.[68] Unfortunately, there is no journal of Hinderer's for the period in which Kukomi most likely became a Christian,[69] but there are two sharply contrasting sources for what occurred. The first is the testimony which Kukomi himself gave at a prayer meeting in 1872:

> He had long suffered from dropsy so severe that he could not walk the few miles to his farm; he spent much money on doctors to little effect; he became Christian and was cured. Whenever a fresh attack occurs, he lays it before the Lord, who hears him. . . . "Now, my brethren," he added, "if any of you fall into trouble, and you go to Him for deliverance, he will answer you. And if He does not answer you, then examine yourself and be sure your sin is mixed up with unbelief and doubtings, and sin lies at the door."[70]

The other is a tradition current among Kukomi's descendants about his early encounters with Hinderer:

> When Hinderer first preached at Oke Ofa, where Kukomi lived in the eastern part of Ibadan, Kukomi would not go to hear him, nor did he want his sons to. He thought his stories were fit only for women and girls. Once when Hinderer visited, some children in the compound started throwing sand at him, and in the course of this one girl fell over. Kukomi (who was watching unobserved) thought she would get slapped, but Hinderer picked her up and patted her. Could it be, thought Kukomi, that he was the Prince of Peace he was always preaching about? Next time he came, Hinderer treated the girl's grazed knee from his first-aid kit, and she hit him when it stung. Kukomi was again impressed that he did not smack her back. The third time Hinderer came, Kukomi asked him if he was the Prince of Peace. So they came to talk, and Kukomi agreed to send his eldest son Oyebode to go and board with the Hinderers at Kudeti for schooling.[71]

Kukomi's testimony is uncompromisingly Christian, yet it still strongly endorses the Yoruba view that religions are proved by their capacity to deliver pragmatic benefits such as healing. It was thus very well suited to the context in which it was delivered, which was intended to convince Yoruba Christians of the power of their adopted religion. But is this a sufficient explanation of Kukomi's conversion? Against his cure from dropsy, which in any case seems to have been far from complete, has to be set the loss of conventional status entailed by his giving up all but one of his wives. Why would he make this sacrifice—quite extraordinary for an Ibadan man of his standing—if there was not more to his decision than the palliation of his dropsy? Hinderer's message of the Prince of Peace—which we know from other evidence was a dominant theme in his preaching at this time—was not merely one of gentle forbearance in personal relations, but also had clear political implications. The epithet comes from Isaiah's great prophecy of the coming of the Messiah and of his peaceable kingdom (Isaiah 9:6), and is very likely to have been at least partially understood by Kukomi in terms of the expectation of many Yoruba in the mid-1850s that the missionaries brought *atunṣe aiye* [restoration of the world], a peaceful resolution of the conflicts of the age.[72] (Ironically, the year of Kukomi's conversion saw the outbreak of the Ijaye War and the deferment of hopes of lasting peace for a whole generation.) Can we resist the view that Kukomi was swayed by attraction to the broader ethical, and beyond that political, vision summed up by the image of the Prince of Peace?

Kukomi's rejection of the polygamous lifestyle of a warrior compound-head, and Oderinde's fascination with a text which legitimates the breaking of conventional social obligations in the name of Christ, both run counter to the general rule that I proposed earlier, that conversion has to be first understood in terms of the cultural continuities which underlie it. Both men were *somehow*—for we cannot pretend to be able to unravel the root causes at the personal level—moved from within their culture to reject a significant part of it. One presumes that this happened in other cases too. But it is a noteworthy (but understandable) paradox that the operation of ethical ideals in conversion should show up most incontrovertibly in the narratives of those who had the least *interest* in breaking from the system, not of the many poorer and lower-status converts whose interests coincided more closely with the missionaries' critique of it.

SOCIAL STATUS AND SOCIAL SANCTIONS

In nearly all cases, conversion involved a balance or trade-off between the attractions of becoming a Christian and its costs. The costs were mainly to do with the various kinds of social severance which becoming a Christian was likely to entail, or with the social sanctions—ranging from physical force through material deprivation to moral censure—which might be deployed to stop it happening. This implies that conversion would be least attractive and feasible for those who were already well-integrated or of high status in the community, for they would have more to lose; and, so we should find, that strangers and slaves would be disproportionately present among the first waves of converts. Of all forms of social differentiation the most fundamental were age and gender. It is only analytically that age can be treated separately from gender, since it is the age-sex conjunction in every individual which is the most important variable affecting conversion. So I shall begin with gender, then gender as modified by age, before moving to the more contingent social attributes.

The idea that Christianity, at least when initially presented, might be more attractive to women, has been raised not only with respect to Africa in general,[73] but is also prompted by the commonly expressed view of Yoruba men that it was a "womanly" religion.[74] That women, *ceteris paribus,* had less power and status than men, and were more likely, through in-marriage, to be strangers to the town where they lived, should certainly have given women some greater inclination toward Christianity than men; and it is true that women were much more assiduous than men at church attendance in well-established congregations. But the crucial point about women's status here is not that it was lower than men's, but that it was complementary to it in a specific way, which centered on their reproductive and domestic roles. Their concern to bear and successfully rear children made women anxious seekers after any spiritual agency available to help them and, as we have seen, sometimes led them to turn to the mission. Yet it was precisely this need which initially locked them much more deeply into the *orișa* cults than most men were. In early days at Abeokuta, Samuel Crowther commented on "the superstitious fears of parents, especially the mothers, that their children should no longer worship the country fashion to whom they imagine the children owe their births and preservation."[75] White found the same at Ota in 1859:

> "The male population . . . are more disposed to listen to the preaching of the Gospel than the female, who are too bigotted [*sic*] and deep-rooted in their superstitious belief." There is the case of Daniel Oguntolu, whose wife wants him to give up being a Christian. Knowing his attachment to her, she washed and dressed beautifully, put his books next to her, and told him to choose between her and them. "Daniel, to her astonishment . . . seized his books saying, indeed I love you, but God forbid that I should put you in the place of God. This woman at once thought that there must be some mystery in the new religion . . . as formerly at the least threat to forsake the husband he is seized with anxiety, and would earnestly implore her not to leave him. . . . This woman still continues the wife of Daniel."[76]

Here we might surmise that Daniel's wife was having difficulty in conceiving, and thought that his Christianity was not helping matters. A few years later, White was especially pleased to have converted a woman "since it is a rare thing for the female population of [Ota] to attend the things of God, and they are the obstacles in the way of the male population."[77] James Johnson reported a case from Ogbomosho where a Christian was divorced by his wife on the grounds of neglecting her welfare by forsaking the *orișa*.[78] Even Ogunbona, the mission's great patron at Abeokuta and all but Christian in his own religious practice, could not stop the *orișa* devotions of his wives, which were closely bound in with their view of what was good for their children.[79] Though some women were prominent among the early converts at Abeokuta—such as Susannah Kuti, "a crown of our infant church"[80]—women were far fewer than men in Hinderer's class of 109 candidates early in 1849.[81] In 1850 Thomas King baptized twenty-four men (by implication no women), several of whom had been persecuted or fined by the Ogboni for their decision to become Christian.[82] Very partial evidence from Ondo suggests a similar picture, of women being less forward than men in the first wave of inquirers and converts. Only four out of the eleven first converts there were women, and three of them were strangers, two being redeemed slaves who were mission dependents; but six out of the seven male converts were Ondo natives.[83]

But how far was it a matter of women being less able to exercise their preferences rather than one of Christianity appealing less to them? Mrs. Phillips and Mrs. Young once asked the female inquirers at Ondo why they were so slow in declaring for Christianity, and concluded that fear of their men held them back;[84] and when about twelve girls, drawn by friendship with Julie, Young's daughter, started coming to church and even abandoning their *orişa,* their parents by quiet concert moved to stop the association.[85] But persecution in Ondo in the 1880s was nothing to what it had been earlier in Abeokuta (which, apart from the *Ifóle* in 1867, had seen a severe wave of it in 1849) and Ibadan (where it was continual, if sporadic, from the mid-1850s till the late 1870s).[86] Hinderer once asked his candidates what was the greatest evil in the world, expecting the answer *Sin,* but "one of them entirely betraying the thoughts of their hearts answered *Persecution.*"[87] Except for the two waves of publicly sponsored persecution at Abeokuta, the great bulk of it was endured at the hands of close relatives, particularly parents, husbands, or in-laws, and, to a much lesser extent, neighbors. It might take many forms: flogging and beating, confinement in the compound (often in chains or stocks) or expulsion from it, seizure or damage of clothes or property, economic boycott, denial of routine forms of neighborly assistance,[88] charges of divulging Oro or Egungun secrets or, worst of all, of attempting to poison or causing the death of relatives.[89] Yet despite its brutalities, persecution had a real social point. It was directed toward defending the social order from the threat posed by Christianity at the two critical points of its cycle of reproduction: birth and death, of which the first bore on women, the latter mostly on men.

Most references to persecution—about three quarters of reported cases—concern women, young women in particular: mothers of babies, betrothed women, and adolescent girls. It was not just that young women were more susceptible than others to pressure from their elders, but that they were responsible for discharging a key (and, as it seemed, threatened) social function. In the domestic context, the most essential role of the *orişa* was to ensure that the lineage was reproduced; and it was the chief responsibility of the women of the compound to cherish the *orişa* to this end. When Christianity drew women away from this duty, it could only be seen as a blow struck at the vitals of the family:

> In the early days of the Ibadan mission, no case created more disturbance than that of two girls who joined the baptismal class at Kudeti and were beaten by their fathers "for refusing to take part in the usual sacrifice making." A year later, the girls (one of them by now married) ran off to Abeokuta and, their mothers getting no satisfaction from their pleas to Mrs. Hinderer—herself always known as *Iya*, "Mother"—the families complained to the *Bale* of the mission taking away their wives and children.[90]

The final abscondment of the girls took to completion their refusal to be present at the family rituals. Whatever the girls' motives, the complaint of their families was fundamental, that Christianity was a menace to their very future. Feelings about family sacrifices might run very high: when the wife of an Egungun devotee at Ibadan refused to eat her portion of the kola after a sacrifice to Ori, the man threatened to kill both himself and her.[91]

In contrast to this endemic, familial persecution mostly directed at young women, stands the public persecution which burst out at Abeokuta in 1849, which mostly concerned men. It was preceded by the first, fairly modest wave of accessions to Christianity in which males predominated:[92]

> The immediate trigger was the death on 9 October of Idimi, a convert from Itoku township, who had been Hinderer's ostler. Already forsaken by his wife and family on account of his conversion, he had been taken to the mission house to be cared for in his last illness, and was buried in the churchyard (attended by a great crowd), rather than in his family compound. Though the family had sanctioned it, the Christian burial angered the Ogboni because it cut them out from their usual role in funerals (for which it levied a fee from non-initiates) and the next day a good number of Christians were seized and put in chains by order of the Ogboni chiefs. The Itoku converts were whipped, fined, and then released, but by then the movement had started to spread, first to Igbore, where seventy to eighty converts were imprisoned, and then to Igbein and some other townships.[93] By December things were more or less brought to a halt with the help of the mission's patrons among the Ologun (war-chiefs), who appreciated the risk to Abeokuta if it alienated its *oyinbo* allies.

The missionaries held two groups of people chiefly responsible for the persecution: the Ogboni chiefs of certain townships, and *babalawo*. But while some *babalawo* were certainly active—which was interpreted as showing that they felt that they had to defend a heathenism now under powerful threat from the Word of God—it was not the case that *babalawo* as such were committed enemies of Christianity. Hinderer was stopped in the street by one *babalawo* who wanted to justify the persecution, but heard another commend Christianity "as a strong religion, giving strong hearts to the people even in the midst of death," and even met a third whose Ifa had told him that "his wife and children were destined to be Christians."[94] It was in the nature of Ifa divination that *babalawo,* like economic forecasters, should be found on every side in any dispute.

But the Ogboni were committed to the established values of the local community, and the nub of their anxiety was, as Sagbua reported the discussion in the Ake Ogboni house, that

> these book people refuse to obey us by no more making those country fashions which we have received from our fathers, they even expose them, we are their fathers, they are our children, we justly punish our children for this their disobedience.[95]

This note of patriarchal panic was also picked up by the missionaries in the streets: "old people began to curse us, but several young persons would bless us."[96] Even at Ogunbona's township of Ikija, the elders grumbled at "our children because they do too much."[97] It was the behavior of young *men* that the elders were especially concerned about, as witness the indicative charge that the converts had been revealing the secrets of the ancestral cult of Oro to *women.* Critical to the authority of the Ogboni was that they presided over funerals, the rites of passage through which elders became ancestors. And here we see that it was no accident that the flashpoint of the whole episode was the burial of a convert in the churchyard. Disputes over where and how Christians should be buried were to occur repeatedly for many years to come. The mission wanted converts to be buried in "holy ground," separated from their pagan kin but united with their fellow believers. As the Yoruba saw it, this amounted to abandoning the bodies of their kin, who should be intimately available to their descendants in a domestic grave, to the bush, the place for criminals and the untimely dead. To many the idea of burying one's mother "in a box in the bush"[98] was deeply offensive. But behind this lay an issue of the greatest moment for the old Yoruba order, since by separating the dead from their descendants Christian burial custom challenged the very process of social reproduction, in its moral as in its physical aspect. And the missionaries knew it: "There one of their customs has broken through," wrote Crowther, almost gloatingly, of the Christian success in getting Idimi's burial out of the hands of the Ogboni. So the persecution of Christians was undertaken as a cultural defense of public order, of the authority of male elders and of the integrity of the lineage.

If they showed serious signs of interest in Christianity, men in particular were often subject to another form of control, more subtle in its operation than outright persecution and certainly more effective: the pressure of their friends. A young man at Ota threw his Ifa and Esu carelessly to the ground to show White that he had given up their worship, but when asked why he did not come to church, confessed "It is through shame of my companions."[99] A man who helped Ogunpa church in Ibadan by occasionally supplying labor told Okuseinde that "he was ashamed to come [to church] fearing the reproach of his companions and equals, being a man of some note in the town."[100] A man who had promised Young at Ondo that he would come to church "said he was waiting for his companions and they disappointed him; and he considered it a disrespect to him for going alone; as such he thinks his companions will make a mock of him."[101] These were precisely the pressures that Oderinde and Kukomi had had to resist when they embraced the Gospel. Oderinde met it again from his neighbor whom he almost persuaded to join him as a baptismal candidate; but the man put him off since "he feared shame from his company in the war."[102] Though men were not immune to pressures from above, the most typical force for religious conformity to which they were subject was this from their peers in the community, unlike what young women had to endure from their seniors within the family.

Other social distinctions were connected to religious preference more simply than gender, and may largely be treated as variants of the single characteristic of being low or marginal in the status hierarchy. Foremost here was youth. Young people were clearly attracted in disproportionate numbers to missionary teaching, and the surge of inquirers and converts which provoked the 1849 persecution at Abeokuta (like subsequent waves of religious innovation in Yoruba history[103]) had much of the character of a youth movement. In fact, sympathetic elderly people often expressly told missionaries that Christianity was a thing for the future and their children: "Our children must learn the Word of God, but we old people are too old for changing our fashions."[104] In a gerontocratic society the young both have to bear the brunt of their elders' exercise of power and are the least locked into existing religious institutions. If the young were not "caught" in the period in which they were most available—basically the time before first marriage, which extended much longer for men—they were soon drawn into commitments which raised the costs of conversion greatly—above all men's polygamy, which was an absolute bar to their baptism.[105] (A woman married polygamously, however, was not so debarred). The militaristic public culture of the larger Yoruba towns, strongly upheld by men's *ẹgbẹ*, by whose lights Christianity was seen as a religion more fit for women than men, also acted as a strong deterrent to the conversion of adult males.

Women, by contrast, were not so likely to find that growing older directly made Christianity a less attractive or viable option. Certainly once churches had been in existence for some years, middle-aged or elderly women are found as prominent members of them, and not all of them would have grown to seniority from a youthful conversion. Several of the most bitter burial palavers involved Christian women with pagan children, who wanted their mother to be buried in the house—which strongly suggests that the women did not convert till their children were grown. The social benefits of church membership must also have had great appeal for those post-menopausal women who did not have the security of living children, especially if they were strangers to the town.

But some of these mature female converts were natives and women of standing with children of their own. The most famous such was Matilda Suada at Abeokuta, who received a remarkable tribute from her pastor, Samuel Cole, when she died in 1876:

> Her conversion in 1860 caused great surprise "for she was a woman of no ordinary wealth and had respectable families." She was the only daughter of Efunlola, the richest woman of Ikereku township, who was vehemently hostile to her conversion "for fear she might not give her a worthy heathen burial . . . killing rams to her departed spirit." Matilda gave £20 for the rebuilding of Ikija church, and "anything that was done in this church that required money was done under her Matronage . . . She was a Dorcas to heathens and Christians."
>
> As she got old, she would only attend Ikija church once on a Sunday, for she was so "robust and corpulent" she had to stop three times to rest on the 40-minute walk from her house. Only one relative, her youngest child, Moses Venn, became Christian. During her painful last illness, her family at first refused to allow the church people to read and pray with her. But hundreds, both pagans and Christians, attended her funeral. In their grief, some of the Ikija church women threw themselves to the ground with such violence that they injured themselves.
>
> The Christians negotiated with her family for a church burial. Her eldest son, Ogun, admitted that as a Christian she should have one, but he did not feel that he could propose it to her other relatives. Even if it was allowed, he added, "my companions will for ever abuse me, and the reproach will be too great for me, in as much as I live among them. The only favour I can ask of you is, offer prayer that my mother may be received into that heaven prepared for good people."[106]

Why Matilda decided to become a Christian, we have no idea. But Cole's narrative well brings out the conflicts and compromises, within both family and community, that a decision like hers entailed. To her family, she was no less one of them (and as a result, not in the end entirely her own person, as Western or Christian individualism understands it) even though she had decided to take Christian identity. Her story, in a sense (and rather a Yoruba sense at that), continued after her death:

> Two years later, in 1878, under James Johnson's energetic direction, plans get under way for a new church at Ikereku, Matilda's own township. Her son Ogun is working with "his people" [i.e., largely his slaves], digging clay for the foundations of the building.
>
> By 1883, Ikereku church is well established, with its own catechist, A. B. Green. He reports that Matilda's son [not named, but presumably Ogun], who though still a pagan now regularly attends church, intends to make

a sacrifice to his late mother, as he has done every year since her death. Green preaches Exodus 20:3 ("Thou shalt have no other gods before me") to him, and he says he will give up the practice altogether.[107]

As Matilda was taken to belong to her family, her son now belongs to her, a great woman and a "mother in Israel," as the phrase had it. So "conversion" slips loose from its evangelical moorings and Christianization proceeds on more Yoruba terms.

But Matilda Suada, like David Kukomi, was clearly an exceptional case. If conversion was most likely with those who were marginal or low status in some respect—as the young were temporarily—then mature people were most susceptible if they had some other relevant attribute, such as being poor, unfree, or a stranger. So David Williams reported from Ake in 1881 that most converts—he meant fresh recruits, not the large body of second-generation Christians—came "from foreigners or domestic slaves," and at Osiele, the Egba farm town where there had been a mission for thirty years, most of Cole's congregation were not natives, but people who had converted as slaves and then bought their freedom.[108] At Badagry, the converts were either Yoruba migrants or, if they were Egun indigenes, "poor and having no particular trade in hand to better their temporal condition."[109] Ijesha migrants, traders who included many ex-slaves, formed the main component of a string of congregations along the lagoon, from Iworo in the west to Palma, Leki, and Itebu in the east.[110] Once on a visit to his friend James White at Ota, Samuel Pearse commented that the congregation seemed the same size as it had been nine years before but that he saw few old faces there. So together they compared the class lists of 1864 and 1873, and concluded that, of the 69 people who were no longer there (43 being Ota natives and 26 strangers), 23 had died, 14 had relapsed to idolatry, and 32 had moved on to other towns (14 to Lagos; 14 to Oke Odan, a market town near Badagry; and 4 to Abeokuta).[111] It confirms general impressions of just how mobile nineteenth-century Yoruba populations were, and of how dependent Christianity was on both the outward and the homeward phases of the movement. Of the first seven native Ondo converts, four had had undergone enforced migration through enslavement to other places, where they had first come into contact with the Gospel.[112] The rapid spread of Christianity throughout eastern Yorubaland after 1892 was crucially dependent on the return to their homes of these once-despised migrant members of the congregations of Abeokuta and Ibadan.

There was, of course, a large overlap between the categories of poor or low-status people, and of migrants or strangers, slaves in particular. This prompts the question of whether those of them who became Christians were moved more by their low social status or their being strangers. Religions have often been regarded as addressing the needs of lower-class adherents by promoting the idea that poverty as such places people closer to God, or promising that in a future life the virtuous poor will find compensation for their present sufferings in a posthumous felicity; or they have provided present reward through participating in religious ritual or belonging to a close-knit and supportive cult fellowship, which serve somewhat to offset the "injuries of class" in daily existence (and so, perhaps, reconcile people to them). While the intrinsic satisfactions of ritual and fellowship are common to *oriṣa* cults and Christian churches—it is hard to imagine a viable congregational religion without them—the Yoruba still lacked the key conditions for much religious *ressentiment* to take hold. Despite its inequalities, theirs was not properly a class society; they did not have any *culture* of poverty, any tendency to hallow it as "holy poverty"; and they were only marginally disposed to regard the afterlife as a place for moral redress. George Meakin might have been encouraged to hear the slaves and pawns who attended his school at Oyo, after finishing the day's work for their masters, singing together "There is a happy land far, far away,"[113] but we cannot conclude theirs was a "slave religion" in any essential sense.[114] While it is true that concern about heaven and hell is reported as a motive for conversion in some cases, it seems that this was most often because of the eschatological anxiety aroused by evangelical preaching, which affected Yoruba without regard to their social status, rather than a desire for "pie in the sky" in place of deprivation on earth.

Slaves were not usually hindered by their masters from following their own religious preferences—indeed, they seem to have been much less subject to persecution than young family members. Occasionally, a slave did seek to use Christian connections to alleviate his condition:

> An unnamed slave at Abeokuta was disliked by his master, who kept him out at his farm and did not allow him time to work to earn his own redemption money. When his master threatened to sell him, he contacted a Christian at a nearby farm. The master did put him in the hands of a slave dealer with instructions to sell him far away, but the Christians of Owu quarter managed to redeem him for £13 in cowries. The master was so angry when he saw him going well-dressed to church that he tried to buy him back from the dealer, saying he would sacrifice him to Obalufon. The slave became a Christian.[115]

Quite a few slaves, especially at Abeokuta, became Christian through this kind of experience—William Moore had access to money through the Coral Fund, which was provided by well-wishers in England to redeem slaves—but such cases can only have accounted for a very small proportion of the slaves who did become Christian. And however they came to Christianity, the religious orientation of slaves was hardly different from that of free individuals: a concern to exploit available sources of spiritual and social power in order to enhance their existence. Like voluntary migrants, slaves were more religiously biddable than natives, both because they had lost many of the spiritual supports they had known at home and because, paradoxically, they were freer in the absence of their relatives to make new religious choices. It is plausible, too, that for some slaves their projection into a world of wider horizons would make Christianity (as also Islam) ethically and metaphysically, not just instrumentally, appealing to them, as to other migrants.[116]

TOWARD THE MASS MOVEMENTS

No analysis of why Yoruba became Christian in the nineteenth century should conclude without reiterating that the vast majority did not. By 1890 less than 10,000 Yoruba were claimed by the CMS as members of their churches—one might push the figure up by a few thousand if one included "backsliders" and those Christians who had temporarily fallen away from contact with a congregation—and it is doubtful if at that time all the other missions together (Methodist, Baptist, and Roman Catholic) would equal the CMS total. So if around 20,000 Yoruba had become Christian, from a total population of perhaps two million, nearly half a century of missionary effort had succeeded in converting roughly 1 percent of them. Of course vast swathes of Yorubaland were still completely or virtually untouched by missions of any kind, and the Christian presence was much greater in some key centers. In Lagos, where the CMS in 1888 counted 4,229 members (3,642 in seven congregations on Lagos Island, 587 in seven more on the mainland), Christians were estimated in the 1891 census to make up 12 percent of the total population of Lagos. At Abeokuta in 1888, eight congregations headed by Ake with 900 members comprised only 2,020 Christians, though we might push that up to around 3,000 by including small congregations on the farms and making some allowance for backsliders who were not counted. If we double the figure to allow for Christians of other churches, the rough total of 6,000 Christians is 6 percent of a town whose population was estimated at around 100,000. But Ibadan's three CMS churches counted only 443 members, a figure which, in a town estimated to contain 120,000 people in 1891, yields a guesstimate of under 1 percent for the entire body of Christian adherents. Since figures for CMS membership in Abeokuta and Ibadan of just over 2,000 and 400 respectively had been reported in 1878, it seems that there had been virtually no gross overall growth in those towns during the 1880s. Ondo, the fresh start of the 1870s and 1880s—where the CMS was the only mission at this period—rose from only 79 Christians in 1880 to 140 in 1888.[117]

Of course these figures do not express everything that matters. They do not even capture *all* those who fit the definition of "conversion" that I have been using—those who regard themselves and are regarded by others as Christians—because some of these were not considered as Christians by the missionaries who drew up the statistics. Nor do they capture the diffuse influence of Christianity beyond the ranks of accepted Christians. Yet these numbers, unimpressive though they seem, were still the platform upon which spectacular advances were to be made over the next thirty years. By the first general census, in 1921, the proportion of Christians, by province, had risen to: Ijebu, 23.4 percent; Lagos and Colony, 23.1 percent; Ondo, 11.8 percent; Abeokuta (including Egbado and rural areas), 8.2 percent; Oyo and Ibadan, 4.4 percent. It was colonialism that made the difference, not so much through the immediate quickening of interest in Christianity in many towns—"It is God we shall serve"—which followed the display of British military power over the Ijebu in 1892, as from the realization that the good things of life depended so much on the mastery of European knowledge (in which Christianity was included) and the supra-local associations offered by both world religions.

The new appeal of Christianity under colonialism is well conveyed in an account of the life of "Dr." Joseph Odumosu, one of the most celebrated early converts at Ijebu-Ode:

> Before the British occupation of Ijebu-Ode, he was well known as a young man of 'great push', there was much 'go' in him. Whilst engaged in trading adventures to Lagos he was led by curiosity to seek the art of learning to read. The British occupation of Ijebu-Ode was an era that brought on several changes, and he was not slow in availing himself of the opportunities thus offered. Besides trading in goods brought from Lagos European shops of those days, he had learnt Shoe-making, Carpentry, Tailoring and Mud-building. He was the percussor [*sic*] of all present-day shop keepers in Ijebuland, being the first man who exhibited his wares at Oja Oba ["the king's market"] and built the first shop. He was the first Ijebu man to erect a storey building and roof it with corrugated iron sheets. He began the study of English language under Miss Comfort Jekasimi. This study he made considerable use of later on. The first Missionary found regular hospitality and support in him. His house was a regular "'Synagogue' on Sabbath Days for travellers. He travelled round the villages with the Missionaries to preach the Gospel.[118]

Odumosu saw himself as offering to his compatriots not just an example for individual emulation, but also an ideology to inspire "improvement and progress" for the whole country. Over the next few decades this tide of *ọlaju* would spread out to the north and east to embrace virtually the whole of the Yoruba country.

Analysis of the slow and halting advance of Christianity up to the 1890s showed clearly that converts were predominantly drawn from the social periphery: the young, slaves, migrants. But after 1892, it was these peripherals who, in two great waves of movement toward the center of their communities, finally set in motion the mass adoption of Christianity over the next few decades. The first was the reflux of slaves and other migrants back to their towns, particularly in the East, once peace had been established. Their townsmen were not only pleased to see them return to augment the town's strength, but they had prestige in the eyes of their stay-at-home fellows from the knowledge of the wider world, and particularly of the colonial domain, which they had acquired abroad. In the case of Ilesha, for example, the three returnees who played the greatest role in the rapid growth of Christianity were Frederick Haastrup, Peter Apara, and James Gureje Thompson. All in their exile had been associates of the famous *babalawo* convert and Brazilian returnee, Philip Jose Meffre, in the formation first of the Ijesha Association among migrants who had become Christian in Lagos, and then of the Lagos end of the Ekitiparapo, which organized supplies for the anti-Ibadan alliance at Kiriji. Haastrup had been converted in Sierra Leone in the 1840s, and on returning to Lagos set up as a trader along the lagoon.[119] After being made *Owa* in 1895, he opened a school in the palace, to which he pressed his sometimes reluctant chiefs to sent their children. Apara, having redeemed himself from slavery in Ijebu, gravitated to Leki, the trading post on the eastern lagoon which was such a magnet for runaway slaves, where he became the first Christian and got married.[120] By 1884, still described as a "Christian young man," he was at Kiriji where he was in charge of the machine guns, a trusted follower of Ogedengbe, the Ijesha commander. After returning to Ilesha in the mid-1890s, he set up as a large-scale cash-crop farmer, being the first to grow cassava for sale to urban food markets. Thompson was enslaved to Abeokuta where he became a member of the Ake congregation; then, after redeeming himself, he moved to Lagos.[121] He too later joined Ogedengbe, and played a significant role in the Kiriji peace negotiations; and on his return to Ilesha pioneered the growing of cocoa, which would be the source of its later prosperity.[122] For all these men, Christianity was merely part of a general ideology and practice of community and personal development, which they recommended with enthusiasm to their fellow Ijesha. Their success in this stemmed not only from the intrinsic appeal of the cultural package, but from their status in the town. They had all been baptized as young men while still single or monogamous—Apara's Christian marriage to Selina Oni had been the first such at Leki—but all later married more wives, the regular accompaniment of social elderhood. Though this meant they became "backsliders" in the church's eyes—ironically, their pastor was R. S. Oyebode, the son of David Kukomi who had given up all his wives but one in order to be baptized—it did not at all diminish their commitment to the Christian cause.

The second movement was of the young, especially young men. The colonial order brought two great changes to their situation, which together enlarged both their freedom and their influence. Firstly, economic development created a new demand for labor, most but not all of it unskilled, particularly in and near Lagos and on the railway which was built via Abeokuta and Ibadan to northern Nigeria. The railway and the new cash crops such as rubber and later cocoa also brought extensive opportunities for trade. In a fresh wave of migration young men from the interior seized this chance to earn cash incomes and so became much less dependent on their elders at home when they returned. The first charge on their new wealth was to marry outside the traditional betrothal arrangements, which were controlled by lineage elders. The age of men's first marriage started to fall, and young women started to demand a significant say in their choice of husband—and it is not surprising that they found fashionable young men from Lagos with money in their pockets more attractive than older men or stay-at-homes. Christianity was deeply implicated in these social changes: the very fact of migration was strongly conducive to the adoption of a world religion, as the great Ijebu trading diaspora showed most clearly; and in turn Christian individualism gave a ready legitimation for the new cultural choices which now beckoned to the young.

At the same time as it unknowingly stoked up intergenerational conflict, colonial officialdom took away from chiefs and elders the discretionary powers of coercion which they had once used to control religious dissent. There was some persecution: at Ijebu Ode in 1897 converts were subject to "domestic pressures" (i.e., the refusal of elders to betroth their daughters to them);[123] and in 1914 at Aiyede and Egosi, two Ekiti towns, pagans with spears surrounded the church to carry off some Christian girls to the husbands intended for them by their families.[124] But such pressures were a shadow of what converts had once had to endure, and had a sharply declining impact. Indeed, affrays between Christians and pagans were now more likely to result from the provocative acts of young Christians, who felt increasingly confident that the future was theirs. At Ikole in 1900, the Christians were expelled for insisting in beating their drums in celebration of Christmas, even though it clashed with an *orisa* festival where drumming was forbidden.[125] On his tour of Ekiti in 1902, Bishop Phillips found himself mediating in one town after another between intransigent young Christians and the local rulers. At Aisegba, near Ado, they not only refused to participate in *orisa* festivals, but even "claim[ed] that conversion entails an immunity from the customary modes of paying respects to their rulers by prostrating themselves, or from rendering the usual help by manual labour to the rulers or even to their own parents and guardians."[126] Phillips now felt he had to preach Romans 13:1-2 ("Let every soul be subject unto the higher powers") to them. But such texts would not be needed for long. As the young men moved inexorably toward maturity and elderhood, the religion which had been a mark of their rebellion itself shifted from the periphery to the social center.

Young men predominated in the first wave of converts in the eastern towns, as they had in the early days at Abeokuta.[127] But whereas in the 1860s and 1870s the solidarity of young men's *egbe* had mostly worked against Christian conversion, when it was a choice of individuals going against the general run of public opinion, it now started to work strongly for it. This was not just because Christianity provided such an apt ideology for the sectional claims of the young returnees against their elders, but because they sincerely felt it expressed the long-term interests of their communities. In colonial Nigeria, the old ideal of the warrior, while it still had much cultural resonance, was seen to have become functionally redundant; now it was the literate teacher or trader, possessing Christian prowess, who had the attributes needed to make the community prosperous and strong.

The shift in Christianity's social placement was subtly but tellingly evident in the sermon which Daniel Olubi gave at the ordination of his protegé F. L. Akiele at Ibadan in 1898:

> His text was II Timothy 2:1, "Then therefore, my child, be strong in the grace of Christ Jesus." Then he took as the exemplar of the qualities of strength which a Christian pastor would need from the chiefs known as the Ẹṣọ at Old Oyo. Regarded as a corps d'elite or royal bodyguard, they were proverbial for their courage, endurance, and devotion to the Alafin. You must ever be braced and ready for action (pamọra), Olubi enjoined Akiele, you cannot refuse to suffer for the king (iwọ ko gbọdọ ko iya ya), and your dying words must be mo mbọ wa ba ọ [I am coming to meet you]. "You cannot prostrate yourself to the world, you cannot suffer yourself to be turned aside from the path of duty. . . . Even in your death you will still be your master's servant." The sermon had a very powerful effect on the congregation, who deeply appreciated and perfectly understood the reference to the Ẹṣọ.[128]

Here a celebratory seal is set on the church's struggles over nearly fifty years to make itself at home in Ibadan. Olubi had led the Ibadan church for three decades and was now nearing his Biblical span of years. Akiele had been one of its first fruits: his father Olunloyo, the warlord patron of Kudeti mission in its early days, had given him in 1853 as a little boy to live with the Hinderers, who brought him up as a Christian.[129] Following the typical career for an African mission agent, he had spent years as a teacher in Ibadan before rising to catechist in 1885; since 1891, he had been posted to Ogbomosho, which would remain his station as a priest. The really riveting thing about Olubi's sermon was, of course, his assimilation of the pastor to the Ẹṣọ—in effect a transvaluation of the warrior ideal—which boldly turned around Christianity's equation with the marginal and the "womanly." Where their values had been regarded as deeply antithetical to those of Ibadan as ilu jagunjagun, the "warrior town," the Christians now claimed a place for themselves at the center of Yoruba life by means of a symbolic identification with the "classical" warrior ideal of Old Oyo. Only the imposition of the Pax Britannica enabled this to be done, by making real warriors an anachronism and establishing new criteria of prowess in the community. Once Christianity could be plausibly seen as Olubi presented it, as affiliated to the community's past as well as to its presumptive future,[130] then conversion became less a matter of many individual decisions, more a mass movement which swept people along with it.

At this point in our analysis, having examined the antithesis of two religions of a very different character and the movement of some people from one to the other, we need to focus on the emergent synthesis, Yoruba Christianity itself; and that is the subject of the next chapter.

9

LEAF BECOMES SOAP

Bi ewe ba pe l'ara ọsẹ, yio di ọsẹ

"If the leaf stays long upon the soap, it will become soap."

This common proverb alludes to the fact that the soft black soap which was manufactured by the Yoruba from ash and palm oil was kept wrapped in leaves which would over time gradually dissolve into the soap itself. It is used to indicate how people will adapt to the circumstances they are placed in, gradually taking on the characteristics of a new environment. I first came across it in 1965, toward the end of a year's fieldwork in Ibadan: it was a kindly, if hardly deserved, compliment on my adaptation to the ways of the Aladura churches which I was then researching, as if to say "You're almost becoming one of us." A good many proverbs are contained in the CMS journal narratives, but this is the only one to come up twice. The first occasion was when a friendly old man used it—"leaves when they have been long in soap become soap"—to counsel patience to James White in his early days at Ota: it would take a long time before the Yoruba became what the evangelist wanted them to be.[1] The second occasion was when M. J. Luke used it to an old man at a village near Leki in 1881:

> Luke had taught a simple prayer to the villagers of Oniyanrin, who found it too far to walk to the church at Leki for services. "O Lord, make a way for us to serve thee, for Jesus's sake. Amen." An old man asked if they

248

could still worship idols, while still saying the prayer. Luke thought that simply to say yes would confuse the man, so he replied with the proverb. "'If leaf (used in wrapping up soap) continues on soap, it partakes of its quality'. The process is gradual, but sure, worship your idol on as before but remember to say the prayer also, gradually and eventually you will know what to do."[2]

The contextually subtle way in which proverbs were used comes out nicely here. Where the thrust of the old Ota man's remark was to say how long the leaf needed to be on the soap (*Bi ewe ba pe*), Luke used it to express his confidence in the inevitable outcome (*yio di ọsẹ*). More than that, Luke's very use of the proverb implicitly claimed the process of Christianization as yet one more realization of the Yoruba narrative paradigm that the proverb conveys. So though at the explicit level both uses of the proverb treated the Yoruba as the leaf becoming assimilated to Christianity as the soap, at an implicit level the assimilation went the other way: Luke represents Christian conversion in terms of an indigenous narrative precedent, just as Olubi had done in comparing the pastor with the *Ẹsọ*. What we have to deal with is a mutual assimilation of two religious cultures. In this chapter, I shall be treating Christianity as the leaf and Yoruba culture as the soap.

I have already argued that there is no workable alternative to defining Christian conversion in terms of the adoption of the social identity of a Christian, rather than of any particular religious content. Yet the substance of Yoruba Christianity, whether we focus on belief and devotional practice or on the embodied ethics of its life as a community, remains crucial to assessing its historical impact. In trying to balance two very different sets of cultural prescriptions, Yoruba Christians did not quickly find a stable or definitive synthesis. The leaf/soap metaphor gives a misleading impression if it leads us to infer that there is a definitive end state to the adaptive process, a finally "inculturated" Christianity.[3] The process was, of course, a dialectical one; but as it went on, its context kept shifting and its interlocutors changing. As with all conversations its direction was only partially anticipated by those who had started it, the missionaries, so that its very identity *as* a process could only be apprehended retrospectively, and then provisionally. Yet despite all its contingent turns, it still retained enough of the same agenda for later participants to know they were picking up on earlier issues.

Three phases or contexts of Christian adaptation are of concern to us. In the early years, when congregations were almost entirely composed of converts, their Christianity was in good measure an expression of their social marginality. But though it involved some severance from custom and prior social commitments, and even took on some features of a counterculture or an alternative community, the Christian option of the converts still had, at some level, to rest on Yoruba cultural criteria. In a later phase these started to shine through, when second-generation Christians predominated, some of whom were rising to influence in their communities. This was a phase when missionaries often complained about "backsliders," but the lifestyles they slid back into were increasingly affected by Christian influence, and they retained much from their mission formation. A third context emerged with the 1890s, when Christianity began to attract converts on a mass scale. Colonial incorporation meant that although the Christian innovators might still be marginal in local terms, they were not marginal to the new centers of power; and because so many now wanted to follow their example, their Christianity was shaped to the pattern of this popular demand. These three contexts are not pure types, strictly exclusive or sequential: the first two apply especially to the older areas such as Abeokuta or Ibadan in the pre-colonial period and the third mainly to Ijebu and the east; and after the early days there is always some overlap of more than one type of Yoruba Christian—the marginal convert, the second-generation member, and the mass convert—in the same congregation. But the scheme does provide some purchase on the temporally shifting exchanges between Christianity and Yoruba tradition.

EVANGELICALISM AS A RELIGION OF THE HEART

The impressions of the European missionaries are a good place to begin, not because they were unbiased (for emphatically they were not), but because they point up most clearly the contrast between the two religions. What evangelicals wanted above all was a "religion of the heart," a state of living with a continuous sense of the saving presence of Jesus Christ and of the enthusing power of the Holy Spirit. Converts might be intellectually convinced of the scheme of salvation, but the real touchstone of its worth was the "warm" or "lively" inward state of feeling, which came from accepting Christ as Savior. Since their religion was thus validated as much in psychological as in doctrinal terms, the self-reflection of missionaries offers much direct evidence of it, as in the following brief excerpts from the journals of Joseph Carter, a young lay evangelist at Abeokuta:

> Depressed in spirit, felt my own depravity. May I realize the promise of our Saviour when he says I will never leave nor forsake thee . . .
> O may I always feel my responsibility. O may he give me a more earnest desire to glorify him and to seek the salvation of perishing souls around me . . .
> This morning had lively views of my Saviour. O that I could be in this state always.[4]

What is evident here is equally the condition from which this heart-religion offered release—the sense of sin or "depravity," closely associated in missionaries themselves with lassitude or spiritual despair—and the behavior which it was to inspire—an earnest commitment to the active Christian life. No missionary was as candid in revealing his emotional highs and lows as David Hinderer, from his delight at the vivacity of Ibadan's markets or the gaiety of the children to the "frequent flatness of my own heart," which once led him to confide, "Oh how sad my state by nature is! But I don't give in."[5] He used a telling phrase of some of his people, that their Christian belief, though correct, was "cold and dead."[6]

Missionaries were sometimes led by the esteem they accorded to religious feeling to take the paradoxical step of upholding pagans as an example to Christians. Though perverse in effect, pagan devotion itself was often seen as admirable, because it seemed so heartfelt. Thus Mann says of a *babalawo*'s regard for his Ifa palm nuts that "he takes [them] to be more true than many a Christian the living God," while Isaac Smith asks of the much-condemned idolatry of the indigenous Badagrians if it does not teach Christians a lesson: "Oh that Christians in general were more submissive to the requirements of the Gospel . . . more simple and firm [in] their reliance . . . [on] the many precious promises written in the Word of God."[7] Or Joseph Smith, urging greater zeal on the Ibadan converts:

"In conclusion I exhorted them to coppy [*sic*] from the heathen around them in zeal and devotedness to God and in some particulars learn from their example." How well-kept the *oriṣa*-houses were, the paths to them always swept clean, compared with the disrepair of the church and the unkempt graveyard. "I also told them that I often observe that the heathen when sitting in the market place have by their side their favourite idols to give them good success in the disposal of the articles they expose for sale." So must Christians be always mindful of God "and carry him with us in our hearts wherever we go."[8]

The diagnostic phrase here is "in our hearts." That was where Smith placed the wellspring of religious devotion. (We might note in passing that the secular word for "heart," *ọkan*, was used to translate the Christian idea of "soul" into Yoruba). But this was not, and did not need to be, the source of Yoruba attention to their *oriṣa*, which was rather their complete integration into the flow of ordinary life. A Yoruba no more needed to keep the *oriṣa* "in his heart" than he did the *balẹ* of the compound or the chief of the quarter: all were external agents that demanded attention for the plain, practical reason that they produced effects on the local environment of continuous concern to its human denizens. So when Kefer, after passing no less than twenty small *oriṣa*-houses in front of one compound in Ibadan, wrote that he "acknowledge[d] their piety but ask[ed] why there was none for God the Almighty," he was failing to grasp the very different source of what he called "piety."[9] It is noteworthy that virtually all such comments were made by *Europeans* (with the sole exception of James Johnson, who of all the Africans was most deeply imbued with the ethos of mainstream evangelicalism).[10] In general the African clergy were so familiar with the *oriṣa* cults that they were unimpressed with the devotion that they inspired, save perhaps as a measure of how deep was the idolatry which they wished to eradicate. They did not care to use it as a stick to beat the converts with, since they had a much livelier sense of what they had given up and still had to struggle to resist.

The missionary theory of conversion was that it should proceed from the inside outward. While this theory did much to govern how the missionaries proceeded and what they wanted,[11] it did not provide a script that Yoruba drawn to Christianity were bound to follow. And since (it was further assumed) inward conversion must lead to Christian behavior, the latter, in the absence of any other evidence, would allow the former to be inferred. In praising his converts for their steadfastness under persecution, Müller was in effect inferring, in his words, their *"personal* piety" from their *"practical religion"* (i.e., lives lived according to their Christian profession).[12] So when converts began to act in ways that their pastors regarded as falling seriously short of Christian ideals, it was more than a purely pastoral problem. To some extent, it could still be treated as a response to the pressures of a social environment still overwhelmingly non-Christian, or as a problem of the second generation. Indeed it was an evangelical commonplace that, when religion becomes "cold," behavior becomes "worldly."[13]

But some of the longer-serving missionaries adumbrated a more cultural view of why this might happen in the Yoruba case. By 1858, despite the evident successes of the Abeokuta mission, Henry Townsend was less sanguine about how easy it would be to make Christian converts in the evangelical mold:

> I don't think anyone not accustomed to see heathen life can properly understand what it is to become a Christian in the midst of heathenism, and when the subject of Christianity has had his habits and views fixed by a heathen standard since childhood. I can conceive of it's being easy to cast away idols and become Mohammedan, it is only another false system of external form, whilst in spirit it is the same.[14]

He would return obsessively to the contrast of outward form and internal spirit. In 1860, after reviewing several areas of progress in the church at Abeokuta, Townsend again raised the theme of the personal religion of converts: "There is one subject on which I cannot write with satisfaction, viz. personal piety, that is there is no clear and distinct manifestation of it as we would desire."[15] There are some indications of it, it may exist, but he cannot say definitely that it does.

Four years later, he was clear where he should place the burden of his own teaching: "I have . . . especially insisted on the need of the Spirit's influence on the heart, without which the outward form is merely a form."[16] Still exercised by the search for true inner conversion from its outward signs, Townsend described in the same letter the death of a Christian ("of whom we may say he was an Israelite indeed") after a long and painful illness:

> His house was always clean and his countenance denoted inward peace. He never complained, spoke of God as having dealt beautifully with him

and with thankfulness that his providence sustained him." In his last words, "he expressed his belief strongly that the Lord had pardoned him for Jesus' sake, and that death would be a release from suffering and an enterance [*sic*] into the mansion of bliss.

This was a copybook evangelical death.[17] While reports of such "falling asleep in the Lord" come from both African and European missionaries,[18] they seem to have had a particular importance to the Europeans, because they were so anxious to assure themselves that, despite their misgivings, genuine conversions as they understood them were taking place. What happened at the point of death was regarded as likely to furnish the most decisive indication of the Christian's inward state. Recovering from a serious illness himself, Bühler confided to his friend Maser that

> He [Bühler] found he has looked too despairingly on our work; but we should make more allowance on account of the peculiar temptations [the Yoruba converts] were subjected to and our want of knowledge of the character of the natives. When it came to the point of death with them, they never doubted the grace of Christ, but fell asleep simply trusting in their Saviour.[19]

"Spiritual" religion was what the CMS missionaries aimed to produce, one where the in-dwelling of the Holy Spirit would morally and psychologically transform the life of the Christian and energize the Church. Townsend wrote to Venn in 1860:

> We are delighted at hearing of the tokens of a revival of spiritual religion in England, we hope a portion of it will reach to us for we need it from the highest to the lowest—what a difference would be made in our work! How many evils would be removed by it! . . . The young men and women about us are really but little affected by spiritual religion, almost all is outside religion. A gracious revival of the work of the Holy Spirit is what we need.[20]

Townsend's concern was echoed in Mann's three-way categorization of his Aroloya congregation at Lagos. There were the Saro returnees who were "the formal church"; those from the Yoruba interior—many of them refugees from Abeokuta or his own former station at Ijaye—who were "the spiritual church" and his own "joy and blessing"; and the Lagosian ex-slaves, whom he saw as "men without Character, unable to be their own masters yet not willing to submit to the laws of the New Testament."[21] He sets "spirituality" in opposition to, on the one hand, the continuation of "heathen" attitudes and behavior, especially as regards sex and marriage, and on the other, the attraction of Christians to the more "worldly" aspects of Western civilization.

Yet Townsend came to take a more understanding view of how difficult it was for the converts to meet the criteria for the Christian life as laid down by the mission:

> The more experience I have, the more I am inclined to deal tenderly with the faults and sins of the members of the Christian Church here in the midst of heathenism . . . individuals trying to live a new life whilst the atmosphere they breathe is of an opposite character.[22]

He went on to say that in church discipline it was usually wrong to inflict a punishment, and in any case he preferred to leave it to the church elders or class leaders; but it was better if people were governed by their conscience. But here the cultural difficulty, which Townsend registered but did not really articulate—perhaps because it challenged the psychological universalism on which the project of evangelical conversion depended—came again to the fore. For did not the very idea of conscience presuppose just that sense of an inward core to the self which often seemed problematic in the Yoruba converts? The issue was addressed more squarely by a later superintendent of the mission at Abeokuta, J. B. Wood, a good Yoruba-speaker who was deeply experienced in Egba affairs. When in 1887 the CMS secretary sought Wood's views on the holding of slaves by Yoruba Christians, he advised a cautious approach, and expressed the hope that "by the power of enlightened conscience" it would come to seem wrong. He went on to say that, though he thought there was a "growing feeling in the right direction," the Yoruba lack of a *notion* of conscience was an obstacle:

> I believe it would not be difficult to produce twenty modes of speech in Yoruba whereby curses can be imprecated on persons; but there is not one settled word for conscience. It is true there are some four or five words used for conscience, but no one of them is a generally accepted word which conveys anything like a definite idea of what is meant by conscience. This will suffice to show that there is much difficulty in the way of calling into healthy exercise the conscience of the people.[23]

Note that Wood still treats "conscience" as a universal organ or faculty: the Yoruba have it though they do not clearly name it, so it is not developed to its full potential.

The CMS missionaries, though well aware of the social obstacles they faced, were not much inclined to theorize about the issues of cultural relativity thrown up by their project. Yet unavoidably they were drawn into a web of variably understood differences between their religious ethos and that which the converts brought from their Yoruba background. Evangelicalism, despite its firm roots in the Protestant Reformation, was the first distinctively post-Enlightenment form of Christianity, in that its experiential base—not the same as its scriptural or theological warrant—was cut off both from any theory of the material world (left to natural philosophy or science) and from any traditional socio-religious order, that is from the orders of knowledge and of society respectively.[24] The first of these pushed it decisively toward the ethical/other-worldly pole from the instrumental/this-worldly pole of religious action, while the second confirmed its Protestant disposition toward an individualist, rather than a collectivist, ethics. The saliency of conscience, a sort of moral gyroscope that was presumed to be internal to each individual, was a close corollary of these shifts. Moreover, without the old external supports, evangelicalism had to be self-referentially veridical, grounding itself directly in the believer's own "heartfelt" conviction.

Yoruba religion was almost as different from this as could be imagined. It *was* closely integrated with, if not the very articulation of, the Yoruba orders of natural and social knowledge, which meant that its validation was realist rather than psychological; its orientation was markedly this-worldly and instrumental; and its ethics (while giving much recognition to individual distinctiveness) strongly backed communal values. The social embedding of ethics (of which the curses mentioned by Wood were an aspect) is intrinsically a rather more reliable way of controlling behavior than conscience, which tends to emerge when the loosening of social controls creates both the occasion and the need for the development of more internal controls. It was those who were marginal to the cognitive and social order who were most likely to become Christian, drawn by the persuasive things that the missionaries had to say about the spaces within the self and beyond the social here and now—spaces given new saliency by their marginality—where traditional knowledge fell short. Yet however responsive they were to the new moral world offered by the missionaries, the converts were still deeply subject to the promptings of Yoruba culture. As their numbers grew and as they became less special, as their children grew up in the community as well as the church, and as whole cohorts of the population began to turn to Christianity for what they saw in it, they could not help but make of it something more fully their own.

YORUBA SPIRITUALITY

At one level, "spirituality" is no more than a conventional label under which to consider the particular way in which the Yoruba, at the core of their practice, made Christianity their own. At a deeper level, it points to how the Yoruba did this by putting their own distinctive interpretation on a concept— "spirit"—that was, we have just seen, central to evangelical discourse. Until the past decade or so, it was especially through the study of independent churches that attempts were made to examine empirically (as against the normative constructions of African theology) what it might mean for Christianity to be Africanized.[25] Too often was it blandly assumed that the Christianity of the members of "mainline" or ex-mission churches must follow closely along the lines of the parent mission and so be less culturally authentic than that of the independent churches. But the same principle of method applies here as in the analysis of conversion to Christianity: the explanation of change has to be grounded in an appreciation of the continuities through change. Though the independent churches broke away from the mission churches, they still took their origin from existing Yoruba Christian values, just as the Christianity of the first converts was deeply grounded in some basic values of the old religion. So it should not surprise us that the distinctive spirituality of the early Yoruba Christians shows itself most decisively in a form of religious action—*adura*, or prayer—which both became the keynote of the greatest wave of later independent churches, the Aladura, and was recognized as the closest Christian equivalent to the central category of pagan religious action: *ẹbọ*, or sacrifice.[26] This perception was not new: back in 1878, Charles Phillips wrote of an old woman in the candidates' class at Ondo, who after her husband and her brother recovered from illness, was "convinced that prayer is more efficacious than sacrifice."[27]

It did not come readily to European missionaries to recognize religious difference in their converts without finding fault with it, but David Hinderer proved an exception. Toward the end of his time at Ibadan, he commented at the end of a report of the three days of prayer, held in the first week of the New Year, which brought all the three churches together: "Our people, who have essentially a spiritual as well as a temporal sphere of their own, find it hard to pray ex praescripto."[28] Here he alludes to both the importance of prayer for the Yoruba converts, and to its forceful, impromptu character, a very "talking with God."[29] The centrality of prayer to the converts' life as Christians comes out repeatedly in the CMS journals. Phillips again was touched by the "simple and earnest pleadings" in prayer of the members of St Jude's Ebute Meta, on the Lagos mainland, as well as by their great love of quoting the Bible in application to the circumstances of their lives.[30] Of his parishioners at Ota, James White wrote:

> "One of the proofs of the sincerity of our converts . . . is the habit of prayer which they have acquired. Nothing of importance is taken by them without first seeking God's assistance in prayer. Before leaving for a journey—before commencing their daily work—before taking or administering medicine, they would ask God's blessing, protection and assistance."

White goes on to tell how his new convert Erubami told him, "in a very solemn and earnest manner," how he had recently forgotten to say his prayers before setting out for his farm. On the way he remembered, took off his cap and prayed. But later he had an accident—his foot struck a thorn, giving him a troublesome injury—which he considered "a just punishment from God for my sin."[31]

White addresses the quality of his converts' faith in rather different terms from, say, Townsend, and in a way which expresses a distinctively African perspective. He is less concerned about whether their inward state corresponds to the outward forms of their religion than with the manifest overall consistency of their lives. What really matters to him is that the exercise of Christian faith should be integrated with the quotidian or "secular" business of life. For it remained the case for Yoruba Christians, clergy as well as laity, that their faith was more importantly anchored in public and social tokens and usages, both among their fellow Christians and before the non-Christian mass of the community, than in the inward recesses of the individual's soul. That was why the very public act of handing over one's idols or Ifa nuts to the pastor for their destruction played such a large role in becoming a Christian—and why African agents were much more likely to record the details of it in their journals than Europeans were.

So some of the best evidence for Yoruba spirituality is to be found in spontaneous public prayer and testimony, where converts disclosed their hopes and histories before their co-religionists and thus consolidated their Christian self-definition. Special prayer meetings, often on a weekday evening or quarterly over several days or during the New Year season, were a vital addition to the formal Sunday liturgy of the Anglican Prayer Book. The longest prayer—nearly 500 words—preserved in the CMS archive is from Akibode, a *babalawo* of probably Oyo origin who migrated to Badagry, where he was first attracted by the preaching of Gollmer around 1848. He gave his children to board with Gollmer and they duly became Christian. But for long years he himself stayed as an inquirer, unable to renounce his Ifa; only in 1869 did he at last accept baptism from his pastor, Samuel Pearse. It was in January 1863 that Pearse reported Akibode at a prayer meeting, adding "Oh! how touching was his prayer. May the Lord show him mercy." Pearse thought the prayer so noteworthy that he sent an English translation of it (done by Akibode's son Simeon Kester) to Henry Venn himself.[32]

The prayer falls into four sections, though they are not divided as such in the text as we have it:

1. After invoking God Almighty, Akibode confesses himself a sinner. Then, appealing to God's promise in His Holy Word to hearken to his sinner's prayer, he beseeches Him "to send forth thy Holy Spirit in my heart that it may take away all worldly things and set it fast to spiritual things." He has sinned all his life, but especially "it is very hard for me, O Lord, to put away all these wives which is quite abominable to thee." He asks for God's strength to help him to be free: "O do not let me die in my sins."

So far all is impeccably evangelical and, save for the reference to his polygamy, might have come from a European. But then he moves to a narrative figuration of his predicament, which is in a much more Yoruba idiom:

2. "Mine is quite a wonder. It is just as when a strong man comes to another strong man's house and fights with him so much that the former [overcomes] the latter, so that he takes him and ties him well with his chain, digs a pit and throws him in; and then takes the children and ties them separately, but not so much as the father. So the father tries chance and looses the children one by one, telling them to run away home, till the children [are] all gone and only the father remains in the pit. When the

strong man came and peeped into the pit and found the children are got out by the father, he tied him more and more so that the father couldn't move. So it is with me, O Lord, so it is with me. I found that thy word is true and sent all my children to thee from the devil, but I remain there."[33]

Thus Akibode describes in parable form how he sent his children to become Christian, without being able to commit himself. Then he returns from testimony to prayer:

> 3. "Save me O Lord from the hand of the devil." He now refers to Christ's miracles on earth in healing the blind, the deaf and the lame. But his own sickness is far worse: "There is no soundness but wounds and bruises and putrifying sores."[34] One pole would not reach him "in the depth where I am," but he calls on the Lord to tie one pole to another until he reaches him.

From this *De profundis clamavi*, which stands well within a long Christian tradition of penitential devotion, he then turns once again to an expression of his Yoruba life-world:

> 4. Though God has saved him, he confesses, "from all dangers of land and water," he has "given the glory to another God." [He means Ifa.] "It is true, O Lord, that the devil has power, for when we [*babalawo*] say anything, it must come to pass, but thy word says 'it is the power of darkness' and that is the way to destruction. Be with the ministers of thy word who are guiding us in thy way with all those who are now kneeling before thee. Do thou open thy merciful ears to my unworthy prayers, for Jesus Christ sake. Amen."

Thus the prayer ends on the note of evangelical humility with which it began.

It is artificial to separate out, as I have done, the "Yoruba" and the "evangelical" portions of this prayer, as if to imply that it did not express a unified personal outlook on the world, or that Yoruba attitudes should be set in antithesis to Christian, rather than to European, ones. Yet without prejudice to this unity, it is possible to discern those strands in the prayer where Akibode was most fully at one with his fellow Yoruba of all religions. This perspective comes over most strongly in the prayer's recurring reference to mundane power, which is the more striking because overall it was decisively oriented toward the other world: Akibode's main expressed desire was not to die in his sins. There is the vivid metaphor of Akibode's spiritual torment: a struggle between two strong men—*alagbara* must have been the original Yoruba rendering—Akibode being one, and his stronger opponent, the Devil, the other. Implicit here is the common Yoruba idea of a personal enemy (*ọta*) as the source of one's troubles, as in the pagan Yoruba prayer from Ijaye quoted in Chapter 4.[35] Then, the signs he adduces of God's power are his own past deliverances from "dangers of land and water" and Christ's miracles of healing—not what he is praying for here, but the common object of countless Yoruba prayers of all religions. Finally, hinting back to the story of the Devil as adversary, there is the insistence that what the Devil does through the *babalawo* is not a mere empty deception (as Europeans nearly always argued), but a real "power of darkness."

This was an exceptional prayer by an exceptional convert. As a successful *babalawo* Akibode was indeed a "strong man," and he had more cogent reasons *not* to become a Christian than to become one. Like Kukomi at Ibadan, he was swayed by issues of meaning rather than of power: a professional master of the past and guide to the future, he was seized by the force of Christianity's scheme of redemptive history. But however much this may have lain in the background of the more typical convert's thinking, the primary concern of their day-to-day prayers was to enlist the power of God for the same kind of help and protection which the *oriṣa* provided for their devotees. A continuing affinity with other forms of Yoruba religious feeling is clearly indicated in Cole's brief account of the Easter service at Ake church in 1876, when fears of a Dahomean invasion for that year had relaxed, but still many pagans attended church to join in the prayers:

> Oluwa gba wa, Oluwa ran wa l'ọwọ, k'a le ṣegun ọta wa
>
> "Lord save us, Lord help us, that we may vanquish our enemies."[36]

The complement of prayer was testimony, where public witness was given of the effectiveness of prayer, of the power of God working in converts' lives. Particularly at prayer meetings, Christians told their stories, which often included accounts of special providences they had received. Kukomi's testimony in 1872 was accompanied by one from his close friend Isaac Atere, and rounded off with remarks about prayer.[37] At another in 1882, after "interesting stories of missionary work" from the younger agents, the elders were asked "to encourage the people," and Abraham Adebiyi told "the old but still alarming" story—which makes it sound as if it had been told a few times before!—of his escape from a fire at Igangan which had killed over 600 people.[38] In 1884, the embryo historian Samuel Johnson even read a paper at a meeting of the three Ibadan churches "enumerating some of the special mercies vouchsafed to us as a church during the past year."[39] These included the protection of the houses of Kukomi and others from pillage by the sword-bearers of the straitened war-chiefs at Kiriji, the rescue of Alice Omiyuke from enslavement, and the happy outcome of the lightning strike on the mission house at Aremo, when the demands of the Sango people had been repulsed.[40] Deliverance from these "dangers of land and water" was a much-needed assurance to the Ibadan Christians that theirs was a powerful God who hearkened to the prayers of His faithful.

How far did these hostile powers include not only "secular" ones like the marauding Ibadan warboys or the Dahomean army, but also the whole range of "spiritual" powers of the old cosmology, from the *oriṣa* to a multitude of smaller entities such as *oogun* (charms or "medicines") or *iwin* (sprites)? In their efforts to persuade Yoruba that Christ was the *only* mediator between God and man, missionaries drew upon a mix of European common sense, technological effects, and popular science to challenge the view that behind mundane phenomena lay a myriad of hidden forces. But how far did they succeed in persuading Yoruba converts that the *orisa* were nothing but "dumb idols" and "imaginary invisible beings"? And to the extent that their success at this task of disenchantment fell short, what were the consequences for the character of Yoruba Christianity? The conspicuous surrender of idols which African missionaries, in particular, required and reported of their converts may tell us something about their practice, but it does not tell us about how the abandoned *orisa* and other spirits then stood in the converts' eyes.

This is a topic where the evidence is particularly sparse and sketchy. In reports destined for the CMS secretary in London, missionaries were more concerned to document conversion than the survival of old beliefs in the converts; these were, moreover, beliefs which converts may well have wanted to conceal from missionaries who they knew regarded them as superstitious; and it is in any case doubtful how deep a knowledge most European missionaries had of the personal beliefs of Yoruba Christians. The African agents, by contrast, had much more intimate contact with them and shared many of their personal concerns; and here the question must be how much of traditional belief about the spirit world they too retained. The difficulty of coming to a just view of these elusive matters is nicely conveyed by Daniel Coker's description of an *orisa* called Agba, worshipped by the fishermen near Lagos, as an "imaginary deity . . . [which] means Esu the Devil."[41] Here Coker sends out two contradictory messages: one, as if to assure the CMS that he shares the modern view, asserts that *orisa* have no external reality; the other, which is more likely his own opinion, implies that Agba *is* a real force, to be identified with Christianity's own prince of darkness and further (by hallowed mistranslation) with the *orisa* Esu.

Other evidence points to the continued reality of much of the old spirit world for many mission agents, and so a fortiori for ordinary lay Christians. One of Mann's assistants at Ijaye expressed his firm conviction that recent lightning strikes in the town were due to "the bad tricks of Are," that is, to Kurunmi's credited ability to call down Sango's anger on the houses of people whom he wanted to mulct.[42] Maser reported a tragic incident at Abeokuta in 1864, when one night the wife of the Wesleyan teacher and two of her children were found dead, and everyone else in the house became sick. Maser and his colleagues at first suspected poison, but on investigation concluded they had died from the fumes of a coal-pot taken inside the house, the windows and door having been shut for fear. All the mission agents, however, were convinced that the minor spirits known as *iwin* were responsible.[43]

The idiom of stories about strange or untoward events that was constantly circulating in the community as part of its narrative self-constitution carried with it causal assumptions in terms of hidden spiritual agency which would have been nearly impossible for the Yoruba pastors to be free of—even though they did not often think it was suitable material for their journal extracts. Even the sage Olubi told a story which implies that he did not altogether write off the *orisa* as fantasies:

> Isaac Atere, a notable elder of the Ibadan church who had just died, had previously been a devotee of Sango. He had once had a slave known as Dada. [Dada was a name given to babies born with curly hair, which indicated their spiritual affinity to an *orisa* also called Dada, said to have been Sango's older brother, or his predecessor as a king of Oyo. Olubi here elides the historical gap to identify Atere's slave with his *orisa* eponym.] This Dada was once caught by the Ijayes in a war in Oluyole's time [before 1850]. Dada escaped through guidance in a dream, and Atere was told in a dream by Sango that he would return that day. So it happened. "A singular case and power of darkness."[44]

So Olubi treats dreams from *orisa* as genuine messages, just as Akibode did the predictions of his Ifa, as giving a Yoruba content to a Christian category of concrete powers of evil.

Yet this was an uncertain sphere of constant questioning, with no uniform line being taken among either Africans or Europeans. In 1875 Young reported an extraordinary incident from Ondo:

> A young man, the nephew of their landlord, suddenly went missing from a farm some five miles to the southeast of Ondo. A search party went out and sacrifices were made, to no avail. Twelve days later he turned up near Okeigbo, a dozen miles to the northwest, where he was promptly enslaved. The man could not say how he had got there, save that while at his farm-work "he heard a sound like a bugle and at once he was moved with his feet going." As he passed through the forest, it all seemed dark behind him and clear in front. This was said to be the work of Babaji, the *orisa* of the whirlwind, which often made people or animals go walkabout in this way.[45]

Young's conclusion—that he "[could] not easily be persuaded to believe that the whirlwind could take such a young man as that away to such a distance as that"—seems to include a note of equivocation in its denial. Would it have been more credible if it had been a child or the distance less? Young avers that he had never before heard of such an incident, and leaves it as a mystery as to how the young man got to Okeigbo. The Yoruba term that comes closest to "mystery"—*awo*—does not convey the common English sense of an odd event that defies explanation, but rather a hidden cause only to be known by esoteric procedures. Most Yoruba Christians, especially laypeople living in their own towns—and Young was a newly arrived stranger—would have found it hard not to have gone along with the prevailing view that the young man's removal had a "spiritual" cause. For the Yoruba pagan such extraordinary events were not insignificant but supersignificant, since they were precisely how *orìṣa* manifested themselves. Moreover, the idea that by the right *awo* a man might be made invisible or instantly whisked to another place was not bizarre. Hardheaded warlords spent large sums of cowries to buy charms to enable them to do just that—and everyone, Christians included, feared them for it. One of the most eloquent—if incidental—testimonies for the continuing persuasiveness of traditional explanations of mishap comes from Hinderer himself, commenting on Ogunpa church in Ibadan:

> Ogunpa station has always struggled. Kefer laboured here and was cursed by a *babalawo*, who said he would never return, and that the church would not flourish. "Strange to say," Kefer died soon afterward [1855]. Barber [an African catechist] worked here, but collapsed and died [1858]. Two men looked as if they would become the nucleus of the church, but both died and their families scattered. A "notoriously bad woman" joined but her following fell away. These experiences bring his mind back, against his will, to "that wicked old Babalawo and his curses."[46]

Here Hinderer does not so much assert as reluctantly adumbrate a view very similar to one which the ex-*babalawo* Akibode had forcefully expressed in his prayer, that the powers of diviners were genuine, but diabolical. He was surely moved in this direction, not only by his experiences in Ibadan (including the opinions of nearly everyone around him), but by his own prior conviction that the Devil was a real person.

Now the Devil had an crucial cognitive function in the emergence of Yoruba Christianity. He permitted the converts to incorporate old beliefs, which they could not yet or wholly abandon, in the active existence of *orìṣa* and other spirits, into the framework of their new religion.[47] For this to happen, something had to give on either side. The *orìṣa* had to be demonized, morally negated by the criteria of Christianity; but evangelical Christianity had to yield to an essentially Yoruba view of what might be called "spiritual causation." This harmonization took place on the terrain of the ordinary converts' own experience, as we see from the case of an unnamed female member of M. J. Luke's congregation at Leki:

> This woman became irregular in her attendance, she told Luke, because "her former idols (or devil according to her own narration) appeared in ghostly shape in her dreams." Luke encouraged her with the parable of a slave escaping by canoe to avoid a cruel master, who, knowing he could not touch him on British soil, chased him with redoubled effort. Would the slave look back and let up on his effort when so close to safety?[48]

The idols/Devil equation was clearly a spontaneous expression of the woman. So it was too in the prayer of a young man at a valedictory service for Hinderer at Ibadan:

> We have received grace to hear thy word, we like it, it is good for us, we want to follow it; then comes the devil and tries to spoil it all, give him warning to leave us alone, it is no use him troubling us so; we do not want to follow him again. And as to ourselves, we pray thee furnish us with the right sword and put the proper *kumo* (club) into our right hand that we may fight him manfully.[49]

Hinderer added his approval of "the clear consciousness of the personality of the devil" shown in the prayer. Now while converts will certainly have had the Devil presented to them in the teaching of the missionaries, he was not anything like as salient in them as in the examples we have of converts' own prayers. In fact the nineteenth century saw a general decline in the Devil's importance within mainstream European Christianity,[50] and Hinderer's seriousness about the Devil as a personality, not merely a principle of evil, may perhaps have been rather old-fashioned, the product of his rural Pietist background.

For opinions in the Yoruba Mission varied, as the following episode at Ibadan in 1883 shows:

> Olubi went with all the mission agents to pay courtesy calls on the leading chiefs, including the *Araba,* the senior Ifa priest of the town. "He being a lively and funning [*sic*] man . . . began to make some fun which we soon converted into a spiritual conversation." When Olubi criticized their mode of worship, the *Araba* interrupted to say, "Of all the idols which we worship, there is none of importance, not even Sango for he was only a man and for bad conduct he was driven from Oyo. But Esu . . . you must help us to beg God to bind him fast and give him no chance to plague us, he being the only object we dread." Foster [the catechist from Iseyin, who was a Lagos man] then said there is no Devil but in man's own actions: "When you are insulted, it is the work of the Devil, and when you draw your knife in revenge, it is still the work of the Devil, for he does not use force but by urging and persuasion." Oyebode then enlarged upon Foster's words.[51]

It is interesting that here (if Olubi's reportage is accurate) the *Araba* had adopted the long-established identification, standard among Yoruba Christians, of the Devil with the *orişa* Esu.[52] What also seems to have been in the *Araba*'s mind was Esu's role as the trickster who might spoil any sacrifice, and by extension the author of the social disorder of the Age of Confusion (well evoked in Foster's reference to quarrels of honor among the warboys). The other striking feature is how similar the *Araba*'s image of the Devil was to the one that recurs in the prayers of the Christian laity considered above, as a powerful personal enemy who must be fought and bound. In challenging it, the clergy sought to render the Devil in immanent, ethical terms, rather than the external, physical ones in which Yoruba Christians were disposed to figure him. It is not surprising that people who found the evangelical tenet of humanity's intrinsic sinfulness so alien to their thinking should be drawn to a concept of evil as a spoiling, external force.[53] But the Christian rendering of the Devil as Esu also went beyond a simple equation of Satan with that one *oriṣa*, for Esu qua the Devil took on a wider meaning which he did not have before, to denote the *oriṣa* in general, the collective works of Satan. So the Devil stood for several things at once for Yoruba Christians: he was their grand Enemy, the sum and source of all their particular enemies; he was those parts of their old belief system which the missionaries proscribed as idolatrous, essentially the *oriṣa;* and he was the principle of Evil, present in all immoral and disorderly acts.

The clearest token of a new and distinctive tenor in the Yoruba converts' religion is found in the modified concept of "spirit" which started to emerge, taking elements from both its parent traditions. The "spiritual" religion aspired to by the missionaries was a faith that was inward, ethical, and strongly oriented toward eternal or "otherworldly" goals. Its main conceptual underpinning was a marked dualism between body and spirit, or worldly and spiritual things—on that, the first section of Akibode's prayer was as orthodox as his missionary teachers might have wished. This was not easy to render in existing Yoruba terminology. Crowther translated "spirit" as *ẹmi*, a word which derives from the verb *mí*, "breathe," and has a close cognate in *imi*, "breath" or "breathing." So *emi* essentially meant spirit in the sense of the thing which made the difference between a person or animal living and one dead, the thing which left the body at death. The *ẹmi* is put into man by God, and can have a wraithlike existence after death, but it does not connote the enduring quality of a person as he proceeds from life into the afterlife and subsequent rebirth. Nor does it have anything of the generic quality of the English "spirits," the whole category of unseen or non-mundane beings. *Ẹmi Mimọ,* "the Holy Spirit," must have seemed a very strange coinage to those Yoruba who heard it for the first time. In two places the CMS archive provides evidence for the nineteenth-century Yoruba understanding of *ẹmi*, and in both of them it seems to mean just "life." Kurunmi's chiefs greeted him with the words *"Ki Ọlọrun bun ọ li ẹmi* [May God grant you life]";[54] and a dying orphan, when asked what he prays for, replies *"Ẹmi ni."*[55] I think he was simply praying not to die.

How ordinary Yoruba Christians understood "spirit," or rather how they came to appropriate evangelical language to say something very different, is implicit rather than directly stated in the CMS journals. Here let me take an anthropologist's liberty with historical method and fast forward to a twentieth-century context where this understanding had fully declared itself and found its language. By the 1920s the term "spiritual" had taken on a new strand of meaning in Nigerian English, essentially as "powerful in spirit." It had this currency particularly among, and with reference to, a group of independent churches, the Aladura, whose claim was that by enlisting the power of the Holy Spirit, healing, prophecy, and other blessings (the "gifts of the Spirit") could be attained. A "spiritualist" was not someone who communicates with the dead, but an *alagbara ẹmi* [literally, someone "strong in spirit" or "of spiritual power"], someone who is effective in prayer, visions, healing, and so forth. This perspective also made use of the dualism of body/spirit or earth/heaven, but in a different way from classic evangelicalism. There the relationship was rather metaphorical: the spheres were parallel but also opposed, with the Christian striving to escape from the world and its snares to the realm of spirit. But "spiritualism," like the traditional cosmology, treated the dualism more metonymically: the realm of spirit is the true source of life, and empowerment in the world depends on drawing on it to enhance life.

Though a religious practice based four-square on this perspective was fully articulated only in Aladura, it was clearly present in the outlook of the early converts. Indicative idioms crop up in the CMS journals, as with the sick farm slave of a Christian elder at Ibadan who began to imitate his master by praying to God; he started to feel better, and "from that time I became a praying man."[56] The Yoruba original of this last phrase must have been something like *"mo di aladura,"* and the implication is that the slave was using *aladura* as a virtual synonym of *Onigbagbọ* (Christian). This made much sense, granted that *adura* (prayer) was for Christians what *ẹbọ* (sacrifice) was for the pagan (*aborisa*), both means for accessing "spiritual" power. At the heart of the spirituality of the Yoruba converts was their sense that they had a great power on whom they could call with confidence, for the needs both of this world and of the next.

COMMUNICANTS AND BACKSLIDERS

The spiritual ethos that has just been described was formed over time within congregations that were themselves evolving as moral communities. Morality has two aspects here, though they were closely connected: the rules for living which Christians received from their pastors or from the prevailing norms of their society, and the moral bonds which constituted and expressed the church as a community. Morality was also connected, but ambiguously, with the power which was the prime objective of religious action. In non-Christian practice, there was a rough continuum—as from moral to amoral—between a sacrifice to an *orisa* for the welfare of the household, in which the sharing of the meal expressed and confirmed the moral values of kinship, and an *oogun* or *tira*, a "juju," bought from a specialist to deal with one's enemies, whose use was entirely unfettered by moral conditions. While the prayers of Yoruba Christians were also strongly oriented toward practical results, heavy emphasis was also laid on the moral conditions imposed by God for the success of prayer, as in the prayer which James Okuseinde used for the sick at Ibadan:

Ọlọrun ṣanu fun mi, dari ẹṣẹ mi ji mi, l'orukọ Jesu ọmọ rẹ

"God have mercy on me, forgive me my sins, in the name of Jesus thy son."[57]

The moral conditions of effective prayer were often emphasized to the point of implying a mutual obligation between God and the believer, very similar to how relations between the *oriṣa* and their devotees were construed: I will do what *you* want, and then you will give me what *I* want. Samuel Johnson reported how David Kukomi gave moral instruction to his children, telling them stories about "those who perished from immorality . . . [and] those who prospered by cultivating good moral habits. . . . It is very peculiar with him to turn every incident to good account, and [he] is a regular chaplain to his people."[58] Kukomi's solution for unanswered prayers—to "examine yourself and be sure your sin is mixed up with unbelief and doubtings, and sin lies at the door"[59]—presumes the same direct link between well-being (*alafia*) and morality.

The CMS missionaries, like many missionaries at other times and places, wanted of their converts a virtuoso religious practice, even moral heroism. James Johnson pointed up the moral condition of the Abeokuta church in 1878 (about which he was scathing) by means of a highly idealized portrayal of its early years (which he had not personally known):

> Then the Christian community was a real brotherhood and each man looked not only on his own things but also on the things of others. It was as if the Brethren had all things in common. All were single-minded, loving and confiding. Then it seemed to them as it did to the Thessalonian Christians that the day of Christ was at hand: the journey was soon to be ended and the race brought to a close. . . . It did not enter the minds of many that the struggle might be long and the conflict with flesh protracted, and that the faith which showed itself able to breast itself at one time against a concentration of foes might yet fail in repelling a long and detail[ed] attack [by] some other form of opposition. Then the brethren spake one to another in psalms and hymns and spiritual songs, singing and making melody in their hearts to the Lord. . . . There was a devouring of scripture portions as fast as missionaries increased translations. . . . Zeal was ardent and love great; and both stood in scripture basis. Some of our old converts are wont to allude in their conversation to the good olden days when they and their fellows first knew the Lord and tested of his grace.[60]

It is very unlikely that the persecuted converts of 1849 really lived in imminent expectation of the *parousia*—there is nothing whatever to suggest it in the contemporary journals—and Johnson appears to have been carried away by a romantic identification of the early Egba Christians with those of New Testament times.

We get a more reliable glimpse of the religious outlook of Egba Christians at roughly this time through the unusual medium of some short sentences used in his literacy classes by a convert called Dunkuru. Wanting to illustrate particular two-letter phonemes (such as *bi*, *le*, or *we*) in use, he chose examples of informal religious speech as he might have found it among the members of his class. Some telling examples, chosen from twenty-four in all:

Pin ẹsẹ rẹ l'atijọ silẹ, "Abandon your former sins."

Irọ yi a npa l'atijọ, "We told these lies in former times."

Ọlọrun naa k'a maa sin titi, k'a ma su ni, "It is God we should serve always, let us not be weary."

K'a di ẹru, k'a mu giri, "Let us tie our load and hold it fast."

Owo li a mọ li Egba, a ko mọ ọrọ Ọlọrun, "We Egbas know only money, we do not know God's word."

Bi o ba nṣe panṣaga, k'a le ọ lọ, "If you commit adultery, let us drive you out."

A ṣe ṣe, a ti i, "We try and try again, but we fail."

Wẹ ẹsẹ rẹ nu, wẹ nu, wẹ nu, "Wash off your sins, wash them, wash them."

Ẹniti ko gbagbọ, o wo, "Who believes not is broken down."

Bi igbagbọ ko si, igbe li a o ke l'igbẹyin Ye! Ye!, "If we have no faith, what we cry out at the last will be Woe! Woe!"[61]

These few sentences—so much the expression of group attitudes that they are cast as exhortations of converts to one another—say much about the moral experience of the life of a Yoruba Christian. It is seen as a tiring process of practical learning, like a trader's journey in which the trader carries a load (*ẹru*) which needs to be tied on well but has expectation of a rich reward.[62] The sin (*ẹsẹ*) and falsity (*irọ*) of the past must be left behind. The key to success is faith (*igbagbọ*), by which the Christian (*Onigbagbọ*) can hold to what the word of God (*ọrọ Ọlọrun*), mentioned four times in the document as a whole, requires of him. Yet there is repeated failure and a recurrent need for the washing away of sin. The whole set of maxims conveys a *process* of becoming Christian, set between two great historical markers, the past left behind (*atijọ*) and the judgment which will come at the end (*igbẹyin*). Thus the missionary narrative of redemption is realized in the consciousness of the converts.

Though the down-to-earthness of Dunkuru's examples is much more convincing than James Johnson's idyll of the primitive church, it is still true that mission Christianity's heavy moral demands were more likely to be realized where the Christians were a tight-knit minority, their zeal enhanced by persecution, sustaining a countercultural ethos. The best environment for this was the localities called *Wasimi* [literally "Come and rest"] which grew up next to the main mission stations at Abeokuta as places of refuge for those driven out of their family compounds by persecution or for strangers who had nowhere else to go.[63] Those who lived there were regarded as falling under direct church control rather than under the chiefs of their own township. But even these did not long provide much of a barrier against influence from the wider society. It is significant that the two sins which are highlighted in Dunkuru's examples—adultery and love of money—were of large social consequence, since they involved just those human and material means—women and cowries—which were essential for maintaining large personal followings and so realizing the standard prestige values of Yoruba men. The tone in which Dunkuru and his fellows encouraged one another to stand fast by their Christian counter-values strongly suggests that by 1855 the moral resolve of 1849, celebrated by Johnson, was already slackening.

As the church discipline of the early days gradually relaxed, Christians, young men especially, moved back toward behavioral norms which the missionaries had proscribed. No area gave rise to greater pastoral problems than sex and marriage. The values upheld by the mission—premarital sexual abstinence, followed by lifelong marriage to one exclusive partner—were commonly breached even in their place of origin, "Christian England," where they were backed, not just by social and legal sanctions, but by widespread cultural attitudes absent from Yoruba, such as a "puritan" attitude toward bodily pleasures, romantic love, and an ideal of "companionate marriage."[64] References to "immorality"—the term nearly always refers to sexual relations outside marriage—were common, particularly in the letters of the European agents. Bühler wrote of the "fearful immorality" of "some of our young, educated, unmarried African merchants," and after seeing a parishioner who was unrepentant about an affair, opined that "adulterers . . . are bound with stronger chains by Satan than even idolators."[65] In Abeokuta and, later, Lagos, Roper considered sexual irregularity the besetting sin of "our young men" and refused to baptize the child of a man not married to its mother.[66] African lay Christians were inclined to take a more lenient view of sexual peccadilloes than were their pastors, and there was "great sorrow" in the Ake congregation when Thomas King struck two members off the list of communicants for having had sex together before marriage while away in Lagos.[67]

Much more serious, and at times a general scandal both within the Christian body and beyond it, was sexual misconduct by mission agents, especially young male schoolteachers. Adultery by one of the Aremo teachers led non-Christians to taunt Kukomi for the disgrace, and a group of younger men in the church, feeling exposed to temptation, formed themselves "into a closer kind of union for mutual protection and to watch over each other's conduct."[68] At Abeokuta in 1881, the Church Council had to spend much time investigating the "irregularities" alleged of mission agents, and several had to be dismissed.[69] One Ake member refused to take communion from William Moore because he was ineffective in checking the misconduct of a teacher.[70] Yet still lay Christians were often prepared to take a forgiving view of the faults of pastors whom they felt had served them well: when James Garber, a lay visitor who after the Outbreak of 1867 had rallied the Iporo Christians and erected a chapel for them at his own expense, was suspended for adultery with his housemaid, his people wrote on behalf of "our beloved visitor," praying for his reformation and reinstatement.[71]

These cases of adultery and fornication mostly involved unmarried young men, or monogamously married mission agents. But polygamy presented a much more intractable problem than adultery, since it was less an individual impropriety than a structural feature of the social order, and an honorable institution at that. In September 1882, there died in his seventies John Okenla, *Balogun* of Egba Christians. One of the earliest converts and an exemplary member of Ake church, a monogamist and a communicant, Okenla had led the Christian company in many campaigns over the previous twenty years. A great crowd of all faiths attended his funeral, at which a choir sang an anthem in his praise, and the warboys fired a salute, holding their guns in one hand and wiping away their tears with the other. It was not at all easy to find a suitable replacement for him, since (as Faulkner, the then superintendent put it) "the greater part of our strong and brave men have become polygamists," or (in the delicate wording of S. W. Doherty) "our young men of high standing hav[e] all become inconsistent members."[72] The man they eventually chose as *Balogun,* Joseph Olumide, was an Osiele convert in his late sixties, described as good and sensible but not especially strong; and he was never able to command the respect that Okenla had.[73]

At this period it was not so common for *converts* to marry further wives, since the decision to become a Christian had often carried high costs and implied a high level of commitment. Lacking this defining experience, it was their baptized sons who typically became polygamists, not allowing their Christian identity to stand in the way of their advance up the Yoruba status system. At Abeokuta this compromise began with some of the Saro returnees of the 1840s, who found that plural marriages, slaveholding, and membership in associations such as Ogboni and Parakoyi—with all the ritual obligations and pressures to cultural conformity that that entailed—were useful for their trading interests. Such Saro, even if they were Christians from Sierra Leone, never became deeply attached to the mission congregations, and the missionaries were very critical of their mode of life. Many of them, indeed, were strongly opposed to the influence of European missionaries in Egba affairs, up to the 1867 *Ifọle* and beyond. And as early as the 1850s, some mission Christians were seeking to integrate themselves more closely into Egba affairs, above all by getting initiated into the Ogboni society. Since the Ogboni were the very guardians of "country fashion" (*oro ibilẹ*) and had been at the root of the persecution in 1849, this was an alarming development. It came to a head in 1861, when John King, Gollmer's schoolmaster at Ikija, whom he regarded as a future leader of the church, joined the Ogboni, as most of the other teachers and promising young men of the Ake congregation had done.

The missionary response to this—for little could be done to stop it—split two ways. Treating the Ogboni as a "religious" institution, they might explain its pulling power as a sign that the Devil had been "specially busy these last few years . . . in contaminating, ensnaring, and corrupting."[74] On the other hand, they might take the line of Thomas King (no relative to John), who contended that "Ogboni in this country . . . is nothing but civil constitution or political community; or in other words African freemasonry."[75] This went with a secular or pragmatic explanation of the desire to join Ogboni: to gain privileges and to avoid molestation. The aim of King's tendentious interpretation of Ogboni as a purely secular society with a direct European equivalent was to enable Yoruba Christians to feel at home in institutions whose charter was indeed "heathen." This intention was all of a piece with the missionary attempts to secularize other areas of Yoruba culture. Here the forensic interests of the African agents stood close to those of educated second-generation Christians generally, whereas the view of the European agents concurred with that of most first-generation converts, though from a very different starting point. King did not deny that many Christian converts viewed Ogboni with "dread and disgust," and Maser went further, insisting that converts who were former Ogboni members avoided the Ogboni house as much as they did their abandoned idols.[76] He even cites an ex-Ogboni Muslim at Ibadan who told Hinderer that the Ogboni oath was "too horrible and filthy even to utter it." In sum, those who had known Ogboni *as religion* mostly found it incompatible with their new monotheistic faith, and only those who were distanced from it could mentally reconstruct it as a kind of freemasonry. Membership in Ogboni and other "secret societies" has continued to be a vexatious issue among Christians and Muslims down to the Nigerian present.

The movement of young Christian men to join the Ogboni society did have one undeniable payoff for the Christian body as a whole. It greatly moderated the wave of Egba hostility to the Christians which broke out in 1867: the Ogboni chiefs of some townships spoke up for their local Christians and gave support when they started to rebuild their churches. It is fitting that the journals of John King himself, by then a catechist, give the best close account of this process. The sacred precedent of the Jews' return from captivity in Babylon often occurred to him: the renewed sound of the church bell at Igbore led him to quote Zechariah 4:10 ("For who hath despised the day of small things?," a favorite text) and, asked suddenly to preach at the re-opened Ogbe Wesleyan chapel, he improvised from Ezra 1: 2–3, where Cyrus, King of Persia, is charged "to build [the Lord] an house at Jerusalem."[77] The dependence of God's people on the goodwill of a pagan king was necessarily much in his mind too: when the old *Baṣọrun* Somoye died later in the year, King prayed that God would "raise up another such one to be a nursing father to his church; for the hearts of kings are in his hands as the rivers of water."[78] But the consummation came when he was posted to Igbein, the nerve center of anti-Christian feeling in 1867; and at the rebuilding of its church, representatives of each group of chiefs, as well as the sword-bearer of Solanke, head of Igbein and *Balogun* of the Egba, joined in the laying of a new foundation stone.[79] These images of reunion and restoration, which so affected King, ran both ways: the town took Christianity more into itself, and the Christians recovered more of a sense of themselves as Egba.

An inevitable effect of the decisions of Christians to join Ogboni was to encourage them to take their non-Christian fellow members as a reference group—so that polygamy and slaveholding, the usual correlates of social standing, became normalized among them. By the mid-1870s a very anomalous situation had developed in the Abeokuta church: most influential Christian men were disqualified—for their polygamy, not their slaveholding—from being communicants or lay officeholders, while women and low-status men (including slaves) formally predominated in these central church activities. Briefly back in Abeokuta for his last tour in 1875, Townsend addressed the problem of these "inconsistent" Christians with his usual realism:

> I want the cooperation of a class of men whom we cannot receive as members of the Church [i.e., as communicants]. They are men engaged in trade who have been baptized and taught, and fallen into sinful habits, but who attend church regularly and are often seen at prayer meetings. They are no better and no worse than the majority of church goers in England. Their children are baptized and attend our schools here or at Lagos. As a body they have been our enemies and certainly did not prevent the Outbreak . . . and now many of them are against us as [whites].[80]

He wanted to keep these influential but excommunicated men attached to the church by involving them as "money helpers" on school boards of which they would form half the membership.

When James Johnson arrived in 1877, the tone of his comments was much more severe than Townsend's. He was seeing the Abeokuta church, which Townsend had known from its birth, for the first time, and was impatient with its compromises, especially over slaveholding by Christians. As an outsider, he expressed more clearly than anyone else just how fully church life had become suffused with the hierarchical values of Egba society at large. Slaves in the church, he felt, "really have no equal locus standi with the freeborn or freed members, . . . [are] less likely to be elected to committees or are simply a numerical complement there. . . . [They] must see with other men's eyes and can have no consciences of their own."[81] The corollary of the slaves' position was the "worldliness" of their Christian owners, slaves being the principal form of wealth. A wealthy man was esteemed in the Christian community, he was outraged to find, "though his life be a flagrant violation of Christian morality . . . by the maintenance of large harems whose inmates are Christians and heathens together." To these "gospel hardened" Christians, as he called them, Johnson still preached the need to "maintain a difference between themselves and the world"—precisely the old evangelical ideal which had had to be severely trimmed to enable the church to survive under Egba conditions. It was, of course, these powerful polygamists, in alliance with the chiefs (and with some collusion from the Egba agents of the CMS), who finally succeeded in driving Johnson from Abeokuta.

The story of the last few paragraphs has been largely a story of Abeokuta, which is not exactly replicated elsewhere. Lagos and Ibadan can be added to make up a triangle of contrasts. Links between Lagos and Abeokuta were close, with Egba forming by far the largest "tribal" constituency within the Lagos churches, and there was continuous movement between the two towns. Though there were other forms of social dependence, there was formally no slavery in Lagos, and Christians were mainly involved in commerce, bureaucratic employment, or various kinds of wage labor. But even without the powerful structural inducements to polygamy which held in the interior, the culture of plural marriage exercised a strong pull on the Christian elite in Lagos, despite the social prestige attaching to presumptively monogamous marriage in church. After arguing the case against polygamy for several hours with two Christians at Leki—a trader and a clerk—Charles Phillips reported that "the generality of our Lagos young men begin to think that polygamy is not opposed to the principles of Christianity."[82] It was in Lagos that there emerged in the 1880s an articulated challenge to the missions' insistence on monogamy—one strand (though not the main one) of the discontent with missionary policy which led to the African Church secessions of 1891 and 1901.[83] In her study of elite marriage patterns in Lagos over the period 1880–1915, Kristin Mann found that no less than 60 percent of elite men entered into customary or polygamous unions or had informal liaisons with "outside wives" during their lives, mostly in addition to their church unions.[84]

At Ibadan, there was a much wider social gap than at Abeokuta between the mission and the town. On the one side, the ethos of the church bore the imprint of Hinderer's Pietism, with its marked sense of withdrawal from the world. On the other, the public culture of the town, embodied in its chiefs with their turbulent warboys and slave-filled households, was starting to take on an Islamic flavor through the influence of *Arẹ* Latosisa. Nor was there a large mediating group such as the Saro returnees or a Christian company under its own *Balogun* to help defend the town, or any movement of Christians to take titles and of titleholders to become Christians, even nominal ones, as was happening in Abeokuta by the 1870s. The sharp separation of the Ibadan church both served as more of a barrier against easy backsliding and made it more likely, when its young men came under pressure from the ambient culture of the warboys, that they would leave Christianity altogether. The option of being "inconsistent" Christians, that capacious penumbra which took in so many of the second-generation at Abeokuta, was less viable at Ibadan.

The strains became evident in the mid to late 1870s, when the second generation of Christians began to come through and (at the end of the decade) the Ibadan war machine started to falter. A series of linked episodes, involving the families of several prominent converts, showed up how hard it was for a Christian to meet the criteria for a man of public standing (ọlọọla) in the town. Islam might then appear to be an attractive alternative. An early indication of the strains came in 1873 when Cornelius Adesolu, a leading elder of Aremo, poured out his heart at a prayer meeting about the wickedness of his four sons.[85] Whatever it was that they had done, the vehemence of Adesolu's testimony strongly points to something more than routine backsliding. But the most embarrassing case—so much so that Olubi and Okuseinde pass over it in silence—was over the apostasy of the sons of James Oderinde, the head man of the Ibadan Christians. The following reconstruction is based mostly on entries from the private diary of Robert Oyebode, Kukomi's son, and the journal of Samuel Johnson:

> The old man died on 17 March 1877 after a long illness. Within the month occurred two signs that his sons, John and Abel, were not happy with the public identity they had received from their father: they refused to take "Oderinde" as their surname, which was the usual Christian practice; and Abel, at least, had his face cut with Ibadan marks. But in July, John married Nancy Oja, and the feast was held at Samuel Johnson's house. Still, there must have been worries about what he was up to, since a few days later, Oyebode had a "fine talk" with Rev. Daniel Olubi about him.
>
> Then on 10 October a serious fight broke out at Adesolu's compound, where many Christians lived. A Muslim convert from Christianity, Bakare, attacked two members of the compound, Akintayo and his Christian brother Akinyele. The next Sunday, Oderinde's people did not come to church as usual, presumably because Bakare had taken refuge with Oderinde's sons after the affray. After Akintayo died of his wounds, Bakare was arrested and publicly executed a week later. On 16 October, Oyebode makes the enigmatic entry, "I had no joy of heart the whole day and understood that all was done through Mohammedan charms," and early in November notes without further comment that John Oderinde was now allowed to be called Bakare. The following March he publicly declared for Islam.[86]

Two days after Bakare's execution, while his headless corpse was still being picked over by the vultures at the central market, Johnson wrote a deft pen-portrait of him, which also brings out much of the culture of the Ibadan warboys:

He recalls that it was he who had once taught Bakare (or Molara as he was then known) the Yoruba alphabet. His winning manners made him a favorite pupil. His father and elder brother had been converts, but fell away during the Ijaye War, and after their deaths he turned Muslim. He became angry and truculent, taking up his cutlass at the slightest offense and boasting that he would end up being given to the vultures, meaning he would die in battle. [A writer like Johnson is not likely to have been unaware of the irony in the way that this prediction came to pass.] He was prone to pick quarrels with the Christians in the compound, "accusing them before the chiefs of not going to war."[87]

A significant charge, this reiterated the common Ibadan view of Christianity as a "womanly" religion. And it also meshed with the earnest pleas that his relatives made to Josiah Akinyele, now that the death of his senior brother Akintayo put him in line as the next compound head (*bale*). He recoiled from its obligations, and his relatives in turn urged him to renounce his religion:

Christianity, they argued, was "not for one of his capacity but for beggars or slaves." He must not let his father's house fall into ruins, he must inherit his father's and brother's wives and be their leader in war. Then he would receive all "honour and respect."

Then they sought to challenge his Christian faith: "He cannot be happy in heaven, for he will go there alone as neither his parents nor his brothers and relatives have any portion there." But their concerns were practical, and they could be flexible: "You can even embrace Mohammedanism and we shall embrace it with you, only be not a Christian."

His kinsfolk begged him with tears in their eyes, and got his father's companions, elderly men, to come in a company to prostrate to the ground to persuade him [this was a signal reversal of Yoruba etiquette]. He found this hard to resist, but the Spirit gave him no rest. He asked his wife [Kukomi's daughter Lapemo] to pray with him, but broke down with emotion and could not continue. . . . His relatives then turned to "threats and persecutions and all sorts of epithets were lavished on him."

The Christians were meanwhile remembering him "at the throne of grace." He resolved he had to leave his father's house: "I had rather gain my soul and lose the world than otherwise."[88]

Samuel Johnson concluded this Journal with unusual solemnity, quoting Isaiah 43:2 ("When thou passest through the waters, I will be with thee"), and began his next one by reporting that Akinyele's troubles seemed to be over, "his relatives . . . [leaving] him to himself whether madly or stupidly to follow the religion which obliges him to be a monogamist."[89] He moved from the compound of his father Bolude and built a new house at Alafara, the seat of the Akinyeles to this day.

The final act of the Oderinde saga, in two scenes, again showed up the intensity of the Christian dilemma in Ibadan, as well as its highly gendered character:

> In May 1881 Abel, the junior brother of John, died of what Samuel Johnson called "female disease." He was in no doubt as to the reason: "seduced by the lusts of the flesh and by what he was seduced Satan used as an instrument of his punishment." His family wanted him to have a Christian burial, as his mother had wished, so that he might "sleep near his father that he might be where his father is in the next world." The clergy said they dare not read the burial service over an apostate, and that anyway it could not benefit his soul. His brother John [now Bakare] then sent for the Muslims, and they buried him.[90]

In a reversal of the usual burial palaver, where both the pagan family and the Christians would want to claim the dead person as their own, here the Christians refused to claim in death someone who had rejected them in life, despite the wishes of the still-Christian widow of their former head man, Abel's mother.

It was above all the problems of *men* in Ibadan which led to apostasy, and the *women* who were most likely to remain loyal. As if to strengthen the point, Johnson ends this journal with the uplifting story of the escape from slavery of the other person in the family who stayed Christian, the "lawful" wife whom John had married in 1877:

> After John abandoned Christianity and took other wives, his first wife [Nancy Oja], though she had a baby by him, found herself neglected. To support herself she took up work as "a carrier from place to place," and was doing this when she was kidnapped with some other women at Ife, then sold on to Okeigbo. Here she was chained up, destined to be resold to Ondo. But her jailer was so struck by her bold assertion, "I am a child of God," that he helped her by seeing she was sold back to the Yoruba country. Fetching up at Iwo, she was sent to Oyo—presumably working as a carrier—where she was severely reprimanded by her owner for speaking to a "Christian sister." Resolving to escape from Iwo, she prayed God to send a deep sleep on her mistress, and slipped away at cockcrow. With a man's help she crossed over the river Oba, and with her two-year old son finally got back to Ibadan.[91]

With his comment, "That mighty Name was her protector," Johnson reasserts a trust in providence that must have been severely tried by the apostasy of the sons of Oderinde.

While the phenomena of backsliding and apostasy serve usefully to remind us that the process of religious change was not one of smooth forward motion, we must not assume either that those who, in some way or to some extent, went "back" from their Christian profession were unaffected by their experience of it. Paradoxically, the virtuoso standards of missionaries led them often to understate their impact, precisely because it often took forms that the Yoruba, rather than they, had determined. Even James Johnson did not deny, though it seems to have baffled him, that many of his Abeokuta reprobates were "regular at church, able to read the scriptures themselves, punctual in sabbath observances and some in family devotion also and attentive at church sermons."[92] Backsliders come up in many forms and contexts. Many are identified as Saro returnees, about whom the missionaries were particularly scathing, for their ingratitude to God despite His delivery of them. "The dog is turned to his own vomit again" is a harsh text applied to them more than once (II Peter 2:22, quoting Proverbs 26:11). James Okuseinde quizzes one at Ibadan about why he stays away from church, like many others of his kind. He mentions polygamy and persecution, and perhaps more revealingly, that Christianity "do[es] not admit an undecided man."[93] Sometimes the pragmatic motives which first brought people into Christianity took them away again, as with Thomas Okiji, an Ake communicant who became a Christian after a missionary cured him of a chronic illness and then reverted in order to secure an inheritance from his brother.[94] Circumstances suggest that many relapsed simply as an aspect of moving away from the church community they had known into another social environment where they readapted to the local cults. William George met many such on his tour of the villages to the southeast of Abeokuta in 1879, including a Saro called Joseph Marsh, who was head of the Egungun cult but also still said his prayers. To needle George—but in the gentlest of ways, one might think—they called out an *egungun* who greeted him *"Oyinbo, o ku!* [Greetings, white man]."[95]

But if migration here took people away from Christianity (as mostly it brought them to it), they often carried something of their abandoned religion with them. An apostate whom Maser met among the market women in Lagos was still called Onigbagbo [Christian] by her companions.[96] Often it was more than just a label. George was shown the way to Isan by a backsliding Christian called James Osoko, a polygamist and a "magician," who asked him to pray for him; George told him he could pray for himself, and quoted Isaac Watts's hymn, "Backsliding sons return and come / Cast off despair, there yet is room"; and Osoko was silent for a long time as they walked along.[97]

Though we might suspect the missionaries of wanting to find it, a sense of regret or shame is quite often reported of these backsliders, such as a woman whom George met in Abeokuta at a friend's house:

A communicant member of Igbein church fifteen years before, she is ashamed to see George, who asks her, "Mamma, why do you stoop your head as you see me?" She replies that she has had too many discouragements, with her husband and two children dying. George tells her not to murmur against this, for it was God's chastening hand; by sin came death into the world. "Will she be able to say to her maker that because he had deprived her of husband and children therefore this is the cause of her being kept back from serving him?" She begins to weep. George reminds her that she has a soul to save. He sits by her to comfort her and begs her to attend church again.[98]

The emotional gulf between Christian theodicy and Yoruba (or perhaps just human) need comes over painfully here, and one wonders if it was not a sense of being abandoned by God in the cardinal project of her life—her children—which led the woman to abandon the church. Some apostates seem to have accepted a Christian view of their predicament with stoical despair, like the former Lagos policeman, now with Sango beads around his neck, who said (in English) "I am lost";[99] or the dying John Cole, a Saro polygamist who had played a role in the persecution at Abeokuta, whose last words to his wife, herself a communicant, were reported as "I am lost, I am for ever lost. O put me out a little in order to have some dew fall on me." Was this last request less a plea for physical relief than a prayer for the mercy of God, mediated by the dew?[100]

It is easier to distinguish apostasy and backsliding conceptually than empirically. Apostasy, we might say, is essentially an act of saying "No" to Christianity after having accepted it. Backsliding results from a Christian's inability to say "No" to aspects of Yoruba culture and religion, defined as incompatible with it. So it tends to what has been called syncretism: the attempt to combine elements from two distinct cultural systems.[101] In fact this is what *all* Yoruba Christians had to do, in one way or another, almost the whole time: "backsliders" were merely those who chose to do it in ways that fell outside the limits prescribed by the mission. So it is not surprising that we come across backsliders promoting Christianity in their own way, like the man at a farm hamlet near Ibadan, a polygamist, whom Oyebode admired for teaching the elements of Christianity to his pagan wives and nephews.[102] Or there was Deroye, once the wealthiest trader in his township at Abeokuta, who was drawn to Christianity by a business partner, started coming to church, and sent his son to school, but broke off when his trade failed and he had to take to farming. He still felt Christianity to be the true religion and that *orisa*-worship was "not clean," but he never left in the morning without praying to God, calling his wives to witness. However, he had no conviction of sin or concern with the last things.[103] People like these, so far from being tokens of where the missions had failed, were in a larger sense among the builders of Yoruba Christianity.

10

THE MAKING OF THE YORUBA

The last chapter dealt with what is now sometimes called "inculturation": the embodiment of Christianity in the forms of a particular local culture. Words from a fine hymn by Isaac Watts, "Let every creature rise and bring / Peculiar honours to our king," remind us that this has been a normal and repeated process in Christian history. It *can* only happen through ordinary Yoruba becoming Christians, not as an exercise performed by missionaries from outside the culture; and it *has* to start happening as soon as they do, not requiring the admonitions of African theologians to tell them that it is needed. It always entails, too, a complementary process by which Christianity exerts an influence on the culture that receives it. In the Yoruba case, the influence of the incoming religion on the cultural identity of those who adopted it (as well as on many who did not) went much further, since the very ethnic category "Yoruba," in its modern connotation, was the product of missionary "invention." If many Yoruba have found this an unpalatable idea,[1] the deep reason seems to be because, as commonly represented, the ethnic designation "Yoruba" belongs to a pre-colonial, traditional, or even primordial order, while Christianity belongs to an opposed global or modern order. So how could the latter engender the former? But the plain fact is that the person who has the best claim to be considered *the* proto-Yoruba—in the sense of being the first Yoruba effectively to so ascribe himself—namely Samuel Ajayi Crowther, was also the first Yoruba Christian of any significance. Over the subsequent century and a half, what it has meant to be Yoruba and what it has meant to be Christian have evolved in continuous interaction with one another, and neither can be regarded as having reached a definitive resting point. But a study of the first half-century of the encounter of Christianity and the Yoruba ought to conclude by showing how this course was decisively set.

RELIGION, NATION, AND "CULTURAL NATIONALISM"

The political effects of the creation of a Yoruba identity worked themselves out during the colonial period and afterward, and are not our concern here, except insofar as they have influenced later perceptions of how the process began. Here, much of the material to be considered has most often been treated as belonging to a movement of "cultural nationalism," between the late 1880s and the First World War. This has never been sharply defined, but the received account goes roughly as follows. In response to new levels of racial discrimination and social exclusion, as well as to the disparagement of their culture and collective achievements, educated or "bourgeois" Africans reasserted their dignity as a race/nation by a new insistence on the worth of what was distinctive of them. So they cultivated the Yoruba language; adopted African dress; in many cases changed their European names to Yoruba ones; collected the ancestral wisdom of their communities in the form of proverbs, stories, and poetry; compiled historical narratives from oral traditions; and even started to find merit in some aspects of traditional religion.

The key question to be addressed here concerns the place of Christianity in this movement, which opens out into the broader issue of the relationship between Christianity and nationalism, whether Yoruba or any other. The place to start is J. F. Ade Ajayi's seminal article of 1961, "Nineteenth-Century Origins of Nigerian Nationalism," where the term "cultural nationalism" seems to occur for the first time.[2] Ajayi argues that nationalism had its roots in the missionary movement, which he explicitly contrasts in this respect with the movement of Islamic reform that led to the foundation of the Sokoto Caliphate. But whereas the Sokoto jihadists drew their inspiration from the transnational religious ideals of classical Islam, the missionaries were the bearers of the European idea of nation-states. As Ajayi noted, "They could not conceive of Christianity flourishing in a social or economic or even political environment that differed in essentials from the European environment."[3] Though they themselves did not take up the task of nation-building, they sought to do so through the educated Christian class which they created.

The viewpoint from which Ajayi wrote was that of a nationalist intellectual in a newly independent Nigeria who was concerned to trace the antecedents of his country's situation as well as of his own intellectual forbears. Ajayi avoided the danger of teleology here by pointing out that this was really a "nationalism" before the nation, certainly before the Nigerian nation. Not only was the term "Nigeria" still to be invented, but the Yoruba educated class, whose project this was, had at this stage little or no sense of identification with the non-Yoruba peoples of what would become the hinterland of colonial Nigeria.[4] Externally, the educated circles in Lagos and Abeokuta that created "cultural nationalism" had closer links with similar groups among the Christian bourgeoisie along the coast from Freetown to Calabar, with the Creole diaspora, and even with Blacks across the Atlantic than with the non-Yoruba interior. What all these people had in common, apart from a varying mix of African and Euro-Christian cultural traditions, was a consciousness shaped by their dealings with Europeans in social settings increasingly structured by racial criteria which excluded and disparaged them. So their "nationalism" was not focused on a given political or cultural entity, but on "the African nation" ("the Negro race") in general. It was because they saw the British Empire as a valuable instrument by which Africa could be elevated to take its place among the respected nations of the earth that so many of them—Edward Blyden most conspicuously—strongly supported it.[5] An unusual nationalism, that had so much of a disappointed imperialism about it!

But any nationalism has to have *some* distinctive cultural content. Ajayi's essay, dealing with the whole trajectory from the mid-nineteenth to the mid-twentieth centuries, gives relatively small weight to the twenty years when "cultural nationalism" per se — "a minor cultural renaissance," he calls it[6]—was at its height. The cultural ferment of these years received much more extended treatment from E. A. Ayandele,[7] and it is from him that most later discussion has taken its rise. While Ayandele is sometimes inclined to read too much of the later Nigerian nationalism into the movement of the 1890s,[8] he does vividly bring out the contradictory impulses which cultural nationalism displayed—to validate African tradition and to promote the assimilation of European modernity—perhaps because the issues are often so alive and unresolved in his own texts.[9] Yet at the same time Ayandele rarely loses sight of the Christian agenda that underlay so much of the project of the cultural nationalists. Their criticism of European missionaries, for example, did not make them less enthusiastic for mission as such, since they saw the more effective evangelization of their non-Christian compatriots as the essential foundation of cultural advance. Few figures of the movement were as assertive of the claims of the African nation as was Mojola Agbebi, but he wanted studies of traditional religion to be undertaken not as an antidote to missionary Christianity, but as "useful instruments in the hands of the aggressive missionary."[10]

In recent years there has seemed to be some danger that the importance of the specifically Christian filiation of cultural nationalism might slip from sight. Farias and Barber, for example, describe the cultural nationalists as having to "deal . . . culturally, politically and intellectually with the incursions of European powers"—which elides the central *religious* terrain of argument, and rather implies that they were not themselves in many ways part of the "incursions."[11] They acknowledge that "most of [the participants] were Christians," which makes it sound as if some were not, or as if this was an incidental aspect of the movement. But at its height, 1890–1914, virtually all the key figures of cultural nationalism were clergymen or active Christian laymen. Ironically, the best witness for the Christian inspiration of cultural nationalism is the one Muslim whose ideas are discussed in their book, the Yoruba Arabist, Shaikh Adam al-Iluri, who criticized it for making compromises with idolatry.[12]

Christianity was integral to cultural nationalism in two main ways. First, as Ajayi argued, there was its strong link with the idea of "nation" as such. But this has much deeper roots than the somewhat contingent one that he emphasized: the missionaries' adoption of the nation-state, as it had come to exist in early modern Western Europe, as the political norm, the "natural" environment for their kind of Christianity. After all, Christianity had existed for centuries in many other political settings. But still underlying Christianity's endorsement of the nation-state was its readiness from its earliest years to valorize the idea of the *ethnos,* which is the pre-political foundation of the nation state.[13] The impulse of Christianity to translate its Gospel implies its acceptance of peoples or "nations" as naturally given units to which the Church must speak: in the New Testament the Church's mission "to the Gentiles" was literally "to the nations/peoples" (*pros ta ethnē*).[14] A work such as Bede's *Ecclesiastical History of the English People* (completed in A.D. 731, well before England had become a single political entity) is an authentic outcome of this deep disposition of the Christian religion. Islam's *ideal* situation stands in sharp contrast: the confessional group, or *umma,* was to displace the nation, and the Arabic language of its revelation was to transcend its ethnic origins and have a supra-national status.[15]

Relationships that grow up between particular religions and peoples cannot but be reciprocal. And as peoples become nations, they tend to look toward religions in very specific ways. Since nations virtually always see themselves as standing in comparison (if not overt rivalry) with other nations, they need not only those features such as language and culture which define their uniqueness, but also some qualities that distinguish them from the others in terms of more widely shared values. Variants of the world religions are ideal for this purpose, since they offer higher, transcendent values, which can give an external, moral drive to nationhood that it is much harder to derive from mere cultural distinctiveness. From the sixteenth to the nineteenth centuries, the Protestant identity of the British nation (Scots and Welsh as well as English) did much to solidify loyalties, uniting the political class and the people, justifying action against the Catholic enemy both within (the rebellious Irish) and without (their French rivals).[16] Modern nations are essentially in a condition of becoming, rather than of being. And the more they depend on religion for the definition of their project, the more it is that what presents itself for analysis is an articulation of two projects: the national one and the dynamic of the religion itself.

This brings us to the second way in which Christianity was integral to cultural nationalism, and also back again to the basic question of just which nation was at issue. The nation envisaged in the missionary project was an ethno-linguistic one: the Yoruba. The nation which arose from the social predicament of the Christian bourgeoisie in the towns of coastal West Africa—the "African nation"—was another name for a racial category. James Johnson gave plaintive expression to the fact that this "nation" had so little positive substance to it:

> Our life in British settlements has not been a national one, we are not a nation but a collection of individuals of different tribes, though of the same race, under a foreign government with divergent feelings and aspirations, and whom it has been difficult to fuse into one and make one great nation of. We have no national sentiment, ambition or aspiration, and no national pride and thankfulness for our great men.[17]

Since this category had no intrinsic cultural content, the nationalists of Lagos naturally turned to the rich culture and historical experience that *could* give it substance, their own as Yoruba. So *cultural* nationalism was in effect largely concerned with consolidating Yoruba identity. Much of its historical writing, even on particular groups (and a fortiori in the pan-Yoruba studies such as those of J. O. George and Samuel Johnson), had as a motive to "foster unity, instead of tribal feelings,"[18] and as such gelled with the active CMS involvement in negotiations to bring the "intertribal" wars to an end. At the same time, many of its typical manifestations had their roots in the long-term process of Christian mission rather than in the specific roots of the racial nationalism that began to show itself in the 1880s. It is thus not at all surprising that two of the early venues of "cultural nationalist" discussion were the Young Men's Christian Association of Breadfruit Church, whose pastor was then James Johnson, and the Abeokuta Patriotic Association, based at Ake Church and under the patronage of the English missionary J. B. Wood. If Robin Law is right in suggesting that it was the enactment of the Lagos Education Ordinance of 1882 which more than anything else triggered cultural nationalism,[19] then the cause of Yoruba-language instruction was a missionary cause long before it was a "nationalist" one. Its aim was simply to enable Yoruba Christians to read the Bible in their mother tongue. In later sections of this chapter my aim will be to show that so-called nationalist initiatives in the areas of language, music, the investigation of traditional religion, and the writing of history derived their primary impetus from the necessities of Christian inculturation.

Nowadays the Yoruba have to be considered both a nation and an "ethnic group." The first, which came first, is what they are in their own ideal self-conception, potentially a free-standing political entity with all the classic features of a modern nation save that of having their own state.[20] The second is what they are in relation to Nigeria, where "ethnicity" refers to the competition between ethnic groups for access to the resources of the state, a related pattern of clientelist politics, and the instrumental use of culture for political ends.[21] The contrast is perhaps overdrawn, since both nations and ethnic groups have two faces: an external, "political" one, pragmatically oriented toward rival groups, and an internal, "moral" one, focused on the constitutive values of the group itself.[22] It is for this latter face of ethnicity, a relatively unexplored aspect, that Christianity is likely to be especially important. Since modern ethnicity (or its higher projection, nationalism) always involves making the "traditional" relevant to political concerns, the world religions have a vital mediating role to play here. "Moral ethnicity" certainly involves communal values, concepts of selfhood, ideals of the successful life, and so on, that have their roots in pre-Christian, pre-colonial times: the mode and meaning of being Igbo, for example, still differ strikingly from being Yoruba. But as people became Christian (or in the case of many Yoruba, Muslim), traditional values were in various ways transmuted by new understandings, or else blended with new values related, above all, to progressive concepts of time and new ideas of personal and social development. The world religions have been the principal vehicle for this negotiation between past and present in the lives of Yoruba.

YORUBA, AKU, OYO, AND OTHERS

How, then, *did* the Yoruba come to be so called? There is no doubt that the word immediately comes from the Hausa, and that it was applied to that Yoruba entity with which they were most involved, namely Oyo. So it appears in what is the earliest general account of Yoruba origins, the Sokoto Sultan Bello's *Infaq al-Maysur* (1812), a general history of Islamic West Africa.[23] The word has also been linked with the name of Ya'rub, a prestigious figure in early Arab genealogies, from which it is most likely to be derived.[24] From Hausa sources, the name (in several variants like "Yarriba") passed to travelers and diplomats, such as Clapperton, the Landers, Bowdich, and Dupuis (who had it from Hausa traders at Kumasi), who from the 1820s gave it some currency in England.[25] But the earliest direct acquaintance of Europeans with Yoruba-speaking people had taken place earlier on the coast, where they were known by the indigenous names of the various sub-groups or "tribes," such the Oyo [Eyeo, Hio, etc.] or the Ijebu [Jaboo].[26]

There is no evidence that the Yoruba-speaking peoples, despite the affinities of their dialects, their shared customs, and their widespread traditions of origin from Ife, used an all-embracing name for themselves in their homeland, where the "others" were the speakers of other Yoruba dialects, Egba to Ijebu, Ijesha to Oyo. But it is telling that a common name based on linguistic and cultural resemblances did emerge wherever the Yoruba were in diaspora, and the others were Igbo, Kongo, or Mandinka. Lucumi in Cuba, Nago in Brazil, it is their appellation Aku in Sierra Leone—said to be from their mode of greeting, "*o ku*"—which concerns us here. In Freetown the Aku were well known for their strong "compatriotism," and in 1843 they were involved in communal riots against the Igbo[27]—a circumstance which may help to explain why the Igbo parents of James White's first wife were so opposed to her marrying an Aku man.[28] The CMS missionaries in Sierra Leone followed the prevalent usage, and the pioneer of Yoruba language study, Rev. John Raban (who received help from the young Samuel Crowther), published his *Vocabulary of the Eyo or Aku Language, a Dialect of Western Africa* in 1830–1832. Here he implicitly treats as equivalent Oyo and all the cognate dialects, just as the term "Yoruba" would do. Yet these CMS scholars became rather attached to "Aku" as the designation of all Yoruba-speakers. The greatest of them, S. W. Koelle, was severely critical of his fellows for adopting the term "Yoruba." It was, he said, "unhistorical, having never been used of the whole Aku nation by anybody, except for the last few years conventionally by missionaries"; it would confuse, since the same word applied both to the whole and a part; and, being incorrect, "[could] never be received by the different tribes as a name for the whole nation."[29] Koelle makes two telling assumptions here: that the unit of evangelism must be the nation; and that there must have been a "proper national name" for the people called Aku in Sierra Leone, which it was the job of missionaries to identify correctly. Yet there *was* no prior Aku/Yoruba nation until it began to emerge in exile and was later re-imported to its homeland by the mission. What seems to have been decisive for the final adoption of "Yoruba" was Crowther's use of it in the title of his *Vocabulary of the Yoruba Language* (1843). In 1836, Crowther was still describing his home-town near Iseyin as being "in the Eyo Country."[30] If we ask why he finally opted for the Hausa term used by travelers to the interior, rather than the one in use by his colleagues in the Sierra Leone Mission, the answer may perhaps be found in his participation in the 1841 Niger expedition. Here he and his colleague Schön spoke of the "Yaruba" when they encountered them along the Niger upstream from the confluence—both for non-Oyo groups such as "the Yagba . . . a dialect of Yaruba," and for the Oyo of the old "Yaruba kingdom."[31] The term Aku hardly made it back to Yorubaland.[32]

So the Yoruba Mission it became, the Bible was translated into Yoruba, and Yoruba was what the converts came to understand themselves to be. They did not abandon their previous self-ascriptions as Egba, Lagosian (*ọmọ Eko*), Ijesha, and so forth—what missionaries (and soon literate Yoruba) often called "tribes," in the sense of sub-divisions of the nation, like the tribes of Israel. These remained the focus of people's primary loyalties, as Gollmer observed while planning, from Abeokuta, a mission station at Ijaye:

"The 'feeling' which exists between the different tribes of the Yoruba nation is a drawback to the extension of mission work. Friends at home may say, if there are so many openings in the Yoruba country, why not send some of the Abbeokuta converts to these places? This can be done and is being done. But if the Chief of Ijaye [Kurunmi] tells us, 'These Egba boys [Phillips the catechist and Wilhelm the visitor] I know not', but 'Thompson [the interpreter] that Yoruba man, I know he is my family', we understand what a feeling exists . . . more or less among all the tribes. . . . However[,] we trust ere long the Gospel will heal this wound and reciprocity of affection [will be] cherished among all, cementing the many Yoruba tribes into one great Christian nation."[33]

But the tribe/nation distinction was not consistently employed, and our witnesses sometimes shift between levels in naming the nation. So Olubi, an Egba living in Ibadan, writes in one place of "the unhappy suspicions between the Egba and Yoruba nations, which had begun over sixty years ago."[34] But then an impending human sacrifice at Ibadan leads him to pray "on behalf of our wretched country and [its] disgusting customs," where what is implied is not Egba or Oyo-Yoruba but the "neo-Yoruba" nation of the Christian imaginary.[35]

As the above remarks of Olubi and Gollmer imply, the foreign term "Yoruba" did not only come to designate the "supra-tribal" nation which the missionaries wanted to help into existence, but also the Oyo sub-group or "tribe" to which the Hausa had originally applied it. For this latter usage there was strictly no semantic need, since the Oyo were already known as such by themselves and others, and continued to be so.[36] This double reference can be confusing, though the context usually makes it clear which level of reference was intended. It went back to the earliest days of the mission, as when Crowther wrote in one phrase of "a man of the Egba tribe" and "a Yoruba man,"[37] and led to the use of the tendentious expression (again apparently coined by Crowther), "Yoruba Proper," to denote the Oyo.[38] It was the Egba, unsurprisingly, who were the most sensitive to the status implications of this. The vernacular newspaper *Iwe Irohin*, first published at Abeokuta in 1859, was subtitled *"fun awọn ara Ẹgba ati Yoruba* [for Egba and Yoruba people]." Egba dislike of the name Yoruba being applied to include them reached its climax in the years after the *Ifọle* of 1867 (which had arisen from what they saw as the partiality of Governor Glover for their Oyo enemy, Ibadan). In 1868, the Egba chiefs told William Moore, the senior pastor and himself Egba, that they objected to the "Yoruba translation," and wanted English to be used in schools. Their reason was "because it is called the Yorubas' and not the Egbas' [book], by so doing preference is given to the Oyos who are chiefly called Yorubas." Moore defended the translation: "By Yoruba the good people of England mean the whole of the tribes who understood each other's speech in this part of the globe." Asalu, the senior Ogboni chief, finally relented when it was agreed to refer to the Primer as the "Egba Book."[39] Ten years later, James Johnson—a Saro of mixed Ijebu/Ijesha ancestry—was dismayed by the way that the Egba "look[ed] with a sour contempt on other tribes, and [met] them with a patronizing air," especially toward "Yorubans."[40]

In the late 1890s Bishop Charles Phillips offered what has become the standard definition of the Yoruba in terms of two coincident criteria, "(1) having a common language, (2) holding the tradition of a common origin, regarding Ile-Ife as the cradle of the race."[41] Language was an important marker of sub-group identity, and people were highly sensitive to its nuances. While still in Freetown on his way out, Adolphus Mann got himself an Aku interpreter who was able to point out to him dialect variations, saying "that is Yoruba and this Egba."[42] James White commented on small differences between the speech of two Awori towns barely thirty miles apart: for "It is me," they said *Emi la* at Ota, but *Omi la* at Igbesa, while the Egba said *Emi re a* and the Yoruba said *Emi ni* (which is the form in today's Standard Yoruba).[43] The language of the Yoruba Primer and the Bible was based on Oyo, but it was modified with a number of forms from Egba and coastal speech. Within the full spectrum of Yoruba dialect differences, the Egba and Oyo dialects are far from the extremes, both belonging to the "North Western" (NWY) dialect area.[44] What seems to have annoyed the Egba in 1868 was not the hybridity or relative Oyo-ness of the written language, but the mere fact that it was *called* Yoruba. On the other hand, Mann at Ijaye felt he had to get hymns translated or newly composed, since the existing collection could not be used in that proudly Oyo town because of their "English-Egba jargon."[45]

The notion of a "pure" Yoruba speech seems to have been cherished among the Oyo—Samuel Johnson was once commended by a traveling companion, Bishop Oluwole, for the "purity of his Yoruba," as well as for "his thorough knowledge of the manners and customs of the people."[46] Unmixed speech in other dialects was more commonly said to be "deep," and "the thorough Ijesha language" of George Vincent was noted when he preached at Ondo.[47] When the CMS opened up its Eastern District in the mid-1870s, it encountered the much more divergent dialects of Southeastern Yoruba. Yet Europeans were also agreeably surprised that Lagos interpreters could still be used as far as Ondo, and even in the creeks of the Ilaje country. "Here I can hardly understand the people," wrote Roper from Igbobini, "but many of them readily understand us; the further north we go [toward Ife and Ilesha], the more pure does the dialect become."[48] The new eastern trade route rapidly became a two-way conduit for travelers between Lagos and the north, and NWY forms of speech tended to become its lingua franca. The CMS Standard Yoruba, itself an artifact of NWY components, was thus introduced to Ondo and the east as part of a general, and broadly welcomed, "opening up" of the country. Lacking the Egbas' history of intimacy with and oppression by the Oyo, the Ondo never thought to object to the use of the "Yoruba" language in schools.

Just as the Oyo provided normative standards in language for the new Yoruba identity, so too there were standards to be forged in "culture." Here the picture is more complicated. Oyo pride was a factor here, too, but that tended to be rather retrospective, as with the Ibadan woman who told Samuel Johnson that "she is of no mixed breed, but of a pure Yoruba blood; and as such, she should not change her father's religion."[49] But a certain notion of "Yoruba Proper" affected even Europeans. Maser speculated—on very slight acquaintance and quite mistakenly—that "the fact that the royal family of Ondo have Oyo and not Ondo marks cut in their face seems to show that they were sent in ancient times as Governors by the Alafin or King of Yoruba into this province."[50] When it came to cultural legitimation through origins, Ife had the edge over Oyo, and was anyway attractive to invoke because its power had been in the legendary past, rather than in recent history.

But such backward-looking appeals to prestigious centers of power needed somehow to be combined with ideologies of progress. The missionaries saw themselves as raising the level of civilization, but not as being its originators. Following the social evolutionary doctrine of the age, they assessed the communities they knew in terms of how far they had advanced along a fairly universal scale of "improvement." So when Hinderer first passed through Ijebu, he commented on the lower standard of its agriculture compared with what he had seen around Ibadan, concluding that the people were "much more degraded and less civilized than the Yoruba [Oyo]."[51] On the other hand, when Townsend had to be ferried across the upper Ogun River near Iseyin in a large calabash, he compared it unfavorably with the Egbas' use of canoes. It was, he thought, "an extraordinary instance of [Oyo-Yoruba] faithfulness to old usages and dislike to innovations . . . in spite of a better plan known to them."[52] By implication Egba openness to Christianity, and Oyo resistance to it, were each grounded in a general disposition toward progress, and there was an inverse relationship between openness to change and cultural pride.

More instructive than these early comments by Europeans on Oyo/Egba differences are the responses of the mainly Egba and Oyo missionaries to the peoples of the east, who differed much more from both the Oya and the Egba than they did from one another. Young's characterization of the Ondo institution of concubinage as "one thing which is too peculiar to these people . . . quite different from the Egbas and the Yorubas, I believe from that of other nations,"[53] was to be echoed in much later comment on Ondo customs, particularly by Phillips.[54] These cultural differences were readily graded in a hierarchy of value. The Ondo, opined J. B. Wood, "were socially lower than [other] Yoruba-speaking tribes," and had some customs "which must be a hindrance to their elevation."[55] But Ondo was still a major kingdom, with a dynasty of recognized Ife origin. When the Oyo Samuel Johnson passed south through Ikale in 1880, his judgment was trenchant and unabashed:

> The Ikales [are] . . . still inferior to the Ondos in intellect and mode of life. They are a half-naked, greasy-bodied, dirty and covetous people, occupying a vast portion of land but living in thickets without any regular town.

> Each village consists of a family or families, and the headman is their chief. One of such chiefs [is] chosen as the head, . . . living in a similar village or hamlet in a thicket somewhere. No sign of royalty to distinguish them, they are all in their primitive state.[56]

Later that year, after traveling the same route, Johnson's Egba colleague Olubi expressed views so similar that one feels they must have compared notes. He added two further details to the cultural indictment: that the Ikale had no local markets and that their women went to the farm just like the men.[57] So although the Ikale were Yoruba by the criterion of language, by the cultural standards of "Yoruba Proper" they were judged to fall severely short: they did not live in "regular towns" or have a king, they lacked markets, their womenfolk did not do proper women's work, they did not come up to the moral or aesthetic norms of Yoruba life. But there was more to this than the mere expression of prejudice. Johnson and Olubi married a Yoruba scale of cultural value, itself without intrinsic temporality, to the developmental scheme (cf. "primitive state") brought in the intellectual baggage of the missionaries. So a unified project was sketched out, in which the Ikale would be drawn further into the circle of Yorubaness and, as an aspect of this process, Christianity would be made integral to the destiny of the emergent nation. Some two decades later, this is just what would be attempted by E. M. Lijadu, a CMS pastor from Abeokuta who founded his own mission, mostly among the Ikale and Ilaje. Lijadu was as zealous a "nationalist" as he was an evangelist, a man much in the mould of James Johnson, who set it as the grand aim of his mission to make Christianity "the home religion of our Nation."[58] He was under no illusions that his attack on the cults of Ikale was regarded by their chiefs as "exposing the [Ikale] nation to the wrath of [its] national gods." It was the inevitable corollary of his labors to make the Ikale Christian that he had also to make them understand that they belonged to the Yoruba nation.

SING UNTO THE LORD A NEW SONG

In the unusual situation that a mission is the midwife of a nation, its ability to perform this role must depend on its success in writing itself into a pre-national history to which it has not belonged. Especially when the mission has not entered as the spiritual arm of imperial conquest, a language to persuade has to be the first crucial step in this process of Christian inscription. At first it is a purely instrumental matter: people cannot become Christian in the way that a Protestant mission intends unless the Bible, simple tracts, and devotional materials such as the Prayer Book are translated into their language. It was the great good fortune of the CMS that the problem of finding a suitable linguistic medium for its Word was offset by the availability of a chief translator with the exceptional background, aptitude, and skill of

Crowther. Even more fortunate was the wider niche provided for this language by the historical circumstances, first in Sierra Leone and then in colonial Nigeria, which created the practical opportunity for an Aku or Yoruba nation to crystallize as a shared subjective reality. That, above all, underwrote the process by which the missions, which articulated this nation-defining language, were able to write themselves into Yoruba history.

Missionaries, and the African clergy in particular, were never in doubt about the culture- and nation-forming potential of their language work, its religious content as well as its linguistic form. When James Johnson claimed in 1878 that "the Bible in the native tongue" was the greatest achievement of the Yoruba Mission, the evangelical in him was in complete harmony with the nationalist: "This Book must influence the religion, the coming literature, the thought, the language, the phraseology and the life of the country, if it be diligently and extensively used."[59] If this is seen as an early showing of the "cultural nationalism" to come, it is also no more than the expression of an outlook that arises directly from the logic of mission that had been around for more than twenty years. Already in 1855 Samuel Crowther the younger had concluded his admiring account of the methods used by the Egba convert Dunkuru in his literacy classes by remarking:

> We may hope and not vainly for native *linguists* and *grammarians* who[,] although at present for want of sufficient information to enable them to develop their talents, remain hidden in the mass of the people who daily flock to us for instruction. Yet we doubt not that in proportion as literature thrives among the Egbas and Yorubas, men will not be wanting to come forth with their talents and embellish the pages of African history.[60]

These aspirations were all of a piece with the outlook that led to the formation in 1858 of an Abbeokuta Road Improvement Society and an Abeokuta Lyceum, held in the Ake school room, where Robert Campbell lectured on the "Dignity of Labour," and Crowther on "How Can the African Improve his Country?"[61] None of this was at all out of line with CMS official policy.

On the more narrowly "cultural" front, the outstanding early figure among the African mission agents was James White. This may come as a surprise to those readers who have noticed in these pages that few evangelists were as harsh in their opposition to idolatry or as strenuous in the assertion of the Gospel as he was. Yet White also showed an exceptional awareness of the aesthetic dimensions of life in Ota, the stony vineyard where he labored for over twenty years. In his first journal from Ota in 1855 he gave the earliest extant account of the Gelede masquerade, describing both the costumes and performance and the appreciative responses of the audience.[62] So impressed was White with the Ota passion for Gelede that he even thought that "their industry at trade and agriculture is not prompted so much for the sake of satisfying their wants as to be enabled to join in these games."

Fifteen years later he again mentioned Gelede in his journal, pointing out "the skill of the artists in producing the best workmanship in carving and painting" and the competition between the different quarters of the town to produce the most gorgeous displays.[63] But the evangelical in White still led him to the view that the enthusiasm that went into Gelede was essentially misdirected:

> It is a great pity to see the interest and zeal manifested by each individual and the considerable amount of money lavished on mere fleeting, momentary and unprofitable pursuits and gratifications, whereas the great and important truth of their being great sinners in the sight of God . . . is treated with as much indifference as a child's play thing. How forcible are the words of Scripture, "They spend their money for that which is not bread and their labour for that which satisfieth not."

Interestingly, White's critique of Gelede does not touch on its religious aspect—as a cult to assuage the power of female witches—but focuses entirely on its entertainment value. Here his evangelicalism shows both in the privilege he accords to utility over play and display and in his distinct preference for verbal and musical art over the visual and plastic. There is a clear rationale for this preference: White regarded language and music as media more detachable from a specific informational content than painting and sculpture, and so more adaptable to the Christian project.

The problem that so much of Yoruba culture came embedded in unacceptable religious practices showed up acutely when White succeeded in converting a drummer named Ajaka. He was an unlikely convert, being a grandson of the *Ọlọta,* and as the best drummer in town he was in much demand to play at ceremonies and festivals. But though he had wealth, wives, and slaves, he was childless, and it was this which most probably led him to become a Christian.[64] White conveys vividly the perceived power of Ajaka's drum to bring worship alive, and (whether intentionally or not) expresses this in terms which he almost might have applied to the Holy Spirit and the evangelical search for a heartfelt religion. Without his drumming, "the idolatrous . . . devotion of the pagans would be cold and devoid of life, for them it was necessary to drum the attributes of the various deities and awake them to be propitious to them." On becoming a Christian, Ajaka renounced his *orisa* but kept his drum, "one of his inquiries always being whether our religion forbad drumming." White knew that drumming was more than just music, and could not but regard Ajaka's relationship with his drum as incompatible with his Christian profession:

> "Finding that a direct answer would be repulsive to his feelings and occasion a relapse (for he loves it as his god and actually sacrifices to it),[65] I told him not to be in a hurry about that, but he should not beat it on the Lord's day." For a while Ajaka did sometimes secretly break this rule, but found that if he did it for any length of time, the leather would break, as

if "God saw him and his hand was against him." So he gave up drumming on Sundays.

Some months later, Ajaka again asked if Christianity forbad drumming. White now decided that he was mature enough in his faith to be told. The exchange went as follows. "Whose praise do you celebrate with those sounds you make with your drum?" "The gods." "How would you like to have a child who sides with your enemies and uses all [his] efforts to extol and magnify them?" "I would be very indignant." "Can you be a true child of God when you espouse the cause of his greatest enemy, the Devil, and do you not in effect recognize the idols to be something?" White told Ajaka he could not compel him to renounce drumming, but asked him to ponder whether it really became him. He soon stopped altogether, despite the appeals of many friends.

Six months later, he surrendered the drum to White, along with two smaller ones that went with it, saying: "God is great. I never thought anyone could take my affections from this my favourite pursuit but God has done so." The drums were eventually handed over to Townsend, who offered to pay for them—they had cost fifteen heads of cowries—but Ajaka refused: "Abraham of old [this was Ajaka's baptismal name] sacrificed his only son to God, I have no child but give this."[66]

This poignant story underscores the cultural dilemma of Yoruba Christians, who found some of the most powerful media too bound in with *orisa*-worship for them to adopt them without feeling very queasy. Yet White was still anxious both for his converts to be able to express their Christian faith in ways congenial to them and for the Yoruba to develop their arts to higher levels. Very much a words-and-music man, he soon came to feel at Ota that the musical side of the services did not work well. The trouble was with the translated hymns sung to English tunes. Their sense was generally too "squeezed and half-expressed for the sake of rhyme"; and their sequences of verses, different in meaning but always with the same tune, was incompatible with the tonal character of Yoruba, which requires that words and tune be matched.[67] But a solution occurred to him:

> While meditating on what way music can best be taught, so that men and women, adults and children, can unite with heart and voice, the thought came into my mind that the Otas are spoken of as superior to the [other] tribes of the Yoruba nation in these things. . . . Our converts, when heathens, certainly had hymns and songs of praise in honour of their gods— might they not also, now that they are Christians, compose songs and hymns in honour of the GOD of gods and LORD of lords?

His people responded enthusiastically to the proposal. "The women too [were] not backward in assisting in the matter," so much so that a woman who came to be treated for a bad sore, "a poetess and a musician," composed a hymn while she was with him.[68] Instead of the fixed pattern of verses of

English hymns, the Ota hymns had a looser, more fluid structure. Unfortunately, they were only reported in English translation, such as this one quoted approvingly by Townsend:

> We have served the creature more than the Creator
> We have served the blind
> We have served the lame
> We served him who had no ears
> They could not save themselves, still less save us
> Come and serve the creator of all of us
> Come and serve God the Saviour
> Come and serve him who carries all our sins away.[69]

They sang "soberly" till "Come and serve," then as loudly and animatedly as they could.

So began the notable tradition of popular church music in Nigeria, "native airs" and choruses which not only gave a distinctive voice to the worship of Yoruba Christians but would in years to come be a major influence on the development of secular popular music.[70] White's initiative became widely known, and whether from his example or independently, was soon emulated elsewhere. The choruses were often sung in local dialect and to local styles of music. Charles Phillips, not long after reaching Ondo, was charmed by the Christmas songs sung by women in the "pathetic" Ondo style:

> This is the day on which Thou art born
> This is thy own day
> We bow in worship to Thee
> We are in thy hand / Our children are in thy hand
> Drive the Devil from us, do!
> Take away the world's sins, do!
> The world is in Thy hand.[71]

Or a song of Ijesha Christians:

> Persevere, Jesus' children
> Persevere, we won't deal with the Devil
> Persevere that we may all meet on high
> Persevere for our home is on high.[72]

From the dozen or so examples that we have, these virtually spontaneous expressions of popular faith evince much the same religious outlook that was present in the impromptu prayers examined in the last chapter. Other individuals were also later credited with pioneering the use of short choruses in public Christian witness, such as the well-known CMS evangelist Joseph Fadipe, based at the southern Egba town of Isan, in the 1880s, or the flamboyant Methodist lay preacher, Ademuyiwa Haastrup, in Lagos in the 1890s, or, most famously, Rev. J. J. Ransome-Kuti of Abeokuta, in the years after 1900.[73] (Of these pioneers, the uneducated evangelist Fadipe appears to have been the subject of the first biography of a Nigerian ever written by a Nigerian).[74] The efflorescence of indigenous church music toward the end of the century has been seen as a product of "cultural nationalism," and Ademuyiwa (once Joseph Pythagoras) Haastrup is reckoned to be a major figure in that movement.[75] But the work of the 1890s stands in a far longer trajectory, which began much earlier and went on longer than can be accounted for by the specific determinants of the 1890s. Its roots are Christian rather than nationalist (or rather, nationalist only insofar as they are Christian), and the trajectory is simply that of Christianity's Yoruba inculturation. The new style eventually moved upward, being adopted in hymns, anthems, and choruses composed by countless organists and choirmasters, as far as Christ Church Cathedral in Lagos.[76] Independent churches are sometimes credited with critical innovation here in this field; but while their achievements are not to be denied, they should be seen as a development of what had been begun within the mission churches, rather than a departure from it.

How far should White's "cultural nationalism," in the sense of an assertion of the value of African culture, be seen as a response to the depreciation of Africans by Europeans? His dealings with Gollmer, under whom he had first served in Lagos, had led him as early as 1860 to write one of the most forthright critiques of "the spirit of distinction of color" (as he put it) among European missionaries that the CMS archive contains:

> The doctrine delivered from the pulpit is denied and contradicted by the inconsistent walk of the missionaries. . . . They pretend to be anxious for the salvation of our souls whilst they are mortified to see improvement in our temporal condition. . . . The lowest class of people, the ignorant, those that will be ruled by them, are by them loved and pass with them for the best of men, but all such as are rising into reputation and influence, the intelligent and civilized Africans, are by them judged proud and any other epithet but good.[77]

Thirty years later, this kind of sentiment would be regularly expressed in the radical newspapers of Lagos. The case for seeing him as a cultural nationalist seems to be clinched by the broader project that White outlined in the letter in which he reported the hymns of the Ota converts: "It seems natural . . . that every nation should, if possible, have its own hymns of music."[78] He follows this with the assertion that "the fine arts of the Yoruba nation are in a very rude and unfinished state," but "the preference is generally given to the Egbadoes,"[79] which is the basis on which improvement can be made. But what underpins both these judgments of White's is less a claim for the unique value of *local* culture than a commitment to Africa's right of access to what is presumed to be of *universal* value. What White particularly condemns in his European colleagues is their disparagement of Africans as they grow in civilization, which he correctly sees as inconsistent with the general tenor of CMS ideology. His remarks about Yoruba musical culture makes the same assumption as Johnson and Olubi had done in their judgments on the Ikale way of life: that there is an objective scale of cultural attainment, on which the different tribes of the Yoruba nation are variably placed; and, if the lower emulate the higher, the level of the lower and of the whole will be raised.

The main problem with "cultural nationalism" is now revealed as having less to do with its national than with its cultural component. If the teleology of the concept was initially disquieting, hardly less so must be the anachronism of the implicit notion of culture. Neither White nor any of his contemporaries used the term "culture" in relation to any of their projects. In speaking of "cultural nationalism" or of White's "cultural" interests, we follow the most common modern referent of "culture," which is to a range of expressive or aesthetic activities and products—roughly those that White himself called the "fine arts" (including the verbal and musical arts)—rather than the usage of cultural anthropology, where culture refers to the whole set of a people's "lifeways" and the technology that underpins them. But in separating off what we may be pleased to call White's *cultural* interests from the larger scheme within which he framed his prescriptions for the Yoruba nation, we fail to grasp the integrity of his vision. While he might not have been entirely consistent, any elements of a relativistic notion of culture (which we have to read into him) were well subordinated to a normative concept of civilization (which he and his colleagues expressly avowed on many occasions). From this it followed that his conviction that Christianity needed to be expressed in the terms of African culture never led him to consider repudiating European knowledge, techniques, skills, styles, or products if he thought that they brought improvement, which overwhelmingly he did. Indeed, he used them as evidence for the truth of the Europeans' religion. In his delight at the completion of his house, which many came to marvel at, he commented:

> I have always advanced the fact of the superiority and excellency of English workmanship not only in architecture but in everything to our own as evident and decided proof of the excellence and superiority of the religion of Jesus Christ to the religion of our fathers.[80]

Where culture is limited to the expressive sphere, it can be treated relativistically and so serves more easily as an ethnic or national marker. The corollary of this is that the cognitive and practical sphere can still be treated in a non-relativist way. White may have yearned for modernity—of which the separation of the expressive from the practical and cognitive is a decisive sign—but he was not wholly a modern man. For all his regard for "English" achievements, his Yorubaness showed in a deeper way, in his pre-Enlightenment conviction that the fine and the useful arts formed a unity, which was intimately bound in with moral value and spiritual power. Most so-called cultural nationalists took a similar view. Their high-profile adoption of Yoruba names and African dress—tokens or expressive gestures of the African race or the Yoruba nation—did not signalize any rejection of education or Christianity, the twin motors of civilization. If they criticized white missionaries, it was because they wanted more, not less, effective mission to their unenlightened compatriots.

BACK TO THE FUTURE: FIVE MODES OF CHRISTIAN INSCRIPTION

The area where the inscription of Christianity proved most difficult was, of course, religion itself. Here the missionary challenge had been concentrated, and many very hard things were said about "heathenism." Yet this was manifestly an area of central importance within Yoruba culture: it inspired its highest artistic achievements and it was intimately bound in with group identity at all levels. When Yoruba spoke, as they often did, of the difficulty of abandoning "the religion of our fathers," they were saying more than that it was their "traditional religion," as the modern cant term has it. For the *orişa* were regarded as quasi-ancestral, and the most common idiom of community membership was in terms of being fellow descendants of such a more-than-mortal person. What fueled the interest of ardent Christians, both clergy and laity, in traditional religion was the desire to find ways of reducing the apparently stark incompatibility between Christianity and Yoruba social being. Their reflections arose first in the context of religious encounter and finally gave rise at the end of the century to a number of articles, pamphlets, and short books, of which the most notable were by E. M. Lijadu and James Johnson.

Yoruba religion was not all of a piece and did not need to be condemned wholesale by even the most dismissive missionary. It was the least historical part of it, in one sense, that presented fewest problems: the Supreme Being. Nearly all of what Yoruba, at least in the center and west of the country, asserted of God could be taken up and developed by Christian missionaries. The heart of the argument revolved around what to do about the *orişa*, which were the main form in which Yoruba religion was concretely realized in daily life and showed small potential for reworking into evangelical Christianity. The Christian task had two complementary sides: to find the cultural leverage within pagan belief and motivation to move the Yoruba along a path of religious change, and to find ways to represent Christianity as the realization of Yoruba historical destiny. Five main modes of Christian inscription resulted: euhemerism, restoration, evolution, anticipation, and prophecy.

Euhemerism is the theory that those who are worshipped as gods were once merely men who have been raised to divine status in recognition of their great deeds.[81] Its appeal for a Yoruba evangelist was that it enabled him to accept the ancestral, heroic, or royal character of figures treated with respect by pagans while at the same time removing their status as *orişa*. There is no evidence that it was a tactic much employed by European missionaries, nor even that Africans learned it from European teachers. Rather it was adopted because it made such practical sense to reduce the area of unhelpful disagreement between the evangelists and their pagan interlocutors; and also because the simple reduction of *oriṣa* to total non-existence would have created cognitive problems even for African pastors, since *oriṣa* often figured in overtly "secular" forms such as genealogies and foundation narratives. White commented after reporting an argument with an Osanyin priest that "with the exception of Ifa, every individual god they worship was once a creature as well as ourselves"; and on another occasion tried to convince the Ota elders that "orishas are mortal men deified after their death."[82] The *oriṣa* who was most conspicuously subject to this treatment was Sango. Lashite, a Scripture reader at Abeokuta, "related the history of Shango the deified man and Oya his deified wife" in order to deflate an Oya devotee; and during the great confrontation with the Sango people at Ibadan in 1883, Samuel Johnson made polemical use of Sango's history.[83] This must have been the famous story of how Sango, an early *Alafin* of Oyo, hanged himself from a shea-butter tree after causing much destruction to his people by his magical powers.[84] It was reported from Bahia, the main center of Yoruba settlement in Brazil, around the turn of the century, that local people of Yoruba origin attributed certain versions of Sango myths to the euhemeristic interpretation promoted by Protestant evangelists in Lagos.[85]

A less prominent yet more effective case of euhemerism, whose motive was less to devalue a deity than to preserve the respect felt for an ancestor, concerned Oduduwa. As already shown in Chapter 4,[86] the earliest accounts we have of Oduduwa represent her/him as a refraction of the Supreme Being, in the aspect of ancestor. In southwest Yoruba, Oduduwa was invariably represented as a female ancestor, the consort or counterpart of the male creator-demiurge, Obatala. In central Yorubaland, Oduduwa was usually held to be male, but was still regarded both as a facet of God and as an ancestor. People spoke of themselves as *ọmọ Oduduwa* [child of Oduduwa] when they wanted to represent their relationship to God in terms of descent. This idea was itself quite unacceptable to Christians (as it must have been earlier to Muslims too), so Oduduwa could only be retained as an ancestor if s/he was reduced to humanity. Though the steps by which this was done are not traceable in detail, the outcome starts to emerge in Samuel Johnson's *History*. Here Oduduwa appears both as a "mythical personage," sent by his father Olodumare to create dry land on earth and to propagate the human race, and as an idolatrous migrant from the east who established himself as a king at Ife, where he died and was deified.[87] After Johnson, Oduduwa's de-apotheosis gathered pace. In the mid-nineteenth century the priests of Ife had insisted that the entire human race had originated there,[88] but a hundred years later this claim had contracted: Oduduwa was now the more particular ancestor of the Yoruba through the kingdoms set up by his sons.[89] So the foundation in 1947 of *Ẹgbẹ Ọmọ Oduduwa* [Society of the Descendants of Oduduwa], a Yoruba cultural organization which prefigured the Action Group party, showed the confluence of two strands: the Christian reworking of religious tradition and the formation of the Yoruba as an ethnic group within Nigeria. By the 1990s it had become an academic orthodoxy, bolstered by the findings of archaeology and art history, that Oduduwa was an essentially historical figure, a king of Ife who established his rule over an aboriginal population and created the classical form of its social institutions, a proto-Yoruba order.[90] And when Obatala as well is euhemerized to being the ruler of pre-Oduduwa Ife, we realize how far we have been brought from the versions of these myths first encountered by Christian evangelists.[91]

Closely allied to a euhemerist view of the gods is the notion that idolatry represents a decline from a religion that was previously without corruption or misunderstanding, a primordial monotheism, which it was the objective of missionary endeavor to restore. So White preached that "Christianity [is] the only true religion from God and heathenism [is] man's invention, [so] that the former is more ancient than the latter and therefore should not be regarded as new."[92] This was an ingenious ploy—to reverse the old and the new—and one that he came back to more than once in his untiring attempts to counter the "religion of our fathers" response to Christian evangelism. And what else could that pure, ancient religion have been, but the one to which Adam and Eve had spontaneously adhered in the time of man's innocence, and which had left echoes in the religion of the Israelites of old?[93]

The recognition of self in the narratives of the Old Testament often occurs in the CMS agents' journals, particularly of the Africans. It mostly takes the form of Scriptural precedents for incidents in their own lives, but sometimes of parallels between Hebrew and Yoruba customs—for example in sacrifices, burial, or marriage practices—which might be read as survivals from the presumed ancestral order of things. Some of the more sophisticated agents realized that these were areas of academic controversy. A detail in the manner of an Ifa sacrifice made James Johnson wonder if it might not be "a dim and confused remnant of the Jewish paschal sacrifice," but he at once disavowed any suggestion "of any African connection with the lost ten tribes [of Israel]."[94] But the theological education of nearly all the African agents, untouched by the Higher Criticism, had taught them that all human beings were literally descended from Adam and Eve through the genealogies contained in the Old Testament. Pinnock's *Scripture History,* for example, concluded its discussion of the effects of Noah's curse of Ham's son Canaan, by telling how many Canaanites were "obliged . . . to fly, some into Africa and others into various countries—their present condition in Africa we now know."[95]

In fact, it was not Christians but Muslims who first introduced this mode of thinking to the Yoruba. Samuel Johnson derived from the "national historians" (*arǫkin*) at Oyo a story that Oduduwa was the son of one Lamurudu, king of Mecca, who relapsed into idolatry and was driven into exile, eventually settling at Ile-Ife.[96] Again we encounter the idea that Yoruba paganism is a falling away from a prior monotheism, coupled with the implication that the Yoruba themselves must have migrated from the east. Johnson's ultimate Muslim source clearly drew upon the same tradition of linking all peoples to a common Hebraic stem: "Lamurudu" is a Hausa vocalization of Nimrod, "the mighty hunter before the Lord," the son of Cush and grandson of Ham. While Johnson is quite happy to work within the idiom of this story, he cannot as a Christian bring himself to accept the Meccan origin. The customs of the Yoruba prove that they came from the east, he agrees, but they "are certainly not of the Arabian family." On various grounds, he concludes that they most likely sprang from upper Egypt, had been subjects of the Phoenician Nimrod, and may well have been image-worshipping Coptic Christians (hence their expulsion as idolators from Mecca). That this is a speculative historical jumble should not conceal from us the ideological neatness of Johnson's solution: the Yoruba are given an eastern origin that points to a Christian destiny, with garbled memories of Bible stories and a religious practice in need of Protestant reform.

This notion of a return to the pure, ancient religion was also combined with a seemingly opposite idea, that of religious evolution or development. A substantial account of Yoruba religion along these lines appeared in 1894 in Ellis's *Yoruba-speaking Peoples of the Slave Coast,* which argued that Yoruba religious conceptions represented a higher evolutionary stage than those of the Akan and the Ewe to their west.[97] But a more instructive book—because, unlike Ellis, it does not stand outside Yoruba society but is so intensely involved in it—is James Johnson's *Yoruba Heathenism* (1899). In both purpose and form this work bears the deep imprint of Johnson's missionary background. He says he wrote it for young Yoruba Christians, especially those born in the faith like most of his flock at Breadfruit, to enable them to be more effective in winning converts and to help them feel "sympathy with those who are through this heathenism groping their way in the dark to find their Lord and their God."[98] It takes the form of a catechism, the information set out as the answers to a sequence of 125 questions in seven sections, posed as if for an examination.

Yoruba Heathenism opens with a section on "the Divine Being," reverence for whom by means of worship and moral practice is what constitutes religion. Johnson asserts that the knowledge of God is universal, "as coextensive with human existence as the light of the sun is," and that it derives from revelation handed down.[99] Since he only cites Genesis in this regard, the presumption must be that all knowledge of God comes down from a single, unmediated, original religion. Its corruption, in paganism, arises from natural human inclinations, such as man's feeling that he can most effectively approach God through a mediator, or to his preference for deities that are visible, material, and temporal over a God who is invisible, spiritual, and eternal. Paganism is thus a generic type of religion, and Johnson traces many parallels between the Yoruba *orişa* and the deities of the Canaanites and Phoenicians, the Greeks and Romans, the Anglo-Saxons and others. It is moreover a normal thing, a stage in the general history of humanity, from which advance can be expected. Johnson is optimistic that in the Yoruba case much ground has already been covered: they possess some notion of heaven and future judgement, and their "moral code . . . only waits for the superior enlightenment of Christianity to raise it to a higher level."[100]

Two of the many parallel cases have, by implication, a greater normative significance than the rest. One is the Anglo-Saxons, because their paganism was ancestral to the main contemporary exemplar of religious and social advancement, Christian England. So Johnson informs his readers that the names of the days of the week are a "standing monument . . . to the Heathen Idolatry of the Saxon race, of whom the great English nation is a section"; and at once follows it with the question "Is there anything similar to this among Yorubans?" answering it with the *orisa*-names of the four-day Yoruba week.[101] If the English mattered more as a secular reference group, parallels with the ancient Hebrews had a special religious significance. After all, the English were one of many pagan peoples who became Christian and raised themselves up, but Hebrew religion was uniquely the forerunner of Christianity. Johnson actually gave one of the aims of *Yoruba Heathenism* as being to explain how "the Jewish ritual of worship detailed in the Books of Moses . . . prepared the way for the Christian."[102] So when he discusses the place of sacred groves and trees in ancient religions, for example, the detail he gives to the palm tree, sacred to Ifa in Yoruba religion and extensively used at Hebrew festivals, strongly hints both at Hebrew survivals in Yoruba paganism and at the precedent for its evolution into Christianity.[103]

No less than three of the seven sections of *Yoruba Heathenism* deal exclusively with Ifa, and they contain much of its richest material. While this certainly reflects the influence of the man whom Johnson names as his chief informant, a *babalawo* convert to Christianity called Philip Jose Meffre, it also indicates how deeply Christian evangelists in general had been touched by their contact with the priests of Ifa, the intellectuals of Yoruba society. With the possible exception only of David Kukomi, Meffre was the most significant lay convert of the nineteenth century. He was an Ijesha by birth, named Arije, perhaps of the lineage of Chief Odole, who fell into slavery and was taken to Brazil, where he acquired the name by which he was later known and presumably received formal Catholic baptism. Still, he seems to have been in no very real sense a Christian when after his return he met Samuel Pearse, who brought him to conversion at Badagry in 1863.[104] After moving to Lagos he became an active member of Johnson's Breadfruit congregation and a licensed lay preacher. In 1876, he and James Johnson went to see the ex-king of Lagos and his chiefs, and Meffre

> endeavoured to show them the folly and sinfulness of adhering to the customs of their forefathers for the simple reason that they were their *fathers'* customs, and rejecting Christianity which their fathers had no opportunity

of knowing. He [based] his remarks upon the traditional saying of an old Ijesha heathen man [reputed] in wisdom. This man, when asked in a time of difficulty by his king to say what the people of old were accustomed to do in cases of emergency, advised in effect, we have nothing to do with the customs and views of the times that are past, but we are to move onward with time and follow its changes.[105]

At a later meeting Meffre took a more theological line, basing his remarks on

descriptive significant names of Ifa, such as 'The Great and Mighty One, 'The Child of God', 'The One who came down from the Heavens to the Earth', 'The One whom men have put to death with cudgels ceaselessly', 'The One who is the brightest among the gods and prevailed to do in a certain occasion what they could not' . . . and brought it up with eloquent references to Scripture. . . . He reminded them of a prayer Ifa priests were wont to pray, 'That Ifa may bring white men into their country with their good things'. This prayer was doubtless offered for the goods of Europe and America, but Mr Jose showed them that their wish had been through the mercy of God granted.[106]

The Lagos chiefs, reported Johnson, were "entranced" by this, and "listened to it with breathless attention." At the end, when Meffre challenged the ablest *babalawo* present to show how Ifa was better than Christianity, he prudently stayed silent.

Here we have the fourth and fifth modes by which Christianity sought to inscribe itself into Yoruba history and culture: anticipation and prophecy. They were closely related, even complementary to one another; and both particularly involved Ifa and the *babalawo*. Anticipation is where Christian Yoruba claim to find, within the traditional religious repertory, elements pointing toward Christ or Christian teaching as their fulfillment. Above all it was Orunmila, the *oriṣa* of Ifa, who was argued to prefigure Christ. On the other hand, there were prophecies of the coming of the Europeans and their religion, or of how they would bring order and restoration to the country— prophecies whose main and most authoritative source was *babalawo*. As is usual with historically significant prophecies, the evidence for them is entirely post hoc, but the important thing for the present argument is that it should have been widely believed that they were made. It is that which produced the effect with which we are concerned, the sense that Christianity was providentially written into Yoruba history even before it had arrived. Since Ifa was essentially a projective system, in which the diviner's clients played a key role in selecting the revelatory message that made sense to them, it typically worked in practice to sanction courses of action that they were already inclined to take or felt to be unavoidable. As Meffre's remarks to the Lagos chiefs imply, the role of *babalawo* must often have been to reconcile their clients, the Yoruba people at large, to the historical necessities of their times. There was thus, in the outcome, a large degree of collusion between their prophecies and the anticipations of the Christians.

So Samuel Johnson supported his providentialist reading of Yoruba history by referring to "an old . . . prophecy that as ruin and desolation spread from the interior to the coast, so light and restoration will be from the coast interiorwards," in a contrastive allusion to the Fulani jihad and the Christian missions.[107] Though Johnson is here unspecific about the source and circulation of the alleged prophecy, several concrete examples occur in the CMS journals. A man at Abeokuta in 1853 replied to T. B. Macaulay's urging him to give up Ifa, by saying it always spoke the truth: had not it foretold the coming of white men in the time of Sodeke?[108] Alluding to what looks like a related prophecy, an old Ogboni chief, a friend of Townsend's, told David Williams that the *babalawo* from whom he first received his Ifa, years before in Old Ake, had predicted "that after many years had passed, white people would come and dwell among them, that out of them I would form a friendship on which would depend my prosperity."[109] Sometimes Ifa was used to confirm an anticipatory dream, as when Ajaka the Ota drummer saw a person resembling James White, telling him (as in waking life) that all was true in God's book; but he still continued to feel "very uneasy . . . till he consulted his Ifa which told him all was for the good."[110] So he continued on his path toward Christianity.

But while such endorsement from Ifa was no doubt practically very helpful, it could also be a serious embarrassment:

> C. N Young was talking with a *babalawo* and chief at Ondo, who said that years before it happened, his Ifa had told him that white men would come and "put things in their proper order." When he went and told the chiefs, they had said he must be mad. A few months later, Glover's messenger Obayomi had come, and the events that led to Ondo's restoration got under way. "All these [things] were said to prove that Ifa really does see and can predicts future events. Then I told him that he must have heard from someone that [the] white man was about to visit them."[111]

Ifa's reputation for giving accurate predictions, even among Christians, was such that James Johnson felt he had to address the issue in *Yoruba Heathenism*. After insisting that no human being has the right to divine for others—a sure and definite knowledge of the future lies with God alone—he agrees that divination sometimes works. This might variously be due to "a synchronizing of divinely ordered events with the diviner's predictions" (i.e., chance), or to God's use of the agency of the Devil, or to His "pity and paternal sympathy" for those who seek the diviner's help.[112]

But the sense that Ifa was special, not to be simply dismissed with the rest of idolatry, could not be overruled. Here anticipation came to the aid of prophecy. Again, Meffre seems to have broken the ground. Whereas his fellow *babalawo*-convert Akibode had unequivocally represented his diviner's art as a Satanic power to be left behind,[113] Meffre treated the pagan past much more as a springboard into a Christian future. To a village congregation near Lagos in 1876 he showed "from many country sayings and parables that the natives of this country had a faint idea of God, but that we had not the true and full knowledge of Him till Christianity was introduced."[114] A few years later, he was bolder in asserting the growth potential of tradition. His sermon from John 1:12 ("As many as received him, to them gave he power to become the sons of God") was "enlivened by . . . parallelisms drawn from the heathen priesthood, showing that its fulfilment was in Christ and not in Ifa."[115] Meffre's influence is very evident in the rich collection of epithets in *Yoruba Heathenism* which present Ifa as a deity of salvation: *Okitibiri a-pa-ọjọ-iku-da* [Being who, turning himself over as it were in a struggle, postpones the day of death]; *Ẹla ni nwọn mbo la n'ilẹ wa* [Ela (Orunmila) is the one we sacrifice to for salvation in our house]; *Ko t'ina, ko to ro, bẹẹni on nii gba ni la n'Ifẹ* [He is of no account, is too small to be talked of, yet he is the one who saved us in Ife]; and many others.[116]

But the fullest exposition of Ifa as an anticipation, almost a "pre-revelation," of Christ comes in the writings of E. M Lijadu.[117] Born in 1862 at Osiele, the son of a catechist, Lijadu had his secondary schooling in Lagos and attended Breadfruit church, where he was strongly influenced by James Johnson and had the spiritual experience which "led [him] to the habit of sacred prayer and devotion."[118] Evangelicalism led to evangelism. He was strenuous in his commitment to mission, and (as we have already seen) he was uncompromising in his assault on the idolatry of the Ikale and Ilaje, among whom he chiefly worked. Yet his credentials as a "cultural nationalist" were strong: he early made a pioneering collection of the poetry of the Egba poet Aribiloso and later undertook researches into native medicine.[119] It was after he went to Ondo in 1890, first as catechist and then as priest, that the two sides of him—Christian and nationalist—came together, in a passionate conviction that Africans must bear the responsibility for evangelizing Africa. This would entail some serious adjustments of practice: "Africa is not going to rise while her sons sit down theorizing and quoting rules which admit of no adaptation to local environments."[120] Ironically, his strong views on the need for African self-reliance in mission got their strongest support from an English missionary, Tom Harding, and brought him into collision with his African superior at Ondo, Bishop Charles Phillips. The issue was resolved by Lijadu going independent: in 1900 he set up his own organization, the Self-Supporting Evangelists Band (*Ẹgbẹ Ajihinrere-lofẹ*). While no longer working directly under the CMS, Lijadu stayed fully in communion with the Church of England and maintained its order in the churches that he founded.[121]

Lijadu wrote two books on Ifa.[122] The first (1897) was frankly polemical—its foreword by Phillips is along the lines of "Know your enemy"—and commented critically on short excerpts from Ifa divination verses, in order to show that Ifa did not yield "a knowledge of the God of truth." In his journal for 1896 he described an Ifa consultation by local people near Ondo as "troubling a dumb idol," but five years later reported that he had been "pursuing [his] Investigations in native Theology," taking instruction from a *babalawo*.[123] The fruits are to be seen in his second book, *Orunmla!* (1908), which takes quite an opposite tack. Now all the emphasis is laid on how closely the *oriṣa* Orunmila—the god of Ifa[124]—anticipated the attributes of Christ. Beginning in the favored etymological mode, he interprets Orunmila's name as *Ọrun li o mọ ilaja* [It is Heaven which knows reconciliation], thus picking up on those numberless encounters in which Christian evangelists had sought to persuade Yoruba that Jesus Christ was *the* mediator that they had been looking for. Then he turns to a number of epithets or praise-names of Orunmila, using them to argue for his uniquely close relationship with God. Thus Orunmila is *Ẹlẹẹri ipin* [Witness to the allocation of destiny], the coeval and confident of God in the process by which all other gods and men receive their destiny; and he is *Igbakeji Olodumare* [Deputy to Olodumare]. Now Lijadu assumes, like all Yoruba Christians both lay and clerical, that the Olodumare of the Ifa verses may be unproblematically identified with the God of the Christian creeds. If what may be said of the relationship of Orunmila to Olodumare is also true of the relationship of Christ to God, it follows that Orunmila is to be identified with Christ. Lijadu does not shrink from the inference that "the pagans of our land had a knowledge of the existence of Jesus Christ."[125] When James Johnson (who had not gone so far in *Yoruba Heathenism*) spoke in his address to the Pan-Anglican Congress in 1908 of an indigenous African belief in "a second Person in the Godhead . . . often described as the Son of God, who in the form of a man came down from heaven to earth in order to correct the evils in it and reform a degenerate race," he was surely taking his cue from Lijadu.[126]

Lijadu probably went as far as an evangelical missionary could go. For having put so much emphasis on the mediatory and salvific attributes of Orunmila, how could he persuade the reader that conversion to Christianity was still necessary to win salvation? In any case, his tactic was to assimilate Orunmila to Christ, not the other way round, as if to suggest that the potential convert's journey was already begun and only needed completion. So, for example, he presented Orunmila as the conqueror of evil, in the person of the *oriṣa* Esu, and drove his point home by citing not only Ifa verses, but also Bible texts (such as Hebrews 2:14–15, and 1 John 3:8) in which the standard (mis)translation of "the Devil" as Esu occurs.[127] But in the end he had to insist that only Christ, by his redemptive sacrifice, could fully wash away mankind's sin and effect reconciliation with God.[128]

Twenty years later others did take Lijadu's argument further. The historical circumstances were very different: the colonial order was well installed, mass conversions to Christianity were under way, and the beginnings of Nigerian nationalism were evident in Lagos, nourished by a new current of international pan-Africanism. The initiative mostly came from members of the independent African churches. Adeniran Oke, self-styled "messenger to Ethiopians," argued that Orunmila was God's prophet to Africans, just as Jesus was to Europeans and Mohammed to the Arabs.[129] Rev. D. O. Epega insisted that Ifa was "the embodiment of the soul of the Yoruba nation and the repository of their knowledge, religious, historical and medical."[130] These tendencies came to fruition in an *Ijǫ Ǫrunmila* [Church of Orunmila], founded in 1934, which established a liturgy and a holy book (*Iwe Odu Mimǫ*), whose form was modeled on those of the mainline churches but whose content was drawn from Ifa. The Church of Orunmila was never more than a minor strand in Yoruba religious life and declined after the 1950s. Its present interest is that it *does* at last furnish us with an unambiguous case of cultural nationalism, in the shape of a religion constructed to an African (namely Yoruba) nationalist agenda. By contrast, the labors of Lijadu, White, James and Samuel Johnson, and their fellows were directed to the implantation of Christianity and to the reworking of local culture the better to receive it.

HISTORY REDEEMED

Without doubt the greatest work that came out of cultural nationalism was Samuel Johnson's massive 684-page *History of the Yorubas*. It not only provides us with far more information about pre-colonial Yorubaland than any other single source, but it has profoundly shaped our perception of the pattern of Yoruba history. More than that, it is the only one of the texts of cultural nationalism that can truly be considered a work of literature, and arguably the fount of the modern Nigerian canon at that.[131] Its author has often figured in these pages, not as the historian he became toward the end of his life, but as preacher and teacher, diplomat and social observer. A work as singular and unprecedented as Johnson's *History* must obviously be traced to a unique personality and experience. Yet there is a remarkable personal reticence in the writing of this most eloquent and voluminous of the Yoruba CMS authors—we get a much more vivid sense from the letters and journals of, say, James White or Moses Lijadu, of what kind of men they inwardly were. Compare Johnson's terse record of his marriage—"Today I was coupled. May she truly prove a help meet. May we both be enabled to adourn [*sic*] our profession by our example and also be enabled as long as life permits to labour the vineyard"[132]—with the intense expression of White's grief at the death of his first wife Anne.[133] It is not surprising that the more self-confident of the African clergy should express feelings of dismay at their experience of the racist attitudes of Europeans or their own subaltern status within the mission; but while White, James Johnson, and Lijadu all on occasion do, Samuel Johnson preserves an unbroken discreet silence on what he may have thought about such things. He reveals himself not through introspection but by the particularity of his outward gaze, which evinces two powerful attachments—

to the project of Christian evangelism and to the making (or as he conceived it, the restoration) of Yoruba unity and greatness. Johnson sought to reconcile the contradictory claims of Christian faith and Yoruba identity, not by any kind of theological argument about what either of them essentially was, but by a narrative of their providential resolution on the terrain of historical practice.

The process by which Johnson grew into being a historian has left some clear traces in his journals over nearly thirty years.[134] Though there is reference to the days of Old Oyo even in his awkwardly written first journal—in 1870, when he was a young schoolmaster of twenty-four—what soon distinguishes Johnson's journals from those of his contemporaries is the zest and detail with which he records the contemporary history of the late 1870s in Ibadan. But the great project of his *History* does not seem to have crystallized until around 1882, when he became deeply involved in the high politics of his country and his diplomatic mission to the camps at Kiriji brought him up against the rival claims of the warring Yoruba states. Back in Ibadan later that year he asserted the authority of his own historical knowledge in an argument with a Muslim: "I can now tell you the names and histories of the kings of Yoruba since it was a kingdom, generations before King Abiodun."[135] Here Johnson showed his strong sense of being an Oyo or "Yoruba Proper"; and moreover, as he proudly claimed, a descendant of Abiodun, already proverbial as the *Alafin* of Oyo at its apogee. In terms of a personal agenda, the *History* may be read as a resolute bid by a man who had been involuntarily torn from his roots—his parents were enslaved and became Christian in Sierra Leone, returning to Yorubaland in 1858, when Samuel was eleven—to re-plant himself in his native soil; and who realized that his homeland needed to be re-imagined and re-configured for him to be truly at home there. The memory of Abiodun's vanished Oyo had to be connected to the new, extended category of "Yoruba" introduced by the CMS, and Christianity needed somehow to be integrated into its history.

Though Johnson completed his *History* at Oyo, where he was pastor for the last fifteen years of his life (1886–1901), his historical imagination was formed in Ibadan, which took a pivotal role in its narrative. Now in terms of the fourfold typology of modes of emplotment which Hayden White has applied to nineteenth-century historiography, Johnson's *History* is a Romance. That is to say, it is to be read as "a drama of self-identification symbolized by the hero's transcendence of the world of experience, and his final liberation from it, . . . a drama of the triumph of good over evil, of virtue over vice, of light over darkness, . . . [a] a drama of redemption."[136] Of the four modes which White discusses—the others are Tragedy, Comedy, and Satire—Romance is the only one with a Christian, rather than a Classical, source. It is not surprising that Johnson was drawn to this mode of emplotment, since he had clear such precedents for it in the "plan of redemption" expounded in Scripture History and in the testimonies that converts gave of the work-

Figure 10.1. Rev. Samuel Johnson and his wife at their wedding. Courtesy of Dr. Michael Doortmont.

ing of divine providence in their own lives. The hero of Johnson's *History* was the Yoruba people, whose fall and redemption he figured by means of a three-part scheme. In the first stage, Oyo is founded by Oduduwa's grandson Oranyan and grows and prospers, up to the reign of Abiodun. "He was the last of the Kings that held the different parts of the Kingdom together in one universal sway, and with him ended the tranquillity and prosperity of the Yoruba country."[137] In the second stage Yorubaland disintegrates, with the incursions of the Fulani and the breakaway of its "provinces," the sacking of many towns, and the enslavement of their people. The third stage is summarized as "Arrest of disintegration—Ilorins checkmated—Attempts at reconstruction—Intertribal wars—British Protectorate."[138] Though Johnson begins this third stage with an account of the foundation of New Oyo by Atiba, a son of Abiodun who had himself installed as *Alafin*, he could not doubt that the real "new Oyo" was Ibadan: the sprawling, kingless, heterogeneous town that would become the metropolis of the "neo" Yoruba. After the late 1830s, he wrote, "the history of the Yorubas centred largely at Ibadan which, down to the time of the British Protectorate continued to attract to itself ardent spirits from every tribe and family all over the country, so that while the rest of the country was quiet, Ibadan was making history."[139]

The key to Johnson's *History* is his strategy for reconciling Ibadan and Christianity. Of all the towns where the CMS operated, none had an ethos more inimical to the values of missionary Christianity than Ibadan. For all that he thrilled to the drama and heroism of Ibadan's history, Johnson did not stint on his condemnation of the way of life that it represented. Writing of Ibadan's early years, he remarks that it "really lived by plunder and rapine . . . violence, oppression, robbery, man-stealing were the order of the day ."[140] He returns to the theme at later points in the narrative, as in recounting the deadly internal politics of the 1870s, or the domestic ravages of the warboys in the 1880s. Yet even in all this, Ibadan serves a divine purpose, so in the last analysis it works with Christianity:

> Yet [Ibadan was] destined by God to play a most important part in the history of the Yorubas, to break the Fulani yoke and to save the rest of the country from foreign domination; in short to be a protector as well as a scourge in the land. . . .
>
> A nation born under such strenuous circumstances cannot but leave the impress of its hardihood and warlike spirit on succeeding generations, and so we find it in Ibadan to this day. It being the Divine prerogative to use whomsover He will to effect His Divine purpose, God uses a certain nation or individual as the scourge of another nation and when His purposes are fulfilled he casts the scourge away."[141]

The theme of Ibadan as God's "scourge" was not original with Johnson, but was drawn from a theodicy long in use among the African missionaries at Ibadan. Hinderer's catechist James Barber had written back in 1856 that the Ibadans "are proud of the conquering power which the Lord has lent them for a time [but] . . . they do not know themselves to be [anything] but a whip in the hand of God to chastise their fellow sinners."[142] So Ibadan served a dual purpose in God's plan for the Yoruba. It was a punishment for their sins, an incentive to make them turn to the Word of God and "make their country good." At the same time the military strength of Ibadan made it into the bulwark of Yoruba country against the Fulani at Ilorin, and so the immediate guarantor of the mission's own freedom to operate. In the religious geopolitics of Yorubaland, which Johnson did so much to articulate, Ibadan—though its own indigenes were starting to become mainly Muslim—was thus aligned with the forces of peace and enlightenment from the south, against the "ruin and destruction" brought by the Fulani from the north.[143] Yoruba history would thus be redeemed through the providential interaction of a new community and a new religion, each of which presented itself as the means to recover the best of the old.

The history of Johnson's *History* proved to be almost as providential itself. It was completed in the first half of 1897, and despite the preference expressed at the Finance Committee—the local executive body—of the Mission in Lagos for a shorter book in Yoruba for use in schools, the 1,000-page manuscript was forwarded to London for consideration by the CMS Parent Committee.[144] By the end of 1898 it was on the desk of R. N. Cust, a liberal-minded member of the Committee, who quickly perused it but did not have the time to read it properly. Though he was highly impressed with what he saw, he did not think it was a viable publishing proposition:

> It speaks volumes in favour of the degree of culture to which Negro missionaries have attained when they can compile in so complete and orderly a manner such a gigantic work. I look at it with admiration—no native convert of India could produce such a work. Unluckily it is so very prolix, and the subject matter so very unimportant both from a secular and a religious point of view that I have not what to recommend.[145]

Much worse than this cavalier dismissal was to follow. Cust returned the manuscript to the CMS, which sent it on to their publisher Elliott Stock, who first said he had never received it, but later acknowledged that he had "mislaid" it![146] It seems that the CMS authorities made no effort to recover the manuscript that had been entrusted to their care by an obscure African pastor. What Samuel Johnson made of this indifference to his labor of so many years we do not know; but he was already a sick man, and in April 1901 he died at Lagos. It was left to his younger brother, Dr. Obadiah Johnson, to reconstitute the manuscript from Samuel's notes and drafts. Exactly how much of the present version is Samuel's and how much Obadiah's is beyond speculation. Suffice it to say that only Samuel could have collected the material and formed the judgments that make the *History* as we know it, and that Obadiah, having helped his brother complete the first version, was uniquely placed to put it together again. Obadiah was a busy man, and the work took a further fifteen years. Then the boat taking the new version to England was captured by a German warship and taken to the United States, the manuscript took two years longer to get to the printers, and the high cost of paper further delayed its production. It was finally delivered to the public in 1921.

So the *History* was reborn into another world. Nigeria had come into being, and the colonial order was well in place. In direct response the first movements of political nationalism were starting to find their voice: the National Congress of British West Africa (1920) and the Nigerian National Democratic Party, active in Lagos from 1923 under the leadership of Bishop Crowther's grandson, Herbert Macaulay. In their scope the former of these was wider, the latter (despite its name) much narrower, than the later phase of nationalism after 1945 which eventually led to Nigerian independence; but still both challenged the British colonial administration of Nigeria. How did Johnson's *History*, as a work of "cultural nationalism," relate to them? Here we have to return to a question posed earlier in this chapter: was it African (i.e., of the "Negro race"), Nigerian, or Yoruba nationalism that was at issue? Samuel Johnson knew nothing of Nigeria—even Obadiah's "Editor's Preface," written after 1916, makes no allusion to it—and his work shows few traces of that anxiety to vindicate Africans as a race in the face of British prejudice and disparagement that was so much felt by educated Africans on the coast. There is little of that pained critique of the doings of Europeans or missionaries that might be regarded as the hallmark of *African* nationalist discourse. The *History* is dedicated in the warmest tones to the mentor of Johnson's youth, Rev. David Hinderer, described as "the pioneer missionary of the C. M. S. in Yoruba Proper." The English and the Yoruba are even compared as races to their mutual advantage—"it would appear that what the one is amongst the whites, the other is among the blacks." With a certain note of caution, Johnson welcomed British overrule as the framework within which the future "prosperity and advancement" of the *Yoruba* nation might come about. So when the *History* was received by the public, its direct contribution was less to the nascent Nigerian nationalism than to the shaping of Yoruba ethnicity within Nigeria.

11

LOOKING BACK

   That human beings construct society though telling stories, and then trying to implement them, has been the theoretical basis of this book. Christian mission is about the effective telling of a story, and conversion occurs when people are prepared to take that story as their own. In practice, things are more complicated because the mission's story always has to be aligned or reconciled with other, ongoing stories current among those who receive it; and stories of all kinds have competitors, rival versions of how things might go. In any case, however powerful may be the sense that stories and lives correspond—so that, as the Psalmist says, "We spend our years as a tale that is told"[1]—an irreducible gap still lies between them, since real lives and histories have to respond to unforeseen material contingencies and the clashing projects of others. Nearly a century later, Yoruba are still engaged in the unfinished project of making themselves, now as Nigerians as well as Yoruba, and so have fresh stories to tell, which necessarily involve them in reconfiguring their past. No part it of it has engaged them more than the religious encounter through which they first knew themselves as a people desiring to be modern. It is no accident than the two founding classics of modern Yoruba historiography, both conceived in the bright morning of

Nigerian nationalism—Ajayi's *Christian Missions* and Ayandele's *Missionary Impact*—took this as their subject.

Four decades after independence, Nigeria's history evokes responses of disappointment and hopes deferred. The giant of Black Africa, standing alongside South Africa as a major regional focus for the continent's development, its potential has been thwarted by conflicts arising from its great regional and cultural diversity (culminating in the Civil War of 1967–1970) and by appalling misgovernment, mostly at the hands of the military regimes which have predominated since independence. Perhaps the most galling thing of all has been that the revenue from Nigeria's vast oil reserves, whose value surged in the early 1970s, yielded so little in terms of improved social infrastructure or standards of living. The Yoruba, with the rest of southern Nigeria—now mainly Christian, with higher levels of education and wealth— were especially alienated from a national power structure dominated by a military that was largely northern and Muslim in its highest echelons and connected with the ruling class of the northern emirates. With the continued growth of both Christianity and Islam—to the point where only a declining residuum of Nigerians (and very few Yoruba indeed) do not adhere to either of them—religion has joined region and ethnicity as a basis for conflict at the national level. By the 1990s there was a strong and widespread feeling that the national project of Nigeria was faltering. I shall conclude with two narratives of the present that reflect critically on this predicament.

Wole Soyinka is Nigeria's leading intellectual, and in 1986 became the first African to win the Nobel Prize for Literature.[2] Since the 1960s he has been an unsparing and courageous critic of the abuses of Nigeria's rulers, and he has endured periods of imprisonment or exile because of it. Through his mother, Soyinka's lineage ascends to his great-great-grandfather Daniel Olubi; he was born in the CMS compound at Ake, Abeokuta, where his father was the headmaster of the primary school; his wider family is replete with connections in the Anglican Church in which he grew up; and he remains intensely (and critically) aware of this heritage and its responsibilities. No modern African writer is as versatile as Soyinka—drama, poetry, novels, critical essays on culture and politics—but it is in his autobiographical works that he most vividly holds up a mirror to the public life of his country.[3] Of these the best-known is the delightful *Ake: The Years of Childhood*, whose theme is the widening world of the growing boy, out from the enclosed microcosm of the church compound—where to the teacher's son the malevolent *iwin* sprites[4] seemed as real as the resident shades of Bishop Crowther or Rev. Canon Delumo—to the bustling, essentially non-Christian town beyond its gates. This transit seems to prefigure Soyinka's own eventual abandonment of Christianity as a young adult in the nationalist climate of the late 1950s:

he judged Christian missions severely for their destructive attitude towards African culture, and he adopted Ogun as an icon of his own values as an artist committed to African liberation.[5]

But it is in *Ìsarà: A Voyage around "Essay,"* a quasi-fictional exploration of the social world of his father ("Essay"), named after his home-town in Ijebu, that Soyinka reaches furthest and deepest into the past. The book's main story line is based on a real episode in 1941–1943, the successful attempt of a group of youngish, educated sons of Isara, most of them working away from home—hence their name for themselves, the "ex-Ilés"[6]—to get Akinsanya, a nationalist trade union leader in Lagos, elected as king of the little town. The contest between the two candidates is portrayed as one of progressives against traditionalists, for the ex-Iles are all Christians, and speak the language of Christian "enlightenment." They reminisce and dream about their time at college together—it is modeled on St Andrew's College, Oyo, which S. A. Soyinka entered in 1910 to train as a teacher—and they put on a play to commemorate the centenary of Rev. Henry Townsend's first visit to Abeokuta in 1843. But the importance of religion to the narrative—and especially of the tension between Christianity and Yoruba cultural identity—emerges most strongly at the climax of the book, when the two factions confront one another. The traditionalist view is expressed as the thoughts of the ancient chief Odubona, last survivor of the old regime swept away by the British conquest of Ijebu in 1892, which at last let in the missionaries. He sees that defeat as essentially a spiritual catastrophe—"Was it not enough that that the missionaries strutted through the proud land, their churches and schools everywhere?"—and the educated man whom the ex-Iles want to see put on the throne of Isara as "their way of finishing off what they began forty years before."[7] As if mindful of the two sides of his own family, Soyinka has Odubona contrast Ijebu's gallant attempt to control its cultural destiny by keeping missionaries out with the Egba decision to let them in, with all its fateful consequences. The case for the progressives' man Akinsanya is put by the suave Opeilu, adept at settling church disputes. It is simply that these are modern times, and that Akinsanya has the cultural skills to promote Isara's interests effectively: "He knows the white man but he belongs to Isara. He has sworn to preserve the ways of Isara while carrying our voice to the highest councils of the land, and beyond the seas." Akinsanya succeeds in becoming king of Isara.

The tone of *Ìsarà* is very genial, even in its treatment of Christianity. Since Soyinka elsewhere makes no bones about his distaste for "alien religions,"[8] the reason is surely that in Isara they have been so well domesticated. When there is a public dedication, a prayer from a church elder, a reading from the Koran, and a libation to the ancestors or the *orişa* are offered alongside one another. Christians, even the modernizing ex-Iles, are not averse to consulting oracles or getting charms made, if the need arises. The main criterion by which Christianity is valued is what it will contribute to the welfare of the town as a whole. But Soyinka's celebration of what Isara stands for goes further than the tolerance and eclecticism of the Yoruba outlook on religion (which itself may be a little overstated).[9] He is looking back from the late 1980s, by which time years of corrupt, incompetent, and increasingly brutal military dictatorship had done much to erode the institutions of civil society and spoil the hopes of Nigerian nationalism. The ex-Iles of Isara, whom Soyinka intends to stand for their kind "all over the nation," are compared favorably with their successors: "[Their] life . . . was lived robustly, but was marked also by an intense quest for a place in the new order, and one of a more soul-searching dimension than the generation they spawned would later undertake."[10] The personal ambitions of the ex-Iles are balanced and checked by their public-spiritedness and by the moral values of their small community.[11] In *Ìsarà* Soyinka seems to look back to a time where nationalist ideals were still unsullied by the political practices of later years, and to a place where civility was underwritten by the pragmatic, live-and-let-live ethos of the old religion. Such has been the intensification of conflict between Christianity and Islam in Nigeria over the past thirty years[12]—even among the Yoruba who are supposed to go happily to one another's festivals—that Soyinka addressed it directly in a public lecture in 1991.[13] The audience must have been a largely Christian one, and Soyinka (while as usual not mincing words about the "holy frenzy" of both monotheisms) reserves his sharpest remarks for some Muslim manifestations of it. However, an oblique reference to the "born-again" suggests that Soyinka had another religious force at the back of his mind, the surge of born-again Christianity, which has a very different story to tell of Nigeria.[14]

The history of Yoruba Christianity has not proceeded evenly, but by challenge and reaction, by lulls and revivals. The very process by which it became domesticated and subject to routine cultural demand gave rise to feelings that its original *élan* had been lost and its spiritual power depleted. Soyinka evokes it well in words he attributes to his mother, known as Wild Christian, in *Ake*. "The period of faith is gone," she says, "There was faith among our early christians. Faith. *Igbagbọ*. And it is out of that faith that real power comes." It is power to drive back evil spirits that she has in mind.[15] It may be that the pattern of religious revivals that we find in Yoruba history expresses a cultural dynamic very widespread in west-central Africa, whereby periodic outbreaks of social malaise gives rise to movements of renewal, when new spiritual means are found to expel evil and restore social and bodily well-being;—until things again run down, and the cycle is repeated.[16] But a model of simple repetition will hardly do for the Yoruba case, since superimposed on any local-level determinations is the pattern of its colonial and post-colonial history; and they in turn are now affected by influences and conditions constituted at the global or transnational level.

The greatest single force on the Yoruba religious scene today, and indeed throughout most of southern and central Nigeria, is the charismatic or neo-Pentecostal movement, whose members are colloquially called born-agains. Pentecostalism first made its appearance in Nigeria in 1930–1931, when the leaders of the Aladura revival, so far easily the most important movement of renewal in Yoruba Christianity, made contact with the Apostolic Church, a British Pentecostal body. Thus emerged a grouping of churches distinguished by the practices of "tarrying" for the Holy Spirit and speaking with tongues, as well as by a concern for effective prayer and visionary guidance, and for a more spontaneous, African style of music and worship. These were the original Aladura hallmarks. Over the 1950s and 1960s, the influence of American Pentecostalism grew, with leading evangelists conducting revivals in Nigeria and Nigerians visiting their various headquarters in the United States. But the movement did not take off until the 1970s, that period after the Civil War when vastly increased public revenues from oil permitted a great expansion of higher education and fueled urban growth. According to Matthews Ojo, its leading historian, the charismatic movement had its deepest roots, and found most of its effective leaders, among university staff and students.[17] It later moved with them off campus and continued to grow in the urban centers, still strongest among the educated young, but with a broadening social base; and it expanded even faster as economic and political conditions worsened in the 1980s. The born-agains have tended to dominate the religious airwaves, excelling in the use of the new electronic media; and the leaders of their main churches or "ministries," like Deeper Life or the Redeemed Christian Church of God, are major public figures. By the mid-1990s Redeemed's monthly "Holy Ghost Nights" at its campground off the Lagos-Ibadan expressway had become perhaps the largest regular gatherings of any kind—about 30,000–40,000 people attend—ever to have been held in Nigeria.

The question of how neo-Pentecostal or born-again churches relate to the older independent churches such as the Aladura, marked by an earlier Pentecostal impulse, is complicated. The born-agains themselves stress how different they are, and there *are* striking differences in style, idiom, and emphasis. Whereas the Aladura were proud that theirs was an authentically African Christianity, the born-agains see themselves as belonging to the most dynamic movement of world Christianity, members of a Christian internationale. The preferred language for their services is English, rather than Yoruba; African styles of music, drums, and so forth find less favor than American gospel-type music, with electric guitars; dress, particularly of the mass of youthful members, is most often fashionable Western style. The keynote throughout is one of global modernity, which is both expressed in, and made possible by, the born-agains' effective use of electronic media. Yet basically the born-agains and the Aladura share the same worldview, with its deep Yoruba (or Nigerian, or African) roots. Its positive side is that God is available to answer the prayers of His faithful people in their daily needs for heal-ing, prosperity, guidance, success. On the negative side, the world is affected by a plurality of hidden forces—demons, ancestral spirits, powers of the old religion such as *oriṣa*—which impede progress and from which protection and deliverance may need to be sought. The very vehemence of born-again attacks on the Aladura churches—"white-garment churches" (*alaṣofunfun*) they contemptuously call them—is paradoxically a token of how close they stand on many essentials. The trump card of the born-agains is that they can address these perennial needs in the terms of doctrinal formulations (e.g., "faith gospel," deliverance theology)[18] that have an international currency among Pentecostalists, and that in an attractively modern style.

Perhaps what most distinguishes the born-agains from the Aladura is sim-ply the strength of their commitment to the idea of making over anew. That is also why the stories by which they place themselves in time are so reveal-ing. They have two complementary stories to tell: a sacred or canonical one which they aim to replicate, and a concrete history of Nigeria, which is less to do with tracing their origins than with clarifying what it is that they have come to redeem. The first narrative is, of course, their own theological char-ter, the account in Acts 2 of what happened "when the day of Pentecost was fully come": the greatest of all Christian miracles, when the Holy Spirit de-scended upon the Apostles and enabled them to speak in tongues, so that the heteroglot mass of visitors to Jerusalem heard them, "every man . . . in his own language." It is a story of the weak become strong, of the establish-ment of universal communication and of the mandate of mission. The im-mediate application of this potent story is in the renewal of *individual* lives stunted or dislocated by the vicissitudes of experience, and it is true that Pen-tecostalism has not always given rise to much of a *social* gospel. Yet the grow-ing comparative literature suggests that Pentecostalism is a protean phe-nomenon, whose exact public import will depend on other features of the context in which it gains adherents.[19] The very idea of being "born again" has great potency as a metaphor of radical renewal, and by the 1980s Niger-ian born-agains regularly applied it to the condition of their nation.

So the second born-again narrative is a spiritual history of Nigeria. Its ba-sic premise is that Nigeria is a land spoiled, its God-given bounty squandered, by the misrule of those who, mostly by force and fraud, have wielded power since independence. Ruth Marshall-Fratani sums up the general lines of the born-again diagnosis of the problem:

> Pentecostalist discourses engage with the history of the present, ques-tioning the social, political and cultural forms they see as historical ground for the present crisis. This questioning focuses not on external interven-tions such as colonialism or capitalism, but rather on the *practices* of local agents—"What is basically wrong with us as a people?" Pentecostalism's fierce rejection of all forms of socio-cultural practice which are seen as par-ticularly "Nigerian," "traditional" and "local" expresses not only a form of

socio-political critique which emphasizes individual agency—it is individual sin and the personal rejection of Christ that opens up the space in which the failure of the nation is manifested—but also reinforces its resolutely, "modern," transnational character.[20]

If the born-agains take for granted the concept of Nigeria as a nation, they reject the nationalist precept that the nation's growth depended on establishing a continuity with its pre-colonial cultural roots, for they are above all anxious to put its past behind them.

One way in which they do this is to stigmatize certain dates in Nigerian history as taking it away from its proper destiny. One of these is 1804, the date of the foundation of the Sokoto Caliphate. In recent years "the Caliphate" has become a common sobriquet among the Yoruba for the Muslim political class of northern Nigeria, whose hegemony they so much resent. It was often adduced in explanation of why the Yoruba politician Chief M. K. Abiola was prevented from taking office, despite winning the most votes in the presidential election of 1993.

Another negative date is 1977. What is felt to be at stake here are not just symbols of a negative past, but real powers of evil which underlie the practices of Nigeria's rulers and hold the nation back. The symbolic revival of tradition was a pronounced feature of the public culture of nationalism, reaching a high point in the holding of the Second World Festival of Black and African Arts and Culture (FESTAC) at Lagos in 1977. Born-agains often single it out as a milestone on Nigeria's downward path, since many of its performances were associated with traditional cults that they regard as demonic. For just as an individual may only reach fulfillment through his deliverance from ancestral spirits and demons, so Nigeria must be spiritually delivered from its past. In Samuel Johnson's *History,* the Yoruba were joined to the stock of Adam through Oduduwa's affiliation to Nimrod (Lamurudu). In an address by a Pentecostal leader cited by Marshall-Fratani, Nimrod is given a very different meaning:

> Nimrod, he was a hunter . . . and there's a hunting spirit that has come all the way down from Nimrod. Now notice that Nimrod was a man who dealt a lot into sorcery, he was into all kinds of things. And most of the continent of Africa, you notice, are the people of the descendants of Ham, and the things you find in the life of Nimrod, you find all over the continent. . . . The man was actually possessed of a leopard spirit, a hunting spirit. . . . Many African leaders seem to have something in common with the leopard."[21]

The speaker goes on to compare the theft of the animals' life by the hunter to the spoliation of national resources by corrupt rulers; and it is more than a mere analogy, for "there is something at work—it's not necessarily poverty only, there's a spirit behind it." The redemption of Nigeria from its past history, in the view of the new Pentecostals, is more than a secular struggle; it is a battle against the principalities and powers of darkness.

While Soyinka and the born-agains may touch hands in their condemnation of the conduct of Nigeria's rulers, the narratives in which they figure the Nigerian predicament could hardly be more different. If Soyinka is a nationalist disappointed, he is a nationalist still, especially in the cultural sphere where his main achievements lie, but the born-agains are in important ways post-nationalist. Yet neither of them, in telling their stories of religion and nationhood, can avoid situating themselves in relation to the Christian missions and the religious encounter of the nineteenth century, where the cultural dilemma which the narratives address was first put squarely on the Yoruba agenda.

At its most general the dilemma was and is how to achieve the most effective and viable mix of the traditional and the modern: a temporal antithesis once severely criticized by anthropologists but rendered fashionable again by its transposition into a spatial mode, as local and global. In Yoruba eyes the two dimensions have always been strongly coordinated with one another, as their cardinal concept of modernity—*olaju*—indicates precisely: it means "sophistication," "civilization," most literally "enlightenment," where it carries the connotation that progress depends on opening oneself to the wider world, forward movement on spatial enlargement. It is a quality which the Yoruba have prided themselves on possessing, compared with other Nigerian peoples. *Olaju* began with the missionary metaphor of bringing light to darkness, and missionaries have always stood as the paradigm of imposing external, in fact relatively global, definitions of value. Yet mission can only succeed if its message is translated into local terms: even the concept of *olaju* took root as deeply as it did because, more perhaps than its missionary originators realized, it also drew potently on Yoruba symbols and ideas.[22] And though missionaries may well be taken as (in Mudimbe's words) "the best symbol of the colonial enterprise," it is still true that the primary motive of the "cultural nationalism" of the late nineteenth century was to write Christianity into Yoruba culture and history.

In relating themselves to this heritage, the main strategic choice faced by contemporary Yoruba has been where to place the continuities and where the ruptures from what has gone before. As always with making history, it is a decision which hinges on existential choices in the present as much as on the interpretation of the past. Wole Soyinka, as much born in the CMS purple as any Nigerian, chooses to sever those links for an emphasis on his prior Yoruba roots, though his vision of a democratic, religiously tolerant Nigeria also chimes well with the secular tendency of evangelicalism, whenever it turns theologically liberal. Pentecostalism, in its American origins, was a protest against such liberal Protestantism, and its spread in Africa has been facilitated by the decidedly un-secular character of African worldviews, even after conversion to Christianity. The born-agains, more in accord with the popular spirit of the times at the end of the century throughout Africa, reach for the fruits of modernity through a vehement rejection of their "traditional" heritage. In effect, they revive the modernizing challenge presented to African institutions by the evangelical missions of the last century, one of the great transnational religious movements of their day; and their criticism of the mainstream Protestant churches for "deadness" uses the same language in which ardent missionaries criticized their congregations for becoming formal and complacent in their religious life. Yet at the same time, when a leading born-again advocate of the fashionable "gospel of prosperity" defines it as a "state of well-being in your spirit and body . . . a life of plenty and fulfilment . . . life on a big scale," his idea of it hardly differs from the traditional notion of *alafia*. And their project for individual and national renewal continues to presume the existence of a plurality of spiritual powers, demonic as well as divine, a reminder that the missionaries, while they could require the converts to hand in their idols for destruction, were less successful in persuading them that they represented nothing but their own imaginings. When modernity is offered on these premises, old demands for inculturation lose much of their appeal. The pendulum of cultural change, which for many decades has swung toward Africanization, now swings back to more transnational idioms such as Pentecostalism provides. So this complex history moves forward, with its ebbs and flows, its splits and convergences, and its successive reconfigurations of the relations of past, present, and future. The storyteller is tempted to bring things to a satisfying finality; but the historian knows he must refuse the sense of an ending.

NOTES

1. NARRATIVES OF RELIGION AND OF EMPIRE

1. As argued by K. Bediako, *Christianity in Africa: The Renewal of a Non-Western Religion* (Edinburgh, 1995).

2. J. D. Y. Peel, *Aladura: A Religious Movement among the Yoruba* (London, 1968).

3. See, for example, M. Carrithers, *Why Humans Have Cultures* (Oxford, 1992) esp. Chapter 5; and R. Finnegan, *Tales of the City: A Study of Narrative and Urban Life* (Cambridge, 1998), both of which cite especially J. Bruner, *Actual Minds, Possible Worlds* (Cambridge, Mass., 1986); "Life As Narrative," *Social Research* 54 (1987): 1–32; and "The Narrative Construction of Reality," *Critical Enquiry* 18 (1991): 1–21.

4. Apart from his many writings on Zimbabwe, see especially his contributions to two important collections which he edited: (with I. Kimambo) *The Historical Study of African Religion* (London, 1972); and (with J. Weller) *Themes in the Christian History of Central Africa* (London, 1975). His magisterial survey, "Religious Movements and Politics in Sub-Saharan Africa," *African Studies Review* 29 (1986): 1–69, was important in marking the change in intellectual climate which he had done much to bring about.

5. J. F. Ade Ajayi and E. A. Ayandele, "Writing African Church History," in *The Church Crossing Frontiers: Essays in Honour of Bengt Sundkler,* ed. P. Beyerhaus and C. F. Hallencreuz (Uppsala, 1969), 90–108; J. F. Ade Ajayi, *Christian Missions in Nigeria 1841–1941: The Making of a New Elite* (London, 1965); E. A. Ayandele, *The Missionary Impact on Modern Nigeria 1842–1914: A Social and Political Analysis* (London, 1966).

6. Their study had been pioneered by mission-linked scholars, notably by B. G. M. Sundkler in his *Bantu Prophets in South Africa* (London, 1949), one of the truly original books in African studies. For an important attempt at synthesis, see D. B. Barrett, *Schism and Renewal in Africa: An Analysis of Six Thousand Contemporary Religious Movements* (London, 1968).

7. R. Horton, "African Conversion," *Africa* 41 (1971): 85–108, which was followed up by a fuller double article, "On the Rationality of Conversion," *Africa* 45 (1975): 219–35, 373–99.

8. H. J. Fisher, "Conversion Reconsidered: Some Historical Aspects of Religious

Conversion in Black Africa," *Africa* 43 (1973): 27–40; and "The Juggernaut's Apologia: Conversion to Islam in Black Africa," *Africa* 55 (1985): 153–73.

9. A point made in J. D. Y. Peel, "History, Culture and the Comparative Method," in *Comparative Anthropology*, ed. L. Holy (Oxford, 1987), a testing of Horton's theory against the cases of Yoruba and Akan. For an assessment of Horton in an even wider comparative context, see R. W. Hefner, ed., *Conversion to Christianity: Historical and Anthropological Perspectives on a Great Transformation* (Berkeley, 1993).

10. See, for example, J. Fabian, *Language and Colonial Power: The Appropriation of Swahili in the Belgian Congo, 1880–1938* (Cambridge, 1986); V. L. Rafael, *Contracting Colonialism: Translation and Christian Conversion in Tagalog Society under Early Spanish Rule* (Ithaca, N.Y., 1988); N. B. Dirks, *Colonialism and Culture* (Ann Arbor, 1992); N. Thomas, *Colonialism's Culture: Anthropology, Travel and Government* (London, 1994); B. S. Cohn, *Colonialism and its Forms of Knowledge: The British in India* (Princeton, 1996); and a useful review by P. Pels, "The Anthropology of Colonialism," *Annual Review of Anthropology* 26 (1997): 168–83.

11. A. Hastings, *A History of African Christianity, 1950–1975* (Cambridge, 1979) gives a fine overview of church history over this crucial period without neglecting the continuing (though changing) role of missionaries; and R. Gray, *Black Christians and White Missionaries* (New Haven, 1990) sets the revived discussion in a longer historical span. Among anthropologists, who had severely neglected missions, T. O. Beidelman's *Colonial Evangelism* (Bloomington, 1982) opened a new chapter.

12. V. Y. Mudimbe, *The Invention of Africa* (Bloomington, 1988), 45–47.

13. J. and J. L. Comaroff, *Of Revelation and Revolution: Christianity, Colonialism and Consciousness in South Africa* (Chicago, 1991), 11.

14. Ibid., 8–9.

15. Comaroffs, *Of Revelation*, 10–12, 36.

16. See B. Stanley, "Commerce and Christianity, Providence Theory, the Missionary Movement and Free Trade," *Historical Journal* 26 (1983): 71–94; A. N. Porter, "Commerce and Christianity: The Rise and Fall of a Nineteenth-Century Missionary Slogan," *Historical Journal* 28 (1985): 587–621.

17. Mudimbe, *Invention of Africa*, 47–48.

18. Ibid., 48–51.

19. On which see also A. Hastings, *The Church in Africa, 1450–1950* (Oxford, 1994), 73–75.

20. On Boniface, see R. Fletcher, *The Conversion of Europe: From Paganism to Christianity in Europe 371–1386 AD* (London, 1997), 204–216.

21. Such as the use of Christian missionaries to help consolidate his kingdom by Khama, king of the Ngwato, from the 1870s. See P. Landau, *The Realm of the Word: Language, Gender and Christianity in a Southern African Kingdom* (Portsmouth, N.H., 1995).

22. Fletcher, *Conversion of Europe*, 126–29, referring to King Moshoeshoe of Lesotho; and N. J. Higham, *The Convert Kings: Power and Religious Affiliation in Early Anglo-Saxon England* (Manchester, 1997), whose first chapter, "Out of Africa," takes off from the conversion debate launched by Horton.

23. See, for example, W. A. Chaney, *The Cult of Kingship in Anglo-Saxon England: The Transition from Paganism to Christianity* (Manchester, 1970).

24. See C. R. Boxer, *The Church Militant and Iberian Expansion, 1440–1770* (Baltimore, 1978). Also T. Todorov, *The Conquest of America* (London, 1984), esp. 43, 107;

and Thomas, *Colonialism's Culture*, 72–75, on the religious framework of "Renaissance colonialism," where paganism is the decisive mark of the other, in contrast to post-Enlightenment colonialism, where lack of civilization is.

25. There is no substantial modern treatment of the origins of the modern missionary movement overall, but for a splendid brief overview in relation to Africa see Hastings, *The Church in Africa*, Chapter 7, "The Victorian Missionary." On the more specific question of the links between missions and empire, see B. Stanley, *The Bible and the Flag: Protestant Missions and British Imperialism in the Nineteenth and Twentieth Centuries* (Leicester, 1990); and A. N Porter, *Religion and Empire: British Expansion in the Long 19th Century, 1780–1914* (London, 1991).

26. From a large literature, see B. Hilton, *The Age of Atonement: The Influence of Evangelicalism on Social and Political Thought, 1795–1865* (Oxford, 1988); D. W. Bebbington, *Evangelicalism in Modern Britain: A History from the 1730s to the 1980s* (London, 1989); and W. R. Ward, *The Protestant Evangelical Awakening* (London, 1992).

27. R. Anstey, *The Atlantic Slave Trade and British Abolition, 1760–1810* (London, 1975); and J. Peterson, *Province of Freedom: A History of Sierra Leone, 1787–1870* (London, 1969).

28. See P. van der Veer, ed., *Conversion to Modernities: The Globalization of Christianity* (New York, 1996).

29. On the history of the CMS see E. Stock, *A History of the Church Missionary Society*, 3 vols. (London, 1899); G. Hewitt, *The Problem of Success: A History of the CMS, 1910–1942*, 2 vols. (London, 1971, 1977); J. Murray, *Proclaim the Good News: A Short History of the CMS* (London, 1985); C. P. Williams, *The Ideal of the Self-Governing Church: A Study in Victorian Missionary Strategy* (Leiden, 1990); and K. Ward and B. Stanley, eds., *The Church Mission Society and World Christianity* (Grand Rapids and London, 1999).

30. J. T. Kefer, Journal, 13–27 August, 1854, CMS, CA2/O/58; W. Allen, Journal, 5 February, 1865, CMS, CA2/O/18. An obtuse CMS editor of Kefer's manuscript, preparing it for publication, crossed out "Bonifacius" for "Benefactor," presumably feeling that a lay English audience would miss the allusion. St. Cyprian (d. 258) was Bishop of Carthage.

31. D. Coates to Mr and Mrs Wilson, 18 Sept. 1832, CN/L2/220. I am grateful to Miss Rosemary Keen, former archivist of the CMS, for this and the following reference.

32. Revd W. Jowett to Revd G. Pettit, 4 June 1934, CI/L2/401.

33. The nearest case we have is the published selections made after her death from the private journal kept by David Hinderer's wife: R. B. Hone, *Seventeen Years in the Yoruba Country: Memorials of Anna Hinderer . . . Gathered from Her Journals and Letters* (London, 1872). This work is often cited as if she was its author, even though it gives an account of her death.

34. D. Olubi to Parent Committee, 27 Dec. 1869, from Ibadan; J. A. Lahanmi, Journal, Jan.–June, from Ijaye, Abeokuta.

35. C. A. Gollmer, Journal, 12 Dec. 1859. Scripture readers were the grade of African mission agent below catechists.

36. F. L Akiele, then schoolmaster of Kudeti, mentions his reading over, correcting, and copying out the journals of his two senior colleagues. "Met together with the Revd Mr Olubi's for the reading of our journals and left off at 4 p.m.," he writes on 9 June 1885. In fact, many days seem to have been principally devoted to this literary work: 4, 22, 25 April and 9, 12 13, 15, 16 June. See his personal diaries in Box 1, Bishop A. B. Akinyele Papers, Ibadan University Library.

37. Such as *The Church Missionary Intelligencer, The Church Missionary Gleaner* (though this does contain line drawings and photographs of interest), or the published volumes of *Letters of the Missionaries,* which are edited, sometimes much shortened, versions of the originals.

38. Apart from Hone's *Seventeen Years,* based on Anna Hinderer's journals, the most useful is M. A. S. Barber, *Oshielle; or Village Life in the Yoruba Country* (London, 1857), based on early journals of the African catechist William Moore which are not now in the CMS archive. J. Page, *The Black Bishop: Samuel Adjai Crowther* (London, 1908), is useful for the traditions collected from family members, but the few biographies of European missionaries are very disappointing: G. Townsend, *Memoir of the Rev. Henry Townsend* (Exeter, 1887); [C. H. V. Gollmer], *Charles A. Gollmer, His Life and Missionary Labours in West Africa* (London, 1889). Miss [Sarah] Tucker's *Abbeokuta; or Sunrise within the Tropics: An Outline of the Origin and Progress of the Yoruba Mission* (London 1853) is a work entirely derivative from published CMS material by a popular writer of books on missions.

39. For a fuller view see J. D. Y. Peel, "Problems and Opportunities in an Anthropologist's Use of a Missionary Archive," in *Missionary Encounters: Sources and Issues,* ed. R. A. Bickers and R. Seton (London, 1996), 70–94.

40. The outstanding exception here is the work of Peter McKenzie, who has lately crowned a string of articles over many years with a large-scale study of Yoruba traditional religion: *Hail Orisha! A Phenomenology of a West African Religion in the Mid-Nineteenth Century* (Leiden, 1997). Also valuable is Bernard Salvaing, *Les Missionaires à la Rencontre de l'Afrique au XIXe Siècle: Côte des Esclaves et Pays Yoruba, 1840–1891* (Paris, 1994), which is more based on published sources, but also makes many telling comparisons between British Protestants (CMS and Wesleyan Methodists) and the French Catholics of the SMA.

41. Fletcher, *Conversion of Europe,* 9–10: "Very nearly all the surviving written narratives were composed by what might be called professional Christians for a primary audience of other professional Christians."

42. E. Le Roy Ladurie, *Montaillou: Cathars and Catholics in a French Village 1294–1324* (London, 1978); C. Ginzburg, *The Cheese and the Worms: The Cosmos of a Sixteenth-Century Miller* (London, 1980).

43. In this, they were less sophisticated than the Spanish missionaries to Mexico in the sixteenth century, on whom see A. Pagden, *The Fall of Natural Man* (Cambridge, 1982).

44. One result of this was that no European missionary published any "anthropological" account of Yoruba religion—with one significant exception. This was S. S. Farrow's *Faith, Fancies, and Fetich, being Some Account of the Religious Beliefs of the West African Negroes, particularly of the Yoruba Tribes of Southern Nigeria* (London, 1926). Farrow had been a CMS missionary for about five years in the late 1880s—not an especially notable one—so the book was written long after he left the field. By then, of course, the concept of culture had come in, and was made extensive use of by such missionary-ethnographers as E. W. Smith. R. R. Marett, professor of anthropology at Oxford, wrote a foreword for Farrow's book.

45. Such as A. Apter, *Black Critics and Kings: The Hermeneutics of Power in Yoruba Society* (Chicago, 1992); and H. J. and M. T. Drewal, *Gelede: Art and Female Power among the Yoruba* (Bloomington, 1983).

46. On which see J. D. Y. Peel, "The Pastor and the *Babalawo:* The Encounter of Religions in Nineteenth-Century Yorubaland," *Africa* 60 (1990): 338–69.

47. On which see Elizabeth Tonkin, *Narrating Our Pasts: The Social Construction of Oral History* (Cambridge, 1992), Chapter 3.

48. R. S. Oyebode, Diary for 1877, Oba I. B. Akinyele Papers, University of Ibadan Library.

49. Here I am indebted to D. Carr, *Time, Narrative, and History* (Bloomington, 1991), 57–65, especially for his insistence that "narrative form is . . . the structure inherent in human experience and action." His critique is here directed against H. White, "The Value of Narrativity in the Representation of Reality" (1980), reprinted in *The Content of the Form: Narrative Discourse and Historical Representation* (Baltimore, 1987), 1–25. More generally see S. Chatman, *Story and Discourse: Narrative Structure in Fiction and Film* (Ithaca, 1978).

50. S. W. Doherty, Journal to 31 Dec. 1881, at Igbore, Abeokuta.

51. J. Smith, Journal for Half-year to 25. Dec. 1865, at Ibadan.

52. J. A. T. Williams, Report for Half-year to 30 June 1882, at Muroko, near Lagos.

53. R. S. Oyebode, Diary, 25 October to 28 November 1877; 17–25 March 1877. For a fuller discussion of the latter sequence, see Chapter 9, p. 273.

54. For a fuller account, see below Chapter 6, p. 155.

55. C. Phillips Sr., Journal, 22 March 1855, comparing the tyrant Kurunmi of Ijaye to Herod.

56. J. A. Maser to H. Venn, 30 August 1867, likening him to the king of Dahomey.

57. S. W. Doherty, Journal, 16–17 May 1876, at Iganna. For a fuller account, see Chapter 6, p. 171.

58. J. Okuseinde, Journal, 20 Jan. 1878.

59. S. Pearse to H. Venn, 31 Dec. 1859. The quotation (Isaiah 1:8, but not so identified by Pearse) refers to the bereft condition of Judah.

60. S. Pearse, Annual Letter, 13 Jan. 1868. This text (Luke 5:5) yields a further interpretation. The words are addressed by Peter to Jesus as "Master," after he had been told to cast the net on the other side of the boat. Likewise Pearse addressed them to the man whom he revered as the "master" of the mission, its clerical secretary, Henry Venn. The passage concludes with the commissioning of the Galilean fishermen, including Peter, as missionaries: "From henceforth thou shalt catch men."

61. S. Johnson, Journal, 1 May, 6 June 1874. A fuller version, with different emphases, appears in his *History of the Yorubas,* 391–94. See further, Chapter 4, p. 77. J. White, Journal, 6 March 1870.

62. C. Phillips Sr., Journal, April 1855.

63. For the record, these are from S. Cole, Journal, 13 Dec. 1877, at Abeokuta; and D. Olubi, Journal, 26 June 1866, at Ibadan.

64. See J. D. Y. Peel, "*Olaju:* A Yoruba Concept of Development," *Journal of Development Studies* 14 (1978): 135–65.

65. J. Okuseinde, Journal, 26 July 1876.

66. D. Olubi, Journal, 8 May 1868. The proverb literally goes: "Whoever knows the road to Ofa, does not [want to] hear Ifa; whoever [wants to] hear Ifa, does not know the road to Ofa." Ofa, near Ilorin, was a town known for its Ifa diviners (*babalawo*). In Olubi's gloss, "foreign and clever priests" would want to visit it, but would not know the way there.

67. J. A. Maser, Journal, 13 Aug. 1855; I. Smith, Journal, 12 Sept. 1855; S. Crowther Jr., Journal to 25 Sept. 1855; T. King, Journal, 15 Sept. 1855. See also the analysis of P. R. McKenzie, "Was the Priestess of Yemoja Also among the Prophets?" *Orita* 9 (1975): 67–71.

68. On which see Peel, *Aladura*, 91–95.

69. S. Crowther Jr., Journal to 25 Dec. 1855; T. King, Journal, 3 March 1856.

70. A. F. C. Wallace, *The Death and Rebirth of the Seneca* (New York, 1969); M. Sahlins, *Historical Metaphors and Mythical Realities* (Ann Arbor, 1981); *Islands of History* (Chicago, 1985); and (with P. V. Kirch) *Anahulu: The Anthropology of History in the Kingdom of Hawaii* (Chicago, 1992).

71. Comaroff and Comaroff, *Of Revelation and Revolution*, vol. 1.

72. Cf. F. Kermode, *The Sense of an Ending: Studies in the Theory of Fiction* (New York, 1966), 7: "Men like poets rush 'into the middest', *in medias res*, when they are born; they also die *in mediis rebus*. They need fictive constructs with origins and ends, such as give meanings to lives and to poems."

73. Among recent work on the anthropology of memory, see P. Antze and M. Lambek, eds., *Tense Past: Cultural Essays in Trauma and Memory* (New York, 1996); R. Werbner, ed., *Memory and the Postcolony: African Anthropology and the Critique of Power* (London, 1998).

74. J. Barber, Journal, 4 January 1855, discussed more fully in Peel, "For Who Hath Despised the Day of Small Things: Missionary Narratives and Historical Anthropology," *Comparative Studies in Society and History* 37 (1995): 594–95.

75. T. B. Wright, Journal, 6 January, 1869.

76. See further J. D. Y. Peel, "Two Pastors and their Histories: Samuel Johnson and C. C. Reindorf," in *The Recovery of the West African Past: African Pastors and African History in the Nineteenth Century*, ed. P. Jenkins (Basel, 1996), 69–91.

77. J.-F. Bayart, *The State in Africa: The Politics of the Belly* (London, 1993), 20–32.

2. YORUBALAND AT WAR

1. K. Barber, *I Could Speak Until Tomorrow: Oriki, Women, and the Past in a Yoruba Town* (London, 1991), 195–220.

2. For example, B. Awe, "Militarism and Economic Development in Nineteenth Century Yoruba Country: The Ibadan Example," *Journal of African History* 14 (1973): 65–77.

3. In what is now a large secondary literature, the only *general* modern historical account of Yoruba kingdoms remains R. S. Smith, *Kingdoms of the Yoruba* (London, 1969).

4. The fruitful idea of placing the Yoruba in a wider-than-Yoruba zone was first put forward in I. A. Akinjogbin, *Dahomey and Its Neighbours, 1708–1818* (Cambridge, 1967); and further his "Towards a Historical Geography of Yoruba Civilization," in *Proceedings of the Conference on Yoruba Civilisation*, ed. I. A. Akinjogbin and G. O. Ekemode (University of Ife, 26–31 July, 1976).

5. S. T. Barnes, ed., *Africa's Ogun, Old World and New* (Bloomington, 1989), esp. Chapter 3 by Barnes, and P. G. Ben-Amos, "Ogun, the Empire Builder." No fully comparative study exists for Ifa/Fa/Afa across its range from the Ewe through Dahomey, Yoruba, and Benin even to the trans-Niger cultures of Igbo and Igala; but compare W. R. Bascom, *Ifa Divination: Communication between Gods and Men in West Africa* (Bloom-

ington, 1969); and B. Maupoil, *La Géomancie a l'Ancienne Côte des Esclaves* (Paris, 1943) on Fa in Dahomey.

6. On the cowry zone, which links the Yoruba *oikoumene* to a broad band of the Central and Western Sudan, see J. Hogendorn and M. Johnson, *The Shell Money of the Slave Trade* (Cambridge, 1986), Chapter 8.

7. R. E. Bradbury, *The Benin Kingdom and the Edo-speaking Peoples of South-western Nigeria* (London, 1957).

8. Hounkpatin C. Capo, "Le Gbe est une langue unique," *Africa* 53 (1983): 47–57.

9. On the physical conditioning, see G. J. Afolabi Ojo, *Yoruba Culture: A Geographical Analysis* (Ife, 1966).

10. G. Connah, *African Civilizations: Precolonial Cities and States in Tropical Africa: An Archaeological Perspective* (Cambridge, 1987), 123–49.

11. For a stimulating essay on early state formation, see Ade Obayemi, "The Yoruba and Edo-speaking Peoples and Their Neighbours before 1600," in *History of West Africa*, ed. J. F. A. Ajayi and M. Crowder, vol. I, 2nd ed. (London, 1976), 196–263. There is no synthetic treatment of all the evidence regarding ancient Ife—archaeological, art-historical, ethnographic, oral-traditional, and so forth—but for essays reviewing many aspects, see I. A. Akinjogbin, ed., *The Cradle of a Race: Ife from the Beginning to 1980* (Port Harcourt, 1992). For a sound recent survey of the archaeological data for Ife and Oyo, see B. Agbaje-Williams, "Archeology and Yoruba studies," in *Yoruba Historiography*, ed. T. Falola (Madison, 1991), 5–29.

12. Thus R. Horton, "Ancient Ife: A Reassessment," *Journal of the Historical Society of Nigeria* 9 (1979): 69–150; also A. Obayemi, "Ancient Ile-Ife: Another Cultural Historical Reinterpretation," *Journal of the Historical Society of Nigeria* 9 (1979): 151–85.

13. R. E. Bradbury, *Benin Studies* (London, 1973), 47ff.; A. I. Asiwaju, *Western Yorubaland under European Rule, 1889–1945* (London, 1976), 19; B. A. Agiri and S. Barnes, "Lagos before 1603," in *A History of the Peoples of Lagos State,* ed. A. Adefuye, Babatunde Agiri, and Jide Osuntokun (Lagos, 1987), 18–32.

14. J. D. Y. Peel, *Ijeshas and Nigerians: The Incorporation of a Yoruba Kingdom 1890s–1970s* (Cambridge, 1973), 19–26.

15. The essential work is R. Law, *The Oyo Empire c. 1600–c. 1836: A West African Imperialism in the Era of the Atlantic Slave Trade* (Oxford, 1977).

16. Law, *Oyo Empire,* 56–59.

17. S. A. Akintoye, *Revolution and Power Politics in Yorubaland, 1840–1893* (London, 1971), Chapter 1; F. Afolayan, "Toward a History of Eastern Yorubaland," in Falola, ed., *Yoruba Historiography,* 75–87.

18. S. O. Biobaku, *The Egba and Their Neighbours 1842–1872* (Oxford, 1957), 8–10; Law, *Oyo Empire,* 137–40.

19. Law, *Oyo Empire,* 92–95, 113–17. Biodun Adediran, *The Frontier States of Western Yorubaland 1600–1889* (Ibadan, 1994), 74–80, 124–25, 149–51, shows the role of Oyo migrants in founding the western kingdoms of Sabe and Ketu but argues that the later relationship was one of alliance rather than subordination.

20. P. Morton-Williams, "The Oyo Yoruba and the Atlantic Trade, 1670–1830," *Journal of the Historical Society of Nigeria* 3 (1964): 25–45; R. Law, "The Atlantic Slave Trade in Yoruba Historiography," in Falola, ed., *Yoruba Historiography,* 123–34.

21. Akinjogbin, *Dahomey and Its Neighbours;* Law, *Oyo Empire,* 157–69.

22. On the northeast Obayemi, "Yoruba and Edo-speaking Peoples," 201–209; A. M. O. Ogunsola, "Religious Change and the Reconstruction of Idoani" (Ph.D. the-

sis, University of Liverpool, 1986), Chapter 2, on the Yoruba/Edo border area; and E. P. Renne, *Cloth That Does Not Die: The Meaning of Cloth in Bunu Social Life* (Seattle, 1995), on the Bunu; Adediran, *Frontier States,* Chapter 2, on the pre-dynastic far west; P. Richards, "Landscapes of Dissent: Ikale and Ilaje Country, 1870–1950," in *Empires and Peoples in African History: Essays in Memory of Michael Crowder,* ed. J. F. A. Ajayi and J. D. Y. Peel (London, 1992), 161–84, on the southeast.

23. The comparative analysis of Yoruba social and political institutions is above all indebted to the writings of P. C. Lloyd, such as: "Craft Organization in Yoruba Towns," *Africa* 23 (1953): 30–44; "The Yoruba Lineage," *Africa* 25 (1955): 235–51; "Sacred Kingship and Government among the Yoruba," *Africa* 30 (1960): 221–34; *Yoruba Land Law* (London, 1962), with its comparison of Egba, Ijebu, Ekiti, and Ondo; "Agnatic and Cognatic Descent among the Yoruba," *Man* 1 (1966): 484–500; *The Political Development of Yoruba Kingdoms in the Eighteenth and Nineteenth Centuries* (London, 1971), which applies his theory of conflict between king and commoner lineages to a range of kingdoms. For modern overviews there are W. R. Bascom, *The Yoruba of Southwestern Nigeria* (New York, 1969); E. Krapf-Askari, *Yoruba Towns and Cities* (Oxford, 1969); and (the most critically useful) J. S. Eades, *The Yoruba Today* (Cambridge, 1980)—all of which, however, while treating of "traditional" institutions and drawing on historical sources, are essentially oriented toward the present. In a separate category is N. A. Fadipe, *The Sociology of the Yoruba* (Ibadan, 1970), an edited abridgement of a 1939 London Ph.D. thesis, prepared by F. O. and O. O. Okedeji: a pioneering work that contains much useful material, but not a classic like Johnson's *History.*

24. See, for example, Barber's complete listing of *ile* in Okuku, including their places of origin: *I Could Speak Until Tomorrow,* 292–303.

25. The best overview is A. L. Mabogunje, *Urbanization in Nigeria* (London, 1968), Chapter 2; also W. R. Bascom, "The Early Historical Evidence of Yoruba Urbanism," in *Social Change and Economic Development in Nigeria,* ed. U. G. Damachi and H. D. Seibel (New York, 1973).

26. A parallel that comes to mind is S. J. Tambiah's concept of the "galactic polity" in relation to state formation in medieval Thailand, *World Conqueror and World Renouncer* (Cambridge, 1976), Chapter 7.

27. G. J. A. Ojo, *Yoruba Palaces* (London, 1966), which focuses specially on those of eastern Yorubaland.

28. See P. Wheatley, "The Significance of Traditional Yoruba Urbanism," *Comparative Studies in Society and History* 12 (1970): 393–423.

29. On the cultural significance of the cowry see T. Falola and O. B. Lawuyi, "Not Just a Currency: The Cowry in Nigerian Culture," in *West African Economic and Social History: Studies in Memory of Marion Johnson,* ed. D. Henige and T. C. McCaskie (Madison, 1990), 29–36; and K. Barber, "Money, Self-realization and the Person in Yoruba Texts," in *Money Matters,* ed. J. Guyer (London, 1995), 205–224.

30. Law, *Oyo Empire,* 297. Law reviews the extensive earlier literature on the collapse of Oyo, of which perhaps the most important items are J. F. Ade Ajayi, "The Aftermath of the Fall of Old Oyo," in *History of West Africa,* ed. J. F. A. Ajayi and Michael Crowder, vol. 2 (London, 1974), 129–66; and Abdullahi Smith, "A Little New Light on the Collapse of the Alafinate of Yoruba," reprinted in his *A Little New Light* (Zaria, 1987), 149–91.

31. See especially Law, "The Constitutional Troubles of Oyo in the Eighteenth Century," *Journal of African History* 12 (1971): 25–44, and his later thoughts, "Mak-

ing Sense of a Traditional Narrative: Political Disintegration in the Kingdom of Oyo," *Cahiers d'études africaines* 22 (1982): 387–401.

32. For a further and fuller account of Yoruba Islam, see Chapter 7 below.

33. On Owu, see A. L. Mabogunje and J. Omer-Cooper, *Owu in Yoruba History* (Ibadan, 1971).

34. H. Clapperton, *Journal of Second Expedition into the Interior of Africa* (London, 1829); R. and J. Lander, *Journal of an Expedition to Explore the Course and Termination of the Niger* (London, 1832).

35. As Ajayi argued, in Ajayi and Smith, *Yoruba Warfare*, 124–25, quoting a Baptist missionary at the time: "To re-establish the Yoruba kingdom and make it what it once was, I am quite certain, is the grand cause of this war."

36. R. S. Smith, *The Lagos Consulate, 1851–1861* (London: Macmillan, 1978).

37. A. G. Hopkins, *Economic History of West Africa* (London, 1973), 135–48, for the general picture; T. Falola, *The Political Economy of a Pre-colonial West African State: Ibadan 1830–1900* (Ife, 1984) for the richest Yoruba case study.

38. On Ibadan, the most recent treatment is Ruth Watson, "Chieftaincy Politics and Civic Consciousness in Ibadan History, 1829–1939" (D. Phil. thesis, University of Oxford, 1998), Chapters 2 and 3. See also Toyin Falola, *Political Economy of a Precolonial African State*, which contains extensive oral materials; and Bolanle Awe, "The Rise of Ibadan As a Yoruba Power, 1851–1893" (D. Phil. thesis, University of Oxford, 1964). Studies by local historians are especially valuable: apart from Johnson's *History of the Yorubas*, which is strongly oriented toward Ibadan, the essential figure is I. B. Akinyele (an Ibadan chief from 1936 and *Olubadan* from 1955 to 1964), *Iwe Itan Ibadan* (Ibadan, 1911; and many subsequent editions). Akinyele's history was the basis of a completely reworked English version—really a new book—by his niece Kemi Morgan, *Akinyele's Outline History of Ibadan*, 3 vols. (Ibadan, n.d.). The relationship of Akinyele and Morgan is examined in T. Falola, "Kemi Morgan and the Second Reconstruction of Ibadan History," *History in Africa* 18 (1991): 93–112, though I think he is not entirely fair to Mrs. Morgan's achievement.

39. As Falola, *Political Economy*, 43, is inclined to do, valuable though his account is for its empirical detail.

40. "Warboys" was a direct translation of the Yoruba term *omo-ogun* (literally "sons of war") referring to young warriors. Interestingly, it was also used in Crowther's translation of the Bible in the phrase "Lord of hosts" [*Oluwa awon omo-ogun*].

41. On Ijaye, see G. O. Oguntomisin, "New Forms of Political Organisation in Yorubaland in the Mid-Nineteenth Century: A Comparative Study of Kurunmi's Ijaye and Kosoko's Epe" (Ph.D. diss., University of Ibadan, 1979): also J. F. A. Ajayi in Ajayi and R. S. Smith, *Yoruba Warfare in the Nineteenth Century* (Cambridge, 1964), part II; and Falola and Oguntomisin, *Military in Nineteenth Century Yoruba Politics*, Chapter 3.

42. Which might seem to support Jack Goody's thesis, in his *Technology, Tradition and the State in Africa* (London, 1971), that gunpowder encouraged political centralization in West African states. Not so: as the contrast with Ibadan neatly shows, power monopoly was the condition, not the consequence, of the ability to centralize the control of powder.

43. For example, C. A. Gollmer, Journal, 9 Feb. 1853: Ijaye "far better governed than any other town I have seen in this country." Further examples in Falola and Oguntomisin, *Military*, 70.

44. On Abeokuta, see S. O. Biobaku's pioneering *The Egba and Their Neighbours, 1842–1872* (Oxford, 1957); also (though focused on the later period) A. Pallinder, "Government in Abeokuta, 1830–1914" (Ph.D. thesis, University of Goteborg, 1973). The premier local history is E. Olympus O. Moore, *History of Abeokuta* (London, 1916; second edition, 1924, under the name of A. K. Ajisafe). Also valuable is J. H. Blair, "Abeokuta Intelligence Report" (1937), to be found in the Nigerian National Archives, Ibadan, or in the Ransome-Kuti Papers, University of Ibadan Library.

45. On Badagry, see C. Sorensen, "Badagry, 1784–1863: A Political and Commercial History" (Ph.D. thesis, University of Stirling, 1996).

46. Johnson, *History*, 324–27; D. Hinderer, Half-yearly Report of the Ibadan Station Ending April 1859.

47. A. Mann, Journal, 22 March 1855.

48. On the war, see J. F. Ade Ajayi's masterly "The Ijaye War, 1860–65," part II of his and R. S. Smith's *Yoruba Warfare in the Nineteenth Century* (Cambridge, 1964).

49. On the fate of the Ijaye people, as refugees at Abeokuta and elsewhere, see T. Falola, "The Ijaye in Diaspora, 1862–1895," *Journal of Asian and African Studies* 22 (1987): 67–79.

50. On Ijebu, see M. d'Avezac-Macaya, *Notice sur le pays et le peuple des Yebous en Afrique* (Paris, 1845); O. O. Ayantuga "Ijebu and its Neighbours, 1851–1914" (Ph.D. diss., University of London, 1965); D. R. Aronson, "Cultural Stability and Social Change among the Modern Ijebu" (Ph.D. thesis, University of Chicago, 1970), esp. Chapters 1 and 2; and (though it mostly deals with the period after Ijebu's conquest in 1892) E. A. Ayandele, *The Ijebu of Yorubaland 1850–1950: Politics, Economy, and Society* (Ibadan, 1992). Local histories are not so impressive as for Abeokuta or Ibadan, but see M. B. Okubote, *Iwe Ikekuru ti Itan Ijebu* (Ibadan, 1937).

51. This was produced by such distinctive pan-Ijebu institutions as the triennial age-grades, the Agemo cult, and the economic complementarity of Ijebu Ode and the smaller towns—on which see P. C. Lloyd, *Yoruba Land Law* (London, 1962), 54–59 and Chapter 6—and the awesome prestige of the *Awujale*, the paramount ruler at Ijebu Ode.

52. On Remo, see M. I. Nolte, "Ritualized Interaction and Civic Solidarity: Kingship and Politics in Ijebu-Remo" (Ph.D. thesis, University of Birmingham, 1999).

53. For a fuller account of the *Ifole* see Chapter 5 below, pp. 135–36.

54. For an overview of Ibadan's conquests in the east, see S. A. Akintoye, *Revolution and Power Politics in Yorubaland 1840–1893: Ibadan Expansion and the Rise of the Ekitiparapo* (London, 1871), Chapter 2.

55. This account is mainly indebted to I. A. Akinjogbin's "Ife: The Years of Travail, 1793–1893," in *The Cradle of a Race,* 148–70. In general, the historiography of Ife is especially thin as regards the middle period of Ife's history: the centuries between its "classical age" before the sixteenth century and the early nineteenth century.

56. J. B. Wood to Lang, 19 Oct. 1885.

57. Their depredations are graphically described in Johnson, *History of the Yorubas,* 405–406. See also Akintoye, *Revolution and Power Politics,* 71–75, on the *ajele;* and Falola, *Political Economy,* 145–51, on "Ibadan economic imperialism."

58. On Oyo, see Law, *Oyo Empire,* 108–110; or Peel, *Ijeshas and Nigerians,* 42, on the Ijesha, where the patron-chiefs were called *onile* ("house owner").

59. See B. Awe, "The *Ajele* System: A Study of Ibadan Imperialism in the Nine-

teenth Century," *Journal of the Historical Society of Nigeria* 3 (1964): 47–60. On *ajele* in Old Oyo, see Law, *Oyo Empire,* 110–12.

60. S. A. Akintoye, "The Ondo Road Eastwards of Lagos, c. 1870–1895," *Journal of African History* 10 (1969): 581–98.

61. On which, see R. Smith, "Nigeria-Ijebu," in *West African Resistance: The Military Response to Colonial Occupation,* ed. M. Crowder (London, 1971), 170–204.

62. Peel, *Ijeshas and Nigerians,* 91–92.

63. J. A. Atanda, *The New Oyo Empire: Indirect Rule and Change in Western Nigeria 1894–1934* (London, 1973), 63–74.

64. Studies of Johnson as a historian include T. Falola, ed., *Pioneer, Patriot, and Patriarchy: Samuel Johnson and the Yoruba People* (Madison, 1993), a collection of mostly original essays; R. Law, "Constructing 'A Real National History': A Comparison of Edward Blyden and Samuel Johnson," in *Self-assertion and Brokerage: Early Cultural Nationalism in West Africa,* ed. P. F. de Moraes Farias and K. Barber (Birmingham, 1990); M. Doortmont, "Recapturing the Past: Samuel Johnson and the Construction of the History of the Yoruba" (Ph.D. thesis, Erasmus University, Rotterdam, 1994); and essays by J. F. A. Ajayi and J. D. Y. Peel in *The Recovery of the West African Past: African Pastors and African History in the Nineteenth Century,* ed. P. Jenkins (Basel, 1998).

65. It is no derogation from the achievement of Robin Law's *The Oyo Empire,* the authoritative modern study, that it is so dependent on Johnson. By a rough reckoning, references to Johnson appear in the text or footnotes on six out of every seven pages of the central portion (Chapters 4–6) of Law's book.

3. LIVING IN AN AGE OF CONFUSION

1. See M. Sahlins, *Historical Metaphors and Mythical Realities* (Ann Arbor, 1981); *Islands of History* (Chicago, 1985); and "The Return of the Event, Again; With Reflections on the Beginnings of the Great Fijian War of 1843 to 1855 between the Kingdoms of Bau and Rewa," in *Clio in Oceania: Toward a Historical Anthropology,* ed. A. Biersack (Washington, 1991).

2. W. S. Allen, Journal, 29 April 1885.

3. W. S. Allen, Journal, 24 May 1873. For fuller discussion of the genre of *owe,* which covers both "proverbs" and "parables," see D. LaPin "Story, Medium and Masque: The Idea and Art of Yoruba Storytelling" (Ph.D. diss., University of Wisconsin, 1977), Chapter 1.

4. The first table is comprised of Commandments I through IV, the second table of Commandments V through X. In the standard furnishing of English parish churches between the Reformation and the ecclesiological changes of the Victorian period, it was customary to have boards displaying the two tables set up at the east end of the chancel.

5. W. S. Allen, Journal, 20 and 27 January 1878.

6. Another reference to Afonja was made by a visitor to Allen's house in 1873 (Journal, 13 March), but he was mistakenly described as "a king of Oyo that died some seventy years ago."

7. For example, C. Phillips Sr., Journal, 22 March 1855, at Ijaye; S. W. Doherty, Journal, 20 May 1876, at Okewere in Oke Ogun. Of course, this was only in the Oyo Yoruba areas.

8. *History of the Yorubas*, 642.

9. D. Hinderer, Journal, 4 Oct. 1851.

10. D. Hinderer, Journal, 9 Sept. 1858.

11. D. Hinderer, Journal, 2 May 1856.

12. J. A. Maser, Journal, 3 May 1858.

13. On Esu: E. B. Idowu, *Olodumare: God in Yoruba Belief* (London, 1962), 80–85; J. Pemberton, "Eshu-Elegba: The Yoruba Trickster God," *African Arts* 9 (1975): 21–27, 66–70, 90–91; J. Westcott, "The Sculpture and Myths of Eshu-Elegba, the Yoruba Trickster," *Africa* 32 (1962): 336–53; P. F. Verger, *Orixás: Deuses Iorubás na África e no Novo Mundo* (São Paulo, 1981), 76–85; R. D. Pelton, *The Trickster in West Africa: A Study of Mythic Irony and Sacred Delight* (Berkeley, 1980).

14. J. Barber, Journal, 14 Jan. 1855.

15. From a manuscript history of his family and its farmland, *Iwe Itan Oko Apara*, dictated by Peter Apara in 1919 to his son (Library of Obafemi Awolowo University, Ife). Apara played a large role in supplying Snider rifles to Kiriji and became a principle supporter of Ogedengbe. On Apara, see further below p. 66 and Chapter 8, p. 244.

16. J. A. Maser, Journal, 21 March 1854.

17. T. King, Journal, 14 Dec. 1853. The exact circumstances of the *Alake*'s death (c. 1826) are not clear, but it occurred during or soon after the destruction of the old Egba towns. On the politics of the decision to install a new *Alake*, see Biobaku, *Egba and Their Neighbours*, Chapter 4.

18. T. King, Journal, 25 March 1851.

19. S. Johnson, Journal Extracts 1870–73, n.d.

20. D. Hinderer, Half-yearly Report of the Ibadan Station Ending April 1859. It is a pity that neither Johnson's *History of the Yorubas* nor Kemi Morgan's *Akinyele's Outline History of Ibadan* allude to the Oke'badan oracle. Johnson does, however, document the general sense there was at Ibadan of a need for "social reforms," as he puts it, as a result especially of the great influx of slaves at this time (pp. 324–27).

21. Of which Hinderer gave a vivid description: "running and tumbling over one another, together with the hallooing and bellowing of their female owners quarrelling with their persecutors, and the uproar and confusion of the town was complete. We have now got rid of these dirty creatures but their role as scavengers is sadly needed."

22. Notably in the writings of P. C. Lloyd, who has promoted the concept of the Yoruba town as a "federation of lineages" (cf. Chapter 2, n.23). For an alternative view, see Peel, *Ijeshas and Nigerians*, Chapter 3.

23. A. A. Akiwowo, *Ajobi and Ajogbe: Variations on the Theme of Sociation* (Ile-Ife, 1980), esp. 23–24. "Out of the disharmony in one or more aspects of the relationships and separations of the members of an *ajobi*, comes new forms of sociation such as *ọre* (friendship), *ara* (neigbours) and *ileto* (settlements). When natural bonds *okun-ifa* . . . weaken or are severed, new types of bonds . . . are created, such as *ifọwọsọwọpọ* (co-operatives) . . . *ajọmu* (drinkers' clubs) and so on. . . . These social forms or sociations may emerge in response to constraining pressures by the *ajobi* on its members . . . or to one's need for playmates outside, or to a breakdown in the *ajobi*. . . . [They] may also emerge in response to religious rites."

24. D. Hinderer, Half-yearly Report . . . [to] 25 June 1867. This picture of the intimacy of these elderly men reminds one of the friendship group around Bishop A. B. Akinyele and three of his clerical cousins (all of them grandchildren of Ku-

komi) in their retirement, a hundred years later: T. A. Adebiyi, *The Beloved Bishop* (Ibadan, 1969), 94.

25. S. Johnson, Journal, 28 Sept. 1879, in G3 A2 (1880), 160.

26. W. S. Allen, Journal, 22 March 1870.

27. C. N. Young, Journal, 27 June 1875.

28. C. N. Young, Journal, 2 May 1878.

29. C. N. Young, Journal, 10 Jan., 9 Feb., 18 Feb. 1880.

30. D. Hinderer, Journal, 7–12 May 1856.

31. D. Olubi, Journal, 6 Sept. 1879, G3 A2 (1880) 125.

32. M. F. Willoughby, Journal, 29 July 1870. For a fuller description, see J. D. Y. Peel, "Problems and Opportunities in an Anthropologist's Use of a Missionary Archive," in *Missionary Encounters,* ed. R. A. Bickers and R. Seton (London, 1996), 85–88.

33. S. Pearse, Journal, 12 Nov. 1863.

34. C. Phillips, Sr., Journal, 20 June 1853, at Ijaye; or S. W. Doherty, Journal, 18 May 1876, at Iganna in the Oke Ogun, where the attraction was the evangelist's mechanical wooden snake.

35. See J. A. Maser, Journal, 21 May 1855, at Abeokuta: a man is summoned to the Ogboni house to pay a fine which had been levied on him, by means of "the Elders' staff . . . small brass figures on iron sticks connected by a chain, always a frightful appearance in the house of any native." James White (Report, 25 March 1869) describes how his main chiefly opponent at Ota got the Ogboni of Igbein township at Abeokuta, opposed to Christian influence, to frustrate him by using their *ẹdan* (here named as such) to put an interdict on the completion of his house. On Ogboni and *ẹdan* see further R. F. Thompson, *Black Gods and Kings,* Chapter 6.

36. J. A. Maser to H. Venn, 10 Sept. 1861. He deplored this leveling as preventing capital accumulation and development and even urged that "the system must be exterminated by the gospel."

37. As A. C. Mann described its sound when it came out for the New Yam festival at Iseyin: Journal, 2–3 Aug. 1856.

38. At Oyo, Egungun was headed by the *Alapinni,* one of the *Ọyọmesi* chiefs, and at Ijaiye, Kurunmi headed it (Falola and Oguntomisin, *Military in Nineteenth Century Yoruba Politics,* 71). At Ibadan, the head of Egungun was the *Alaagbaa,* a prestigious figure in the town.

39. See accounts by D. Olubi and W. S. Allen (respective Journals for 23 May 1970) of an incident during the annual festival when a big Egungun with a club blocked their way and Allen was thrown off his horse. Such an offense to dignity was serious, and Olubi demanded, and got, a formal apology from the *Alaagbaa.* The man responsible came with 100 companions to beg forgiveness.

40. S. A. Crowther to T. J. Hutchinson, 10 Sept. 1856.

41. J. C. Muller, Journal, 11 June 1848, at Abeokuta. An Egungun had disturbed Sunday service at Ake church. When protest was made, the senior Egba chief *Sagbua* fined those responsible, saying that Egungun was at all times forbidden to pass through Ake. This may imply that Egungun, as an Oyo cult, was seen as a disruptive presence in Abeokuta, in contrast to the indigenous Oro, subject to Ogboni control. We should therefore probably read "Yoruba" here in the sense of "Oyo."

42. W. S. Allen, Journal, 23 May 1870, at Ibadan. Again, "Yoruba" to be taken in sense of "Oyo."

43. V. Faulkner, Journal of Itinerancy, 10 August 1877.

44. For an Egba account of Lisabi and the Egba as ọmọ Lisabi, see Moore, *History of Abeokuta*, 9–10.

45. The modern desire for a more "fraternal" concept has led to the widespread use in colloquial Yoruba of the English-derived term burọda.

46. For discussion in relation to Ibadan compounds, see Falola, *Political Economy*, 45–46, 58.

47. As noted by Johnson, *History of the Yorubas*, xxxvii.

48. As the son of Hinderer's first friend in Ibadan, the elderly chief *Agbakin* wanted to take his father's place after his death (D. Hinderer, Journal, 22 Aug. 1853). The brother of a deceased Christian insists that his children take up the *orişa* he cast away (W. S. Allen, Journal, 8 Feb. 1866).

49. D. Hinderer, Journal, 4 July 1851.

50. D. Olubi, Journal, 24 Dec. 1870.

51. C. Phillips Jr., Journal, 26 Oct. 1878.

52. C. Phillips Sr., Journal, 10 July 1854. The first of these incidents nearly provoked a civil uprising, since the adulterer belonged to the *Balogun*'s family. Other chiefs intervened to beg Kurunmi off.

53. C. Phillips Sr., Journal, 9 Nov. 1853. About this time eighty heads (£9) was what it cost to redeem a slave (C. A. Gollmer, Journal, 12 Nov. 1857, at Abeokuta).

54. J. White, Journal, 3 March 1855.

55. For example, J. A. Maser, Annual Letter, 31 Jan. 1880 (a newly baptized woman at Leki is so hard pressed by creditors that she tries to cut her throat); or C. Phillips, Journal, 13 June 1877 (a creditor threatens to kill himself to force a party of travelers to which a debtor had joined himself to hand him over); or T. King, Journal, 7 Nov. 1856 (a creditor several times tries to hang himself in the debtor's house, so the debtor goes to stay at *his* debtor's house to pressure him into paying).

56. Like the Sierra Leonian woman seized from Lagos for a debt, whom Thomas King saw held in irons at Abeokuta (Journal, 21 July 1855). She was lucky, since they agreed to send her back to Lagos for the Consul to settle.

57. I. Smith, Journal, 5 Oct. 1854.

58. H. Townsend to Wright, 11 Nov. 1875.

59. C. Phillips, Journal, 5 June 1878.

60. I. Smith, Journal, 7 April 1848.

61. Quoted by D. Williams to J. A. Maser, 24 Nov. 1879, a letter written during the 1879–1880 CMS inquiry into the holding of slaves and pawns by Christians and mission agents at Abeokuta.

62. See "Domestic Slavery. Minutes of a Conference held at Lagos, 16–19, 22–23 March 1880," G3 A2 (1880), 106. The "gentle" view of pawnship was strongly put by the agents of the CMS in the interior, all of whom held them (e.g., Olubi had four, S. Johnson had three, etc.). The benchmark work on Yoruba pawnship is E. A. Oroge, "Iwofa: An Historical Survey of the Yoruba Institution of Indenture," *African Economic History* 14 (1985): 75–106. See also T. Falola and P. E. Lovejoy, eds., *Pawnship in Africa: Debt Bondage in Historical Perspective* (Boulder, 1994), especially the three chapters on the Yoruba by Judith Byfield, Ann O'Hear, and Falola himself.

63. G. Meakin, Journal, 22 June, 8 Aug. 1859.

64. A. C. Mann, Journal, 14 Aug. 1859.

65. D. Olubi, Journal, 21 March 1867.

66. J. Okuseinde, Journal, 18 June 1880, G3 A2 (1880) 165.

67. J. Okuseinde, Journal, 28 Sept. 1879, G3 A2 (1880) 124.

68. On Yoruba slavery, E. A. Oroge's "The Institution of Slavery in Yorubaland, with Particular Reference to the Nineteenth Century" (Ph.D. thesis, University of Birmingham, 1971), though never published, remains the only general study. For a valuable, but rather untypical, case study, see A. O'Hear, *Power Relations in Nigeria: Ilorin Slaves and their Successors* (Rochester, N.Y., 1997), Chapters 2 and 3.

69. J. Johnson, Annual Report for 1879.

70. The general perspective here substantially follows that taken by I. Kopytoff and S. Miers in their introduction, "African 'Slavery' As an Institution of Marginality," to their edited volume *Slavery in Africa: Historical and Anthropological Perspectives* (Madison, 1977).

71. H. Townsend, Journal, 30 Jan. 1851, at Abeokuta.

72. For example, a former slave of the great Egba chief Sodeke is put to death by Oro for selling his own child and other relatives: J. C. Muller, Journal, 8 Nov. 1848.

73. J. A. Maser, Journal, 22 May 1858. The boy was noticed in the slave market at Oke Odan by a Christian convert who perceived that he could read. He had attended the Baptist school at Ijaye and his father was so frightened at the insult to the Egun that he handed him over to Kurunmi, who sold him.

74. A. C. Mann, Journal, 6 July 1856.

75. J. Barber, Journal, 4 April 1856. Cf. D. Hinderer, Journal, 4 Oct. 1855: caravans from Ibadan taking slaves to Epe (Kosoko's town on the Lagoon) and to Porto Novo, along with large quantities of palm oil and livestock.

76. C. Phillips Sr., 17 July 1854.

77. G. F. Bühler to Venn, 5 Jan. 1863, commenting on the stalemate between Ibadan and Abeokuta in the Makun campaign.

78. D. Olubi, Journal, 22 March 1880, G3 A2 (1880), 159. This was in the early years of the Kiriji war, before the forces were stalemated.

79. C. Phillips Sr., Journal, 22 March 1855.

80. See J. A. Maser, Journal, 22 May 1855: two Egba kidnappers, who had operated round Ibadan and captured the sister of Ibadan's ally the *Balogun* of Ipara, are handed over by Ibadan to the Egba Ogboni, who execute them.

81. J. A. Maser, Journal, 11 Oct. 1865. The word comes from the Hausa *samame*, and presumably was a recent adoption, to name a new phenomenon.

82. W. Moore, Journal, 7 July 1851.

83. As in the description by Barber (Journal, 4 Jan. 1855) of how it was done in Ijebu Remo in the 1820s.

84. W. Moore, Journal, 6 Aug. 1855.

85. T. King, 7 April 1850.

86. J. White, Journal, 9 Jan. 1862. The freeing of the women from Lagos was entirely prudential, since otherwise there would have been a major conflict with the British governor. More generally, see T. Falola, "The Ijaye in Diaspora, 1862–1895," *Journal of Asian and African Studies* 22 (1987): 67–79.

87. J. White, Report for Half-year to 25 Sept. 1862.

88. Johnson, *History of the Yorubas*, 381.

89. "Itan idile Apara ati awon omo re," 75–77 ff. of "Iwe Itan Oko Apara," manuscript at Obafemi Awolowo University Library.

90. D. Hinderer, Half-yearly Report of the Ibadan Station Ending April 1855.

91. S. Johnson, Journal, 21 May 1881, G3 A2 (1881), 23; W. S. Allen, Journal, 15 July 1883, G3 A2 (1883), 103; and 11 May 1885 (1885), 36.

92. Unsigned journal from Aremo station (I think by R. S. Oyebode), 18 and 31 Jan. 1886, G3 A2 (1886), 112; also F. L. Akiele, Journal, 30 Jan. 1886, ibid., 114; and Unsigned (in fact D. Olubi, but written by Akiele), 30 Jan. 1886, ibid., 115, which identified "the late *Balogun*'s people" (i.e., slaves) as the culprits.

93. G. Meakin, Annual Letter [for 1858], 29 Jan. 1859; and Journal, 7 Jan. 1959. The road south of Ilorin was infested with the king's slaves who, despite the shackles on their legs, were seen stealing loads from farmers (H. Townsend, Journal, 22 Aug. 1859).

94. For a useful account, see Oroge "Institution of Slavery," Chapter 4.

95. W. Allen to Wright, 19 Nov. 1879.

96. For example, J. Barber, Journal, 30 March 1853, at Ketu: wanting to get the ground cleared for a mission, he asks the *Alaketu* who "fancied it to be impossible to get labourers to hire, because it is not the practice of the country.," but, anxious to help, offers to "beg" his men to clear the bush. Or C. A. Gollmer, Journal, 21 April 1859, at Abeokuta: laments he cannot get servants, despite thousands of people in the town, so he redeems two "Ibari" (i.e., Gwari) slaves recently imported from the interior. Or D. Williams to Maser, 24 Nov. 1879, at Abeokuta: "Commonly looked upon as very mean, the simple name labourer is very odious to people; a pauper would rather be content to go begging about or go to gather sticks or leaves in the bush for the market."

97. As porters, see J. Barber, Journal, 18 Dec. 1853, women carriers from Ibadan to Lagos; or J. Johnson, "From Lagos to Abeokuta," Aug. 1877: "Women are largely employed as porters and are considered less troublesome." As house-builders (insofar as it involved making mud walls, a task linked to women's traditional work as potters), see H. Townsend, Journal, 16 July 1857; or J. Barber, Journal, 13 Jan. 1857, which interestingly mentions slaves and *free* women working together.

98. C. Phillips Jr., Journal, 12 Jan. 1877. The context of these remarks was the poor workmanship shown by thirty-one Ondo male laborers, hired to put up the first church building in Ondo.

99. W. Allan [n.b. not the Egba William Allen], in his report "The Yoruba Mission," G3 A2 (1888), 42. Allan was sent out to report on various issues then affecting the Mission, notably the bishopric question. On slavery, he considered that the 1879 Minute on slavery, which forbade the holding by CMS agents of redeemed slaves as servants and pawns, was a dead letter.

100. J. Johnson representing a common view which he rejected, Annual Report for 1879.

101. D. Hinderer (in retirement in Germany) to Lang, July 1887.

102. H. Townsend to Venn, 27 July 1863.

103. For example, T. B. Macaulay, Journal, 21 Nov. 1855.

104. This document, with a good many others of its kind, papers of the Court of Redemption set up after the 1880 Domestic Slavery Conference, is in "Manumission of Slaves in Abeokuta 1877–1886," CMS(Y), 2/2/3, National Archives, Ibadan.

105. J. White to H. Venn, 2 Feb. 1866.

106. J. Barber, Journal, 10 Sept. and 23 Nov. 1855.

107. J. Johnson, Annual Report for 1879.

108. S. W. Doherty, Journal, 9 March 1875.

109. For an overview of the phenomenon, see R. Law, "Human Sacrifice in Pre-colonial West Africa," *African Affairs* 84 (1985): 53–88. Though it draws most of its data from Benin, Asante, and Dahomey rather than Yoruba, its lucid discussion of the conceptual issues is applicable generally.

110. S. A. Crowther, Journal Ending 25 Dec. 1847.

111. D. Olubi, Journal, 29 March 1867.

112. *Seventeen Years in the Yoruba Country*, 212–13; cf. J. Barber, Journal, 26 Feb. 1854: "There was a perfect silence in the town, for the people were going to offer that abominable sacrifice of human being to their god of war called Oranmiyan."

113. J. Okuseinde, Journal, 21 Dec. 1872.

114. W. S. Allen, Journal, 23 Nov. 1873.

115. A. B. Ellis, *The Yoruba-speaking Peoples of the Slave Coast of West Africa* (London, 1894), 69, says the sacrifice was to Ogun, but Oranyan was the usual recipient. Though this evidence is not strictly contemporary and depends on hearsay, it comes from only a few years later (1894), and the circumstances make it quite plausible.

116. Already in 1848, S. A. Crowther commented, at the news of a man sacrificed to Obalufon at Igbein (the leading township in war), that some other townships, such as Itoko, had commuted the sacrifice to bullocks: Journal, 25 June 1848.

117. C. Phillips, Journal, 20 Nov. 1878. Cf. at Igbesa, where V. Faulkner was accosted by a woman who was about to be bought for sacrifice, crying *Gba mi* ("Save me"). Journal of itinerancy, 17 Sept. 1879.

118. E. M. Lijadu, Journal, 22 Sept. 1892. The Ikale were Ondo's enemies to the south, with whom a disastrous war had recently been fought.

119. J. A. Maser, Journal, 21 July 1866. As Soretire was *Balogun* of Ikereku, it is possible that the mutual regard of warriors played a part in saving the Ijesha. Tinubu, a famous trader and the senior woman of the town, was Owu by birth and the niece of King Akitoye of Lagos.

120. There is an interesting discussion of the logic of human sacrifice, a common enough practice in "archaic" societies (i.e., with states but not world religions) all round the world, in T. Todorov, *The Conquest of America: The Question of the Other* (New York, 1987). Todorov argues, referring to the Aztecs, that in order to perform his mediatory function with the beyond, the ideal victim must be neither a member of the community nor a total cultural stranger. From that viewpoint, an Ijesha might have suited well for an Egba sacrifice. Of course, the Yoruba did not have human sacrifice on anything like the scale of the Aztecs, nor did they fight wars to get victims.

121. This account is drawn from three documents: C. Phillips's letter to the Governor of Lagos, 26 Oct. 1880, reviewing the whole train of events, and the Journals of Phillips, Aug.–Dec. 1880, and C. N. Young, July–Nov. 1880, the latter two in G3 A2 (1881), 11 and 12.

122. On Okeigbo, see R. J. M. Clarke, "Agricultural Production in a Rural Yoruba Community" (Ph.D. thesis, University of London, 1979), esp. Chapter 2, which points out the similarities between Okeigbo and Ibadan in its early days.

123. W. S. Allen, Journal, 23 Nov. 1873.

124. See, for example, Oroge, "Institution of Slavery," Chapter 2, and Barber, *I Could Speak*, Chapter 4, on "big men" and *ologun* households.

125. Quoted by I. O. Delano, *Owe l'Ẹsin Ọrọ: Yoruba Proverbs — Their Meaning and Use*, 1.

126. Part of a saying attributed to the great Ijesha warrior Ogedengbe (d. 1910).

127. For Babaode, "Journal of an Ilesha Evangelist" [i.e., George Vincent], from 6 April 1875, CA2/O11/76. A woman thus saluted Esu, and when Vincent asked her who Babaode was she replied: "Devil [Esu] the father of the gates outside a house." Babaluaye, sometimes Obaluaye or just Babalu, is more widespread. For an example of a worshipper addressing smallpox as simply "Baba," E. W. George, Journal, 15 Aug. 1888.

128. W. Marsh, Journal, 17 April 1850.

129. D. Olubi, Journal, 18 Oct. 1883.

130. S. W. Doherty, Journal, 1 June 1876, quoting people at Oke Amu (a very small place), and 2 Feb. 1877, quoting the *Ṣabiganna* of Iganna, the premier ruler of this, the old Onko province of the Oyo Empire. The latter remark—the point of which was to say that the *ọba* needed to consult his chiefs—arose from Doherty's request for land for what he hoped would become the centre of an Onko District of the CMS. That was not to be.

131. S. W. Doherty, Journal, 18 May 1876, at Iganna. A missionary visiting a town on tour was often referred to as "the king's stranger," to emphasize his special privileged status.

132. D. Hinderer, Journal, 26 May 1856. The remark is quoted by Ajayi, *Yoruba Warfare*, 66–67, who further analyzes the context.

133. C. N. Young to "Rev. and Dear Sir," 26 Feb. 1876.

134. Peel, *Ijeshas and Nigerians*, 84.

135. D. Olubi, Journal, 29 Nov. 1868. What he said was *Kuku o jara o jọlọ*, translated by Olubi as "Rough body hinders a decent look."

136. D. Olubi, Journal, 11 Feb. 1870. Labosinde was a leader of the Ifes in Ibadan's early days, and "was most agreeable and very fatherly in his manners and therefore much respected by all" (Johnson, *History of the Yorubas*, 225).

137. D. Hinderer, Half-yearly Report of the Ibadan Station, to 25 June 1867.

138. Latosa: D. Olubi, Journal, 4 Feb. 1881. Kurunmi: A. C. Mann, Journal, 6 Nov. 1853, 30 Jan. 1854, 9 July 1854; C. Phillips Sr., Journal, 29 March 1853, 3 Nov. 1853, Annual Letter 1857.

139. C. Phillips to Finance Committee, 10 Nov. 1884.

140. C. N. Young, Journal, 28–29 Oct. 1878.

141. C. Phillips, Journal, 26 Oct. 1878. He claimed *Lisa* had a seraglio of some 300–400 women.

142. W. Moore, letters to Parent Committee, 28 Oct. 1869, 27 Jan. 1869, 26 Feb. 1869, and E. O. O. Moore, *History of Abeokuta*, 80–81.

143. In 1878 Ogundipe killed the son of a wife because she absconded (J. A. Maser, Report of Faji Station, 1878), and in 1882 closed the churches because two Christians were suspected of helping another, "the most confidential of his wives," to escape to Lagos (V. Faulkner to J. B. Wood, 18 Apr. 1882; J. B. Wood to C. M. S. Secretaries, 24 Apr. 1882; S. W. Doherty, Journal, 16 Apr. 1882). On the affair of Madarikan's slaves, J. B. Wood to Lang, 18 Aug. 1886, 22 Sept. 1886.

144. Sahlins, *Islands of History*, 35–54.

145. Johnson, *History of the Yorubas*, 384–386 gives the fullest account. Ajobo's fall is also mentioned in Olubi to Finance Committee, 13 Sept. 1871; J. Okuseinde, Journal, 6 July 1871; and W. S. Allen, Journal, 22 July 1871. Allen and Okuseinde mention presents taken from the messengers of Masaba of Nupe (omitted by Johnson), which were the final cause of Ajobo's rejection.

146. Johnson, *History*, 391–94, and Journal, 1 May, 30 June, and 1–10 July 1874.

Johnson was a witness to the slaves' execution. Unfortunately, neither Olubi nor Oku-seinde nor Allen mention this episode in their journals for this period. On Efunse-tan as arms dealer, see Falola, *Political Economy*, 79; and more generally LaRay Den-zer, *The Iyalode in Ibadan Politics and Society, c.1850–1997* (Ibadan, 1998), 10–12.

147. It is the tragic contradictions so arising that have fascinated subsequent Yoruba portrayals of her, as in Akinwumi Isola's play *Efunṣetan Aniwura*.

148. R. S. Oyebode, Diary, 1 Nov. 1877.

149. Johnson, *History*, 407–410. Contemporary references in D. Olubi, Journal, 21–22 Jan. and 12 Feb. 1877 (i.e., the opening and the concluding days of the whole affair); J. Okuseinde, 22, 24, 30 Jan. and 12–13 Feb. 1877; and most fully in John-son himself, Journal, 13, 14, 20–23, 25, 30 Jan. and 12 Feb. 1877. Also R. S. Oye-bode, Diary, 30 October 1877.

150. Johnson, *History*, 410–12, 417–20, and Journal, 26–27 Feb., 23, 26 April 1977. Also J. Okuseinde, Journal, 27 Feb. 1877; D. Olubi, Journal, 1–3, 9, 11 Nov. 1877; W. S. Allen, Journal, 11 Nov. 1877; R. S. Oyebode, Diary, 26 Feb., 1–3, 5, 11 Nov. 1877. Oyebode's diary is the most immediate source but lacks the retrospective sweep of Johnson's narrative. Though it does not add much information, it conveys a vivid sense of how these conflicts may have seemed to an Ibadan man (as Oyebode was) not directly caught up in them. Mostly they rumble like distant thunder behind the more pressing concerns of daily life—such as, in Oyebode's case, his wife's fatal illness at the time of Iyapo's final downfall—but sometimes they burst through like great lightning flashes.

151. Thus Kemi Morgan, *Akinyele's Outline History*, Part III, 32.

152. Ibid., 26–27; and Johnson, *History*, 419–20.

153. I am grateful to Karin Barber for drawing my attention to the importance of *oriki* to I. B. Akinyele's *Iwe Itan Ibadan*, which are much less prominent in Mrs. Mor-gan's reworked English version of her uncle's book. Her *Akinyele's Outline History* is rather like a melding of Johnson and Akinyele, with additional material of her own.

154. On Yoruba fears about "enemies"—which draws mostly on modern data but includes many proverbial sayings, so can substantially be taken as applying to the nine-teenth century too—I am much indebted to an unpublished paper by B. A. Oyetade, "Ọtá: Enemy in Yoruba Belief."

155. S. W. Doherty, Journal, 8 Feb. 1877.

156. C. N. Young, 17 March 1884. It was the powerful Mode family group, who have had many notable members to this day, including the Awosika family. On the social background, see P. C. Lloyd, *Yoruba Land Law*, 102–105.

157. R. S. Oyebode, Diary, 5 Sept. 1977. Who "Aje" was is not clear—an Egba well known for his charms, I suppose. "Aje" surely has nothing to do with *àjẹ́* ("witch"), since *àjẹ́*/witch is never an element in Yoruba personal names, unlike *ajé* ("money, profit") as in *Ajéwọlé* ("Prosperity comes to the house").

158. W. S. Allen, Journal, 15 Jan. 1871.

159. S. W. Doherty, Journal, 9 March 1875.

160. T. King, Journal, 19 July 1861.

161. Rumor reported in Moore, *History of Abeokuta*, 67–68; report of his fatal ill-ness in King, Journal, 19 July 1861, who also suggests the possibility of suicide.

162. K. Barber shows this brilliantly in "Going Too Far in Okuku: Some Ideas About Gender, Excess and Political Power," in *Gender and Identity in Africa*, ed. M. Reh and G. Ludwar-Ene (Munster, 1994).

163. S. W. Doherty, Journal, 3 March 1875.

164. C. Phillips Sr., Journal, 3 Nov. 1853; A. C. Mann, Journal, 6 Nov. 1853. The discrepancy in the dates is not a problem: Phillips expressly says it happened on the 3rd, and gives it as the lead theme of his entry for that day, whereas Mann (who has no entry for the 3rd) relates it as background to an entry for the 6th, when he went to see Kurunmi.

165. A. C. Mann, Journal, 10 Oct. 1853.

166. C. Phillips Sr., Journal, 10 Oct. 1853. Swearing by Kurunmi's sword comes close to identifying him with Ogun. Anyone's "head," or *Ori*, is their guardian spirit, uniquely linked to their own personality.

167. A parallel from outside Africa which comes to mind is Polynesia, and particularly in relation to the debate over whether Captain Cook was really perceived by the Hawaiians as a manifestation of their god Lono. See G. Obeyesekere, *The Apotheosis of Captain Cook* (Princeton, 1992), 139–41, 197–99; M. Sahlins, *How "Natives" Think: About Captain Cook, for example* (Chicago, 1995), esp. 126–28, 136–38, 252–55. Sahlins refutes Obeyesekere, not just because of his superior command of the details of the case, but because he succeeds in showing how particular Hawaiian attributions of the divine to priests and chiefs (and with Cook, an extraordinary sea-borne stranger) fall under an enchanted conception of nature (163–64). See also G. Dening, *Mr Bligh's Bad Language: Passion, Power and Theatre on the Bounty* (Cambridge, 1992), esp. 196–97, on Tahiti.

168. For example, C. Phillips Sr., Journal Ending 30 June 1855.

169. C. Phillips Sr., Journal, 22 March 1855. There is no evidence that Kurunmi was possessed by Sango and so symbolically his "wife" (on possession as analogous to wifely subordination, see Matory's cogent analysis in *Sex and the Empire*). He was "child of Sango" in the same sense that all followers of particular *orișa* were their children.

170. C. Phillips Sr., Journal, 7 Nov. 1856 (he is abused and nearly beaten by Kurunmi's sons, who go about the town with companions making trouble); or A. C. Mann, Journal, 21 Feb. 1855 (a son of Kurunmi's, briefly sent to school, will not allow the other children to sit in his presence).

171. C. Phillips Sr., Journals, 17 June 1858, 14 Jan. 1858, 19 Apr. 1857.

172. A. C. Mann, Annual Letter for 1858, 18 Jan. 1859.

173. T. King, Journal, 17 July 1861.

174. J. B. Wood to Lang, 18 Jan. 1884.

175. Moore, *History of Abeokuta*, 92.

176. J. B. Wood to Lang, 31 July 1884.

177. See J. Iliffe, "Poverty in Nineteenth-Century Yorubaland," *Journal of African History* 25 (1984): 43–57, on the incidence and nature of poverty. On the interpretation of "begging" and attitudes toward giving, see J. D. Y. Peel, "Poverty and Sacrifice in Nineteenth-Century Yorubaland," *Journal of African History* 31 (1990): 465–84, and the further exchange between Iliffe and Peel in *Journal of African History* 32 (1991).

178. H. Townsend, Journal, 16 Aug. 1859.

179. H. Townsend, Journal, 9 Aug. 1857. A Sango priest had called to ask for a present from him at Iseyin. He means "Yoruba" here in the sense of Oyo, in contrast to Egba.

180. J. White to H. Venn, 6 June 1867.

181. J. B. Wood to Lang, 6 Aug. 1890.

4. MAKING COUNTRY FASHION

1. Yoruba religion in the nineteenth century has received very little properly *historical* study, as against the very many accounts of *oriṣa* cults in the twentieth century which tend to carry the assumption that their detail can be retrojected to the past because they deal with the "traditional." The major exception is the work of Peter McKenzie, culminating in *Hail Orisha! A Phenomenology of a West African Religion in the Mid-Nineteenth Century* (Leiden, 1997), which presents a comprehensive digest of the information contained in the CMS archives on Yoruba religion. It will be a great boon to all future students of the subject, whether or not they share McKenzie's phenomenological approach.

2. See, for example, P. Landau, "'Religion' and Christian Conversion in African History," *Journal of Religious History* 23 (1999): 8–30, with particular reference to the Khoikhoi of South Africa.

3. S. Crowther Jr. to H. Straith, 2 Sept. 1858. Whether the tract referred to in this letter was ever published is not clear.

4. J. Johnson to CMS Secretary, 21 June 1878. The phrase "orisha man" (*oloriṣa*) might refer to *oriṣa*-worshippers in general, but more likely to devotees of Orisanla or Obatala.

5. E. O. O. Moore, *History of Abeokuta,* 18.

6. A. C. Mann, document dated 26 June 1856. He cites it purely as a specimen of the idiom of prayer "more fluent than that of the translation." I have retained the idiosyncratic and inconsistent orthography of the original.

7. S. Crowther Sr., Journal Ending 25 Dec. 1846.

8. J. White, Journal, 5 Nov. 1854.

9. T. B. Wright, Journal, 14 Jan. 1869.

10. C. A. Gollmer, Journal, 12 Aug. 1858, at Lower Ijaka.

11. J. C. Müller, Journal, 19 Feb. 1849.

12. W. Moore, Journal, 8 Aug. 1851.

13. S. W. Doherty, Journal, 12 May 1876. One cannot repose as much trust in the diction of this prayer as in the Ijaye prayer quoted in Yoruba by Mann, as it has such distinct echoes of the Book of Common Prayer. But there is nothing un-Yoruba about the sentiments expressed.

14. This point is excellently made in T. C. McCaskie's *State and Society in Pre-Colonial Asante* (Cambridge, 1995), esp. 3–19, against the all-but-complete exclusion of religion from I. Wilks's monumental work, *Asante in the Nineteenth Century: The Structure and Evolution of a Political Order* (Cambridge, 1975).

15. J. Goody, "Religion and Ritual: The Definitional Problem," *British Journal of Sociology* 12 (1961).

16. R. Needham, *Belief, Language, and Experience* (Oxford, 1972).

17. See T. Asad, "The Construction of Religion As an Anthropological Category" [1984], reprinted in his *Genealogies of Religion* (Baltimore, 1993), Chapter 1, which is a critique of C. Geertz's influential "Religion As a Cultural System" [1966], reprinted in his *The Interpretation of Cultures* (New York, 1973), Chapter 4.

18. For a text which summarizes this position with great lucidity, see J. Beattie, *Other Cultures* (London, 1964), Chapters 12 and 13, which treat both magic and religion under the rubric "The Field of Ritual"; and for an exemplary ethnography

along these lines see J. Middleton, *Lugbara Religion* (London, 1960), esp. Chapter 4, "The Field of Ritual Action." See also T. Asad, "Toward a Genealogy of the Concept of Ritual," in *Genealogies of Religion,* Chapter 2.

19. This perspective has been argued most consistently and eloquently by R. Horton, with whose general approach I am much in sympathy. See his collection *Patterns of Thought in Africa and the West: Essays on Magic, Religion and Science* (Cambridge, 1993).

20. Quoted by a convert to D. Olubi, Journal, 16 Dec. 1869. The word *abosa* might refer to *orisa* in general, but more likely to a devotee of Orisanla or Obatala.

21. See M. Gilbert, "Sources of Power in Akuropon-Akuapem: Ambiguity in Classification," in *Creativity of Power: Cosmology and Action in African Societies,* ed. W. Arens and I. Karp (Washington, 1989), 59–90, for an excellent account of one Akan society; and R. Horton, "Social Psychologies: African and Western," published with the reissue of M. Fortes, *Oedipus and Job in West African Religion* (Cambridge, 1983), 41–87, which essays a comparative explanation of variations in the balance between natural and social forces in four West African religions.

22. On the cannon, W. Kirkham, Journal, 25 Sept. 1856: the *Alake*'s slaves at his annual festival were stopped from offering yam and palm oil to it (which suggests it was taken as a token of Ogun). On the bell, A. B. Green, Journal, 6 July, 1883: it fell into the possession of a young man "who . . . has made a god of it," but agreed to give it up for £5, or 150 heads of cowries.

23. H. Townsend, Journal to 25 Dec. 1847.

24. On the heavy symbolic load of the cowrie shell in Yoruba culture, see Toyin Falola and O. B. Lawuyi, "Not Just a Currency: The Cowrie in Nigerian Culture," in *West African Economic and Social History: Studies in Memory of Marion Johnson,* ed. D. Henige and T. C. McCaskie (Madison, 1990), 29–36.

25. S. Johnson, Journal, 29 Feb. 1875. The same vision appears in *The History of the Yorubas,* 28–29, with some small differences in wording.

26. I. Kopytoff, "Ancestors and Elders in Africa," *Africa* 41 (1971), 129–41.

27. C. N. Young, Journal, 20 Apr. 1875.

28. W. S. Allen, Journal, 24 June 1885.

29. J. White, Journal, 3 Sept. 1853, 20 Feb. 1854, 3 Apr. 1854.

30. C. A. Gollmer, Journal, 13 Oct. 1853 (an entry which also mentions his own prayers for success in an expedition to defeat Kosoko at Epe) and 2 Aug. 1854.

31. A comparative linguistic footnote to Kopytoff's thesis, which is mainly based on an ethnography of the Bantu-speaking Suku of Zaire. Though he argued against using the term "worship" for ancestors on the grounds of the continuity between ancestors and elders, Bantu languages do widely have a root [*-zimu*] which distinguishes "ancestors" clearly from living elders. I have argued the opposite for the Yoruba on ethnographic grounds, even though the Yoruba have no distinct word for ancestors: they just refer to them as *baba wa* ("our fathers").

32. *Alapansapa* means "the one who swings his arms to and fro," and is also widespread as an *egungun*'s name. See M. Schiltz, "Egungun Masquerades in Iganna," in *African Arts* 11 (1978): 48. *Oloolu* means "the one with the mallet."

33. S. A. Crowther, Journal, 21 Aug. 1846.

34. J. White, Journal, 31 July 1853.

35. S. Crowther to H. Venn, 4 Nov. 1848.

36. S. Johnson, *History of the Yorubas,* 32.

37. A ritual of this kind is nowhere described in the CMS papers (or any other

nineteenth-century source known to me), but I think it safe to assume that the basic form of the transit from bush shrines to town shrines as described in modern ethnographies is an enduring feature of "country fashion." See the detailed analysis of the Yemoja festival at Ayede given by Apter, *Black Critics and Kings*, 98–114.

38. J. C. Müller, Journal, 10 Feb. 1849.

39. C. N. Young, Journal, 10 Apr. 1877. The *Lisa*'s wives were at first not easily persuaded that Mrs. Phillips and Mrs. Young *were* actually women!

40. See T. J. H. Chappel, "The Yoruba Cult of Twins in Historical Perspective," *Africa* 44 (1974). Nevertheless, something of the old revulsion at the birth of twins seems to have survived even in the west: S. Cole at Abeokuta (Journal, 13 Sept. 1873) reports the case of a women who came begging to Ake mission house because her husband abandoned her when she gave birth to twins.

41. C. Phillips, Journal, 6 Apr. 1885. See the entry for 31 Aug. 1880 and C. N. Young, Journal, 28 Aug. 1880: the case of a Christian, converted at Leki, whose wife bore twins at his hometown, Ado (Ekiti), which was equally opposed to twins, who had to escape to Lagos. Also C. Phillips, Journal, 9 Apr. 1883 and C. N. Young, Journal, 7 Oct. 1885: cases where twins were born to a non-Ondo mission teacher.

42. On the Idoko generally, see C. Phillips, Journal, 19 July 1881 and 11 March 1887 and letter to A. Merensky, 9 Jan. 1889. There were about 200 of them, "rather exclusive in their habits." Their particular *orişa* was Oro Idoko, associated with the wind, and they also venerated the earth. On the purification rituals, see C. Phillips, Journal, 7 July 1885 and 20 Feb. 1890.

43. J. F. King, Journal, 16 Jan. 1871. An almost identical incident happened in Ibadan: the *Arę* Latosisa told William Moore that there was "something supernatural" about his arrival from the interior on the same day that Olubi returned to Ibadan from the coast (Journal, 30 Aug. 1873). The coincidence seems to have put Latosisa in a very elated mood.

44. W. Allen, Journal, 15 May 1859.

45. J. A. Maser, Journal, 18 Dec. 1865.

46. This is still widely said of albinos, who are not infrequently to be seen in Yoruba towns. It appears that they may formerly have been killed as an abomination, like twins in eastern Yorubaland. Olubi reports (Journal, 3 Aug. 1868) an incident in Ibadan in which a white spot, said to be Obatala's mark, appeared on the head of the brother of a boy attending church. The boy's family withdrew him lest Obatala's anger be provoked and the brother go white all over, leading him to be treated as an abomination and killed.

47. W. S. Allen, Journal, 26 July 1867, at Ibadan. The bees were called Sango's "messengers," so kola and cold water were offered to appease him.

48. C. Phillips Sr., Journal, 20 July 1857.

49. On white *orişa*, the group of deities linked to Obatala, see Verger, *Orixas*, Chapter 18, and B. Belasco, *The Entrepreneur As Culture Hero* (New York, 1980), 108–109, 131.

50. J. C. Müller, Journal, 5 Feb. 1849.

51. J. White, Journal, 6, 19 March 1870.

52. J. White, Journal, 23 March 1873.

53. C. N Young, Journal, 31 March, 14, 25 Apr., 2 May, 9 Oct. 1879, 12–13 Feb. 1880. C. Phillips Sr., Journal, 17 July 1879. In fact none of these entries actually names the god of smallpox, most widely called Sopona but also called a variety of other

names. The king whom Young calls "Olukolasi" must be Arilekolasi, in whose reign (1861–1866) civil war broke out between the palace slaves and the town chiefs. Before he died, he is said to have cursed Ondo, saying it would remain desolate—as it did till Captain Glover sponsored its restoration in 1872. But the smallpox made the chiefs in 1880 think that Arilekolasi might still need appeasement. On the Ondo background, see J. K. Olupona, *Kingship, Religion, and Rituals in a Nigerian Community: A Study of Ondo Yoruba Festivals* (Stockholm, 1991), 30–31.

54. Annual letter of J. A. Maser for 1876, from Faji (Lagos).

55. E. M. Lijadu, Journal, Jan.–June 1895.

56. T. B. Macaulay, Journal, 25 Sept. 1855.

57. S. Pearse, Journal, 21 Sept. 1959, at Badagry. "Ifa dust" (*iyerosun*), made by insects from the tree *Baphia nitida,* is put on the divining tray in which the *babalawo* marks the signs dictated by the oracle.

58. Though the tones are different, there seems to be some semantic association between *ètùtù* and the verb *tútù*, "to be cold, wet, or moist," which is associated with calm and good intentions. Abraham's *Dictionary of Modern Yoruba* (p. 658, s.v. *tútù*) gives two examples: *ó fínúntútù bá mi sọrọ*, "he spoke pleasantly to me," and, said as a prayer, *iléémi kó tútù mọn mi*, "may my house be reposeful."

59. W. Moore, Journal, 22 May 1862.

60. This expression is a literal rendering of the Yoruba phrase *ṣere orìṣa;* for a discussion of the concept of "play" (*ere*) in relation to Yoruba performance, see M. T. Drewal, *Yoruba Ritual: Performers, Play, Agency* (Bloomington, 1992), 15–23.

61. The point is well made in K. Barber, "How Man Makes God in West Africa: Yoruba Attitudes towards the *Orisa*," *Africa* 51 (1981): 724–45.

62. Like the *babalawo* Phillips met at Ondo with all his paraphernalia spread out, ready to make a sacrifice for protection: C. Phillips, Journal, 21 July 1887.

63. Thus J. T. Kefer, Journal, 25 Sept. 1853, at Ibadan; J. A. Maser, Journal, 14 Oct. 1853, visiting Osiele.

64. T. King, Journal, 6 Oct. 1850.

65. A. C. Mann, Journal, 25–26 May 1854. Though "his rank [in the cult] entitles him to many honours," Erinle was attracted to Christianity and attended church, but eventually he yielded to family and public pressure.

66. A. B. Green, Journal, 28 Aug. 1883. The man had declined the office—which involved making an annual human sacrifice—two or three years earlier, and now ran to the mission to avoid it.

67. W. R. Bascom, "The Sociological Role of the Yoruba Cult-Group," *American Anthropologist* 46 (1944): 1–75, here 44. This remains the definitive study of recruitment to cult-groups and of the relations between kinship and cult membership. Despite its date and specific location, in general its analysis is compatible with the nineteenth-century CMS data.

68. T. King, Journal, 2 Dec. 1850.

69. "A journal of Mr D. Coker, a catechist at Ido (1873?)."

70. S. A. Crowther, Journal to 16 June 1848. See also Crowther to G. C. Greenway, 15 Sept. 1847, making a similar observation.

71. Crowther, Journal to 16 June 1848. Cf. a case reported by J. White from Lagos (Journal, 6 April 1853): a young female convert asks permission of her mother's husband to give up the idols—Sango, Elegbara, Osanyin, Obatala, and Ifa—which he had helped to procure.

72. J. C. Müller, Journal, 18 April 1848.

73. J. White, Journal, 31 May 1855.

74. T. B. Wright, Journal, 27 Oct. 1867.

75. See J. L. Matory, *Sex and the Empire That is No More: Gender and the Politics of Metaphor in Oyo Yoruba Religion* (Madison, 1994), esp. Chapter 6, for a cogent account of this in relation to the contemporary Sango cult in northwestern Oyo.

76. A. F. Foster, Journal, 23 Feb. 1875. While he is at Ado Awaye, there is a commotion in the middle of the night caused by a "messenger" from Oya to say there is a witch in the town. He says all the women in the town will be killed unless they make a sacrifice.

77. C. A. Gollmer, Journal, 22 Sept. 1859, at Isala, a small Egbado town: "a female *quite frantic . . .* her eye was full of fire and her mind and person appeared to be wrought upon by some supernatural influence." C. Phillips Sr., 25 July 1854, at Ijaye: a devotee (of unspecified sex) is "tipsied with the Sango's spirit" and rushes at Phillips with her/his staff (*oṣe*).

78. C. N. Young, Journal, 13 April 1875. Palm wine was recognized as taboo to Obatala.

79. S. Johnson, Journal, 28 Sept. 1883. Johnson does not identifying the possessing *oriṣa*.

80. For fuller documentation, see J. D. Y. Peel, "Poverty and Sacrifice in Nineteenth-Century Yorubaland," *Journal of African History* 31 (1991): 465–84.

81. W. Moore, Journal, 2 Oct. 1862.

82. I. Smith, Journal, 19 April 1851.

83. For example, "They gave it in order that Obatala may give them wealth and children": T. King, Journal, 31 Dec. 1851, of an Obatala priestess collecting cowries in Kesi market, Abeokuta.

84. H. Townsend, Journal, 9 Jan. 1852, says of an old *Eleṣu* woman who became a Christian at Abeokuta that "she . . . had also given herself the horrible name Esu, i.e. Devil."

85. J. T. Kefer, Journal, 3 Sept. 1854.

86. W. S. Allen, Journal, 17 Aug. 1870.

87. Thus the individuals referred to in notes 97 (case 3) and 95 (case 1).

88. S. Johnson, Journal, 1 July 1879. He doesn't name the woman's *oriṣa* but the description in all its details suggests it was Sango, perhaps the deity most widely worshipped in Ibadan, with the bag called the *laba Ṣango,* as described below (note 90).

89. W. S. Allen, Journal, 5 Feb. 1873.

90. D. Williams, Journal, 19 and 25 July 1873, on a recent convert at Abeokuta. Sango is not named, but see Joan Westcott and P. Morton-Williams, "The Symbolism and Ritual Context of the Yoruba Laba Shango," *Journal of the Royal Anthropological Institute* 92 (1962): 23–37. With the *laba* was also handed in what Williams called "her idol Bayoni, a goddess," a cap made of cowries, with strings of cowries hanging from the rim with a bell on the end of each one, which was also part of the Sango regalia.

91. On Orisa Oko, the outstanding source is a remarkable ethnographic essay which Thomas King had as his Journal entry for 23 June 1861. See too H. Townsend, Journal, 16 January 1855, and J. Johnson, Annual Report for 1879.

92. J. Carter, Journal, 30 Aug. 1857.

93. E. B. Idowu, *Olodumare,* 63, quotes a saying: *Ibiti enia ko si, ko si imale,* "Where there is no man, there is no divinity." J. L. Matory comments that "Shango initiation

'makes an *oriṣa*' (*ṣe oriṣa*) in the neophyte's head," in his "Government by Seduction: History and the Tropes of 'Mounting' in Oyo-Yoruba," in *Modernity and its Malcontents: Ritual and Power in Postcolonial Africa*, ed. J. and J. L. Comaroff (Chicago, 1993), 77.

94. K. Barber, "How Man Makes God."

95. A. C. Mann, Journal, 3 June 1859.

96. J. White, Journal, 23 Aug. 1873. Elere ("owner of the python") may well be another name for Osumare ("the rainbow") who was widely worshipped in western Yorubaland. Agemo, manifest in the chameleon, was also widely worshipped in Ijebu.

97. J. White, Report to 15 Sept. 1867. This account is of special interest since it carefully describes the form most of these *oriṣa* took. Ifa very likely consisted of the sixteen dedicated *ikin* (palm nuts); Iweren was "two snail shells, said to have been the means of their [the palm nuts?] conveyance from the invisible world and to have landed them on earth"; Osanyin, an iron rod with a rounded head; Elegbara, a conical lump of clay with certain leaves pounded in it; Osun, a string of yellow beads, a brass bracelet, and a yellow pebble; Yemoja, white beads and a pebble.

98. D. Williams, Journal, 9 Nov. 1872.

99. D. Williams, Journal, 14 March 1873.

100. S. Pearse to C. C. Fenn (Annual Letter), 13 Oct. 1873.

101. J. Smith, Journal, 24 Sept. 1866.

102. J. Okuseinde, Journal, 2 Apr. 1892. On Bayoni, an *oriṣa* dependent on Sango, see note 90.

103. M. J. Luke, Journal, 30 Sept. 1878, at Leki.

104. S. Pearse, Journal, 30 April 1863, at Badagry. This was the famous Arije, or Phillip Jose Meffre, on whose conversion see J. D. Y. Peel, "The Pastor and the *Babalawo*," *Africa* 60 (1990): 338–69. Olojo, the deity of the day, was at Ilesha particularly worshipped by members of Chief *Odọle*'s lineage.

105. M. J. Luke, Journal, 15 Sept. 1889, G3 A2/1891/O/23–24. This is a very Ijesha list: Orisa Asalu is an *oriṣa funfun* worshipped only by members of Chief *Loro*'s lineage; Olode is the Ilesha smallpox god. Agbure is unknown to me.

106. C. Phillips, "An Account of the Candidates Who Are Baptized at Ode Ondo on Whitsunday, May 13, 1883," G3 A2/1883/O/134.

107. Ibid. Ibaokoigbo was said simply to be a deity of Efon in Ekiti.

108. Ògùn, the river which flows past Abeokuta, has no connection with Ògún, the god of iron.

109. S. Crowther, Journal to 25 Sept. 1845, writes of "the great goddess Obbatalla, also called Odudua, who is supposed to be head of all the deities in the world, in as much as the creating of flesh and bones of children in the womb is the prerogative of this goddess." On the great shrine of the female Oduduwa at Ado Odo, see J. White, Journal, 29 Oct. 1860; and S. Pearse, Journal, 6 Oct. 1863. For an early rendering of the central Yoruba view of Oduduwa, given by Gollmer's Ijesha Scripture reader, as "the great god at Ife and the reputed father of the Yoruba race," see H. Townsend to H. Venn, 19 Dec. 1854.

110. The Ibeji worshipper among the women converts at Ondo (case no. 12) was the only Egba among them.

111. See further J. D. Y. Peel, "A Comparative Analysis of Ogun in Pre-Colonial Yorubaland," in *Africa's Ogun: Old World and New*, ed. Sandra T. Barnes, 2nd ed. (Bloomington, 1997).

112. For example, on Ede, U. Beier, *A Year of Sacred Festivals in One Yoruba Town* (Lagos, 1959); on New Oyo, P. Morton-Williams, "An Outline of the Cosmology and Cult Organisation of the Oyo Yoruba," *Africa* 34 (1964): 243–61; on Ila Orangun, J. Pemberton, "A Cluster of Sacred Symbols: *Orisa* Worship among the Igbomina Yoruba of Ila-Orangun," *History of Religions* 17 (1977): 1–28; on Ondo, J. K. Olupona, *Kingship, Religion, and Rituals in a Nigerian Community* (Stockholm, 1991); on Ayede-Ekiti, A. Apter, *Black Critics and Kings* (Chicago, 1992), 56–68.

113. D. Olubi, Annual Letter to C. C. Fenn, 28 Dec. 1875.

114. J. A. Sunday, Journal, 31 Aug. 1880. One legend of Ogiyan or Ogiriyan described him as a rich man who worshipped Obatala and was made king of Ejigbo, an Oyo town to the northeast of Ibadan, which was the recognized center of the cult: G. F. Bühler, Journal, 3 Sept. 1856. See also "Itinerancy of Bishop Oluwole and the Rev. S. Johnson in the Ibolo District of the Yoruba Country, January 14–21, 1896," in G3 A2/O/1896/74.

115. Journals of C. Phillips, C. N. Young, and E. M. Lijadu, passim. The sequence is confirmed for today and much of the symbolic significance is elaborated in Olupona, *Kingship, Religion, and Rituals*, but as he does not expressly address the question of how their substance may have changed over the past century, care must be taken in simply applying his analysis wholesale to the nineteenth century. Obviously the human sacrifices have gone, and the Ogun festival seems to have modified its character somewhat; for further discussion see J. D. Y. Peel, "Historicity and Pluralism in Some Recent Studies of Yoruba Religion," *Africa* 64 (1994): 157–60.

116. C. N. Young, Journal, 16 July 1876; cf. C. Phillips, Journal, 4 Aug. 1877.

117. Bascom, "Sociological Role of Yoruba Cult-Group," 36–39, on Oramfe at Ife. This function is not mentioned by the CMS authors for Ondo, nor by Olupona, *Kingship, Religion, and Rituals*, Chapter 4, in his account of the modern Oramfe festival at Ondo, which he describes as a ritual of "cosmization."

118. Obalufon was apparently treated by some households at Ibadan as the New Yam deity (J. Barber, Journal, 3 Aug. 1856), and he was called "god of yams" at Akure (E. M. Lijadu, Journal, June 1985).

119. See above, Chapter 1, pp. 20–21.

120. By a rough count, among 253 references to *orisa* in CMS journals from Abeokuta, there were fifteen (6 percent) to Osun and twelve (5 percent) to Yemoja.

121. Apter, *Black Critics and Kings*, 60–65.

122. J. R. O. Ojo, "Orisa Oko, the Deity of 'the Farm and Agriculture' among the Ekiti," *African Notes* 7 (1973): 25–61.

123. M Schiltz, "Yoruba Thunder Deities and Sovereighty: Ara versus Sango," *Anthropos* 80 (1985): 67–84.

124. For the *Elesu*, C. N. Young, Journal, 27 Dec. 1878 and 2 May 1879, where he expressly says they were "Yorubas" (i.e., in this context, Oyo) who had some support from Obayomi (see Chapter 3, p. 55). For the *Ologun*, who are said to have come from Ife (probably, in fact, Modakeke), C. Phillips, Journal, 19–20 Aug. 1878.

125. Such as the sixty followers of one priestess in Abeokuta: T. King, Journal, 8 January 1853.

126. W. S. Allen, Journal, 2 Jan. 1885, at Ibadan; T. B Macaulay, Journal, 9 Apr. 1853, at Abeokuta.

127. C. Phillips to C. C. Fenn, 23 Nov. 1877.

128. C. Phillips, Journal, 26 Dec. 1879.

129. C. N. Young, Journal, 19 Jan., 2 Feb., 31 March, 2, 14, 16, 25, 28 Apr., 2 May, 9 Oct., 5 Dec. 1879; 4, 21 Jan. 1880.

130. C. Phillips, Journal, 17 July 1879. Further reference is made to this incident by C. N. Young, Journal, 13 Feb. 1880, and in C. Phillips, Annual Letter for 1880, in G3 A2/1881/O/10a.

131. C. Phillips, Journal, 1 Sept. 1879.

132. C. N. Young, Journal, 13 Feb. 1880.

133. C. N. Young, Journal, 29 July, 5 Nov. 1884, in G3 A2/1885/O/7.

134. For full descriptions see Wande Abimbola, *Ifa: An Exploration of Ifa Literary Corpus* (Ibadan, 1976); and W. R. Bascom, *Ifa Divination: Communication between Gods and Men in West Africa* (Bloomington, 1969). Perhaps the earliest detailed description of the method is from the catechist W. Marsh, Journal Ending 25 Dec. 1846.

135. In contrast to the large literature on Ifa (and especially *its* literature), there is relatively little on the *babalawo* themselves beyond the classic work by B. Maupoil, *La Géomancie a l'ancienne Côte des Esclaves*, 3rd ed. (1943; reprint, Paris, 1988), esp. Chapter 4.

136. One cannot say entirely so, though of the very many references to *babalawo* in the CMS papers, none is to a woman. But Maupoil, *Géomancie*, 153, refers to some female *babalawo*, and I have heard of cases in twentieth-century Yorubaland. *Babalawo* does mean "father of mysteries," and the existence of the odd female one tells us more about how Yoruba gender roles could be stretched than it undermines the concept of Ifa as an essentially male cult.

137. Cf. the Igbadu, protective calabashes without which "one has not yet arrived to perfection in the worship of Ifa" (T. King to H. Venn, 25 April 1853) or the elaborate dedicatory ritual called *Pinodu* (J. Johnson to CMS Secretary, Jan. 1879). Again the fullest and most systematic account is Maupoil, *Géomancie*, Chapter 7, which although based on fieldwork in Dahomey deals with practices directly adopted from the Yoruba. M. T. Drewal, *Yoruba Ritual*, Chapter 5, gives a useful account of the Itefa rituals, a stage of initiation mainly for adolescents.

138. M. J. Luke, Journal, 8 Nov. 1888, in G3 A2/1891/O/23–24.

139. J. White, Journal, 2 June 1870.

140. For example, a *babalawo* in Abeokuta said "that Ifa was sent by God as his messenger and the means of man's being": S. Crowther Jr., Journal Ending 25 March 1854, which contains vivid pen portraits of six named *babalawo* who attended for treatment at Crowther's dispensary.

141. I. A. Braithwaite, Journal, 28 Feb. 1878, at Leki.

142. See G. O. Gbadamosi, "'Odu Imale': Islam in Ifa Divination and the Case of Predestined Muslims," *Journal of the Historical Society of Nigeria* 8 (1977): 77–93.

143. S. W. Doherty, Journal, 16 Sept. 1877.

144. See M. O. A. Abdul, "Yoruba Divination and Islam," *Orita* 4 (1970): 17–25. The similarity of the signs marked by the *babalawo* in the dust of the divining tray to those found widely in Islamic West Africa and Madagascar was noted by B. Maupoil, *La Géomancie a l'Ancienne Côte des Esclaves* (Paris, 1943), 430, citing earlier work by R. Trautmann. For the wider diffusion of the system elsewhere in Africa, see W. van Binsbergen, "Regional and Historical Connections of Four-Tablet Divination in Southern Africa," *Journal of Religion in Africa* 26 (1996): 2–29.

145. S. Pearse, Journal, 14 Dec. 1865.

146. D. Hinderer, Journal, 15 June 1853. This was a variant of a well-known saying, *Riro ni t'enia, ṣiṣe ni t'Ọlọrun* ("People will think about something, but God will do it"), which came into J. B. Wood's mind as he listened to the intransigence of the *Arẹ* Latosisa during the Kiriji negotiations. Wood to Lang, 19 Aug. 1885.

147. J. F. King, 13 Aug. 1868. Cf. W. Allen's report of the same conversation—the two men must have gone together, though neither says so—in very similar terms: Journal, 13 Aug. 1868.

148. W. S. Allen, Journal, 2 June 1880.

149. J. A. Lahanmi, Journal, 10 Aug. 1888, at Abeokuta.

150. W. S. Allen, Journal, 8 Dec. 1871. The literal "God exists" does not really catch the force of the remark, which is closer to "God is great" or "God is powerful."

151. S. Johnson, Journal, 27 March 1870, at Ibadan.

152. Cf. Idowu, *Olodumare*, 61: "He [Olodumare] is indisputably *not* one among the divinities [*orìṣa*]."

153. H. Townsend, Journal to 25 Dec. 1847.

154. S. W. Doherty, Journal, 18 May 1876, at Iganna.

155. J. T. Kefer, Journal, 3 Dec. 1854. It was not proper for an ordinary person to approach the head-chief directly, only through a subordinate chief as mediator.

156. Thus R. C Abraham, *Dictionary of Modern Yoruba*, s.v. *orìṣa*.

157. M. J. Luke, Journal, 27 May 1889.

158. C. Phillips to A. Merensky, 9 Jan. 1889, in G3 A2/1889/O/29. Similar letters were written by D. Coker from Badagry and T. Harding from Abeokuta (G3 A2/1888/O/162, 172 respectively), but they are not as interesting and detailed as Phillips's.

159. On Edo and Itsekiri terms see R. E. Bradbury, *The Benin Kingdom and the Edo-speaking Peoples of South-Western Nigeria* (London, 1957), 52–53, included in which is a section on the Itsekiri by P. C. Lloyd, 199–200. The Itsekiri language is so close to Yoruba as to be virtually a dialect of it. Cf. Bishop James Johnson's comments on an epithet of the Supreme Being at Benin, *Orisabuniwa*, which he renders as "*Orìṣa* who gives us being," adding that they "[apply] to him the term 'Orisha' which in Yoruba is used exclusively [for] imaginary and inferior divinities and which takes the place of 'Olorun.'": Report from Benin, 2 Dec. 1902, G3A2/O/1903/2.

On Gbe terms, see M. J. Herskovits, *Dahomey: An Ancient West African Kingdom*, vol. 2 (New York, 1938), Chapter 26: Lisa is the male half of a God in two persons, the female half being Mawu. Mawu is plausibly identified with Yemowo, the wife of Orisanla/Obatala, who alone of the *orìṣa* could be called Orisa *tout court*: O. Yai, "From Vodun to Mawu: Monotheism and History in the Fon Cultural Area," in *L'invention religieuse en Afrique*, ed. J.-P. Chrétien (Paris, 1993), 241–265.

160. Idowu, *Olodumare*, 61–62, on *imọlẹ*. He treats *imọlẹ* as interchangeable and synonymous with *orìṣa*, but also suggests that "earlier on, the word was used in a restricted sense of divinities . . . connected in a specific way with earth." Lloyd (in Bradbury, *Benin Kingdom*, 199–200) notes that among the Itsekiri, *umalẹ* (which continues their sole generic term) are "deified early inhabitants of the country," which fits with the connection with the earth.

161. For his role as God's deputy in creation, his purity and serenity, see further, Idowu, *Olodumare*, 71–75.

162. A phrase used by B. I. Belasco, *The Entrepreneur As Culture Hero: Preadaptations in Nigerian Economic Development* (New York, 1980), 121–23, referring to the myth of how Obatala fragmented and produced the various white *orișa*, which he interprets as a response to the social impact of the Atlantic trade and the introduction of cowry currency on Yoruba society.

163. M. J. Luke, Journal, 7 Oct. 1888. A European missionary, F. G. Toase, was told by the chief (*Oloja*) "that he never worshipped idols but that he simply spread out his hands to the God of heaven whom he called Aramufe and to whom he offered kola nuts." "Diary of an Itinerating Tour in the Ijesha Country," in G3 A2/1894/O/171. These ritual details are confirmed in modern accounts of Oramfe's worship at Ife: M. A. Fabunmi, *Ife Shrines* (Ile-Ife, 1969), 3. Aramufe is merely the Ijesha pronunciation of Oramfe.

164. Bascom, "Sociological Role of the Yoruba Cult-Group," 36–37. See also the brief reference to Oramfe as "the special Ife thunder and solar deity" and short description of a ritual like Oramfe's which he ascribes to Olodumare, in Idowu, *Olodumare*, 142–43. Oddly, Idowu omits any reference to Bascom's study.

165. G. A. Vincent, Journal, 17 May 1885, in G3 A2/1886/O/35. Olojo also had a great festival at the Ife-dominated town of Okeigbo, where he was felt especially to govern the destinies of women. E. M. Lijadu, Journal, 16–18 Oct. 1895, in G3 A2/1896/O/42.

166. Idowu, *Olodumare*, 54.

167. See especially Chapters 3–7 in I. A. Akinjogbin, ed., *The Cradle of a Race: Ife from the Beginning to 1980* (Port Harcourt, 1992).

168. See Idowu, *Olodumare*, 24–28, for some report of this variety, which he plainly finds embarrassing and does not resolve convincingly.

169. See J. White, Journal, 29 Dec. 1860: "the goddess Oduduwa." Or S. A. Crowther, Journal Ending 25 Sept. 1845: "the great goddess Obbatalla, also called Odudua, who is supposed to be head of all the deities in the world." The account of Oduduwa given by A. B. Ellis, *The Yoruba-speaking Peoples of the Slave Coast of West Africa* (London, 1894), 41–43, deriving from experience and contacts near the coast, is emphatic about her female gender: "Wife of Obatala but . . . coeval with Olorun," or the female part of an androgynous earth/sky deity. Similar are the views of the Lagosian cleric, J. Olumide Lucas, *The Religion of the Yorubas* (Lagos, 1948), 93–95.

170. J. White, Journal, 11 January 1866, at Ado Odo; and ibid., 20 March 1855, referring to a day sacred to "Odudua (God)" at Ota.

171. C. N. Young, 15 Jan. 1878.

172. Idowu, *Olodumare*, 33–37, on the name.

173. T. B. Macaulay, Journal, 12 Apr. 1855.

174. C. Phillips to A. Merensky, 9 Jan. 1889. It is, however, likely that this should not be taken at face value as a widespread Ondo belief at this time. As I argue below (Chapter 6, p. 173), his account contains traces of two very different eschatologies, one ancient and one recently introduced from central Yorubaland. This picture of Olodumare as heavenly judge may well belong to the latter.

175. J. White, Journal, 17 Jan. 1855.

176. W. Moore, Journal, 1862.

177. One of the best discussions of these issues in West African religions is H. Sawyerr, *God: Ancestor or Creator?* (London, 1970), whose Chapter 3 deals with the Yoruba.

178. There was a subordinate center of the Ifa cult at Ado Awaye in the Oke Ogun, from where the *Alafin* recruited his diviners: J. A. Maser, Journal, 12 Sept. 1854; S. W. Doherty, Journal, 23 Feb. 1875, at Ado.

179. See the saying quoted at the beginning of Chapter 7 below.

5. THE MISSION AND THE POWERS

1. See J. Lonsdale's discussion of "the African race for power" in his "Scramble and Conquest in African History," in R. Oliver and G. N. Sanderson, eds., *Cambridge History of Africa*, Vol. 8 (Cambridge, 1985), 700–722.

2. T. C. McCaskie, "Innovational Eclecticism: The Asante Empire and Europe in the Nineteenth Century," *Comparative Studies in Society and History* 14 (1972): 30–45.

3. The literature on Buganda is large, but A. Hastings, *The Church in Africa: 1450–1950* (Oxford, 1994), 371–85, gives an excellent summary.

4. P. S. Landau, *The Realm of the Word: Language, Gender, and Christianity in a Southern African Kingdom* (Portsmouth, N.H., 1995).

5. S. A. Crowther, Journal ending 25 Sept. 1846. See further Biobaku, *Egba and Their Neighbours*, 31–33; and Pallinder-Law, "Government in Abeokuta," Chapter 1.

6. Moore, *History of Abeokuta*, 51–53.

7. S. Pearse to H. Venn, Annual Letter, 10 Jan. 1871. There is also a 28-page pamphlet by the amateur historian T. O. Avoseh, *The History of St Thomas's Church Badagry, 1842–1970* (Araromi-Apapa, Adeolu Printing Works, n.d.), which attributes the name to Thomas Tickel (d. 1886). He was an English trader who was appointed Civil Commandant of the Western District of the Lagos Colony after its annexation in 1863, and gave much support to the church. Pearse's authority is to be preferred over Avoseh's. For a good account of Badagry at this period see Sorensen, "Badagry, 1784–1863," Chapters 8–9.

8. J. O. Lucas, *History of St Paul's Church Breadfruit Lagos, 1852–1945* (Lagos, 1954), a substantial centenary history by its then pastor. The very first church had been a bamboo shack near the landing stage at Ebute Ero, where Gollmer's catechist James White had first preached. They then moved to a derelict slave barracoon on the site of St Paul's, where breadfruit trees grew.

9. The founding pastor was the Saro William Morgan, and the main pillar of the congregation was a Lagos war-chief, Jacob Ogunbiyi, who could give up his Ifa but not his wives (on whom see Morgan, Annual Letter, 7 Jan. 1861). He was the father of a later Archdeacon of Lagos, T. A. J. Ogunbiyi.

10. J. White, Annual Letter (for 1880), at Ebute Meta.

11. The extent of Gollmer's political involvement in Lagos affairs would not be realized from his mission journals or from his son's biography. But see *Correspondence Relative to the Dispute between Consul Campbell and the Agents of the C. M. S. at Lagos* (Confidential Print 4141, July 1856), and discussion in Ajayi, *Christian Missions*, 76–83.

12. The earliest recorded *aroko*, accompanied by twenty kola nuts, and expressly said to have been called forth by the defeat of Dahomey, was sent by the *Oni* of Ife to Townsend at Abeokuta. H. Townsend, Journal, 24 April 1851. Sometime in the 1850s Gollmer received an elaborate one from the *Owa* of Ilesha, professing friendship and asking for a white man to live with him: [C. V. H. Gollmer], *Charles A. Gollmer, His Life and Missionary Labours in West Africa* (London, 1889), 200–216. In 1854, Hinderer at Ibadan had a "cowrie letter" from the *Awujale* of Ijebu professing "tight friend-

ship" by means of a standard motif of these messages, pairs of cowries strung facing one another to signify amity. Letter to H. Venn, 22 April 1854.

13. S. A. Crowther, "Account of a Journey to Ketu, Jan. 5–19 1853." This visit was soon followed up by the catechist James Barber: J. Barber, Journal, 24 March to 14 April 1853. With the clearing of a plot, it must have seemed that a Ketu station was all but established. But this was not to be. On the religious politics of Ketu, see further Adediran, *Frontier States of Western Yorubaland*, 183–92.

14. D. Hinderer, Journal, 24 Sept. 1849. For more on the curtailment of the CMS's ambitious original expansion plans, see Ajayi, *Christian Missions*, 95–96.

15. D. Hinderer, "Journal of Visit to Ibadan, a Yoruba Town Two Days Journey East from Abbeokuta," 16 May to 11 June 1851, and Journal for Quarter Ending 25 Sept. 1851, esp. his "Final Account of Ibadan."

16. D. Hinderer, Journal for Quarter Ending 25 June 1853, and R. B. Hone, *Seventeen Years in the Yoruba Country: Memorials of Anna Hinderer . . . Gathered from Her Journals and Letters* (London, 1872).

17. H. Townsend, Journal, 25 March, 21 Aug.–7 Sept. 1852.

18. H. Townsend to H. Venn, 14 Nov. 1850.

19. C. A. Gollmer, Journal, 12 Aug. 1859. Also cited in [C. H. V. Gollmer], *Charles A. Gollmer,* 152–53.

20. H. Townsend, Journal, 3 Sept. 1852.

21. C. A. Gollmer, Journal Ending 25 June 1845.

22. A. C. Mann, Journal, 24 July 1856.

23. S. A. Crowther, Journal Ending 25 June 1846.

24. H. Townsend, Journal, 12 June 1851. This offering would have been called *saraa,* on which see further Chapter 7 below.

25. J. T. Kefer, Journal, 25 Oct. 1853.

26. Ibid., 27 Oct. 1853.

27. H. Townsend, Journal, 14 Feb. 1853: he introduces Mann to Kurunmi, whose wives sing his praises, "especially in that he now had a white man dwelling in his town, and white men were his friends"; A. C. Mann, Journal, 2 Dec. 1853.

28. J. Smith, Journal, 4 April 1859, 24 Jan. 1860. Isaga was in fact sacked by the Dahomeans in 1862.

29. D. Hinderer to Knight, 19 May 1853.

30. Thus Samson Yeyeju (an Ake Christian) to Townsend, 12 Sept. 1870, in CA2/O/85/170, H. Townsend to Venn, 21 Jan. 1871; Barber, *Oshielle,* 73.

31. D. Hinderer, Half-yearly Report Ending Sept. 1859.

32. Biobaku, *Egba and Their Neighbours,* 52, credits Townsend with a leading role in the restoration of the *Alake*ship. There is no sign of this in Townsend's journals and letters, and Pallinder-Law, "Government in Abeokuta," 28, is right to express skepticism about it.

33. H. Townsend, Journal, 9–31 July 1853. As an ally of Porto Novo, Ado had threatened Abeokuta's route to the port of Badagry. Now it agreed to be neutral and not to molest Egba traders.

34. For a wide-ranging account of the missions' initiatives in material civilization, see Ajayi, *Christian Missions*, Chapter 5; and specifically on the cotton scheme, 84–86, 167–68.

35. S. Crowther Jr. to T. Clegg, 30 Oct. 1856, on cotton production, listing the

main sources: a mixture of war-chiefs (Ogunbona, Atambala, Sokenu), wealthy traders, several Saro and Christians, and Madam Tinubu.

36. An edition in translation of Scala's *Memorie* is being prepared by Dr. R. S. Smith, to be published in the British Academy's *Fontes Historiae Africanae* series. See also T. King, Journal, 26 Nov. 1856; T. B. Macaulay, Journal, 27, 29 Aug., 20 Nov. 1856; J. A. Maser, Journal, 27 Aug., 28 Oct., 10–20 Nov. 1856; H. Townsend, letters to H. Venn, 28 May, 28 Aug., 18 Oct. 1858; 2 June 1859.

37. Isaac Smith (Journal, 6 June 1850) visits Ogunbona's farm, seven to eight miles out on the Abaka road, with its fine yams and maize, and ground being prepared for cotton and pepper.

38. S. Crowther Jr., Report for the period to 25 Dec. 1856.

39. For a fuller discussion of this see Chapter 9 below.

40. H. Townsend, Journal, 2 Jan. 1854.

41. T. King, Journal, 2 Jan. 1854.

42. H. Townsend to H. Venn, 24 June 1858. He adds a telling detail: the puissant Madam Tinubu, big in the cotton trade but not especially of the missionary party, associated herself with the project by giving 20,000 cowries toward its cost.

43. He was the grandson of Archdeacon William Paley, the author of influential works of Christian apologetics—*View of the Evidences of Christianity* (1794), and *Natural Theology* (1802)—which put the teleological argument for the existence of God in classic form. On the Training Institution, see further Ajayi, *Christian Missions*, 150–52.

44. His brother James established a printing business in their home town, Exeter, which still exists.

45. H. Townsend to H. Venn, 6 Feb., 4 May 1860.

46. H. Townsend, Annual Letter, 8 Jan. 1858, and D. J. May, "Journey in the Yoruba and Nupe Countries in 1858," *Journal of the Royal Geographical Society* 30 (1860): 212–33.

47. H. Townsend, Journal, 20 Jan. 1853. "All our new friends ill," he comments laconically two days later, referring to the fresh arrivals. Of the thirty European mission agents (excluding wives) who had come out to West Africa up to the end of 1860, ten had already died in post, while five had retired (often on doctor's orders). Of the fifteen in post at the end of 1860, another four would shortly die.

48. D. Hinderer, Half-yearly Reports Ending April and September 1859.

49. D. Hinderer to Knight, 11 June 1860. The plan was that the agents would come to Ibadan to report every two months.

50. The period 1850–1856 saw the recruitment from Sierra Leone of ten Yoruba agents at the catechist level or above, that is, literate enough in English to be able to write journals. These were James White, Sam. Crowther Jr., William Moore, T. B. Macaulay, Charles Phillips Sr., William Morgan, James Barber, Sam. Pearse, William Allen, and Thomas King.

51. Thus E. G. Irving to "My dear sir" (Straith or Venn), 20 Jan. 1854. Dr Irving was a naval surgeon, appointed by the CMS with Foreign Office support as a political agent and adviser to the Egba chiefs.

52. See discussions by Biobaku, *Egba and Their Neighbours*, 52–56; and Ajayi, *Christian Missions*, 80–83.

53. R. F. Burton, *Abeokuta and the Camaroons Mountains* (London, 1863), vi: "We

have petted our bantling Abeokuta, and . . . the spoiled child has waxed fat and kicked against the foreign pricks." And 171: "The weak outlying states of El Islam, Ilori [*sic*] for instance—now the last ripple of the mighty wave urged southwards by an irresistible current—though at present unable to sweep away the barriers of Paganism, is strong enough to resist any encroachments. And the day will come when the Law of the Prophet shall rule throughout the lands, when Ethiopia shall stretch forth her hands unto Allah, and shall thus rise to her highest point of civilization. Meanwhile those who support Abeokuta are but shoring up a falling wall."

54. H. Townsend to H. Venn, 4 Oct. 1860.

55. D. Hinderer to H. Venn, 25 April 1860; 10 March 1863.

56. J. A. Maser to H. Venn, 10 Sept. 1861: "The Baloguns have always assisted us, whilst the Ogbonis have always acted against us."

57. See S. A. Crowther to H. Venn, 3 Nov. 1849; D. Hinderer, Journal, 10–24 Oct. 1849; J. C. Muller, 17–29 Oct. 1849; H. Townsend, Journal, 8 April 1850. The persecution broke out in Itoku, and was taken up in Igbore, Igbein, Itori, Oba, Imo, and Ijeun. For a fuller analysis see Chapter 9, pp. 236–37.

58. Burton, *Abeokuta and the Camaroons*, 286.

59. H. Townsend to H. Venn, 2 July 1862, represents Egbas as saying, at the time when a Consul for Abeokuta was being discussed, "Better we had never received a white man, the Ijebus were wiser than we were." J. A. Maser to H. Venn, 3 March 1864, says feelings against Europeans were so high that the mission had suspended public preaching.

60. Best details of the aftermath to Ikorodu are in J. A. Maser to H. Venn, 9 March ("a storm is blowing over us"), 2 June, 3 Aug. 1865. Maser was very critical of Glover's policy.

61. The earliest reference to him is J. A. Maser, Journal, 24 Oct. 1865, who says he was "called 'Reversible' from his invention of a new pattern of handkerchiefs which can be used on both sides as headdress for women." Later he was contrasted with two CMS clergy: "Holy" (James) Johnson and "Eloquent" (Henry) Johnson.

62. J. A. Maser to H. Venn, 31 July 1867.

63. H. Townsend to H. Venn, 3 April 1966.

64. J. A. Maser, Journal, 24 June 1866. Igbein, which regarded tolls on the river trade with Lagos as its perquisite, had always been a focus of anti-missionary feeling.

65. V. Faulkner to H. Venn, 18 April 1868, tracing the 1867 *Ifọle* back to the assault on Lieb; on the arson, H. Townsend to H. Venn, 25 Jan. 1867.

66. J. A. Maser, "The second persecution of the Abeokuta Mission, October 1867," CA2/O/68/163. Maser was at Ikija. W. Allen, who was Faulkner's catechist at Igbein, gives a slightly different version of the bellman's message (Journal, 12 Oct. 1867): that the white men, the Saro, and the native Christians should worship separately. His comment that the *Baṣọrun* did not mean to stop the worship of God would seem to imply that this was indeed said, and perhaps widely believed.

67. This was the English missionary Edward Roper, on whom see below, p. 139.

68. *Christian Missions*, 201.

69. W. Allen, Journal, 13 Oct. 1867.

70. W. Allen, Journal, 23 Nov. 1869. Their participation was the more significant because the head of the Parakoyi at Igbore, Akigbogun, had been so prominent in the 1849 persecution. H. Townsend, Journal, 16 May 1850.

71. An elderly chief, the *Agbakin,* looked after him on his first visit in 1851 (D. Hinderer, Journal, 23 May 1851). After his death, Olunloyo, who was the main figure in the Kudeti neighborhood, was the "chief warrior under whom we're placed," as the catechist James Barber put it. Journal, 14 Oct. 1856, an entry which gives a good example of how important it was to have such a patron. Olunloyo died in 1857, and thereafter Ajobo, who rose to *Balogun* but fell from power in 1871, was a major patron at a higher level.

72. Having said this, I don't want to imply a constant and unmediated influence of theology on social action. Gollmer shared Hinderer's Pietist religious background, and few CMS missionaries liked political involvement better than him.

73. D. Hinderer to H. Venn, 29 Sept. 1863, translating it amid the shortages of the war. J. Johnson, Report, Aug. 1877, notes its popularity. R. S. Oyebode was given an English text and a dictionary to help him learn English: "Life of R. S. Oyebode," G3A2/O/1893/95, referring to his youth in the 1860s. On the other hand, Daniel Coker, Journal, Sept. 1876, reported of a woman reading it at Badagry, that it was "not agreeable with native modes of thought"—which was surely so.

74. D. Hinderer, Journal, 1 Oct. 1855.

75. D. Hinderer, Journal, 7, 12 May 1856.

76. H. Townsend to H. Venn, 6 April 1863, referring to the aborted Dahomean invasion of that year, and ibid., 25 Feb. 1864. Also to Major Straith, 31 May 1864: "The war [vs. the Ibadans at Makun] is bringing the Christians into a political position the end of which we don't yet see." The idea had been on the agenda some years back: in 1857, some converts had tried "to unite themselves and assist in the war as a church," leading Townsend to speak to them on "the duty of Christians . . . in the time of war" (Journal, 5 Sept. 1857).

77. During the siege of Ilesha in 1870, some young warriors called to see Daniel Olubi (Hinderer's successor), full of joyful anticipation of its surrender. Olubi gave them an impromptu address from James 4:1–3—"From whence come wars and fightings among you? Come they not hence, even of your lusts that war in your members?"

78. J. Johnson, Annual Report for 1879, referring to 1 Nov. 1878. In 1864, Hinderer had had trouble over the seizure of converts for refusing to go to war: extract of letter from J. A. Maser to J. A. Lamb, Feb. 1868, CA2/O/68/108. Hinderer reported (letter to H. Venn, 30 March 1865) that ten young Christians retired to the farms to avoid being press-ganged. For more on the effects of the strains between Christian and warrior values at Ibadan, see Chapter 9, pp. 272–74.

79. S. Johnson, Journal, 5 April 1876.

80. D. Hinderer to H. Venn, 15 Sept. 1862. Roper's own full account in letters to H. Venn, 24 March and 22 April 1862. He was based in Ibadan, but went to Ijaye in Mann's place to allow Mann to escort his wife and other refugees to Abeokuta. See also A. C. Mann to H. Venn, 15 May 1865, and narrative in Ajayi, "The Ijaye War," 109–110.

81. The period 1863–1865 saw almost continuous blockade. See especially E. Roper to H. Venn, 7 Oct. 1863, which gives a month-by-month account of their privations, which forced him to spend most of his time as a subsistence farmer because cowries were so short. He had no paper to write anything for the whole of 1864, and the next letter to Venn was dated 1 March 1865. No wonder it was bitter about the Egba bias of *Iwe Irohin.*

82. D. Hinderer, Half-yearly Report to 25 June 1869.

83. The earliest reference to him is D. Hinderer, Journal, 21 Oct. 1849, which puts him at fourteen to fifteen years old. Olubi himself reviews his early life in the Journal entry (6 Feb. 1867) which records his mother's death. She was an *oriṣa* priestess and Olubi assisted her, "called early to the service of the Temple, like Samuel." At first he was indignant at missionary attacks on *oriṣa*, but was moved by the preaching of J. C. Müller, which he heard while laid up with a neck injury when he was eighteen.

84. The party came to be known, in the oral traditions of the Ibadan church, as *Ekeje l'ẹṣin* ("The seventh was a horse," i.e., Hinderer's mount).

85. See Kemi Morgan, *Akinyele's Outline History of Ibadan*, Part II, 108–110.

86. 20: "The Lord hear thee in the day of trouble; the Name of the God of Jacob defend thee." 45: "My heart is inditing of a good matter; I will speak of the things which I have made touching the king." 118: "O give thanks unto the Lord, for he is gracious; because his mercy endureth for ever."

87. D. Olubi, Journal, 11 Nov. 1970; W. S. Allen, Journal, 11 Nov. 1870.

88. Taking as a measure the year in which African agents first appear as authors of journals (which indicates a definite level of education and responsibility), the period 1857–1863 saw no accessions. Thereafter: 1864 (T. B. Wright), 1865 (W. S. Allen, W. George), 1866 (S. W. Doherty, J. F. King, D. Williams, D. Olubi, J. Okuseinde, T. John), 1867 (N. Johnson), 1870 (S. Johnson, S. Cole), 1872 (C. N. Young), 1873 (C. Phillips Jr.), 1874 (A. F. Foster, J. Johnson), 1876 (H. Johnson), 1877 (I. A. Braithwaite, M. J. Luke, D. O. Williams), 1879 (J. A. Williams).

89. A. C. Mann, Letter from Lagos, 6 Sept. 1866; N. Johnson, Annual Letter for 1877.

90. See N. O. Sogunle, *History of St Jude's Church, Ebute Metta* (Lagos, 1968), a good centenary history, by a member of one of the old Egba families of the church.

91. G. F. Bühler, Journal, 25 June, 1857; J. A. Maser, Journal, 3 May, 1858; Bühler to Dawes, 29 Nov. 1864; and J. O. Lucas, *History of St Paul's*. It is a great pity that Nicholson's own letters—there are no journals—are so exiguous.

92. One feels this is a topic which yet awaits its definitive study, but see M. J. C. Echeruo, *Victorian Lagos* (London, 1977).

93. A nice anecdote of this was recorded by Herbert Macaulay (1864–1946), the "father of Nigerian nationalism," in a short autobiographical manuscript, Box 57, Herbert Macaulay Papers, University of Ibadan Library. Governor Glover used to take a ride around Lagos every evening, and would regularly call to greet HM's father, the Rev. T. B. Macaulay, Principal of the CMS Grammar School. HM as a little boy had a pair of velvet knickerbockers whose knees were worn bare by kneeling on the floor at family prayers. Noticing this, Glover one day asked him: "Little Herbert, what has spoilt your royal purple knickers on the knee like that?" "Let-us-pray has done it, Sir." Glover roared with laughter and gave him a silver sixpence, and then always asked after the "let-us-pray chap."

94. The officers were J. P. L. Davies, President; Charles Foresythe (lawyer, also of Breadfruit), Secretary; Rev. T. B. Wright and Rev. T. B. Macaulay, Vice-Presidents; Rev. W. Morgan, Treasurer. Also active was J. A. Payne (court clerk, of Christ Church Faji). See various letters in CA2/O/11/57–64.

95. J. A. Maser to Finance Committee, 25 Sept. 1873, CA2/O/11/64B.

96. E. Roper to Hutchinson, 10, 20, Oct. 1873.

97. For a biography see E. A. Ayandele, *Holy Johnson: Pioneer of Nigerian National-*

ism, 1836–1917 (London, 1970), which is stronger on the political than the religious side of Johnson. On the latter, see J. D. Y. Peel, "Between Crowther and Ajayi: The Religious Origins of the Nigerian Intelligentsia," in *African Historiography: Essays in Honour of Jacob Ade Ajayi*, ed. T. Falola (Lagos, 1993), 64–79.

98. This example—it may be apocryphal—is given in Lucas's *History of St Paul's*, Chapter 4.

99. For an excellent account of the ecclesiastical politics of all this, see Ajayi, *Christian Missions*, Chapter 7. The anomalies went further: Ota (on the road from Lagos to Abeokuta) and its out-stations did fall under Crowther's jurisdiction, because the missionary there, James White, was an African.

100. D. Hinderer to Wright, 18 May 1875. Townsend would still have preferred a capable white missionary, but "I have taken in review all my white fellow labourers at home and here, but there is a want of tact and of practical wisdom in dealing with heathen chiefs and . . . also with our native helpers among them," and thought Johnson the better choice. Letters to Wright, 25 Nov., 20 Dec. 1875.

101. Venn died early in 1873. For the modulation of his ideals in official CMS circles, see C. P. Williams, *The Ideal of the Self-Governing Church: A Study in Victorian Missionary Strategy* (Leiden, 1990), esp. 90–94.

102. J. Johnson, "From Ibadan to Oyo and Ogbomoso" (26 Apr. to 3 July 1877); "A Visit of Inspection to Ilaro and Itinerancies (Jan. 1879); and report headed "Ibadan, Oyo, Iseyin, Ogbomoso, Ilesa" (1878). All enclosed in letter to CMS Secretary, Jan. 1879; letter to CMS Secretary, 21 June and 2 July 1878. His particular desire to develop Ijebu and Ilesha would seem to arise from the two sides of his ancestry.

103. J. Johnson to CMS Secretary, 2 Aug. 1879.

104. J. Johnson to CMS Secretary, 30 Jan. 1878.

105. On the argument about slavery, see Chapter 5 and Chapter 11.

106. J. Johnson to CMS Secretary, 10 Nov. 1879; Minutes of a Conference on Domestic Slavery held at Lagos, 16–23 March 1880, which contains several accounts of the events of 1879; W. Moore to H. Townsend, 26 Jan. 1880, accusing Johnson of "divid[ing] the Egba church into parts." Also file "Manumission of Slaves at Abeokuta, 1877–1886," CMS(Y) 2/2/3, National Archives, Ibadan.

107. Ajayi, *Christian Missions*, 237–38, notes that at first the CMS Committee had been minded to keep Johnson in post, but later changed its mind. He puts this down to a general decline of confidence in African leadership. This may well be so, but the dependence of the mission on the goodwill of the Egba chiefs and the fear of another *Ifọle* must also have weighed strongly. Johnson was replaced by Faulkner, who had been pastor of St Jude's, which had a largely Egba congregation. In 1883 J. B. Wood took over and continued till his death in 1897, becoming almost as adept in Egba politics as Townsend had been.

108. "Journal of J. A. Maser During a Journey to Countries East of Lagos in December 1873"; D. Hinderer to H. Wright, 15 Dec. 1874, 9 Feb. 1875.

109. D. Hinderer to H. Wright, 14 May 1875.

110. C. Phillips, "Short Account of Himself," 10 May 1875.

111. At the Yoruba Language Conference held in 1875, he was so forward in his views for "such a *young* man" (as Olubi put it)—"self-opinionated," thought Faulkner, though he had a history of hostility to Phillips—that he was rebuked by the always mild Crowther: V. Faulkner to H. Wright, 17 May 1875.

112. M. J. Luke, Journal, 2 Aug. 1888. This phrase was usually used to refer to the

local *ọba*, as when Luke was once called "my father's stranger" by a son of the king of Otun-Ekiti (Journal, 9 June 1893).

113. J. A. Maser, Journal, 24 Dec. 1873.

114. C. N. Young to "Rev. and Dear Sir," 26 Feb. 1976.

115. C. Phillips, Journal, Sept.–Dec. 1888. "High Chiefs" is the term used at Ondo to refer in English to the five senior non-royal title-holders (*Iwarefa*).

116. See E. A. Ayandele, *The Missionary Impact on Modern Nigeria, 1842–1914* (London, 1966), Chapters 6–8; and P. F. de Moraes Farias and K. Barber, *Self-Assertion and Cultural Brokerage: Early Cultural Nationalism in West Africa* (Birmingham, 1990). For further critical discussion, see Chapter 10 below.

117. See the full treatments of this cardinal episode, very different in tone but complementary in substance, in Ajayi, *Christian Missions,* Chapter 8; and Ayandele, *Missionary Impact,* Chapter 7.

118. On the African church movement, the standard work is still J. B. Webster, *The African Churches among the Yoruba, 1891–1922* (Oxford, 1964).

119. S. Johnson to Governor, 6 Jan. 1882.

120. F. L. Akiele and J. Okuseinde, Journal, 29 Aug. 1886.

121. As president of the Native Pastorate Association, which raised funds to make the Lagos churches financially independent of the CMS, Payne worked closely with James Johnson, its secretary. He added "Otonba" to his name in 1889 to indicate his descent from the royal lineage of Ijebu Ode. His position was delicate, since besides being an Ijebu patriot he was, as the supreme court registrar, a servant of the British Crown.

122. "Beginning of Missionary Work in Ijebu Ode," manuscript account by the teacher, 4/1/9, CMS(Y), National Archives, Ibadan.

123. For a fuller account of the maneuvers which led up to the Ijebu campaign, see Ayandele, *Missionary Impact,* 54–68. His main omission is that his focus on the *white* missionaries leads him to ignore the significance of the Ijebu hatred of Olubi.

124. Ayandele, *Missionary Impact,* 65.

125. Harding was called "the surveyor" by the Ijebu: M. D. Coker, Journal, 12 Feb. 1892. This journal gives a vivid picture of the tense atmosphere in Ijebu Ode in the run-up to the invasion.

126. T. Harding to Lang, 11 April 1892; W. S. Allen, Journal, 2–3 April 1892; R. S. Oyebode, Journal, 4, 7–16 April 1892.

127. On the campaign, see R. S. Smith, "Nigeria—Ijebu," in M. Crowder, *West African Resistance: The Military Response to Colonial Occupation* (London, 1971), 170–204.

128. W. S. Allen, Journal, 26 May 1892. In fact, the news, arriving just before that of the chiefs' decision from Kiriji to expel Harding and Olubi, seemed miraculous: "and so the tongues of the messengers were made to cleave in a wondrous manner to the roofs of their mouths" (J. Okuseinde Jr., Journal, 23 May 1892).

129. W. S. Allen, 7 Aug. 1892. Cf. E. M. Lijadu at Ondo, Journal, 5 June 1892: "Christianity has become contagious."

130. For two comparative accounts, drawn on here, see J. D. Y. Peel, "Conversion and Tradition in Two African Societies: Ijebu and Buganda," *Past and Present* 77 (1977): 108–141; and "Religious Change among the Yoruba," *Africa* 37 (1967): 292–306.

131. For this reason it is much less well documented than most other Yoruba areas,

since the missionaries (all of them Africans in the early years) were not CMS agents and so did not have to report their activities to London.

132. Islam, through its long-established trading links with Ibadan and also with the mixed Ijebu-Lagosian town of Epe on the Lagoon (where Kosoko had taken refuge), had a much firmer pre-1892 foothold than Christianity. This was consolidated when the main political figure of the post-1892 era, *Balogun* Kuku (who had been in exile in Ibadan), joined Islam with a huge following in 1902. Where Christianity won out was in the peripheral Ijebu towns, which did not have many prior links with Islam and used Christianity after 1892 to loosen the hold of Ijebu Ode over them.

133. J. Johnson to Baylis, Annual Letter, Feb. 1902.

134. Further on Ilesha, see Peel, *Ijeshas and Nigerians*, 92–97, 164–74.

135. "Life of R. S. Oyebode," G3A2/o/1893/95. His father was David Kukomi, the most important early convert at Ibadan.

136. T. Harding, "Journal of Tour," 21 Nov. to 3 Jan. 1900. Gollmer was called *Alapako* ("Owner of the plank house") from the old mission house at Badagry which he had reassembled at the CMS Lagos headquarters. As Gollmer retired in 1862, *Oni* Adelekan must have been quite an elderly man. After early suspicion of Christianity because the first church was sited at Modakeke, Adelekan encouraged its expansion after 1900, especially when an Ife man, E. A. Kayode, was put in charge. See "Bishop Phillips' Report on the Ife Church Troubles," CMS(Y), 2/2/8, National Archives, Ibadan.

137. "Ondo and Ilesha Districts; Papers Relating to Development of Churches and Schools, 1907–1923," 2/2/11; and "Papers on Ekiti District, 1923–1928," 2/2/16, both CMS(Y), National Archives, Ibadan.

138. James Johnson was eventually made an assistant bishop in 1901 and given charge of the Niger Delta pastorate. It was a sad comment on the CMS Yoruba Mission that its two most able African clergy of the century—Crowther and Johnson—were in the end dispatched to work outside Yorubaland.

139. F. Melville Jones (the Principal of the Oyo Training Institution) to Baylis, 10 Jan. 1907, on the issue of whether more Europeans should be transferred into training work: "I quite believe that Native Agents can well be utilized in Evangelizing new districts, but where we should feel the lessening of European Agency would be in the work of Superintendence." While he went on to say that some native workers might be capable of it, such as Bishop Phillips, he felt that for a good while to come there would be a need for European superintendence.

6. PREACHING THE WORD

1. See Chapter 5.

2. *A Memoir of the Revd. W. A. B. Johnson* (London, 1852) was read by J. T. Kefer while recovering from his first bout of fever (Journal, 14 April 1853), and J. A. Maser was sent a copy a little later (Journal, 23 Sept. 1853). G. Meakin read it, as well as a life of Martyn, while on the boat out (Journal, 27 Oct. 1856). On Johnson's ministry at Regent in Sierra Leone (1816–1823), see J. Peterson, *Province of Freedom*, 103–117; it was the reason why "Johnson" became such a common name among liberated Africans.

3. E. Roper to H. Venn, 15 Feb. 1861.

4. E. Roper to H. Venn, 3 Dec. 1861.

5. J. T. Kefer, Journal, 13 June 1853.

6. T. Harding and H. Tugwell, "Report of a Visit to the Ondo and Ilesha Missions," 31 July 1890, G3A2/O/1890/145.

7. A. C. Mann, "Journal of the Mission Station, Ijaye, from February 17 to March 30, 1853." For another discussion of missionary journeys "to the field," see Comaroff and Comaroff, *Of Revelation*, 172–78.

8. D. Olubi, Annual Letter to Parent Committee, 7 Dec. 1870.

9. D. Hinderer, Journals, passim, 1849–1850.

10. J. T. Kefer, Journal for Quarter Ending 25 March 1855, passim; D. Hinderer, Journal, 31 Aug. 1853.

11. C. A. Gollmer, Journal, 22 Dec. 1859.

12. W. S. Allen, Journal extracts for half-year to December 1870. On the indifference of the war-chiefs, D. Hinderer, Half-yearly Report to April 1859.

13. S. Johnson, Journal extracts, 1870–1873.

14. W. S. Allen, Journal for Half-year to December 1868, passim. This new stand was opened in response to Hinderer's decision to abandon one under a tree at Isale Ijebu, on the same side of town. That had over many years seen many sermons, by different people, to small avail.

15. C. N. Young, Journal, 2 July 1876.

16. See Chapter 7, pp. 206.

17. Examples: D. Hinderer, Journal up to 13 Feb. 1851; H. Townsend, Journal, 29 Jan. 1855.

18. D. Olubi to Parent Committee, 26 June 1871.

19. S. Pearse, Journal, 3 Aug. 1863. Pearse himself translates *igede* as "a mystery," but this is much too mild. When the catechist William Marsh was first reunited with his family at Abeokuta, some people were afraid to approach him, fearing lest he "speak some supernatural word which is termed 'Igedi'": Journal from 9 June to 21 Dec. 1845. In the same journal, Marsh instances two men who were condemned to death for killing people through threats interpreted as curses.

20. J. Johnson, "A Visit of Inspection to Ilaro and Itinerancies," 1878.

21. W. S. Allen, Journal, 3 April 1868.

22. J. Barber (Hinderer's catechist), Journal, 2 Sept. 1855. Barber certainly did not tell this story against Hinderer, since he went on to drive the nail in deeper, telling the man that he would be judged as "hating God which is worse than hearing the word of God and not doing it."

23. C. A. Gollmer, Journal, 15 June 1854.

24. S. Cole, Journal, 13 Dec. 1877. The "deceiving" alluded to by the speaker was probably no more telling the missionary that you would come to church with no intention of so doing, just to get rid of him. Missionary journals often complain of this.

25. S. Pearse, Journal, 23 Nov. 1859.

26. J. White, Journal, 31 Aug. 1855.

27. J. A. Maser, Journal, 20 Nov. 1864.

28. J. White, Journal, 19 October 1862 at Ota; 4 Aug. 1852 at Lagos.

29. W. Moore, Annual letter for 1879.

30. J. White, Journal, 7 July 1857.

31. J. Smith, Journal, 10 Nov. 1859.

32. S. W. Doherty, Journal, 9–23 Dec. 1878.

33. J. T. Kefer, Journal, 31 Aug. 1853.

34. Thus a case reported by W. S. Allen, Journal, 4 Oct.1885.

35. D. Hinderer, Journal, 27 March 1855.

36. J. Smith, Journal, 10 May 1860, at Isaga.

37. J. White, Journal, 2–4 July 1857.

38. J. D. Y. Peel, "The Pastor and the *Babalawo*," *Africa* 60 (1990): 338–69.

39. J. F. King, Journal, 24 March 1867.

40. Family tradition recounted by Mrs. Kemi Morgan, the Ibadan historian and great-granddaughter of Kukomi, interview, 23 Nov. 1994.

41. T. King, Journal, 1 Jan. 1852. Twenty-one years later another Dahomean attack produced just the same analogy. D. Williams, Journal, 28 April 1873: "the wonderful interposition of God in the time of King Hezekiah, when after all the boastings, braggings and threatenings of Sennacherib the Assyrian king against Judah, his host was thrown into confusion and himself fled back home with great shame. Thus it happened with the Dahomean king and his host."

42. B. Meyer, *Translating the Devil: Religion and Modernity among the Ewe in Ghana* (Edinburgh, 1999), 38–40.

43. D. Hinderer, Journal, 28–29 April 1856.

44. J. C. Müller, Journal, 18 Aug. 1849. J. Smith (Journal, 18 Sept. 1858) reported of Gollmer that "to make the Word more plaintive and expressive, he took many illustrations from the objects around." Smith was English but was supervised by Gollmer, so this report implies that *Transgression* was a distinctively German preaching style.

45. C. A. Gollmer, Journal, 26 Jan. 1853.

46. W. S. Allen, Journal, 7 July 1869. Allen is told the cloth is so called "because it is a valuable cloth and whoever you find using it is freed from poverty." Allen replies there is something of great value which is available to the poor as well as the rich, and concludes: "You may have your store full of etu, [but] if you have not the etu of God in you, you are still in poverty." Cloth was extremely important to Yoruba as an item and an indicator of social value. See further E. P. Renne, *Cloth That Does Not Die* (Seattle, 1995); and D. P. Clarke, "Aso Oke: The Evolving Tradition of Hand-Woven Textile Design among the Yoruba of South-Western Nigeria" (Ph.D. thesis, School of Oriental and African Studies, London, 1998), esp. Chapter 6.

47. W. S. Allen, Journal, 26 June 1872.

48. V. Faulkner, Journal of Itinerary to the West and Northwest of Lagos, 23 Jan. 1877.

49. J. C. Müller, Journal, 25, 29 Jan. 1849.

50. On *aroko* see C. A. Gollmer, "African Symbolic Messages," *Journal of the Royal Anthropological Institute* 14 (1885): 169–82.

51. S. W. Doherty, Journal, 9 Sept. 1875.

52. J. White, Journal, 2 June 1870.

53. D. Olubi. Journal, 27 Oct. 1867.

54. D. Hinderer, Journal, 12 April 1855.

55. J. Okuseinde, Journal, 13 March 1866.

56. V. Faulkner, Journal of Itinerary to West and Northwest of Lagos, 23 Jan. to 1 March 1877, at Ajelike village (Egbado); C. A. Gollmer, Journal, 24 Sept. 1850, at Ajido, on the lagoon east of Badagry.

57. C. A. Gollmer, Journal, 6 Nov. 1859.

58. C. A. Gollmer, Journal, 12 Aug. 1858, at Lower Ajaka.

59. See above, pp. 90–91.

60. J. C. Müller, Journal, 9 Oct. 1849.

61. Thus D. Hinderer, Journal to 13 Feb. 1851, at Osiele, eliciting the response, "we never heard the like before": D. Olubi, Journal, 2 July 1868.

62. On Yoruba attitudes toward death, the article by P. Morton-Williams, "Yoruba Responses to the Fear of Death," *Africa* 30 (1960): 34–40, though based on field-work in the 1950s, sheds much light on data from the last century.

63. C. Phillips, Journal for Half-year to 31 March 1874.

64. C. Phillips, Annual Letter for 1880, G3A2/O/1881/10a. His catechist, Charles Young, reported the children's deaths in his journal (15, 20 Feb. 1880), but "[did] not know what to say about the repeated trials of Mr Phillips."

65. It was used by White in his long letter to Henry Venn reporting his first wife's death, 6 June 1867; and by D. Williams in relation to a dying member of his Ake con-gregation, Journal, 2 Oct.1868.

66. The works most used by the CMS were by the Pinnocks—father (d. 1843) and son (d. 1885)—either William Pinnock's *Catechism of Scripture History* (London, 1825), which expounded it in a simple question-and-answer form, or Rev. W. H. Pinnock's fuller *Analysis of Scripture History* (Cambridge, 1853). The latter (which still employed Archbishop Ussher's chronology, dating the creation to 4004 B.C.) was used by stu-dents preparing for the Cambridge theological examinations. G. F. Bühler wrote to Venn, 30 Sept. 1858, asking for some copies of Pinnock's *Analysis* for use in the Train-ing Institution, and White included it in a report of his reading to Venn, 10 June 1864.

67. C. N. Young, Journal, 5 April 1875.

68. Pinnock, *Analysis of Scripture History*, 50, 58–60, 85–86.

69. D. Hinderer, Journal, 10 Aug. 1855.

70. J. White, Journal, Report for Half-year to 25 Sept. 1862; Journal, 2 July 1856.

71. W. George, Journal, 20 Jan. 1879.

72. C. N. Young, Journal, 27 Sept. 1876.

73. Thus S. Johnson, Journal, 1 Oct. 1883. After lightning struck the Aremo mis-sion house, he sought to demystify Sango ideology by a two-pronged assault: he ex-plained "the problem of electricity" and he gave a secular history of Sango as a king of Oyo posthumously made into a god by the people.

74. C. A. Gollmer, Journal, 10 Aug. 1858, at Igbogila.

75. J. B. Read to Wright, 23 Oct. 1877. Read was a young lay evangelist who went to Leki as his first post in September 1877 and died of fever only three months later. He was an enthusiastic and effective missionary—he introduced some of the new Ira D. Sankey hymns—and Isaac Braithwaite, the African schoolmaster, was evidently very attached to him.

76. I. A. Braithwaite, Quarterly Report, 29 Dec. 1877.

77. W. S. Allen, Journal, 21 July 1869: sugar was standard for sweetness, or good relations, while salt recalled the covenant of salt forever (Numbers 18:19).

78. S. W. Doherty, Journal, 14 Aug. 1875. The analogy between the two offerings was very precise: in both cases a vehicle of sacred power (Bible, water) is enclosed in a container whose white color symbolizes that sacredness. Water was itself regarded as symbolically white.

79. On Yoruba color symbolism, see A. Buckley, *Yoruba Medicine* (Oxford, 1985).

One should emphasize that the connotations of black in Yoruba thought, while they include negative ideas, such as darkness, also include some positive ideas, such as fertility.

80. V. W. Turner, *The Forest of Symbols* (Ithaca, N.Y., 1967), especially Chapters 1 and 3. Cf. also A. Jakobson-Widding, *Red-White-Black As a Mode of Thought: A Study of Triadic Classification in the Ritual Symbolism and Cognitive Thought of the People of the Lower Congo* (Stockholm, 1978).

81. On the contrast of systematic and narrative theology, see G. W. Stroup, *The Promise of Narrative Theology* (London, 1984), esp. Chapter 3. For a narrative theology conceived in postmodernist terms, but against the "nihilist postmodernism" of a Don Cupitt, see G. Loughlin, *Telling God's Story: Bible, Church, and Narrative Theology* (Cambridge, 1996).

82. S. W. Doherty, Journal, 16–17 May 1876.

83. No link with "archaeological," in either the common or Foucault's sense of the word—from *archē* ("origin") not *archaia* ("ancient things"). Perhaps "archeotropic" would be better, if it existed.

84. "Reincarnation," while it is a term often applied to Yoruba belief, is not entirely the right word here. In the classic Hindu case, souls may reincarnate themselves in any living thing whose level relates to the moral deserts of the preceding life, so that the doctrine provides the functions of a theodicy. The Yoruba idea that ancestors are reborn in their descendants is more limited and without ethical implications (except insofar as Christian authors like James Johnson or Idowu have interpreted it to say that only the *good* dead are reborn). For a useful discussion of the literature, see R. Hallgren, *The Good Things of Life* (Loberod, 1988), 62–64.

85. This is not to imply any sort of "Whorfian" view of how language might constrain culture, rather that the way Yoruba talk about the remoter past and future seems to express their cultural disposition to identify them. For a further discussion of Yoruba temporal ideas in relation to anthropological debates about the cultural relativity of time, see J. D. Y. Peel, "Making History: The Past in the Ijesha Present," *Man* 19 (1984): 111–32. On the wider issues, A. Gell, *The Anthropology of Time* (Oxford, 1992), esp. Chapters 10–14, is excellent.

86. For brief comments to this effect see C. N. Young, Journal, 5 June 1877; C. Phillips, Journal, 29 Sept. 1881; 12 March 1888.

87. C. Phillips, Journal, 6 Aug. 1879.

88. For example, E. B. Coker, Journal, 7 April 1890, reporting the view that "there is no place where one can go after death; women's womb are heaven to us here [*sic*]," which he found "disgusting and painful." Cf. a conversation with a friend of the Christian sympathizer Chief *Oyegbata*, who replied to Phillips and Young that "the womb of women . . . is the place where everybody goes when he or she dies. . . . They had never considered that there is another world besides in which persons go after death": C. N. Young, Journal, 6 Aug. 1879.

89. C. N. Young, Journal, 13 Sept. 1877.

90. C. Phillips to A. Merensky, 9 January 1889, in G3A2/O/1889/29.

91. P. Morton-Williams's classic article, "An Outline of the Cosmology and Cult Organization of the Oyo Yoruba," *Africa* 34 (1964): 362–74, shows how these two views of the ancestors, respectively linking them with earth and heaven, were still current in New Oyo in the 1950s.

92. W. Moore, Journal, 8 Aug. 1851, at Osiele.

93. S. Pearse to H. Venn, 6 Dec. 1862, reporting the words of Philip Jose Meffre, the Brazilian returnee, who *did* soon convert.

94. A. C. Mann, Journal, 12 May 1856.

95. W. S. Allen, Journal, 10 Oct. 1865, 8 June 1868.

96. G. F. Bühler, Journal, 28 April, 1856.

97. I. Smith to "Dear brethren," 12 March 1848. On *ipin* (from *pin*, "divide"), see E. B. Idowu, *Olodumare: God in Yoruba Belief,* Chapter 13; and Wande Abimbola, *Ifa: An Exposition of Ifa Literary Corpus,* Chapter 5. R. Hallgren, *The Good Things in Life,* 60–83, is a full and useful survey of the literature. A person's *ipin* is in effect their *ori* ("head, personality, guiding spirit"), which they might worship in the form of a small cowrie-covered shrine throughout their life. This destiny is also known by the compound name *iponri.*

98. William Allen, Journal, 19 Sept. 1859.

99. C. Phillips Sr., Journal, April–June 1855. Cf. a priest in Ibadan to David Hinderer (Journal, 26 March 1855): "'How can any body know and believe what you call the word of God, unless come one [who] has been to the other world to fetch it from there[?]' This was unanswerable in the poor man's opinion."

100. J. White, Journal, 17 Feb. 1867.

101. S. W. Doherty, Journal, 6 Oct. 1878.

102. H. Townsend, Journal Ending 25 Dec. 1845.

103. J. White, Journal, 31 Dec. 1863.

104. D. Olubi, Journal, 1 Sept. 1870.

105. W. Moore, Journal, 24 Sept. 1851, at Osiele.

106. The cognitive situation was like that diagnosed by Paul Veyne in *Did the Greeks Believe in Their Myths?: An Essay on the Constitutive Imagination* (Chicago, 1988), 23–27. Myth was treated not as revealed or arcane knowledge, but as information that filled a gap, taken on the basis of respect for its human source's competence and sincerity. The issue of its truth or falsehood was undeterminable and secondary. It is notable that Veyne cites as comparable another case from the nineteenth-century mission field: the readiness of the Tibetans to receive the Christian mytho-history presented to them by the famous French missionary, Father Huc.

107. W. Moore, Journal, 19 Feb. 1866.

108. G. Meakin, Journal, 9 Sept. 1858.

109. J. C. Müller, Journal, 21 Feb. 1849.

110. T. King, Journal, 14 June 1861.

111. D. Olubi, Journal, 12 Feb. 1885.

112. W. Marsh, Journal, 16 May 1850.

113. A. C. Mann, Journal, 13 March 1853.

114. Samuel Johnson, Journal, 2 Feb. 1877.

115. Thus Idowu, *Olodumare,* 21–22. What is questionable in Idowu's account is how casually he subjects the myths to the kind of Judeo-Christian gloss which I am here calling into question. In particular the offense (*ẹṣẹ*) which produced the estrangement is tendentiously described as "man sinned against the Lord of Heaven."

116. For other examples see E. W. Smith, *African Ideas of God* (London, 1949).

117. H. Townsend to C. C. Fenn, 29 Nov. 1864, from Abeokuta.

118. W. Moore, Journal, 21 June 1866.

119. J. White, Journal, 27 May 1852.

120. S. W. Doherty, Journal, 18 May 1876. The expression "make the gods" echoes the Yoruba phrase *şe orişa,* on which see Chapter 4 above, p. 106.

121. J. T. Kefer, Journal, 8 June 1853.

122. D. Hinderer, Journal, 18 Oct. 1855.

123. A. C. Mann, Journal, 25 April 1854.

124. J. A. Lahanmi, Journal, 4 Aug. 1886, Ijaye (Abeokuta).

125. G. A. Vincent, Journal, Jan.–March 1885.

126. J. White, Journal, 20 July 1868. One cannot rule out that such representations of Ifa by *babalawo* were partly stimulated by the unique claims made on behalf of their respective founders by Muslims and Christians.

127. C. Phillips, Journal, 20 July 1884. For another case where this etymology of Orunmila is brought into play (as "heaven's reconciliation"), this time by a *babalawo,* see I. A. Braithwaite, Journal, 28 Feb. 1878, at Leki. See further below, Chapter 10, p. 303.

128. In this I am greatly indebted to E. A. A. Adegbola, "Ifa and Christianity among the Yoruba: A Study in Symbiosis and the Development of Yoruba Christology, 1890–1940" (Ph.D. thesis, University of Bristol, 1976).

129. J. C. Müller, Journal, 23 June 1849.

130. G. Meakin, Journal, 20 May 1858, at Oyo.

131. J. White, Journal, 14 May 1865. Other instances: T. B. Macaulay, 13 March 1853, at Osiele; C. N. Young, Journal, 10 July and 4 Sept. 1878, at Ondo; and Charles Phillips, at Ondo, as reported by E. M. Lijadu, Journal, June–Nov. 1895.

132. J. White, Journal, 16 Aug. 1852, at Lagos.

133. J. White, Journal, 10 Nov. 1863. Cf. the special sacrifice to Ifa (*pinodu*), in which none of the victim's bones were broken, which struck James Johnson as possibly "a dim and confused remnant of a tradition of the Jewish paschal sacrifice": letter to CMS Secretary, Jan. 1879, from Abeokuta.

134. R. S. Oyebode, Journal, 4 June.

135. J. Smith, Journal, 12 Nov. 1859.

136. The anthropological literature on sacrifice is vast, but the main theories are usefully reviewed from a structuralist perspective in L. de Heusch, *Sacrifice in Africa* (Manchester, 1985), Chapter 1.

137. The argument of this paragraph is diffusely indebted to M. Bloch, *Prey into Hunter: The Politics of Religious Experience* (Cambridge, 1992), esp. Chapter 3.

7. ENGAGING WITH ISLAM

1. See above Chapter 4, pp. 115,121, and Chapter 6, pp. 172–75.

2. Notably E. W. Blyden, *Christianity, Islam and the Negro Race* (1887; reprint Edinburgh, 1967).

3. See S. Vryonis, *The Decline of Medieval Hellenism in Asia Minor* (Berkeley, 1971); I. M. Lapidus, "The Conversion of Egypt to Islam," *Israel Oriental Studies* 2 (1972): 248–62; P. Crone and M. Cook, eds., *Hagarism: The Making of the Islamic World* (Cambridge, 1977), esp. Chapters 9 and 10; N. Levtzion, ed., *Conversion to Islam* (New York, 1979); R. Bulliet, *Conversion to Islam in the Medieval Period* (Cambridge, Mass., 1979).

4. Lamin Sanneh, *Translating the Message: The Missionary Impact on Culture* (Mary-

knoll, N.Y., 1989). See also the critical discussion by Marilyn Waldman and Olabiyi Yai, with response by Sanneh, in *Journal of Religion in Africa* 22 (1992): 159–72; and Sanneh's further essay, "Translatability in Islam and Christianity in Africa: A Thematic Approach," in T. D. Blakely, W. van Beek, and D. L. Thomson, eds., *Religion in Africa: Experience and Expression* (London and Portsmouth, N.H., 1994), 22–45.

5. H. J. Fisher, "Conversion Reconsidered: Some Historical Aspects of Religious Conversion in Black Africa," *Africa* 43 (1973): 27–40.

6. Patrick J. Ryan, *Imale: Yoruba Participation in the Muslim Tradition* (Missoula, 1978), esp. Chapter 5. This rather neglected work is quite the best overall study of Yoruba Islam, particularly because of its precise and situated account of the views of Yoruba clerics of different persuasions.

7. S. Reichmuth, "Songhay-Lehnwörter im Yoruba und ihr historischer Kontext," *Sprache und Geschichte in Afrika* 9 (1988): 269–99.

8. A term current in Nigerian English, deriving from the Hausa for an Arabic teacher or literate.

9. John Adams, in West Africa between 1786 and 1800, saw many Muslims at Porto Novo, tributary to Old Oyo, and its coastal outlet. Its richest inhabitant was a former Hausa slave who spoke "Hio" (Oyo) as well as Hausa and French. See his *Remarks on the Country Extending from Cape Palmas to the River Congo* (London, 1823), 78ff.

10. On early Yoruba Islam, see T. G. O. Gbadamosi, *The Growth of Islam among the Yoruba, 1841–1908* (London: Longman, 1978), Chapter 1; and Ryan, *Imale*, Chapter 3.

11. See H. O. A. Danmole, "The Frontier Emirate: A History of Islam in Ilorin" (Ph.D. thesis, University of Birmingham, 1980); and S. Reichmuth, *Islamische Bildung und soziale Integration in Ilorin (Nigeria) seit ca 1800* (Muenster, 1998).

12. The first was the American Baptist T. J. Bowen, in 1855 (*Adventures and Missionary Labours in the Interior of Africa 1849–1857*, Charleston, 1857). He was followed by A. C. Mann, the first CMS visitor, a few months later (Journal for Quarter Ending 25 Sept. 1855); by W. H Clarke, who made three visits between 1855 and 1858 (*Travels and Explorations in Yorubaland, 1854–1858*, Ibadan 1972); and by H. Townsend (Journal, 18–21 Aug. 1859), after which visits became less frequent till much later in the century. See further Danmole, "Frontier Emirate," 104–110.

13. Cf. the testimony of the senior convert at Ibadan, James Oderinde, of a severe persecution of Muslims which he had seen, some of whom were publicly executed in the market of an unnamed town: D. Olubi, Journal, 5 June 1876.

14. For example, Buraimo Aina, Ota's first Muslim, who returned there via Lagos in 1847, according to oral tradition reported in I. A. A. Seriki, "Islam among the Egba and Ijebu Peoples, 1841–1982" (Ph.D. thesis, University of Ibadan, 1986), 62. J. White (Journal, 7 March 1855) is visited by what he calls the only native Ota Muslim—this Buraimo?—whom he says became a Muslim after Ifa advised it to his parents.

15. Gbadamosi, *Growth of Islam*, 23. Seriki "Islam among Egba and Ijebu," 75–77, dates Islam at Ilaro from the activities of Alfa Musa Kannike, a Kanuri slave of the *Olu*, c. 1860, but Law (*Oyo Empire*, 258) shows it to have been influential much earlier, in the 1830s.

16. G. Meakin, Journal, 15 Jan. 1857. On the local background, see E. D. Adelowo, "Islam in Oyo and its Districts in the Nineteenth Century" (Ph.D. thesis, University of Ibadan, 1978); and P. F. de Moraes Farias, "'Yoruba Origins' Revisited by

Muslims," in P. F. Farias and K. Barber, *Self-Assertion and Brokerage: Early Cultural Nationalism in West Africa* (Birmingham, 1990), esp. 114–15.

17. Law, *Oyo Empire*, 204, 280.

18. H. Townsend, Journal, 14–15 Sept. 1853; G. F. Bühler, Journal, 17 April 1856; D. Olubi, Journal, 25 Nov. 1880.

19. Townsend, Journal, 14–15 Sept. 1853, referring to Chief Ajinia.

20. D. Olubi, Journal, 3 Dec. 1877: he met the son, Oyewo by name, plundering compounds at Fiditi near Ibadan on his way back to Ibadan.

21. J. Johnson, "Report of a Journey from Ibadan to Oyo and Ogbomoso, 1877," CA2/O/56.

22. G. Meakin, Journal, 28 April 1858; D. Hinderer, Journal, 5 Sept. 1858; W. Clark, *Travels and Explorations in Yorubaland, 1854–1858*, ed. J. A. Atanda (Ibadan, 1972), 97–98. Clark, an American Baptist missionary, visited Iwo in 1855. For more on the origins of Islam in relation to politics at Iwo, see P. C. Lloyd, *The Political Development of Yoruba Kingdoms in the Nineteenth Century* (London, 1971), Chapter 7.

23. D. Hinderer, Journal, 10–11 Sept. 1858. Presumably this man was the successor to the *Timi* with whom Hinderer had exchanged gifts in Ibadan a few years earlier (Journal, 16 July 1851). On Ede Muslims, see also Clarke, *Travels*, 115–16.

24. On Islam in Ibadan generally see F. H. El-Masri, "Islam," in *The City of Ibadan*, ed. P. C. Lloyd, A. L. Mabogunje, and B. Awe (Cambridge, 1967), 249–57; Gbadamosi, *Growth of Islam*, 25, 52–53, 67–68; and Ryan, *Imale*, 123–28.

25. Kemi Morgan, *Akinyele's Outline History of Ibadan*, Part I, 107–108.

26. D. Hinderer, Journal, 23 May 1851.

27. D. Hinderer to Knight, 19 May 1853.

28. See Hinderer to Venn, 24 Sept. 1858, reporting the current suspicion that the *Bale*'s recent death was due to Muslim poison, as well as rumors that two other senior chiefs were in danger.

29. Biobaku, *Egba and their Neighbours*, 12–14.

30. Seriki, "Islam among the Egba," 58–60.

31. H. Townsend, Quarterly Journal to 25 Dec. 1846.

32. S. Crowther to H. Venn, 3 Nov. 1849, reporting an assessment of Ogunbona, the main mission supporter among the chiefs. Cf. also J. C. Müller, Journal, 29 Oct. 1849.

33. On Lagos Islam, see Gbadamosi, *Growth of Islam*, 27–31, 50–51, 69–70, 159–60; and "Patterns and Developments in Lagos Religious History," in *Lagos: The Development of an African City*, ed. A. B. Aderibigbe (London, 1975), 173–96; Ryan, *Imale*, 118f.; Titilola Euba, "Muhammad Shitta Bey and the Lagos Muslim Community (1850–1895)," *Nigerian Journal of Islam* 2 (1871): 21–30.

34. See J. White to Straith, 16 June 1853, estimating (with much exaggeration) that perhaps half of Lagos was Muslim owing to Ajinia's influence; and again to Straith, 18 April 1854, referring to the desperate announcement by Kosoko's rival Akitoye, shortly before his death in September 1853, that "he would have no more of Mohammedanism in the country and that whoever wishes to serve God should go to receive book from the English."

35. See P. D. Cole, "Lagos Society in the Nineteenth Century," in *Lagos: The Development of an African City*, ed. A. B. Aderibigbe (Lagos, 1975), Chapter 2.

36. Peel, *Ijeshas and Nigerians*, 170–71.

37. C. N. Young, Journal, 15 Aug. 1875.

38. H. Townsend, Quarterly Journal to 25 Dec. 1847. He goes on to note, "Our own dress is now being imitated and I suppose many will adopt it." Interestingly, he disapproved of this, arguing as the "cultural nationalists" would later do, that "their native costume is very becoming."

39. See Reichmuth, "Songhay Lehnwörter," 288–92; Gbadamosi, *Growth of Islam*, Appendix II, "Arabic Loan Words in Yoruba"; I. A. Ogunbiyi, "Arabic Loan Words in the Yoruba Language," *Arabic Journal of Language Studies* [Khartoum] 3 (1984).

40. Apter suggests (*Black Critics and Kings*, 200) that Crowther "took great pains to find 'deep' Yoruba equivalents of Christian vocabulary . . . [from] 'traditional priests,'" but he gives no examples of any of these alleged equivalents.

41. On Crowther's role, see J. F. A. Ajayi, "Bishop Crowther: An Assessment," *Odu* (N. S.) 4 (1970).

42. Arabic *wali*, hereditary possessors of divine blessing (*baraka*), deemed able to perform miracles. Associated especially with the Sufi brotherhoods, they were not as important in Yoruba as elsewhere in Islamic West Africa, so I wonder if the term did not have a notional more than an empirical reality, which may have eased its adoption. If a Yoruba Muslim wanted particular spiritual aid, he went to the *alufa* for a charm (*tira*) or for special prayers. For more on *wali*, see J. S. Trimingham, *A History of Islam in West Africa* (Oxford, 1962), 155–58; and R. Launay, *Beyond the Stream: Islam and Society in a West African Town* (Berkeley, 1992), 220–21.

43. See Ryan, *Imale*, 228–38, on Muslim prayer, and 245–46, on Crowther's engagement with the Muslim vocabulary. There were differences of opinion about some of these Muslim-derived terms. C. A. Gollmer (letter to Venn, 9 Nov. 1847) was happy with *alufa* as "priest of God," but proposed Yoruba-based neologisms for "prayer" (*ibaolorunso*, "talking with God") and for "prophet" (*olusotele*, "one who foretells").

44. Reichmuth, "Songhay Lehnwörter," 277–78.

45. In his *Vocabulary of the Yoruba Language* (1852), Crowther rendered it as "a coming to pass." For modern discussions, see H. J and M. T. Drewal, *Gelede: Art and Female Power among the Yoruba* (1983) esp. 5–6; R. Abiodun, "*Ase*: Verbalizing and Visualizing Creative Power through Art," *Journal of Religion in Africa* 24 (1994): 309–322.

46. *Esu* does, however, appear in the translation of some of the Epistles, which were among the last books to be translated, and then not by Crowther but by other African clergy working under him.

47. I am grateful to my colleague Dr. Akin Oyetade for drawing my attention to this difference between the 1884 and later editions of the Yoruba Bible. R. D. Abubakre, "The Contribution of Yorubas to Arabic Literature" (Ph.D. thesis, University of London, 1980), Vol. II, 92, quotes an expression from an *ijala* (hunter's chant)—*Esu kukuru biliisi*—in which *biliisi* is taken to mean the same as *Esu*, so as to redouble its force: "an extraordinarily short devil."

48. Olubi once chanced on a sacrifice in progress, specified as an *etutu*, at a chief's house in Ibadan. When the goat was killed, its acceptance was indicated by the standard formula used for any *orisa*, but the actual phrase used was *maleka gba* ("the angel has taken it"). Since there were Muslims present as well as pagans, I surmise the term *maleka* might have been used out of regard for the Muslims present. See D. Olubi, Journal, 8 May 1867.

49. S. W. Doherty, Journal, 24 Nov. 1878.

50. J. F. King, Journal, 13 Sept. 1868. King must have been accompanied by William Allen, since his Journal for the same day gives a briefer corroborative account, in-

cluding Akodu's remark about God's two books of remembrance and the phrase *"Baba mimọ ti ko ni ẹẹri."* His translation of the invocation is: "The Lord, the merciful king, the pure and holy king."

51. G. P. Bargery, *A Hausa-English Dictionary* (London, 1934), s.v. *ubangiji*, gives 1. The owner of a slave or of any object, 2. Lord (God).

52. Abubakre, "Contribution of Yorubas to Arabic Literature," Vol. I, 261–65, discusses the difficulties that Yoruba Muslims have felt in translating the credal assertion *La ilaha illa Allah* ("There is no god but God"), on account of the fact that the equivalent of *ilah* ("god") would most naturally be *orisa*. To say "There is no *orisa* but Olorun" is semantically impossible in Standard Yoruba, since it places Olorun in the class of *orisa*. So the solution in popular discourse has been to adopt a secular metaphorical approximation, and say *ọba* ("king") rather than *orisa: Ko si ọba kan ayafi Ọlọrun,* or more pithily, as you often see it nowadays painted on lorries, in Yoruba or English, *Ọba bi Ọlọrun ko si* ("No king but God"). Abubakre notes that Yoruba Muslims are reluctant to apply the name "Olodumare," common in the Ifa corpus, to God, as Christians do ("Almighty"); and Ryan, *Imale,* 98, comments that Muslims prefer to say *Ọlọrun Ọba.*

53. S. A. Crowther, Journal, 9 Jan. 1844, CA1 (Sierra Leone Mission), O 79. See also J. F. Ade Ajayi, "How Yoruba Was Reduced to Writing," *Odu* 8 (1960): 49–58.

54. S. Crowther, *Vocabulary of the Yoruba Language* (London, 1843), 177. Here he translates the second petition of the Prayer rather abruptly as *Ohworh l'orukoh reh* ("Respect[worthy] is your name"). What was later published in the full translation of the Bible was smoother—*Ki a bọwọ fun orukọ rẹ* ("May we give respect to your name")—but here the word *ọwọ* was retained.

55. In exemplary fashion by Max Weber, *The Sociology of Religion,* trans. E. Fischoff (London, 1965).

56. A. C. Mann, Journal, 24 July 1855.

57. C. A. Gollmer, Journal, 11 April 1859. A "sherriff" [*sic*] or *sharif* is a man of accepted descent from the Prophet, here perhaps a recognized leader in one of the Sufi orders originating from Morocco. On the political situation in Ketu at this time, see Adediran, *Frontier States of Western Yorubaland* (Ibadan, 1994), 187–88.

58. S. W. Doherty, Journal, 14 Aug. 1875.

59. As at Abeokuta in 1851 (T. King, Journal, 9 July), in this case alongside the *babalawo.*

60. As at Iseyin, by means of a solemn reading of the Koran at the mosque, with an offering of a goat and a few heads of cowries: A. F. Foster, 10, 13 Jan. 1881. At Ota, the chiefs rejected the Muslims' request for an offering to enable them to perform a ritual to prevent fire, but a few years later did turn to them to stop smallpox: J. White, Journal, 6 March 1870; 23 March 1873.

61. S. W. Doherty, Journal, 28 Feb. 1877, at Iseyin. At Ota, J. White (Journal, 16 Oct. 1859) persuaded the *Ọlọta* not to accede to the Muslims' request for the materials for a sacrifice, on the grounds that only God knows the time of the Last Judgment.

62. H. Townsend, Journal, 7 May 1851.

63. A. C. Mann, Journal, 12 Oct. 1855, 29 Oct. 1854, 7 Nov. 1855. He was intending to have him killed like a common criminal, with his head exposed in the market, but when his chiefs told him this had never been done before with an *alufa,* the sentence was commuted to burial alive. Since Kurunmi was then on very bad terms with the *Alafin* of Oyo, it is probable that the *alufa* was acting at the *Alafin's* instance.

64. J. Johnson, "A Visit of Inspection to Ilaro and Itinerancies, Jan. 1879," CA2/O/56.

65. A. F. Foster, Journal, 15 July 1880.

66. H. Townsend, Journal, 22 Sept. 1851.

67. D. Olubi, Journal, 11 Sept. 1884, reporting what he had been told by a Muslim neighbor. The oral Muslim source of the story leaves its trace in its starting with "Musa," the Muslim version of the name, which then reverts to "Moses" in Olubi's re-telling.

68. A. C. Mann, Journal, 29 Oct. 1854.

69. J. White, Journal, 6 June 1852, at Lagos. The use of black and white thread together is common in Yoruba medicines, and expresses a theory—in no way Islamic in its origin—that power was generated by this combination of opposites: see Renne, *Cloth That Does Not Die*, 42–44.

70. That is, of dark (*dudu*) or light (*pupa*) complexion.

71. S. W. Doherty, Journal, 11 Feb. 1875. While it may not be verbatim accurate, I see no reason to doubt the general tenor and expression of the prayer as Doherty reports it, particularly the invocations at the end: it was repeated some twenty times. "Misimilahi" is a corruption of the opening of the Arabic formula *Bismillah ar-Rahmani ar-Rahim* ("In the name of God, the Merciful, the Compassionate"), pronounced at the beginning of significant acts; while "Alahaududulai" is a version of the phrase *Al-hamdu lillahi* ("Praise be to God"). "Deku Allah" is less clear, but perhaps it is a corruption of the Arabic *Thiqu billahi* ("Have confidence in God"). I am grateful to Professor I. A. Ogunbiyi and to Dr. Paulo Farias for the elucidation of these and other matters of Arabic language.

72. In this shift of meaning the Yoruba are far from unique. In his great comparative word-list, *Polyglotta Africana* (1854), the CMS missionary S. W. Koelle gave words derived from *sadaqa* (*saraka, saraha, sadara, sada, sadaka, sadaga,* etc.) to mean "sacrifice" in nearly fifty languages, mostly in Upper Guinea or Central Sudan. For an excellent ethnographic account of *saraka*/sacrifice in one of these cultures, the Dyula of the northern Ivory Coast, see R. Launay, *Beyond the Stream* (Berkeley, 1992), Chapter 9.

73. J. Okuseinde, Journal, 2 March 1875. This remark shows a Muslim term being used (in preference to *ẹbọ* or *etutu*) in order to make the act more acceptable to a Christian.

74. S. Johnson, Journal, 17 April 1870.

75. J. Okuseinde, Journal, 16 Nov. 1869, probably referring to Chief Aiyejenku, who praised the Muslims to him "because their way and the heathens are much in an equal match"; D. Olubi, Journal, 12 April 1880.

76. M. J. Luke, Journal, 19 May 1877. This woman had been to Mecca. Since very few Yoruba at all performed the pilgrimage in the nineteenth century, according to Gbadamosi (*Growth of Islam*, 61), this *alhaja* must have been very exceptional indeed.

77. W. S. Allen, Journal, 9 July 1882. He declined, saying that they were not like the Muslims. A similar incident happened to William Marsh at Badagry in 1848. Marsh then defined *saraa* as "a kind of offering given to the Mahomedans to pray for the people," and went on to say that God wanted men to offer themselves as a living sacrifice, thus playing on the *saraa*/sacrifice link in another way: Journal, 19 Nov. 1848.

78. Thus a priest of Buruku: J. Kefer, Journal, 3 Sept. 1854.

79. W. S. Allen, Journal, 31 July 1879.

80. Cf. Ryan, *Imale,* 17: "It would seem that more than once Islam emerged from Quarantine first of all as a clerical style of worship and petitionary prayer that was seen to be of great benefit to a king or nation in distress. The first apprehension of Islam in West Africa has often been pragmatic: its prayer worked, especially when made in the context of the peculiar ritual worship of Muslims. It was not the ideal Islam of egalitarian worship that attracted West Africans at first. Rather they perceived Islam as the prayer of these gifted holy men who could write and heal and make amulets for others."

81. W. Moore, Journal, 30 July 1851.

82. A. F. Foster, Journal, 1879.

83. Moore, Journal, 30 July 1851.

84. For a vivid account of a modern rendering of the Yoruba Muslim appropriation of this style—in the celebration of *Ileya* at Ijebu Ode—see M. T. Drewal, *Yoruba Ritual: Performers, Play, Agency* (Bloomington, 1992), Chapter 8.

85. T. B. Wright, Journal, 21 April 1867, in Lagos. Cf. R. S. Oyebode's comment, on not finding hearers for his outdoors preaching at Ibadan, that "heathens and Mohammedans [were] busy at feasts" for the end of Ramadan.

86. D. Olubi, Journal, 14 July 1869.

87. S. Johnson, Journal, 17 June 1880.

88. The ritual acknowledgement of the incomparable uniqueness of God and the prophethood of Mohammed, which formally makes a person a Muslim.

89. A. C. Mann to CMS Secretary, 6 Oct. 1866.

90. W. Marsh, Journal, 1849.

91. A. F. Foster, Journal, 12 Aug. 1881.

92. J. Johnson to E. Hutchinson, 3 June 1875.

93. T. B. Macaulay, Journal, 15 May 1853, Owu, Abeokuta.

94. T. King, Account of Journey to Ota, 8 Jan. 1852.

95. D. Olubi, Journal, 23 Sept. 1869.

96. J. Okuseinde, Journal, 9 May 1866.

97. S. W. Doherty, Journal, 30 May 1876.

98. S. W. Doherty, Journal, 7 Feb. 1875.

99. T. B. Wright, Journal, 23 June 1866.

100. T. B. Wright, Journal, 1866.

101. T. B. Wright, Journal, 29 Sept. 1869. Also at Faji, J. A. Maser was told to go and preach to the *ibogibope* ("worshippers of wood and palm trees") instead: Annual Letter, 1876.

102. W. S. Allen, Journal, 24 Dec. 1877.

103. J. White, Journal for Half-year to 25 March 1860. Some years later he reports that a young man whom he had persuaded to abandon his Ifa and Elegbara was exposed to persuasion by his neighbor to become Muslim instead: Journal, 34 April 1874.

104. J. A. Maser to Hutchinson, 11 April 1870; similarly in his Annual Letter for 1877, 6 Feb. 1878.

105. S. W. Doherty, Journal, 18 June 1876. The reference is to Acts 13:8, where Elymas the sorcerer seeks to turn aside the Roman governor of Cyprus (here implicitly equated with the *Bale* of Okeho) from his desire to hear the word of God from Paul and Barnabas.

106. W. S. Allen, Journal, 22 October 1889.

107. G. Meakin, Journal, 1–2 Sept. 1858.

108. J. A. Maser, Journal, 4 April 1855.

109. S. W. Doherty, Journal, 2 May, 1876.

110. D. Hinderer, Journal, 28 April 1858.

111. M. D. Coker, Journal, 20 July 1892. Coker was then in temporary charge of Ogunpa church in Okuseinde's absence. He was so keen to display his knowledge of Arabic that in his journal he wrote Aminu's name exclusively in Arabic script.

112. S. Johnson, Journal, 7 Aug. 1876.

113. C. A. Gollmer, Journal, 14 Dec. 1847.

114. S. Crowther Sr., Journal for Quarter Ending 25 Sept. 1845.

115. S. Crowther, Jr., Journal, 30 Sept. 1852.

116. C. A. Gollmer, Journal, 3–4 June 1852.

117. C. A. Gollmer, Journal, 9 Dec. 1847.

118. J. Okuseinde, Journal, 12 Jan. 1872.

119. D. Hinderer, Journal, 8 March 1850.

120. D. Hinderer, Journal, 15 April 1855.

121. Gbadamosi, *Growth of Islam*, 132–33.

122. C. A. Gollmer, Journal, 14 Dec. 1847.

123. See above, p. 196.

124. J. Barber, Journal, 9 May 1855.

125. S. Cole, Journal, 18 Dec. 1877.

126. W. S. Allen, Journal, 14 Sept. 1873.

127. J. White, Journal, 30 May 1858.

128. S. Cole, Journal, 18 Dec. 1877, 21 Aug. 1876. Similar arguments made by W. Marsh, Journal, 25 Dec. 1848; 9 Jan. 1850, at Badagry; and by C. Phillips Sr., Journal, 25 Oct. 1853 at Ijaye.

129. R. S. Oyebode, Journal, 5 July 1890.

130. Mary Douglas's *Purity and Danger* (London, 1966), Chapters 1 and 2, sheds much light on these Yoruba debates. Her sympathy for the "bog Irish" view aligns her more with the Yoruba Muslim than the evangelical Christian position. See also P. Burke, "Historians, Anthropologists and Symbols," in *Culture through Time: Anthropological Approaches,* ed. E. Ohnuki-Tierney (Stanford, 1990), 268–83, on the origins of that distrust of "mere ritual" strong among evangelicals, and of its links with another of their traits: literal-mindedness.

131. J. T. Kefer, Journal, 7 Feb. 1855. One wonders whether anyone ever made a pun of Kefer's name, pronounced in its proper German way, with *Keferi* ("pagan"). It is the kind of thing that his Yoruba Muslim opponents would have found hard to resist.

132. W. Marsh, Journal, 25 Aug. 1849. Marsh reports several other discussions with Muslims about Jesus Christ: Ibid., 25 Dec. 1849; 3 Apr. 1850.

133. F. L. Akiele, 20 Jan. 1891.

134. E. W. George, Journal, 4 March 1890.

135. For example, C. A. Gollmer, Journal, 14 Dec. 1847.

136. A. F. Foster, Journal Ending 10 Dec. 1879, at Iseyin; C. Phillips Jr., Journal, 9 June 1887, at Ondo.

137. For full details see J. D. Y. Peel, "The Pastor and the *Babalawo:* The Interaction of Religions in Nineteenth-Century Yorubaland," *Africa* 60 (1990): 338–69; and

"Between Crowther and Ajayi: The Religious Origins of the Yoruba Intelligentsia," in *African Historiography: Essays Presented to Jacob Ade Ajayi*, ed. T. Falola (Lagos, 1993), 64–79; and Chapter 10, pp. 302–303.

138. J. White, Journal, 12 Aug. 1870; T. King, Journal, 7 March 1855. Other instances of this argument: W. Marsh, Journal Ending 25 June 1847, at Badagry; J. White, Journal, 7 Aug. 1852, of a group of Muslims admiring the first church building erected in Lagos, at Oko Faji; S. Johnson, Journal, 7 Aug. 1876, at Ibadan.

139. E. M. Lijadu, Journal, 18–22 July 1891.

140. R. S. Oyebode, Journal, 17 March 1892. The English Muslim must have been Abdullah Quilliam, a Liverpool lawyer of Manx origin and president of the Moslem Association there. He visited Lagos in 1894 as the representative of the Ottoman Sultan and was present at the opening of the Shitta Bey mosque. This made a great stir: see *Lagos Weekly Record*, 30 June 1894; D. Coker, Annual Letter, 23 Nov. 1894; and Gbadamosi, *Growth of Islam*, 167–68.

8. THE PATH TO CONVERSION

1. For recent discussion, much of which is in response to Horton's theory (see above, Chapter 1, pp. 3–4) see R. W. Hefner, ed., *Conversion to Christianity: Historical and Anthropological Perspectives on a Great Transformation* (Berkeley, 1993); P. van der Veer, ed., *Conversion to Modernities: The Globalization of Christianity* (New York, 1996); and G. A. Oddie, ed., *Religious Conversion Movements in South Asia: Continuities and Change, 1800–1900* (London, 1997). On issues around religious conversion more generally, see L. R. Rambo, *Understanding Religious Conversion* (New Haven, Conn., 1993).

2. As in William James's classic analysis of conversion, *The Varieties of Religious Experience* (New York, 1902), Lectures 9 and 10.

3. Both were *babalawo* in Ibadan, so they might have been the same man: J. Johnson, Report headed "Ibadan, Oyo, Iseyin, Ogbomoso, Ilesa," 1879; and W. S. Allen, Journal, 21 May 1878. Allen had a dispute with the latter, and used his name against him, saying that the *oyinbo* got their sense from the Word of God.

4. W. S. Allen, Journals, 30 Nov. 1877, 5 Jan. 1880, 6 Jan. 1886.

5. S. Crowther Jr., Journal, June 1855.

6. J. White, Journal, 2 July 1852, at Lagos: he explains the form of the *oṣe* as being "from the notion (being ignorant of the electric power) that the deity splits trees and damages houses with an axe." Also D. Williams, Journal, 25 Dec. 1871, at Abeokuta, explaining to a bystander that lightning "is the rapid motion of vast quantities of electric matter." One wonders how this would have been expressed, or understood, in Yoruba.

7. V. Faulkner, Journal, 10 July 1863.

8. "Reversed thunder" is one of the images used in George Herbert's wonderful sonnet "Prayer" (published 1633).

9. See above Chapter 5, p. 140.

10. S. Crowther, Journal, 13 Oct. 1852.

11. J. White, Journal, 18 Jan. 1855, gives a detailed account. He shamed the priest by showing bystanders how the trick was done, and even imitated it by using a wooden duck attached to some bellows to imitate the sound which the Osanyin priest interpreted.

12. J. White, Journal, 14 April 1855.

13. S. W. Doherty, Journal, 29–30 April 1876.

14. W. Moore, Journal, 5 July 1851.

15. The *Aladura* or "praying" churches, on which see H. W. Turner, *African Independent Church* (Oxford, 1967); J. D. Y. Peel, *Aladura: A Religious Movement among the Yoruba* (London, 1968); and J. A. Omoyajowo, *Cherubim and Seraphim* (New York, 1982).

16. See, for example, A. E. Southon, *Ilesha—and Beyond! The Story of the Wesley Guild Medical Work in West Africa* (London, n.d. [c. 1932]).

17. C. A. Gollmer, Journal to 25 Sept. 1861, at Abeokuta.

18. H. Townsend, Journal, 10 April 1853.

19. The earliest reference to "a strange sleeping sickness" is J. A. Maser, Journal, 25 July 1864, at Abeokuta. D. Hinderer, Journal, 31 May 1869, records a convert's death, and says it is "very prevalent in Ibadan at present, whereas it was hardly known a few years ago." Olubi refers to "the incurable disease of drowsiness" several times in the 1870s.

20. C. A. Gollmer, Journal, 10 Oct. 1857.

21. C. A. Gollmer, Journal, 31 March, at Badagry.

22. H. Townsend, Journal, 16 Aug. 1850.

23. See above Chapter 3, p. 48.

24. A. C. Mann, Journal, 30 Nov. 1856.

25. S. Crowther Jr., Journals between 1852 and 1858, passim. The dispensary was originally to be run by Hensman, but after his death in 1853 Crowther (who had had several years' medical training in London) took it over. A journal of particular interest is CA2/O/32/58, Quarter Ending 25 March 1854, which gives details of six *babalawo* who attended, having failed in their own search for remedies: as one said, "*Ọwọ Ifa ko ka* [Ifa's hand does not reach it]."

26. S. Crowther Jr., Journal to 25 March 1854.

27. J. White, Journal Ending 25 March 1860.

28. J. White, Journal to 25 March 1861; 23 June 1870; 28 Nov. 1871. Little did these sufferers know they were contributing to the cause of women's higher education in England: Sir Thomas Holloway of the Ointment used his fortune to endow Royal Holloway College in the University of London.

29. W. S. Allen, Journals, 24 June 1877; 1 Jan., 22 Feb., 16 Oct. 1885; 16–17 March 1886.

30. C. Phillips, Journals, 4, 11 Aug. 1879. Nasi was the staunchest early patron of Christianity among the Ondo chiefs, with ten members of his house under Christian instruction at the time of his death.

31. S. Pearse to H. Venn, Annual Letter, 10 Jan. 1871. The indigenous Egun or Popo population of Badagry were notoriously resistant to evangelization, so the disappointment over Afresi's death was especially acute.

32. Something like this was expressed by Crowther (Journal, 29 Sept. 1852) when he quotes a man, come to look at the bottles of medicine in his dispensary, saying to his friend: "One great difference between Egba and English medicines, in the former there must . . . be medicines of deceit with the true ones, but among the English medicines there is no deceitful drug intermixed, for the identical effect that their doctors assign to any of their medicines at its administration . . . is exactly what will be subsequently be experienced by the patient."

33. C. N. Young, Journal, 31 March 1879.

34. D. Olubi, Journal, 26 June 1866.

35. J. Okuseinde, Journal, 27 June 1866.

36. D. Hinderer, Journal, 14 Aug. 1855.

37. W. S. Allen, Journal, 17 Oct. 1880. The name which Christians adopted for themselves was *Onigbagbo*, "Believers," which remains standard today. *Buku*, taken popularly from the English, is not the standard word for "book," which is *iwe*.

38. H. Townsend, Journal, 7 Jan. 1851.

39. J. Okuseinde, Journal, 11 Feb. 1880. Cf. D. Williams, Journal, 12 Feb. 1867, at Abeokuta: a pagan admires communication by letter above all.

40. C. Phillips, Journal, 19 Jan. 1877.

41. W. Marsh, Journal, 15 May 1848.

42. W. Marsh, Journal to 21 Dec. 1845.

43. W. S. Allen, Journal, 2 Nov. 1873. The reference to the Koran is more likely to imply that the men were not Muslims than that they were. For Muslims (unless they were very ignorant) would not have thought that Christians had the Koran, but Yoruba pagans might well have supposed that *Alukurani* was the name of any holy book. In any case, there would have been very few Muslims in Ejigbo at this period.

44. J. White, Journal, 4 Dec. 1863.

45. J. White reports a conversation with a young man who has just "received Ifa," but who still professes that the time will come "when we do receive book" (Journal, 10 July 1855).

46. S. A. Crowther, Journal to 25 June 1848.

47. S. Crowther Jr., Journal, 15 Nov. 1852.

48. R. S. Oyebode, Journal, 12 Jan. 1889, G3A2/O/1890/48.

49. S. Johnson, Journal, 7 Aug. 1875.

50. J. White, Journal, 16 July 1852, at Lagos.

51. J. C. Müller, Journal, 26 July 1849, at Abeokuta: a group of chiefs are "astonished above measure" to hear a little boy read from the primer—"he knows more than all our wise men." Cf. D. Williams, Journal, 12 Feb. 1867: a man says "aged people are no more capable of learning [to read], but children," and asks if women can learn to read; he is assured they can.

52. G. Meakin, Journal, 15 June 1858.

53. J. Okuseinde, Journal, 28 April 1873.

54. A. C. Mann, Journal, 3 April 1855.

55. A. C. Mann, Journal, 10 July 1854.

56. T. King, Journal, 1 Oct. 1856.

57. T. King, Journal, 23 June 1856.

58. J. White, Journal, 26 April 1870. A similar argument was used by E. W. George to a poor Sango devotee at Leki, Journal, 25 March 1890, in G3A2/0/1891/18.

59. J. Okuseinde, Journal, 9 May 1870.

60. D. Coker, Annual Letter, 9 Nov. 1876.

61. T. King, Journal, 15 May 1857.

62. J. Okuseinde, Journal, 18 April 1870.

63. J. Okuseinde, Journal, 9 April 1875.

64. R. S. Oyebode, Journal, 30 March 1889.

65. A. C. Mann, Journal, 25–26 May 1864.

66. J. White, Journals, 25 Aug. to 24 Sept. 1873, passim.

67. G. F. Bühler, Journal, 23 Nov. 1856. Other references to Oderinde in D. Hinderer, Journal, 10 April 1855 (as a candidate); W. Moore to H. Venn, 7 June 1869 (for the detail about Yemoja); D. Olubi, Journals, 11 Nov. 1870 (when he gave the address to *Bale* Orowusi on the Christians' formal visit); and 17 March 1877 (his death).

68. D. Hinderer, Half-yearly Report of the Ibadan Station, 25 June 1867. He established a large compound for these ex-wives near his own, and told them to let him know if they were "in any pressing temporal need," in which case he would try to help them: D. Olubi, Journal, 1 Jan. 1868.

69. Hinderer's last set of Journal Extracts (CA2/o/49/115) is dated 26 Oct. 1858. The next two documents (/116 and /117) take the form of Half-yearly Reports, ending respectively April and September 1859, which do not take the "chronicle" form of the Journals and so contain much less day-to-day detail. The last three months of 1859, when Kukomi's conversion most likely occurred, are not covered at all.

70. D. Olubi, Journal, 2 Dec. 1872.

71. Mrs. Kemi Morgan, interview, 23 Nov. 1994. Mrs. Morgan was the great-granddaughter of Kukomi, through his daughter Lapemo, who married her grandfather Josiah Akinyele.

72. While preaching in the southeast outskirts of Ibadan in 1856, Hinderer was told by a man that people were concerned "lest our preaching peace among them should be only a covering under which we watch for an opportunity to make a war upon the country," which would be worse than the one started by the Fulani. Journal, 1 May 1856.

73. See F. Bowie, D. Kirkwood, and S. Ardener, eds., *Women and Missions, Past and Present: Anthropological and Historical Perspectives* (Providence and Oxford, 1993), especially Bowie's Introduction, 1–17; and A. Hastings, "Were Women a Special Case?" 109–125.

74. This was an insult sometimes thrown at young Christian men in Ibadan (see above Chapter 5, p. 138), and was David Kukomi's initial view (p. 232 above).

75. S. Crowther, Journal, 16 June 1848.

76. J. White, Annual Letter to H. Venn, 31 Dec. 1860.

77. J. White, Journal, 22 Dec. 1862.

78. J. Johnson, "Ibadan, Oyo, Iseyin, Ogbomoso, Ilesa," CA2/O/56.

79. G. F. Bühler, Half-yearly Report, Jan.-July 1862, reports that one wife, "a very careless, fierce woman, never willing to listen to nor be influenced by the Word of God," took her 7-year-old son away from school for "heathen" medical treatment. This was a year after Ogunbona's death, but one wonders if she was the same woman as the "saucy" wife who a few years earlier took her daughter by Ogunbona—baptized as Honora—away from the mission, wanting her to worship her own *orişa*. In exasperation, Ogunbona had the girl put in the stocks, but it did not work—she kept running away. T. B. Macaulay, Journal, 25 Feb. to 22 March, passim.

80. J. C. Müller, Journal, 1 Oct. 1848, reporting her baptism, alongside two men.

81. D. Hinderer, first Journal in form of letter to "My dear brethren," 9 June 1849. This may have been the same cohort of candidates who went forward to baptism at Ake the following year, which was comprised of sixty-one males and forty-four females: H. Townsend, 17 June 1850.

82. T. King, Journal, 1 Dec. 1850.

83. C. Phillips, "An Account of the Candidates Who Are Baptised at Ode Ondo

on Whitsunday, May 13, 1883," G3 A2/O/1883/134. This list—giving name, origin, age, previous cult, and brief biography of the first batch of converts—is unfortunately unique.

84. C. Phillips, Journal, 2 April 1878.

85. C. N. Young, Journal, 22 April 1884.

86. On the persecution of early Christian converts see P. R. McKenzie, "The Persecution of Early Nigerian Converts," *Orita* 11 (1977): 3–14, which ranges widely over West Africa; and J. Iliffe, "Persecution and Toleration in Pre-Colonial Africa: Nineteenth-Century Yorubaland," *Studies in Church History* 21 (1984): 352–378.

87. D. Hinderer, Journal, 26–27 Oct. 1855.

88. Such as house roofing: J. Okuseinde, Journal, 23 Dec. 1874. The man was persecuted for letting two of his wives attend church.

89. D. Olubi, Journal, 2 May 1870: an elderly man annoys his sister for continually pressing her to abandon her *oriṣa*. She finds an *atare* pepper in the water pot and accuses him of putting poison there. The compound head expels him, he collapses in the street on the way to Kudeti, and boys pelt him with stones. James Johnson, Annual Report, Jan. 1880: a woman seeks protection from the *Arẹ* Latosisa when her father accuses her of having killed her sister by taking her to *Igbagbọ* (the Christians).

90. D. Hinderer, Journals, 13–14 Oct. 1854; 2 Oct., 13 Dec. 1855.

91. S. Johnson, Journal, 22 June 1876.

92. Sources on the persecution: D. Hinderer, Journal for Quarter Ending 25 Dec. 1849, passim; J. C. Müller, Journal, Nov.–Dec. 1849, passim; S. A. Crowther to H. Venn, 3 Nov. 1849, giving an analysis.

93. Other townships where persecution occurred were Itori, Imo, and Oba. Attitudes in some of these townships, like Igbein, arose from the strength there of the pro-Kosoko slave trade party and burst out again in the 1867 *Ifọle*.

94. D. Hinderer, Journals, 8 Nov. 1849, 4 Nov. 1849, and 12 Feb. 1850 respectively.

95. D. Hinderer, Journal, 13 Oct. 1849. Ake, the premier township as well as the seat of the mission, did not have any systematic persecution, so it is likely that this meeting was a general one for all Ogboni throughout Abeokuta.

96. Thus J. C. Müller at Ijeun: Journal, 18 Oct. 1849.

97. J. C. Müller, Journal, 29 Oct. 1849.

98. Thus C. Phillips Sr., Journal, 3 Aug. 1852, quoting a woman at Abeokuta otherwise attracted to Christian "fashions." For Christians (and eventually for other Yoruba too), burial in a coffin was a token of respect. Of many reports of burial palavers, one of the fullest concerns a Christian woman of Igbore township, whose pagan relatives "would not suffer the body of the old woman to be taken away by the oiboes and to be interred in the [cemetery] which they called thrown to the bush," and managed to get the Ogboni to perform the funeral. J. Barber, Journal, 27 Oct. 1853.

99. J. White, Journal, 23 April 1874.

100. J. Okuseinde, Journal, 9 July 1866.

101. C. N. Young, Journal, 14 May 1879.

102. D. Hinderer, Journal, 10 April 1855.

103. Such as the various mass movements to Christianity after 1892, the Aladura movement of the 1920s and the 1930s, and the "born-again" movement of the 1980s and 1990s.

104. D. Hinderer, Journal, 30 July 1849, at Abeokuta. In his Half-yearly Report, Sept. 1859, from Ibadan, he gave it as a one of the standard objections that people made: "We are too old to change, our children will follow the new way."

105. On the problem of men taking additional wives after baptism, which occurred much more often with second-generation Christians, see Chapter 9, pp. 269–72.

106. S. Cole, Journal, 21 Dec. 1876.

107. S. Cole, Journal, 25 Jan. 1878; [A. B. Green], "Report of Ikereku," G3A2/O/1883/191.

108. D. Williams to C. C. Fenn, Annual Letter, 15 Jan. 1881; S. Cole, Journal, 21 April [1881], G3A2/O/1882/28.

109. S. Pearse to H. Venn, Annual Letter, 10 July 1871.

110. S. Pearse to C. C. Fenn, 23 Feb. 1875, on Iworo, where the Ijesha ex-*babalawo* Philip Jose Meffre was the converts' patron, having himself been converted by Pearse at Badagry (on which see Peel, "Pastor and *Babalawo*"); C. Phillips "Account of Visit . . . to Itebu, Leke and Palma Stations," esp. 17 April 1880; J. B. Wood to Lang, 14 July 1885: almost all of the Itebu congregation of thirty to fifty are Ijesha. Wood went on to generalize this observation: "I have often had occasion to observe in this land that those away from their own homes are much more readily got at than those at home in their own towns."

111. J. White, Annual Letter for 1873. This analysis seems to be the only one of its kind.

112. C. Phillips, "An Account of the Candidates Who Are Baptised at Ode Ondo on Whitsunday, May 13, 1883."

113. G. Meakin, Journal, 14 June 1858.

114. For example, J. J. Raboteau, *Slave Religion: The "Invisible Institution" in the Antebellum South* (New York, 1978), who, however, emphasizes that it was not just a matter of compliance.

115. C. F. Lieb, Journal, 14 July 1862.

116. As with the basic argument of R. Horton, "African Conversion," *Africa* 41 (1971): 85–108.

117. Sources for these figures: Annual Reports in G3A2/O/1881–1890; P. Amaury Talbot, *The Peoples of Southern Nigeria* (London, 1926); and A. L. Mabogunje, *Urbanization in Nigeria* (London, 1968), Chapter 4.

118. "A Brief Life Review of the Late Dr Joseph Odumosu," a commemorative eulogy composed by an educated granddaughter, printed as an appendix to *Iwosan* ["Healing"] (Liverpool, for the Odumosu family, n.d. but c. 1941–1942), 377–80. Odumosu was the youngest son of Odubela, whose house sheltered a covert group of Christian adherents even before 1892. His wider kindred, known as Iyan Ijefa, came to include many of the Christian elite of Ijebu-Ode, including Dr. N. T. Olusoga, the first Ijebu qualified as a medical doctor, and Bishop S. O. Odutola, the first Ijebu to be an Anglican bishop.

119. His unusual surname must have come at baptism from a Danish CMS missionary, Rev. Niels Christian Haastrup, who died in 1849 in the ninth year of his service and is buried in St Patrick's Kissy, Freetown. By 1883, he is noted as attending church at the lagoon port of Itebu, and is respectfully described as "Mr. F. Haastrop" by C. N. Young, Journal, 24 June 1883.

120. I. A. Braithwaite, Journal, 6 May 1878. We may infer that this was the famous

Peter Apara of later years, since the name, date, and place fit exactly with later information about him.

121. I surmise that he took his surname from Mr. John Thompson, the recognized headman of Lagos Ijeshas, a member of St Peter's Faji (C. Phillips, Journal, 16 Feb. 1884). Gureje's grandson Chief S. O. Thompson told me in 1974 that the family were "connected somehow" to the Lagos Thompsons.

122. A. F. Foster, Journal, 26–27 Sept. 1884, meets Thompson at Kiriji, while accompanying the peace mission of J. B. Wood.

123. R. A. Coker, Annual Letter, 19 Dec. 1897.

124. Ekiti District Report, G3A2/O/1914/86.

125. Executive Committee Minutes, G3A2/O/1901/43.

126. "Journal of Bishop Phillips' Tour, Apr. 22 to June 19, 1902," G3A2/O/1902/126.

127. For example, Aisegba's early Christians were sixteen men and three women, Unyin's were twelve men, Iperindo's were thirty-three men and four women.

128. Bishop H. Tugwell to Baylis, 5 Feb. 1898. Tugwell did not understand Yoruba, but Harding, who spoke it well, translated it for him.

129. F. L. Akiele, "Short Account of My Life," G3A2/O/1893/130. On his life with the Hinderers, see R. B. Hone, *Seventeen Years in the Yoruba Country*, esp. 62–76. Bishop A. B. Akinyele Papers, University of Ibadan Library, contain a genealogy of Olunloyo's descendants (box 39, folder 32), as well as several of his diaries, going back to 1885. Though "Akiele" is the same name as "Akinyele" (the correct form), there is no connection between the two families.

130. As Samuel Johnson did in *The History of the Yorubas*, finished just the year before, a work which does on the grandest scale what Olubi's sermon did in miniature. Interestingly Johnson refers specifically (pp. 73–74) to the pride people still felt in being descended from an *Eṣọ*.

9. LEAF BECOMES SOAP

1. J. White, Journal, 11 April 1856.

2. M. J. Luke, Journal, 17 March 1881.

3. It has emerged from the modern debate about African theology, where "inculturation" has been a key concept among Roman Catholics, that this concept should not be allowed to imply a final outcome, where Christianity would be at last "incarnate" in African culture. That could only be imaginable if African culture itself were regarded as static or as only authentic in the state it was in on the eve of the European impact. For a representative set of views see P. Turkson and F. Wijsen, eds., *Inculturation: Abide by the Otherness of Africa and the Africans* (Kampen, 1994); and, more critical, T. Bamat and J.-P. Wiest, *Popular Catholicism in a World Church: Seven Case Studies in Inculturation* (Maryknoll, N.Y., 1999).

4. J. Carter, Journals, 9 Dec. 1856; 25 Feb, 29 March 1857. Because he was still learning the language, Carter's few journals tell us much more about his own feelings than his impressions of life in Abeokuta. He succumbed to fever after less than ten months.

5. D. Hinderer, Journals, 12 June, 19 Aug. 1851; 11 Aug. 1850.

6. D. Hinderer, Journal, 14 Aug. 1855.

7. A. C. Mann, Journal, 5 July 1858, at Ijaye; I. Smith, Journal, 28 Feb. 1850, at Badagry.

8. J. Smith, Journal, 1 Jan. 1866.

9. J. T. Kefer, Journal, 29 Dec. 1855.

10. J. Johnson, "A Visit of Inspection to Ilaro and Itinerancies," Jan. 1879, CA2/O/56: "However much one may dislike and reprobate heathenism, one can hardly fail to be struck by the excessive religiousness of the people."

11. Compare above their views on Islamization, Chapter 7, pp. 203–204.

12. J. C. Müller, Journal, 3 Dec. 1849. His emphasis in the original.

13. Cf. the observation of the father of evangelicalism, John Wesley, that the religion of the heart, though it flourish "as a green bay tree," tended to decline with prosperity, famously quoted in *The Protestant Ethic and the Spirit of Capitalism,* trans. T. Parsons (London, 1930), 175.

14. H. Townsend, Annual Letter, 8 Jan. 1858.

15. H. Townsend, Annual Letter, 31 Jan. 1860.

16. H. Townsend, Annual Letter, 4 Feb. 1864.

17. For a good discussion of the European model, see Pat Jalland, *Death in the Victorian Family* (Oxford, 1996), Part 1.

18. An especially poignant Yoruba instance is R. S. Oyebode's questioning of his first wife Comfort, who died from the effects of childbirth, as reported by his friend Samuel Johnson, Journal, 23 Nov. 1877. He asks her if she knows Jesus, and is satisfied when she says she is going to him. Later he asks her why she is so composed about dying. "It is very sweet to die," she replies. Oyebode, "very inquisitive to know her state, then . . . asked 'Is it like sleep?' 'No', she replied, 'It is sweeter than sleep or any thing imaginable.'" In his own Diary, not composed for sending to the CMS, Oyebode gives a much more factual, day-by-day account of his wife's death (Oba I. B. Akinyele Papers, University of Ibadan Library).

19. J. A. Maser, Journal, 21 Sept. 1864, at Abeokuta. It was rather unusual for one missionary thus to report a conversation with another.

20. H. Townsend to H. Venn, 28 Feb. 1860. The movement of 1859–1860, which began in the United States in 1857 and spread first to Ulster and Scotland, was the most important evangelical revival for decades, "a nationwide and sustained revival," says D. W. Bebbington, *Evangelicalism in Modern Britain* (London, 1989), 116–17. Fullest treatment is in J. E. Orr, *The Second Evangelical Revival* (London, 1949).

21. A. C. Mann, Annual Letter, 1875, CA2/O/66/111.

22. H. Townsend, Annual Letter, 1 Feb. 1866.

23. J. B. Wood to Lang, 14 Sept. 1887. There is a modern term for conscience, *eri-ọkan.* This literally means "witness of the soul," and looks like a Christian coinage, since it appears to build on the Yoruba Bible's use of *ọkan* ("heart") to render "soul" (Idowu, *Olodumare,* 170). At the same time it echoes one of the epithets of Ifa or Orunmila, *Ẹlẹẹri-ipin* ("the one who witnesses destiny"), that is, was present when God assigned to each person before birth their own destiny, identified with their *ori* ("head," "personality"). Another possibility, suggested by B. Hallen and J. O. Sodipo, *Knowledge, Belief, and Witchcraft: Analytic Experiments in African Philosophy* (London, 1986), 61–62, is that *eri-ọkan*'s original meaning was something like "self-consciousness" or "judgment" (i.e., witness of *ọkan* in another sense as "mind"). Hallen and Sodipo suggest that this meaning has been widely overlaid by the Christian use of it to mean "conscience." Either way, it seems there was no exact pre-Christian equivalent of "conscience."

24. The latter was vestigially present in the CMS, being an Anglican society, but the readiness with which it took in German Pietists and cooperated with the

Methodists in campaigns and revivals shows that the mission was much freer of its historical links with the Establishment than was its parent church.

25. Such as A. Hastings, "Ganda Catholic Spirituality," in *African Catholicism* (London, 1989), 68–81; or D. Gaitskell, "Prayer and Preaching: The Distinctive Spirituality of African Women's Church Organizations," in *Missions and Christianity in South African History*, ed. H. Bredekamp and R. Ross (Johannesburg, 1995), 211–32. More immediately relevant is B. C. Ray, "Aladura Christianity: A Yoruba Religion," *Journal of Religion in Africa* 23 (1993): 266–91.

26. *Adura l'ẹbọ* ("Prayer is the sacrifice") was the headline in one newspaper reporting the activities of Prophet Babalola in the Aladura revival of 1930–1931: Peel, *Aladura*, 91–96. My colleague Dr. Akin Oyetade recalls a popular religious chorus which went "*Adura l'ẹbọ mi, Bi mo ba ji n o ru u* [Prayer is the sacrifice, When I wake up I will offer it]"—*ru* being the term standardly used for to "offer" a sacrifice.

27. C. Phillips, Journal, 9 March 1878.

28. D. Hinderer, Half-yearly Report to 25 June 1868.

29. One thinks here of the word by which Gollmer proposed to translate "prayer," *ibaọlọrunsọ*, which literally means just that.

30. C. Phillips, Journal, 12 March to 30 June 1876. He had just moved there as his first independent posting, and would leave within the year to go to Ondo. Being largely composed of "simple"—he uses the word twice, in warm commendation—Christian farmers, who had left Abeokuta after the *Ifọle* less than a decade before, the tone of St Jude's would be like what Mann had called the "spiritual" part of his congregation at Palm Church Aroloya (see note 21 above).

31. J. White, Journal, 28 May 1874.

32. S. Pearse, Journal, 10 Jan. 1863. There is a minor dating problem in that the report of the prayer, in a separate document, "My father's prayer or Akibode's prayer in the annual prayer meeting" (CA2/O/11/26), attributes it to 7 January 1863. Pearse had been reporting his meetings with Akibode to Venn for several years, so this prayer was deemed likely to be of great interest, and an edited version of it appeared in the *Church Missionary Gleaner* for 1864. For a fuller account of Akibode's conversion see Peel, "The Pastor and the *Babalawo*," *Africa* 60 (1990).

33. I have tidied up the punctuation and tenses of this passage, partly following the CMS editors, in order to make the story flow without distraction to the reader.

34. Though not identified as such, this is a quotation from Isaiah 1:6. Interestingly, it was this same text, encountered in a printed tract, which inspired the leader of the quasi-Christian Taiping Rebellion in China in the 1840s. See J. Spence, *God's Chinese Son: The Taiping Heavenly Kingdom of Hong Xiuquan* (New York, 1996), 55.

35. See pp. 90–91 above.

36. S. Cole, Journal, 7 April 1876.

37. D. Olubi, Journal, 2 Dec. 1872, quoted above Chapter 8, p. 232.

38. D. Olubi, Journal, 4 Dec. 1882, G3A2/O/1884/100.

39. D. Olubi, Journal, 14 Jan. 1884, G3A3/O/1886/38.

40. Described vividly in S. Johnson, Journal, 29 Sept. 1883, G3A2/O/1884/101.

41. D. Coker, Journal up to Feb. 1873. He was then catechist at Ido island.

42. A. Mann, Journal, 7 Nov. 1859.

43. J. A. Maser, Journal, 1 July 1864. Maser adds a detail which he does not explicate: the family had been disturbed by the nocturnal cries of a bird which had perched on a tree near the house. Since this was a standard sign that a witch was

about, it was probably the reason why the family, in fear, had tightly closed the doors and windows.

44. D. Olubi, Journal, 14 April 1885. An earlier version of this dream was reported in Atere's testimony over ten years before: Olubi, Journal, 2 Dec. 1872. For traditions of Dada, sometimes known as Ajaka, see A. B. Ellis, *The Yoruba-speaking Peoples of the Slave Coast of West Africa* (London, 1894), 76; P. Verger, *Orixás* (São Paulo, 1981), 134; A. Isola, "Yoruba Beliefs about Sango as a Deity," *Orita* 11 (1977): 106. On dreams more generally, see P. R. McKenzie, "Dreams and Visions from Nineteenth-Century Yoruba Religion," in *Dreaming, Religion and Society in Africa,* ed. M. C. Jedrej and R. Shaw (Leiden, 1992), 126–34.

45. C. N. Young, Journal, 13 May 1875. Babaji literally means just "Father of the whirlwind (*iji*)."

46. D. Hinderer, Half-yearly Report of the Ibadan Mission Station, Ending 25 June 1867. It is a pity that one cannot tell from Kefer's own journals which of his many encounters with *babalawo* led to this curse.

47. For a striking parallel case, see B. Meyer, *Translating the Devil: Religion and Modernity among the Ewe in Ghana* (Edinburgh, 1999), Chapter 4.

48. M. J. Luke, Journal, 23 August 1883. Leki was a haven for runaway slaves throughout eastern Yorubaland.

49. D. Hinderer, Half-yearly Report to 25 June 1869.

50. On which see J. B. Russell, *Mephistopheles: The Devil in the Modern World* (Ithaca, N.Y., 1986), Chapters 4 and 5, the last of a trilogy of works on the cultural history of the Devil; and *The Prince of Darkness: Radical Evil and the Power of Good in History* (London, 1989), Chapters 13 and 14, which cover much the same ground. Despite its value, in terms of the history of ideas, Russell's work is not as refined as D. P. Walker's *The Decline of Hell* (London, 1964), which covers a related topic at an earlier period.

51. D. Olubi, Journal, 18 Oct. 1883, G3A2/O/1884/100.

52. This identification long pre-dated the foundation of the Yoruba Mission, and seems to have been widespread along the Slave Coast, among liberated Africans in Sierra Leone, and in the Afro-Catholic cults of Brazil and Cuba. It still awaits serious historical treatment.

53. For a valuable comparative study of concepts of evil, see D. Parkin, ed., *The Anthropology of Evil* (Oxford, 1985).

54. C. Phillips Sr., Journal, 1 Jan. 1854.

55. H. Townsend to H. Venn, 18 Oct. 1858.

56. R. S. Oyebode, Journal, 12 Jan. 1889.

57. J. Okuseinde, Journal, 23 Feb. 1875.

58. S. Johnson, Journal, 18 July 1881, G3A2/O/1884/101.

59. D. Olubi, Journal, 2 Dec. 1872.

60. J. Johnson to CMS Secretary, Report, 30 Jan. 1878.

61. Quoted by S. Crowther Jr., Journal, 11 March 1855. I have slightly modified the Yoruba orthography and translation. His purpose in quoting them was not to show off their religious content, but to draw attention to Dunkuru's intelligence and to suggest the scope for "native *linguists* and *grammarians,* who . . . at present for want of sufficient information to enable them to develop their talents, remain hidden in the mass of people who daily flock to us for instruction."

62. This likening of Christianity as a burden which must be carried to the end contrasts sharply with the well-known metaphor of Christian's burden in *The Pilgrim's*

Progress, which represents sin, and falls off before the Cross at any early point in the journey.

63. The largest one was at Ake, and the Owu one had only seven houses (J. A. Maser, Journal, 20 July 1864). At the little town of Isaga, the few Christians wanted their own Wasimi, as at Abeokuta (C. A. Gollmer, Journal, 1 Feb. 1858). Townsend was right to assert that even the Ake Wasimi was not like the "Christian villages" found elsewhere in Africa (Annual Letter, 1 Feb. 1866), and the so-called Christian village of Sunren, founded by the *Balogun* John Okenla, soon contained many pagans and Muslims. Ibadan did not have a Wasimi as such.

64. For the emergence of some of these attitudes in England, see L. Stone, *The Family, Sex and Marriage in England, 1500–1800* (London, 1977), particularly on the growth of "affective individualism" and "the companionate marriage."

65. G. F. Bühler to H. Venn, 24 Feb. 1860, from Adelberg in Germany, reporting on information in letters from his African agents; and Journal, 30 Sept. 1858.

66. E. Roper, Annual Letter, 31 Dec. 1860, from Abeokuta; and to E. Hutchinson, 10 Oct. 1873.

67. T. King, Journal, 30 Oct. 1852.

68. D. Hinderer, Half-yearly Report to 25 June 1869. H. Townsend to H. Venn, 17 Aug. 1871, mentions unproved allegations against two ordination candidates, confessing himself puzzled.

69. V. Faulkner, Annual Letter, 28 Jan. 1881.

70. Faulkner, ibid.

71. Thomas Cole and five other members of Isale Iporo chapel to H. Townsend, 7 Feb. 1870, CA2/O/85/151.

72. V. Faulkner to R. Lang, 14 Sept. 1882; S. W. Doherty, Journal, 7 Sept. 1882, G3A2/O/1883/73.

73. J. B. Wood to R. Lang, 18 Jan. 1884.

74. Thus Gollmer, Journal to 25 Sept. 1861. Cf. Maser to H. Venn, 10 Sept. 1861, describing Ogboni as "a kind of authorized freemasonry *and much more* [emphasis added]."

75. T. King to H. Straith, 5 Oct. 1861.

76. J. A. Maser to H. Venn, 10 Sept. 1861.

77. J. F. King, Journals, 28 June, 9 Aug. 1868.

78. J. F. King, Journal, 25 Aug. 1868.

79. J. F. King, Journal, 1, 9 Jan. 1871.

80. H. Townsend to H Wright, 9 Feb. 1875.

81. J. Johnson, Annual Report for 1879, Jan. 1880.

82. C. Phillips, Journal, 10 Jan. 1880, G3A2/O/1891/74.

83. J. Johnson (by then back at Breadfruit) to F. E. Wigram, 12 Aug. 1881, enclosing an anonymous pamphlet, *The Hamite's General Economy,* supposedly written by a Black American former employee of the Baptist Mission who later lived polygamously in Lagos. The pamphlet (which itself does not survive) justified polygamy with Biblical precedents and urged Africans to form "a church for themselves on their own racial and national lines, in which both polygamy and slavery should be fully tolerated." Johnson added that the view that "practical Christianity" was consistent with polygamy was growing in Lagos. Since Johnson was a passionate racial nationalist himself, he must have found it discomforting that this stance was combined with support for institutions which the evangelical in him abhorred.

84. K. Mann, *Marrying Well: Marriage, Status and Social Change among the Educated Elite in Colonial Lagos* (Cambridge, 1985), esp. Chapter 2 and p. 55.

85. W. S. Allen, Journal, 7 Jan. 1873.

86. R. S. Oyebode, Diary for 1877, passim; S. Johnson, Journals, esp. 10, 22, 25 Oct. 1877 (the fight and its aftermath), 20 March 1878. According to Mrs. Kemi Morgan, Akinyele's granddaughter, Cornelius Adesolu was the younger brother of a *babalawo* called Bolude, the father of Akintayo and Akinyele (interview, 23 Nov. 1994).

87. S. Johnson, Journal, 22 Oct. 1877.

88. S. Johnson, Journal, 24 Dec. 1877.

89. S. Johnson, Journal, 1 Jan. 1878.

90. S. Johnson, Journal, 14 May 1881, G3A2/O/1882/23. A quiet irony of this account is how strong the Yoruba assumptions are beneath the Christian/Muslim opposition—in Abel's mother's desire to see the lineage reunited in heaven, and in Johnson's portrayal of Satan as an agent of God, like an *oriṣa*.

91. S. Johnson, Journal, 25 June 1881. Johnson does not give her name, which comes from R. S. Oyebode's Diary entry for 2 July 1877.

92. J. Johnson, Annual Report for 1879.

93. Thus J. Okuseinde, Journal, 25 July 1872, at Ibadan.

94. J. A. Maser, Journal, 21 Oct. 1854.

95. W. George, Journal, 17–19 Jan. 1879. George was an Egba, not a European; *oyinbo* was more cultural than racial in its connotations.

96. J. A. Maser, Annual Letter for 1876.

97. W. George, Journal, 22 Jan. 1879.

98. W. George, Journal, 15 Jan. 1877.

99. J. A. Lahanmi, Journal, 3 Jan. 1888, at Ijaye, Abeokuta.

100. T. King, Journal, 2 Sept. 1851. King does not further interpret the request in any way, but compare the role of dew or fine rain in response to the *etutu* described in Chapter 4 above, p. 100.

101. Syncretism itself is a far from unproblematic notion. For a valuable recent review, see R. Shaw and C. Stewart, *Syncretism/Anti-Syncretism* (London, 1994).

102. R. S. Oyebode, Journal, 21 April 1888, G3A2/O/1889/131.

103. S. W. Doherty, Journal, 10 Oct. 1877.

10. THE MAKING OF THE YORUBA

1. More than once, in giving lectures on the subject, in England, Nigeria, or the United States, I have met Yoruba members of the audience who found the very idea of it paradoxical, if not absurd. For them, "Yoruba" was given in the language and in their legendary descent from Oduduwa, which was the very cultural nature of things.

2. *Journal of the Historical Society of Nigeria* 2 (1961): 196–211.

3. Ibid., 198.

4. The name was proposed in an article in *The Times* by Flora Shaw (later Lady Lugard) in 1900, and started to appear in official documents later the same year: J. C. Anene, *Southern Nigeria in Transition, 1885–1906* (Cambridge, 1966), 213. The Colony and Protectorate of Lagos (which took in the great bulk of the Nigerian Yoruba) was united with Southern Nigeria (i.e., the non-Yoruba peoples lying to the east) in 1906, and that again was amalgamated with Northern Nigeria in 1914.

5. As Ajayi put it ("Nineteenth-Century Origins," 209–210): "The driving force of nationalism in Nigeria was not loyalty to Nigeria as such, but racial consciousness as Africans." See further the discussion by Robin Law, "Local Amateur Scholarship in the Construction of Yoruba Ethnicity, 1880–1914," in *Ethnicity in Africa*, ed. Louise de la Gorgendière, Kenneth King, and Sarah Vaughan (Centre of African Studies, University of Edinburgh, 1996).

6. Ajayi, "Nineteenth-Century Origins," 208.

7. E. A. Ayandele, "Missionary Enterprise and the Awakening of Nigerian Cultural Nationalism, 1875–1914," *Missionary Impact*, Chapter 8.

8. For example, he exaggerates the extent of educated African opposition to British military conquests, as of Ijebu.

9. On this, see the extremity of Ayandele's judgement of many of the cultural nationalists whom he had earlier celebrated in his *The Educated Elite in the Nigerian Society* (Ibadan, 1974), esp. Chapter 2: "Deluded Hybrids" and Chapter 3: "Collaborators."

10. Ayandele, *Missionary Impact*, 264. Agbebi's original name was David B. Vincent. He was the son of George Vincent, the long-time CMS agent at Ilesha, but became a Baptist. Ayandele, even describes him as "the only educated African who approximated to a practical cultural nationalist," since he regarded such leading lights as Blyden and James Johnson as such only in theory (p. 254).

11. P. F. de Moraes Farias and K. Barber, eds., *Self-Assertion and Brokerage: Early Cultural Nationalism in West Africa* (Birmingham, 1990), 1–2.

12. P. F. Moraes de Farias, "'Yoruba Origins' Revisited by Muslims: An Interview with the Arọkin of Oyo and a Reading of the *Asl Qabail Yuruba* of Al-Hajj Adam al-Iluri," in Farias and Barber, *Self-Assertion and Brokerage*, 109–147, here 132. On Adam al-Iluri (1917–1992) see also P. J. Ryan, *Imale*, 213ff.

13. See A. D. Smith, *The Ethnic Origins of Nations* (Oxford, 1986).

14. The connections between Christianity and nationalism are well explored in Adrian Hastings, *The Construction of Nationhood: Ethnicity, Religion, and Nationalism* (Cambridge, 1997). Hastings argues persuasively against the "modernism"—and its associated neglect of the role of religion—of such well-known theorists of nationalism as E. Gellner, *Nations and Nationalism* (Oxford, 1983); Benedict Anderson, *Imagined Communities* (London, 1983); and E. J. Hobsbawm, *Nations and Nationalism since 1780* (Cambridge, 1990).

15. This has not, of course, remained so, even from quite early on in Islam's history. For a modern view, see J. P. Piscatori, *Islam in a World of Nation-States* (Cambridge, 1986).

16. See Linda Colley, *Britons: Forging the Nation, 1707–1837* (London, 1992).

17. Speech given at the unveiling of a memorial window to Dr. N. T. King, *Eagle and Lagos Critic* 12 (26 Sept. 1885), copy in G3A2/O/1885/172.

18. Thus the Methodist Rev. Hezekiah Atundaolu, "A Short Traditional History of the Ijeshas and other Hinterland Tribes," *Lagos Weekly Record*, 27 July 1901.

19. Law, "Local Amateur Scholarship."

20. As the leading Yoruba among Nigerian nationalist politicians, Obafemi Awolowo put it in his *Path to Nigerian Freedom* (London, 1947).

21. See, for example, R. A. Joseph, *Democracy and Prebendal Politics in Nigeria* (Cambridge, 1987), esp. Chapters 4 and 5; and J.-F. Bayart, *The State in Africa* (London, 1993), Chapter 1.

22. See J. Lonsdale's seminal discussion of the place of civic virtue in the Kikuyu

sense of ethnic identity in B. Berman and J. Lonsdale, *Unhappy Valley: Conflict in Kenya and Africa* (London, 1992), 326ff.

23. Muhammad Bello, *Infaq al-Maysur*, ed. C. J. Whiting (1912; reprint, London, 1951).

24. The matter is discussed with subtlety by Farias, "'Yoruba Origins' Revisited," 140–44.

25. See Law, *Oyo Empire*, 5–6, on these sources.

26. For example, J. Adams, *Remarks on the Country Extending from Cape Palmas to the River Congo: Including Observations on the Customs and Manners of the Inhabitants* (London, 1823), 92–97.

27. J. Peterson, *Province of Freedom*, 212–26.

28. In 1849, she came to be a teacher at Charlotte, White's village. "But there was a difficulty in the way of both of us and this was tribal feelings. Her parents are of the Ibo tribe and my parents are of the Yoruba, and the difficulty was not so much on the part of my family as with hers." J. White to H. Venn, 6 June 1867.

29. S. W. Koelle, *Polyglotta Africana* (London, 1854), 5.

30. Letter to the Rev. William Jowett, recounting his early life, included as Appendix III in [J. F. Schön and S. Crowther,] *Journals of the Rev. James Frederick Schön and Mr Samuel Crowther, who . . . accompanied the Expedition up the River Niger in 1841* (London, 1842), 372.

31. [Schön and Crowther], *Journals*, 307, 317–18. Here Crowther still chiefly equates "Yoruba" with Oyo, as when he writes of "Katunga the capital of Yaruba after the death of Abiohdung," and gives a list of its principal towns which is, with the sole exception of "Illah," purely Oyo. He then refers to "Abbeh Okuta" as belonging to the "Egba dialect," which implies the broader meaning of Yoruba. His use of the term "Katunga" for Oyo-Ile—a word of unknown origin and very un-Yoruba appearance, used by Clapperton and Lander but never by Yoruba—shows the influence of the European travel literature upon him.

32. A case which underscores how much "Aku" remained a Sierra Leone designation is the reference to an Akoo Benevolent Committee of Freetown sending a large quantity of ammunition to Abeokuta against the danger of another Dahomean attack, and a letter to Ibadan urging cooperation with the Egba: I. Smith, Journal, 1 Oct. 1851.

33. C. A. Gollmer, Journal, 30 Jan. 1853.

34. D. Olubi to C. C. Fenn, 15 Nov. 1872 (Annual Letter).

35. D. Olubi, Journal, 28 Feb. 1873.

36. It has to be that in the incident reported by Gollmer (Journal, 30 Jan. 1853), Kurunmi did not actually use the term "Yoruba" in referring to the Oyo "tribe" to which he and the mission interpreter Thompson belonged.

37. S. A. Crowther, Journal to 25 June 1845.

38. S. A. Crowther to T. J. Hutchinson, 10 Sept. 1856, which gives a very overextended account of the former dominion of the "King of Yoruba": from Benin in the east to Dahomey in the west, as well as "Yoruba Proper northward in the plain, Ife, Ijesha, Ijamo, Efon, Ondo, Idoko, Igbomna [*sic*] and Ado"—an oddly skewed area. Ijamo was an old name for the Ondo kingdom, and the Idoko were an aboriginal group within Ondo. Efon at this time was often used to refer to Ekiti generally. Apart from Ado Odo in the southwest, Ado might refer to the Ekiti town or even to Benin.

39. W. Moore to Parent Committee, 28 Oct. 1868.

40. J. Johnson to CMS Secretary, 18 Sept. 1879.

41. Report of CMS Conference of Clergy, Ibadan, 23–26 Jan. 1899, G3A2/O/1899/75. The phrase "cradle of the race" was also used by Johnson, *History of the Yorubas*, 232, who put it into the mouth of Ogunmola of Ibadan; and it was adopted by I. A. Akinjogbin for the title of his book on Ife history (Port Harcourt, 1992).

42. A. C. Mann to H. Venn, 13 Oct. 1852.

43. J. White, Journal, 16 Feb. 1862. The occasion for his telling us this was a visit by a choir from the Ota church, where White had pioneered songs in the local dialect, to sing at Igbesa.

44. A. Adetugbo, "The Yoruba Language in Western Nigeria: Its Major Dialect Areas" (Ph.D. diss., Columbia University, 1967). The main dividing line between dialect areas runs from the southwest to the northeast, with a central area of relative overlap (CY) running from Ife and Ilesha into Ekiti. SEY, which includes Ijebu, Ondo, Ikale, Ilaje, Owo, and Akoko, has over the past century been under pressure from NWY, largely because of the influence of Standard Yoruba. The NWY/SEY contrast would seem linked to other cultural/ecological ones, such as savannah-versus-forest or Oyo-versus-Benin influence.

45. A. C. Mann, Annual Letter, Dec. 1861.

46. "Itinerancy by Bishop Oluwole and the Rev. Samuel Johnson in the Ibolo district of the Yoruba country," Jan. 14–21, 1896.

47. C. N. Young, Journal, 29 March 1875.

48. E. Roper to T. J. Hutchinson, 2 July 1873; and Mrs. A. Roper to same, quoting her husband, 27 Dec. 1873.

49. S. Johnson, Journal, 8 Jan. 1881.

50. J. A. Maser, Journal, 24 Dec. 1873. Ondo marks were one vertical slash on each cheek. What Maser supposed to be Oyo marks may have three or four horizontal ones—but marks were not always uniform or unique for each town. See further Johnson, *History*, 106–109.

51. D. Hinderer, Journal, 14 Oct. 1855. Ijebu's poor soils do in fact result in a less productive agriculture than the land farther north.

52. H. Townsend, Journal, 23 July 1857.

53. C. N. Young, Journal, 27 June 1875.

54. For example, C. Phillips to Lang, 16 June 1885.

55. J. B. Wood to Lang, 14 July 1885. Wood was English and did not know Ondo, so can be presumed to have gotten his views from Phillips. What they had particularly in mind were human sacrifice and twin-killing, which had been abandoned by the Oyo and Egba.

56. S. Johnson, Journal, 8–9 March 1880.

57. D. Olubi, Journal, 13 Dec. 1880. For a positive modern view of Ikale cultural forms, see P. Richards, "Landscape of Dissent: Ikale and Ilaje Country, 1870–1950," in *People and Empires in African History: Essays in Memory of Michael Crowder,* ed. J. F. Ade Ajayi and J. D. Y. Peel (London, 1992), 161–84.

58. E. M. Lijadu, Journal, Apr.–Oct. 1902, G3A2/O/1903/117.

59. J. Johnson, Report to CMS Secretary, 30 Jan. 1878.

60. S. Crowther Jr., Journal, 11 March 1855. On Dunkuru, see above, Chapter 9, pp. 266–67.

61. Handbill and notices for these activities in CA2/O/32/34–35. R. Campbell

was a Jamaican who wrote *Pilgrimage to My Motherland: An Account of a Journey among the Egbas and Yorubas of Central Africa* (Philadelphia, 1861).

62. J. White, Journal, 31 Dec. 1855. For richly detailed modern accounts of Gelede (neither of which draws upon White's testimony), see H. J. and M. T. Drewal, *Gelede: Art and Female Power among the Yoruba* (Bloomington, 1983); and Babatunde Lawal, *The Gelede Spectacle: Art, Gender and Social Harmony in an African Culture* (Seattle, 1996).

63. J. White, Journal, 13 Jan. 1871. White was also, I think, the first writer to name an individual Yoruba artist, Kudoro, "a celebrated Otta Artist who carves masks for public amusement": Journal, 30 Sept. 1862. See too his description of a woman's pottery, "beautifully ornamented with intersecting lines." (Journal, 2 March 1858); of the "theatres" (*ile awo*) at Igbesa, where "public plays and amusements" were put on (Journal, 16 Feb. 1862).

64. J. White, Journal, 24 Feb., 29 May, 5 July, 2 Aug. 1855, and 12 July 1856, mentioning various stages in the process; and especially J. White to H. Venn, 1 Sept. 1857, which narrates the final conversion.

65. This bracketed clause of White's letter was crossed out in pencil in the manuscript by the editor who prepared it for publication in the printed volume of missionaries' letters. It seems an odd thing to have done, since only the reference to the sacrifices makes it fully clear why White felt he had to take what otherwise seems a very unfeeling action.

66. H. Townsend—not a great cultural commentator himself—refers to the episode in a letter to H. Venn, 30 Aug. 1857, who says of the drum: "I never saw a drum in England equal to an African war drum, rude and barbarous as it is in some respects."

67. J. White to H. Straith, 31 Dec. 1857.

68. J. White, Report for Half-year to 25 March 1861.

69. H. Townsend to H. Venn, 30 Aug. 1857.

70. See Chris Waterman, *Juju* (Chicago, 1991).

71. C. Phillips, Journal, 25 Dec. 1877.

72. C. Phillips, Journal, 21 Jan. 1885.

73. See jottings in Yoruba in a notebook containing reminiscences and memoranda by A. B. Akinyele, Box 29, Bishop Akinyele Papers, University of Ibadan Library; and I. O. Delano, *The Singing Minister of Nigeria: The Life of the Rev. Canon J. J. Ransome-Kuti* (London, c. 1942).

74. I have not come across a copy, but a "Life of Fadipe" is mentioned as an earlier work on the title page of E. O. O. Moore's *History of Abeokuta* (London, 1916)— I cannot think of what other Fadipe it might have dealt with. Moore (a close relative of Rev. W. Moore) was enough of a cultural nationalist to have later renamed himself Abiodun Kolawole Ajisafe.

Fadipe wrote no document in the CMS archive himself, but his activities around Isan are celebrated in a report by the pastor at Ake, D. O. Williams, "A Visit to Isan," G3A2/O/1897/12, and his death in January 1906 is reported in a letter of Bishop I. Oluwole to Baylis, 19 Jan. 1906, G3A2/O/1906/17. A former *babalawo*, Fadipe had no schooling but could read the Bible in Yoruba. He had begun as a voluntary evangelist in the early 1880s: "powerful in the Scriptures, a man of prayer . . . his sermons were original and powerful."

75. On whom see Ayandele, *Missionary Impact*, 65, 257–58, 270. He got his sur-

name from an association with Frederick Haastrup, later *Owa* of Ilesha, but he was paternally a "prince" of Ijebu Remo. An auctioneer by profession, he played a large role in introducing the Methodist Mission to his homeland. He fits Ayandele's thesis well since unlike most Yoruba Christians he protested vigorously at the British invasion of Ijebu.

76. For many years its organist was T. K. E. Phillips, the son of Bishop Charles Phillips of Ondo. In 1926, he successfully proposed a motion to the Synod of the Diocese of Lagos (see *Proceedings*) in support of the use of "native airs" in worship. See also his pamphlet, *Yoruba Church Music: The Beauty of Yoruba Music, Its Relation and Similarity to the European Medieval Music and Its Development for Worship* (Lagos, 1914).

77. J. White to H. Venn, 4 Dec. 1860. Most of the detail of the letter concerns Gollmer's relations with the African agents, but Townsend is also mentioned.

78. J. White to H. Straith, 31 Dec. 1857.

79. White obviously intends to include Ota, from where he was writing, in the category of "Egbadoes." Ota is now (and was then) regarded as falling in the Awori subgroup, rather than Egbado. But Egbado was not an exact ethnonym—it literally means "the lower Egba," or the people lying between the Egba and the sea.

80. J. White, Journal, 3 March 1869. Expressive of the same outlook is a favorite analogy: as coins are a lighter, more convenient, and more advanced currency than cowries, so is Christianity superior to paganism. Journal, 1 March 1869, 4 Oct. 1873.

81. From Euhemerus of Messene (fl. 300 B.C.), who made use of the theory in a novel of fabulous travel. It fitted the rationalism of the age, as well as the sense of blurred boundaries between men and gods, which the career of Alexander the Great had encouraged. It passed to the Romans and was used by Lactantius (fl. A.D. 300), "the Christian Cicero," as an instrument to desacralize pagan deities. Paul Veyne, *Did the Greeks Believe in Their Myths? An Essay on the Constitutive Imagination* (Chicago, 1988), 46–57, argues that it arose in the context of an attempt to reconcile two contradictory principles: "the rejection of the marvelous and the conviction that legends had a true basis." Many educated Yoruba regard their traditional myths and legends—known simply as *itan*, "histories"—in a very similar way.

82. J. White, Journals, 19 May 1857, 24 April 1870. Ifa he treated purely as the misconceived deification of palm nuts.

83. D. Williams, Journal, 28 Dec. 1878; S. Johnson, Journal, 18 April 1881, G3A2/O/1882/23.

84. S Johnson, *History of the Yorubas,* 148–50. This story, as retold in the CMS's *Iwe Kika Ekerin* ("Fourth Reading Book"), has been criticized as a clerical distortion of genuine Sango traditions by Akinwumi Isola, "Religious Politics and the Myth of Sango," in J. K. Olupona, ed., *African Traditional Religions in Contemporary Society* (St. Paul, Minn., 1991), 93–100, though he does not explain exactly how.

85. R. Nina Rodrigues, *Os Africanos no Brasil,* 2nd ed. (São Paulo, 1935), 333. I am grateful to Dr. Paulo de Moraes Farias for this reference.

86. See above, p. 119, especially the assertions of Derin, the *Oni*-elect of Ife.

87. S. Johnson, *History,* 3–8, 143. Johnson's ontological equivocation—cf. his title for the first period of Yoruba history, "Mythological Kings and Deified Heroes"—closely recalls the outlook of the Greco-Roman elite on their mytho-history, as discussed by Veyne.

88. For example, David Hinderer's report of Ife traditions, collected during his first visit to Ibadan, that "from [Ife] the sun and moon rises, where they are buried in the ground, and all the people of this country and even white men spring from that town." Journal, 7 June 1851. Or C. Phillips Sr., reporting a *babalawo* at Abeokuta, who said "from Ife white people derived their original" and told the myth of Obatala having two children, the younger one of whom was the ancestors of the whites, who disobeyed him. Journal, 24 Oct. 1852.

89. An early version of this view appears in the comments of M. J. Luke on his visit to Ife (then deserted and in ruins) in 1889, when Oduduwa is described as the deified ancestor of the "Yorubas, Egbas, Ekitis, Ijesas and Ados" (Journal, 21 Nov. 1889). Here "Ados" is most likely to refer to Benin (Edo), so Luke's original must have been traditions of the Oduduwa descent of the royal lineages of these groups, extending beyond the ethnic Yoruba. See also R. C. C. Law, "The Heritage of Oduduwa: Traditional History and Political Propaganda among the Yoruba," *Journal of African History* 14 (1973): 207–222.

90. Among the major research findings in this work, it says on the back cover of Akinjogbin's *The Cradle of the Race* (1992), "that Oduduwa started a period of sociopolitical revolution in Ile-Ife and that the system has continued with various modifications till today." Ulli Beier's "Before Oduduwa," *Odu* 3 (1956): 25–32, was an influential early statement of the view.

91. O. B. Lawuyi, "The Obatala Factor in Yoruba History," *History in Africa* 19 (1992): 369–75.

92. J. White, Journal, 13 Jan. 1878. Cf. ibid., 20 Nov. 1874.

93. Cf. J White, Journal, 24 April 1870, where he argues that since *orişa* were deified former mortals, Adam and Eve could not have been idolators.

94. J. Johnson to CMS Secretary, Jan. 1879.

95. W. H. Pinnock, *An Analysis of Scripture History,* 19–20. The story in Genesis 9 and 10 of the curse which Noah laid on Canaan on account of his father Ham's sight of Noah's nakedness seems to carry no direct implication of the servitude of Africans or Black people. Most of the peoples descended from Ham were Middle Eastern, such as the Canaanites, Philistines, and Akkadians. And since the curse fell on Canaan and not his brother Cush, later taken to be the ancestor of Africans, it is hard to see why the story was ever adapted to justify the servitude of Africans. Its very evident function is to legitimate the Israelites' takeover of the land of Canaan. On the story of the curse, see E. Isaac, "Genesis, Judaism, and the 'Sons of Ham,'" in J. R. Willis, *Slaves and Slavery in Muslim Africa,* Vol. 1 (London, 1985), 75–91. For a good full account of the wider intellectual setting in West Africa see P. S. Zachernuk, "Of Origins and Colonial Order: Southern Nigerian Historians and the 'Hamitic Hypothesis,'" *Journal of African History* 35 (1994): 427–55.

96. S. Johnson, *History,* 3–7.

97. A. B. Ellis, *The Yoruba-speaking Peoples of the Slave Coast of West Africa* (London, 1894). This followed earlier works on the *Tshi-speaking Peoples of the Gold Coast* (1887) and *The Ewe-speaking peoples of the Slave Coast* (1890). Ellis was a colonel in the West India Regiment who served extensively in West Africa.

98. J. Johnson, *Yoruba Heathenism* (Exeter, 1899), Introduction. For ease and exactness, references to this book will be to the section or Chapter and the number of each question/answer.

99. Ibid., 1:3.

100. Ibid., 7:10.

101. Ibid., 2:17.

102. Ibid., Introduction.

103. Ibid., 2:25–27.

104. For a fuller account of Meffre's conversion, see J. D. Y. Peel, "The Pastor and the *Babalawo*," *Africa* 60 (1990): 339–69.

105. J. Johnson to Secretary CMS, 2 Sept. 1876, reporting incident of 16 June 1876.

106. Ibid., 1 July 1876.

107. Johnson, *History of the Yorubas*, 296.

108. T. B. Macaulay, Journal, 12 May 1853. It was Sodeke (the leading chief of Abeokuta from its foundation around 1830 till his death in 1845) who first invited the missionaries to Abeokuta. Townsend was always known as "Sodeke's white man."

109. D. Williams, Journal, 26 Sept. 1867. This was less than a month before the *Ifole*.

110. J. White, Journal, 12 July 1856.

111. C. N. Young, Journal, 2 July 1878. The "put things in their proper order" of the prophecy was taken up in the way the CMS Mission was welcomed in 1875: see Chapter 5, pp. 144–45 above.

112. Johnson, *Yoruba Heathenism*, 4:20–21.

113. See Chapter 9, pp. 258–59. Very different life experiences must largely account for the contrasting attitudes of the two men. Meffre, who had been to Brazil, became a Christian only three years after meeting Pearse. It took Akibode, who did not leave Yoruba country, twenty-one years after first hearing the Gospel to convert.

114. C. Phillips to CMS Secretary, 1 Sept. 1876. This was at Iwaiya village on the Lagos mainland, where many Ondo migrants were settled.

115. S. Johnson, Journal, 25 Dec. 1881, G3A2/1883/101. More generally, see E. G. Parrinder, "An African Saviour God," in *The Saviour God: Comparative Studies in the Concept of Salvation*, ed. S. G. F. Brandon (Manchester, 1963), 117–28.

116. J. Johnson, *Yoruba Heathenism*, 3:9, 4:1–4.

117. This account of Lijadu is based on Peel, "Between Crowther and Ajayi" in T. Falola, ed., *African Historiography*, 64–80, though that makes fairly uncritical use of the concept of "cultural nationalism." The theological importance of Lijadu was first seriously recognized in E. A. A. Adegbola, "Ifa and Christianity among the Yoruba: A Study in Symbiosis and in the Development of Yoruba Christology, 1890–1940" (Ph.D. thesis, University of Bristol, 1976).

118. E. M. Lijadu, "Account of Himself," 13 Feb. 1894, G3A2/O/1894/67.

119. On Lijadu's cultural work, see R. Law, "A Pioneer of Yoruba Studies: Moses Lijadu (1862–1926)," in *Studies in Yoruba History and Culture: Essays in Honour of Professor S. O. Biobaku*, ed. G. O. Olusanya (Ibadan, 1983), 108–115.

120. "Rev. E. M. Lijadu's Apology," G3A2/O/1901/116.

121. Lijadu did eventually break with the Anglican Church, in 1920. His eldest son, whom he wanted to succeed him as head of the Evangelists' Band, had attended the CMS training college at Oyo but was turned down for ordination. When Lijadu ordained him himself, the Bishop of Lagos withdrew his Anglican priest's license.

122. *Ifa: Imole re ti ise Ipile Isin ni Ile Yoruba* (London: Religious Tract Society, 1901). Bishop Phillips's foreword is dated 1897, so I surmise it was completed by then but

took some time to find a publisher. *Ọrunmla!* (1908; reprint Ado Ekiti: Omolayo Standard Press, 1972).

123. Journal, Jan.–June 1896, G3A2/O/1896/160; "Apology," G3A2/O/1901/116.

124. Lijadu understood Orunmila as the name of the deity and Ifa as the messages or the oracle of which Orunmila was the author. However, the two names are also widely used as synonyms: see Wande Abimbola, *Ifa: An Exposition of Ifa Literary Corpus* (Ibadan, 1976), 3–4.

125. *Ọrunmla!* 16: "*awọn keferi ilẹ wa ti ni imọ wiwa Jesu Kristi.*"

126. J. Johnson, "Relation of Mission Work to Native Customs," *Pan-Anglican Papers: Political and Social Conditions of Missionary Work* (London: SPCK, 1908). Lijadu also attended this conference.

127. *Ọrunmla!* 21–22. In "traditional" belief (which lacked a concept of absolute evil), Esu and Orunmila were interdependent rather than radically opposed: see Idowu, *Olodumare*, 81.

128. *Ọrunmla!* 78–80.

129. S. A. Oke, *The Ethiopian National Church: A Necessity* (Ibadan, 1923).

130. D. O. Epega, *The Mystery of Yoruba Gods* (Ode Remo, 1932).

131. So it is treated by A. Quayson, *Strategic Transformations in Nigerian Writing: Orality and History in the Work of Rev. Samuel Johnson, Amos Tutuola, Wole Soyinka and Ben Okri* (Oxford, 1997).

132. S. Johnson, Journal, 19 Jan. 1975. His wife was Lydia, daughter of James Okuseinde, who was in charge of the Ogunpa station. On Johnson's family background, see the full account in M. Doortmont, "Recapturing the Past: Samuel Johnson and the Construction of Yoruba History" (Ph.D. Thesis, Erasmus University, Rotterdam, 1994), Chapter 2, esp. p. 22, commenting on the paucity of our knowledge of the details of Johnson's personal life.

133. J. White to H. Venn, 6 June 1867.

134. For a fuller version of the following account of Johnson's achievement as a historian, see J. D. Y. Peel, "Two Pastors and their Histories: Johnson and Reindorf," in *The Recovery of the West African Past: African Pastors and African History in the Nineteenth Century*, ed. P. Jenkins (Basel, 1998), 69–81.

135. S. Johnson, Journal, 16 Nov. 1882.

136. H. White, *Metahistory: The Historical Imagination in Nineteenth-Century Europe* (Baltimore, 1973), 7–11.

137. Johnson, *History*, 187.

138. Ibid., 274.

139. Ibid., 293.

140. Ibid., 245.

141. Ibid., 246.

142. J. Barber to H. Venn, 23 Dec. 1856. Cf. D. Olubi to H. Wright, 22 April 1878, quoting a view that the Ibadans were "made as rods by God to correct these nations, and when he pleases to finish with them, there will be an end."

143. Cf. the "old tradition . . . of a prophecy" to this effect (*History*, 296), discussed above, p. 301.

144. Finance Committee Minutes, February 1987, G3A2/O/1897/33; S. Johnson asks for leave to enable him to go through his history with his brother (Obadiah). Finance Committee Minutes, July 1898, G3A2/O/1898/136: Dr. Obadiah Johnson (a member of the Committee) raises the issue of his brother's *History*, which

is to be sent to the Parent Committee in London; the Finance Committee expresses its hope to see a Yoruba edition.

145. R. N. Cust to CMS, 3 January 1899.

146. Proof that Johnson's manuscript had passed through the CMS office is the slip in the Precis Book, recording that it had been taken out: G3A2/O/1898/4. For its later vicissitudes, see O. Johnson to Baylis (CMS Secretary), 2 Dec. 1899; and to Cust, 2 Dec. 1899. There was evidently a plan to get the manuscript printed at the expense of "Mr Blaize," presumably the Lagos merchant R. B. Blaize. The Precis Book adds a laconic entry: "[N. B.—Mr Elliott Stock has lately acknowledged receipt of the MS, and states that he mislaid it]."

11. LOOKING BACK

1. The evocative title of Isabel Hofmeyr's fine study, *We Spend Our Years As a Tale That Is Told: Oral Historical Narrative in a South African Chiefdom* (Johannesburg, 1993).

2. The literature on Soyinka is huge, but see E. Jones, *The Writing of Wole Soyinka* (London, 1973); D. Wright, *Wole Soyinka Revisited* (New York, 1993); O. Ogunba, ed., *Soyinka: A Collection of Critical Essays* (Ibadan, 1994); A. Maja-Pearce, ed., *Wole Soyinka: An Appraisal* (London, 1994).

3. *The Man Died* (1969), *Akẹ: The Years of Childhood* (1981), *Ìsarà: A Voyage around "Essay"* (1989), *Ibadan, The Penkelemes Years: A Memoir, 1946–1965* (1994).

4. Soyinka agreeably renders them in English or Tolkienish as "ghommids."

5. See especially his "The Fourth Stage: Through the Mysteries of Ogun to the Origin of Yoruba Tragedy" (1973), in *Art, Dialogue and Outrage: Essays on Literature and Culture* (London, 1993), 27–39.

6. It makes a pun on *ile*, "house, home."

7. *Ìsarà*, 228–37.

8. "Neo-Tarzanism: The Poetics of Pseudo-Tradition" (1975), in *Art, Dialogue and Outrage*, 302.

9. Ibid.: "Yoruba society is full of individuals who worship the Anglican God on Sundays, sacrifice to Sango every feastday, consult Ifa before any new project and dance with the Cherubim and Seraphims every evening." This sort of view has become rather an academic commonplace: see D. Laitin, *Hegemony and Culture: Politics and Religious Change among the Yoruba* (Chicago, 1986).

10. *Ìsarà*, vi.

11. One might in fact take *Ìsarà* to illustrate the thesis argued by P. P. Ekeh in his influential paper, "Colonialism and the Two Publics in Africa: A Theoretical Statement," *Comparative Studies in Society and History* 17 (1975).

12. For an overall account, see T. Falola, *Violence in Nigeria: The Crisis of Religious Politics and Secular Ideologies* (Rochester, N.Y., 1998). For an indicative episode over the issue of the cross and the mosque at the University of Ibadan in 1985–1986, see Ayo Banjo, *In The Saddle: A Vice-Chancellor's Story* (Ibadan, 1997), 69–77.

13. W. Soyinka, *The Credo of Being and Nothingness* (Ibadan, 1991), the first of the Olufosoye Annual Lectures on Religions at the University of Ibadan.

14. Ibid., 20: a critical reference to Professor Ali Mazrui as "islam's born-again revisionist of history" for adopting the thesis, in a television series of lectures, "that the contest for the African soul, on African soil, between christianity and islam took place in a virtual spiritual vacuum."

15. *Aké,* 7.

16. W. de Craemer, J. Vansina, and R. Fox, "Religious Movements in Central Africa: A Theoretical Study," *Comparative Studies in Society and History* 18 (1976): 458–75; and W. MacGaffey, *Religion and Society in Central Africa: The BaKongo of Lower Zaire* (Chicago, 1986), Chapter 8.

17. M. A. Ojo, "The Contextual Significance of Charismatic Movements in Independent Nigeria," *Africa* 58 (1988): 172–92. I am also grateful to Dr. Ojo for showing me a copy of the typescript of his forthcoming book, *End-Time Army: The Charismatic Movements in Modern Nigeria.*

18. Paul Gifford, "The Complex Provenance of Some Elements of African Pentecostal Theology," in *Between Babel and Pentecost: Transnational Pentecostalism in Africa and Latin America,* ed. A. Corten and R. Marshall-Fratani (Bloomington: Indiana University Press, 2000).

19. D. Martin, *Tongues of Fire: The Explosion of Protestantism in Latin America* (Oxford, 1990): H. Cox, *Fire from Heaven: The Rise of Pentecostal Spirituality and the Reshaping of Religion in the Twenty-First Century* (New York, 1994): K. Poewe, ed., *Charismatic Christianity As a Global Culture* (Columbia, S.C., 1994); P. Gifford, *African Christianity: Its Public Role* (London, 1998). Two fine recent African case studies are D. Maxwell, *Christians and Chiefs in Zimbabwe: A Social History of the Hwesa People, c 1870s–1990s* (Edinburgh, 1999); and B. Meyer, *Translating the Devil: Religion and Modernity among the Ewe in Ghana* (Edinburgh, 1999).

20. R. Marshall-Fratani, "Mediating the Global and the Local in Nigerian Pentecostalism," *Journal of Religion in Africa* 28 (1998): 278–315.

21. Ibid., 305.

22. See above Chapter 6, p. 169; and Peel, "Olaju: A Yoruba Concept of Development," *Journal of Development Studies* 14 (1978): 135–65.

SOURCES AND REFERENCES

PRIMARY SOURCE MATERIAL

The principal source, the papers of the Church Missionary Society, are now held in Birmingham University Library. I have not usually given full references in the end-notes, but the great bulk of relevant documents are from the Incoming Papers, Series O. Up to 1879, documents are classified under the heading CA2 (for the Yoruba Mission), with a numbered file for each missionary. From 1880 the papers are classified under the heading G3A2, ordered by year in the sequence of their receipt; and are easiest located in the Precis Books (Series P) which summarize their contents.

The mission agents whose letters and journals have been of most value are grouped below by racial or national origin, since this is not always evident from their names alone. For those active before 1879, their file numbers in the CA2/O series are as follows:

African: F. L. Akiele, William Allen (18), W. S. Allen (19), James Barber (21), I. A. Braithwaite (22), Daniel Coker (28), E. B. Coker, M. D. Coker, Samuel Cole (29), Samuel Ajayi Crowther (31), S. Crowther Jr. (32), S. W. Doherty (35), A. F. Foster (40), E. W. George, William George (41), A. B. Green, Thomas John (54), James Johnson (56), Samuel Johnson (58), J. F. King (60), Thomas King (61), J. A. Lahanmi, E. M. Lijadu, M. J. Luke (64), T. B. Macaulay (65), William Marsh (67), William Moore (70), William Morgan (71), James Okuseinde (74), Daniel Olubi (75), Isaac Oluwole, R. S. Oyebode, Samuel Pearse (76), Charles Phillips Sr. (77), Charles Phillips Jr. (78), George Vincent, James White (87), Andrew Wilhelm (89), David Williams (90), D. O. Williams (91), J. A. T. Williams, T. B. Wright (97), C. N. Young (98).

English: Joseph Carter (26), Valentine Faulkner (37), Edward Irving (52), J. A. Lamb (99), George Meakin (69), J. B. Read (79), Edward Roper (81), Isaac Smith (82), Joseph Smith (83), Henry Townsend (85), J. B. Wood (96).

German: F. Bühler (23), C. A. Gollmer (43), David Hinderer (49), J. T. Kefer (59), J. A. Mann (66), J. A. Maser (68), J. C. Müller (72).

Other unpublished sources were consulted in Nigeria: local Church Missionary Society records, reference CMS(Y), held at the Nigerian National Archives, Ibadan; documents in the Bishop A. B. Akinyele Papers, the Oba I. B. Akinyele Papers, the Lijadu Papers, the Herbert Macaulay Papers, the Phillips Papers, and the Ransome-Kuti papers, all held in the Kenneth Dike Library, University of Ibadan; and the Apara Papers, Obafemi Awolowo University, Ile-Ife.

A number of near-contemporary published works by or about members of the Yoruba Mission contain some primary source material, though in general they add very little to the unpublished letters and journals of mission agents:

Barber, M. A. S. *Oshielle; or Village Life in the Yoruba Country.* London, 1857.

[Gollmer, C. H. V.]. *Charles A. Gollmer: His Life and Missionary Labours in West Africa.* London, 1889.

Hone, R. B. *Seventeen Years in the Yoruba Country: Memorials of Anna Hinderer . . . Gathered from her Letters and Journals.* London, 1872.

Page, J. *The Black Bishop: Samuel Adjai Crowther.* London, 1908.

Roper, E. *Facts about Foreign Missions in West Africa.* London, 1871–1872.

Townsend, G. *Memoir of the Rev. Henry Townsend.* Exeter, 1887.

Tucker, [S.]. *Abbeokuta; or Sunrise within the Tropics: An Outline of the Origin and Progress of the Yoruba Mission.* London, 1853.

SECONDARY SOURCES ON THE YORUBA AND NIGERIA

Abdul, M. O. A. "Yoruba Divination and Islam." *Orita* 4 (1970): 17–25.

Abimbola, W. *Ifa: An Exposition of Ifa Literary Corpus.* Ibadan, 1976.

Abiodun, R. "*Aṣẹ:* Verbalizing and Visualizing Creative Power through Art." *Journal of Religion in Africa* 24 (1994): 309–322.

Abraham, R. C. *Dictionary of Modern Yoruba.* London, 1958.

Abubakre, R. D. "The Contribution of Yorubas to Arabic Literature." Ph.D. thesis, University of London, 1980.

Adams, J. *Remarks on the Country extending from Cape Palmas to the River Congo.* London, 1823.

Adebiyi, T. A. *The Beloved Bishop.* Ibadan, 1969.

Adediran, B. *The Frontier States of Western Yorubaland, 1600–1899.* Ibadan, 1994.

Adegbola, E. A. A. "Ifa and Christianity among the Yoruba: A Study in Symbiosis and the Development of Yoruba Christology, 1890–1940." Ph.D. thesis, University of Bristol, 1976.

Adelowo, E. D. "Islam in Oyo and Its Districts in the Nineteenth Century." Ph.D. thesis, University of Ibadan, 1978.

Aderibigbe, A. B., ed. *Lagos: The Development of an African City.* Lagos, 1975.

Adetugbo, A. "The Yoruba Language in Western Nigeria: Its Major Dialect Areas." Ph.D. diss., Columbia University, 1967.

Afolayan, F. "Towards a History of Eastern Yorubaland." In *Yoruba Historiography,* edited by T. Falola, 75–87. Madison, 1991.

Agbaje-Williams, B. "Archaeology and Yoruba studies." In *Yoruba Historiography,* edited by T. Falola. Madison, 1991.

Agiri, B. A., and Barnes, S. T. "Lagos before 1603." In *A History of the Peoples of Lagos State*, edited by A. Adefuye, Babatunde Agiri, and Jide Osuntokun. Lagos, 1987.

Ajayi, J. F. A. "How Yoruba Was Reduced to Writing." *Odu* 8 (1960): 49–58.

———. "Nineteenth Century Origins of Nigerian Nationalism." *Journal of the Historical Society of Nigeria* 2 (1961): 196–211.

———. *Christian Missions in Nigeria, 1841–1891: The Making of a New Elite.* London, 1965.

———. "Bishop Crowther: An Assessment." *Odu* 4 (1970): 3–17.

———. "The Aftermath of the Fall of Old Oyo." In *History of West Africa,* vol. II, edited by J. F. A. Ajayi and M. Crowder, 129–66. London, 1974.

———, and R. S. Smith. *Yoruba Warfare in the Nineteenth Century.* Cambridge, 1964.

Akinjogbin, I. A. *Dahomey and Its Neighbours, 1708–1818.* Cambridge, 1967.

———. "Towards a Historical Geography of Yoruba Civilization." In *Proceedings of the Conference on Yoruba Civilisation,* edited by I. A. Akinjogbin and G. O. Ekemode. Ile-Ife, 1976.

———, ed. *The Cradle of a Race: Ife from the Beginning to 1980.* Port Harcourt, 1992.

Akintoye, S. A. "The Ondo Road Eastwards of Lagos, c. 1970–1895." *Journal of African History* 3 (1964): 110–12.

———. *Revolution and Power Politics in Yorubaland, 1840–1893: Ibadan Expansion and the Rise of the Ekitiparapo.* London, 1971.

Akinyele, I. B. *Iwe Itan Ibadan.* Ibadan, 1911.

Akiwowo, A. A. *Ajobi and Ajogbe: Variations on the Theme of Sociation.* Ile-Ife, 1980.

Anene, J. C. *Southern Nigeria in Transition, 1885–1906.* Cambridge, 1966.

Apter, A. *Black Critics and Kings: The Hermeneutics of Power in Yoruba Society.* Chicago, 1992.

Aronson, D. A. "Cultural Stability and Social Change among the Modern Ijebu." Ph.D. diss., University of Chicago, 1970.

Asiwaju, A. I. *Western Yorubaland under European Rule, 1889–1945.* London, 1987.

Atanda, J. A. *The New Oyo Empire: Indirect Rule and Change in Western Nigeria, 1894–1934.* London, 1973.

Atundaolu, H. "A Short Traditional History of the Ijeshas and Other Hinterland Tribes." *Lagos Weekly Record,* 27 July 1901.

Avoseh, T. O. *History of St Thomas's Church, Badagry.* Araromi-Apapa, n.d.

Awe, B. "The Rise of Ibadan as a Yoruba Power, 1851–1893." D.Phil. thesis, University of Oxford, 1964.

———. "The Ajẹlẹ System: A Study of Ibadan Imperialism in the Nineteenth Century." *Journal of African History* 3 (1964): 47–60.

———. "Militarism and Economic Development in Nineteenth-Century Yoruba Country: The Ibadan Example." *Journal of African History* 14 (1973): 65–77.

Awolowo, O. *Path to Nigerian Freedom.* London, 1947.

Ayandele, E. A. *The Missionary Impact on Modern Nigeria, 1842–1914: A Social and Political Analysis.* London, 1966.

———. *Holy Johnson: Pioneer of Nigerian Nationalism, 1836–1917.* London, 1970.

———. *The Educated Elite in the Nigerian Society.* Ibadan, 1974.

———. *The Ijebu of Yorubaland, 1850–1950: Politics, Economy and Society.* Ibadan, 1992.

Ayantuga, O. O. "Ijebu and Its Neighbours, 1851–1914." Ph.D. thesis, University of London, 1965.

Banjo, A. *In the Saddle: A Vice-Chancellor's Story.* Ibadan, 1997.

Barber, K. "How Man Makes God in West Africa: Yoruba Attitudes towards the *Orisa*." *Africa* 51 (1981): 724–45.

———. "Discursive Strategies in the Texts of Ifa and in the 'Holy Book of Odu' of the African Church of Orunmila." In *Self-Assertion and Brokerage: Early Cultural Nationalism in West Africa,* edited by P. F. Farias and K. Barber, 196–224. Birmingham, 1990.

———. *I Could Speak Until Tomorrow: Oriki, Women, and the Past in a Yoruba Town.* London, 1991.

———. "Going Too Far in Okuku: Some Ideas about Gender, Excess, and Political Power." In *Gender and Identity in Africa,* edited by M. Reh and G. Ludwar-Ene. Muenster, 1994.

———. "Money, Self-Realization and the Person in Yoruba Texts." In *Money Matters,* edited by J. Guyer, 205–224. London, 1995.

Bargery, G. P. *A Hausa-English Dictionary.* London, 1934.

Barnes, S. T., ed. *Africa's Ogun: Old World and New.* 2nd ed. Bloomington, 1997.

Bascom, W. R. "The Sociological Role of the Yoruba Cult Group." *American Anthropologist* 46 (1944): 1–75.

———. *Ifa Divination: Communication between Gods and Men in West Africa.* Bloomington, 1969.

———. *The Yoruba of Southwestern Nigeria.* New York, 1969.

———. "The Early Historical Evidence of Yoruba Urbanism." In *Social Change and Economic Development in Nigeria,* edited by U. G. Damachi and H. D. Siebel. New York, 1973.

Beier, U. "Before Oduduwa." *Odu* 3 (1956): 25–32.

———. *A Year of Sacred Festivals in One Yoruba Town.* Lagos, 1959.

Belasco, B. *The Entrepreneur as Culture Hero: Preadaptations in Nigerian Economic Development.* New York, 1980.

Biobaku, S. O. *The Egba and Their Neighbours, 1842–1872.* Oxford, 1957.

Bowen, T. J. *Adventures and Missionary Labours in the Interior of Africa, 1849–1857.* Charleston, 1957.

Bradbury, R. E. *The Benin Kingdom and the Edo-speaking Peoples of South-western Nigeria.* London, 1957.

———. *Benin Studies.* London, 1973.

Buckley, A. *Yoruba Medicine.* Oxford, 1985.

Burton, R. F. *Abeokuta and the Camaroons Mountains.* London, 1863.

Campbell, R. *Pilgrimage to My Motherland: An Account of a Journey among the Egbas and Yorubas of Central Africa.* Philadelphia, 1861.

Chappel, T. J. H. "The Yoruba Cult of Twins in Historical Perspective." *Africa* 44 (1974): 250–65.

Clapperton, H. *Journal of a Second Expedition into the Interior of Africa.* London, 1829.

Clarke, D. P. "*Aṣọ Oke:* The Evolving Tradition of Hand-Woven Textile Design among the Yoruba of South-western Nigeria." Ph.D. thesis, University of London, 1998.

Clarke, R. J. M. "Agricultural Production in a Rural Yoruba Community." Ph.D. thesis, University of London, 1979.

Clarke, W. H. *Travels and Explorations in Yorubaland, 1854–1858.* Ibadan, 1972.

Cole, P. D. "Lagos Society in the Nineteenth Century." In *Lagos: The Development of an African City,* edited by A. B. Aderibigbe, 27–58. Lagos, 1975.

Connah, G. *African Civilizations: Precolonial States and Cities in Tropical Africa.* Cambridge, 1987.

Crowther, S. *Vocabulary of the Yoruba Language.* London, 1843.

Danmole, H. O. A. "The Frontier Emirate: A History of Islam in Ilorin." Ph.D. thesis, University of Birmingham, 1980.

d'Avezac-Macaya, M., *Notice sur le pays at le peuple des Yebous en Afrique.* Paris, 1945.

Delano, I. O. *The Singing Minister of Nigeria: The Life of the Rev. Canon J. J. Ransome-Kuti.* London, c.1942.

————. *Òwe l'Ẹsin Ọrọ Yoruba: Yoruba Proverbs, Their Meaning and Usage.* Ibadan, 1966.

Denzer, L. *The Iyalode in Ibadan Politics and Society, c.1850–1997.* Ibadan, 1998.

Doortmont, M. "Recapturing the Past: Samuel Johnson and the Construction of the History of the Yoruba." Ph.D. thesis, Erasmus University, Rotterdam, 1994.

Drewal, H. J., and M. T. *Gelede: Art and Female Power among the Yoruba.* Bloomington, 1983.

Drewal, M. T. *Yoruba Ritual: Performers, Play, Agency.* Bloomington, 1992.

Eades, J. S. *The Yoruba Today.* Cambridge, 1980.

Ellis, A. B. *The Yoruba-speaking Peoples of the Slave Coast of West Africa.* London, 1984.

El-Masri, F. H. "Islam." In *The City of Ibadan,* edited by P. C. Lloyd, A. L. Mabogunje, and B. Awe. Cambridge, 1967.

Epega, D. O. *The Mystery of Yoruba Gods.* Ode Remo, 1932.

Euba, T. "Muhammad Shitta Bey and the Lagos Muslim Community (1850–1895)." *Nigerian Journal of Islam* 2 (1971): 21–30.

Fabunmi, M. A. *Ife Shrines.* Ile-Ife, 1969.

Falola, T. *The Political Economy of a Pre-colonial West African State: Ibadan, 1830–1900.* Ile-Ife, 1984.

————. "The Ijaye in Diaspora, 1862–1895." *Journal of Asian and African Studies* 22 (1987): 67–79.

————. "Kemi Morgan and the Second Reconstruction of Ibadan History." *History in Africa* 18 (1991): 93–112.

————, ed. *Pioneer, Patriot and Patriarch: Samuel Johnson and the Yoruba People.* Madison, 1993.

————. *Violence in Nigeria: The Crisis of Religious Politics and Secular Ideologies.* Rochester, 1998.

————, and O. B. Lawuyi. "Not Just a Currency: The Cowry in Yoruba Culture." In *West African Economic and Social History: Studies in Memory of Marion Johnson,* edited by D. Henige and T. C. McCaskie, 29–36. Madison, 1990.

————, and P. E. Lovejoy, eds. *Pawnship in Africa: Debt Bondage in Historical Perspective.* Boulder, 1994.

————, and G. O. Oguntomisin. *The Military in Nineteenth Century Yoruba Politics.* Ibadan, 1984.

Farias, P. F. de Moraes, "'Yoruba Origins' Revisited by Muslims: An Interview with the Arokin of Oyo and a Reading of the *Asl Qabail Yuruba* of Al-Hajj Adam al-Iluri." In *Self-Assertion and Brokerage: Early Cultural Nationalism in West Africa,* edited by P. F. Farias and K. Barber, 109–147. Birmingham, 1990.

————, and K. Barber, eds. *Self-Assertion and Brokerage: Early Cultural Nationalism in West Africa.* Birmingham, 1990.

Farrow, S. S. *Faith, Fancies, and Fetich, being Some Account of the Religious Beliefs of the West African Negroes, Particularly of the Yoruba Tribes of Southern Nigeria.* London, 1926.

Gbadamosi, [T]. G. O. "Patterns and Developments in Lagos Religious History." In *Lagos: The Development of an African City,* edited by A. B. Aderibigbe, 173–96. Lagos, 1975.

————. "'Odu Imale': Islam in Ifa Divination and the Case of Predestined Muslims." *Journal of the Historical Society of Nigeria* 8 (1977): 77–93.

————. *The Growth of Islam among the Yoruba, 1841–1908.* London, 1978.

Gollmer, C. A. "African Symbolic Messages." *Journal of the Royal Anthropological Institute* 14 (1885): 169–82.

Hallen, B. and J. O. Sodipo. *Knowledge, Belief, and Witchcraft: Analytic Experiments in African Philosophy.* London, 1986.

Hallgren, R. *The Good Things of Life: A Study of the Traditional Religious Culture of the Yoruba People.* Loberod, 1988.

Hogendorn, J., and M. Johnson. *The Shell Money of the Slave Trade.* Cambridge, 1986.

Hopkins, A. G. *An Economic History of West Africa.* London, 1973.

Horton, R. "Ancient Ife: A Reassessment." *Journal of the Historical Society of Nigeria* 9 (1976): 69–150.

Idowu, E. B. *Olodumare: God in Yoruba Belief.* London, 1962.

Iliffe, J. "Poverty in Nineteenth-Century Yorubaland." *Journal of African History* 25 (1984): 43–57.

————. "Persecution and Toleration in Pre-Colonial Africa: Nineteenth-Century Yorubaland." *Studies in Church History* 21 (1984): 352–378.

Isola, A. "Yoruba Beliefs about Sango as a Deity." *Orita* 11 (1977): 106.

————. "Religious Politics and the Myth of Sango." In *African Traditional Religions in Contemporary Society,* edited by J. K. Olupona, 93–100. St. Paul, 1991.

Johnson, J. *Yoruba Heathenism.* Exeter, 1899.

————. "The Relation of Mission Work to Native Customs." In *Pan-Anglican Papers: Political and Social Conditions of Missionary Work.* London, 1908.

Johnson, S. *The History of the Yorubas.* Lagos, 1921.

Joseph, R. A. *Democracy and Prebendal Politics in Nigeria.* Cambridge, 1987.

Koelle, S. W. *Polyglotta Africana.* London, 1854.

Krapf-Askari, E. *Yoruba Towns and Cities.* Oxford, 1969.

Laitin, D. *Hegemony and Culture: Politics and Religious Change among the Yoruba.* Chicago, 1986.

Lander, J. *Journal of an Expedition to Explore the Course and Termination of the Niger.* London, 1832.

LaPin, D. "Story, Medium and Masque: The Idea and Art of Yoruba Storytelling." Ph.D. thesis, University of Wisconsin, 1977.

Law, R. "The Constitutional Troubles of Oyo in the Eighteenth Century." *Journal of African History* 12 (1971): 25–44.

————. "The Heritage of Oduduwa: Traditional History and Political Propaganda among the Yoruba." *Journal of African History* 14 (1973): 207–222.

————. *The Oyo Empire c.1600–c.1836: A West African Imperialism in the Era of the Atlantic Slave Trade.* Oxford, 1977.

————. "Making Sense of a Traditional Narrative: Political Disintegration in the Kingdom of Oyo." *Cahiers d'etudes africaines* 22 (1982): 387–401.

————. "A Pioneer of Yoruba Studies: Moses Lijadu (1862–1926)." In *Studies in Yoruba History and Culture: Essays in Honour of Professor S. O. Biobaku,* edited by G. O. Olusanya, 108–115. Ibadan, 1983.

———. "Human Sacrifice in Pre-colonial West Africa." *African Affairs* 84 (1985): 53–88.

———. "Constructing 'a Real National History': A Comparison of Edward Blyden and Samuel Johnson." In *Self-Assertion and Brokerage: Early Cultural Nationalism in West Africa,* edited by P. F. Farias and K. Barber, 78–100. Birmingham, 1990.

———. "Local Amateur Scholarship in the Construction of Yoruba Ethnicity, 1880–1914." In *Ethnicity in Africa,* edited by Louise de la Gorgendière, Kenneth King, and Sarah Vaughan. Centre of African Studies, University of Edinburgh, 1996.

Lawal, B. *The Gelede Spectacle: Art, Gender and Social Harmony in an African Culture.* Seattle, 1996.

Lawuyi, O. B. "The Obatala Factor in Yoruba History." *History in Africa* 19 (1992): 369–75.

Lijadu, E. M. *Ifa: Imọlẹ rẹ ti iṣe Ipilẹ Isin ni Ilẹ Yoruba.* London, 1901.

———. *Ọrunmla!* 1908. Reprint, Ado-Ekiti, 1972.

Lloyd, P. C. "Craft Organization in Yoruba Towns." *Africa* 23 (1953): 30–44.

———. "The Yoruba Lineage." *Africa* 25 (1955): 235–51.

———. "Sacred Kingship and Government among the Yoruba." *Africa* 30 (1960): 221–34.

———. *Yoruba Land Law.* London, 1962.

———. "Agnatic and Cognatic Descent among the Yoruba." *Man* 1 (1966): 484–500.

———. *The Political Development of Yoruba Kingdoms in the Eighteenth and Nineteenth Centuries.* London, 1971.

Lucas, J. O. *The Religion of the Yorubas.* Lagos, 1948.

———. *History of St Paul's Church, Breadfruit, Lagos.* Lagos, 1954.

Mabogunje, A. L. *Urbanization in Nigeria.* London, 1968.

———, and J. Omer-Cooper. *Owu in Yoruba History.* Ibadan, 1971.

Maja-Pearce, A., ed. *Wole Soyinka: An Appraisal.* London, 1994.

Mann, K. *Marrying Well: Marriage, Status and Social Change among the Educated Elite in Colonial Lagos.* Cambridge, 1985.

Marshall-Fratani, R. "Mediating the Global and the Local in Nigerian Pentecostalism." *Journal of Religion in Africa* 28 (1998): 278–315.

Matory, J. L. "Government by Seduction: History and the Tropes of 'Mounting' in Oyo-Yoruba Religion." In *Modernity and Its Malcontents: Ritual and Power in Postcolonial Africa,* edited by J. and J. L. Comaroff, 58–85. Chicago, 1993.

———. *Sex and the Empire That Is No More: Gender and the Politics of Metaphor in Oyo–Yoruba Religion.* Minneapolis, 1994.

Maupoil, B. *La Géomancie à l'ancienne côte des esclaves.* Paris, 1943.

May, D. J. "A Journey in the Yoruba and Nupe Countries in 1858." *Journal of the Royal Geographical Society* 30 (1860): 212–33.

McKenzie, P. R. "Was the Priestess of Yemoja Also among the Prophets?" *Orita* 9 (1975): 67–71.

———. "The Persecution of Early Nigerian Converts." *Orita* 11 (1977): 3–14.

———. "Dreams and Visions from Nineteenth-Century Yoruba Religion." In *Dreaming, Religion, and Society in Africa,* edited by M. C. Jedrej and R. Shaw, 126–34. Leiden, 1992.

———. *Hail Orisha! A Phenomenology of a West African Religion in the Mid-Nineteenth Century.* Leiden, 1997.

Moore, E. O. O. *History of Abeokuta.* London, 1916.

Morgan, K. *Akinyele's Outline History of Ibadan*. 3 vols. Ibadan, n.d.

Morton-Williams, P. "Yoruba Responses to the Fear of Death." *Africa* 30 (1960): 34–40.

———. "The Oyo Yoruba and the Atlantic Trade, 1670–1830." *Journal of the Historical Society of Nigeria* 3 (1964): 25–45.

———. "An Outline of the Cosmology and Cult Organization of the Oyo Yoruba." *Africa* 34 (1964): 243–61.

Nina Rodrigues, R. *Os Africanos no Brasil*. 2nd ed. São Paulo, 1935.

Nolte, M. I. "Ritualized Interaction and Civic Solidarity: Kingship and Politics in Ijebu-Remo." Ph.D. thesis, University of Birmingham, 1999.

Obayemi, A. "The Yoruba and Edo-Speaking Peoples and Their Neighbours before 1600." In *History of West Africa*, 2nd ed., vol. I, edited by J. F. A. Ajayi and M. Crowder. London, 1976.

[Odumosu family]. *Iwosan*. Liverpool, n.d. [c. 1941–1942].

Ogunba, O., ed. *Soyinka: A Collection of Critical Essays*. Ibadan, 1994.

Ogunbiyi, I. A. "Arabic Loan Words in the Yoruba Language." *Arabic Journal of Language Studies* 3 (1984).

Ogunsola, A. M. O. "Religious Change and the Reconstruction of Idoani." Ph.D. thesis, University of Liverpool, 1986.

Oguntomisin, G. O. "New Forms of Political Organization in the Mid-Nineteenth Century: A Comparative Study of Kurunmi's Ijaye and Kosoko's Epe." Ph.D. thesis, University of Ibadan, 1979.

O'Hear, A. *Power Relations in Nigeria: Ilorin Slaves and Their Successors*. Rochester, N.Y., 1997.

Ojo, G. J. A. *Yoruba Culture: A Geographical Analysis*. Ile-Ife, 1966.

———. *Yoruba Palaces*. London, 1966.

Ojo, J. R. O. "Orisa Oko: The Deity of 'the Farm and Agriculture' among the Ekiti." *African Notes* 7 (1973): 25–61.

Ojo, M. A. "The Contextual Significance of Charismatic Movements in Independent Nigeria." *Africa* 58 (1988): 172–92.

———. "End-Time Army: The Charismatic Movements in Modern Nigeria." Unpublished ms.

Oke, S. A. *The Ethiopian National Church: A Necessity*. Ibadan, 1923.

Olupona, J. K. *Kingship, Religion, and Rituals in a Nigerian Community: A Study of Ondo Yoruba Festivals*. Stockholm, 1991.

Omoyajowo, J. A. *Cherubim and Seraphim*. New York, 1982.

Oroge, E. A. "The Institution of Slavery in Yorubaland, with Particular Reference to the Nineteenth Century." Ph.D. thesis, University of Birmingham, 1971.

———. "*Iwofa*: An Historical Survey of the Yoruba Institution of Indenture." *African Economic History* 14 (1985): 75–106.

Oyetade, B. A. "*Ota*: Enemy in Yoruba Belief." Unpublished ms.

Pallinder, A. "Government in Abeokuta, 1830–1914." Ph.D. thesis, University of Goteborg, 1973.

Parrinder, E. G. "An African Saviour God." In *The Saviour God: Comparative Studies in the Concept of Salvation*, edited by S. G. F. Brandon, 117–28. Manchester, 1963.

Peel, J. D. Y. "Religious Change among the Yoruba." *Africa* 37 (1967): 292–306.

———. *Aladura: A Religious Movement among the Yoruba*. London, 1968.

———. "Conversion and Tradition in Two African Societies: Ijebu and Buganda." *Past and Present* 77 (1977): 108–141.

———. "Olaju: A Yoruba Concept of Development." *Journal of Development Studies* 14 (1978): 135–65.

———. *Ijeshas and Nigerians: The Incorporation of a Yoruba Kingdom, 1890s–1970s.* Cambridge, 1983.

———. "Making History: The Past in the Ijesha Present." *Man* 19 (1984): 111–32.

———. "The Pastor and the *Babalawo:* The Encounter of Religions in Nineteenth-Century Yorubaland." *Africa* 60 (1990): 338–69.

———. "Poverty and Sacrifice in Nineteenth-Century Yorubaland." *Journal of African History* 31 (1990): 465–84.

———. "Between Crowther and Ajayi: The Religious Origins of the Nigerian Intelligentsia." In *African Historiography: Essays in Honour of Jacob Ade Ajayi,* edited by T. Falola, 64–79. Lagos, 1993.

———. "Historicity and Pluralism in Some Recent Studies of Yoruba Religion." *Africa* 64 (1994): 157–60.

———. "For Who Hath Despised the Day of Small Things: Missionary Narratives and Historical Anthropology." *Comparative Studies in Society and History* 37 (1995): 581–607.

———. "Problems and Opportunities in an Anthropologist's Use of a Missionary Archive." In *Missionary Encounters: Source and Issues,* edited by R. A. Bickers and R. Seton, 70–94. London, 1996.

———. "A Comparative Analysis of Ogun in Precolonial Yorubaland." In *Africa's Ogun: Old World and New,* 2nd ed., edited by S. T. Barnes, 63–289. Bloomington, 1997.

———. "Two Pastors and Their Histories: Samuel Johnson and C. C. Reindorf." In *The Recovery of the West African Past,* edited by P. Jenkins, 69–81. Basel, 1998.

Pelton, R. D. *The Trickster in West Africa: A Study of Mythic Irony and Sacred Delight.* Berkeley, 1980.

Pemberton, J. "Eshu-Elegba: The Yoruba Trickster God." *African Arts* 9 (1975): 21–27, 66–70.

———. "A Cluster of Sacred Symbols: Orisa Worship among the Igbomina Yoruba of Ila-Orangun." *History of Religions* 17 (1977): 1–28.

Phillips, T. K. E. *Yoruba Church Music: The Beauty of Yoruba Music, Its Relation and Similarity to the European Medieval Music and Its Development for Worship.* Lagos, 1914.

Quayson, A. *Strategic Transformations in Nigerian Writing: Orality and History in the Work of Rev. Samuel Johnson, Amos Tutuola, Wole Soyinka and Ben Okri.* Oxford, 1997.

Ray, C. "Aladura Christianity: A Yoruba Religion." *Journal of Religion in Africa* 23 (1993): 266–91.

Reichmuth, S. "Songhay-Lehnwörter im Yoruba und ihr historischer Kontext." *Sprach und Geschichte in Afrika* 9 (1988): 269–99.

———. *Islamischer Bildung und soziale Integration in Ilorin (Nigeria) seit ca 1800.* Muenster, 1998.

Renne, E. P. *Cloth That Does Not Die: The Meaning of Cloth in Bunu Life.* Seattle, 1995.

Richards, P. "Landscapes of Dissent: Ikale and Ilaje Country, 1870–1950." In *Empires and Peoples in African History: Essays in Memory of Michael Crowder,* edited by J. F. A. Ajayi and J. D. Y. Peel, 161–88. London, 1992.

Ryan, P. J. *Imale: Yoruba Participation in the Muslim Tradition.* Missoula, 1978.

Salvaing, B. *Les missionaires à la rencontre a l'Afrique au XIXe siècle: Côte des esclaves et pays Yoruba, 1840–1891.* Paris, 1994.

Schiltz, M. "Egungun masquerades in Iganna." *African Arts* 11 (1978).

———. "Yoruba Thunder Deities and Sovereignty: Ara Versus Sango." *Anthropos* 80 (1985): 67–84.

[Schön, J. F., and S. Crowther.] *Journals of the Rev. James Frederick Schon and Mr Samuel Crowther, who . . . accompanied the Expedition up the River Niger in 1841.* London, 1842.

Smith, A. [H. F. C.] "A Little New Light on the Collapse of the Alafinate of Yoruba." In *A Little New Light,* 149–91. Zaria, 1987.

Smith, R. S. *Kingdoms of the Yoruba.* London, 1969.

———. "Nigeria-Ijebu." In *West African Resistance: The Military Response to Colonial Occupation,* edited by M. Crowder, 170–204. London, 1971.

———. *The Lagos Consulate, 1851–1861.* London, 1978.

Sogunle, N. O. *History of St Jude's Church, Ebute Metta.* Lagos, 1968.

Sorensen, C. "Badagry, 1784–1863: A Political and Commercial History." Ph.D. thesis, University of Stirling, 1996.

Southon, A. E. *Ilesha—and Beyond! The Story of the Wesley Guild Medical Work in West Africa.* London, n.d. [c. 1932].

Soyinka, W. *Ake: The Years of Childhood.* London, 1981.

———. *Isara: A Voyage around "Essay."* New York, 1989.

———. *The Credo of Being and Nothingness.* Ibadan, 1991.

———. *Art, Dialogue, and Outrage: Essays on Literature and Culture.* London, 1993.

Talbot, P. A. *The Peoples of Southern Nigeria.* 4 vols. London, 1926.

Thompson, R. F. *Black Gods and Kings: Yoruba Art at UCLA.* Bloomington, 1976.

Turner, V. W. *African Independent Church.* 2 vols. Oxford, 1967.

Verger, P. *Orixás: Deuses Iorubás na África e no Novo Mundo.* São Paulo, 1981.

Waterman, C. *Juju: A Social History and Ethnography of African Popular Music.* Chicago, 1991.

Watson, R. "Chieftaincy Politics and Civic Consciousness in Ibadan History, 1829–1939." D.Phil. thesis, University of Oxford, 1998.

Webster, J. B. *The African Churches among the Yoruba, 1891–1922.* Oxford, 1964.

Westcott, J. "The Sculpture and Myths of Eshu-Elegba, the Yoruba Trickster." *Africa* 32 (1962): 336–53.

———, and P. Morton-Williams. "The Symbolism and Ritual Context of the Yoruba Laba Shango." *Journal of the Royal Anthropological Institute* 92 (1962): 23–37.

Wheatley, P. "The Significance of Traditional Yoruba Urbanism." *Comparative Studies in Society and History* 12 (1970): 393–423.

Wright, D. *Wole Soyinka Revisited.* New York, 1993.

Yai, O. "From Vodun to Mawu: Monotheism and History in the Fon Cultural Area." In *L'invention religieuse en Afrique,* edited by J.-P. Chrétien, 241–65.

Zachernuk, P. S. "Of Origins and Colonial Order: Southern Nigerian Historians and the 'Hamitic Hypothesis.'" *Journal of African History* 35 (1994): 427–55.

OTHER WORKS CITED

Ajayi, J. F. A., and E. A. Ayandele. "Writing African Church History." In *The Church Crossing Frontiers: Essays in Honour of Bengt Sundkler,* edited by P. Beyerhaus and C. F. Hallencreuz, 90–108. Uppsala, 1969.

Anderson, B. *Imagined Communities*. London, 1983.

Anstey, R. *The Atlantic Slave Trade and British Abolition, 1760–1810*. London, 1975.

Antze, P., and M. Lambek, eds. *Tense Past: Cultural Essays in Trauma and Memory*. New York, 1996.

Asad, T. *Genealogies of Religion*. Baltimore, 1993.

Bamat, T., and J.-P. Wiest. *Popular Catholicism in a World Church; Seven Case Studies in Inculturation*. Maryknoll, 1999.

Barrett, D. B. *Schism and Renewal in Africa: An Analysis of Six Thousand Contemporary Religious Movements*. London, 1968.

Bayart, J.-P. *The State in Africa: The Politics of the Belly*. London, 1993.

Beattie, J. *Other Cultures*. London, 1964.

Bebbington, D. W. *Evangelicalism in Modern Britain: A History from the 1730s to the 1830s*. London, 1989.

Bediako, K. *Christianity in Africa: The Renewal of a Non-Western Religion*. Edinburgh, 1995.

Beidelman, T. O. *Colonial Evangelism*. Bloomington, 1982.

Binsbergen, W. van. "Regional and Historical Connections of Four-Tablet Divination in Southern Africa." *Journal of Religion in Africa* 26 (1996): 2–29.

Bloch, M. *Prey into Hunter: The Politics of Religious Experience*. Cambridge, 1992.

Blyden, E. W. *Christianity, Islam and the Negro Race*. 1887. Reprint; Edinburgh, 1967.

Bowie, F., D. Kirkwood, and S. Ardener, eds. *Women and Missions, Past and Present: Anthropological Perspectives*. Providence, 1993.

Boxer, C. R. *The Church Militant and Iberian Expansion, 1440–1770*. Baltimore, 1978.

Bruner, J. *Actual Minds, Possible Worlds*. Cambridge, Mass., 1986.

———. "Life as Narrative." *Social Research* 54 (1987): 1–32.

———. "The Narrative Construction of Reality." *Critical Enquiry* 18 (1991): 1–21.

Bulliet, R. *Conversion to Islam in the Medieval Period*. Cambridge, Mass., 1979.

Burke, P. "Historians, Anthropologists and Symbols." In *Culture through Time: Anthropological Approaches*, edited by E. Ohnuki-Tierney. Stanford, 1990.

Carr, D. *Time, Narrative, and History*. Bloomington, 1991.

Carrithers, M. *Why Humans Have Cultures*. Oxford, 1992.

Chaney, W. A. *The Cult of Kingship in Anglo-Saxon England*. Manchester, 1970.

Chatman, S. *Story and Discourse: Narrative Structure in Fiction and Film*. Ithaca, N.Y., 1978.

Cohn, B. S. *Colonialism and Its Forms of Knowledge: The British in India*. Princeton, 1996.

Colley, L. *Britons: Forging the Nation, 1707–1837*. London, 1992.

Comaroff, J., and J. L. Comaroff. *Of Revelation and Revolution: Christianity, Colonialism and Consciousness in South Africa*. Vol. I. Chicago, 1991.

Cox, H. *Fire from Heaven: The Rise of Pentecostal Spirituality and the Reshaping of Religion in the Twenty-first Century*. New York, 1994.

Craemer, W. de, J. Vansina, and R. Fox. "Religious Movements in Central Africa: A Theoretical Statement." *Comparative Studies in Society and History* 18 (1976): 458–75.

Crone, P., and M. Cook. *Hagarism: The Making of the Islamic World*. Cambridge, 1977.

Dening, G. *Mr Bligh's Bad Language: Passion, Power, and Theatre on the Bounty*. Cambridge, 1992.

Dirks, N. B. *Colonialism and Culture*. Ann Arbor, 1992.

Douglas, M. *Purity and Danger*. London, 1966.

Fabian, J. *Language and Social Power: The Appropriation of Swahili in the Belgian Congo, 1880–1938*. Cambridge, 1986.

Finnegan, R. *Tales of the City: A Study of Narrative and Urban Life*. Cambridge, 1998.

Fisher, H. J. "Conversion Reconsidered: Some Historical Aspects of Religious Conversion in Black Africa." *Africa* 43 (1973): 27–40.

———. "The Juggernaut's Apologia: Conversion to Islam in Black Africa." *Africa* 55 (1985): 153–73.

Fletcher, R. *The Conversion of Europe: From Paganism to Christianity in Europe, 371–1386 AD*. London, 1997.

Gaitskell, D. "Prayer and Preaching: The Distinctive Spirituality of African Women's Church Organizations." In *Missions and Christianity in South African History*, edited by H. Bredekamp and R. Ross. Johannesburg, 1995.

Geertz, C. "Religion as a Cultural System." In *Anthropological Approaches to The Study of Religion*, edited by M. Banton, 1–46. London, 1966.

Gell, A. *The Anthropology of Time*. Oxford, 1992.

Gellner, E. *Nations and Nationalism*. Oxford, 1983.

Gifford, P. *African Christianity: Its Public Role*. London, 1998.

———. "The Complex Provenance of Some Elements of African Pentecostal Theology." In *From Babel to Pentecost: Pentecostalism and Transnationalism in Africa and Latin America*, edited by A. Corten and R. Marshall-Fratani. London, forthcoming.

Gilbert, M. "Sources of Power in Akuropon-Akuapem: Ambiguity in Classification." In *Creativity of Power: Cosmology and Action in African Societies*, edited by W. Arens and I. Karp, 59–90.

Ginzburg, C. *The Cheese and the Worms: The Cosmos of a Sixteenth-Century Miller*. London, 1980.

Goody, J. "Religion and Ritual: The Definitional Problem." *British Journal of Sociology* 12 (1961): 143–64.

———. *Technology, Tradition, and the State in Africa*. London, 1971.

Gray, R. *Black Christians and White Missionaries*. New Haven, 1990.

Hastings, A. *A History of African Christianity, 1950–1975*. Cambridge, 1979.

———. "Ganda Catholic Spirituality." In *African Catholicism*, by A. Hastings, 68–81. London, 1989.

———. "Were Women a Special Case?" In *Women and Missions, Past and Present: Anthropological Perspectives*, edited by F. Bowie, D. Kirkwood, and S. Ardener, 109–125. Providence, 1993.

———. *The Church in Africa, 1450–1950*. Oxford, 1994.

———. *The Construction of Nationhood: Ethnicity, Religion and Nationalism*. Cambridge, 1997.

Hefner, R. W., ed., *Conversion to Christianity: Historical and Anthropological Perspectives*. Berkeley, 1993.

Herskovits, M. J. *Dahomey: An Ancient West African Kingdom*. 2 vols. New York, 1938.

Heusch, L. de. *Sacrifice in Africa*. Manchester, 1985.

Higham, N. J. *The Convert Kings: Power and Religious Affiliation in Early Anglo-Saxon England*. Manchester, 1997.

Hilton, B. *The Age of Atonement: The Influence of Evangelicalism on Social and Political Thought, 1795–1965*. Oxford, 1988.

Hobsbawm, E. J. *Nations and Nationalism since 1780*. Cambridge, 1990.

Hofmeyr, I. *We Spend Our Years as a Tale That Is Told: Oral Historical Narrative in a South African Chiefdom*. Johannesburg, 1993.

Horton, R. "African Conversion." *Africa* 41 (1971): 85–108.
———. "On the Rationality of Conversion." *Africa* 45 (1975): 219–35, 373–99.
———. "Social Psychologies: African and Western." In M. Fortes, *Oedipus and Job in West African Religion,* 2nd ed., edited by R. Horton, 41–87. Cambridge, 1983.
———. *Patterns of Thought in Africa and the West: Essays on Magic, Religion and Science.* Cambridge, 1993.
Isaac, E. "Genesis, Judaism and the 'Sons of Ham.'" In *Slaves and Slavery in Muslim Africa,* vol. I, edited by J. R. Willis, 75–91. London, 1985.
Jakobson-Widding, A. *Red-White-Black as a Mode of Thought: A Study of Triadic Classification in the Ritual Symbolism and Cognitive Thought of the People of the Lower Congo.* Stockholm, 1978.
Jalland, P. *Death in the Victorian Family.* Oxford, 1966.
James, W. *The Varieties of Religious Experience.* New York, 1902.
Kermode, F. *The Sense of an Ending: Studies in the Theory of Fiction.* New York, 1966.
Kopytoff, I. "Ancestors and Elders in Africa." *Africa* 41 (1971): 129–41.
———, and S. Miers, eds. *Slavery in Africa: Historical and Anthropological Perspectives.* Madison, 1977.
Ladurie, E. Le Roy. *Montaillou: Cathars and Catholics in a French Village, 1294–1324.* London, 1878.
Landau, P. *The Realm of the Word: Language, Gender, and Christianity in a Southern African Kingdom.* Portsmouth, N.H., 1995.
———. "'Religion' and Christian Conversion in African History." *Journal of Religious History* 23 (1999): 8–30.
Lapidus, I. M. "The Conversion of Egypt to Islam." *Israel Oriental Studies* 2 (1972): 248–62.
Launay, R. *Beyond the Stream: Islam and Society in a West African Town.* Berkeley, 1992.
Levtzion, N., ed. *Conversion to Islam.* New York, 1979.
Lonsdale, J. "Scramble and Conquest in African History." In *Cambridge History of Africa,* vol. VIII, edited by R. Oliver and G. N. Sanderson, 700–722. Cambridge, 1985.
———, and B. Berman, *Unhappy Valley: Conflict in Kenya and Africa.* London, 1992.
Loughlin, G. *Telling God's Story: Bible, Church and Narrative Theology.* Cambridge, 1996.
MacGaffey, W. *Religion and Society in Central Africa: The BaKongo of Lower Zaire.* Chicago, 1986.
Martin, D. *Tongues of Fire: The Explosion of Pentecostalism in Latin America.* Oxford, 1990.
Maxwell, D. *Christians and Chiefs in Zimbabwe: A Social History of the Hwesa People, c.1870s–1990s.* Edinburgh, 1999.
McCaskie, T. C. "Innovational Eclecticism: The Asante Empire and Europe in the Nineteenth Century." *Comparative Studies in Society and History* 14 (1972): 30–45.
———. *State and Society in Pre-colonial Asante.* Cambridge, 1995.
Meyer, B. *Translating the Devil: Religion and Modernity among the Ewe in Ghana.* Edinburgh, 1999.
Middleton, J. *Lugbara Religion.* London, 1960.
Mudimbe, V. Y. *The Invention of Africa.* Bloomington, 1988.
Murray, J. *Proclaim the Good News: A Short History of the CMS.* London, 1985.
Needham, R. *Belief, Language and Experience.* Oxford, 1972.
Obeyesekere, G. *The Apotheosis of Captain Cook.* Princeton, 1992.
Oddie, G. A. *Religious Conversion Movements in South Asia: Continuities and Change, 1800–1900.* London, 1997.

Orr, J. E. *The Second Evangelical Revival*. London, 1949.

Pagden, A. *The Fall of Natural Man: The American Indian and the Origins of Comparative Ethnology*. Cambridge, 1982.

Parkin, D., ed., *The Anthropology of Evil*. Oxford, 1985.

Peel, J. D. Y. "History, Culture and the Comparative Method: A West African Puzzle." In *Comparative Anthropology*, edited by L. Holy, 88–108. Oxford, 1987.

Pels, P. "The Anthropology of Colonialism." *Annual Review of Anthropology* 26 (1997): 68–183.

Peterson, J. *Province of Freedom: A History of Sierra Leone, 1878–1870*. London, 1969.

Pinnock, W. *Catechism of Scripture History*. London, 1825.

Pinnock, W. H. *Analysis of Scripture History*. Cambridge, 1853.

Piscatori, J. P. *Islam in a World of Nation-States*. Cambridge, 1986.

Poewe, K., ed. *Charismatic Christianity as a Global Culture*. Columbia, S.C., 1994.

Porter, A. N. "Commerce and Christianity: The Rise and Fall of a Nineteenth-Century Missionary Slogan." *Historical Journal* 28 (1985): 587–621.

———. *Religion and Empire: British Expansion in the Long 19th Century*. London, 1991.

Raboteau, J. J. *Slave Religion: The "Invisible Institution" in the Antebellum South*. New York, 1978.

Rafael, V. L. *Contracting Colonialism: Translation and Christian Conversion in Tagalog Society under Early Spanish Colonial Rule*. Ithaca, 1988.

Rambo, L. R. *Understanding Religious Conversion*. New Haven, 1993.

Ranger, T. O. "Religious Movements and Politics in Sub-Saharan Africa." *African Studies Review* 29 (1986): 1–69.

———, and I. Kimambo, eds. *The Historical Study of African Religion*. London, 1972.

———, and J. Weller, eds. *Themes in the Christian History of Central Africa*. London, 1975.

Russell, J. B. *Mephistopheles: The Devil in the Modern World*. Ithaca, N.Y., 1986.

———. *The Prince of Darkness: Radical Evil and the Power of Good in History*. London, 1989.

Sahlins, M. *Historical Metaphors and Mythical Realities*. Ann Arbor, 1981.

———. *Islands of History*. Chicago, 1985.

———. "The Return of the Event, Again; . . ." In *Clio in Oceania: Toward a Historical Anthropology*, edited by A Biersack, 37–100. Washington, 1991.

———. *How "Natives" Think: About Captain Cook, for Example*. Chicago, 1995.

Sanneh, L. *Translating the Message: The Missionary Impact on Culture*. Maryknoll, 1989.

———. "Translatability in Islam and Christianity in Africa." In *Religion in Africa: Experience and Expression*, edited by T. D. Blakely, W. van Beek, and D. L. Thomson, 22–45. London and Portsmouth, 1994.

Sawyerr, H. *God: Ancestor or Creator?* London, 1970.

Shaw, R., and C. Stewart, eds., *Syncretism/Anti-Syncretism: The Politics of Religious Synthesis*. London, 1994.

Smith, A. D. *The Ethnic Origins of Nations*. Oxford, 1986.

Smith, E. W., ed. *African Ideas of God*. London, 1949.

Spence, J. *God's Chinese Son: The Taiping Heavenly Kingdom of Hong Xiuquan*. New York, 1996.

Stanley, B. "Commerce and Christianity, Providence Theory and Free Trade." *Historical Journal* 26 (1983): 71–94.

————. *The Bible and the Flag: Protestant Missions and British Imperialism in the Nineteenth and Twentieth Centuries.* Leicester, 1990.

Stock, E. *A History of the Church Missionary Society.* 3 vols. London, 1899.

Stone, L. *The Family, Sex and Marriage in England, 1500–1800.* London, 1977.

Stroup, G. W. *The Promise of Narrative Theology.* London, 1984.

Sundkler, B. G. M. *Bantu Prophets in South Africa.* London, 1949.

Tambiah, S. J. *World Conqueror and World Renouncer.* Cambridge, 1976.

Thomas, N. *Colonialism's Culture: Anthropology, Travel, and Government.* London, 1994.

Todorov, T. *The Conquest of America: The Question of the Other.* London, 1984.

Tonkin, E. *Narrating Our Pasts: The Social Construction of Oral History.* Cambridge, 1992.

Trimingham, J. S. *A History of Islam in West Africa.* Oxford, 1962.

Turksen, P., and F. Wijsen, eds., *Inculturation: Abide by the Otherness of Africa and the Africans.* Kampen, 1994.

Turner, V. W. *The Forest of Symbols.* Ithaca, 1967.

van der Veer, P., ed. *Conversion to Modernities: The Globalization of Christianity.* London, 1996.

Veyne, P. *Did the Greeks Believe in Their Myths? An Essay in the Constitutive Imagination.* Chicago, 1988.

Vryonis, S. *The Decline of Medieval Hellenism in Asia Minor.* Berkeley, 1971.

Waldman, M., and O. Yai. "Comments on Sanneh 1989." *Journal of Religion in Africa* 22 (1992): 159–72.

Walker, D. P. *The Decline of Hell.* London, 1964.

Wallace, A. F. C. *The Death and Rebirth of the Seneca.* New York, 1969.

Ward, K., and B. Stanley. *The Church Mission Society and World Christianity.* Grand Rapids, 1999.

Ward, W. R. *The Protestant Evangelical Awakening.* London, 1992.

Weber, M. *The Sociology of Religion.* Trans. E. Fischoff. London, 1965.

————. *The Protestant Ethic and the Spirit of Capitalism.* Trans. T. Parsons. London, 1930.

Werbner, R., ed., *Memory and the Postcolony: African Anthropology and the Critique of Power.* London, 1998.

White, H. *Metahistory: The Historical Imagination in Nineteenth-Century Europe.* Baltimore, 1973.

————. "The Value of Narrativity in the Representation of Reality." In *The Content of the Form: Narrative Discourse and Historical Representation,* by H. White, 1–25. Baltimore, 1987.

Wilks, I. *Asante in the Nineteenth Century.* Cambridge, 1975.

Williams, C. P. *The Ideal of the Self-Governing Church.* Leiden, 1990.

INDEX

J. D. Y. PEEL

is on the faculty of the School of Oriental and African Studies at the University of London. He has held appointments at Nottingham University, the London School of Economics, the University of Ife, Liverpool University, and the University of Chicago. He is author of *Aladura, Herbert Spencer,* and *Ijeshas and Nigerians,* for which he won the Herskovits award. He has been editor of *Africa* and is former president of the African Studies Association of the United Kingdom. He was elected a Fellow of the British Academy in 1991.